MyEconLab PROVIDES THE POWER OF PRACTICE

Optimize your study time with MyEconLab, the online assessment and tutorial system. When you take a sample test online, **MyEconLab** gives you targeted feedback and a personalized Study Plan to identify the topics you need to review.

Study Plan The Study Plan consists of practice problems taken directly from the end-of-chapter Study Plan Problems and Applications in the textbook.

Unlimited Practice As you work each exercise, instant feedback helps you understand and apply the concepts. Many Study Plan exercises contain algorithmically generated values to ensure that you get as much practice as you need.

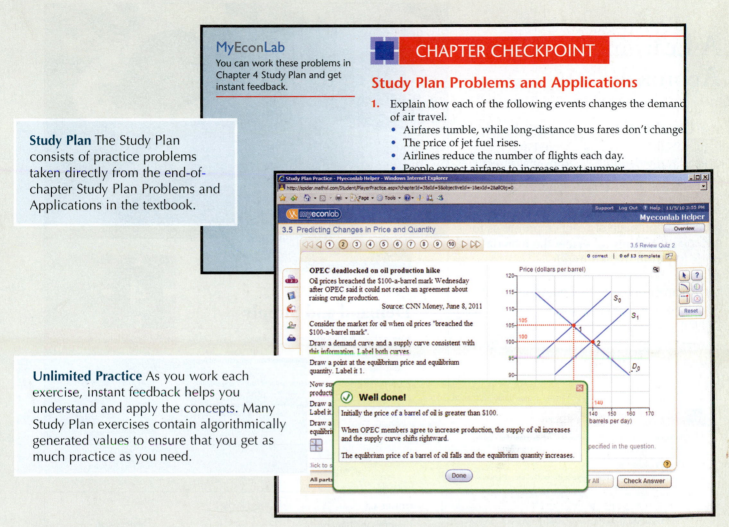

Learning Resources

Study Plan problems link to learning resources that further reinforce concepts you need to master.

- **Help Me Solve This** learning aids help you break down a problem much the same way as an instructor would do during office hours. Help Me Solve This is available for select problems.
- Links to the **eText** promote reading of the text when you need to revisit a concept or explanation.
- **Animated graphs,** with audio narration, appeal to a variety of learning styles.
- A **graphing tool** enables you to build and manipulate graphs to better understand how concepts, numbers, and graphs connect.

MyEconLab

Find out more at www.myeconlab.com

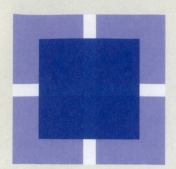

FOUNDATIONS OF ECONOMICS

delivers a complete, hands-on learning system designed around active learning.

A Learning-by-Doing Approach

The **Checklist** that begins each chapter highlights the key topics covered and the chapter is divided into sections that directly correlate to the Checklist.

The **Checkpoint** that ends each section provides a full page of practice problems to encourage students to review the material while it is fresh in their minds.

Each chapter opens with a question about a central issue that sets the stage for the material.

Why did the price of coffee soar in 2010 and 2011?

Demand and Supply

4

When you have completed your study of this chapter, you will be able to

CHAPTER CHECKLIST

1 Distinguish between quantity demanded and demand, and explain what determines demand.

2 Distinguish between quantity supplied and supply, and explain what determines supply.

... supply determine price and quantity in a ... ffects of changes in demand and supply.

 CHECKPOINT 4.1

Distinguish between quantity demanded and demand, and explain what determines demand.

Practice Problems

The following events occur one at a time in the market for cell phones:
- The price of a cell phone falls.
- Everyone believes that the price of a cell phone will fall next month.
- The price of a call made from a cell phone falls.
- The price of a call made from a land-line phone increases.
- The introduction of camera phones makes cell phones more popular.

1. Explain the effect of each event on the demand for cell phones.
2. Use a graph to illustrate the effect of each event.
3. Does any event (or events) illustrate the law of demand?

In the News

Airlines, now flush, fear a downturn
So far this year, airlines have been able to raise fares but still fill their planes.
Source: *The New York Times*, June 10, 2011

MyEconLab
You can work these problems in Study Plan 4.1 and get instant feedback.

Confidence-Building Graphs

use color to show the direction of shifts and detailed, numbered captions guide students step-by-step through the action.

100% of the figures are animated in MyEconLab, with step-by-step audio narration.

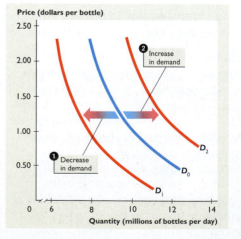

■ **FIGURE 4.3**

Changes in Demand

MyEconLab Animation

A change in any influence on buying plans, other than a change in the price of the good itself, changes demand and shifts the demand curve.

1 When demand decreases, the demand curve shifts leftward from D_0 to D_1.

2 When demand increases, the demand curve shifts rightward from D_0 to D_2.

Real Applications

Eye On Boxes apply theory to important issues and problems that shape our global society and individual decisions.

Eye On boxes that build off the chapter opening question help students see the economics behind key issues facing our world.

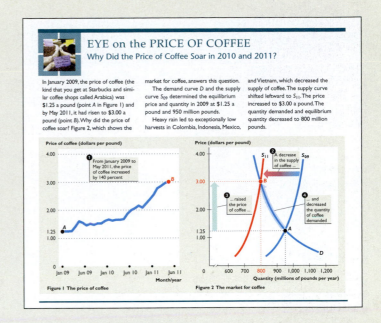

EYE on the PRICE OF COFFEE
Why Did the Price of Coffee Soar in 2010 and 2011?

In January 2009, the price of coffee (the kind that you get at Starbucks and similar coffee shops called Arabica) was $1.25 a pound (point A in Figure 1) and by May 2011, it had risen to $3.00 a pound (point B). Why did the price of coffee soar? Figure 2, which shows the market for coffee, answers this question.

The demand curve D and the supply curve S_{09} determined the equilibrium price and quantity in 2009 at $1.25 a pound and 950 million pounds.

Heavy rain led to exceptionally low harvests in Colombia, Indonesia, Mexico, and Vietnam, which decreased the supply of coffee. The supply curve shifted leftward to S_{11}. The price increased to $3.00 a pound. The quantity demanded and equilibrium quantity decreased to 800 million pounds.

Figure 1 The price of coffee

Figure 2 The market for coffee

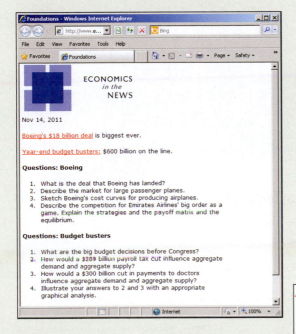

Economics in the News

MyEconLab

To keep you informed about the latest economic news, each day the authors upload two relevant news articles: a microeconomic topic and a macroeconomic topic. Each article includes discussion questions, links to additional online resources, and references to related textbook chapters.

Practice and Learning Aids in MyEconLab

An end-of-chapter problem based on the chapter-opening issue gives students further practice.

All of the Checkpoint problems are in MyEconLab and available for self-assessment or instructor assignment.

Immediate feedback and problem specific learning aids give students support when they need it most.

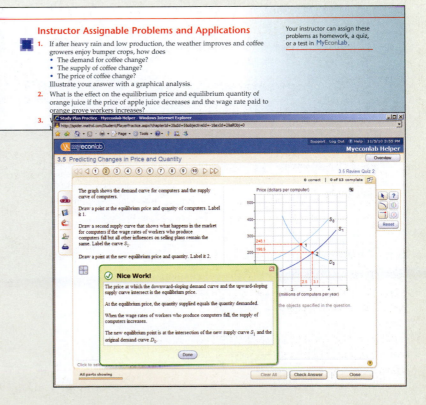

Foundations of
MICROECONOMICS

Robin Bade

Michael Parkin
University of Western Ontario

SIXTH EDITION

PEARSON

Boston   Columbus   Indianapolis   New York   San Francisco   Upper Saddle River
Amsterdam   Cape Town   Dubai   London   Madrid   Milan   Munich   Paris   Montréal   Toronto
Delhi   Mexico City   Sao Paulo   Sydney   Hong Kong   Seoul   Singapore   Taipei   Tokyo

Editor in Chief: Donna Battista
Executive Acquisitions Editor: Adrienne
  D'Ambrosio
Editorial Project Manager: Sarah Dumouchelle
Editorial Assistant: Elissa Senra-Sargent
Executive Marketing Manager: Lori DeShazo
Senior Managing Editor: Nancy Fenton
Production Project Manager: Nancy Freihofer
Media Publisher: Denise Clinton
Content Lead for MyEconLab: Noel Lotz
Senior Media Producer: Melissa Honig

Image Permission Manager: Rachel Youdelman
Photo Researcher: Amy Dunleavy
Art Director, Cover: Jonathan Boylan
Cover Image: Angel_a/Dreamstime.com
Copyeditor: Catherine Baum
Technical Illustrator: Richard Parkin
Project Management, Page Makeup,
  Design: Integra
Printer/Binder: Courier/Kendallville
Cover Printer: Courier/Kendallville
Text Font: 10/12, Palatino-Roman

Credits and acknowledgments borrowed from other sources and reproduced, with permission, in this textbook appear on the appropriate page within text and on pages C-1–C-2.

Library of Congress Cataloging-in-Publication Data

Bade, Robin.
    Foundations of Microeconomics/Robin Bade, Michael Parkin.—6th ed.
      p. cm.
    Includes index.
    ISBN-13: 978-0-13-283088-1
    ISBN-10: 0-13-283088-4
    1. Economics.   I. Parkin, Michael, 1939–   II. Title.
    HB171.5.B155 2013
    330—dc23

                                        2011045330

V011

10 9 8 7 6 5 4 3

ISBN 10:   0-13-283088-4
ISBN 13: 978-0-13-283088-1

To Erin, Tessa, Jack, Abby, and Sophie

About the Authors

Robin Bade was an undergraduate at the University of Queensland, Australia, where she earned degrees in mathematics and economics. After a spell teaching high school math and physics, she enrolled in the Ph.D. program at the Australian National University, from which she graduated in 1970. She has held faculty appointments at the University of Edinburgh in Scotland, at Bond University in Australia, and at the Universities of Manitoba, Toronto, and Western Ontario in Canada. Her research on international capital flows appears in the *International Economic Review* and the *Economic Record*.

Robin first taught the principles of economics course in 1970 and has taught it (alongside intermediate macroeconomics and international trade and finance) most years since then. She developed many of the ideas found in this text while conducting tutorials with her students at the University of Western Ontario.

Michael Parkin studied economics in England and began his university teaching career immediately after graduating with a B.A. from the University of Leicester. He learned the subject on the job at the University of Essex, England's most exciting new university of the 1960s, and at the age of 30 became one of the youngest full professors. He is a past president of the Canadian Economics Association and has served on the editorial boards of the *American Economic Review* and the *Journal of Monetary Economics*. His research on macroeconomics, monetary economics, and international economics has resulted in more than 160 publications in journals and edited volumes, including the *American Economic Review*, the *Journal of Political Economy*, the *Review of Economic Studies*, the *Journal of Monetary Economics*, and the *Journal of Money, Credit, and Banking*. He is author of the best-selling textbook, *Economics* (Addison-Wesley), now in its Ninth Edition.

Robin and Michael are a wife-and-husband team. Their most notable joint research created the Bade-Parkin Index of central bank independence and spawned a vast amount of research on that topic. They don't claim credit for the independence of the new European Central Bank, but its constitution and the movement toward greater independence of central banks around the world were aided by their pioneering work. Their joint textbooks include *Macroeconomics* (Prentice-Hall), *Modern Macroeconomics* (Pearson Education Canada), and *Economics: Canada in the Global Environment*, the Canadian adaptation of Parkin, *Economics* (Addison-Wesley). They are dedicated to the challenge of explaining economics ever more clearly to an ever-growing body of students.

Music, the theater, art, walking on the beach, and five fast-growing grandchildren provide their relaxation and fun.

MICROECONOMICS Brief Contents

Contents

PART 2   A CLOSER LOOK AT MARKETS

PART 3   HOW GOVERNMENTS INFLUENCE THE ECONOMY

PART 4   MARKET FAILURE AND ITS SOLUTIONS

PART 5   A CLOSER LOOK AT DECISION MAKERS

PART 6   PRICES, PROFITS, AND INDUSTRY PERFORMANCE

Preface

Students know that throughout their lives they will make economic decisions and be influenced by economic forces. They want to understand the economic principles that can help them navigate these forces and guide their decisions. *Foundations of Microeconomics* is our attempt to satisfy this want.

The response to our earlier editions from hundreds of colleagues across the United States and throughout the world tells us that most of you agree with our view that to achieve its goals, the principles course must do four things well. It must

- Motivate with compelling issues and questions
- Focus on core ideas
- Steer a path between an overload of detail and too much left unsaid
- Encourage and aid learning by doing

The Foundations icon with its four blocks (on the cover and throughout the book) symbolizes this four-point approach that has guided all our choices in writing this text and creating its comprehensive teaching and learning supplements.

WHAT'S NEW IN THE SIXTH EDITION

The extraordinary events in the U.S. and global economies provide a rich display of economic forces in action through which students can be motivated to discover the economic way of thinking. The global financial crisis, slump, and faltering recovery; headwinds from the European debt crisis; ongoing tensions that result from globalization and international outsourcing; the continued spectacular expansion of China and India in the information-age economy; enhanced concern about the depletion of the world's rainforests and fish stocks; climate change; and the relentless pressure on the federal budget from the demands of an aging population and increased defense and homeland security expenditures; are just a few of these interest-arousing events. All of them feature at the appropriate points in our new edition, and the text and examples are all thoroughly updated to reflect the most recently available data and events.

Every chapter contains many small changes, all designed to enhance clarity and currency. We have also made a few carefully selected major changes that we describe below.

■ New Features

We have simplified the chapter openers to grab student attention and provide instant focus for the chapter. Each chapter opens with a question about a central issue that the chapter addresses and is illustrated with a carefully selected photograph. An *Eye On* box returns to and discusses the question and an end-of-chapter problem, that is also in the MyEconLab Homework and Test Manager, makes the issue available for assignment with automatic grading. This feature enables the student to get the point of the chapter quickly; ties the chapter together; and enables the instructor to focus on a core issue in class and for practice.

The Chapter Checkpoint (the last three pages of each chapter) has been thoroughly revised. The first page contains problems and applications for the student to work, which are replicated in the MyEconLab Study Plan. The second page contains problems and applications for the instructor to assign for homework, quiz, or test. Many of these problems and applications are new to the sixth edtion and include mini case studies from recent news stories. The third page contains a short multiple choice quiz. This quiz, also available in MyEconLab for student practice, hits the high points of the chapter and enables students to test themselves on the types of questions they are likely to encounter on tests and exams.

The Checkpoints at the end of each major section of a chapter have been reorganized to separate practice with basic analysis and "In the News" applications. Worked solutions are provided for both types of questions.

■ Major Content Changes in Introductory Chapters

You're in school! Did you make the right decision? Who makes the iPhone? Is wind power free? Why did the price of coffee soar in 2010 and 2011? These are the questions that motivate the four introductory chapters.

We reworked Chapter 1 to strengthen the explanation and illustration of the economic way of thinking by placing the student center stage and focusing on the decision to remain in school or get a full-time job. Our goal is to engage the student from the outset of the course, grab attention, and show the relevance of economics and its place in everyday life. We also revised and improved our explanation of the scientific method in economics.

Chapter 3 has a more gradual and fully illustrated explanation of the mutual gains from trade arising from comparative advantage and a new *Eye On* box on the power of specialization and trade through the classic story of the production of the pencil.

■ Major Content Changes in Micro Chapters

What do you do when the price of gasoline rises? Should price gouging be illegal? Can the President repeal the laws of supply and demand? Does Congress decide who pays the taxes? Who wins and who loses from globalization? How can we limit climate change? Should America build a high-speed rail network like Europe's? How do you avoid buying a lemon? How much would you pay for a song? Which store has the lower costs: Wal-Mart or 7-Eleven? Why did GM fail? Are Microsoft's prices too high? Which cell phone? Is two too few? Why is a coach worth $6 million? Who are the rich and the poor? These are the motivating questions and features of *Eye On* boxes and end-of chapter problems in the 16 micro chapters.

Overall, these chapters have been well-received and positively reviewed, so for the most part we have limited our changes to refinements and updating data and examples. Beyond these many smaller innovations, we have made two larger structural changes.

The first of these is a reorganization of the chapters that deal with externalities, public goods, and common resources. In the fifth edition, we covered public goods and positive externalities on one chapter and negative externalities and common resources in another. In the sixth edition, we have reverted to our earlier organization of this material. Chapter 10 explains all types of externalities. It explains negative externalities, illustrated with pollution, and positive externalities, illustrated with knowledge (education and research). A new *Eye On* features Caroline Hoxby's research on charter schools and vouchers. Chapter 11 covers public goods and common resources and uses Obama's wish to create a high-speed rail network similar to Europe's to illustrate the efficient and inefficient provision of a public good. The analysis of common resources treats the tragedy of the commons as a type of externality problem.

The second major change in the micro chapters is an entirely new Chapter 12 "Markets with Private Information." This chapter explains the lemons problem and its solutions and the problems that arise from asymmetric information in insurance and health-care markets. A section of this new chapter is devoted to health care and the challenges that arise from asymmetric information, missing insurance markets, and public health externalities. The U.S. health-care market is compared with those in other countries and Laurence Kotlikoff's voucher-based "Medicare Part C for All" is described.

THE FOUNDATIONS VISION

■ Focus on Core Concepts

Each chapter of *Foundations* concentrates on a manageable number of main ideas (most commonly three or four) and reinforces each idea several times throughout the chapter. This patient, confidence-building approach guides students through unfamiliar terrain and helps them to focus their efforts on the most important tools and concepts of our discipline.

■ Many Learning Tools for Many Learning Styles

Foundations' integrated print and electronic package builds on the basic fact that students have a variety of learning styles. In MyEconLab, students have a powerful tool at their fingertips: They can complete all Checkpoint problems online and get instant feedback, work interactive graphs, assess their skills by taking Practice Tests, and receive a personalized Study Plan, and step-by-by help through the feature called "Help Me Solve This."

■ Diagrams That Tell the Whole Story

We developed the style of our diagrams with extensive feedback from faculty focus group participants and student reviewers. All of our figures make consistent use of color to show the direction of shifts and contain detailed, numbered captions designed to direct students' attention step-by-step through the action.

Because beginning students of economics are often apprehensive about working with graphs, we have made a special effort to present material in as many as three ways—with graphs, words, and tables—in the same figure. In an innovation that seems necessary, but is to our knowledge unmatched, nearly all of the information supporting a figure appears on the same page as the figure itself. No more flipping pages back and forth!

■ Real-World Connections That Bring Theory to Life

Students learn best when they can see the purpose of what they are studying, apply it to illuminate the world around them, and use it in their lives.

Eye On boxes offer fresh new examples to help students see that economics is everywhere. Current and recent events appear in *Eye On the U.S. Economy* boxes; we place current U.S. economic events in global and historical perspectives in our *Eye on the Global Economy* and *Eye on the Past* boxes; and we show how students can use economics in day-to-day decisions in *Eye On Your Life* boxes.

The *Eye On* boxes that build off of the chapter-opening question help students see the economics behind key issues facing our world and highlight a major aspect of the chapter's story.

ORGANIZATION

We have organized the sequence of material and chapters in what we think is the most natural order in which to cover the material. But we recognize that there are alternative views on the best order. We have kept this fact and the need for flexibility firmly in mind throughout the text. Many alternative sequences work, and the Flexibility Chart on p. xxxiii explains the alternative pathways through the chapters. In using the flexibility information, keep in mind that the best sequence is the one in which we present the material. And even chapters that the flexibility chart identifies as strictly optional are better covered than omitted.

MYECONLAB   MyEconLab

MyEconLab has been designed and refined with a single purpose in mind: to create those moments of understanding that transform the difficult into the clear and obvious. With comprehensive homework, quiz, test, and tutorial options, instructors can manage all their assessment needs in one program.

- All of the Checkpoint and Chapter Checkpoint Problems and Applications are assignable and automatically graded in MyEconLab.
- Extra problems and applications, including algorithmic, draw-graph, and numerical exercises are available for student practice or instructor assignment.
- Test Item File questions are available for assignment as homework.
- Custom Exercise Builder gives instructors the flexibility of creating their own problems for assignment.
- Gradebook records each student's performance and time spent on the Tests and Study Plan and generates reports by student or by chapter.

Experiments in MyEconLab   Experiments are a fun and engaging way to promote active learning and mastery of important economic concepts. Pearson's Experiments program is flexible and easy for instructors and students to use.

- Single-player experiments allow your students to play against virtual players from anywhere at anytime so long as they have an internet connection.
- Multiplayer experiments allow you to assign and manage a real-time experiment with your class.
- Pre and post-questions for each experiment are available for assignment in MyEconLab.

    For a complete list of available experiments, visit www.myeconlab.com

Economics in the News   Economics in the News is a turn-key solution to bringing daily news into the classroom. Updated daily during the academic year, the authors upload a relevant article and provide discussion questions.

Videos   A comprehensive suite of ABC news videos, which address current topics such as education and energy, is available for classroom use. Video-specific exercises are available for instructor assignment.

AACSB and Learning Outcomes   All end-of-chapter and Test Item File questions are tagged in two ways: to AACSB standards and to discipline-specific Learning Outcomes. These two separate tagging systems allow professors to build assessments around desired departmental and course outcomes and track results in MyEconLab's gradebook.

   We are the authors of the MyEconLab content for *Foundations of Microeconomics* and have worked hard to ensure that it is tightly integrated with the book's content and vision. For more information, visit the online demonstration at www.myeconlab.com.

MyEconLab Also Includes

- Enhanced Pearson eText, available within the online course materials and offline via an iPad app, allows instructors and students to highlight, bookmark, and take notes.
- Advanced Communication Tools enable students and instructors communication through email, discussion board, chat, and ClassLive.
- Customization options provide new and enhanced ways to share documents, add content, and rename menu items.
- Prebuilt courses offer a turn-key way for instructors to create a course that includes pre-built assignments distributed by chapter.
- Temporary Access for students who are awaiting financial aid provides a seventeen-day grace period of temporary access.
- One Place for students to access all their MyLab Courses. Students and instructors can register, create, and access all of their courses, regardless of discipline, from one convenient online location: www.pearsonmylab.com.

SUPPORT MATERIALS FOR INSTRUCTORS AND STUDENTS

Foundations of Microeconomics is accompanied by the most comprehensive set of teaching and learning tools ever assembled. Each component of our package is organized by Checkpoint topic for a tight, seamless integration with both the textbook and the other components. In addition to authoring the MyEconLab and PowerPoint content, we have helped in the reviewing and revising of the Study Guide, Solutions Manual, Instructor's Manual, and Test Item Files to ensure that every element of the package achieves the consistency that students and teachers need.

■ Study Guide

Mark Rush of the University of Florida has prepared the Study Guide, which is available in both print and electronic formats in MyEconLab. It provides an expanded Chapter Checklist that enables the student to break the learning tasks down into smaller, bite-sized pieces; self-test materials; and additional practice problems. The Study Guide has been carefully coordinated with the text, MyEconLab, and the Test Item Files.

■ Solutions Manual

The Solutions Manual, written by Mark Rush, and checked for accuracy by Jeannie Gillmore, contains the solutions to all the Checkpoint Practice Problems and Chapter Checkpoint Problems and Applications. It is available for download in Word and PDF formats.

■ Instructor's Manual

The Instructor's Manual, written by Luke Armstrong and edited by Mark Rush, contains chapter outlines and road maps, additional exercises with solutions, a comprehensive Chapter Lecture resource, and a virtual encyclopedia of suggestions on how to enrich class presentation and use class time efficiently. Both the micro and macro portions have been updated to reflect changes in the main text as well as infused with a fresh and intuitive approach to teaching this course. It is available for download in Word and PDF formats.

■ Three Test Item Files and TestGen

More than 6,000 multiple-choice, numerical, fill-in-the-blank, short answer, essay, and integrative questions make up the three Test Item Files that support *Foundations of Microeconomics*. Mark Rush reviewed and edited questions from three dedicated principles instructors to form one of the most comprehensive testing systems on the market. Our authors are Carol Dole (Jacksonville University); Luke Armstrong (Lee College); and Fola Odebunmi (Cypress College). The entire set of questions is available for download in Word, PDF, and TestGen formats.

All three Test Item Files are available in test generator software (TestGen with QuizMaster). TestGen's graphical interface enables instructors to view, edit, and add questions; transfer questions to tests; and print different forms of tests. Instructors also have the option to reformat tests with varying fonts and styles, margins, and headers and footers, as in any word-processing document. Search and sort features let the instructor quickly locate questions and arrange them in a preferred order. QuizMaster, working with your school's computer network, automatically grades the exams, stores the results on disk, and allows the instructor to view and print a variety of reports.

■ PowerPoint Resources

We have created the PowerPoint resources based on our 20 years of experience using this tool in our own classrooms. Six sets of PowerPoint presentations are available:

- Lecture notes with full-color, animated figures, and tables from the textbook
- Figures and tables from the textbook, animated with step-by-step walk-through for instructors to use in their own personal slides.
- Eye On features
- Checkpoint Practice Problems and solutions
- Alternative lecture notes with full-color, animated figures and tables that use examples different from those in the textbook
- Clicker-enabled slides for your Personal Response System. The slides consist of 10 multiple choice questions from the Study Guide for each chapter. You can use these in class to encourage active learning.

■ Instructor's Resource Disk

This disk contains the Instructor's Manual, Solutions Manual, and Test Item Files in Word and PDF formats. It also contains the Computerized Test Item Files (with a TestGen program installer) and Powerpoint resources. It is compatible with both Windows and Macintosh operating systems.

For your convenience, all instructor resources are also available online via our centralized supplements Web site, the Instructor Resource Center (www.pearsonhighered.com/irc). For access or more information, contact your local Pearson representative or request access online at the Instructor Resource Center.

ACKNOWLEDGMENTS

Working on a project such as this one generates many debts that can never be repaid. But they can be acknowledged, and it is a special pleasure to be able to do so here and to express our heartfelt thanks to each and every one of the following long list, without whose contributions we could not have produced *Foundations.*

Mark Rush again coordinated, managed, and contributed to our Study Guide, Solutions Manual, Instructor's Manual, and Test Item Files. He assembled, polished, wrote, and rewrote these materials to ensure their close consistency with the text. He and we were in constant contact as all the elements of our text and package came together. Mark also made many valuable suggestions for improving the text and the Checkpoint Problems. His contribution went well beyond that of a reviewer, and his effervescent sense of humor kept us all in good spirits along the way.

Working closely with Mark, Luke Armstrong wrote content for the Instructor's Manual. Carol Dole, Luke Armstrong, and Fola Odebunmi authored new questions for the Test Item Files.

The ideas that ultimately became *Foundations* began to form over dinner at the Andover Inn in Andover, Massachusetts, with Denise Clinton and Sylvia Mallory. We gratefully acknowledge Sylvia's role not only at the birth of this project but also in managing its initial development team. Denise has been our ongoing inspiration for more than 10 years. She is the most knowledgeable economics editor in the business, and we are privileged to have the benefit of her enormous experience.

The success of *Foundations* owes much to its outstanding Sponsoring Editor, Adrienne D'Ambrosio. Adrienne's acute intelligence and sensitive understanding of the market have helped sharpen our vision of this text and package. Her value-added on this project is huge. It has been, and we hope it will for many future editions remain, a joy to work with her.

Sarah Dumouchelle, Project Manager, and Elissa Senra-Sargent, Editorial Assistant, ensured that we were provided with outstanding and timely reviews and gave our draft chapters a careful and helpful read and edit.

Jonathan Boylan created the new impressive cover design and converted the raw ideas of our brainstorms into an outstandingly designed text.

Susan Schoenberg, Media Director, Denise Clinton, Media Publisher, Melissa Honig, Senior Media Producer, and Noel Lotz, MyEconLab Content Lead have set a new standard for online learning and teaching resources. Building on the pioneering work of Michelle Neil, Susan worked creatively to improve our technology systems. Melissa managed the building of MyEconLab, and Noel provided reviews of the content. They have all been sources of high energy, good sense, and level-headed advice and quickly found creative solutions to all our technology problems.

Nancy Freihofer, our outstanding, ever calm, Project Manager, worked with a talented team at Integra, Project Editor, Heather Johnson, and designer, art coordinator, and typesetter. Our copy editor, Catherine Baum, gave our work a thorough review and helpful polish, and our proofreader ensured the most error-free text we have yet produced.

Our Executive Marketing Manager, Lori DeShazo, has been a constant source of good judgment and sound advice on content and design issues, ranging over the entire package from text to print and electronic supplements. Dave Theisen reviewed our previous edition and gave excellent advice (much of which we have taken) on areas that needed adjusting to achieve the clarity that we seek.

Richard Parkin, our technical illustrator, created the figures in the text, the dynamic figures in the eText, and the animated figures in the PowerPoint presentations and contributed many ideas to improve the clarity of our illustrations. Laurel Davies provided painstakingly careful work on MyEconLab questions and acted as one of its accuracy checkers.

Jeannie Gillmore, our personal assistant, worked closely with us in creating MyEconLab exercises and guided solutions.

Finally, our reviewers, whose names appear on the following pages, have made an enormous contribution to this text and MyEconLab resources. Once again we find ourselves using superlatives, but they are called for. In the many texts that we've written, we've not seen reviewing of the quality that we enjoyed on this revision. It has been a pleasure (if at times a challenge) to respond constructively to their many excellent suggestions.

Robin Bade
Michael Parkin
London, Ontario, Canada
robin@econ100.com
michael.parkin@uwo.ca

FOUNDATIONS OF ECONOMICS: FLEXIBILITY CHART

Micro Flexibility

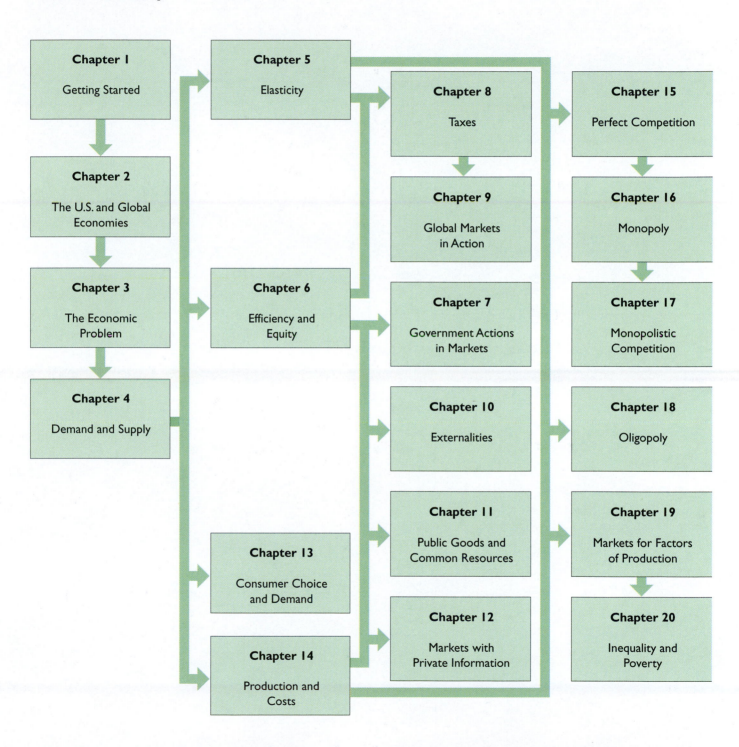

Start here ...   **... then jump to**   **... and jump to any of these after**
          any of these ...   **doing the pre-requisites indicated**

Reviewers

Alfredo A. Romero Aguirre, North Carolina A&T State University

Seemi Ahmad, Dutchess Community College

William Aldridge, Shelton State Community College

Rashid B. Al-Hmoud, Texas Tech University

Neil Alper, Northeastern University

Nejat Anbarci, Deakin University

J.J. Arias, Georgia College & State University

Luke A. Armstrong, Lee College

Leland Ash, Skagit Valley College

Ali Ataiifar, Delaware County Community College

John Baffoe-Bonnie, Pennsylvania State University, Delaware County Campus

A. Paul Ballantyne, University of Colorado

Tyra D. Barrett, Pellissippi State Community College

Sue Bartlett, University of South Florida

Klaus Becker, Texas Tech University

Clive Belfield, Queen's College, City University of New York

William K. Bellinger, Dickinson College

John Bethune, Barton College

Gautam Bhattacharya, University of Kansas

Gerald W. Bialka, University of North Florida

David Bivin, Indiana University–Purdue University at Indianapolis

Geoffrey Black, Boise State University

Carey Anne Borkoski, Arundel Community College

Jurgen Brauer, Augusta State University

Greg Brock, Georgia Southern University

Barbara Brogan, Northern Virginia Community College

Bruce C. Brown, California State Polytechnic University, Pomona

Christopher Brown, Arkansas State University

James O. Brown, Delta State University

Brian Buckley, Clemson University

Donald Bumpass, Sam Houston State University

Seewoonundun Bunjun, East Stroudsburg University

Nancy Burnett, University of Wisconsin at Oshkosh

James L. Butkiewicz, University of Delaware

Barbara Caldwell, Saint Leo University

Bruce Caldwell, University of North Carolina, Greensboro

Joseph Calhoun, Florida State University

Robert Carlsson, University of South Carolina

Shawn Carter, Jacksonville State University

Regina Cassady, Valencia Community College

Jack Chambless, Valencia Community College

Joni Charles, Southwest Texas State University

Anoshua Chaudhuri, San Francisco State University

Robert Cherry, Brooklyn College

Chi-Young Choi, University of New Hampshire

Paul Cichello, Xavier University

Quentin Ciolfi, Brevard Community College

Victor V. Claar, Henderson State University

Jim Cobbe, Florida State University

John Cochran, University of Chicago

Mike Cohick, Collin County Community College

Ludovic Comeau, De Paul University

Carol Conrad, Cerro Coso Community College

Christopher Cornell, Vassar College

Richard Cornwall, University of California, Davis

Kevin Cotter, Wayne State University

Erik Craft, University of Richmond

Tom Creahan, Morehead State University

Elizabeth Crowell, University of Michigan at Dearborn

Susan Dadres, Southern Methodist University

David Davenport, McLennan Community College

Troy Davig, College of William and Mary

Jeffrey Davis, ITT Technical Institute (Utah)

Lewis Davis, Union College

Dennis Debrecht, Carroll College

Al DeCooke, Broward Community College

Vince DiMartino, University of Texas at San Antonio

Vernon J. Dobis, Minnesota State University–Moorhead

Carol Dole, Jacksonville University

Kathleen Dorsainvil, American University

John Dorsey, University of Maryland, College Park

Amrik Singh Dua, Mt. San Antonio College

Marie Duggan, Keene State College

Allen Dupont, North Carolina State University

David Eaton, Murray State University

Kevin J. Egan, University of Toledo

Harold W. Elder, University of Alabama

Harry Ellis, University of North Texas

Stephen Ellis, North Central Texas College

Carl Enomoto, New Mexico State University

Chuen-mei Fan, Colorado State University

Elena Ermolenko Fein, Oakton Community College

Gary Ferrier, University of Arkansas

Rudy Fichtenbaum, Wright State University

Donna K. Fisher, Georgia Southern University

Kaya Ford, Northern Virginia Community College

Robert Francis, Shoreline Community College

Roger Frantz, San Diego State University

Amanda S. Freeman, Kansas State University

Marc Fusaro, East Carolina University

Arthur Friedberg, Mohawk Valley Community College

Julie Gallaway, Southwest Missouri State University

Byron Gangnes, University of Hawaii

Gay GareschÈ, Glendale Community College

Neil Garston, California State University, Los Angeles

Lisa Geib-Gunderson, University of Maryland

Lisa M. George, City University of New York

Linda Ghent, Eastern Illinois University

Soma Ghosh, Bridgewater State College

Kirk Gifford, Ricks College

Scott Gilbert, Southern Illinois University

Maria Giuili, Diablo Valley Community College

Mark Gius, Quinnipiac College

Randall Glover, Brevard Community College

Stephan Gohmann, University of Louisville

Richard Gosselin, Houston Community College

John Graham, Rutgers University

Patricia E. Graham, University of Northern Colorado

Warren Graham, Tulsa Community College

Homer Guevara, Jr., Northwest Vista College

Osman Gulseven, North Carolina State University

Jang-Ting Guo, University of California, Riverside

Dennis Hammett, University of Texas at El Paso

Leo Hardwick, Macomb Community College

Mehdi Haririan, Bloomsburg University

Paul Harris, Camden County Community College

Mark Healy, William Rainey Harper College

Rey Hernandez-Julian, Metropolitan State College of Denver

Gus Herring, Brookhaven College

Michael Heslop, Northern Virginia Community College

Steven Hickerson, Mankato State University

Frederick Steb Hipple, East Tennessee State University

Lee Hoke, University of Tampa

Andy Howard, Rio Hondo College

Yu Hsing, Southeastern Louisiana University

Greg Hunter, California State Polytechnic University, Pomona

Matthew Hyle, Winona State University

Todd Idson, Boston University

Harvey James, University of Hartford

Russell Janis, University of Massachusetts at Amherst

Ricot Jean, Valencia College

Jay A. Johnson, Southeastern Louisiana University

Ted Joyce, City University of New York, Baruch College

Jonathan D. Kaplan, California State University, Sacramento

Arthur Kartman, San Diego State University

Chris Kauffman, University of Tennessee

Diane Keenan, Cerritos College

Brian Kench, University of Tampa

John Keith, Utah State University

Kristen Keith, University of Toledo

Joe Kerkvliet, Oregon State University

Randall Kesselring, Arkansas State University

Gary Kikuchi, University of Hawaii at Manoa

Douglas Kinnear, Colorado State University

Morris Knapp, Miami Dade Community College

Steven Koch, Georgia Southern University

Kate Krause, University of New Mexico

Stephan Kroll, California State University, Sacramento

Joyce Lapping, University of Southern Maine

Tom Larson, California State University, Los Angeles

Robert Lemke, Florida International University

J. Mark Leonard, University of Nebraska at Omaha

Tony Lima, California State University, Hayward

Joshua Long, Ivy Tech Community College

Kenneth Long, New River Community College

Noel Lotz, Middle Tennessee State University

Marty Ludlum, Oklahoma City Community College

Brian Lynch, Lake Land College

Michael Machiorlatti, Oklahoma City Community College

Roger Mack, De Anza College

Michael Magura, University of Toledo

Mark Maier, Glendale College

Svitlana Maksymenko, University of Pittsburgh

Paula Manns, Atlantic Cape Community College

Dan Marburger, Arkansas State University

Kathryn Marshall, Ohio State University

John V. Martin, Boise State University

Drew E. Mattson, Anoka-Ramsey Community College

Stephen McCafferty, Ohio State University

Thomas S. McCaleb, Florida State University

Katherine S. McCann, University of Delaware

William McLean, Oklahoma State University

Diego Mendez-Carbajo, Illinois Wesleyan University

Evelina Mengova, California State University, Fullerton

Thomas Meyer, Patrick Henry Community College

Meghan Millea, Mississippi State University

Michael Milligan, Front Range Community College

Jenny Minier, University of Miami

David Mitchell, Valdosta State University

Dr. Carl B. Montano, Lamar University

Christine Moser, Western Michigan University

William Mosher, Clark University

Mike Munoz, Northwest Vista College

John R. Mundy, St. Johns River State College

Kevin Murphy, Oakland University

Ronald Nate, Brigham Young University, Idaho

Nasrin Nazemzadeh, Rowan Cabarrus Community College

Michael Nelson, Texas A&M University

Rebecca Neumann, University of Wisconsin—Milwaukee

Charles Newton, Houston Community College Southwest

Melinda Nish, Salt Lake Community College

Lee Nordgren, Indiana University at Bloomington

Norman P. Obst, Michigan State University

Inge O'Connor, Syracuse University

William C. O'Connor, Western Montana College–University of Montana

Fola Odebunmi, Cypress College

Victor I. Oguledo, Florida A&M University

Charles Okeke, College of Southern Nevada

Lydia M. Ortega, St. Philip's College

P. Marcelo Oviedo, Iowa State University

Jennifer Pate, Ph.D., Loyola Marymount University

Sanjay Paul, Elizabethtown College

Ken Peterson, Furman University

Tim Petry, North Dakota State University

Charles Pflanz, Scottsdale Community College

Jonathon Phillips, North Carolina State University

Basharat Pitafi, Southern Illinois University

Anthony Plunkett, Harrison College

Paul Poast, Ohio State University

Greg Pratt, Mesa Community College

Fernando Quijano, Dickinson State University

Andy Radler, Butte Community College

Ratha Ramoo, Diablo Valley College

Karen Reid, University of Wisconsin, Parkside

Mary Rigdon, University of Texas, Austin

Helen Roberts, University of Illinois at Chicago

Greg Rose, Sacramento City College

Barbara Ross, Kapi'olani Community College

Elham Rouhani, Gwinnett Technical College

Jeffrey Rous, University of North Texas

June Roux, Salem Community College

Udayan Roy, Long Island University

Nancy C. Rumore, University of Louisiana–Lafayette

Mark Rush, University of Florida

Joseph Santos, South Dakota State University

Roland Santos, Lakeland Community College

Mark Scanlan, Stephen F. Austin State University

Ted Scheinman, Mount Hood Community College

Buffie Schmidt, Augusta State University

Jerry Schwartz, Broward Community College

Gautam Sethi, Bard College

Margaret Anne Shannon, Georgia Southern University

Mushtaq Sheikh, Union County College

Michelle Sheran-Andrews, University of North Carolina at Greensboro

Virginia Shingleton, Valparaiso University

Steven S. Shwiff, Texas A & M University—Commerce

Charles Sicotte, Rock Valley College

Issoufou Soumaila, Texas Tech University

Martin Spechler, Indiana University

Leticia Starkov, Elgin Community College

Stela Stefanova, University of Delaware

John Stiver, University of Connecticut

Richard W. Stratton, The University of Akron

Terry Sutton, Southeast Missouri State University

Janet M. Thomas, Bentley College

Donna Thompson, Brookdale Community College

Deborah Thorsen, Palm Beach State College

James Thorson, Southern Connecticut State University

Marc Tomljanovich, Colgate University

Cynthia Royal Tori, Valdosta State University

Ngoc-Bich Tran, San Jacinto College South

Nora Underwood, University of California, Davis

Jogindar S. Uppal, State University of New York

Va Nee L. Van Vleck, California State University, Fresno

Victoria Vernon, Empire State College / SUNY

Christian Weber, Seattle University

Ethel Weeks, Nassau Community College

Jack Wegman, Santa Rosa Junior College

Jason White, Northwest Missouri State University

Benjamin Widner, Colorado State University

Barbara Wiens-Tuers, Pennsylvania State University, Altoona

Katherine Wolfe, University of Pittsburgh

Kristen Wolfe, St. Johns River State College

William Wood, James Madison University

Ben Young, University of Missouri, Kansas City

Michael Youngblood, Rock Valley College

Bassam Yousif, Indiana State University

Sourushe Zandvakili, University of Cincinnati

Inske Zandvliet, Brookhaven College

Joachim Zietz, Middle Tennessee State University

David W. Zirkle, University of Virginia; Virginia Commonwealth University

Armand Zottola, Central Connecticut State University

You're in school!
Did you make the right decision?

1

Getting Started

When you have completed your study of this chapter, you will be able to

CHAPTER CHECKLIST

1 Define economics and explain the kinds of questions that economists try to answer.

2 Explain the ideas that define the economic way of thinking.

1.1 DEFINITION AND QUESTIONS

We all want more than we can get. We want good health and long lives. We want spacious and comfortable homes. We want running shoes and jet skis. We want the time to enjoy our favorite sports, video games, novels, music, and movies; to travel to exotic places; and just to hang out with friends. Human wants exceed the resources available to satisfy them, and this fact is the source of all economic questions and problems.

■ Scarcity

Our inability to satisfy all our wants is called **scarcity**. The ability of each of us to satisfy our wants is limited by the time we have, the incomes we earn, and the prices we pay for the things we buy. These limits mean that everyone has unsatisfied wants. The ability of all of us as a society to satisfy our wants is limited by the productive resources that exist. These resources include the gifts of nature, our labor and ingenuity, and the tools and equipment that we have made.

Everyone, poor and rich alike, faces scarcity. A student wants Beyonce's latest album and a paperback but has only $10.00 in his pocket. He faces scarcity. Brad Pitt wants to spend a week in New Orleans discussing plans for his new eco-friendly housing and he also wants to spend the week promoting his new movie. He faces scarcity. The U.S. government wants to increase defense spending and cut taxes. It faces scarcity. An entire society wants improved health care, an Internet connection in every classroom, an ambitious space exploration program, clean lakes and rivers, and so on. Society faces scarcity.

Faced with scarcity, we must make choices. We must choose among the available alternatives. The student must choose the album or the paperback. Brad Pitt must choose New Orleans or promoting his new movie. The government must choose defense or tax cuts. And society must choose among health care, computers, space exploration, the environment, and so on. Even parrots face scarcity!

■ Economics Defined

Economics is the social science that studies the choices that individuals, businesses, governments, and entire societies make as they cope with *scarcity*, the *incentives* that influence those choices, and the arrangements that coordinate them.

The subject has two broad parts:

- Microeconomics, and
- Macroeconomics

Microeconomics

Microeconomics is the study of the choices that individuals and businesses make and the way these choices interact and are influenced by governments. Some examples of microeconomic questions are: Will you buy a 3-D television or a standard one? Will Nintendo sell more units of Wii if it cuts the price? Will a cut in the income tax rate encourage people to work longer hours? Will a hike in the gas tax encourage more people to drive hybrid or smaller automobiles? Are MP3 downloads killing CDs?

Scarcity
The condition that arises because wants exceed the ability of resources to satisfy them.

Not only do I want a cracker—we all want a cracker!

© The New Yorker Collection 1985 Frank Modell from cartoonbank.com. All Rights Reserved.

Economics
The social science that studies the choices that individuals, businesses, governments, and entire societies make as they cope with *scarcity*, the *incentives* that influence those choices, and the arrangements that coordinate them.

Microeconomics
The study of the choices that individuals and businesses make and the way these choices interact and are influenced by governments.

Macroeconomics

Macroeconomics is the study of the aggregate (or total) effects on the national economy and the global economy of the choices that individuals, businesses, and governments make. Some examples of macroeconomic questions are: Why did production and jobs expand slowly in the United States during 2010 and 2011? Why are incomes growing much faster in China and India than in the United States? Why are production and incomes stagnating in Japan? Why are Americans borrowing more than $2 billion a day from the rest of the world?

Macroeconomics
The study of the aggregate (or total) effects on the national economy and the global economy of the choices that individuals, businesses, and governments make.

Two big questions provide a useful summary of the scope of economics:

- How do choices end up determining *what, how,* and *for whom* goods and services get produced?
- When do choices made in the pursuit of *self-interest* also promote the *social interest*?

■ What, How, and For Whom?

Goods and services are the objects and actions that people value and produce to satisfy human wants. Goods are *objects* that satisfy wants. Running shoes and ketchup are examples. Services are *actions* that satisfy wants. Haircuts and rock concerts are examples. We produce a dazzling array of goods and services that range from necessities such as food, houses, and health care to leisure items such as Blu-ray players and roller coaster rides.

Goods and services
The objects (goods) and the actions (services) that people value and produce to satisfy human wants.

What?

What determines the quantities of corn we grow, homes we build, and health-care services we produce? Sixty years ago, 25 percent of Americans worked on a farm. That number has shrunk to less than 3 percent today. Over the same period, the number of people who produce goods—in mining, construction, and manufacturing—has also shrunk, from 30 percent to 20 percent. The decrease in farming and the production of goods is matched by an increase in the production of services. How will these quantities change in the future as ongoing changes in technology make an ever-wider array of goods and services available to us?

How?

How are goods and services produced? In a vineyard in France, basket-carrying workers pick the annual grape crop by hand. In a vineyard in California, a huge machine and a few workers do the same job that a hundred grape pickers in France do. Look around you and you will see many examples of this phenomenon—the same job being done in different ways. In some stores, checkout clerks key in prices. In others, they use a laser scanner. One farmer keeps track of his livestock feeding schedules and inventories by using paper-and-pencil records, while another uses a computer. GM hires workers to weld auto bodies in some of its plants and uses robots to do the job in others.

Why do we use machines in some cases and people in others? Do mechanization and technological change destroy more jobs than they create? Do they make us better off or worse off?

In a California vineyard a machine and a few workers do the same job as a hundred grape pickers in France.

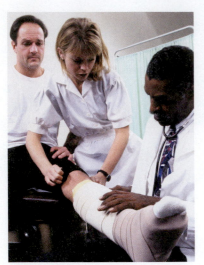

A doctor gets more of the goods and services produced than a nurse or a medical assistant gets.

For Whom?

For whom are goods and services produced? The answer to this question depends on the incomes that people earn and the prices they pay for the goods and services they buy. At given prices, a person who has a high income is able to buy more goods and services than a person who has a low income. Doctors earn much higher incomes than do nurses and medical assistants, so doctors get more of the goods and services produced than nurses and medical assistants get.

You probably know about many other persistent differences in incomes. Men, on average, earn more than women. Whites, on average, earn more than minorities. College graduates, on average, earn more than high school graduates. Americans, on the average, earn more than Europeans, who in turn earn more, on average, than Asians and Africans. But there are some significant exceptions. The people of Japan and Hong Kong now earn an average income similar to that of Americans. And there is a lot of income inequality throughout the world.

What determines the incomes we earn? Why do doctors earn larger incomes than nurses? Why do men earn more, on average, than women? Why do college graduates earn more, on average, than high school graduates? Why do Americans earn more, on average, than Africans?

Economics explains how the choices that individuals, businesses, and governments make and the interactions of those choices end up determining *what*, *how*, and *for whom* goods and services get produced. In answering these questions, we have a deeper agenda in mind. We're not interested in just knowing how many Blu-ray players get produced, how they get produced, and who gets to enjoy them. We ultimately want to know the answer to the second big economic question that we'll now explore.

◼ When Is the Pursuit of Self-Interest in the Social Interest?

Every day, you and 311 million other Americans, along with 7 billion people in the rest of the world, make economic choices that result in *"what," "how,"* and *"for whom"* goods and services are produced.

Are the goods and services produced, and the quantities in which they are produced, the right ones? Do the scarce resources get used in the best possible way? Do the goods and services that we produce go to the people who benefit most from them?

Self-Interest and the Social Interest

Self-interest
The choices that are best for the individual who makes them.

Social interest
The choices that are best for society as a whole.

Choices that are the best for the individual who makes them are choices made in the pursuit of **self-interest**. Choices that are the best for society as a whole are said to be in the **social interest**. The social interest has two dimensions: *efficiency* and *equity.* We'll explore these concepts in later chapters. For now, think of efficiency as being achieved by baking the biggest possible pie, and think of equity as being achieved by sharing the pie in the fairest possible way.

You know that your own choices are the best ones for you—or at least you *think* they're the best at the time that you make them. You use your time and other resources in the way that makes most sense to you. But you don't think much about how your choices affect other people. You order a home delivery pizza because you're hungry and want to eat. You don't order it thinking that the delivery person or the cook needs an income. You make choices that are in your self-interest—choices that you think are best for you.

When you act on your economic decisions, you come into contact with thousands of other people who produce and deliver the goods and services that you decide to buy or who buy the things that you sell. These people have made their own decisions—what to produce and how to produce it, whom to hire or whom to work for, and so on.

Like you, everyone else makes choices that they think are best for them. When the pizza delivery person shows up at your home, he's not doing you a favor. He's earning his income and hoping for a good tip.

Could it be possible that when each one of us makes choices that are in our own best interest—our self-interest—it turns out that these choices are also the best for society as a whole—in the social interest?

Much of the rest of this book helps you to learn what economists know about this question and its answer. To help you start thinking about the question, we're going to illustrate it with four topics that generate heated discussion in today's world. You're already at least a little bit familiar with each one of them. They are

- Globalization
- The Information Age
- Climate change
- A Social Security time bomb

Globalization

Globalization—the expansion of international trade and the production of components and services by firms in other countries—has been going on for centuries. But in recent years, its pace accelerated. Microchips, satellites, and fiber-optic cables have lowered the cost of communication. A video-conference of people who live 10,000 miles apart has become an everyday and easily affordable event.

This explosion of communication has globalized production decisions. When Nike produces more sports shoes, people in Malaysia get more work. When Steven Spielberg wants an animation sequence for a new movie, programmers in New Zealand write the code. And when China Airlines wants a new airplane, Americans who work for Boeing build it.

Globalization is bringing rapid income growth, especially in Asia. China, already the world's second largest economy, will become the largest in the 2020s.

But globalization is leaving some people behind. Jobs in manufacturing and routine services are shrinking in the United States and Europe. And the nations of Africa and parts of South America are not sharing in the prosperity that globalization is bringing to other parts of the world.

Workers in Asia make our shoes.

The owners of multinational firms benefit from lower production costs and consumers benefit from low-cost imported goods. But don't displaced American workers lose? And doesn't even the worker in Malaysia, who sews your new shoes for a few cents an hour, also lose? Is globalization in the social interest, or does globalization just benefit some at the expense of others?

The Information Age

We are living at a time of extraordinary economic change that has been called the *Information Revolution*. This name suggests a parallel with the *Industrial Revolution* that occurred around 1800 and the *Agricultural Revolution* of 12,000 years ago.

The changes that occurred during the last 25 years were based on one major technology: the microprocessor or computer chip. The spin-offs from faster and

The computer chip has transformed our lives.

cheaper computing have been widespread in telecommunications, music and movie recording, and the automation of millions of routine tasks that previously required human decision and action. You encounter these automated tasks every day when you check out at the grocery store, use an ATM, or call a government department or large business. All the new products and processes and the low-cost computing power that made them possible resulted from people pursuing their self-interest. They did not result from any grand design or government plan.

When Gordon Moore set up Intel and started making chips, and Bill Gates quit Harvard to set up Microsoft, they weren't thinking how much easier it would be for you to turn in your essay on time if you had a better computer. Moore and Gates and thousands of other entrepreneurs were in hot pursuit of the big payoffs that many of them achieved. Yet their actions made many other people better off. They advanced the social interest.

But were resources used in the best possible way? Or did Intel and Microsoft set their prices too high and put their products out of reach for too many people? And did they really need to be rewarded with billions of dollars?

Climate Change

The Earth is getting hotter and the ice at the two poles is melting. Since the late nineteenth century, the Earth's surface temperature has increased about 1 degree Fahrenheit, and close to a half of that increase occurred over the past 25 years.

Most climate scientists believe that the current warming has come at least in part from human economic activity—from self-interested choices—and that, if left unchecked, the warming will bring large future economic costs.

Are the choices that each of us makes to use energy damaging the social interest? What needs to be done to make our choices serve the social interest? Would the United States joining with other nations to limit carbon emissions serve the social interest? What other measures might be introduced?

Human activity is raising the Earth's temperature.

A Social Security Time Bomb

Every year since 2001, the U.S. government has run a budget deficit. On average, the government has spent $1.8 billion a day more than it has received in taxes. The government's debt has increased each day by that amount. Over the ten years 2002 through 2011, government debt increased by $6.5 trillion. Your personal share of this debt is $21,600.

Also, since 2001, Americans bought goods and services from the rest of the world in excess of what foreigners have bought from the United States to the tune of $5.7 trillion. To pay for these goods and services, Americans borrowed from the rest of the world.

These large deficits are just the beginning of an even bigger problem. From about 2019 onwards, the retirement and health-care benefits to which older Americans are entitled are going to cost increasingly more than current taxes can cover. With no changes in taxes or benefit rates, the deficit and debt will swell ever higher.

A Social Security time bomb is ticking as benefits grow faster than contributions.

Deficits and the debts they create cannot persist indefinitely, and debts must somehow be repaid. They will most likely be repaid by you, not by your parents. When we make our voter choices and our choices to buy from or sell to the rest of the world, we pursue our self-interest. Do our choices serve the social interest?

We'll return to all these questions at various points throughout this text.

CHECKPOINT 1.1

Define economics and explain the kinds of questions that economists try to answer.

MyEconLab
You can work these problems in Study Plan 1.1 and get instant feedback.

Practice Problems

1. Economics studies choices that arise from one fact. What is that fact?

2. Provide three examples of wants in the United States today that are especially pressing but not satisfied.

3. In the following three news items, find examples of the *what*, *how*, and *for whom* questions: "With more research, we will cure cancer"; "A good education is the right of every child"; "Congress raises taxes to curb the deficit."

4. How does a new Starbucks in Beijing, China, influence self-interest and the social interest?

5. How does Facebook influence self-interest and the social interest?

In the News

1. According to the Bureau of Labor Statistics (BLS), high-paying jobs in health care and jobs in leisure, hospitality, and education will expand quickly over the next five years. How does the BLS expect *what* and for *whom* goods and services are produced to change in the next five years?

2. In May 2011, businesses cut hiring because higher prices of gas pushed up costs and higher food prices forced consumers to cut spending.

    Source: CNNMoney, June 4, 2011

    Did businesses and consumers act in their self-interest or the social interest?

Solutions to Practice Problems

1. The fact is scarcity—human wants exceed the resources available.

2. Security from international terrorism, cleaner air in our cities, better public schools. (You can perhaps think of some more.)

3. More research is a *how* question, and a cure for cancer is a *what* question. Good education is a *what* question, and every child is a *for whom* question. Raising taxes is a *for whom* question.

4. Decisions made by Starbucks are in Starbucks' self-interest but they serve the self-interest of its customers and so contribute to the social interest.

5. Facebook serves the self-interest of its investors, users, and advertisers. It also serves the social interest by enabling people to share information.

Solutions to In the News

1. The BLS expects the goods and services produced by workers in health care, leisure, hospitality, and education to increase. For whom goods and services are produced are the people who work in these expanding industries.

2. Businesses made their decisions on the basis of their costs, so they acted in their self-interest. Consumers' decisions to cut spending was made on the basis of the prices they face, so they acted in their self-interest.

1.2   THE ECONOMIC WAY OF THINKING

The definition of economics and the kinds of questions that economists try to answer give you a flavor of the scope of economics. But they don't tell you how economists *think* about these questions and how they go about seeking answers to them. You're now going to see how economists approach their work.

We'll break this task into two parts. First, we'll explain the ideas that economists use to frame their view of the world. These ideas will soon have you thinking like an economist. Second, we'll look at economics both as a social science and as a policy tool that governments, businesses, and *you* can use.

■ Economic Ideas

Six ideas define the *economic way of thinking*:

- A choice is a *tradeoff*
- People make *rational choices* by comparing benefits and costs.
- *Benefit* is what you gain from something.
- *Cost* is what you *must give up* to get something.
- Most choices are *"how much"* choices made at the *margin*.
- Choices respond to *incentives*.

■ A Choice Is a Tradeoff

Because we face scarcity, we must make choices. And when we make a choice, we select from the available alternatives. For example, you can spend Saturday night studying for your next economics test or having fun with your friends, but you can't do both of these activities at the same time. You must choose how much time to devote to each. Whatever choice you make, you could have chosen something else.

You can think about your choices as tradeoffs. A **tradeoff** is an exchange—giving up one thing to get something else. When you choose how to spend your Saturday night, you face a tradeoff between studying and hanging out with your friends.

Tradeoff
An exchange—giving up one thing to get something else.

■ Rational Choice

The most basic idea of economics is that in making choices, people act rationally. A **rational choice** is one that uses the available resources to best achieve the objective of the person making the choice.

Only the wants and preferences of the person making a choice are relevant to determine its rationality. For example, you might like chocolate ice cream more than vanilla ice cream, but your friend prefers vanilla. So it is rational for you to choose chocolate and for your friend to choose vanilla.

A rational choice might turn out not to have been the best choice after the event. For example, a farmer might decide to plant wheat rather than soybeans. Then, when the crop comes to market, the price of soybeans might be much higher than the price of wheat. The farmer's choice was rational when it was made, but subsequent events made it less profitable than the alternative choice.

The idea of rational choice provides an answer to the first economic question: What goods and services will be produced and in what quantities? The answer is: The goods and services that people rationally choose to buy.

Rational choice
A choice that uses the available resources to best achieve the objective of the person making the choice.

But how do people choose rationally? Why have most people chosen to buy Microsoft's Windows operating system rather than another? Why do more people today choose an iPhone rather than a BlackBerry? Why has the U.S. government chosen to fund the building of an interstate highway system and not an interstate high-speed railroad system?

The answer is that we make rational choices by comparing *benefits* and *costs*.

■ Benefit: What You Gain

The **benefit** from something is the gain or pleasure that it brings and is determined by personal *preferences*—by what a person likes and dislikes and the intensity of those feelings. If you get a huge kick out of "Guitar Hero," that video game brings you a large benefit. And if you have little interest in listening to Yo Yo Ma playing a Vivaldi cello concerto, that activity brings you a small benefit.

Some benefits are large and easy to identify, such as the benefit that you get from being in school. A big piece of that benefit is the goods and services that you will be able to enjoy with the boost to your earning power when you graduate. Some benefits are small, such as the benefit you receive from a slice of pizza.

Economists measure benefit as the most that a person is *willing to give up* to get something. You are willing to give up a lot to be in school. But you would give up only an iTunes download for a slice of pizza.

Benefit
The benefit of something is the gain or pleasure that it brings.

■ Cost: What You *Must* Give Up

The **opportunity cost** of something is the best alternative that must be given up to get it.

To make the idea of opportunity cost concrete, think about your opportunity cost of being in school. It has two components: the things you can't afford to buy and the things you can't do with your time.

Start with the things you can't afford to buy. You've spent all your income on tuition, residence fees, books, and a laptop. If you weren't in school, you would have spent this money on tickets to ball games and movies and all the other things that you enjoy. But that's only the start of the things you can't afford to buy because you're in school. You've also given up the opportunity to get a job and buy the things that you could afford with your higher income. Suppose that the best job you could get if you weren't in school is working at Citibank as a teller

Opportunity cost
The opportunity cost of something is the best thing you *must* give up to get it.

For these students, the opportunity cost of being in school is worth bearing.

For the full-time bank teller, the opportunity cost of remaining in school is too high.

earning $24,000 a year. Another part of your opportunity cost of being in school is all the things that you could buy with that extra $24,000.

As you well know, being a student eats up many hours in class time, doing homework assignments, preparing for tests, and so on. To do all these school activities, you must give up many hours of what would otherwise be leisure time spent with your friends.

So the opportunity cost of being in school is the best alternative things that you can't afford and don't have the spare time to enjoy. You might want to put a dollar value on that cost or you might just list all the items that make up the opportunity cost.

The examples of opportunity cost that we've just considered are *all-or-nothing costs*—you're either in school or not in school. Most situations are not like this one. They involve choosing *how much* of an activity to do.

■ How Much? Choosing at the Margin

You can allocate the next hour between studying and instant messaging your friends, but the choice is not all or nothing. You must decide how many minutes to allocate to each activity. To make this decision, you compare the benefit of a little bit more study time with its cost—you make your choice *at the margin*.

Other words for "margin" are "border" or "edge." You can think of a choice at the margin as one that adjusts the border or edge of a plan to determine the best course of action. Making a choice at the **margin** means comparing the relevant alternatives systematically and incrementally.

Marginal Cost

The opportunity cost of a one-unit increase in an activity is called **marginal cost**. The marginal cost of something is what you *must* give up to get *one additional* unit of it. Think about your marginal cost of going to the movies for a third time in a week. Your marginal cost of seeing the movie is what you must give up to see that one additional movie. It is *not* what you give up to see all three movies. The reason is that you've already given up something for two movies, so you don't count that cost as resulting from the decision to see the third movie.

The marginal cost of any activity increases as you do more of it. You know that going to the movies decreases your study time and lowers your grade. Suppose that seeing a second movie in a week lowers your grade by five percentage points. Seeing a third movie will lower your grade by more than five percentage points. Your marginal cost of moviegoing is increasing as you see more movies.

Marginal Benefit

The benefit of a one-unit increase in an activity is called **marginal benefit**. Marginal benefit is what you gain from having *one more* unit of something. But the marginal benefit from something is *measured* by what you *are willing* to give up to get that *one additional* unit of it.

A fundamental feature of marginal benefit is that it diminishes. Think about your marginal benefit from movies. If you've been studying hard and haven't seen a movie this week, your marginal benefit from seeing your next movie is large. But if you've been on a movie binge this week, you now want a break and your marginal benefit from seeing your next movie is small.

Because the marginal benefit from a movie decreases as you see more movies, you are willing to give up less to see one additional movie. For example, you know that going to the movies decreases your study time and lowers your grade.

Margin
A choice on the margin is a choice that is made by comparing *all* the relevant alternatives systematically and incrementally.

Marginal cost
The opportunity cost that arises from a one-unit increase in an activity. The marginal cost of something is what you *must* give up to get *one additional* unit of it.

Marginal benefit
The benefit that arises from a one-unit increase in an activity. The marginal benefit of something is *measured* by what you *are willing* to give up to get *one additional* unit of it.

You pay for seeing a movie with a lower grade. You might be willing to give up ten percentage points to see your first movie in a week, but you won't be willing to take such a big hit on your grade to see a second movie in a week. Your willingness to pay to see a movie decreases as the number of movies increases.

Making a Rational Choice

So, will you go to the movies for that third time in a week? If the marginal cost of the movie is less than the marginal benefit from it, your rational choice will be to see the third movie. If the marginal cost exceeds the marginal benefit, your rational choice will be to spend the evening studying. As long as the marginal benefit from something exceeds or equals its marginal cost, our choice is rational and our scarce resources are used to make us as well off as possible.

■ Choices Respond to Incentives

The choices we make depend on the incentives we face. An **incentive** is a reward or a penalty—a "carrot" or a "stick"—that encourages or discourages an action. We respond positively to "carrots" and negatively to "sticks." The carrots are marginal benefits; the sticks are marginal costs. A change in marginal benefit or a change in marginal cost changes the incentives that we face and leads us to change our actions.

Most students believe that the payoff from studying just before a test is greater than the payoff from studying a month before a test. In other words, as a test date approaches, the marginal benefit from studying increases and the incentive to study becomes stronger. For this reason, we observe an increase in study time and a decrease in leisure pursuits during the last few days before a test. And the more important the test, the greater is this effect.

A change in marginal cost also changes incentives. For example, suppose that last week, you found your course work easy and you scored 100 percent on your practice quizzes. You figured that the marginal cost of taking an evening off to enjoy a movie was low and that your grade on the next test would not suffer, so you had a movie feast. But this week the going has gotten tough. You're just not getting it, and your practice test scores are low. If you take off even one evening, your grade on next week's test will suffer. The marginal cost of seeing a movie is now high so you decide to give the movies a miss.

A central idea of economics is that by observing *changes in incentives*, we can predict how *choices change*.

Incentive
A reward or a penalty—a "carrot" or a "stick"—that encourages or discourages an action.

Changes in marginal benefit and marginal cost change the incentive to study or to enjoy a movie.

■ Economics as Social Science

Economists try to understand and predict the effects of economic forces by using the *scientific method* first developed by physicists. The scientific method is a commonsense way of systematically checking what works and what doesn't work.

A scientist begins with a question or a puzzle about cause and effect arising from some observed facts. An economist might wonder why computers are getting cheaper and more computers are being used. Are computers getting cheaper because more people are buying them? Or are more people buying computers because they are getting cheaper? Or is some third factor causing both the price of a computer to fall and the quantity of computers bought to increase?

Economic Models

Economic model
A description of some feature of the economic world that includes only those features assumed necessary to explain the observed facts.

A scientist's second step is to build a model that provides a possible answer to the question of interest. All sciences use models. An **economic model** is a description of some feature of the economic world that includes only those features assumed necessary to explain the observed facts.

A model is analogous to a map. If you want to know about valleys and mountains, you use a physical map; if you're studying nations, you use a political map; if you want to drive from *A* to *B* in an unfamiliar city, you use a street map; and if you're a telephone engineer who is wanting to fix a broken connection, you use a map of the wires and tubes under the streets.

Sometimes, in the natural sciences, models are physical objects such as a plastic model of an atom or DNA. But models are also mathematical and often can be visualized in graphs. You can imagine a Lego model of an economy but you can also see that such a model wouldn't be very revealing. So in economics we use mathematical and graph-based models.

The questions we posed about the price and quantity of computers are answered by an economic model called the "demand and supply model" that you will study in Chapter 4.

Check Models Against Facts

A scientist's third step is to check the proposed model against the facts. Physicists can check whether their models correspond to the facts by doing experiments. For example, with a particle accelerator, a physicist can test a model of the structure of an atom.

Economists have a harder time than physicists but they still approach the task in a scientific manner. To check an economic model against the facts, economists use natural experiments, statistical investigations, and economic experiments.

A natural experiment is a situation that arises in the ordinary course of economic life in which the one factor of interest is different and other things are equal (or similar). For example, Canada has higher unemployment benefits than the United States, but the people in the two nations are similar. So to study the effect of unemployment benefits on the unemployment rate, economists might compare the United States with Canada.

Correlation
The tendency for the values of two variables to move together in a predictable and related way.

A statistical investigation looks for a **correlation**—a tendency for the values of two variables to move together (either in the same direction or in opposite directions) in a predictable and related way. For example, cigarette smoking and lung cancer are correlated. Sometimes a correlation shows a causal influence of one variable on the other. Smoking does cause lung cancer. But sometimes the direction of causation is hard to determine.

EYE on the PAST
Adam Smith and the Birth of Economics as a Social Science

Many people had written about economics before Adam Smith did, but he made economics a social science.

Born in 1723 in Kirkcaldy, a small fishing town near Edinburgh, Scotland, Smith was the only child of the town's customs officer. Lured from his professorship (he was a full professor at 28) by a wealthy Scottish duke who gave him a pension of £300 a year—ten times the average income at that time—Smith devoted ten years to writing his masterpiece, *An Inquiry into the Nature and Causes of the Wealth of Nations,* published in 1776.

Why, Adam Smith asked in that book, are some nations wealthy while others are poor? He was pondering these questions at the height of the Industrial Revolution. During these years, new technologies were applied to the manufacture of textiles, iron, transportation, and agriculture.

Adam Smith answered his questions by emphasizing the role of the division of labor and free markets. To illustrate his argument, he used the example of a pin factory. He guessed that one person, using the hand tools available in the 1770s, might make 20 pins a day. Yet, he observed, by using those same hand tools but breaking the process into a number of individually small operations in which people specialize—by the division of labor—ten people could make a staggering 48,000 pins a day. One draws out the wire, another straightens it, a third cuts it, a fourth points it, a fifth grinds it. Three specialists make the head, and a fourth attaches it. Finally, the pin is polished and packaged.

But a large market is needed to support the division of labor: One factory employing ten workers would need to sell more than 15 million pins a year to stay in business!

An economic experiment puts people in a decision-making situation and varies the influence of one factor at a time to discover how they respond.

Disagreement: Normative versus Positive

Economists sometimes disagree about assumptions and models. They also sometimes disagree about what policy should be followed. Some disagreements can be settled by appealing to further facts, but others cannot.

Disagreements that can't be settled by facts are *normative statements*—statements about what *ought to be*. These statements depend on values and cannot be tested. The statement "We *ought to* cut back on our use of coal" is a normative statement. You may agree or disagree with it, but you can't test it. It doesn't assert a fact that can be checked. Economists as social scientists try to steer clear of normative statements.

Disagreements that *can* be settled by facts are *positive statements*—statements about *what is*. A positive statement might be right or wrong and we can discover which by careful observation of facts. "Our planet is warming because of the quantity of coal that we're burning" is a positive statement. It could be right or wrong, and it can be tested.

■ Economics as Policy Tool

Economics is useful, and you don't have to be an economist to think like one and to use the insights of economics as a policy tool. The subject provides a way of approaching problems in all aspects of our lives:

- Personal
- Business
- Government

Personal Economic Policy

Should you take out a student loan? Should you get a weekend job? Should you buy a used car or a new one? Should you rent an apartment or take out a loan and buy a condominium? Should you pay off your credit card balance or make just the minimum payment? How should you allocate your time between study, working for a wage, caring for family members, and having fun? How should you allocate your time between studying economics and your other subjects? Should you leave school after getting a bachelor's degree or should you go for a master's or a professional qualification?

All these questions involve a marginal benefit and a marginal cost. Although some of the numbers might be hard to pin down, you will make more solid decisions if you approach these questions with the tools of economics.

Business Economic Policy

Should Sony make only flat panel televisions and stop making conventional ones? Should Texaco get more oil and gas from the Gulf of Mexico or from Alaska? Should Palm outsource its online customer services to India or run the operation from California? Should Marvel Studios produce *Spider-Man 4,* a sequel to *Spider-Man 3*? Can Microsoft compete with Google in the search engine business? Can eBay compete with the surge of new Internet auction services? Is Alex Rodriguez really worth $32,000,000 to the New York Yankees?

Like personal economic questions, these business questions involve the evaluation of a marginal benefit and a marginal cost. Some of the questions require a broader investigation of the interactions of individuals and businesses. But again, by approaching these questions with the tools of economics and by hiring economists as advisers, businesses can make better decisions.

Government Economic Policy

How can California balance its budget? Should the federal government cut taxes or raise them? How can the tax system be simplified? Should people be permitted to invest their Social Security money in stocks that they pick themselves? Should Medicaid and Medicare be extended to the entire population? Should there be a special tax to penalize corporations that send jobs overseas? Should cheap foreign imports of furniture and textiles be limited? Should the farms that grow tomatoes and sugar beets receive a subsidy? Should water be transported from Washington and Oregon to California?

These government policy questions call for decisions that involve the evaluation of a marginal benefit and a marginal cost and an investigation of the interactions of individuals and businesses. Yet again, by approaching these questions with the tools of economics, governments can make better decisions.

Notice that all the policy questions we've just posed involve a blend of the positive and the normative. Economics can't help with the normative part—the objective. But for a given objective, economics provides a method of evaluating alternative solutions. That method is to evaluate the marginal benefits and marginal costs and to find the solution that brings the greatest available gain.

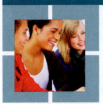

EYE on the BENEFIT AND COST OF SCHOOL
Did You Make the Right Decision?

Did you make the right decision when you chose school over looking for a full-time job? Or, if you have a full-time job and you're studying in what would be your leisure time, did you make the right choice? Does school provide a big enough benefit to justify its cost?

The Benefits of School

Being in school has many benefits but they fall into two broad categories: present enjoyment and a higher future income.

You can easily make a list of all the fun things you do with your friends in school that would be harder to do if you didn't have these friends and opportunities for social interaction that school provides.

Putting a dollar value on the items in your list would be hard but it is possible to put a dollar value, or rather an expected dollar value, on the other benefit—a higher future income.

On average, a high-school graduate earns $40,000 a year. A graduate with a bachelor's degree earns, on average, $76,000 a year.

So by being in school, you can expect (on average) to increase your annual earnings by $36,000 a year.

This number is likely to grow as the economy becomes more productive and prices and earnings rise.

The Costs of School

The costs of being in school for a full-time student are:

- Tuition
- Books
- Other study costs
- Forgone earnings

For a student in state university in her or his home state, tuition runs at around $7,000 per year.

Books and other study costs run at around $1,000 per year.

Forgone earnings are the wage of a high-school graduate in a starter job. That is around $24,000 a year.

So the total annual cost is about $32,000 or $96,000 for a 3-year degree and $128,000 for a 4-year degree.

Benefit-Cost Balance

The benefit of extra earnings alone brings in $36,000 a year or $360,000 in 10 years and $1,440,000 in a working life of 40 years.

The costs are incurred in the present and the benefits accrue in the future, so we need to lower the benefits to be able to compare them properly with the costs. You'll learn how to do that later in your economics course. But even allowing for the fact that the costs are now and the benefits in the future, the net gain is big!

Is School Always Best?

Alex Rodriguez, the highest earning baseball player ($32,000,000 in 2011) ever, turned down a scholarship at the University of Miami and chose instead to sign with the Seattle Mariners right out of high school. With a 0.311 batting average, he quickly rose through the player ranks and played his first Major League game at the age of 18.

Alex Rodriguez's opportunity cost of a college education vastly exceeded the benefit he could expect to get from it. So Alex, like you, made the right decision.

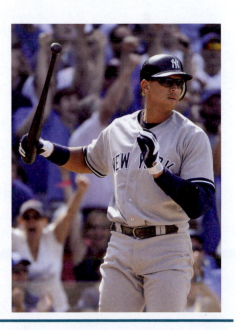

MyEconLab

You can work these problems in Study Plan 1.2 and get instant feedback.

CHECKPOINT 1.2

Explain the ideas that define the economic way of thinking.

Practice Problems

Every week, Kate plays tennis for two hours, and her grade on each math test is 70 percent. Last week, after playing for two hours, Kate considered playing for another hour. She decided to play for another hour and cut her study time by one hour. But last week, her math grade fell to 60 percent. Use this information to work Problems **1** to **4**.

1. What was Kate's opportunity cost of the third hour of tennis?
2. Given that Kate played the third hour, what can you conclude about her marginal benefit and marginal cost of the second hour of tennis?
3. Was Kate's decision to play the third hour of tennis rational?
4. Did Kate make her decision on the margin?

In the News

The *New York Times* reports that cruise lines have been slashing prices and cruise sales are up. It says this surge of interest tells us that despite the uncertain economic climate, people clearly need more fun in their lives and view their vacations as a valuable and necessary part of it.

1. In deciding whether to take a cruise would you face a tradeoff?
2. How would you make a rational choice about taking a cruise?
3. What would be the marginal benefit from a cruise? What would be the marginal cost of a cruise?
4. Why would you expect a lower price to increase the number of people who decide to take a cruise?

Solutions to Practice Problems

1. Kate's opportunity cost of the third hour of tennis was the drop in her grade of ten percentage points.
2. The marginal benefit from the second hour of tennis must have exceeded the marginal cost of the second hour because Kate chose to play the third hour.
3. If marginal benefit exceeded marginal cost, Kate's decision was rational.
4. Kate made her decision on the margin because she compared the benefit and cost of one more hour (marginal benefit and marginal cost).

Solutions to In the News

1. You would face a tradeoff because you would have to forgo something else that you might otherwise do with your resources (time and budget).
2. You would make a rational choice by comparing the marginal benefit from a cruise and the marginal cost of taking one.
3. The marginal benefit from a cruise is the most you are willing to pay for one. The marginal cost is what you would have to pay to take a cruise.
4. With a lower price, more people will have a marginal benefit that exceeds the price and they will chose to take a cruise.

CHAPTER SUMMARY

Key Points

1. Define economics and explain the kinds of questions that economists try to answer.

- Economics is the social science that studies the choices that we make as we cope with scarcity and the incentives that influence and reconcile our choices.
- Microeconomics is the study of individual choices and interactions, and macroeconomics is the study of the national economy and global economy.
- The first big question of economics is: How do the choices that people make end up determining *what, how,* and *for whom* goods and services are produced?
- The second big question is: When do choices made in the pursuit of *self-interest* also promote the *social interest*?

2. Explain the ideas that define the economic way of thinking.

- Six ideas define the economic way of thinking:
  1. A choice is a *tradeoff*.
  2. People make *rational* choices by comparing benefits and costs .
  3. *Benefit* is what you gain when you get something (measured by what you *are willing to* give up to get it).
  4. *Cost* is what you *must* give up to get something.
  5. A "how much" choice is made on the *margin* by comparing *marginal benefit* and *marginal cost*.
  6. Choices respond to *incentives.*
- Economists use the *scientific method* to try to understand how the economic world works. They create economic models and test them using natural experiments, statistical investigations, and economic experiments.
- Economics is a tool for personal, business, and government decisions.

Key Terms

Benefit, 9	Macroeconomics, 3	Rational choice, 8
Correlation, 12	Margin, 10	Scarcity, 2
Economic model, 12	Marginal benefit, 10	Self-interest, 4
Economics, 2	Marginal cost, 10	Social interest, 4
Goods and services, 3	Microeconomics, 2	Tradeoff, 8
Incentive, 11	Opportunity cost, 9	

LIST 1

- Local car sales in India grow at their slowest pace in two years.
- Coffee prices rocket.
- Globalization has reduced African poverty.
- The government must cut its deficit.
- Apple sells 2 million iPhones a month.

LIST 2

- Low-income people pay too much for housing.
- The number of U.S. farms has decreased over the past 50 years.
- Toyota expands parts production in the United States.
- Imports from China are swamping U.S. department stores.
- The population of rural United States is declining.

CHAPTER CHECKPOINT

Study Plan Problems and Applications

1. Provide three examples of scarcity that illustrate why even the 1,210 billionaires in the world face scarcity.

2. Label each entry in List 1 as dealing with a microeconomic topic or a macroeconomic topic. Explain your answer.

Use the following information to work Problems **3** to **6**.

The Social Network had world-wide box office receipts of $225 million. The movie had a production budget of about $70 million and additional marketing costs of about $50 million. Creating a successful movie brings pleasure to millions, generates work for thousands, and makes a few rich.

3. What contribution does a movie like *The Social Network* make to coping with scarcity? When you buy a ticket to see a movie in a theater, are you buying a good or a service?

4. Who decides whether a movie is going to be a blockbuster? How do you think the creation of a blockbuster movie influences *what, how,* and *for whom* goods and services are produced?

5. What are some of the components of marginal cost and marginal benefit that the producer of a movie faces?

6. Suppose that Jesse Eisenberg had been offered a bigger and better part in another movie and that to hire him for *The Social Network,* the producer had to double Jesse's pay. What incentives would have changed? How might the changed incentives have changed the choices that people made?

7. Pam, Pru, and Pat are deciding how they will celebrate the New Year. Pam prefers to take a cruise, is happy to go to Hawaii, but does not want to go skiing. Pru prefers to go skiing, is happy to go to Hawaii, but does not want to take a cruise. Pat prefers to go to Hawaii or to take a cruise but does not want to go skiing. Their decision is to go to Hawaii. Is this decision rational? What is the opportunity cost of the trip to Hawaii for each of them? What is the benefit that each gets?

8. Label each of the entries in List 2 as a positive or a normative statement.

9. What is the social interest? Distinguish it from self-interest. In your answer give an example of self-interest and an example of social interest.

Use the following information to work Problems **10** to **12**.

Hundreds line up for 5 p.m. Eminem ticket giveaway
Hundreds of Eminem fans lined up to get a free ticket to the rapper's secret concert. Although tickets would be released at 5 p.m., people lined up all day. Eminem will release his new album *Relapse* (his first in 5 years) on the same day.
Source: *Detroit Free Press*, May 18, 2009

10. Eminem is giving away tickets to his show in a 1,500-seat theater in Detroit. What is free and what is scarce? Explain your answer.

11. What do you think Eminem's incentive is to give a free show? Was his decision made in self-interest or in the social interest? Explain.

12. Because all the tickets were free, was the marginal benefit from the concert zero? Explain your answer.

Instructor Assignable Problems and Applications

Your instructor can assign these problems as homework, a quiz, or a test in MyEconLab.

1. Which of the following are components of the opportunity cost of being a full-time student? The cost of:
    *   Tuition and books
    *   Residence and a meal plan
    *   A subscription to the *New Yorker* magazine
    *   The income a student will earn after graduating

2. Think about the following news items and label each as involving a *what*, *how*, or *for whom* question:
    *   Today, most stores use computers to keep their inventory records, whereas 20 years ago most stores used paper records.
    *   Health-care professionals and drug companies recommend that Medicaid drug rebates be made available to everyone in need.
    *   A doubling of the gas tax might lead to a better public transit system.

3. On Friday June 16, 2011, the headlines in List 1 appeared in *The Wall Street Journal*. Classify each headline as a signal that the news article is about a microeconomic topic or a macroeconomic topic. Explain your answers.

4. Your school decides to increase the intake of new students next year. To make its decision, what economic concepts would it have considered? Would the school have used the "economic way of thinking" in reaching its decision? Would the school have made its decision on the margin?

5. Provide two examples of monetary and two examples of non-monetary incentives, a carrot and a stick of each, that government policies use to influence behavior.

6. Think about each of the items in List 2 and explain how they affect incentives and might change the choices that people make:

7. Does the decision to make a blockbuster movie mean that some other more desirable activities get fewer resources than they deserve? Is your answer positive or normative? Explain your answer.

8. Provide two examples of economics being used as a tool by each of a student, a business, and a government. Classify your examples as dealing with microeconomic topics and macroeconomic topics.

Use the following news clip to work Problems **9** to **12**.

Obama will drive up miles-per-gallon requirements
Obama's revision of auto-emission and fuel-economy standards will require automakers to boost fuel economy to 35.5 miles per gallon by 2016, notching up 5% each year from 2012, to limit the amount of carbon dioxide cars can emit.

Source: *USA Today*, May 18, 2009

9. What are two benefits of the new miles-per-gallon requirements? Are these benefits in someone's self-interest or in the social interest?

10. What are two benefits of the new auto-emission standards?

11. What costs associated with the new miles-per-gallon requirements arise from decisions made in self-interest and in the social interest?

12. What costs associated with the new auto-emission standards arise from decisions made in self-interest and in the social interest?

LIST 1

*   Apple Opens Locker for Songs.
*   U.S. Household Debt Falls.
*   Indian Carriers Set to Order 60 Airbus Planes.
*   U.S. Trade Gap Narrows.

LIST 2

*   A hurricane hits Central Florida.
*   The World Series begins tonight but a storm warning is in effect for the area around the stadium.
*   The price of a personal computer falls to $50.
*   Unrest in the Middle East sends the price of gas to $5 a gallon.

MyEconLab

You can work this quiz in Chapter 1 Study Plan and get instant feedback.

Multiple Choice Quiz

1. Which of the following describes the reason why scarcity exists?

    A. Governments make bad economic decisions.
    B. The gap between the rich and the poor is too wide.
    C. Wants exceed the resources available to satisfy them.
    D. There is too much unemployment.

2. Which of the following defines economics?
   Economics is the social science that studies _____.

    A. the best way of eliminating scarcity
    B. the choices made to cope with scarcity, how incentives influence those choices, and how the choices are coordinated
    C. how money is created and used
    D. the inevitable conflict between self-interest and the social interest

3. Of the three big questions, *what*, *how*, and *for whom*, which of the following is an example of a *how* question?

    A. Why do doctors and lawyers earn high incomes?
    B. Why don't we produce more small cars and fewer gas guzzlers?
    C. Why do we use machines rather than migrant workers to pick grapes?
    D. Why do college football coaches earn more than professors?

4. Which of the following is not a key idea in the economic way of thinking?

    A. People make rational choices by comparing costs and benefits.
    B. Poor people are discriminated against and should be treated more fairly.
    C. A rational choice is made at the margin.
    D. Choices respond to incentives.

5. A rational choice is _____.

    A. the best thing you must forgo to get something
    B. what you are willing to forgo to get something
    C. made by comparing marginal benefit and marginal cost
    D. the best for society

6. Which of the following best illustrates your marginal benefit from studying?

    A. The knowledge you gain from studying 2 hours a night for a month
    B. The best things forgone by studying 2 hours a night for a month
    C. What you are willing to give up to study for one additional hour
    D. What you must give up to be able to study for one additional hour

7. The scientific method uses models to _____.

    A. clarify normative disagreements
    B. avoid the need to study real questions
    C. replicate all the features of the real world
    D. focus on those features of reality assumed relevant for understanding a cause and effect relationship

8. Which of the following is a positive statement?

    A. We should stop using corn to make ethanol because it is raising the cost of food.
    B. You will get the most out of college life if you play a sport once a week.
    C. Competition among cell phone providers across the borders of Canada, Mexico, and the United States has driven roaming rates down.
    D. Bill Gates ought to spend more helping to eradicate malaria in Africa.

APPENDIX: MAKING AND USING GRAPHS

When you have completed your study of this appendix, you will be able to

1 Interpret graphs that display data.

2 Interpret the graphs used in economic models.

3 Define and calculate slope.

4 Graph relationships among more than two variables.

Basic Idea

A graph represents a quantity as a distance and enables us to visualize the relationship between two variables. To make a graph, we set two lines called *axes* perpendicular to each other, like those in Figure A1.1. The vertical line is called the *y*-axis, and the horizontal line is called the *x*-axis. The common zero point is called the *origin*. In Figure A1.1, the *x*-axis measures temperature in degrees Fahrenheit. A movement to the right shows an increase in temperature, and a movement to the left shows a decrease in temperature. The *y*-axis represents ice cream consumption, measured in gallons per day.

To make a graph, we need a value of the variable on the *x*-axis and a corresponding value of the variable on the *y*-axis. For example, if the temperature is 40°F, ice cream consumption is 5 gallons a day at point *A* in Figure A1.1. If the temperature is 80°F, ice cream consumption is 20 gallons a day at point *B* in Figure A1.1. Graphs like that in Figure A1.1 can be used to show any type of quantitative data on two variables.

■ FIGURE A1.1

Making a Graph   MyEconLab Animation

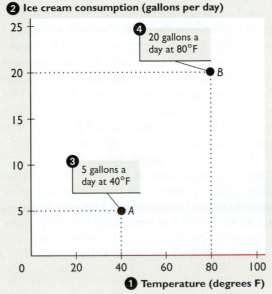

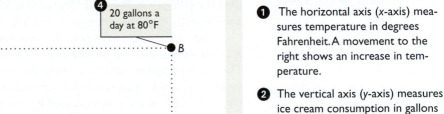

All graphs have axes that measure quantities as distances.

❶ The horizontal axis (*x*-axis) measures temperature in degrees Fahrenheit. A movement to the right shows an increase in temperature.

❷ The vertical axis (*y*-axis) measures ice cream consumption in gallons per day. A movement upward shows an increase in ice cream consumption.

❸ Point *A* shows that 5 gallons of ice cream are consumed on a day when the temperature is 40°F.

❹ Point *B* shows that 20 gallons of ice cream are consumed on a day when the temperature is 80°F.

■ Interpreting Data Graphs

A **scatter diagram** is a graph of the value of one variable against the value of another variable. It is used to reveal whether a relationship exists between two variables and to describe the relationship. Figure A1.2 shows two examples.

Figure A1.2(a) shows the relationship between expenditure and income. Each point shows expenditure per person and income per person in the United States in a given year from 2000 to 2010. The points are "scattered" within the graph. The label on each point shows its year. The point marked 04 shows that in 2004, income per person was $28,990 and expenditure per person was $27,401. This scatter diagram reveals that as income increases, expenditure also increases.

Figure A1.2(b) shows the relationship between the percentage of Americans who own a cell phone and the average monthly cell phone bill. This scatter diagram reveals that as the cost of using a cell phone falls, the number of cell phone subscribers increases.

A **time-series graph** measures time (for example, months or years) on the x-axis and the variable or variables in which we are interested on the y-axis. Figure A1.2(c) shows an example. In this graph, time (on the x-axis) is measured in years, which run from 1980 to 2010. The variable that we are interested in is the price of coffee, and it is measured on the y-axis.

A time-series graph conveys an enormous amount of information quickly and easily, as this example illustrates. It shows when the value is

1. High or low. When the line is a long way from the x-axis, the price is high, as it was in 2008. When the line is close to the x-axis, the price is low, as it was in 1993.

2. Rising or falling. When the line slopes upward, as in 1994, the price is rising. When the line slopes downward, as in 1998, the price is falling.

3. Rising or falling quickly or slowly. If the line is steep, then the price is rising or falling quickly. If the line is not steep, the price is rising or falling slowly. For example, the price rose quickly in 1994 and slowly in 1984. The price fell quickly in 1998 and slowly in 2003.

A time-series graph also reveals whether the variable has a trend. A **trend** is a general tendency for the value of a variable to rise or fall over time. You can see that the price of coffee had a general tendency to rise from 1980 to the late 1990s. That is, although the price rose and fell, it had a general tendency to rise.

With a time-series graph, we can compare different periods quickly. Figure A1.2(c) shows that the period after 1990 was different from the period before 1990. The price of coffee jumped during the early 1990s, remained high for a number of years, then fell quickly before rising again to a new high. This graph conveys a wealth of information, and it does so in much less space than we have used to describe only some of its features.

A **cross-section graph** shows the values of an economic variable for different groups in a population at a point in time. Figure A1.2(d) is an example of a cross-section graph. It shows the percentage of people who participate in selected sports activities in the United States. This graph uses bars rather than dots and lines, and the length of each bar indicates the participation rate. Figure A1.2(d) enables you to compare the participation rates in these ten sporting activities. And you can do so much more quickly and clearly than by looking at a list of numbers.

■ FIGURE A1.2

Data Graphs

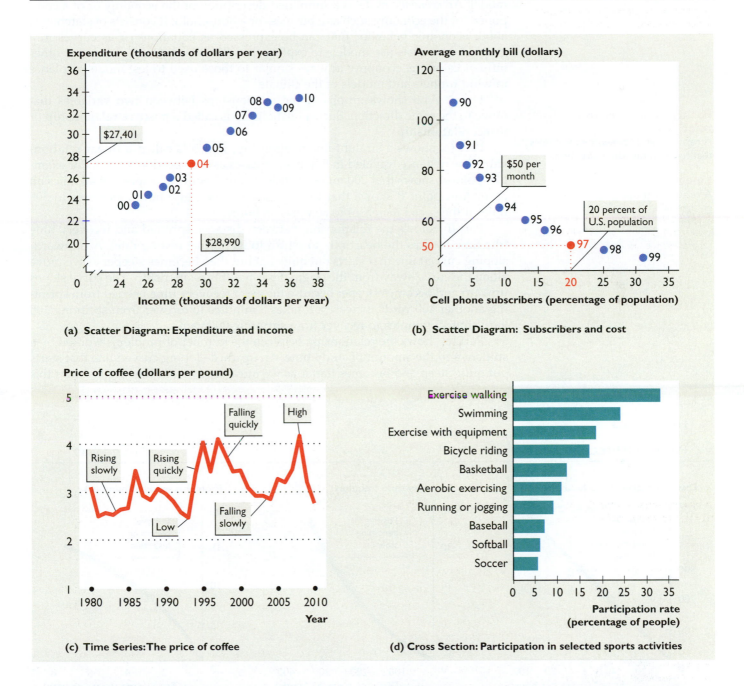

(a) Scatter Diagram: Expenditure and income

(b) Scatter Diagram: Subscribers and cost

(c) Time Series: The price of coffee

(d) Cross Section: Participation in selected sports activities

A scatter diagram reveals the relationship between two variables. In part (a), as income increases, expenditure almost always increases. In part (b), as the monthly cell phone bill falls, the percentage of people who own a cell phone increases.

A time-series graph plots the value of a variable on the *y*-axis against time on the *x*-axis. Part (c) plots the price of coffee each year from 1980 to 2010. The graph shows when the price of coffee was high and low, when it increased and decreased, and when it changed quickly and changed slowly.

A cross-section graph shows the value of a variable across the members of a population. Part (d) shows the participation rate in the United States in each of ten sporting activities.

■ Interpreting Graphs Used in Economic Models

We use graphs to show the relationships among the variables in an economic model. An *economic model* is a simplified description of the economy or of a component of the economy such as a business or a household. It consists of statements about economic behavior that can be expressed as equations or as curves in a graph. Economists use models to explore the effects of different policies or other influences on the economy in ways similar to those used to test model airplanes in wind tunnels and models of the climate.

Figure A1.3 shows graphs of the relationships between two variables that move in the same direction. Such a relationship is called a **positive relationship** or **direct relationship**.

Part (a) shows a straight-line relationship, which is called a **linear relationship**. The distance traveled in 5 hours increases as the speed increases. For example, point *A* shows that 200 miles are traveled in 5 hours at a speed of 40 miles an hour. And point *B* shows that the distance traveled in 5 hours increases to 300 miles if the speed increases to 60 miles an hour.

Part (b) shows the relationship between distance sprinted and recovery time (the time it takes the heart rate to return to its normal resting rate). An upward-sloping curved line that starts out quite flat but then becomes steeper as we move along the curve away from the origin describes this relationship. The curve slopes upward and becomes steeper because the extra recovery time needed from sprinting another 100 yards increases. It takes 5 minutes to recover from sprinting 100 yards but 15 minutes to recover from sprinting 200 yards.

Part (c) shows the relationship between the number of problems worked by a student and the amount of study time. An upward-sloping curved line that starts out quite steep and becomes flatter as we move away from the origin shows this

Positive relationship or direct relationship
A relationship between two variables that move in the same direction.

Linear relationship
A relationship that graphs as a straight line.

■ **FIGURE A1.3**

Positive (Direct) Relationships   MyEconLab Animation

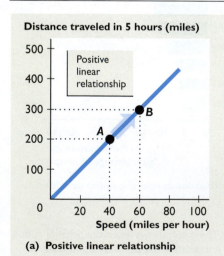

(a) **Positive linear relationship**

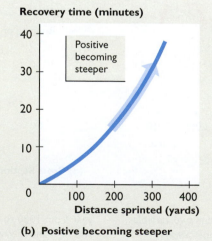

(b) **Positive becoming steeper**

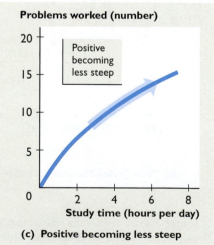

(c) **Positive becoming less steep**

Part (a) shows that as speed increases, the distance traveled in a given number of hours increases along a straight line.

Part (b) shows that as the distance sprinted increases, recovery time increases along a curve that becomes steeper.

Part (c) shows that as study time increases, the number of problems worked increases along a curve that becomes less steep.

relationship. Study time becomes less effective as you increase the hours worked and become more tired.

Figure A1.4 shows relationships between two variables that move in opposite directions. Such a relationship is called a **negative relationship** or **inverse relationship**.

Part (a) shows the relationship between the number of hours spent playing squash and the number of hours spent playing tennis when the total number of hours available is five. One extra hour spent playing tennis means one hour less playing squash and vice versa. This relationship is negative and linear.

Part (b) shows the relationship between the cost per mile traveled and the length of a journey. The longer the journey, the lower is the cost per mile. But as the journey length increases, the fall in the cost per mile becomes smaller. This feature of the relationship is shown by the fact that the curve slopes downward, starting out steep at a short journey length and then becoming flatter as the journey length increases. This relationship arises because some of the costs, such as auto insurance, are fixed, and as the journey length increases, the fixed costs are spread over more miles.

Part (c) shows the relationship between the amount of leisure time and the number of problems worked by a student. Increasing leisure time produces an increasingly large reduction in the number of problems worked. This relationship is a negative one that starts out with a gentle slope at a small number of leisure hours and becomes steeper as the number of leisure hours increases. This relationship is a different view of the idea shown in Figure A1.3 (c).

Many relationships in economic models have a maximum or a minimum. For example, firms try to make the largest possible profit and to produce at the lowest possible cost. Figure A1.5 shows relationships that have a maximum or a minimum.

Negative relationship or inverse relationship
A relationship between two variables that move in opposite directions.

■ **FIGURE A1.4**

Negative (Inverse) Relationships   MyEconLab Animation

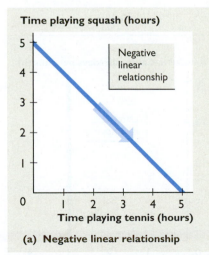

(a) Negative linear relationship

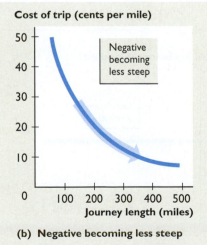

(b) Negative becoming less steep

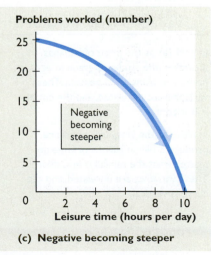

(c) Negative becoming steeper

Part (a) shows that as the time playing tennis increases, the time playing squash decreases along a straight line.

Part (b) shows that as the journey length increases, the cost of the trip falls along a curve that becomes less steep.

Part (c) shows that as leisure time increases, the number of problems worked decreases along a curve that becomes steeper.

■ **FIGURE A1.5**

Maximum and Minimum Points

MyEconLab Animation

In part (a), as the rainfall increases, the curve ❶ slopes upward as the yield per acre rises, ❷ is flat at point A, the maximum yield, and then ❸ slopes downward as the yield per acre falls.

In part (b), as the speed increases, the curve ❶ slopes downward as the cost per mile falls, ❷ is flat at the minimum point B, and then ❸ slopes upward as the cost per mile rises.

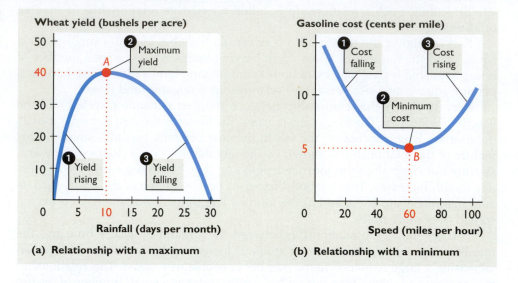

(a) Relationship with a maximum

(b) Relationship with a minimum

Part (a) shows a relationship that starts out sloping upward, reaches a maximum, and then slopes downward. Part (b) shows a relationship that begins sloping downward, falls to a minimum, and then slopes upward.

Finally, there are many situations in which, no matter what happens to the value of one variable, the other variable remains constant. Sometimes we want to show two variables that are unrelated in a graph. Figure A1.6 shows two graphs in which the variables are unrelated.

■ **FIGURE A1.6**

Variables That Are Unrelated

MyEconLab Animation

In part (a), as the price of bananas increases, the student's grade in economics remains at 75 percent. These variables are unrelated, and the curve is horizontal.

In part (b), the vineyards of France produce 3 billion gallons of wine no matter what the rainfall is in California. These variables are unrelated, and the curve is vertical.

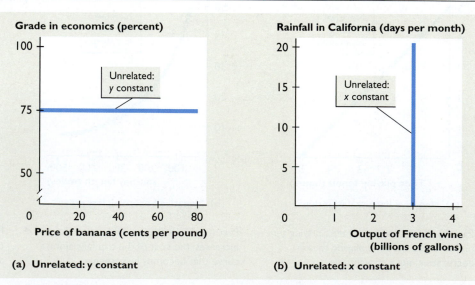

(a) Unrelated: y constant

(b) Unrelated: x constant

The Slope of a Relationship

We can measure the influence of one variable on another by the slope of the relationship. The **slope** of a relationship is the change in the value of the variable measured on the y-axis divided by the change in the value of the variable measured on the x-axis. We use the Greek letter Δ (delta) to represent "change in." So Δy means the change in the value of y, and Δx means the change in the value of x. The slope of the relationship is

$$\Delta y \div \Delta x$$

If a large change in y is associated with a small change in x, the slope is large and the curve is steep. If a small change in y is associated with a large change in x, the slope is small and the curve is flat.

Figure A1.7 shows you how to calculate slope. The slope of a straight line is the same regardless of where on the line you calculate it—the slope is constant. In part (a), when x increases from 2 to 6, y increases from 3 to 6. The change in x is 4—that is, Δx is 4. The change in y is 3—that is, Δy is 3. The slope of that line is 3/4. In part (b), when x increases from 2 to 6, y *decreases* from 6 to 3. The change in y is *minus* 3—that is, Δy is -3 The change in x is plus 4—that is, Δx is 4. The slope of the curve is $-3/4$.

In part (c), we calculate the slope at a point on a curve. To do so, place a ruler on the graph so that it touches point A and no other point on the curve, then draw a straight line along the edge of the ruler. The slope of this straight line is the slope of the curve at point A. This slope is 3/4.

Slope
The change in the value of the variable measured on the y-axis divided by the change in the value of the variable measured on the x-axis.

FIGURE A1.7

Calculating Slope

MyEconLab Animation

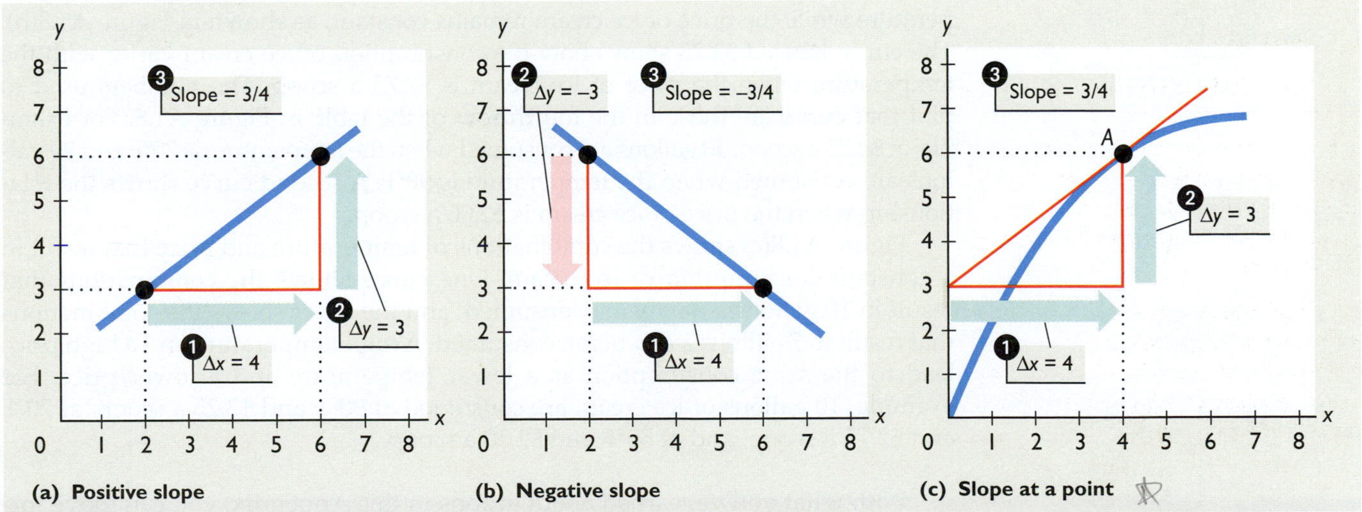

(a) **Positive slope**

(b) **Negative slope**

(c) **Slope at a point**

In part (a), ➊ when Δx is 4, ➋ Δy is 3, so ➌ the slope ($\Delta y \div \Delta x$) is 3/4.

In part (b), ➊ when Δx is 4, ➋ Δy is -3, so ➌ the slope ($\Delta y \div \Delta x$) is $-3/4$.

In part (c), the slope of the curve at point A equals the slope of the red line. ➊ When Δx is 4, ➋ Δy is 3, so ➌ the slope ($\Delta y \div \Delta x$) is 3/4.

■ Relationships Among More Than Two Variables

All the graphs that you have studied so far plot the relationship between two variables as a point formed by the x and y values. But most of the relationships in economics involve relationships among many variables, not just two. For example, the amount of ice cream consumed depends on the price of ice cream and the temperature. If ice cream is expensive and the temperature is low, people eat much less ice cream than when ice cream is inexpensive and the temperature is high. For any given price of ice cream, the quantity consumed varies with the temperature; and for any given temperature, the quantity of ice cream consumed varies with its price.

Figure A1.8 shows a relationship among three variables. The table shows the number of gallons of ice cream consumed per day at various temperatures and ice cream prices. How can we graph these numbers?

To graph a relationship that involves more than two variables, we use the *ceteris paribus* assumption.

Ceteris Paribus

The Latin phrase *ceteris paribus* means "other things remaining the same." Every laboratory experiment is an attempt to create *ceteris paribus* and isolate the relationship of interest. We use the same method to make a graph.

Figure A1.8(a) shows an example. This graph shows what happens to the quantity of ice cream consumed when the price of ice cream varies while the temperature remains constant. The curve labeled 70°F shows the relationship between ice cream consumption and the price of ice cream if the temperature is 70°F. The numbers used to plot that curve are those in the first and fourth columns of the table in Figure A1.8. For example, if the temperature is 70°F, 10 gallons are consumed when the price is $2.75 a scoop and 18 gallons are consumed when the price is $2.25 a scoop. The curve labeled 90°F shows the relationship between consumption and the price when the temperature is 90°F.

We can also show the relationship between ice cream consumption and temperature while the price of ice cream remains constant, as shown in Figure A1.8(b). The curve labeled $2.75 shows how the consumption of ice cream varies with the temperature when the price of ice cream is $2.75 a scoop. The numbers used to plot that curve are those in the fourth row of the table in Figure A1.8. For example, at $2.75 a scoop, 10 gallons are consumed when the temperature is 70°F and 20 gallons are consumed when the temperature is 90°F. A second curve shows the relationship when the price of ice cream is $2.00 a scoop.

Figure A1.8(c) shows the combinations of temperature and price that result in a constant consumption of ice cream. One curve shows the combinations that result in 10 gallons a day being consumed, and the other shows the combinations that result in 7 gallons a day being consumed. A high temperature and a high price lead to the same consumption as a lower temperature and a lower price. For example, 10 gallons of ice cream are consumed at 90°F and $3.25 a scoop, at 70°F and $2.75 a scoop, and at 50°F and $2.50 a scoop.

With what you've learned about graphs in this Appendix, you can move forward with your study of economics. There are no graphs in this textbook that are more complicated than the ones you've studied here.

FIGURE A1.8

Graphing a Relationship Among Three Variables   MyEconLab Animation

Price (dollars per scoop)	Ice cream consumption (gallons per day)			
	30°F	50°F	70°F	90°F
2.00	12	18	25	50
2.25	10	12	18	37
2.50	7	10	13	27
2.75	5	7	10	20
3.00	3	5	7	14
3.25	2	3	5	10
3.50	1	2	3	6

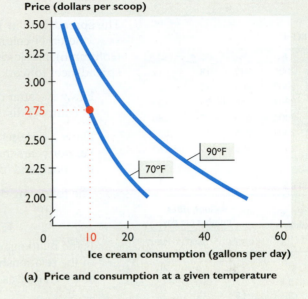

(a) Price and consumption at a given temperature

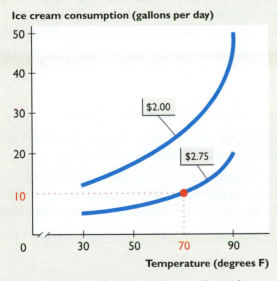

(b) Temperature and consumption at a given price

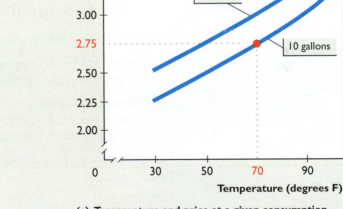

(c) Temperature and price at a given consumption

The table tells us how many gallons of ice cream are consumed at different prices and different temperatures. For example, if the price is $2.75 a scoop and the temperature is 70°F, 10 gallons of ice cream are consumed. This set of values is highlighted in the table and each part of the figure.

Part (a) shows the relationship between price and consumption when temperature is held constant. One curve holds temperature at 90°F, and the other at 70°F.

Part (b) shows the relationship between temperature and consumption when price is held constant. One curve holds the price at

$2.75 a scoop, and the other at $2.00 a scoop.

Part (c) shows the relationship between temperature and price when consumption is held constant. One curve holds consumption at 10 gallons a day, and the other at 7 gallons a day.

TABLE 1

	A	B	C	D
1	2000	943	18	19
2	2002	803	15	51
3	2004	767	33	139
4	2006	620	23	586
5	2008	385	13	1,033
6	2010	226	9	1,162

TABLE 2

Price (dollars per ride)	Balloon rides (number per day)		
	50°F	70°F	90°F
5	32	50	40
10	27	40	32
15	18	32	27
20	10	27	18

TABLE 3

Price (dollars per cup)	Hot chocolate (number per week)		
	50°F	70°F	90°F
2.00	40	30	20
2.50	30	20	10
3.00	20	10	0
3.50	10	0	0

APPENDIX CHECKPOINT

Study Plan Problems

The spreadsheet in Table 1 provides data on the U.S. economy: Column A is the year; the other columns are quantities sold in millions per year of compact discs (column B), music videos (column C), and singles downloads (column D). Use this spreadsheet to work Problems **1** and **2**.

1. Draw a scatter diagram to show the relationship between the quantities sold of compact discs and music videos. Describe the relationship.

2. Draw a time-series graph of the quantity of compact discs sold. Say in which year or years the quantity sold (a) was highest, (b) was lowest, (c) increased the most, and (d) decreased the most. If the data show a trend, describe it.

3. The following data shows the relationship between two variables x and y.

x	0	1	2	3	4	5
y	32	31	28	23	16	7

   Is the relationship between x and y positive or negative? Calculate the slope of the relationship when x equals 2 and when x equals 4. How does the slope change as the value of x increases?

4. Table 2 provides data on the price of a balloon ride, the temperature, and the number of rides a day. Draw graphs to show the relationship between

   • The price and the number of rides, when the temperature is 70°F.

   • The number of rides and the temperature, when the price is $15 a ride.

Instructor Assignable Problems

Use the following information in Table 1 to work Problems **1** and **2**.

1. Draw a scatter diagram to show the relationship between quantities sold of music videos and singles downloads. Describe the relationship.

2. Draw a time-series graph of the quantity of music videos sold. Say in which year or years the quantity sold (a) was highest, (b) was lowest, (c) decreased the most, and (d) decreased the least. If the data show a trend, describe it.

Use the following data on the relationship between two variables x and y to work Problems **3** and **4**.

x	0	1	2	3	4	5
y	0	1	4	9	16	25

3. Is the relationship between x and y positive or negative? Explain.

4. Calculate the slope of the relationship when x equals 2 and x equals 4. How does the slope change as the value of x increases?

5. Table 3 provides data on the price of hot chocolate, the temperature, and the number of cups a week. Draw graphs to show the relationship between

   • The price and the number of cups of hot chocolate, when the temperature is constant.

   • The temperature and the number of cups of hot chocolate, when the price is constant.

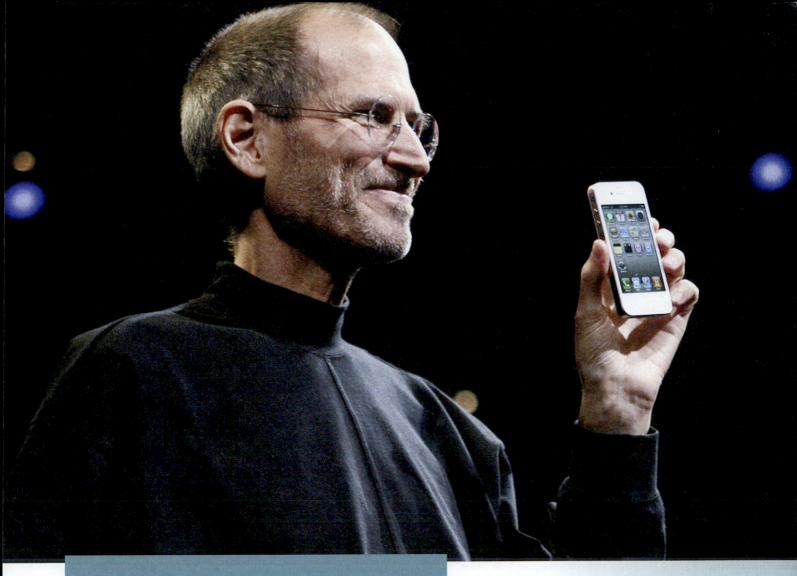

The U.S. and Global Economies

2

CHAPTER CHECKLIST

When you have completed your study of this chapter, you will be able to

1 Describe what, how, and for whom goods and services are produced in the United States.

2 Describe what, how, and for whom goods and services are produced in the global economy.

3 Use the circular flow model to provide a picture of how households, firms, and governments interact in the U.S. economy and how the U.S. and other economies interact in the global economy.

31

2.1   WHAT, HOW, AND FOR WHOM?

Walk around a shopping mall and pay close attention to the range of goods and services that are being offered for sale. Go inside some of the shops and look at the labels to see where various items are manufactured. The next time you travel on an interstate highway, look at the large trucks and pay attention to the names and products printed on their sides and the places in which the trucks are registered. Open the Yellow Pages and flip through a few sections. Notice the huge range of goods and services that businesses are offering.

You've just done a sampling of *what* goods and services are produced and consumed in the United States today.

■ What Do We Produce?

We place the goods and services produced into four large groups:

- Consumption goods and services
- Capital goods
- Government goods and services
- Export goods and services

Consumption goods and services
Goods and services that are bought by individuals and used to provide personal enjoyment and contribute to a person's quality of life.

Capital goods
Goods that are bought by businesses to increase their productive resources.

Government goods and services
Goods and services that are bought by governments.

Export goods and services
Goods and services that are produced in one country and sold in other countries.

Consumption goods and services are items that are bought by individuals and used to provide personal enjoyment and contribute to a person's quality of life. They include items such as housing, SUVs, bottled water and ramen noodles, chocolate bars and Po' Boy sandwiches, movies, downhill skiing lessons, and doctor and dental services.

Capital goods are goods that are bought by businesses to increase their productive resources. They include items such as auto assembly lines, shopping malls, airplanes, and oil tankers.

Government goods and services are items that are bought by governments. Governments purchase missiles and weapons systems, travel services, Internet services, police protection, roads, and paper and paper clips.

Export goods and services are items that are produced in one country and sold in other countries. U.S. export goods and services include the airplanes produced by Boeing that Singapore Airlines buys, the computers produced by Dell that Europeans buy, and licenses sold by U.S. film companies to show U.S. movies in European movie theaters.

Of the four groups of goods and services that we've just defined, consumption goods and services have the largest share and a share that doesn't fluctuate much. The volume of capital goods produced fluctuates as the economy cycles from boom to recession. Goods and services bought by governments are close to a fifth of total production and export goods around one tenth.

Breaking the goods and services down into smaller categories, health services is the largest category, with 17 percent of the value of total production. Real estate services come next at 12 percent. The main component of this item is the services of rental and owner-occupied housing. Education is the next largest service, followed by retail and wholesale trades and transportation and storage.

The categories of goods production are smaller than those of services. The largest category of goods—construction—accounts for only 4 percent of the value of total production, and the next three—utilities, food, and chemicals—each accounts for 2 percent or less.

EYE on the U.S. ECONOMY
What We Produce

In 2011, consumption goods and services accounted for 61 percent of total production, both capital goods and export goods and services accounted for 11 percent, and government goods and services for 17 percent.

Health-care and real estate services, education, retail and wholesale trades, and transportation and storage are the six largest services produced. Construction, utilities, food, and chemicals are the largest categories of goods produced.

The production of services greatly exceeds goods production and is growing faster.

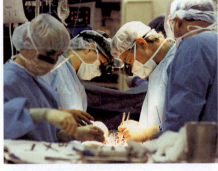

Health-care services …

education services …

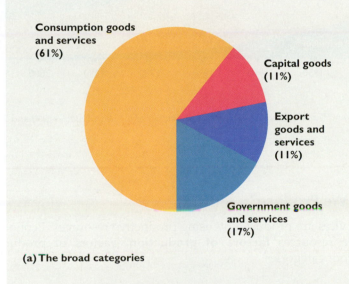

Consumption goods and services (61%)

Capital goods (11%)

Export goods and services (11%)

Government goods and services (17%)

(a) The broad categories

Services
- Health
- Real estate
- Education
- Retail trades
- Wholesale trades
- Transportation and storage

Goods
- Construction
- Utilities
- Food
- Chemicals

0   5   10   15   20
Percentage of total production

(b) Some of the details

retail trades …

and chemicals are among the largest categories of goods and services produced.

SOURCE OF DATA: Bureau of Economic Analysis.

EYE on the PAST
Changes in What We Produce

Seventy years ago, one American in four worked on a farm. That number has shrunk to one in thirty-five. The number of people who produce goods—in mining, construction, and manufacturing—has also shrunk, from one in three to one in five. In contrast, the number of people who produce services has expanded from one in two to almost four in five. These changes in employment reflect changes in what we produce—services.

We hear a lot about globalization and American manufacturing jobs going overseas, but the expansion of service jobs and shrinking of manufacturing jobs is not new. It has been going on over the past 60 years and is likely to continue.

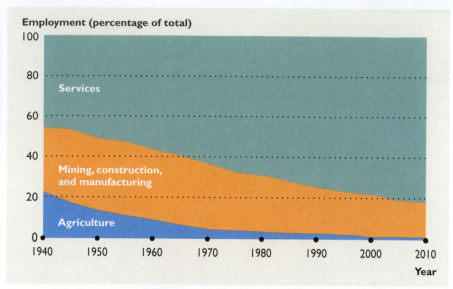

SOURCE OF DATA: U.S. Census Bureau, *Statistical Abstract of the United States*, 1999 and 2010.

■ How Do We Produce?

Goods and services are produced by using productive resources. Economists call the productive resources **factors of production**. Factors of production are grouped into four categories:

- Land
- Labor
- Capital
- Entrepreneurship

Factors of production
The productive resources that are used to produce goods and services—land, labor, capital, and entrepreneurship.

Land

In economics, **land** includes all the "gifts of nature" that we use to produce goods and services. Land is what, in everyday language, we call *natural resources*. It includes land in the everyday sense, minerals, energy, water, air, and wild plants, animals, birds, and fish. Some of these resources are renewable, and some are non-renewable. The U.S. Geological Survey maintains a national inventory of the quantity and quality of natural resources and monitors changes to that inventory.

The United States covers almost 2 billion acres. About 45 percent of the land is forest, lakes, and national parks. In 2009, almost 50 percent of the land was used for agriculture and 5 percent was urban, but urban land use is growing and agricultural land use is shrinking.

Our land surface and water resources are renewable, and some of our mineral resources can be recycled. But many mineral resources can be used only once. They are nonrenewable resources. Of these, the United States has vast known reserves of coal but much smaller known reserves of oil and natural gas.

Land
The "gifts of nature," or *natural resources*, that we use to produce goods and services.

34

Labor

Labor is the work time and work effort that people devote to producing goods and services. Labor includes the physical and mental efforts of all the people who work on farms and construction sites and in factories, shops, and offices. The Census Bureau and Bureau of Labor Statistics measure the quantity of labor at work every month.

In the United States in April 2011, 153 million people had jobs or were available for work. Some worked full time, some worked part time, and some were unemployed but looking for an acceptable vacant job. The total amount of time worked during 2011 was about 250 billion hours.

The quantity of labor increases as the adult population increases. The quantity of labor also increases if a larger percentage of the population takes jobs. During the past 50 years, a larger proportion of women have taken paid work and this trend has increased the quantity of labor. At the same time, a slightly smaller proportion of men have taken paid work and this trend has decreased the quantity of labor.

The *quality* of labor depends on how skilled people are. A laborer who can push a hand cart but can't drive a truck is much less productive than one who can drive. An office worker who can use a computer is much more productive than one who can't. Economists use a special name for human skill: human capital. **Human capital** is the knowledge and skill that people obtain from education, on-the-job training, and work experience.

You are building your own human capital right now as you work on your economics course and other subjects. Your human capital will continue to grow when you get a full-time job and become better at it. Human capital improves the *quality* of labor and increases the quantity of goods and services that labor can produce.

Labor
The work time and work effort that people devote to producing goods and services.

Human capital
The knowledge and skill that people obtain from education, on-the-job training, and work experience.

Capital

Capital consists of the tools, instruments, machines, buildings, and other items that have been produced in the past and that businesses now use to produce goods and services. Capital includes hammers and screwdrivers, computers, auto assembly lines, office towers and warehouses, dams and power plants, airplanes, shirt factories, and shopping malls.

Capital also includes inventories of unsold goods or of partly finished goods on a production line. And capital includes what is sometimes called *infrastructure capital*, such as highways and airports.

Capital, like human capital, makes labor more productive. A truck driver can produce vastly more transportation services than the pusher of a hand cart; the Interstate highway system enables us to produce vastly more transportation services than was possible on the old highway system that preceded it.

The Bureau of Economic Analysis in the U.S. Department of Commerce keeps track of the total value of capital in the United States and how it grows over time. Today, the value of capital in the U.S. economy is around $50 trillion.

Capital
Tools, instruments, machines, buildings, and other items that have been produced in the past and that businesses now use to produce goods and services.

Financial Capital Is Not Capital

In everyday language, we talk about money, stocks, and bonds as being capital. These items are *financial capital*, and they are not productive resources. They enable people to provide businesses with financial resources, but they are *not* used to produce goods and services. They are not capital.

EYE on the U.S. ECONOMY
Changes in How We Produce in the Information Economy

The information economy consists of the jobs and businesses that produce and use computers and equipment powered by computer chips. This information economy is highly visible in your daily life.

The pairs of images here illustrate two examples. In each pair, a new technology enables capital to replace labor.

The top pair of pictures illustrate the replacement of bank tellers (labor) with ATMs (capital). Although the ATM was invented almost 40 years ago, when it made its first appearance, it was located only inside banks and was not able to update customers' accounts. It is only in the last decade that ATMs have spread to corner stores and enable us to get cash and check our bank balance from almost anywhere in the world.

The bottom pair of pictures illustrate a more recent replacement of labor with capital: self-check-in. Air passengers today issue their own boarding pass, often at their own computer before leaving home. For international

flights, some of these machines now even check passport details.

The number of bank teller and airport check-in clerk jobs is shrinking,

but these new technologies are creating a whole range of new jobs for people who make, program, install, and repair the vast number of machines.

Entrepreneurship
The human resource that organizes labor, land, and capital to produce goods and services.

Entrepreneurship

Entrepreneurship is the human resource that organizes land, labor, and capital to produce goods and services. Entrepreneurs are creative and imaginative. They come up with new ideas about what and how to produce, make business decisions, and bear the risks that arise from these decisions. If their ideas work out, they earn a profit. If their ideas turn out to be wrong, they bear the loss.

The quantity of entrepreneurship is hard to describe or measure. During some periods, there appears to be a great deal of imaginative entrepreneurship around. People such as Sam Walton, who created Wal-Mart, one of the world's largest retailers; Bill Gates, who founded the Microsoft empire; and Mark Zuckerberg, who founded Facebook, are examples of extraordinary entrepreneurial talent. But these highly visible entrepreneurs are just the tip of an iceberg that consists of hundreds of thousands of people who run businesses, large and small.

■ For Whom Do We Produce?

Who gets the goods and services depends on the incomes that people earn. A large income enables a person to buy large quantities of goods and services. A small income leaves a person with a small quantity of goods and services.

People earn their incomes by selling the services of the factors of production they own. **Rent** is paid for the use of land, **wages** are paid for the services of labor, **interest** is paid for the use of capital, and entrepreneurs receive a **profit** (or incur a **loss**) for running their businesses. What are the shares of these four factor incomes in the United States? Which factor receives the largest share?

Figure 2.1(a) answers these questions. It shows that wages were 69 percent of total income in 2010 and rent, interest, and profit were 31 percent of total income. These percentages remain remarkably constant over time. We call the distribution of income among the factors of production the *functional distribution of income.*

Figure 2.1(b) shows the *personal distribution of income*—the distribution of income among households. Some households, like that of Carlos Rodriguez, earn many million of dollars a year. These households are in the richest 20 percent who earn 51 percent of total income. Households at the other end of the scale, like those of fast-food servers, are in the poorest 20 percent who earn only 3 percent of total income. The distribution of income has been changing and becoming more unequal. The rich have become richer. But it isn't the case, on the whole, that the poor have become poorer. They just haven't become richer as fast as the rich have.

Rent
Income paid for the use of land.

Wages
Income paid for the services of labor.

Interest
Income paid for the use of capital.

Profit (or loss)
Income earned by an entrepreneur for running a business.

■ **FIGURE 2.1**

For Whom in 2010?   MyEconLab Animation

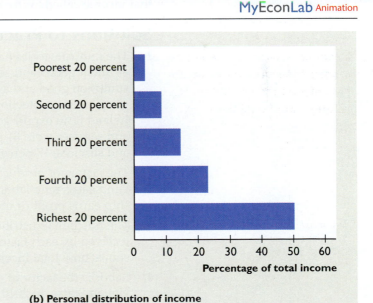

(a) Functional distribution of income   (b) Personal distribution of income

SOURCES OF DATA: Bureau of Economic Analysis, *National Income and Product Accounts*, Table 1.10 and U.S. Census Bureau, *Income, Poverty, and Health Insurance in the United States*: 2010, Current Population Reports P60-235, 2010.

In 2010, wages (the income from labor) were 69 percent of total income. Rent, interest, and profit (the income from the services of land, capital, and entrepreneurship) totaled the remaining 31 percent.

In 2010, the 20 percent of the population with the highest incomes received 51 percent of total income. The 20 percent with the lowest incomes received only 3 percent of total income.

CHECKPOINT 2.1

Describe what, how, and for whom goods and services are produced in the United States.

Practice Problems

1. Name the four broad categories of goods and services that we use in economics. Provide an example of each (different from those in the chapter) and say what percentage of total production each accounted for in 2011.

2. Name the four factors of production and the incomes they earn.

3. Distinguish between the functional distribution of income and the personal distribution of income.

4. In the United States, which factor of production earned the largest share of income in 2010 and what percentage did it earn?

In the News

What microloans miss

The 2006 Nobel Peace Prize winner Muhammad Yunus has said that "all people are entrepreneurs" and that microloans will pull poor people out of poverty. Only 14 percent of Americans are entrepreneurs while almost 40 percent of Peruvians are.

Source: James Surowiecki, *The New Yorker*, March 17, 2008

With only 14 percent of Americans earning their income from entrepreneurship, from what factor of production do most Americans earn their income? What is that income called? Why might so many people in Peru be entrepreneurs?

Solutions to Practice Problems

1. The four categories are consumption goods and services, capital goods, government goods and services, and export goods and services. A shirt is a consumption good and a haircut is a consumption service. An oil rig is a capital good, police protection is a government service, and a computer chip sold to Ireland is an export good. Of total production in 2011, consumption goods and services were 61 percent; capital goods, 11 percent; government goods and services, 17 percent; and export goods and services, 11 percent.

2. The factors of production are land, labor, capital, and entrepreneurship. Land earns rent; labor earns wages; capital earns interest; and entrepreneurship earns profit or incurs a loss.

3. The functional distribution of income shows the percentage of total income received by each factor of production. The personal distribution of income shows how total income is shared among households.

4. Labor is the factor of production that earns the largest share of income in the United States. In 2010, labor earned 69 percent of total income.

Solution to In the News

Most Americans earn their income from labor and the income they earn is called a wage. Peru is a poor country in which jobs are more limited than in the United States. So to earn an income, many people are self-employed and work as small entrepreneurs.

2.2 THE GLOBAL ECONOMY

We're now going to look at *what, how,* and *for whom* goods and services get produced in the global economy. We'll begin with a brief overview of the people and countries that form the global economy.

■ The People

Visit the Web site of the U.S. Census Bureau and go to the population clocks to find out how many people there are today in both the United States and the entire world.

On the day these words were written, June 5, 2011, the U.S. clock recorded a population of 311,495,726. The world clock recorded a global population of 6,923,027,156. The U.S. clock ticks along showing a population increase of one person every 12 seconds. The world clock spins faster, adding 30 people in the same 12 seconds.

■ The Countries

The world's 7 billion (and rising) population lives in 176 countries, which the International Monetary Fund classifies into two broad groups of economies:

- Advanced economies
- Emerging market and developing economies

Advanced Economies

Advanced economies are the richest 29 countries (or areas). The United States, Japan, Italy, Germany, France, the United Kingdom, and Canada belong to this group. So do four new industrial Asian economies: Hong Kong, South Korea, Singapore, and Taiwan. The other advanced economies include Australia, New Zealand, and most of the rest of Western Europe. Almost 1 billion people (15 percent of the world's population) live in the advanced economies.

Emerging Market and Developing Economies

Emerging market economies are the 28 countries in Central and Eastern Europe and Asia that were, until the early 1990s, part of the Soviet Union or one of its satellites. Russia is the largest of these economies. Others include the Czech Republic, Hungary, Poland, Ukraine, and Mongolia.

Almost 500 million people live in these countries—only about half of the number in the advanced economies. But these countries are important because they are emerging (hence the name) from a system of state-owned production, central economic planning, and heavily regulated markets to a system of free enterprise and unregulated markets.

Developing economies are the 119 countries in Africa, Asia, the Middle East, Europe, and Central and South America that include China, India, Indonesia, and Brazil. These economies have not yet achieved high average incomes for their people. Average incomes in these economies vary a great deal, but in all cases, these average incomes are much lower than those in the advanced economies, and in some cases, they are extremely low. More than 5 billion people—almost four out of every five people—live in developing economies.

■ *What* in the Global Economy?

First, let's look at the big picture. Imagine that each year the global economy produces an enormous pie. In 2011, the pie was worth about $70 trillion! To give this number some meaning, if the pie were shared equally among the world's 6.9 billion people, each of us would get a slice worth a bit more than $10,145.

Where Is the Global Pie Baked?

Figure 2.2 shows us where in the world the pie is baked. The advanced economies produce 53 percent—20 percent in the United States, 15 percent in the Euro area, and 18 percent in the other advanced economies. The emerging market economies produce another 8 percent. These economies, which produce 61 percent of the world's output (by value) are home to only 20 percent of the world's population.

Most of the rest of the global pie comes from Asia. China produces 13 percent of the total and other developing Asian economies produce 10 percent. The developing countries of Africa and the Middle East produce 7 percent, and the Western Hemisphere—Mexico and South America—produces the rest.

The sizes of the slices in the global production pie are gradually changing—the U.S. share is shrinking and China's share is expanding.

Unlike the slices of an apple pie, those of the global pie have different fillings. Some slices have more oil, some more food, some more clothing, some more housing services, some more autos, and so on. Let's look at some of these different fillings, and at some similarities too.

■ **FIGURE 2.2**

What in the Global Economy in 2010   MyEconLab Animation

If we show the value of production in the world economy as a pie, the United States produces a slice that is 20 percent of the total. The Euro zone and other advanced economies produce 33 percent of the total.

Most of the rest of the global pie comes from Asia. China produces a slice that is 13 percent of the total, and the rest of the developing Asian economies produce 10 percent. The developing countries of Africa, the Middle East, and the Western Hemisphere produce 16 percent, and the emerging market economies produce the rest.

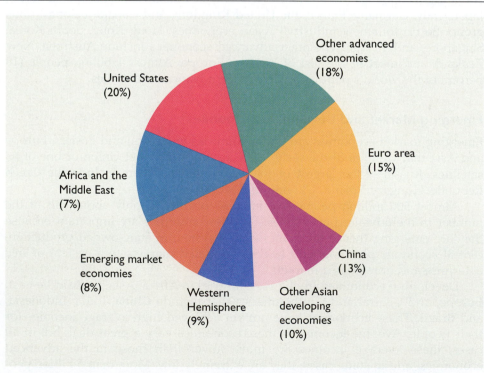

SOURCE OF DATA: International Monetary Fund, World Economic Outlook Database, April 2011.

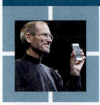

EYE on the iPHONE
Who Makes the iPhone?

Apple designed and markets the iPhone but it doesn't make it. Apple wants to get the iPhone manufactured at the lowest possible cost. It achieves this goal by assigning the task to more than 30 companies on 3 continents who employ thousands of workers. The table identifies some of the companies and the costs of the components they make.

Apple and these firms make decisions and pay their workers, investors, and raw material suppliers to influence *what*, *how*, and *for whom* goods and services are produced.

4Gbyte iPhone costs and producers

Item	Cost	Producer (incomplete list)	Country
Processing chips	31.40	Taiwan Semiconductor	Taiwan
		United Microelectronics Corp	Taiwan
		Samsung	Korea
		Marvell	United States
		Micron	United States
Memory chips	45.80	Intel, SST	United States
Bluetooth	19.10	Cambridge Silicon Radio	United Kingdom
Printed circuit board	36.05	Cheng Uei, Entery	Taiwan
		Cyntec	Taiwan
Phone interface	19.25	Infineon Technology	Germany
Camera module	11.00	Largan Precision	Taiwan
		Altus-Tech, Primax, Lite On	Taiwan
		National Semiconductor	United States
Display	33.50	Novatek	Taiwan
		Sanyo, Epson, Sharp, TMD	Japan
Touch screen controller	1.15	Balda	Germany
		Broadcom	United States
Battery and power management	8.60	Delta Electronics	Taiwan
Case	8.50	Catcher, Foxconn Tech	Taiwan
Assembly	15.50	Foxconn Quanta	Taiwan
Royalties	15.98		
Total cost	**245.83**		

Some Differences in What Is Produced

What is produced in the developing economies contrasts sharply with that of the advanced economies. Manufacturing is the big story. Developing economies have large and growing industries producing textiles, footwear, sports gear, toys, electronic goods, furniture, steel, and even automobiles and airplanes.

Food production is a small part of the U.S. and other advanced economies and a large part of the developing economies such as Brazil, China, and India. But the advanced economies produce about one third of the world's food. How come? Because *total* production is much larger in the advanced economies than in the developing economies, and a small percentage of a big number can be greater than a large percentage of a small number!

Some Similarities in What Is Produced

If you were to visit a shopping mall in Canada, England, Australia, Japan, or any of the other advanced economies, you would wonder whether you had left the United States. You would see Starbucks, Burger King, Pizza Hut, Domino's Pizza, KFC, Kmart, Wal-Mart, Target, the United Colors of Benetton, Gap, Tommy Hilfiger, Tie Rack, the upscale Louis Vuitton and Burberry, and a host of other familiar names. And, of course, you would see McDonald's golden arches. You would see them in any of the 119 countries in which one or more of McDonald's 30,000 restaurants are located.

The similarities among the advanced economies go beyond the view from main street and the shopping mall. The structure of *what* is produced is similar in these economies. As percentages of the total economy, agriculture and manufacturing are small and shrinking whereas services are large and expanding.

McDonald's in Shanghai.

■ *How* in the Global Economy?

Goods and services are produced using land, labor, capital, and entrepreneurial resources, and the combinations of these resources used are chosen to produce at the lowest possible cost. Energy production illustrates this point.

Energy is produced from oil, coal, natural gas, waterfalls and dams, nuclear reactors, windmills, and solar panels. Each of these sources of power uses different combinations of land (which includes natural resources), labor, and capital.

Figure 2.3 shows some interesting facts about energy use and production. Some 80 percent of the energy we use is in the form of electricity. The other 20 percent is for transportation—part (a). Most of the world's electricty is generated using coal (33 percent), natural gas (29 percent), and oil (21 percent), and only 1 percent is generated using wind and solar power —part (b). And almost all the world's transportation is powered by oil (gasoline and diesel), and only 2 percent is powered by ethanol—part (c).

Each country or region has its own blend of land, labor, and capital. But there are some interesting common patterns and crucial differences between the advanced and developing economies that we'll now examine.

Human Capital Differences

The proportion of the population with a degree or that has completed high school is small in developing economies. And in the poorest of the developing economies, many children even miss out on basic primary education. They just don't go to school at all. On-the-job training and experience are also much less extensive in the developing economies than in the advanced economies.

■ **FIGURE 2.3**

How Energy is Used and Produced in the Global Economy   MyEconLab Animation

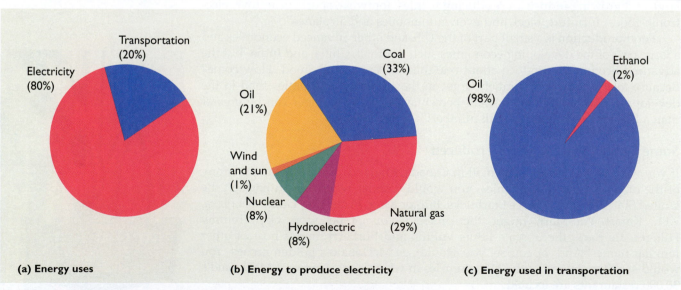

(a) Energy uses   (b) Energy to produce electricity   (c) Energy used in transportation

Sources of data: Energy Information Administration and BP Review of World Energy, June 2011.

Energy is used to generate electricity (80 percent) and for transportation (20 percent) shown in part (a).

Most electricity is produced using coal, natural gas, and oil. Only 9 percent comes from water, wind, and sun power—in part (b).

Almost all transportation is powered by oil (gasoline and diesel) and only 2 percent is powered by ethanol—in part (c).

Physical Capital Differences

The major feature of an advanced economy that differentiates it from a developing economy is the amount of capital available for producing goods and services. The differences begin with the basic transportation system. In the advanced economies, a well-developed highway system connects all the major cities and points of production. You can see this difference most vividly by opening a road atlas of North America and contrasting the U.S. interstate highway system with the sparse highways of Mexico. You would see a similar contrast if you flipped through a road atlas of Western Europe and Africa.

But it isn't the case that the developing economies have no highways. In fact, some of them have the newest and the best. But the new and best are usually inside and around the major cities. The smaller centers and rural areas of developing economies often have some of the worst roads in the world.

The contrast in vehicles is perhaps even greater than that in highways. You're unlikely to run across a horse-drawn wagon in an advanced economy, but in a developing economy, animal power can still be found, and trucks are often old and unreliable.

The contrasts in the transportation system are matched by those on farms and in factories. In general, the more advanced the economy, the greater are the amount and sophistication of the capital equipment used in production. But again, the contrast is not all black and white. Some factories in India, China, and other parts of Asia use the very latest technologies. Furniture manufacture is an example. To make furniture of a quality that Americans are willing to buy, firms in Asia use machines like those in the furniture factories of North Carolina.

Again, it is the extensiveness of the use of modern capital-intensive technologies that distinguishes a developing economy from an advanced economy. All the factories in the advanced economies are capital intensive compared with only some in the developing economies.

The differences in human and physical capital between advanced and developing economies have a big effect on who gets the goods and services.

Beijing has a highway system to match that of any advanced country. But away from the major cities, many of China's roads are unpaved and driving on them is slow and sometimes hazardous.

■ *For Whom* in the Global Economy?

Who gets the world's goods and services depends on the incomes that people earn. So how are incomes distributed across the world?

Personal Distribution of Income

You saw earlier (on p. 37) that in the United States, the lowest-paid 20 percent of the population receives 3 percent of total income and the highest-paid 20 percent receives 51 percent of total income. The personal distribution of income in the world economy is much more unequal. According to World Bank data, the lowest-paid 20 percent of the world's population receives 2 percent of world income, and the highest-paid 20 percent receives about 70 percent of world income.

International Distribution

Much of the greater inequality at the global level arises from differences in average incomes among countries. Figure 2.4 shows some of these differences. It shows the dollar value of what people can afford each day on average. You can see that in the United States, that number is $129 a day—an average person in the United States can buy goods and services that cost $129. This amount is around five times the world average. Canada is close to the United States at $126 a day and Japan at $116 a day. The United Kingdom and Euro zone have average incomes of around 80 percent of that of the United States. Income levels fall off quickly as we move farther down the graph, with Africa achieving an average income of only $4 a day and India only $3 a day.

As people have lost well-paid manufacturing jobs and found lower-paid service jobs, inequality has increased in the United States and in most other advanced economies. Inequality is also increasing in the developing economies. People with skills enjoy rapidly rising incomes but the incomes of the unskilled are falling.

A Happy Paradox and a Huge Challenge

Despite the increase in inequality inside most countries, inequality across the entire world has decreased during the past 20 years. And most important, according to Xavier Sala-i-Martin, an economics professor at Columbia University, extreme poverty has declined. Professor Sala-i-Martin estimates that between 1976 and 1998, the number of people who earn $1 a day or less fell by 235 million and the number who earn $2 a day or less fell by 450 million. This happy situation arises because in China, the largest nation, incomes have increased rapidly and lifted millions from extreme poverty. Incomes are growing quickly in India too.

Lifting Africa from poverty is today's big challenge. In 1960, 11 percent of the world's poor lived in Africa, but in 1998, 66 percent did. Between 1976 and 1998, the number of people in Africa who earn $1 a day or less rose by 175 million, and the number who earn $2 a day or less rose by 227 million.

■ **FIGURE 2.4**

For Whom in the Global Economy in 2010   MyEconLab Animation

In 2010, the average income per person per day in the United States was $129. It was $126 in Canada and $99 in the United Kingdom. It was $116 in Japan and $100 in the Euro area. The number falls off rapidly to $29 in Russia, $12 in China, $4 in Africa, and $3 in India.

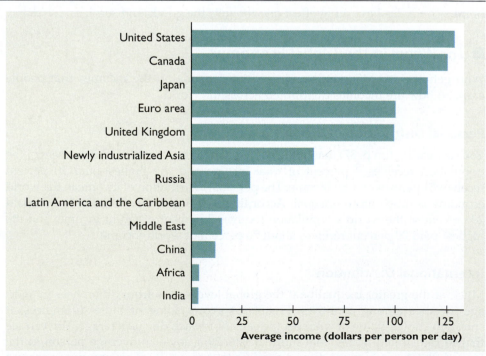

SOURCE OF DATA: International Monetary Fund, World Economic Outlook Database, April 2011.

EYE on YOUR LIFE
The U.S. and Global Economies in Your Life

You've encountered a lot of facts and trends about what, how, and for whom goods and services are produced in the U.S. economy and the global economy. How can you use this information? You can use it in two ways:

1. To inform your choice of career
2. To inform your stand on the politics of protecting U.S. jobs

Career Choices

As you think about your future career, you are now better informed about some of the key trends. You know that manufacturing is shrinking. The U.S. economy is what is sometimes called a *post-industrial economy*. Industries that provided the backbone of the economy in previous generations have fallen to barely a fifth of

the economy today, and the trend continues. It is possible that by the middle of the current century, manufacturing will be as small a source of jobs as agriculture is today.

So, a job in a manufacturing business is likely to lead to some tough situations and possibly the need for several job changes over a working life.

As manufacturing shrinks, so services expand, and this expansion will continue. The provision of health care, education, communication, wholesale and retail trades, and entertainment are all likely to expand in the future and be sources of increasing employment and rising wages. A job in a service-oriented business is more likely to lead to steady advances in income.

Political Stand on Job Protection

As you think about the stand you will take on the political question of protecting U.S. jobs, you are better informed about the basic facts and trends. When you hear that manufacturing jobs are disappearing to China, you will be able to place that news in historical perspective. You might reasonably be concerned, especially if you or a member of your family has lost a job. But you know that trying to reverse or even halt this process is flying in the face of stubborn historical trends.

In later chapters, you will learn that there are good economic reasons to be skeptical about any form of protection and placing limits on competition.

CHECKPOINT 2.2

Describe what, how, and for whom goods and services are produced in the global economy.

MyEconLab
You can work these problems in Study Plan 2.2 and get instant feedback.

Practice Problems

1. Describe what, how, and for whom goods and services are produced in developing economies.
2. A Clinton Foundation success story is that it loaned $23,000 to Rwandan coffee growers to support improvements to coffee washing stations and provided technical support. What was the source of the success?

Solutions to Practice Problems

1. In developing countries, agriculture is the largest percentage, manufacturing is an increasing percentage, and services are a small percentage of total production. Most production does not use modern capital-intensive technologies, but some industries do. People who work in factories have rising incomes while those who work in rural industries are left behind.
2. Rwandan coffee growers improved their knowledge of coffee farming, which increased their human capital. The improvements to washing stations was a change in physical capital that allowed farmers to increase the quantity of washed coffee.

Circular flow model
A model of the economy that shows the circular flow of expenditures and incomes that result from decision makers' choices and the way those choices interact to determine what, how, and for whom goods and services are produced.

Households
Individuals or groups of people living together.

Firms
The institutions that organize the production of goods and services.

Market
Any arrangement that brings buyers and sellers together and enables them to get information and do business with each other.

Goods markets
Markets in which goods and services are bought and sold.

Factor markets
Markets in which the services of factors of production are bought and sold.

We can organize the data you've just studied using the **circular flow model**—a model of the economy that shows the circular flow of expenditures and incomes that result from decision makers' choices and the way those choices interact to determine what, how, and for whom goods and services are produced. Figure 2.5 shows the circular flow model.

■ Households and Firms

Households are individuals or groups of people living together. The 118 million households in the United States own the factors of production—land, labor, capital, and entrepreneurship—and choose the quantities of these resources to provide to firms. Households also choose the quantities of goods and services to buy.

Firms are the institutions that organize the production of goods and services. The 20 million firms in the United States choose the quantities of the factors of production to hire and the quantities of goods and services to produce.

■ Markets

Households choose the quantities of the factors of production to provide to firms, and firms choose the quantities of the services of the factors of production to hire. Firms choose the quantities of goods and services to produce, and households choose the quantities of goods and services to buy. How are these choices coordinated and made compatible? The answer is: by markets.

A **market** is any arrangement that brings buyers and sellers together and enables them to get information and do business with each other. An example is the market in which oil is bought and sold—the world oil market. The world oil market is not a place. It is the network of oil producers, oil users, wholesalers, and brokers who buy and sell oil. In the world oil market, decision makers do not meet physically. They make deals by telephone, fax, and the Internet.

Figure 2.5 identifies two types of markets: goods markets and factor markets. Goods and services are bought and sold in **goods markets**; and the services of factors of production are bought and sold in **factor markets**.

■ Real Flows and Money Flows

When households choose the quantities of services of land, labor, capital, and entrepreneurship to offer in factor markets, they respond to the incomes they receive—rent for land, wages for labor, interest for capital, and profit for entrepreneurship. When firms choose the quantities of factor services to hire, they respond to the rent, wages, interest, and profits they must pay to households.

Similarly, when firms choose the quantities of goods and services to produce and offer for sale in goods markets, they respond to the amounts that they receive from the expenditures that households make. And when households choose the quantities of goods and services to buy, they respond to the amounts they must pay to firms.

Figure 2.5 shows the flows that result from these choices made by households and firms. The flows shown in orange are *real flows:* the flows of the factors of production that go from households through factor markets to firms and of the goods and services that go from firms through goods markets to households. The flows in the opposite direction are *money flows:* the flows of payments made in exchange for the services of factors of production (shown in blue) and of expenditures on goods and services (shown in red).

Lying behind these real flows and money flows are millions of individual choices about what to consume and what and how to produce. These choices result in buying plans by households and selling plans by firms in goods markets. And the choices result in selling plans by households and buying plans by firms in factor markets that interact to determine the prices that people pay and the incomes they earn, and so determine for whom goods and services are produced. You'll learn in Chapter 4 how markets coordinate the buying plans and selling plans of households and firms and make them compatible.

Firms produce most of the goods and services that we consume, but governments provide some of the services that we enjoy. Governments also play a big role in modifying for whom goods and services are produced by changing the personal distribution of income. We're now going to look at the role of governments in the U.S. economy and add them to the circular flow model.

FIGURE 2.5

The Circular Flow Model   MyEconLab Animation

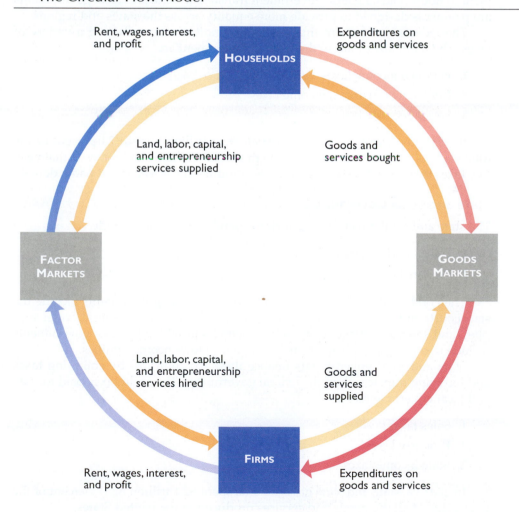

The orange flows are the services of factors of production that go from households through factor markets to firms and the goods and services that go from firms through goods markets to households. These flows are *real* flows.

The blue flow is the income earned by the factors of production, and the red flow is the expenditures on goods and services. These flows are *money* flows.

The choices that generate these real and money flows determine *what*, *how*, and *for whom* goods and services are produced.

■ Governments

More than 86,000 organizations operate as governments in the United States. Some are tiny like the Yuma, Arizona, school district and some are enormous like the U.S. federal government. We divide governments into two levels:

- Federal government
- State and local government

Federal Government

The federal government's major expenditures provide

1. Good and services
2. Social Security and welfare payments
3. Transfers to state and local governments

The goods and services provided by the federal government include the legal system, which protects property and enforces contracts, and national defense. Social Security and welfare benefits, which include income for retired people and programs such as Medicare and Medicaid, are transfers from the federal government to households. Federal government transfers to state and local governments are payments designed to provide more equality across the states and regions.

The federal government finances its expenditures by collecting a variety of taxes. The main taxes paid to the federal government are

1. Personal income taxes
2. Corporate (business) income taxes
3. Social Security taxes

In 2010, the federal government spent $3.5 trillion—about 24 percent of the total value of all the goods and services produced in the United States in that year. The taxes they raised were less than this amount—the government had a deficit.

State and Local Government

The state and local governments' major expenditures are to provide

1. Goods and services
2. Welfare benefits

The goods and services provided by state and local governments include the state courts and police, schools, roads, garbage collection and disposal, water supplies, and sewage management. Welfare benefits provided by state governments include unemployment benefits and other aid to low-income families.

State and local governments finance these expenditures by collecting taxes and receiving transfers from the federal government. The main taxes paid to state and local governments are

1. Sales taxes
2. Property taxes
3. State income taxes

In 2007-08, state and local governments spent $2.1 trillion or 17 percent of the total value of all the goods and services produced in the United States.

■ Governments in the Circular Flow

Figure 2.6 adds governments to the circular flow model. As you study this figure, first notice that the outer circle is the same as in Figure 2.5. In addition to these flows, governments buy goods and services from firms. The red arrows that run from governments through the goods markets to firms show this expenditure.

Households and firms pay taxes to governments. The green arrows running directly from households and firms to governments show these flows. Also, governments make money payments to households and firms. The green arrows running directly from governments to households and firms show these flows. Taxes and transfers are direct transactions with governments and do not go through the goods markets and factor markets.

Not part of the circular flow and not visible in Figure 2.6, governments provide the legal framework within which all transactions occur. For example, governments operate the courts and legal system that enable contracts to be written and enforced.

■ **FIGURE 2.6**

Governments in the Circular Flow

MyEconLab Animation

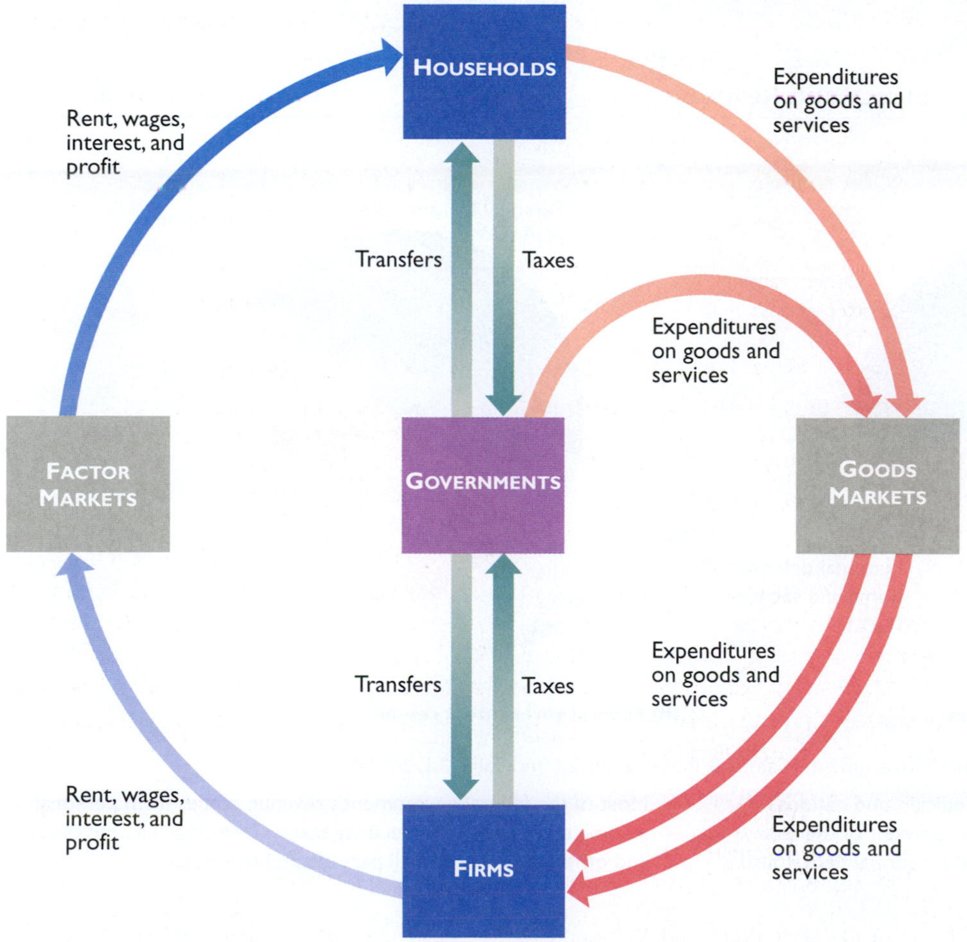

The green flows from households and firms to governments are taxes, and the green flows from governments to households and firms are money transfers.

The red flow from governments through the goods markets to firms is the expenditure on goods and services by governments.

■ Federal Government Expenditures and Revenue

What are the main items of expenditure by the federal government on goods and services and transfers? And what are its main sources of tax revenue? Figure 2.7 answers these questions.

Three items of expenditure are similar in magnitude—and large. They are Social Security benefits, Medicare and Medicaid, and national defense and homeland security. The combined total of these items is 64 percent of the government's expenditures. Other transfers to persons, which includes unemployment benefits, are also large. The "Others" category covers a wide range of items and includes transfers to state governments, NASA's space program, and the National Science Foundation's funding of research in the universities.

The interest payment on the national debt is another significant item. The **national debt** is the total amount that the federal government has borrowed to make expenditures that exceed tax revenue—to run a government budget deficit. The national debt is a bit like a large credit card balance, and paying the interest on the national debt is like paying the minimum required monthly payment.

Most of the tax revenue of the federal government comes from personal income taxes and Social Security taxes. Corporate income taxes and other taxes are a small part of the federal government's revenue.

National debt

The total amount that the federal government has borrowed to make expenditures that exceed tax revenue—to run a government budget deficit.

■ FIGURE 2.7

Federal Government Expenditures and Revenue

MyEconLab Animation

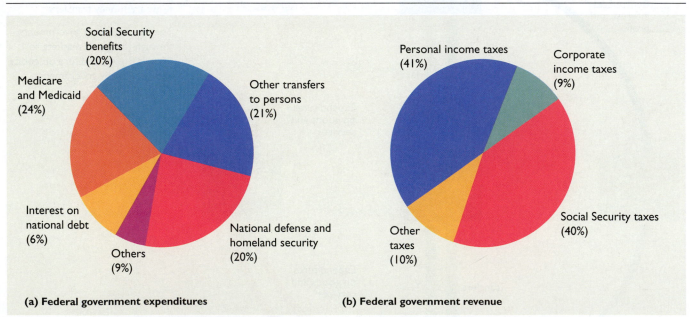

(a) Federal government expenditures

(b) Federal government revenue

SOURCE OF DATA: Budget of the United States Government, Historical Tables, Table 2.1 and Table 3.1, 2010 data.

Social Security benefits, Medicare and Medicaid, and national defense and homeland security absorb 64 percent of the federal government's expenditures. Interest on the national debt is also a significant item.

Most of the federal government's revenue comes from personal income taxes and Social Security taxes. Corporate income taxes and other taxes are a small part of total revenue.

■ State and Local Government Expenditures and Revenue

What are the main items of expenditure by the state and local governments on goods and services and transfers? And what are the main sources of state and local government revenue? Figure 2.8 answers these questions.

You can see that education is by far the largest part of the expenditures of state and local governments. This item covers the cost of public schools, colleges, and universities. It absorbs 34 percent of total expenditures—approximately $826 billion, or $2,650 per person.

Public welfare benefits are the second largest item and they take 17 percent of total expenditures. Highways are the next largest item, and they account for 6 percent of total expenditures. The remaining 43 percent is spent on other local public goods and services such as police services, garbage collection and disposal, sewage management, and water supplies.

Sales taxes and transfers from the federal government bring in similar amounts—about 18 percent and 20 percent of total revenue, respectively. Property taxes account for 17 percent of total revenue. Individual income taxes account for 13 percent, and corporate income taxes account for 2 percent. The remaining revenue comes from other taxes such as those on gasoline, cigarettes, and beer and wine.

■ FIGURE 2.8

State and Local Government Expenditures and Revenue

MyEconLab Animation

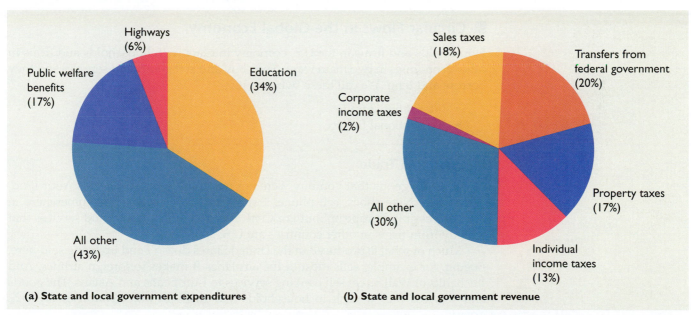

(a) State and local government expenditures

(b) State and local government revenue

SOURCES OF DATA: *Economic Report of the President 2009,* Table B-86, 2007–2008 data.

The largest slices of state and local government expenditures are education (34 percent of total expenditure), public welfare benefits (17 percent), and highways (6 percent).

Most of the state and local government revenue comes from sales taxes (18 percent of total revenue), property taxes (17 percent), and transfers from the federal government (20 percent).

EYE on the PAST
Growing Government

One hundred years ago, the federal government spent 2 cents out of each dollar earned. Today, the federal government spends 23 cents. Government grew during the two world wars and during the 1960s and 1970s as social programs expanded.

Only during the 1980s and 1990s did big government begin to shrink in a process begun by Ronald Reagan and continued by Bill Clinton. But 9/11 saw the start of a new era of growing government, and fiscal stimulus and bailouts to cope with the global financial crisis sent spending soaring.

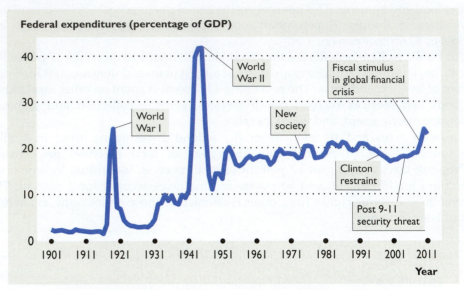

SOURCE OF DATA: Budget of the United States Government, Historical Tables, Table 1.1.

■ Circular Flows in the Global Economy

Households and firms in the U.S. economy interact with households and firms in other economies in two main ways: They buy and sell goods and services and they borrow and lend. We call these two activities:

- International trade
- International finance

International Trade

Many of the goods that you buy were not made in the United States. Your iPod, Wii games, Nike shoes, cell phone, T-shirt, and bike were made somewhere in Asia or possibly Europe or South or Central America. The goods and services that we buy from firms in other countries are U.S. *imports.*

Much of what is produced in the United States doesn't end up being sold here. Boeing, for example, sells most of the airplanes it makes to foreign airlines. And the banks of Wall Street sell banking services to Europeans and Asians. The goods and services that we sell to households and firms in other countries are U.S. *exports.*

International Finance

When firms or governments want to borrow, they look for the lowest interest rate available. Sometimes, that is outside the United States. Also, when the value of our imports exceeds the value of our exports, we must borrow from the rest of the world.

Firms and governments in the rest of the world behave in the same way. They look for the lowest interest rate at which to borrow and the highest at which to lend. They might borrow from or lend to Americans.

Figure 2.9 shows the flows through goods markets and financial markets in the global economy. Households and firms in the U.S. economy interact with those in the rest of the world (other economies) in goods markets and financial markets.

The red flow shows the expenditure by Americans on imports of goods and services, and the blue flow shows the expenditure by the rest of the world on U.S. exports (other countries' imports). The green flow shows U.S. lending to the rest of the world, and the orange flow shows U.S. borrowing from the rest of the world.

It is these international trade and international finance flows that tie nations together in the global economy and through which global booms and slumps are transmitted.

■ FIGURE 2.9

Circular Flows in the Global Economy   MyEconLab Animation

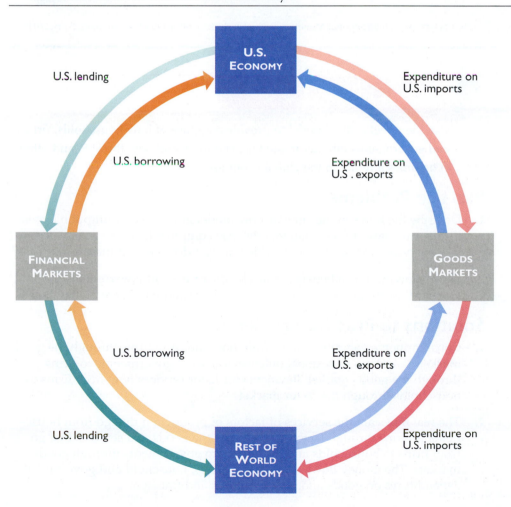

Households and firms in the U.S. economy interact with those in the rest of the world (other economies) in goods markets and financial markets.

The red flow shows the expenditure by Americans on imports of goods and services, and the blue flow shows the expenditure by the rest of the world on U.S. exports (other countries' imports).

The green flow shows U.S. lending to the rest of the world, and the orange flow shows U.S. borrowing from the rest of the world.

International trade has expanded rapidly during the past 25 years. At an average growth rate of close to 7 percent a year, world trade has doubled every decade.

In 2001, a mini-recession in the United States slowed world trade growth to a crawl.

But the 2001 slowdown looks mild compared to the collapse in world trade during the 2009 global economic slump. Despite the slump in 2009, world trade was back to a normal level in 2010 and 2011.

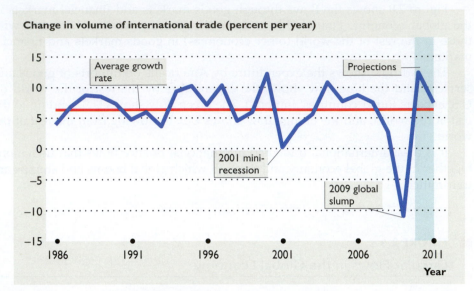

SOURCE OF DATA: International Monetary Fund, World Economic Outlook Database, April 2011.

MyEconLab
You can work these problems in Study Plan 2.3 and get instant feedback.

CHECKPOINT 2.3

Use the circular flow model to provide a picture of how households, firms, and governments interact in the U.S. economy and how the U.S. and other economies interact in the global economy.

Practice Problems

1. Describe the flows in the circular flow model in which consumption expenditure, purchases of new national defense equipment, and payments for labor services appear. Through which market does each of these flows pass?

2. Of the flows that run between households, firms, and governments in the circular flow model, which ones are real flows and which are money flows?

Solutions to Practice Problems

1. Consumption expenditure flows from households to firms through the goods market. Purchases of national defense flow from governments to firms through the goods market. Payments for labor services flow from firms to households through the factor market.

2. The real flows are the services of factors of production that go from households to firms through factor markets and the goods and services that go from firms to households and from firms to governments through goods markets. The money flows are factor incomes, household and government expenditures on goods and services, taxes, and transfers.

CHAPTER SUMMARY

Key Points

1. Describe what, how, and for whom goods and services are produced in the United States.

- Consumption goods and services represent 61 percent of total production; capital goods represent 11 percent.
- Goods and services are produced by using the four factors of production: land, labor, capital, and entrepreneurship.
- The incomes people earn (rent for land, wages for labor, interest for capital, and profit for entrepreneurship) determine who gets the goods and services produced.

2. Describe what, how, and for whom goods and services are produced in the global economy.

- Sixty-one percent of the world's production (by value) comes from the advanced industrial countries and the emerging market economies.
- Production in the advanced economies uses more capital (both machines and human), but some developing economies use the latest capital and technologies.
- The global distribution of income is more unequal than the U.S. distribution. Poverty has fallen in Asia but has increased in Africa.

3. Use the circular flow model to provide a picture of how households, firms, and governments interact in the U.S. economy and how the U.S. and other economies interact in the global economy.

- The circular flow model of the U.S. economy shows the real flows of factors of production and goods and the corresponding money flows of incomes and expenditures.
- Governments in the circular flow receive taxes, make transfers, and buy goods and services.
- The circular flow model of the global economy shows the flows of U.S. exports and imports and the international financial flows that result from lending to and borrowing from other countries.

Key Terms

Capital, 35
Capital goods, 32
Circular flow model, 46
Consumption goods and services, 32
Entrepreneurship, 36
Export goods and services, 32
Factor markets, 46

Factors of production, 34
Firms, 46
Goods markets, 46
Government goods and services, 32
Households, 46
Human capital, 35
Interest, 37

Labor, 35
Land, 34
Market, 46
National debt, 50
Profit (or loss), 37
Rent, 37
Wages, 37

MyEconLab

You can work these problems in Chapter 2 Study Plan and get instant feedback.

CHAPTER CHECKPOINT

Study Plan Problems and Applications

1. Explain which of the following items are *not* consumption goods and services:
   - A chocolate bar
   - A ski lift
   - A golf ball

2. Explain which of the following items are *not* capital goods:
   - An auto assembly line
   - A shopping mall
   - A golf ball

3. Explain which of the following items are *not* factors of production:
   - Vans used by a baker to deliver bread
   - 1,000 shares of Amazon.com stock
   - Undiscovered oil in the Arctic Ocean

4. Which of the four factors of production earns the highest percentage of total U.S. income? Define that factor of production. What is the income it earns called?

5. With more job training and more scholarships to poor American students, which special factor of production is likely to grow faster than in the past?

6. Define the factor of production called capital. Give three examples of capital, different from those in the chapter. Distinguish between the factor of production capital and financial capital.

7. A Job Creation through Entrepreneurship Act, debated in the House of Representatives in 2009, would award grants to small business owners, some of which would be aimed at women, Native Americans, and veterans. The Act would provide $189 million in 2010 and $531 million between 2010 and 2014. Explain how you would expect this Act to influence *what*, *how*, and *for whom* goods and services are produced in the United States.

8. Indicate on a graph of the circular flow model, the real or money flow in which the following items belong:
   - You pay your tuition.
   - The University of Texas buys some Dell computers.
   - A student works at FedEx Kinko's.
   - Donald Trump rents a Manhattan building to a hotel.
   - You pay your income tax.

9. **For-profit colleges may face aid cuts**

   The Obama administration proposes a new rule: Federal aid to for-profit colleges will be cut if students in vocational programs graduate with worthless degrees. Millions of low-income students are borrowing heavily to attend colleges and too many of them are dropping out, and failing to get a job.

   Source: *USA Today*, June 2, 2011

   How do you think the personal distribution of income would change if all graduates could obtain a well-paying job that uses their knowledge gained in college?

Instructor Assignable Problems and Applications

Your instructor can assign these problems as homework, a quiz, or a test in MyEconLab.

1. Buzz surrounds Apple's iPhone. Can you explain:
- Why doesn't Apple manufacture the iPhone at its own factory in the United States?
- Why doesn't Apple offer a cheaper version of the iPhone with no camera?
- In view of the cost of producing an iPhone (in the table on p. 41), why do you think the price of an iPhone is so high? What other costs must be incurred to bring the iPhone to market other than the cost of manufacturing it?

2. The global economy has three cell phone users for every fixed line user. Two in every three cell phone users lives in a developing nation and the growth rate is fastest in Africa. In 2000, 1 African in 50 had a cell phone; in 2009, it was 14 in 50. Describe the changes in *what, how,* and *for whom* telecommunication services the global economy produces.

3. Which of the entries in List 1 are consumption goods and services and which are government goods? Explain your choice.

4. Which of the entries in List 1 are capital goods? Explain your choice.

5. Which of the entries in List 1 are factors of production? Explain your choice.

6. In the African nation of Senegal, to enroll in school a child needs a Birth Certificate that costs $25. This price is several weeks' income for many families. Explain how this requirement is likely to affect the growth of human capital in Senegal.

7. China's prosperity brings income gap

The Asian Development Bank [ADB] reports that China has the largest gap between the rich and the poor in Asia. Ifzal Ali, the ADB's chief economist, claims it is not that the rich are getting richer and the poor are getting poorer, but that the rich are getting richer faster than the poor.

Source: *Financial Times*, August 9, 2007

Explain how the distribution of personal income in China can be getting more unequal even though the poorest 20 percent are getting richer.

8. Compare the scale of agricultural production in the advanced and developing economies. In which is the percentage higher? In which is the total amount produced greater?

9. On a graph of the circular flow model, indicate in which real or money flow each entry in List 2 belongs.

Use the following information to work Problems **10** and **11**.

Poor India makes millionaires at fastest pace

India, with the world's largest population of poor people, also paradoxically created millionaires at the fastest pace in the world. Millionaires increased by 22.7 percent to 123,000. In contrast, the number of Indians living on less than a dollar a day is 350 million and those living on less than $2 a day is 700 million. In other words, there are 7,000 very poor Indians for every millionaire.

Source: *The Times of India*, June 25, 2008

10. How is the personal distribution of income in India changing?

11. Why might incomes of $1 a day and $2 a day underestimate the value of the goods and services that these households actually consume?

LIST 1

- An interstate highway
- An airplane
- A school teacher
- A stealth bomber
- A garbage truck
- A pack of bubble gum
- President of the United States
- A strawberry field
- A movie
- An ATM

LIST 2

- General Motors pays its workers wages.
- IBM pays a dividend to its stockholders.
- You buy your groceries.
- Chrysler buys robots.
- Southwest rents some aircraft.
- Nike pays Roger Federer for promoting its sports shoes.

Multiple Choice Quiz

1. Which of the following classifications is correct?

   A. City streets are consumption goods because they wear out with use.
   B. Stocks are capital goods because when people buy and sell them they make a profit.
   C. The coffee maker in the coffee shop at an airport is a consumption good because people buy the coffee it produces.
   D. White House security is a government service because it is paid for by the government.

2. Which of the following statements about U.S. production is correct?

   A. Government goods and services and export goods and services each account for the same percentage of total production.
   B. Capital goods account for a larger percentage of total production than do consumption goods and services.
   C. Most of U.S. production is consumption goods and services.
   D. Most of what the United States produces is goods not services.

3. Which of the following items is *not* a factor of production?

   A. An oil rig in the Gulf of Mexico
   B. A ski jump in Utah
   C. A bank loan to a farmer
   D. An orange grove in Florida

4. What is human capital?

   A. Immigrant labor
   B. Someone who operates heavy equipment
   C. Your professor's knowledge of the economy
   D. A car assembly line robot

5. Which of the following statements is correct?

   A. Labor earns wages and entrepreneurship earns bonuses
   B. Land earns interest and capital earns rent
   C. Entrepreneurship earns interest and capital earns profit
   D. Capital earns interest and labor earns wages

6. How are goods and services produced in the global economy?

   A. Developing countries use less human capital but just as much physical capital as advanced economies.
   B. Emerging economies use more capital-intensive technology than do developing economies.
   C. Human capital in all economies is similar.
   D. Advanced economies use less capital than developing economies.

7. In the circular flow model, which of the following items is a real flow?

   A. The flow of government expenditures to firms for the goods bought
   B. The flow of income from firms to households for the services of the factors of production hired
   C. The flow of U.S. borrowing from the rest of the world
   D. The flow of labor services from households to firms

Is wind power free?

The Economic Problem

3

CHAPTER CHECKLIST

When you have completed your study of this chapter, you will be able to

1 Explain and illustrate the concepts of scarcity, production efficiency, and tradeoff using the production possibilities frontier.

2 Calculate opportunity cost.

3 Explain what makes production possibilities expand.

4 Explain how people gain from specialization and trade.

3.1 PRODUCTION POSSIBILITIES

Every working day in mines, factories, shops, and offices and on farms and construction sites across the United States, we produce a vast array of goods and services. In the United States in 2011, 250 billion hours of labor equipped with $50 trillion worth of capital produced $15 trillion worth of goods and services.

Although our production capability is enormous, it is limited by our available resources and by technology. At any given time, we have fixed quantities of the factors of production and a fixed state of technology. Because our wants exceed our resources, we must make choices. We must rank our wants and decide which to satisfy and which to leave unsatisfied. In using our scarce resources, we make rational choices. And to make a rational choice, we must determine the costs and benefits of the alternatives.

Your first task in this chapter is to learn about an economic model of scarcity, choice, and opportunity cost—a model called the production possibilities frontier.

■ Production Possibilities Frontier

Production possibilities frontier
The boundary between the combinations of goods and services that can be produced and the combinations that cannot be produced, given the available factors of production and the state of technology.

The **production possibilities frontier** is the boundary between the combinations of goods and services that can be produced and the combinations that cannot be produced, given the available factors of production—land, labor, capital, and entrepreneurship—and the state of technology.

Although we produce millions of different goods and services, we can visualize the limits to production most easily if we imagine a simpler world that produces just two goods. Imagine an economy that produces only DVDs and cell phones. All the land, labor, capital, and entrepreneurship available gets used to produce these two goods.

Land can be used for movie studios and DVD factories or cell-phone factories. Labor can be trained to work as movie actors, camera and sound crews, movie producers and DVD makers or as cell-phone makers. Capital can be used for making movies, making and coating disks, and transferring images to disks, or for the equipment that makes cell phones. Entrepreneurs can put their creative talents to managing movie studios and running electronics businesses that make DVDs or to running cell-phone businesses. In every case, the more resources that are used to produce DVDs, the fewer are left to produce cell phones.

Suppose that if no factors of production are allocated to producing cell phones, the maximum number of DVDs that can be produced is 15 million a year. So one production possibility is no cell phones and 15 million DVDs. Another possibility is to allocate sufficient resources to produce 1 million cell phones a year. But these resources must be taken from DVD factories. Suppose that the economy can now produce only 14 million DVDs a year. As resources are moved from producing DVDs to producing cell phones, the economy produces more cell phones but fewer DVDs.

The table in Figure 3.1 illustrates these two combinations of cell phones and DVDs as possibilities *A* and *B*. Suppose that *C, D, E,* and *F* are other combinations of the quantities of these two goods that the economy can produce. Possibility *F* uses all the resources to produce 5 million cell phones a year and allocates no resources to producing DVDs. These six possibilities are alternative combinations of the quantities of the two goods that the economy can produce by *using all of its resources, given the technology.*

The graph in Figure 3.1 illustrates the production possibilities frontier, *PPF*, for cell phones and DVDs. Each point on the graph labeled *A* through *F* represents the possibility in the table identified by the same letter. For example, point *B* represents the production of 1 million cell phones and 14 million DVDs. These quantities also appear in the table as possibility *B*.

The *PPF* shows the limits to production *with the available resources and technology*. If either resources or technology change, the *PPF* shifts. More resources or better technology shift it outward and a loss of resources shifts it inward.

The *PPF* is a valuable tool for illustrating the effects of scarcity and its consequences. The *PPF* puts three features of production possibilities in sharp focus. They are the distinctions between

- Attainable and unattainable combinations
- Efficient and inefficient production
- Tradeoffs and free lunches

■ **FIGURE 3.1**

The Production Possibilities Frontier

MyEconLab Animation

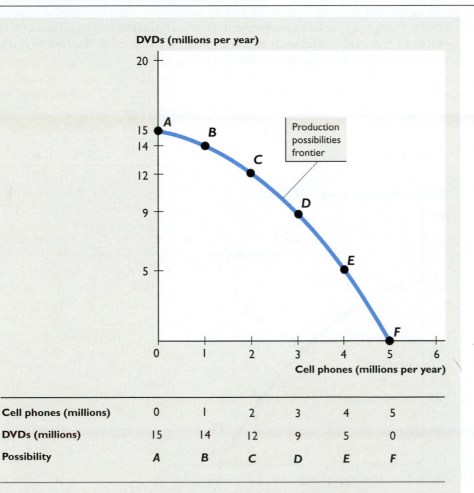

The table and the graph show the production possibilities frontier for cell phones and DVDs.

Point *A* tells us that if the economy produces no cell phones, the maximum quantity of DVDs it can produce is 15 million a year. Each point *A, B, C, D, E,* and *F* on the graph represents the possibility in the table identified by the same letter. The line passing through these points is the production possibilities frontier.

Cell phones (millions)	0	1	2	3	4	5
DVDs (millions)	15	14	12	9	5	0
Possibility	A	B	C	D	E	F

Attainable and Unattainable Combinations

Because the *PPF* shows the *limits* to production, it separates attainable combinations from unattainable ones. The economy can produce combinations of cell phones and DVDs that are smaller than those on the *PPF*, and it can produce any of the combinations *on* the *PPF*. These combinations of cell phones and DVDs are attainable. But it is impossible to produce combinations that are larger than those on the *PPF*. These combinations are unattainable.

Figure 3.2 emphasizes the attainable and unattainable combinations. Only the points on the *PPF* and inside it (in the orange area) are attainable. The combinations of cell phones and DVDs beyond the *PPF* (in the white area), such as the combination at point *G*, are unattainable. These points illustrate combinations that cannot be produced with the current resources and technology. The *PPF* tells us that the economy can produce 4 million cell phones and 5 million DVDs at point *E or* 2 million cell phones and 12 million DVDs at point *C*. But the economy cannot produce 4 million cell phones and 12 million DVDs at point *G*.

Efficient and Inefficient Production

Production efficiency
A situation in which the economy is getting all that it can from its resources and cannot produce more of one good or service without producing less of something else.

Production efficiency occurs when the economy is getting all that it can from its resources. When production is efficient it is not possible to produce more of one good or service without producing less of something else. For production to be efficient, there must be full employment—not just of labor but of all the available factors of production—and each resource must be assigned to the task that it performs comparatively better than other resources can.

■ **FIGURE 3.2**

Attainable and Unattainable Combinations

MyEconLab Animation

The production possibilities frontier, *PPF*, separates attainable combinations from unattainable ones. The economy can produce at any point *inside* the *PPF* (the orange area) or at any point *on* the frontier. Any point outside the production possibilities frontier, such as point *G*, is unattainable.

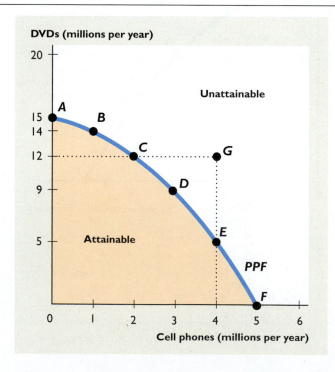

Figure 3.3 illustrates the distinction between efficient and inefficient production. With *inefficient* production, the economy might be producing 3 million cell phones and 5 million DVDs at point *H*. With an *efficient* use of the economy's resources, it is possible to produce at a point on the *PPF* such as point *D* or *E*. At point *D*, there are more DVDs and the same quantity of cell phones as at point *H*. And at point *E*, there are more cell phones and the same quantity of DVDs as at point *H*. At points *D* and *E*, production is efficient.

Tradeoffs and Free Lunches

A **tradeoff** is an exchange—giving up one thing to get something else. You trade off income for a better grade when you decide to cut back on the hours you spend on your weekend job and allocate the time to extra study. The Ford Motor Company faces a tradeoff when it cuts the production of trucks and uses the resources saved to produce more hybrid SUVs. The federal government faces a tradeoff when it cuts NASA's space exploration program and allocates more resources to homeland security. As a society, we face a tradeoff when we decide to cut down a forest and destroy the habitat of the spotted owl.

The production possibilities frontier illustrates the idea of a tradeoff. The *PPF* in Figure 3.3 shows how. If the economy produces at point *E* and people want to produce more DVDs, they must forgo some cell phones. In the move from point *E* to point *D*, people trade off cell phones for DVDs.

Economists often express the central idea of economics—that choices involve tradeoff—with the saying "There is no such thing as a free lunch." A *free lunch* is a gift—getting something without giving up something else. What does the

Tradeoff
An exchange—giving up one thing to get something else.

■ **FIGURE 3.3**

Efficient and Inefficient Production, Tradeoffs, and Free Lunches   MyEconLab Animation

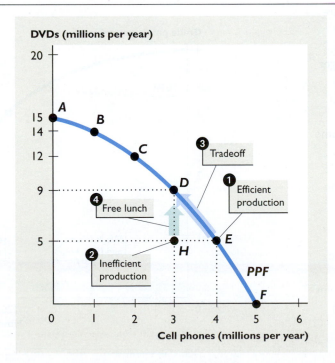

❶ When production occurs at a point on the *PPF*, such as point *E*, resources are used efficiently.

❷ When production occurs at a point inside the *PPF*, such as point *H*, resources are used inefficiently.

❸ When production is efficient—on the *PPF*—the economy faces a tradeoff. To move from point *E* to point *D* requires that some cell phones be given up for more DVDs.

❹ When production is inefficient—inside the *PPF*—there is a free lunch. To move from point *H* to point *D* does not involve a tradeoff.

famous saying mean? Suppose some resources are not being used or are not being used efficiently. Isn't it then possible to avoid a tradeoff and get a free lunch?

The answer is yes. You can see why in Figure 3.3. If production is taking place *inside* the *PPF* at point *H,* then it is possible to move to point *D* and increase the production of DVDs by using currently unused resources or by using resources in their most productive way. Nothing is forgone to increase production—there is a free lunch.

When production is efficient—at a point on the *PPF*—choosing to produce more of one good involves a tradeoff. But if production is inefficient—at a point inside the *PPF*—there is a free lunch. More of some goods and services can be produced without producing less of any others.

So "there is no such thing as a free lunch" means that when resources are used efficiently, every choice involves a tradeoff. Because economists view people as making rational choices, they expect that resources will be used efficiently. That is why they emphasize the tradeoff idea and deny the existence of free lunches. We might *sometimes* get a free lunch, but we *almost always* face a tradeoff.

EYE on YOUR LIFE
Your Production Possibilities Frontier

Two "goods" that concern you a great deal are your grade point average (GPA) and the amount of time you have available for leisure or earning an income. You face a tradeoff. To get a higher GPA you must give up leisure or income. Your forgone leisure or forgone income is the opportunity cost of a higher GPA. Similarly, to get more leisure or more income, you must accept a lower grade. A lower grade is the opportunity cost of increased leisure or increased income.

The figure illustrates a student's *PPF.* Any point on or beneath the *PPF* is attainable and any point above the *PPF* is unattainable. A student who wastes time or doesn't study efficiently ends up with a lower GPA than the highest attainable from the time spent studying. But a student who works efficiently achieves a point *on* the *PPF* and achieves production efficiency.

The student in the figure allocates the scarce 168 hours a week between studying (class and study hours) and other activities (work, leisure, and sleep hours). The student attends class and studies for 48 hours each week and works or has fun (and sleeps) for the other 120 hours. With this allocation of time, and studying efficiently, the student's GPA is 3.

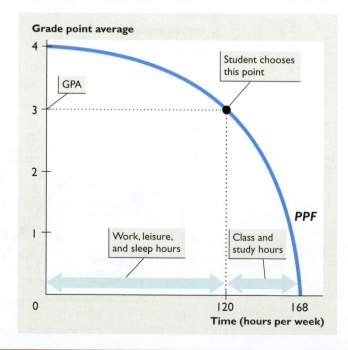

CHECKPOINT 3.1

Explain and illustrate the concepts of scarcity, production efficiency, and tradeoff using the production possibilities frontier.

MyEconLab
You can work these problems in Study Plan 3.1 and get instant feedback.

Practice Problems

1. Table 1 sets out the production possibilities of a small Pacific island economy. Draw the economy's *PPF*.

Figure 1 shows an economy's *PPF* and identifies some production points. Use this figure to work Problems **2** to **4**.

2. Which points are attainable? Explain why.

3. Which points are efficient and which points are inefficient? Explain why.

4. Which points illustrate a tradeoff? Explain why.

In the News

Loss of honeybees is less but still a threat

Honeybees are crucial for the pollination of almonds in California's Central Valley. During 2008, 30 percent of U.S. honeybees died.

Source: *USA Today*, May 20, 2009

Explain how this loss of honeybees affected the Central Valley's *PPF*.

Solutions to Practice Problems

1. The *PPF* is the boundary between attainable and unattainable combinations of goods. Figure 2 shows the economy's *PPF*. The graph plots each row of the table as a point with the corresponding letter.

2. Attainable points: Any point on the *PPF* is attainable and any point below (inside) the *PPF* is attainable. Points outside the *PPF* (*F* and *G*) are unattainable. In Figure 1, the attainable points are *A*, *B*, *C*, *D*, and *E*.

3. Efficient points: Production is efficient when it is not possible to produce more of one good without producing less of another good. To be efficient, a point must be attainable, so points *F* and *G* can't be efficient. Points inside the *PPF* can't be efficient because more goods can be produced, so *D* and *E* are not efficient. The only efficient points are those *on* the *PPF*—*A*, *B*, and *C*.

   Inefficient points: Inefficiency occurs when resources are misallocated or unemployed. Such points are *inside* the *PPF*. These points are *D* and *E*.

4. Tradeoff: Begin by recalling that a tradeoff is an exchange—giving up something to get something else. A tradeoff occurs when moving along the *PPF* from one point to another point. So moving from any point *on* the *PPF*, point *A*, *B*, or *C*, to another point *on* the *PPF* illustrates a tradeoff.

Solution to In the News

Honeybees are a resource used in the production of almonds. At the start of 2008, Central Valley farmers were at a point on their *PPF*. A 30 percent drop in honeybees reduced the quantity of almonds produced by about 30 percent. With no change in the quantity of other crops produced, the Central Valley *PPF* shifted inward.

TABLE 1

Possibility	Fish (pounds)		Berries (pounds)
A	0	and	20
B	1	and	18
C	2	and	15
D	3	and	11
E	4	and	6
F	5	and	0

FIGURE 1

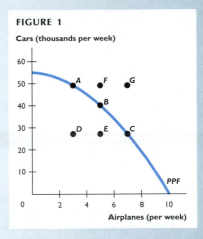

FIGURE 2

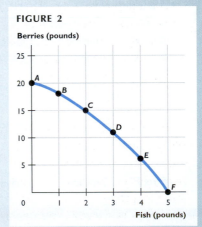

3.2 OPPORTUNITY COST

You've seen that moving from one point to another on the *PPF* involves a trade-off. But what are the terms of the tradeoff? *How much* of one item must be forgone to obtain an additional unit of another item—a large amount or a small amount? The answer is given by opportunity cost—the best thing you must give up to get something (see p. 9). We can use the *PPF* to calculate opportunity cost.

■ The Opportunity Cost of a Cell Phone

The opportunity cost of a cell phone is the number of DVDs forgone to get an additional cell phone. It is calculated as the number of DVDs forgone divided by the number of cell phones gained.

Figure 3.4 illustrates the calculation. At point *A*, the quantities produced are zero cell phones and 15 million DVDs; and at point *B*, the quantities produced are 1 million cell phones and 14 million DVDs. To gain 1 million cell phones by moving from point *A* to point *B*, 1 million DVDs are forgone, so the opportunity cost of 1 cell phone is 1 DVD.

At point *C*, the quantities produced are 2 million cell phones and 12 million DVDs. To gain 1 million cell phones by moving from point *B* to point *C*, 2 million DVDs are forgone. Now the opportunity cost of 1 cell phone is 2 DVDs.

If you repeat these calculations, moving from *C* to *D*, *D* to *E*, and *E* to *F*, you will obtain the opportunity costs shown in the table and the graph.

■ **FIGURE 3.4**

Calculating the Opportunity Cost of a Cell Phone

MyEconLab Animation

Movement along PPF	Decrease in quantity of DVDs	Increase in quantity of cell phones	Decrease in DVDs divided by increase in cell phones
A to **B**	1 million	1 million	1 DVD per phone
B to **C**	2 million	1 million	2 DVDs per phone
C to **D**	3 million	1 million	3 DVDs per phone
D to **E**	4 million	1 million	4 DVDs per phone
E to **F**	5 million	1 million	5 DVDs per phone

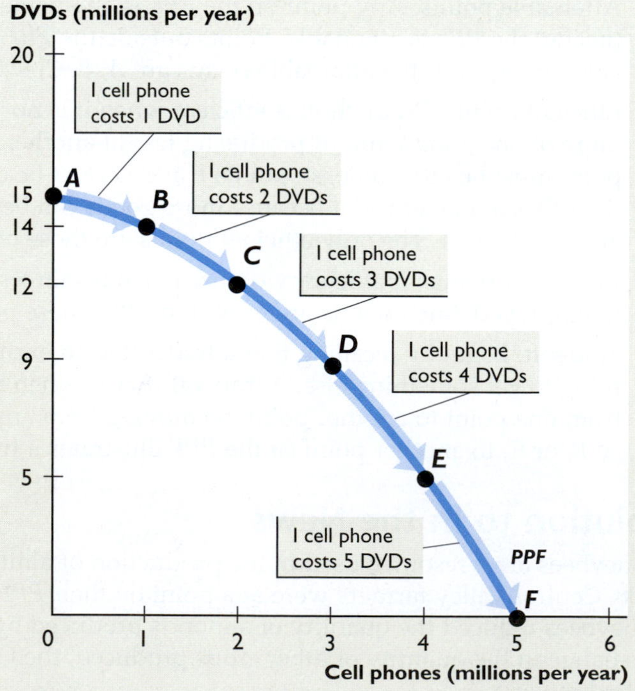

Along the *PPF* from *A* to *F*, the opportunity cost of a cell phone increases as the quantity of cell phones produced increases.

■ Opportunity Cost and the Slope of the *PPF*

Look at the numbers that we've just calculated for the opportunity cost of a cell phone and notice that they follow a striking pattern. The opportunity cost of a cell phone increases as the quantity of cell phones produced increases.

The magnitude of the *slope* of the *PPF* measures the opportunity cost. Because the *PPF* in Figure 3.4 is bowed outward, its slope changes and gets steeper as the quantity of cell phones produced increases.

When a small quantity of cell phones is produced—between points *A* and *B*—the *PPF* has a gentle slope and the opportunity cost of a cell phone is low. A given increase in the quantity of cell phones costs a small decrease in the quantity of DVDs. When a large quantity of cell phones is produced—between points *E* and *F*—the *PPF* is steep and the opportunity cost of a cell phone is high. A given increase in the quantity of cell phones costs a large decrease in the quantity of DVDs. Figure 3.5 shows the increasing opportunity cost of a cell phone.

■ Opportunity Cost Is a Ratio

The opportunity cost of a cell phone is the *ratio* of DVDs forgone to cell phones gained. Similarly, the opportunity cost of a DVD is the *ratio* of cell phones forgone to DVDs gained. So the opportunity cost of a DVD is equal to the inverse of the opportunity cost of a cell phone. For example, moving along the *PPF* in Figure 3.4 from *C* to *D* the opportunity cost of a cell phone is 3 DVDs. Moving along the *PPF* in the opposite direction, from *D* to *C,* the opportunity cost of a DVD is 1/3 of a cell phone.

■ FIGURE 3.5

The Opportunity Cost of a Cell Phone

MyEconLab Animation

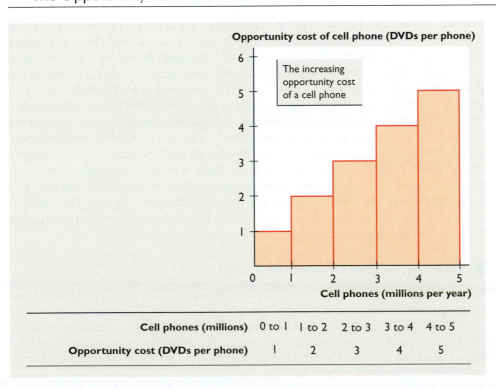

Because the *PPF* in Figure 3.4 is bowed outward, the opportunity cost of a cell phone increases as the quantity of cell phones produced increases.

Cell phones (millions)	0 to 1	1 to 2	2 to 3	3 to 4	4 to 5
Opportunity cost (DVDs per phone)	1	2	3	4	5

EYE on the ENVIRONMENT
Is Wind Power Free?

Wind power is not free. To use it, we must give up huge amounts of other goods and services to build wind turbines and transmission lines.

Wind turbines can produce electricity only when there is wind, which turns out, at best, to be 40 percent of the time and, on average, about 25 percent of the time. Also some of the best wind farm locations are a long way from major population centers, so transmission lines would be long and power transmission losses large.

If we produced 55 percent of our electricity using South Dakota wind power, we would be operating inside the *PPF* at a point such as *Z*.

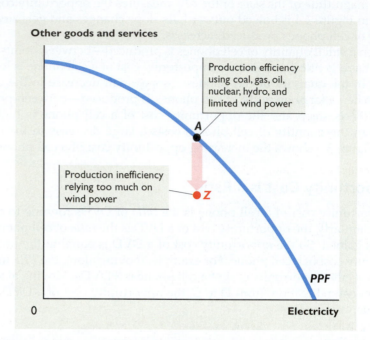

Increasing Opportunity Costs Are Everywhere

Just about every production activity that you can think of has increasing opportunity cost. We allocate the most skillful farmers and the most fertile land to producing food, and we allocate the best doctors and the least fertile land to producing health-care services. Some resources are equally productive in both activities. If we shift these equally productive resources away from farming to hospitals, we get an increase in health care at a low opportunity cost. But if we keep increasing health-care services, we must eventually build hospitals on the most fertile land and get the best farmers to become hospital porters. The production of food drops drastically and the increase in the production of health-care services is small. The opportunity cost of a unit of health-care services rises. Similarly, if we shift resources away from health care toward farming, we must eventually use more skilled doctors and nurses as farmers and more hospitals as hydroponic tomato factories. The decrease in the production of health-care services is large, but the increase in food production is small. The opportunity cost of a unit of food rises.

Your Increasing Opportunity Cost

Flip back to the *PPF* in *Eye on Your Life* on page 64 and think about its implications for your opportunity cost of a higher grade.

What is the opportunity cost of spending time with your friends in terms of the grade you might receive on your exam? What is the opportunity cost of a higher grade in terms of the activities you give up to study? Do you face increasing opportunity costs in these activities?

EYE on the U.S. ECONOMY
Guns Versus Butter

Guns versus butter is the classic economic tradeoff. "Guns" stand for defense goods and services and "butter" stands for food and more generally for all other goods and services. Recently, the U.S. economy has been producing more guns and less butter.

Figure 1 shows the fluctuations in the quantity of defense goods and services produced. (The quantity is measured by expenditure on defense using the prices in 2005 to remove the effects of price changes.) The quantity of defense goods and services produced increases in times of war and decreases in times of peace.

Figure 2 illustrates the recent changes in the production of defense goods and services using the *PPF*.

During the late 1980s and the 1990s, the *PPF* was *PPF*$_0$. President Reagan raised the stakes in the Cold War between the United States and the (former) Soviet Union by a big expansion of military expenditure and we were at point *A*. By the mid-1990s, the Soviet Union had collapsed and we enjoyed a peace dividend by moving along *PPF*$_0$ to *B*.

During the next decade, production possibilities expanded from *PPF*$_0$ to *PPF*$_1$. Defense production and the production of other goods and services increased, and in 2001 we operated at point *C*. Then, in response to the attacks of September 11, 2001, defense spending increased again and by 2011 we had moved along *PPF*$_1$ to point *D*.

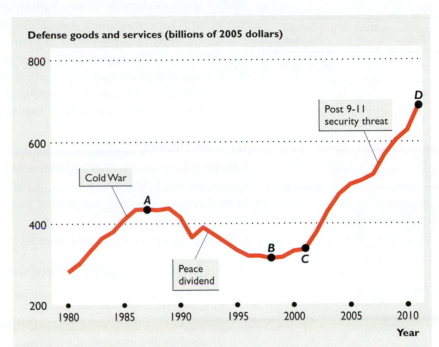

Figure 1 The quantity of defense goods produced

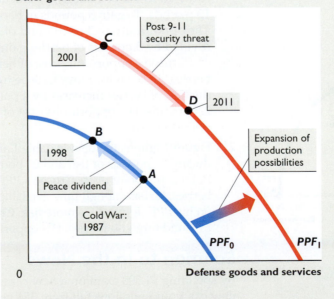

Figure 2 The guns versus butter tradeoff

SOURCE OF DATA: Budget of the United States Government and Bureau of Economic Analysis.

TABLE 1

Possibility	Fish (pounds)		Berries (pounds)
A	0	and	36
B	4.0	and	35
C	7.5	and	33
D	10.5	and	30
E	13.0	and	26
F	15.0	and	21
G	16.5	and	15
H	17.5	and	8
I	18.0	and	0

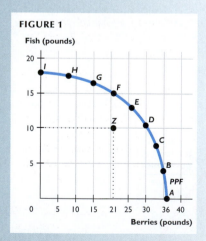

FIGURE 1

CHECKPOINT 3.2

Calculate opportunity cost.

Practice Problems

Table 1 shows Robinson Crusoe's production possibilities.

1. What is his opportunity cost of a pound of berries when Crusoe increases the quantity of berries from 21 pounds to 26 pounds and production is efficient? Does this opportunity cost increase as he produces more berries?

2. If Crusoe is producing 10 pounds of fish and 21 pounds of berries, what is his opportunity cost of an extra pound of berries? And what is his opportunity cost of an extra pound of fish? Explain your answers.

In the News

Obama drives up miles-per-gallon requirements

Emissions from all new vehicles must be cut from 354 grams to 250 grams. To meet this new standard, the price of a new vehicle will rise by $1,300.

Source: *USA Today*, May 20, 2009

Calculate the opportunity cost of reducing the emission level by 1 gram.

Solutions to Practice Problems

1. If Crusoe's production is efficient, he is producing at a point *on* his *PPF*. His opportunity cost of an extra pound of berries is the quantity of fish he must give up to get the berries. It is calculated as the decrease in the quantity of fish divided by the increase in the quantity of berries as he moves along his *PPF* in the direction of producing more berries.

   To increase the quantity of berries from 21 pounds to 26 pounds (from row *F* to row *E* of Table 1), production of fish decreases from 15 pounds to 13 pounds. To gain 5 pounds of berries, Crusoe must forgo 2 pounds of fish. The opportunity cost of 1 pound of berries is the 2 pounds of fish forgone divided by 5 pounds of berries gained—2/5 of a pound of fish.

   Crusoe's opportunity cost of berries increases as he produces more berries. To see why, move Crusoe from row *E* to row *D* in Table 1. His production of berries increases by 4 pounds and his production of fish falls by 2.5 pounds. His opportunity cost of 1 pound of berries increases to 5/8 of a pound of fish.

2. Figure 1 graphs the data in Table 1 and shows Crusoe's *PPF*. If Crusoe is producing 10 pounds of fish and 21 pounds of berries, he is producing at point Z. Point Z is a point *inside* Crusoe's *PPF*. When Crusoe produces 21 pounds of berries, he has enough time available to produce 15 pounds of fish at point *F* on his *PPF*. To produce more fish, Crusoe can move from Z toward *F* on his *PPF* and forgo no berries. His opportunity cost of a pound of fish is zero.

Solution to In the News

By spending $1,300 extra on a new car, you forgo $1,300 of other goods. With a new car, your emissions fall from 354 grams to 250 grams, a reduction of 104 grams. The opportunity cost of a 1-gram reduction in emissions is $1,300 of other goods divided by 104 grams, or $12.50 of other goods.

3.3   ECONOMIC GROWTH

Economic growth is the sustained expansion of production possibilities. Our economy grows when we develop better technologies for producing goods and services; improve the quality of labor by education, on-the-job training, and work experience; and acquire more machines to help us produce.

Economic growth
The sustained expansion of production possibilities.

To study economic growth, we must change the two goods and look at the production possibilities for a consumption good and a capital good. A cell phone is a consumption good and a cell-phone factory is a capital good. By using today's resources to produce cell-phone factories, the economy can expand its future production possibilities. The greater the production of new capital—number of new cell-phone factories—the faster is the expansion of production possibilities.

Figure 3.6 shows how the *PPF* can expand. If no new factories are produced (at point *L*), production possibilities do not expand and the *PPF* stays at its original position. By producing fewer cell phones and using resources to produce 2 new cell-phone factories (at point *K*), production possibilities expand and the *PPF* rotates outward to the new *PPF*.

But economic growth is *not* free. To make it happen, consumption must decrease. The move from *L* to *K* in Figure 3.6 means forgoing 2 million cell phones now. The opportunity cost of producing more cell-phone factories is producing fewer cell phones today.

Also, economic growth is no magic formula for abolishing scarcity. Economic growth shifts the *PPF* outward, but on the new *PPF* we continue to face opportunity costs. To keep producing capital, current consumption must be less than its maximum possible level.

■ **FIGURE 3.6**

Expanding Production Possibilities

MyEconLab Animation

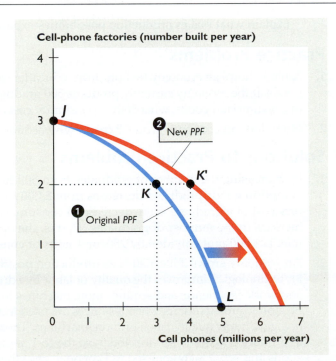

❶ If firms allocate no resources to producing cell-phone factories and produce 5 million cell phones a year at point *L*, the *PPF* doesn't change.

❷ If firms decrease cell-phone production to 3 million a year and produce 2 cell-phone factories, at point *K*, production possibilities will expand. After a year, the *PPF* shifts outward to the new *PPF* and production can move to point *K'*.

EYE on the GLOBAL ECONOMY
Hong Kong's Rapid Economic Growth

Hong Kong's production possibilities per person were 25 percent of those of the United States in 1960. By 2011, they had grown to become equal to U.S. production possibilities per person. Hong Kong grew faster than the United States because it allocated more of its resources to accumulating capital and less to consumption than did the United States.

In 1960, the United States and Hong Kong produced at point *A* on their respective *PPF*s. In 2011, Hong Kong was at point *B* and the United States was at point *C*.

If Hong Kong continues to produce at a point such as *B*, it will grow more rapidly than the United States and its *PPF* will eventually shift out

beyond the *PPF* of the United States. But if Hong Kong produces at a point

such as *D*, the pace of expansion of its *PPF* will slow.

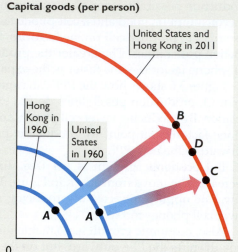

MyEconLab

You can work these problems in Study Plan 3.3 and get instant feedback.

CHECKPOINT 3.3

Explain what makes production possibilities expand.

Practice Problems

TABLE 1

Possibility	Education services (graduates)	Consumption goods (units)
A	1,000	0
B	750	1,000
C	500	2,000
D	0	3,000

1. Table 1 shows an economy that produces education services and consumption goods. If the economy currently produces 500 graduates a year and 2,000 units of consumption goods, what is the opportunity cost of one additional graduate?

2. How does an economy grow? Explain why economic growth is not free.

Solutions to Practice Problems

1. By increasing the number of graduates from 500 to 750, the quantity of consumption goods produced decreases from 2,000 to 1,000 units. The opportunity cost of a graduate is the decrease in consumption goods divided by the increase in the number of graduates. That is, the opportunity cost of a graduate is 1,000 units divided by 250, or 4 units of consumption goods.

2. An economy grows if it expands its production possibilities—if it develops better technologies; improves the quality of labor by education, on-the-job training, and work experience; and acquires more machines to use in production. Economic growth occurs when resources are used today to produce better technologies, better quality labor, or more machines. Those resources cannot be used to produce goods and services today, so the cost of economic growth is the goods and services forgone today. Economic growth is not free.

3.4 SPECIALIZATION AND TRADE

When Adam Smith visited a pin factory (see p. 13), he discovered that 10 people, each specializing in a small task, could make 48,000 pins a day. By dividing pin-making into small parts, what he called the *division of labor*, he found that people were 240 times as productive as they would be if each person performed all the tasks needed to make a pin.

In an 18th century pin factory ...

You can see the productivity of specialization and the division of labor in many everyday places. One of these is a fast-food restaurant. One person specializes in keeping the kitchen stocked with bread, salad materials, meat, sauces, boxes, and wrappers. One works the grill and another the fry maker. Another specializes in assembling the meals. Yet another takes the customers' orders and handles payment. Another has the job of keeping things clean and hygenic.

Imagine how long you would have to wait for your burger if one person performed all these tasks. You place your order and then wait while your friendly server disappeared into the kitchen and emerged 15 minutes later with your not-so-fast-food order.

... and a 21st century fast-food kitchen, specialization boosts productivity.

The productivity gain from specialization makes some people more productive than others. The server at McDonald's can take orders and payment in less time than the grill operator would take to do the same job. And the grill operator can make more burgers per hour than the server could make.

When one person (or nation) is more productive than another—needs fewer inputs or takes less time to produce a good or perform a production task, we say that person (or nation) has an **absolute advantage**.

You are going to discover another way in which people gain by specializing: by producing the good in which they have a *comparative advantage*.

Absolute advantage
When one person (or nation) is more productive than another—needs fewer inputs or takes less time to produce a good or perform a production task.

EYE on the U.S. ECONOMY
No One Knows How to Make a Pencil

Not many products in today's world are as simple as a pencil. Yet the story of how the pencil in your hand got there illustrates the astonishing power of specialization and trade.

When you hold a pencil, you're holding cedar grown in Oregon, graphite mined in Sri Lanka, clay from Mississippi, wax from Mexico, rapeseed oil grown in the Dutch East Indies, pumice from Italy, copper from Arizona and zinc from Alaska.

These materials were harvested and mined by thousands of workers

equipped with hundreds of specialized tools, all of which were manufactured by thousands of other workers using hundreds more specialized tools. These tools were in turn made of steel, itself made from iron ore, and from other minerals and materials.

Rail, road, and ocean transportation systems moved all these things to custom-built factories that made graphite "leads," erasers, brass to hold the erasers, paint, and glue.

Finally, all these components were bought by a pencil factory, which, with

its millions of dollar's worth of custom machinery, put them all together.

Millions of people contributed to making that pencil, many of whom don't even know what a pencil is and *not one of whom knows how to make a pencil*. No one directed all these people. Each worker and business went about its self-interested specialized task trading with each other in markets.

Adapted from *I Pencil*, by Leonard Read, Foundation for Economic Education, 1958.

Comparative advantage
The ability of a person to perform an activity or produce a good or service at a lower opportunity cost than anyone else.

TABLE 3.1   LIZ'S PRODUCTION POSSIBILITIES

Item	Minutes to produce 1	Quantity per hour
Smoothies	2	30
Salads	2	30

TABLE 3.2   JOE'S PRODUCTION POSSIBILITIES

Item	Minutes to produce 1	Quantity per hour
Smoothies	10	6
Salads	2	30

■ Comparative Advantage

A person has a **comparative advantage** in an activity if that person can perform the activity at a lower opportunity cost than anyone else. Notice the contrast between *absolute* advantage and *comparative* advantage. Absolute advantage is about productivity—how long does it take to produce a unit of a good. Comparative advantage is about opportunity cost—how much of some other good must be forgone to produce a unit of a good.

Let's explore the idea of comparative advantage and make it more concrete by looking at production in two quite different smoothie bars: one operated by Liz and the other operated by Joe.

Liz's Smoothie Bar

Liz produces smoothies and salads. In Liz's high-tech bar, she can turn out *either* a smoothie *or* a salad every 2 minutes. If she spends all her time making smoothies, she produces 30 an hour. If she spends all her time making salads, she also produces 30 an hour. If she splits her time equally between the two, she can produce 15 smoothies *and* 15 salads an hour. For each additional smoothie Liz produces, she must decrease her production of salads by one, and for each additional salad Liz produces, she must decrease her production of smoothies by one. So

> **Liz's opportunity cost of producing 1 smoothie is 1 salad,**

and

> **Liz's opportunity cost of producing 1 salad is 1 smoothie.**

Liz's customers buy smoothies and salads in equal quantities, so Liz splits her time equally between the items and produces 15 smoothies and 15 salads an hour.

Joe's Smoothie Bar

Joe also produces both smoothies and salads. Joe's bar is smaller than Liz's, and he has only one blender—a slow, old machine. Even if Joe uses all his resources to produce smoothies, he can produce only 6 an hour. But Joe is pretty good in the salad department, so if he uses all his resources to make salads, he can produce 30 an hour. Joe's ability to make smoothies and salads is the same regardless of how he splits an hour between the two tasks. He can make a salad in 2 minutes or a smoothie in 10 minutes. For each additional smoothie Joe produces, he must decrease his production of salads by 5. And for each additional salad Joe produces, he must decrease his production of smoothies by 1/5 of a smoothie. So

> **Joe's opportunity cost of producing 1 smoothie is 5 salads,**

and

> **Joe's opportunity cost of producing 1 salad is 1/5 of a smoothie.**

Joe's customers, like Liz's, buy smoothies and salads in equal quantities. Joe spends 50 minutes of each hour making smoothies and 10 minutes of each hour making salads. With this division of his time, Joe produces 5 smoothies and 5 salads an hour.

Liz's and Joe's *PPFs*

The *PPFs* in Figure 3.7 illustrate the situation we've just described. In part (a), Liz faces a *PPF* that enables her to produce 15 smoothies and 15 salads. In part (b), Joe

■ **FIGURE 3.7**

Production Possibilities Frontiers

MyEconLab Animation

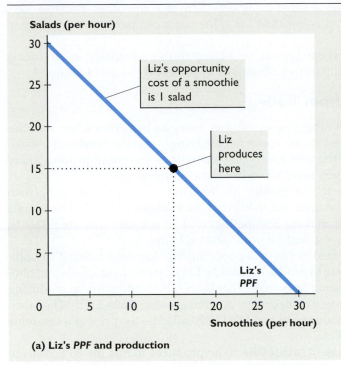

(a) Liz's *PPF* and production

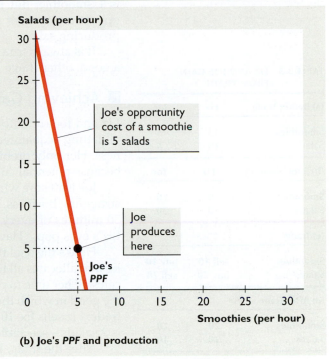

(b) Joe's *PPF* and production

Liz can produce 30 smoothies per hour or 30 salads per hour or any other combination along her *PPF* in part (a). Liz chooses to produce 15 smoothies and 15 salads per hour.

Joe can produce 6 smoothies per hour or 30 salads per hour or any other combination along his *PPF* in part (b). Joe chooses to produce 5 smoothies and 5 salads per hour.

faces a *PPF* that enables him to produce 5 smoothies and 5 salads. On Liz's *PPF*, one smoothie costs one salad. On Joe's *PPF*, one smoothie costs 5 salads.

Liz's Greater Productivity

You can see from the numbers that describe the two smoothie bars that Liz is three times as productive as Joe—her 15 smoothies and 15 salads an hour are three times Joe's 5 smoothies and 5 salads. Liz is more productive than Joe in producing both smoothies and salads. But Liz has a comparative advantage in only one of the activities.

Liz's Comparative Advantage

In which of the two activities does Liz have a *comparative* advantage? Recall that comparative advantage is a situation in which one person's opportunity cost of producing a good is lower than another person's opportunity cost of producing that same good.

You've seen that Liz's opportunity cost of a smoothie is 1 salad, whereas Joe's opportunity cost of a smoothie is 5 salads. To produce 1 smoothie, Liz must forgo 1 salad, while Joe must forgo 5 salads. So, because Liz forgoes fewer salads to make a smoothie, she has a comparative advantage in producing smoothies.

What about Joe? Doesn't he have a comparative advantage at anything? He does as you're about to see.

Joe's Comparative Advantage

Look at the opportunity costs of producing salads. For Liz, that opportunity cost is 1 smoothie. But for Joe, a salad costs only 1/5 of a smoothie. Because Joe's opportunity cost of a salad is less than Liz's, Joe has a comparative advantage in producing salads.

It is always true that if one person has a comparative advantage in producing a good, others have a comparative advantage in producing some other good.

■ Achieving Gains from Trade

Liz and Joe run into each other one evening in a singles bar. After a few minutes of getting acquainted, Liz tells Joe about her amazingly profitable smoothie business. Her only problem, she tells Joe, is that she wishes she could produce more because potential customers leave when her lines get too long.

Joe isn't sure whether to risk spoiling his chances by telling Liz about his own struggling business. But he takes the risk. When he explains to Liz that he spends 50 minutes of every hour making 5 smoothies and 10 minutes making 5 salads, Liz's eyes pop. "Have I got a deal for you!" she exclaims.

Here's the deal that Liz sketches on a paper napkin. Joe stops making smoothies and allocates all his time to producing salads. Liz stops making salads and allocates all her time to producing smoothies. That is, they both specialize in producing the good in which they have a comparative advantage—see Table 3.3(b). They then trade: Liz sells Joe 10 smoothies and Joe sells Liz 20 salads—the price of a smoothie is 2 salads—see Table 3.3(c).

After the trade, Joe has 10 salads (the 30 he produces minus the 20 he sells to Liz) and the 10 smoothies that he buys from Liz. So Joe doubles the quantities of smoothies and salads he can sell. Liz has 20 smoothies (the 30 she produces minus the 10 she sells to Joe) and the 20 salads she buys from Joe. See Table 3.3(d). From specialization and trade, each gains 5 smoothies and 5 salads—see Table 3.3(e).

TABLE 3.3 LIZ AND JOE GAIN FROM TRADE

(a) Before Trade	Liz	Joe
Smoothies	15	5
Salads	15	5
(b) Specialization	**Liz**	**Joe**
Smoothies	30	0
Salads	0	30
(c) Trade		
Smoothies	sell 10	buy 10
Salads	buy 20	sell 20
(d) After Trade		
Smoothies	20	10
Salads	20	10
(e) Gains from Trade		
Smoothies	+5	+5
Salads	+5	+5

EYE on YOUR LIFE
Your Comparative Advantage

What you have learned in this chapter has huge implications for the way you organize your life. It also has implications for the position that you take on the controversial issue of offshore outsourcing.

Just as an economy expands its production possibilities by accumulating capital, so also will you expand your production possibilities by accumulating human capital. That is what you're doing right now in school.

By discovering your comparative advantage, you will be able to focus on producing the items that make you as well off as possible. Think hard about what you enjoy doing and that you do comparatively better than others. That, most likely, is where your comparative advantage lies.

In today's world, it is a good idea to try to remain flexible so that you can switch jobs if you discover that your comparative advantage has changed.

Looking beyond your own self-interest, are you going to be a voice that supports or opposes offshore outsourcing?

You've learned in this chapter that regardless of whether outsourcing remains inside the United States, as it does with Liz and Joe at their smoothie bars, or is global like the outsourcing of jobs by U. S. producers to India, both parties gain from trade.

Americans pay less for goods and services and Indians earn higher incomes. But some Americans lose, at least in the short run.

Liz draws a figure (Figure 3.8) to illustrate her idea. The blue *PPF* is Liz's and the red *PPF* is Joe's. They are each producing at the points marked *A*. Liz's proposal is that they each produce at the points marked *B*. They then trade smoothies and salads.

There is a range of prices at which they might trade. If the price is 5 salads per smoothie (or equivalently, 1/5 smoothies per salad), Liz gets all the gains. If the price is 1 salad per smoothie (1 smoothie per salad), Joe gets all the gains.

Liz suggests that they trade at a price of 2 salads per smoothie (1/2 a smoothie per salad). This price turns out to give each of them equal gains.

Liz gets salads for 1/2 a smoothie each, which is less than the 1 smoothie that it costs her to produce them. Joe gets smoothies for 2 salads each, which is less than the 5 salads it costs him to produce them. Each moves to the points marked *C* where Liz has 20 smoothies and 20 salads, 5 of each more than she has producing only for herself. And Joe has 10 smoothies and 10 salads, also 5 more of each than he has producing only for himself. Because of the gains from trade, total production increases by 10 smoothies and 10 salads.

Notice that the points *C* are *outside* Liz's and Joe's *PPFs*. This is the magic of the gains from trade. Everyone gains and everyone can enjoy quantities of goods and services that exceed their own ability to produce.

FIGURE 3.8

The Gains from Specialization and Trade   MyEconLab Animation

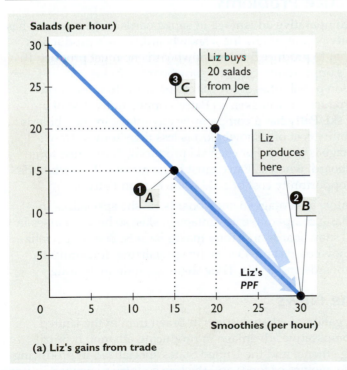

(a) Liz's gains from trade

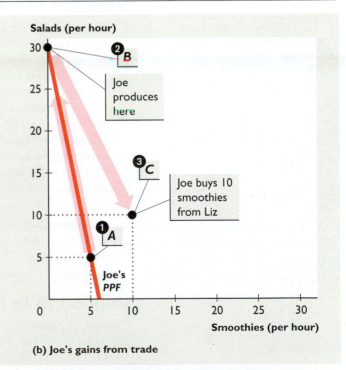

(b) Joe's gains from trade

❶ Liz and Joe each produce at point *A* on their respective *PPFs*. Liz has a comparative advantage in producing smoothies, and Joe has a comparative advantage in producing salads.

❷ Joe specializes in salads and Liz specializes in smoothies, so they each produce at point *B* on their respective *PPFs*.

❸ They exchange smoothies for salads at a price of 2 salads per smoothie. Each goes to point *C*—a point *outside* their individual *PPFs*. They each gain 5 salads and 5 smoothies—the quantities at point *C* minus the quantities at point *A*.

MyEconLab

You can work these problems in Study Plan 3.4 and get instant feedback.

TABLE 1	TONY'S PRODUCTION POSSIBILITIES	
Snowboards (per week)		**Skis (per week)**
25	and	0
20	and	10
15	and	20
10	and	30
5	and	40
0	and	50

TABLE 2	PATTY'S PRODUCTION POSSIBILITIES	
Snowboards (per week)		**Skis (per week)**
20	and	0
10	and	5
0	and	10

CHECKPOINT 3.4

Explain how people gain from specialization and trade.

Practice Problems

Tony and Patty produce skis and snowboards. Tables 1 and 2 show their production possibilities. Each week, Tony produces 5 snowboards and 40 skis and Patty produces 10 snowboards and 5 skis.

1. Who has a comparative advantage in producing snowboards? Who has a comparative advantage in producing skis?

2. If Tony and Patty specialize and trade, what are the gains from trade?

In the News

With big boost from sugar cane, Brazil is satisfying its fuel needs
Brazil is almost self-sufficient in ethanol. Brazilian ethanol is made from sugar and costs 83¢ per gallon whereas U.S. ethanol, made from corn, costs $1.14 per gallon. The United States does not import ethanol.

Source: *The New York Times*, April 12, 2006

Which country has a comparative advantage in producing ethanol? Explain why both the United States and Brazil can gain from specialization and trade.

Solutions to Practice Problems

1. The person with a comparative advantage in snowboards is the one who has the lower opportunity cost of producing a snowboard. Tony's production possibilities show that to produce 5 more snowboards he must produce 10 fewer skis. So Tony's opportunity cost of a snowboard is 2 skis.

    Patty's production possibilities show that to produce 10 more snowboards, she must produce 5 fewer skis. So Patty's opportunity cost of a snowboard is 1/2 a ski. Patty has a comparative advantage in snowboards because her opportunity cost of a snowboard is less than Tony's. Tony's comparative advantage is in skis. For each ski produced, Tony must forgo making 1/2 a snowboard, whereas Patty must forgo making 2 snowboards for a ski. So Tony's opportunity cost of a ski is lower than Patty's.

2. Patty has a comparative advantage in snowboards, so she specializes in snowboards. Tony has a comparative advantage in skis, so he specializes in skis. Patty makes 20 snowboards and Tony makes 50 skis. Before specializing, they made 15 snowboards and 45 skis. By specializing, total output increases by 5 snowboards and 5 skis. They share this gain by trading.

Solution to In the News

The cost of producing a gallon of ethanol is less in Brazil than in the United States, so Brazil has a comparative advantage in producing ethanol. If Brazil specialized in producing ethanol and the United States specialized in producing other goods (for example, movies or food) and the two countries engaged in free trade, each country can gain because it would get to a point outside its own *PPF*.

CHAPTER SUMMARY

Key Points

1. Explain and illustrate the concepts of scarcity, production efficiency, and tradeoff using the production possibilities frontier.

- The production possibilities frontier, *PPF*, describes the limits to what can be produced by using all the available resources efficiently.
- Points inside and on the *PPF* are attainable. Points outside the *PPF* are unattainable.
- Production at any point on the *PPF* achieves production efficiency. Production at a point inside the *PPF* is inefficient.
- When production is efficient—on the *PPF*—people face a tradeoff. If production is at a point inside the *PPF*, there is a free lunch.

2. Calculate opportunity cost.

- Along the *PPF*, the opportunity cost of x (the item measured on the x-axis) is the decrease in y (the item measured on the y-axis) divided by the increase in x.
- The opportunity cost of Y is the inverse of the opportunity cost of X.
- The opportunity cost of producing a good increases as the quantity of the good produced increases.

3. Explain what makes production possibilities expand.

- Technological change and increases in capital and human capital expand production possibilities.
- The opportunity cost of economic growth is the decrease in current consumption.

4. Explain how people gain from specialization and trade.

- A person has a comparative advantage in an activity if he or she can perform that activity at a lower opportunity cost than someone else.
- People gain by increasing the production of the item in which they have a comparative advantage and trading.

Key Terms

Absolute advantage, 73
Comparative advantage, 74
Economic growth, 71

Production efficiency, 62
Production possibilities frontier, 60
Tradeoff, 63

MyEconLab
You can work these problems in Chapter 3 Study Plan and get instant feedback.

TABLE 1

Corn (bushels)		Beef (pounds)
250	and	0
200	and	300
100	and	500
0	and	600

TABLE 2

Labor (hours)	Entertainment (units)		Good food (units)
0	0	or	0
10	20	or	30
20	40	or	50
30	60	or	60
40	80	or	65
50	100	or	67

FIGURE 1

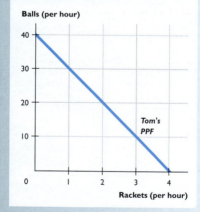

FIGURE 2

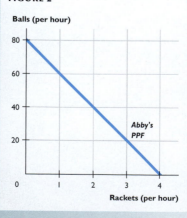

CHAPTER CHECKPOINT

Study Plan Problems and Applications

1. Table 1 shows the quantities of corn and beef that a farm can produce in a year. Draw a graph of the farm's *PPF*. Mark on the graph:
   • An inefficient combination of corn and beef—label this point *A*.
   • An unattainable combination of corn and beef—label this point *B*.
   • An efficient combination of corn and beef—label this point *C*.

Use the following information to work Problems **2** and **3**.

The people of Leisure Island have 50 hours of labor a day that can be used to produce entertainment and good food. Table 2 shows the maximum quantity of *either* entertainment *or* good food that Leisure Island can produce with different quantities of labor.

2. Is an output of 50 units of entertainment and 50 units of good food attainable and efficient? With a production of 50 units of entertainment and 50 units of good food, do the people of Leisure Island face a tradeoff?

3. What is the opportunity cost of producing an additional unit of entertainment? Explain how the opportunity cost of producing a unit of entertainment changes as more entertainment is produced.

Use the following information to work Problems **4** and **5**.

Malaria can be controlled
The World Health Organization's malaria chief says that it is too costly to try to fully eradicate the disease. He says that by using nets, medicine, and DDT it is possible to eliminate 90 percent of malaria cases. But to eliminate 100 percent of cases would be extremely costly.

Source: *The New York Times*, March 4, 2008

4. Make a graph of the production possibilities frontier with malaria control on the *x*-axis and other goods and services on the *y*-axis.

5. Describe how the opportunity cost of controlling malaria changes as more resources are used to reduce the number of malaria cases.

6. Explain how the following events influence U.S. production possibilities:
   • Some retail workers are re-employed building dams and wind farms.
   • More people take early retirement.
   • Drought devastates California's economy.

Use the following information to work Problems **7** and **8**.

Figure 1 shows Tom's production possibilities and Figure 2 shows Abby's production possibilities. Tom uses all his resources and produces 2 rackets and 20 balls an hour. Abby uses all her resources and produces 2 rackets and 40 balls an hour.

7. What is Tom's opportunity cost of producing a racket? What is Abby's opportunity cost of a racket? Who has a comparative advantage in producing rackets? Who has a comparative advantage in producing balls?

8. If Tom and Abby specialize and trade 15 balls for 1 racket, what are the gains from trade?

Instructor Assignable Problems and Applications

Your instructor can assign these problems as homework, a quiz, or a test in MyEconLab.

Use the following information to work Problems **1** to **4**.

Representatives Waxman of California and Markey of Massachusetts proposed a law to limit greenhouse gas emissions from electricity generation and require electricity producers to generate a minimum percentage of power using renewable fuels, with some rights to emit to be auctioned. The Congressional Budget Office estimated that the government would receive $846 billion from auctions and would spend $821 billion on incentive programs and compensation for higher energy prices. Electricity producers would spend $208 million a year to comply with the new rules. (Think of these dollar amounts as dollars' worth of other goods and services.)

1. Would the Waxman-Markey law achieve production efficiency?

2. Is the $846 billion that electricity producers would pay for the right to emit greenhouse gasses part of the opportunity cost of producing electricity?

3. Is the $821 billion that the government would spend on incentive programs and compensation for higher energy prices part of the opportunity cost of producing electricity?

4. Is the $208 million that electricity producers will spend to comply with the new rules part of the opportunity cost of producing electricity?

5. The people of Foodland have 40 hours of labor a day to bake pizza and bread. Table 1 shows the maximum quantity of *either* pizza *or* bread that Foodland can bake with different quantities of labor. Can Foodland produce 30 pizzas and 30 loaves of bread a day? If it can, is this output efficient, do the people of Foodland face a tradeoff, and what is the opportunity cost of producing an additional pizza?

TABLE 1

Labor (hours)	Pizzas		Bread (loaves)
0	0	or	0
10	30	or	10
20	50	or	20
30	60	or	30
40	65	or	40

Use Table 2, which shows a farm's production possibilities, to work Problems **6** and **7**.

6. If the farm uses its resources efficiently, what is the opportunity cost of an increase in chicken production from 300 pounds to 500 pounds a year? Explain your answer.

7. If the farm adopted a new technology, which allows it to use fewer resources to fatten chickens, explain how the farm's production possibilities will change. Explain how the opportunity cost of producing a bushel of soybean will be affected.

TABLE 2

Soybean (bushels per year)		Chicken (pounds per year)
500	and	0
400	and	300
200	and	500
0	and	400

8. In an hour, Sue can produce 40 caps or 4 jackets and Tessa can produce 80 caps or 4 jackets. Who has a comparative advantage in producing caps? If Sue and Tessa specialize and trade, who will gain?

Use the following information to work Problems **9** to **11**.

Cheap broadband's a winner

Inexpensive broadband access has created a new generation of television producers and the Internet is their native medium.

Source: *The New York Times*, December 2, 2007

9. How has inexpensive broadband changed the production possibilities of video entertainment and other goods and services?

10. Sketch a *PPF* for video entertainment and other goods and services before broadband.

11. Explain how the arrival of inexpensive broadband has changed the *PPF*.

MyEconLab

You can work this quiz in Chapter 3 Study Plan and get instant feedback.

TABLE 1

Possibility	Fish (pounds)		Berries (pounds)
A	0	and	40
B	1	and	36
C	2	and	30
D	3	and	22
E	4	and	12
F	5	and	0

Multiple Choice Quiz

1. Table 1 shows the *PPF* of an island community. Choose the best statement.
   A. This community has enough resources to produce 2 pounds of fish and 36 pounds of berries.
   B. This community cannot produce 2 pounds of fish and 36 pounds of berries because this combination is inefficient.
   C. This community will waste resources if it produces 2 pounds of fish and 22 pounds of berries.
   D. This community can produce 2 pounds of fish and 30 pounds of berries but this combination is inefficient.

2. Table 1 shows the *PPF* of an island community. Choose the best statement.
   A. Suppose that this community produces 3 pounds of fish and 20 pounds of berries. If it decides to gather more berries, it faces a tradeoff.
   B. When this community produces 4 pounds of fish and 12 pounds of berries it faces a tradeoff, but it is inefficient.
   C. Suppose that this community produces 5 pounds of fish and 0 pounds of berries. If it decides to gather some berries, it will get a free lunch.
   D. If this community produces 3 pounds of fish and 22 pounds of berries, production is efficient but to produce more fish it faces a tradeoff.

3. Table 1 shows the *PPF* of an island community. This community's opportunity cost of producing 1 pound of fish _____.
   A. is the increase in the quantity of berries gathered as the quantity of fish increases by 1 pound
   B. increases as the quantity of berries gathered increases
   C. is 10 pounds of berries if the quantity of fish increases from 2 to 3 pounds
   D. increases as the quantity of fish caught increases

4. Table 1 shows the *PPF* of an island community. Choose the best statement.
   A. When a drought hits the island, its *PPF* shifts outward.
   B. When the islanders discover a better way of catching fish, the island's *PPF* shifts outward.
   C. When islanders reduce the time they spend gathering berries, the *PPF* shifts inward.
   D. If the islanders decide to spend more time gathering berries but continue to spend the same amount of time fishing, they face a tradeoff.

5. Mary makes 10 pies and 20 cakes a day and her opportunity cost of a cake is 2 pies. Tim makes 20 pies and 10 cakes a day and his opportunity cost of a cake is 4 pies. If they specialize in the good in which they have a comparative advantage _____.
   A. Mary produces pies
   B. Tim produces pies and cakes
   C. Mary produces cakes while Tim produces pies
   D. Tim produces cakes while Mary produces pies

Why did the price of coffee soar in 2010 and 2011?

Demand and Supply

4

CHAPTER CHECKLIST

When you have completed your study of this chapter, you will be able to

1 Distinguish between quantity demanded and demand, and explain what determines demand.

2 Distinguish between quantity supplied and supply, and explain what determines supply.

3 Explain how demand and supply determine price and quantity in a market, and explain the effects of changes in demand and supply.

COMPETITIVE MARKETS

When you need a new pair of running shoes, want a bagel and a latte, or need to fly home for Thanksgiving, you must find a place where people sell those items or offer those services. The place where you find them is a *market*.

You learned in Chapter 2 that a market is any arrangement that brings buyers and sellers together. A market has two sides: buyers (demanders) and sellers (suppliers). There are markets for *goods* such as apples and hiking boots, for *services* such as haircuts and tennis lessons, for *resources* such as computer programmers and tractors, and for other manufactured *inputs* such as memory chips and auto parts. There are also markets for money such as Japanese yen and for financial securities such as Yahoo! stock. Only imagination limits what can be traded in markets.

Some markets are physical places where buyers and sellers meet and where an auctioneer or a broker helps to determine the prices. Examples of this type of market are the New York Stock Exchange; wholesale fish, meat, and produce markets; and used car auctions.

Some markets are virtual spaces where buyers and sellers never meet face-to-face but connect over telephone lines or the Internet. Examples include currency markets, e-commerce Web sites such as Amazon.com and bananarepublic.com, and auction sites such as eBay.

But most markets are unorganized collections of buyers and sellers. You do most of your trading in this type of market. An example is the market for basketball shoes. The buyers in this $3-billion-a-year market are the 45 million Americans who play basketball (or who want to make a fashion statement) and are looking for a new pair of shoes. The sellers are the tens of thousands of retail sports equipment and footwear stores. Each buyer can visit several different stores, and each seller knows that the buyer has a choice of stores.

Markets vary in the intensity of competition that buyers and sellers face. In this chapter, we're going to study a *competitive market* that has so many buyers and so many sellers that no single buyer or seller can influence the price.

Markets for running shoes …

coffee and bagel …

and airline travel.

4.1 DEMAND

First, we'll study the behavior of buyers in a competitive market. The **quantity demanded** of any good, service, or resource is the amount that people are willing and able to buy during a specified period at a specified price. For example, when spring water costs $1 a bottle, you decide to buy 2 bottles a day. The 2 bottles a day is your quantity demanded of spring water.

The quantity demanded is measured as an amount *per unit of time*. For example, your quantity demanded of water is 2 bottles *per day*. We could express this quantity as 14 bottles per week, or some other number per month or per year. A particular number of bottles without a time dimension has no meaning.

Many things influence buying plans, and one of them is price. We look first at the relationship between quantity demanded and price. To study this relationship, we keep all other influences on buying plans the same and we ask: How, other things remaining the same, does the quantity demanded of a good change as its price varies? The law of demand provides the answer.

■ The Law of Demand

The **law of demand** states

> **Other things remaining the same, if the price of a good rises, the quantity demanded of that good decreases; and if the price of a good falls, the quantity demanded of that good increases.**

So the law of demand states that when all other things remain the same, if the price of an iPhone falls, people will buy more iPhones; or if the price of a baseball ticket rises, people will buy fewer baseball tickets.

Why does the quantity demanded increase if the price falls, all other things remaining the same?

The answer is that, faced with a limited budget, people always have an incentive to find the best deals available. If the price of one item falls and the prices of all other items remain the same, the item with the lower price is a better deal than it was before, so some people buy more of this item. Suppose, for example, that the price of bottled water fell from $1 a bottle to 25 cents a bottle while the price of Gatorade remained at $1 a bottle. Wouldn't some people switch from Gatorade to water? By doing so, they save 75 cents a bottle, which they can spend on other things they previously couldn't afford.

Think about the things that you buy and ask yourself: Which of these items does *not* obey the law of demand? If the price of a new textbook were lower, other things remaining the same (including the price of a used textbook), would you buy more new textbooks? Then think about all the things that you do not now buy but would if you could afford them. How cheap would a PC have to be for you to buy *both* a desktop and a laptop? There is a price that is low enough to entice you!

■ Demand Schedule and Demand Curve

Demand is the relationship between the quantity demanded and the price of a good when all other influences on buying plans remain the same. The quantity demanded is *one* quantity at *one* price. *Demand* is a *list of quantities at different prices* illustrated by a demand schedule and a demand curve.

Quantity demanded
The amount of any good, service, or resource that people are willing and able to buy during a specified period at a specified price.

Demand
The relationship between the quantity demanded and the price of a good when all other influences on buying plans remain the same.

Demand schedule

A list of the quantities demanded at each different price when all the other influences on buying plans remain the same.

Demand curve

A graph of the relationship between the quantity demanded of a good and its price when all the other influences on buying plans remain the same.

A **demand schedule** is a list of the quantities demanded at each different price when *all the other influences on buying plans remain the same*. The table in Figure 4.1 is one person's (Tina's) demand schedule for bottled water. It tells us that if the price of water is $2.00 a bottle, Tina buys no water. Her quantity demanded is 0 bottles a day. If the price of water is $1.50 a bottle, her quantity demanded is 1 bottle a day. Tina's quantity demanded increases to 2 bottles a day at a price of $1.00 a bottle and to 3 bottles a day at a price of 50 cents a bottle.

A **demand curve** is a graph of the relationship between the quantity demanded of a good and its price when all the other influences on buying plans remain the same. The points on the demand curve labeled *A* through *D* represent the rows *A* through *D* of the demand schedule. For example, point *B* on the graph represents row *B* of the demand schedule and shows that the quantity demanded is 1 bottle a day when the price is $1.50 a bottle. Point *C* on the demand curve represents row *C* of the demand schedule and shows that the quantity demanded is 2 bottles a day when the price is $1.00 a bottle.

The downward slope of the demand curve illustrates the law of demand. Along the demand curve, when the price of the good *falls*, the quantity demanded *increases*. For example, in Figure 4.1, when the price of a bottle of water falls from $1.00 to 50 cents, the quantity demanded increases from 2 bottles a day to 3 bottles a day. Conversely, when the price *rises*, the quantity demanded *decreases*. For example, when the price rises from $1.00 to $1.50 a bottle, the quantity demanded decreases from 2 bottles a day to 1 bottle a day.

■ **FIGURE 4.1**

Demand Schedule and Demand Curve

The table shows Tina's demand schedule that lists the quantity of water demanded at each price if all other influences on buying plans remain the same. At a price of $1.50 a bottle, the quantity demanded is 1 bottle a day.

The demand curve shows the relationship between the quantity demanded and price, other things remaining the same. The downward-sloping demand curve illustrates the law of demand. When the price falls, the quantity demanded increases; and when the price rises, the quantity demanded decreases.

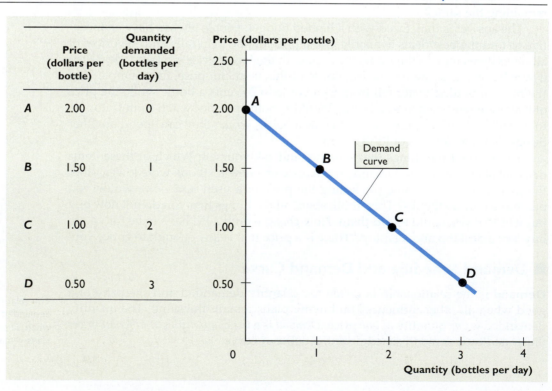

	Price (dollars per bottle)	Quantity demanded (bottles per day)
A	2.00	0
B	1.50	1
C	1.00	2
D	0.50	3

Individual Demand and Market Demand

The demand schedule and the demand curve that you've just studied are for one person. To study a market, we must determine the market demand.

Market demand is the sum of the demands of all the buyers in a market. To find the market demand, imagine a market in which there are only two buyers: Tina and Tim. The table in Figure 4.2 shows three demand schedules: Tina's, Tim's, and the market demand schedule. Tina's demand schedule is the same as before. It shows the quantity of water demanded by Tina at each different price. Tim's demand schedule tells us the quantity of water demanded by Tim at each price. To find the quantity of water demanded in the market, we sum the quantities demanded by Tina and Tim. For example, at a price of $1.00 a bottle, the quantity demanded by Tina is 2 bottles a day, the quantity demanded by Tim is 1 bottle a day, and so the quantity demanded in the market is 3 bottles a day.

Tina's demand curve in part (a) and Tim's demand curve in part (b) are graphs of the two individual demand schedules. The market demand curve in part (c) is a graph of the market demand schedule. At a given price, the quantity demanded on the market demand curve equals the horizontal sum of the quantities demanded on the individual demand curves.

Market demand
The sum of the demands of all the buyers in the market.

FIGURE 4.2

Individual Demand and Market Demand

MyEconLab Animation

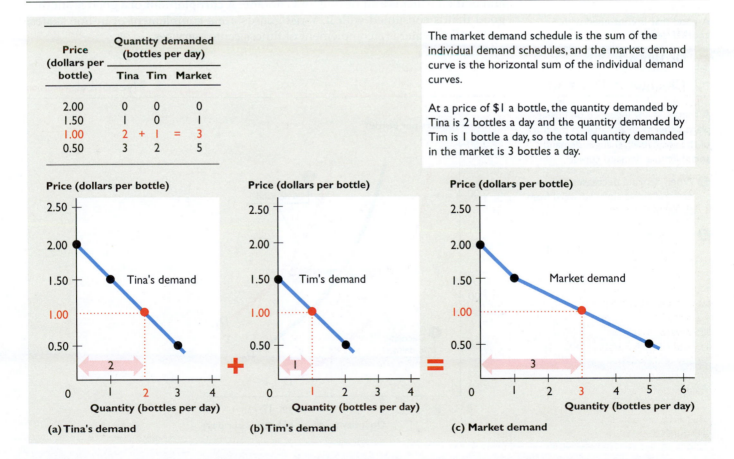

(a) Tina's demand (b) Tim's demand (c) Market demand

Change in demand

A change in the quantity that people plan to buy when any influence on buying plans other than the price of the good changes.

■ Changes in Demand

The demand curve shows how the quantity demanded changes when the price of the good changes but *all other influences on buying plans remain the same.* When any of these other influences on buying plans change, there is a **change in demand**, which means that there is a new demand schedule and new demand curve. *The demand curve shifts.*

Demand can either increase or decrease and Figure 4.3 illustrates the two cases. Initially, the demand curve is D_0. When demand decreases, the demand curve shifts leftward to D_1. On demand curve D_1, the quantity demanded at each price is smaller. When demand increases, the demand curve shifts rightward to D_2. On demand curve D_2 the quantity demanded at each price is greater.

The main influences on buying plans that change demand are

- Prices of related goods
- Expected future prices
- Income
- Expected future income and credit
- Number of buyers
- Preferences

Prices of Related Goods

Substitute

A good that can be consumed in place of another good.

Complement

A good that is consumed with another good.

Goods have substitutes and complements. A **substitute** for a good is another good that can be consumed in its place. Chocolate cake is a substitute for cheesecake, and bottled water is a substitute for Gatorade. A **complement** of a good is another good that is consumed with it. Wrist guards are a complement of in-line skates, and bottled water is a complement of fitness center services.

■ FIGURE 4.3

Changes in Demand

MyEconLab Animation

A change in any influence on buying plans, other than a change in the price of the good itself, changes demand and shifts the demand curve.

❶ When demand decreases, the demand curve shifts leftward from D_0 to D_1.

❷ When demand increases, the demand curve shifts rightward from D_0 to D_2.

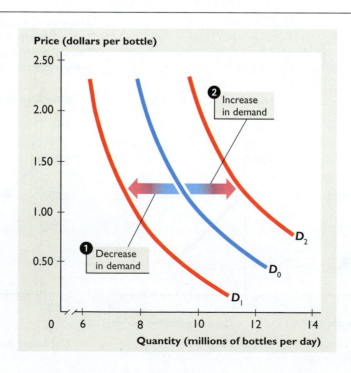

The demand for a good and the price of one of its substitutes move in the *same direction*. The demand for a good *increases* if the price of one of its substitutes *rises* and *decreases* if the price of one of its substitutes *falls*. For example, the demand for cheesecake increases when the price of chocolate cake rises.

The demand for a good and the price of one of its complements move in *opposite directions*. The demand for a good *decreases* if the price of one of its complements *rises* and *increases* if the price of one of its complements *falls*. For example, the demand for wrist guards decreases when the price of in-line skates rises.

Expected Future Prices

A rise in the expected *future* price of a good increases the *current* demand for that good and a fall in the expected *future* price decreases *current* demand. If you expect the price of noodles to rise next week, you buy a big enough stockpile to get you through the next few weeks. Your demand for noodles today has increased. If you expect the price of noodles to fall next week, you buy none now and plan to buy next week. Your demand for noodles today has decreased.

Income

A rise in income brings an increase in demand and a fall in income brings a decrease in demand for a **normal good**. A rise in income brings a *decrease* in demand and a fall in income brings an *increase* in demand for an **inferior good**. For example, if your income increases and you decide to buy more chicken and less pasta, for you, chicken is a normal good and pasta is an inferior good.

Normal good
A good for which demand increases when income increases and demand decreases when income decreases.

Inferior good
A good for which demand decreases when income increases and demand increases when income decreases.

Expected Future Income and Credit

When income is expected to increase in the future, or when credit is easy to get and the cost of borrowing is low, the demand for some goods increases. And when income is expected to decrease in the future, or when credit is hard to get and the cost of borrowing is high, the demand for some goods decreases.

Changes in expected future income and the availability and cost of credit has the greatest effect on the demand for big ticket items such as homes and automobiles. Modest changes in expected future income or credit availability bring large swings in the demand for these items.

Number of Buyers

The greater the number of buyers in a market, the larger is demand. For example, the demand for parking spaces, movies, bottled water, or just about anything is greater in New York City than it is in Boise, Idaho.

Preferences

Tastes or *preferences,* as economists call them, influence demand. When preferences change, the demand for one item increases and the demand for another item (or items) decreases. For example, preferences have changed as people have become better informed about the health hazards of tobacco. This change in preferences has decreased the demand for cigarettes and has increased the demand for nicotine patches. Preferences also change when new goods become available. For example, the development of MP3 technology has decreased the demand for CDs and has increased the demand for Internet service and MP3 players.

■ Change in Quantity Demanded Versus Change in Demand

The influences on buyers' plans that you've just seen bring a *change in demand*. These are all the influences on buying plans *except for the price of the good*. To avoid confusion, when *the price of the good changes* and all other influences on buying plans remain the same, we say there has been a **change in the quantity demanded**.

Change in the quantity demanded

A change in the quantity of a good that people plan to buy that results from a change in the price of the good with all other influences on buying plans remaining the same.

The distinction between a change in demand and a change in the quantity demanded is crucial for figuring out how a market responds to the forces that hit it. Figure 4.4 illustrates and summarizes the distinction:

- If the price of bottled water *rises* when other things remain the same, the quantity demanded of bottled water *decreases* and there is a *movement up* along the demand curve D_0. If the price *falls* when other things remain the same, the quantity demanded *increases* and there is a *movement down* along the demand curve D_0.
- If some influence on buyers' plans other than the price of bottled water changes, there is a change in demand. When the demand for bottled water *decreases*, the demand curve *shifts leftward* to D_1. When the demand for bottled water *increases*, the demand curve *shifts rightward* to D_2.

When you are thinking about the influences on demand, try to get into the habit of asking: Does this influence change the quantity demanded or does it change demand? The test is: Did the price of the good change or did some other influence change? If the price changed, then quantity demanded changed. If some other influence changed and the price remained constant, then demand changed.

■ **FIGURE 4.4**

Change in Quantity Demanded Versus Change in Demand   MyEconLab Animation

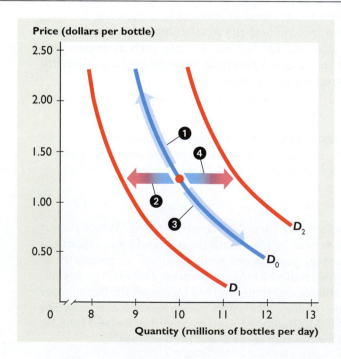

❶ A decrease in the quantity demanded

If the price of a good rises, *cet. par.*, the quantity demanded decreases. There is a movement up along the demand curve D_0.

❷ A decrease in demand

Demand decreases and the demand curve shifts leftward (from D_0 to D_1) if

- The price of a substitute falls or the price of a complement rises.
- The price of the good is expected to fall.
- Income decreases.*
- Expected future income or credit decreases.
- The number of buyers decreases.

* Bottled water is a normal good.

❸ An increase in the quantity demanded

If the price of a good falls, *cet. par.*, the quantity demanded increases. There is a movement down along the demand curve D_0.

❹ An increase in demand

Demand increases and the demand curve shifts rightward (from D_0 to D_2) if

- The price of a substitute rises or the price of a complement falls.
- The price of the good is expected to rise.
- Income increases.
- Expected future income or credit increases.
- The number of buyers increases.

CHECKPOINT 4.1

MyEconLab
You can work these problems in Study Plan 4.1 and get instant feedback.

Distinguish between quantity demanded and demand, and explain what determines demand.

Practice Problems

The following events occur one at a time in the market for cell phones:
- The price of a cell phone falls.
- Everyone believes that the price of a cell phone will fall next month.
- The price of a call made from a cell phone falls.
- The price of a call made from a land-line phone increases.
- The introduction of camera phones makes cell phones more popular.

1. Explain the effect of each event on the demand for cell phones.

2. Use a graph to illustrate the effect of each event.

3. Does any event (or events) illustrate the law of demand?

In the News

Airlines, now flush, fear a downturn
So far this year, airlines have been able to raise fares but still fill their planes.
Source: The New York Times, June 10, 2011
Does this news clip imply that the law of demand doesn't work in the real world? Explain why or why not.

Solutions to Practice Problems

1. A fall in the price of a cell phone increases the quantity of cell phones demanded but has no effect on the demand for cell phones.
   An expected fall in the price of a cell phone next month decreases the demand for cell phones today as people wait for the lower price.
   A fall in the price of a call from a cell phone increases the demand for cell phones because a cell phone call and a cell phone are complements.
   A rise in the price of a call from a land-line phone increases the demand for cell phones because a land-line phone and a cell phone are substitutes.
   With cell phones more popular, the demand for cell phones increases.

2. Figure 1 illustrates the effect of a fall in the price of a cell phone as a movement along the demand curve D.
   Figure 2 illustrates the effect of an increase in the demand for cell phones as the shift of the demand curve from D_0 to D_1 and a decrease in the demand for cell phones as the shift of the demand curve from D_0 to D_2.

3. A fall in the price of a cell phone (other things remaining the same) illustrates the law of demand. Figure 1 illustrates the law of demand. The other events change demand and do not illustrate the law of demand.

Solution to In the News

The law of demand states: If the price of an airline ticket rises, other things remaining the same, the quantity demanded of airline tickets will decrease. The demand curve for airline tickets slopes downward. The law of demand does work in the real world. Airlines can still fill their planes because "other things" did not remain the same. Some event increased the demand for air tickets.

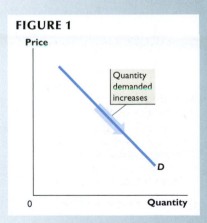

FIGURE 1

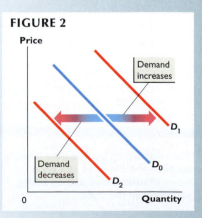

FIGURE 2

4.2 SUPPLY

A market has two sides. On one side are the buyers, or demanders, that we've just studied. On the other side of the market are the sellers, or suppliers. We now study the forces that determine suppliers' plans.

Quantity supplied
The amount of any good, service, or resource that people are willing and able to sell during a specified period at a specified price.

The **quantity supplied** of a good, service, or resource is the amount that people are willing and able to sell during a specified period at a specified price. For example, when the price of spring water is $1.50 a bottle, a spring owner decides to sell 2,000 bottles a day. The 2,000 bottles a day is the quantity supplied of spring water by this individual producer. (As in the case of demand, the quantity supplied is measured as an amount *per unit of time*.)

Many things influence selling plans, and one of them is the price. We look first at the relationship between quantity supplied of a good and its price. To study this relationship, we keep all other influences on selling plans the same, and we ask: Other things remaining the same, how does the quantity supplied of a good change as its price varies? The law of supply provides the answer.

■ The Law of Supply

The **law of supply** states

> **Other things remaining the same, if the price of a good rises, the quantity supplied of that good increases; and if the price of a good falls, the quantity supplied of that good decreases.**

So the law of supply states that when all other things remain the same, if the price of bottled water rises, spring owners will offer more water for sale; if the price of a flat panel TV falls, Sony Corp. will offer fewer flat panel TVs for sale.

Why, other things remaining the same, does the quantity supplied increase if the price rises and decrease if the price falls? Part of the answer lies in the principle of increasing opportunity cost (see p. 68). Because factors of production are not equally productive in all activities, as more of a good is produced, the opportunity cost of producing it increases. A higher price provides the incentive to bear the higher opportunity cost of increased production. Another part of the answer is that for a given cost, the higher price brings a larger profit, so sellers have greater incentive to increase production.

Think about the resources that you own and can offer for sale to others and ask yourself: Which of these items does *not* obey the law of supply? If the wage rate for summer jobs increased, would you have an incentive to work longer hours and bear the higher opportunity cost of forgone leisure? If the bank offered a higher interest rate on deposits, would you have an incentive to save more and bear the higher opportunity cost of forgone consumption? If the used book dealer offered a higher price for last year's textbooks, would you have an incentive to sell that handy math text and bear the higher opportunity cost of visiting the library (or finding a friend) whenever you needed the book?

■ Supply Schedule and Supply Curve

Supply
The relationship between the quantity supplied and the price of a good when all other influences on selling plans remain the same.

Supply is the relationship between the quantity supplied and the price of a good when all other influences on selling plans remain the same. The quantity supplied is *one* quantity at *one* price. *Supply is a list of quantities at different prices* illustrated by a supply schedule and a supply curve.

A **supply schedule** lists the quantities supplied at each different price when all the other influences on selling plans remain the same. The table in Figure 4.5 is one firm's (Agua's) supply schedule for bottled water. It tells us that if the price of water is 50 cents a bottle, Agua plans to sell no water. Its quantity supplied is 0 bottles a day. If the price of water is $1.00 a bottle, Agua's quantity supplied is 1,000 bottles a day. Agua's quantity supplied increases to 2,000 bottles a day at a price of $1.50 a bottle and to 3,000 bottles a day at a price of $2.00 a bottle.

A **supply curve** is a graph of the relationship between the quantity supplied of a good and its price when all the other influences on selling plans remain the same. The points on the supply curve labeled *A* through *D* represent the rows *A* through *D* of the supply schedule. For example, point *C* on the supply curve represents row *C* of the supply schedule and shows that the quantity supplied is 1,000 bottles a day when the price is $1.00 a bottle. Point *B* on the supply curve represents row *B* of the supply schedule and shows that the quantity supplied is 2,000 bottles a day when the price is $1.50 a bottle.

The upward slope of the supply curve illustrates the law of supply. Along the supply curve, when the price of the good *rises*, the quantity supplied *increases*. For example, in Figure 4.5, when the price of a bottle of water rises from $1.50 to $2.00, the quantity supplied increases from 2,000 bottles a day to 3,000 bottles a day. And when the price *falls*, the quantity supplied *decreases*. For example, when the price falls from $1.50 to $1.00 a bottle, the quantity supplied decreases from 2,000 bottles a day to 1,000 bottles a day.

Supply schedule
A list of the quantities supplied at each different price when all the other influences on selling plans remain the same.

Supply curve
A graph of the relationship between the quantity supplied of a good and its price when all the other influences on selling plans remain the same.

FIGURE 4.5

Supply Schedule and Supply Curve

	Price (dollars per bottle)	Quantity supplied (thousands of bottles per day)
A	2.00	3
B	1.50	2
C	1.00	1
D	0.50	0

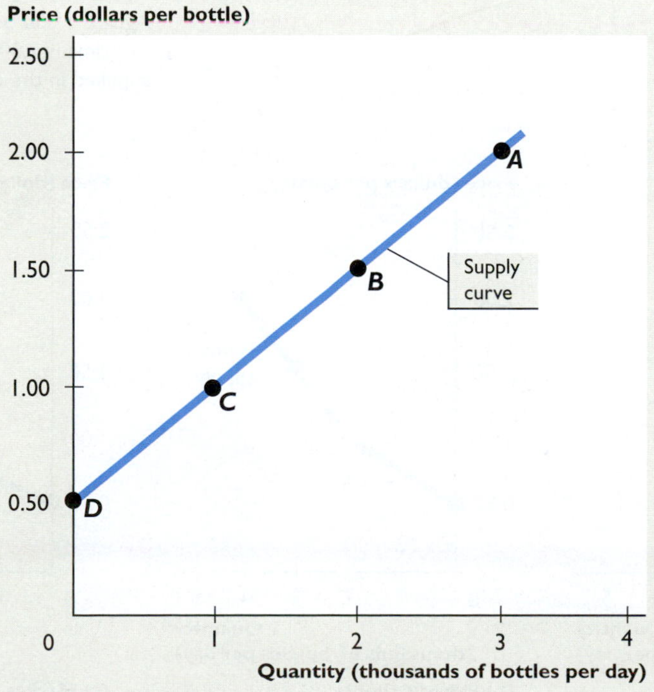

The table shows a supply schedule that lists the quantity of water supplied at each price if all other influences on selling plans remain the same. At a price of $1.50 a bottle, the quantity supplied is 2,000 bottles a day.

The supply curve shows the relationship between the quantity supplied and price, other things remaining the same. The upward-sloping supply curve illustrates the law of supply. When the price rises, the quantity supplied increases; and when the price falls, the quantity supplied decreases.

■ Individual Supply and Market Supply

The supply schedule and the supply curve that you've just studied are for one seller. To study a market, we must determine the market supply.

Market supply is the sum of the supplies of all the sellers in the market. To find the market supply of water, imagine a market in which there are only two sellers: Agua and Prima. The table in Figure 4.6 shows three supply schedules: Agua's, Prima's, and the market supply schedule. Agua's supply schedule is the same as before. Prima's supply schedule tells us the quantity of water that Prima plans to sell at each price. To find the quantity of water supplied in the market, we sum the quantities supplied by Agua and Prima. For example, at a price of $1.00 a bottle, the quantity supplied by Agua is 1,000 bottles a day, the quantity supplied by Prima is 2,000 bottles a day, and the quantity supplied in the market is 3,000 bottles a day.

Agua's supply curve in part (a) and Prima's supply curve in part (b) are graphs of the two individual supply schedules. The market supply curve in part (c) is a graph of the market supply schedule. At a given price, the quantity supplied on the market supply curve equals the horizontal sum of the quantities supplied on the individual supply curves.

Market supply
The sum of the supplies of all the sellers in the market.

■ **FIGURE 4.6**

Individual Supply and Market Supply

MyEconLab Animation

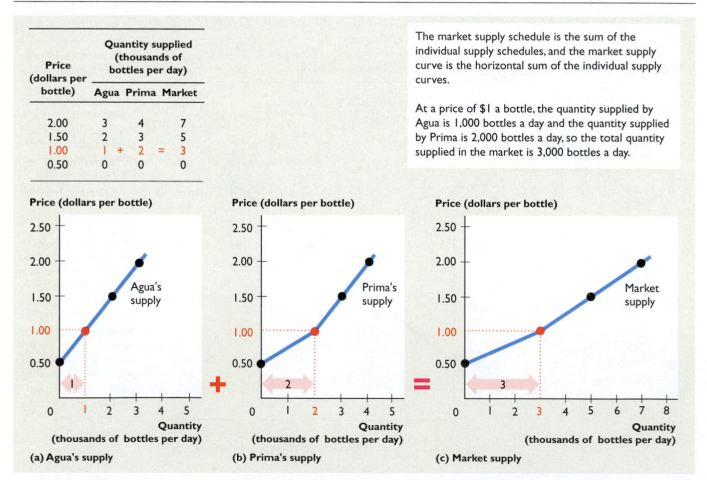

Price (dollars per bottle)	Quantity supplied (thousands of bottles per day)		
	Agua	Prima	Market
2.00	3	4	7
1.50	2	3	5
1.00	1 +	2 =	3
0.50	0	0	0

The market supply schedule is the sum of the individual supply schedules, and the market supply curve is the horizontal sum of the individual supply curves.

At a price of $1 a bottle, the quantity supplied by Agua is 1,000 bottles a day and the quantity supplied by Prima is 2,000 bottles a day, so the total quantity supplied in the market is 3,000 bottles a day.

(a) Agua's supply

(b) Prima's supply

(c) Market supply

Changes in Supply

The supply curve shows how the quantity supplied changes when the price of the good changes but *all other influences on selling plans remain the same.* When any of these other influences on selling plans change, there is a **change in supply,** which means that there is a new supply schedule and new supply curve. *The supply curve shifts.*

Supply can either increase or decrease, and Figure 4.7 illustrates the two cases. Initially, the supply curve is S_0. When supply decreases, the supply curve shifts leftward to S_1. On supply curve S_1, the quantity supplied at each price is smaller. When supply increases, the supply curve shifts rightward to S_2. On supply curve S_2 the quantity supplied at each price is greater.

The main influences on selling plans that change supply are

- Prices of related goods
- Prices of resources and other inputs
- Expected future prices
- Number of sellers
- Productivity

Prices of Related Goods

Related goods are either substitutes *in production* or complements *in production.* A **substitute in production** for a good is another good that can be produced in its place. Skinny jeans are substitutes in production for boot cut jeans in a clothing factory.

A **complement in production** of a good is another good that is produced along with it. Cream is a complement in production of skim milk in a dairy.

Change in supply
A change in the quantity that suppliers plan to sell when any influence on selling plans other than the price of the good changes.

Substitute in production
A good that can be produced in place of another good.

Complement in production
A good that is produced along with another good.

■ **FIGURE 4.7**

Changes in Supply

MyEconLab Animation

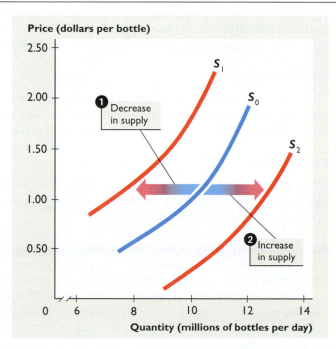

A change in any influence on selling plans other than a change in the price of the good itself changes supply and shifts the supply curve.

❶ When supply decreases, the supply curve shifts leftward from S_0 to S_1.

❷ When supply increases, the supply curve shifts rightward from S_0 to S_2.

A Change in the Price of a Substitute in Production   The supply of a good *decreases* if the price of one of its substitutes in production *rises;* and the supply of a good *increases* if the price of one of its substitutes in production *falls.* That is, the supply of a good and the price of one of its substitutes in production move in *opposite directions.* For example, a clothing factory can produce cargo pants or button-fly jeans, so these goods are substitutes in production. When the price of button-fly jeans rises, the clothing factory switches production from cargo pants to button-fly jeans, so the supply of cargo pants decreases.

A Change in the Price of a Complement in Production   The supply of a good *increases* if the price of one of its complements in production *rises;* and the supply of a good *decreases* if the price of one of its complements in production *falls.* That is, the supply of a good and the price of one of its complements in production move in the *same direction.* For example, when a dairy produces skim milk, it also produces cream, so these goods are complements in production. When the price of skim milk rises, the dairy produces more skim milk, so the supply of cream increases.

Prices of Resources and Other Inputs

Supply changes when the price of a resource or other input used to produce the good changes. The reason is that resource and input prices influence the cost of production. The more it costs to produce a good, the smaller is the quantity supplied of that good at each price (other things remaining the same). For example, if the wage rate of bottling-plant workers rises, it costs more to produce a bottle of water, so the supply of bottled water decreases.

Expected Future Prices

Expectations about future prices influence supply. For example, a severe frost that wipes out Florida's citrus crop doesn't change the production of orange juice today, but it does decrease production later in the year when the current crop would normally have been harvested. Sellers of orange juice will expect the price to rise in the future. To get the higher future price, some sellers will increase their inventory of frozen juice, and this action decreases the supply of juice today.

Number of Sellers

The greater the number of sellers in a market, the larger is the supply. For example, many new sellers have developed springs and water-bottling plants in the United States, and the supply of bottled water has increased.

Productivity

Productivity is output per unit of input. An increase in productivity lowers the cost of producing the good and increases its supply. A decrease in productivity has the opposite effect and decreases supply.

Technological change and the increased use of capital increase productivity. For example, advances in electronic technology have lowered the cost of producing a computer and increased the supply of computers. Technological change brings new goods such as the iPod, the supply of which was previously zero.

Natural events such as severe weather and earthquakes decrease productivity and decrease supply. For example, the tsunami of 2004 decreased the supply of agricultural products and seafood in many places surrounding the Indian Ocean.

■ Change in Quantity Supplied Versus Change in Supply

The influences on sellers' plans you've just considered bring a *change in supply*. These are all the influences on sellers' plans *except the price of the good*. To avoid confusion, when the *price of the good changes* and all other influences on selling plans remain the same, we say there has been a **change in the quantity supplied**.

The distinction between a change in supply and a change in the quantity supplied is crucial for figuring out how a market responds to the forces that hit it. Figure 4.8 illustrates and summarizes the distinction:

- If the price of bottled water *falls* when other things remain the same, the quantity supplied of bottled water *decreases* and there is a *movement down* along the supply curve S_0. If the price *rises* when other things remain the same, the quantity supplied *increases* and there is a *movement up* along the supply curve S_0.
- If any influence on water bottlers' plans other than the price of bottled water changes, there is a change in the supply of bottled water. When the supply of bottled water *decreases*, the supply curve *shifts leftward* to S_1. When the supply of bottled water *increases*, the supply curve *shifts rightward* to S_2.

When you are thinking about the influences on supply, get into the habit of asking: Does this influence change the quantity supplied or does it change supply? The test is: Did the price change or did some other influence change? If the price of the good changed, then quantity supplied changed. If some other influence changed and the price of the good remained constant, then supply changed.

Change in the quantity supplied
A change in the quantity of a good that suppliers plan to sell that results from a change in the price of the good.

■ FIGURE 4.8

Change in Quantity Supplied Versus Change in Supply   MyEconLab Animation

❶ **A decrease in the quantity supplied**

If the price of a good falls, *cet. par.*, the quantity supplied decreases. There is a movement down along the supply curve S_0.

❷ **A decrease in supply**

Supply decreases and the supply curve shifts leftward (from S_0 to S_1) if

- The price of a substitute in production rises.
- The price of a complement in production falls.
- A resource price or other input price rises.
- The price of the good is expected to rise.
- The number of sellers decreases.
- Productivity decreases.

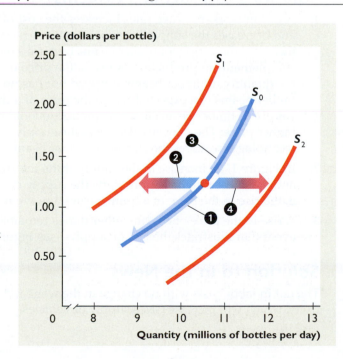

❸ **An increase in the quantity supplied**

If the price of a good rises, *cet. par.*, the quantity supplied increases. There is a movement up along the supply curve S_0.

❹ **An increase in supply**

Supply increases and the supply curve shifts rightward (from S_0 to S_2) if

- The price of a substitute in production falls.
- The price of a complement in production rises.
- A resource price or other input price falls.
- The price of the good is expected to fall.
- The number of sellers increases.
- Productivity increases.

CHECKPOINT 4.2

Distinguish between quantity supplied and supply, and explain what determines supply.

Practice Problems

Lumber companies make timber beams from logs. In the process of making beams, the mill produces sawdust, which is made into pressed wood. In the market for timber beams, the following events occur one at a time:

- The wage rate of sawmill workers rises.
- The price of sawdust rises.
- The price of a timber beam rises.
- The price of a timber beam is expected to rise next year.
- A new law reduces the amount of forest that can be cut for timber.
- A new technology lowers the cost of producing timber beams.

1. Explain the effect of each event on the supply of timber beams.

2. Use a graph to illustrate the effect of each event.

3. Does any event (or events) illustrate the law of supply?

In the News

GM, UAW reach crucial cost-cutting pact

GM and the UAW agree on restructuring workers' jobs. This restructuring, with no change in the wage rate, will save GM billions in labor costs.

Source: *Wall Street Journal*, May 22, 2009

How will this cost-cutting agreement change GM's supply of vehicles? Explain.

Solutions to Practice Problems

1. A rise in workers' wage rates increases the cost of producing a timber beam and decreases the supply of timber beams. A rise in the price of sawdust increases the supply of timber beams because sawdust and timber beams are complements in production. A rise in the price of a timber beam increases the quantity of timber beams supplied but has no effect on the supply of timber beams. An expected rise in the price of a timber beam decreases the supply of timber beams today as producers hold back and wait for the higher price. The new law decreases the supply of timber beams. The new technology increases the supply of timber beams.

2. In Figure 1, an increase in the supply shifts the supply curve from S_0 to S_1, and a decrease in the supply shifts the supply curve from S_0 to S_2. In Figure 2, the rise in the price of a beam creates a movement along the supply curve.

3. A rise in the price of a beam, other things remaining the same, is the only event that illustrates the law of supply—see Figure 2.

Solution to In the News

The cut in labor costs with no change in the wage rate is an increase in productivity, which will increase GM's supply of vehicles.

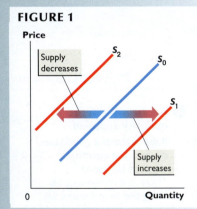

FIGURE 1

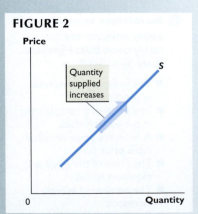

FIGURE 2

4.3 MARKET EQUILIBRIUM

In everyday language, "equilibrium" means "opposing forces are in balance." In a market, demand and supply are the opposing forces. **Market equilibrium** occurs when the quantity demanded equals the quantity supplied—when buyers' and sellers' plans are in balance. At the **equilibrium price,** the quantity demanded equals the quantity supplied. The **equilibrium quantity** is the quantity bought and sold at the equilibrium price.

In the market for bottled water in Figure 4.9, equilibrium occurs where the demand curve and the supply curve intersect. The equilibrium price is $1.00 a bottle, and the equilibrium quantity is 10 million bottles a day.

■ Price: A Market's Automatic Regulator

When equilibrium is disturbed, market forces restore it. The **law of market forces** states

> **When there is a surplus, the price falls; and when there is a shortage, the price rises.**

A *surplus* is a situation in which the quantity supplied exceeds the quantity demanded. If there is a surplus, suppliers must cut the price to sell more. Buyers are pleased to take the lower price, so the price falls. Because a surplus arises when the price is above the equilibrium price, a falling price is exactly what the market needs to restore equilibrium.

A *shortage* is a situation in which the quantity demanded exceeds the quantity supplied. If there is a shortage, buyers must pay a higher price to get more. Sellers are pleased to take the higher price, so the price rises. Because a shortage arises when the price is below the equilibrium price, a rising price is exactly what is

Market equilibrium
When the quantity demanded equals the quantity supplied—buyers' and sellers' plans are in balance.

Equilibrium price
The price at which the quantity demanded equals the quantity supplied.

Equilibrium quantity
The quantity bought and sold at the equilibrium price.

■ **FIGURE 4.9**

Equilibrium Price and Equilibrium Quantity

MyEconLab Animation

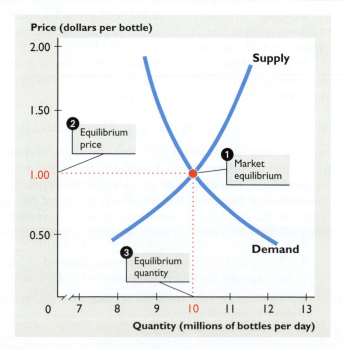

Price (dollars per bottle)

Quantity (millions of bottles per day)

❶ Market equilibrium occurs at the intersection of the demand curve and the supply curve.

❷ The equilibrium price is $1.00 a bottle.

❸ At the equilibrium price, the quantity demanded and the quantity supplied are 10 million bottles a day, which is the equilibrium quantity.

■ **FIGURE 4.10**

The Forces That Achieve Equilibrium

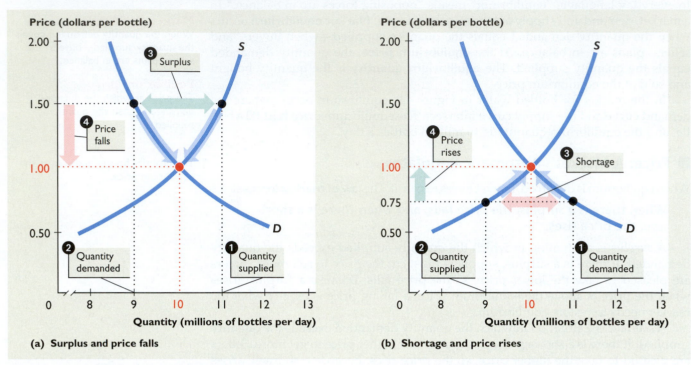

(a) Surplus and price falls

(b) Shortage and price rises

At $1.50 a bottle, ❶ the quantity supplied is 11 million bottles, ❷ the quantity demanded is 9 million bottles, ❸ the surplus is 2 million bottles, and ❹ the price falls.

At 75 cents a bottle, ❶ the quantity demanded is 11 million bottles, ❷ the quantity supplied is 9 million bottles, ❸ the shortage is 2 million bottles, and ❹ the price rises.

needed to restore equilibrium.

In Figure 4.10(a), at $1.50 a bottle, there is a surplus: The price falls, the quantity demanded increases, the quantity supplied decreases, and the surplus is eliminated at $1.00 a bottle.

In Figure 4.10(b), at 75 cents a bottle, there is a shortage of water: The price rises, the quantity demanded decreases, the quantity supplied increases, and the shortage is eliminated at $1.00 a bottle.

■ Predicting Price Changes: Three Questions

Because price adjustments eliminate shortages and surpluses, markets are normally in equilibrium. When an event disturbs an equilibrium, a new equilibrium soon emerges. To explain and predict changes in prices and quantities, we need to consider only changes in the *equilibrium* price and the *equilibrium* quantity. We can work out the effects of an event on a market by answering three questions:

1. Does the event influence demand or supply?
2. Does the event *increase* or *decrease* demand or supply—shift the demand curve or the supply curve *rightward* or *leftward*?
3. What are the new *equilibrium* price and *equilibrium* quantity and how have they changed?

■ Effects of Changes in Demand

Let's practice answering the three questions by working out the effects of an event in the market for bottled water: A new study says that tap water is unsafe.

1. With tap water unsafe, the demand for bottled water changes.

2. The demand for bottled water *increases*, and the demand curve *shifts rightward*. Figure 4.11(a) shows the shift from D_0 to D_1.

3. There is now a *shortage* at $1.00 a bottle. The *price rises* to $1.50 a bottle, and the quantity increases to 11 million bottles.

Note that there is *no change in supply*; the rise in price brings an *increase in the quantity supplied*—a movement along the supply curve.

Let's work out what happens if the price of a zero-calorie sports drink falls.

1. The sports drink is a substitute for bottled water, so when its price changes, the demand for bottled water changes.

2. The demand for bottled water *decreases*, and the demand curve *shifts leftward*. Figure 4.11(b) shows the shift from D_0 to D_2.

3. There is now a *surplus* at $1.00 a bottle. The price *falls* to 75 cents a bottle, and the quantity decreases to 9 million bottles.

Note again that there is *no change in supply*; the fall in price brings a *decrease in the quantity supplied*—a movement along the supply curve.

■ FIGURE 4.11

The Effects of a Change in Demand   MyEconLab Animation

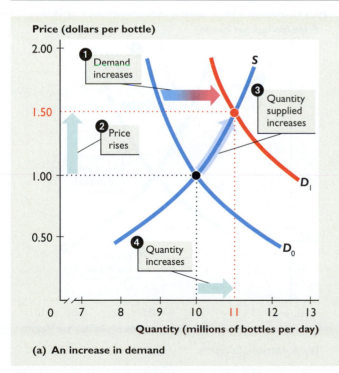 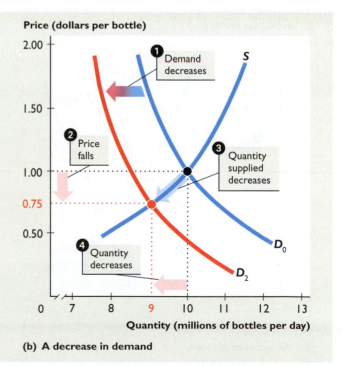

(a) An increase in demand

(b) A decrease in demand

❶ An increase in demand shifts the demand curve rightward to D_1 and creates a shortage. ❷ The price rises, ❸ the quantity supplied increases, and ❹ the equilibrium quantity increases.

❶ A decrease in demand shifts the demand curve leftward to D_2 and creates a surplus. ❷ The price falls, ❸ the quantity supplied decreases, and ❹ the equilibrium quantity decreases.

◼ Effects of Changes in Supply

You can get more practice working out the effects of another event in the market for bottled water: European water bottlers buy springs and open new plants in the United States.

1. With more suppliers of bottled water, the supply changes.

2. The supply of bottled water *increases*, and the supply curve *shifts rightward*. Figure 4.12(a) shows the shift from S_0 to S_1.

3. There is now a *surplus* at $1.00 a bottle. The *price falls* to 75 cents a bottle, and the quantity increases to 11 million bottles.

Note that there is *no change in demand*; the fall in price brings an *increase in the quantity demanded*—a movement along the demand curve.

What happens if a drought dries up some springs?

1. The drought is a change in productivity, so the supply of water changes.

2. With fewer springs, the supply of bottled water *decreases*, and the supply curve *shifts leftward*. Figure 4.12(b) shows the shift from to S_0 to S_2.

3. There is now a *shortage* at $1.00 a bottle. The *price rises* to $1.50 a bottle, and the quantity decreases to 9 million bottles.

Again, there is *no change in demand*; the rise in price brings a *decrease in the quantity demanded*—a movement along the demand curve.

◼ **FIGURE 4.12**

The Effects of a Change in Supply   MyEconLab Animation

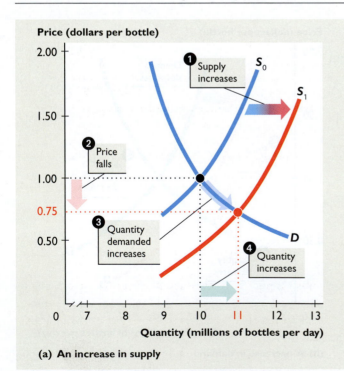

(a) An increase in supply

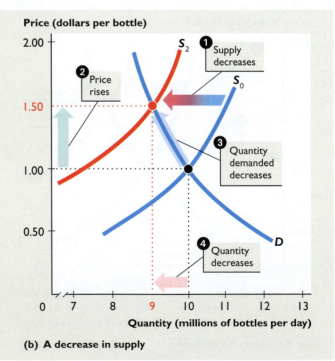

(b) A decrease in supply

❶ An increase in supply shifts the supply curve rightward to S_1 and creates a surplus. ❷ The price falls, ❸ the quantity demanded increases, and ❹ the equilibrium quantity increases.

❶ A decrease in supply shifts the supply curve leftward to S_2 and creates a shortage. ❷ The price rises, ❸ the quantity demanded decreases, and ❹ the equilibrium quantity decreases.

EYE on the PRICE OF COFFEE
Why Did the Price of Coffee Soar in 2010 and 2011?

In January 2009, the price of coffee (the kind that you get at Starbucks and similar coffee shops called Arabica) was $1.25 a pound (point A in Figure 1) and by May 2011, it had risen to $3.00 a pound (point B). Why did the price of coffee soar? Figure 2, which shows the

market for coffee, answers this question.

The demand curve D and the supply curve S_{09} determined the equilibrium price and quantity in 2009 at $1.25 a pound and 950 million pounds.

Heavy rain led to exceptionally low harvests in Colombia, Indonesia, Mexico,

and Vietnam, which decreased the supply of coffee. The supply curve shifted leftward to S_{11}. The price increased to $3.00 a pound. The quantity demanded and equilibrium quantity decreased to 800 million pounds.

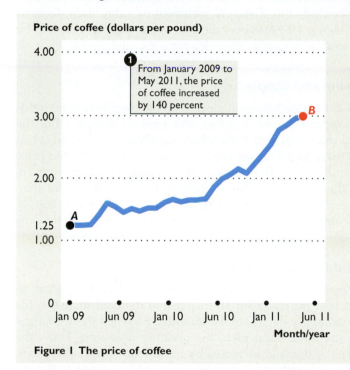

1 From January 2009 to May 2011, the price of coffee increased by 140 percent

Figure 1 The price of coffee

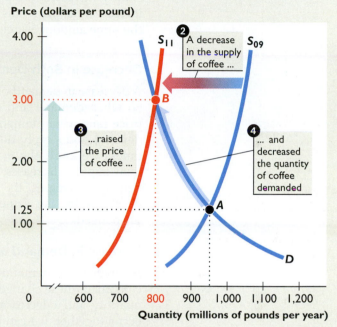

2 A decrease in the supply of coffee ...

3 ... raised the price of coffee ...

4 ... and decreased the quantity of coffee demanded

Figure 2 The market for coffee

EYE on YOUR LIFE
Using Demand and Supply

The demand and supply model is going to be a big part of the rest of your life!

First, you will use it again and again during your economics course. The demand and supply model is one of your major tools, so having a firm grasp of it will bring an immediate payoff.

But second, and much more important, by understanding the laws of demand and supply and being aware of how prices adjust to balance these two opposing forces, you will have a much better appreciation of how your economic world works.

Every time you hear someone complaining about a price hike and blaming it on someone's greed, think about the law of market forces and how demand and supply determine that price.

As you shop for your favorite clothing, music, and food items, try to describe how supply and demand influence the prices of these goods.

■ Changes in Both Demand and Supply

When events occur that change *both* demand and supply, you can find the resulting change in the equilibrium price and equilibrium quantity by combining the cases you've just studied. Figure 4.13 summarizes all the possible cases.

Increase in Both Demand and Supply

An increase in demand or an increase in supply increases the equilibrium quantity. So when demand and supply increase together, the *quantity increases*. But the price rises when demand increases and falls when supply increases. So when demand and supply increase together, we can't say what happens to the price unless we know the magnitudes of the changes. If demand increases by more than supply increases, the price rises. But if supply increases by more than demand increases, the price falls. Figure 4.13(e) shows the case when supply increases by the same amount as demand increases, so the price remains unchanged.

Decrease in Both Demand and Supply

A decrease in demand or a decrease in supply decreases the equilibrium quantity. So when demand and supply decrease together, the *quantity decreases*. But the price falls when demand decreases and rises when supply decreases. So when demand and supply decrease together, we can't say what happens to the price unless we know the magnitudes of the changes. If demand decreases by more than supply decreases, the price falls. But if supply decreases by more than demand decreases, the price rises. Figure 4.13(i) shows the case when supply decreases by the same amount as demand decreases, so the price remains unchanged.

Increase in Demand and Decrease in Supply

An increase in demand or a decrease in supply raises the equilibrium price, so combined, these changes *raise the price*. But an increase in demand increases the quantity, and a decrease in supply decreases the quantity. So when these changes occur together, we can't say what happens to the quantity unless we know the magnitudes of the changes. If demand increases by more than supply decreases, the quantity increases. But if supply decreases by more than demand increases, the quantity decreases. Figure 4.13(h) shows the case when demand increases by the same amount as supply decreases, so the quantity remains unchanged.

Decrease in Demand and Increase in Supply

A decrease in demand or an increase in supply lowers the equilibrium price, so combined, these changes *lower the price*. But a decrease in demand decreases the quantity, and an increase in supply increases the quantity. So when these changes occur together, we can't say what happens to the quantity unless we know the magnitudes of the changes. If demand decreases by more than supply increases, the quantity decreases. But if supply increases by more than demand decreases, the quantity increases. Figure 4.13(f) shows the case when demand decreases by the same amount as supply increases, so the quantity remains unchanged.

For the cases in Figure 4.13 where you "can't say" what happens to price or quantity, make some examples that go in each direction.

FIGURE 4.13

The Effects of All the Possible Changes in Demand and Supply

MyEconLab Animation

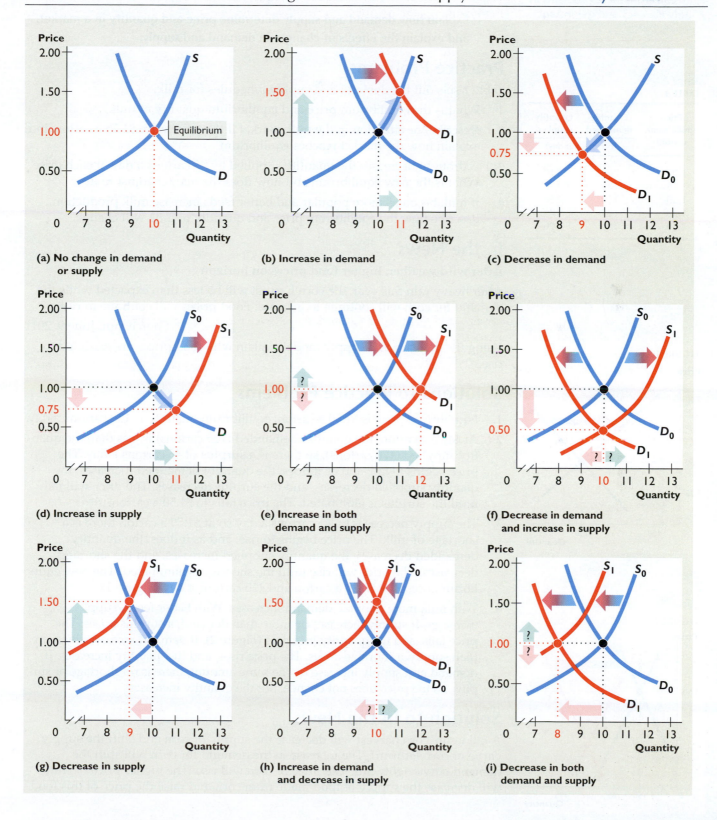

(a) **No change in demand or supply**

(b) **Increase in demand**

(c) **Decrease in demand**

(d) **Increase in supply**

(e) **Increase in both demand and supply**

(f) **Decrease in demand and increase in supply**

(g) **Decrease in supply**

(h) **Increase in demand and decrease in supply**

(i) **Decrease in both demand and supply**

MyEconLab

You can work these problems in Study Plan 4.3 and get instant feedback.

TABLE 1

Price (dollars per carton)	Quantity demanded	Quantity supplied
	(cartons per day)	
1.00	200	110
1.25	175	130
1.50	150	150
1.75	125	170
2.00	100	190

FIGURE 1

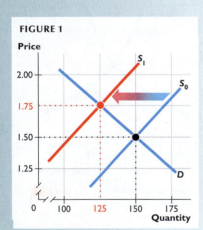

FIGURE 2

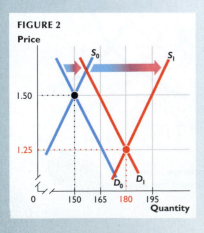

CHECKPOINT 4.3

Explain how demand and supply determine price and quantity in a market, and explain the effects of changes in demand and supply.

Practice Problems

Table 1 sets out the demand and supply schedules for milk.

1. What is the equilibrium price and equilibrium quantity of milk?
2. Describe the situation in the milk market if the price were $1.75 a carton and explain how the market reaches equilibrium.
3. A drought decreases the quantity supplied by 45 cartons a day at each price. What is the new equilibrium and how does the market adjust to it?
4. If milk becomes more popular and better feeds increase milk production, describe how the equilibrium price and quantity of milk will change.

In the News

After wild weather, higher food prices on horizon

After heavy rain this year, the corn harvest will be less than expected while the demand for corn will continue to increase. Food prices will continue to rise.

Source: npr, June 9, 2011

Using the demand and supply model explain why food prices are expected to rise.

Solutions to Practice Problems

1. Equilibrium price is $1.50 a carton; equilibrium quantity is 150 cartons a day.
2. At $1.75 a carton, the quantity demanded (125 cartons) is less than the quantity supplied (170 cartons), so there is a surplus of 45 cartons a day. The price begins to fall, and as it does, the quantity demanded increases, the quantity supplied decreases, and the surplus decreases. The price will fall until the surplus is eliminated. The price falls to $1.50 a carton.
3. The supply decreases by 45 cartons a day so at $1.50 a carton there is a shortage of milk. The price begins to rise, and as it does, the quantity demanded decreases, the quantity supplied increases, and the shortage decreases. The price will rise until the shortage is eliminated. The new equilibrium occurs at $1.75 a carton and 125 cartons a day (Figure 1).
4. With milk more popular, demand increases. With better feeds, supply increases. If supply increases by more than demand, a surplus arises. The price falls, and the quantity increases (Figure 2). If demand increases by more than supply, a shortage arises. The price rises, and the quantity increases. If demand and supply increase by the same amount, there is no shortage or surplus, so the price does not change, but the quantity increases.

Solution to In the News

A fall in the corn harvest will decrease the supply of corn and shift the supply curve of corn leftward. The increase in the demand for corn will shift the demand curve rightward. The price of corn will rise. The higher price of corn will decrease the supply of food made from corn and raise the price of this food.

CHAPTER SUMMARY

Key Points

1. Distinguish between quantity demanded and demand, and explain what determines demand.

- Other things remaining the same, the quantity demanded increases as the price falls and decreases as the price rises—the law of demand.

- The demand for a good is influenced by the prices of related goods, expected future prices, income, expected future income and credit, the number of buyers, and preferences. A change in any of these influences changes the demand for the good.

2. Distinguish between quantity supplied and supply, and explain what determines supply.

- Other things remaining the same, the quantity supplied increases as the price rises and decreases as the price falls—the law of supply.

- The supply of a good is influenced by the prices of related goods, prices of resources and other inputs, expected future prices, the number of sellers, and productivity. A change in any of these influences changes the supply of the good.

3. Explain how demand and supply determine price and quantity in a market, and explain the effects of changes in demand and supply.

- The law of market forces brings market equilibrium—the equilibrium price and equilibrium quantity at which buyers and sellers trade.

- The price adjusts to maintain market equilibrium—to keep the quantity demanded equal to the quantity supplied. A surplus brings a fall in the price to restore market equilibrium; a shortage brings a rise in the price to restore market equilibrium.

- Market equilibrium responds to changes in demand and supply. An increase in demand increases both the price and the quantity; a decrease in demand decreases both the price and the quantity. An increase in supply increases the quantity but decreases the price; and a decrease in supply decreases the quantity but increases the price.

Key Terms

CHAPTER CHECKPOINT

Study Plan Problems and Applications

1. Explain how each of the following events changes the demand for or supply of air travel.
   • Airfares tumble, while long-distance bus fares don't change.
   • The price of jet fuel rises.
   • Airlines reduce the number of flights each day.
   • People expect airfares to increase next summer.
   • The price of train travel falls.
   • The price of a pound of air cargo increases.

Use the laws of demand and supply to explain whether the statements in Problems **2** and **3** are true or false. In your explanation, distinguish between a change in demand and a change in the quantity demanded and between a change in supply and a change in the quantity supplied.

2. The United States does not allow oranges from Brazil (the world's largest producer of oranges) to enter the United States. If Brazilian oranges were sold in the United States, oranges and orange juice would be cheaper.

3. If the price of frozen yogurt falls, the quantity of ice cream consumed will decrease and the price of ice cream will rise.

4. Table 1 shows the demand and supply schedules for running shoes. What is the market equilibrium? If the price is $70 a pair, describe the situation in the market. Explain how market equilibrium is restored. If a rise in income increases the demand for running shoes by 100 pairs a day at each price, explain how the market adjusts to its new equilibrium.

5. "As more people buy fuel-efficient hybrid cars, the demand for gasoline will decrease and the price of gasoline will fall. The fall in the price of gasoline will decrease the supply of gasoline." Is this statement true? Explain.

6. **OPEC deadlocked on oil production hike**
   Oil prices breached the $100-a-barrel mark Wednesday after OPEC said it could not reach an agreement about raising crude production.
   Source: CNN Money, June 8, 2011

   Draw a graph to show the oil market in equilibrium. Suppose that OPEC members had agreed to increase production. Show on your graph, the effect of this decision on the market equilibrium.

Use the following information to work Problems **7** and **8**.

Pricier bread and cereal. Coming soon?
Wheat and corn prices surged about 10 percent last week and could hit the items in your grocery basket by mid-summer. It's a case of two extremes: dry weather conditions in parts of the southern United States and in Europe have sparked fears of a supply crunch of wheat, while supplies of corn are being threatened by flooding and heavy rain in the Midwest.
Source: CNN Money, May 19, 2011

7. Explain why the dry weather will lead to a rise in the price of bread.

8. Use graphs to show why the price of corn has risen and show its effect on the price of cereals.

TABLE 1

Price (dollars per pair)	Quantity demanded	Quantity supplied
	(pairs per day)	
60	1,000	400
70	900	500
80	800	600
90	700	700
100	600	800
110	500	900

Instructor Assignable Problems and Applications

Your instructor can assign these problems as homework, a quiz, or a test in MyEconLab.

1. If after heavy rain and low production, the weather improves and coffee growers enjoy bumper crops, how does
    *   The demand for coffee change?
    *   The supply of coffee change?
    *   The price of coffee change?
    Illustrate your answer with a graphical analysis.

2. What is the effect on the equilibrium price and equilibrium quantity of orange juice if the price of apple juice decreases and the wage rate paid to orange grove workers increases?

3. What is the effect on the equilibrium in the orange juice market if orange juice becomes more popular and a cheaper robot is used to pick oranges?

Table 1 shows the demand and supply schedules for boxes of chocolates in an average week. Use this information to work Problems **4** and **5**.

4. If the price of chocolates is $17.00 a box, describe the situation in the market. Explain how market equilibrium is restored.

5. During Valentine's week, more people buy chocolates and chocolatiers offer their chocolates in special red boxes, which cost more to produce than the everyday box. Set out the three-step process of analysis and show on a graph the adjustment process to the new equilibrium. Describe the changes in the equilibrium price and the equilibrium quantity.

6. After a severe bout of foreclosures and defaults on home loans, banks made it harder for people to borrow. How does this change influence
    *   The demand for new homes?
    *   The supply of new homes?
    *   The price of new homes?
    Illustrate your answer with a graphical analysis.

TABLE 1

Price (dollars per box)	Quantity demanded	Quantity supplied
	(boxes per week)	
13.00	1,600	1,200
14.00	1,500	1,300
15.00	1,400	1,400
16.00	1,300	1,500
17.00	1,200	1,600
18.00	1,100	1,700

7. **Alabama food prices jump in May**
    Alabama Farmers Federation announced that food prices in May will increase. In previous unprofitable years, farmers reduced their herds with the result that in 2009 meat production will fall. Bacon is expected to rise by 32 cents a pound to $4.18 and steaks by 57 cents to $8.41 a pound.

    Source: *The Birmingham News*, May 21, 2009

    Explain why the reduction of herds will lead to a rise in meat prices today. Draw a graph to illustrate.

8. "As more people buy computers, the demand for Internet service increases and the price of Internet service decreases. The fall in the price of Internet service decreases the supply of Internet service." Is this statement true or false? Explain.

9. **Steel output set for historic drop**
    Steel producers expect to cut output by 10 percent in 2009 in response to cancelled orders from construction companies and car and household appliance producers.

    Source: *Financial Times*, December 28, 2008

    Does the cancellation of orders change the demand for steel, the quantity demanded, the supply of steel, or the quantity supplied? What happens to the equilibrium price of steel?

MyEconLab

You can work this quiz in Chapter 4 Study Plan and get instant feedback.

Multiple Choice Quiz

1. Which of the following events illustrates the law of demand: Other things remaining the same, a rise in the price of a good will _____ .

   A. decrease the quantity demanded of that good
   B. increase the demand for a substitute of that good
   C. decrease the demand for the good
   D. increase the demand for a complement of that good

2. In the market for jeans, which of the following events increases the demand for a pair of jeans?

   A. rise in the wage rate paid to garment workers
   B. rise in the price of a denim skirt (a substitute for jeans)
   C. fall in the price of denim cloth
   D. new technology, which reduces the time it takes to make a pair of jeans

3. Other things remaining the same, a fall in the price of peanuts will _____.

   A. increase the supply of peanuts
   B. decrease the supply of peanut butter
   C. decrease the quantity supplied of peanuts
   D. decrease the supply of peanuts

4. In the market for cell phones, which of the following events increases the supply of cell phones?

   A. New technology lowers the cost of making a cell phone
   B. Rise in the price of an e-book reader (a substitute in production)
   C. An increase in people's incomes
   D. A rise in the wage rate paid to electronics workers

5. When floods wiped out the banana crop in Central America, the equilibrium price of bananas _____ and the equilibrium quantity of bananas _____.

   A. rose; increased
   B. rose; decreased
   C. fell; increased
   D. fell; decreased

6. A decrease in the demand for chocolate with no change in the supply of chocolate will create a _____ of chocolate at today's price, but gradually the price will _____.

   A. surplus; fall
   B. shortage; fall
   C. surplus; rise
   D. shortage; rise

7. Many Americans are selling their used cars and buying new fuel-efficient hybrids. Other things remaining the same, in the market for used cars, _____ and in the market for hybrids _____.

   A. supply increases and the price falls; demand increases and the price rises
   B. demand decreases and the price rises; supply increases and the price falls
   C. both demand and supply decrease and the price might rise, fall, or not change; demand increases and the price rises
   D. demand decreases, supply increases, and the price falls; supply increases and the price falls

What do you do when the price of gasoline rises?

Elasticities of Demand and Supply

5

When you have completed your study of this chapter, you will be able to

1 Define the price elasticity of demand, and explain the factors that influence it and how to calculate it.

2 Define the price elasticity of supply, and explain the factors that influence it and how to calculate it.

3 Define the cross elasticity of demand and the income elasticity of demand, and explain the factors that influence them.

5.1 THE PRICE ELASTICITY OF DEMAND

A decrease in supply of gasoline brings a large rise in its price and a small decrease in the quantity that people buy. The reason is that buying plans for gasoline are not very responsive to a change in price. But an increase in the supply of airline services brings a small decrease in its price and a large increase in the quantity of air travel. In the case of air travel, buying plans are highly sensitive to a change in price. By knowing how sensitive or responsive buying plans are to price changes, we can predict how a given change in supply will change price and quantity.

But we often want to go further and predict by how much a price will change when an event occurs. To make more precise predictions about the magnitudes of price and quantity changes, we need to know more about a demand curve than the fact that it slopes downward. We need to know how responsive the quantity demanded is to a price change. Elasticity provides this information.

Price elasticity of demand
A measure of the responsiveness of the quantity demanded of a good to a change in its price when all other influences on buyers' plans remain the same.

The **price elasticity of demand** is a measure of the responsiveness of the quantity demanded of a good* to a change in its price when all other influences on buyers' plans remain the same.

To determine the price elasticity of demand, we compare the percentage change in the quantity demanded with the percentage change in price. But we calculate percentage changes in a special way.

◼ Percentage Change in Price

Suppose that Starbucks raises the price of a latte from $3 to $5 a cup. What is the percentage change in price? The change in price is the new price minus the initial price. The percentage change is calculated as the change in price divided by the initial price, all multiplied by 100. The formula for the percentage change is

$$\text{Percentage change in price} = \left(\frac{\text{New price} - \text{Initial price}}{\text{Initial price}} \right) \times 100.$$

In this example, the initial price is $3 and the new price is $5, so

$$\text{Percentage change in price} = \left(\frac{\$5 - \$3}{\$3} \right) \times 100 = \left(\frac{\$2}{\$3} \right) \times 100 = 66.67 \text{ percent.}$$

Now suppose that Starbucks cuts the price of a latte from $5 to $3 a cup. Now what is the percentage change in price? The initial price is now $5 and the new price is $3, so the percentage change in price is calculated as

$$\text{Percentage change in price} = \left(\frac{\$3 - \$5}{\$5} \right) \times 100 = \left(\frac{-\$2}{\$5} \right) \times 100 = -40 \text{ percent.}$$

The same price change, $2, over the same interval, $3 to $5, is a different percentage change (different absolute value or magnitude) depending on whether the price rises or falls.

Because elasticity compares the percentage change in the quantity demanded with the percentage change in price, we need a measure of percentage change that does not depend on the direction of the price change. The measure that economists use is called the *midpoint method*.

---

*What you learn in this chapter also applies to services and factors of production.

The Midpoint Method

To calculate the percentage change in price using the midpoint method, we divide the change in the price by the *average price*—the *average* of the new price and the initial price—and then multiply by 100. The average price is at the midpoint between the initial and the new price, hence the name *midpoint method*.

The formula for the percentage change using the midpoint method is

$$\text{Percentage change in price} = \left(\frac{\text{New price} - \text{Initial price}}{(\text{New price} + \text{Initial price}) \div 2}\right) \times 100.$$

In this formula, the numerator, (New price − Initial price), is the same as before. The denominator, (New price + Initial price) ÷ 2, is the average of the new price and the initial price.

To calculate the percentage change in the price of a Starbucks latte using the midpoint method, put $5 for new price and $3 for initial price in the formula:

$$\text{Percentage change in price} = \left(\frac{\$5 - \$3}{(\$5 + \$3) \div 2}\right) \times 100 = \left(\frac{\$2}{\$8 \div 2}\right) \times 100$$

$$= \left(\frac{\$2}{\$4}\right) \times 100 = 50 \text{ percent.}$$

Because the average price is the same regardless of whether the price rises or falls, the percentage change in price calculated by the midpoint method is the same (absolute value or magnitude) for a price rise and a price fall. In this example, it is 50 percent.

■ Percentage Change in Quantity Demanded

Suppose that when the price of a latte rises from $3 to $5 a cup, the quantity demanded decreases from 15 cups to 5 cups an hour. The percentage change in the quantity demanded using the midpoint method is

$$\text{Percentage change in quantity} = \left(\frac{\text{New quantity} - \text{Initial quantity}}{(\text{New quantity} + \text{Initial quantity}) \div 2}\right) \times 100$$

$$= \left(\frac{5 - 15}{(5 + 15) \div 2}\right) \times 100 = \left(\frac{-10}{20 \div 2}\right) \times 100$$

$$= \left(\frac{-10}{10}\right) \times 100 = -100 \text{ percent.}$$

When the price of a good *rises*, the quantity demanded of it *decreases*—a *positive* change in price brings a *negative* change in the quantity demanded. Similarly, when the price of a good *falls*, the quantity demanded of it *increases*—this time a *negative* change in price brings a *positive* change in the quantity demanded.

To compare the percentage change in the price and the percentage change in the quantity demanded, we use the absolute values or magnitudes of the percentage changes and we ignore the minus sign.

■ Elastic and Inelastic Demand

To determine the responsiveness of the quantity of Starbucks latte demanded to its price, we need to compare the two percentage changes we've just calculated. The percentage change in quantity is 100 and the percentage change in price is 50, so the percentage change in quantity demanded is twice the percentage change in price. If we collected data on the prices and quantities of a number of goods and services (and we were careful to check that other things had remained the same), we could calculate lots of percentage changes. Our calculations would fall into three groups: The percentage change in the quantity demanded might exceed the percentage change in price, equal the percentage change in price, or be less than the percentage change in price. Which of these three possibilities arises depends on the elasticity of demand:

Elastic demand
When the percentage change in the quantity demanded exceeds the percentage change in price.

Unit elastic demand
When the percentage change in the quantity demanded equals the percentage change in price.

Inelastic demand
When the percentage change in the quantity demanded is less than the percentage change in price.

Perfectly elastic demand
When the quantity demanded changes by a very large percentage in response to an almost zero percentage change in price.

Perfectly inelastic demand
When the percentage change in the quantity demanded is zero for any percentage change in the price.

- When the percentage change in the quantity demanded exceeds the percentage change in price, demand is **elastic.**
- When the percentage change in the quantity demanded equals the percentage change in price, demand is **unit elastic.**
- When the percentage change in the quantity demanded is less than the percentage change in price, demand is **inelastic.**

Figure 5.1 shows the different types of demand curves that illustrate the range of possible price elasticities of demand. Part (a) shows an extreme case of an elastic demand called a **perfectly elastic demand**—an almost zero percentage change in the price brings a very large percentage change in the quantity demanded. Consumers are willing to buy any quantity of the good at a given price but none at a higher price. Part (b) shows an elastic demand—the percentage change in the quantity demanded exceeds the percentage change in price. Part (c) shows a unit elastic demand—the percentage change in the quantity demanded equals the percentage change in price. Part (d) shows an inelastic demand—the percentage change in the quantity demanded is less than the percentage change in price. Finally, part (e) shows an extreme case of an inelastic demand called a **perfectly inelastic demand**—the percentage change in the quantity demanded is zero for any percentage change in price.

■ Influences on the Price Elasticity of Demand

What makes the demand for some things elastic and the demand for others inelastic? The influences on the price elasticity of demand fall into two groups:

- Availability of substitutes
- Proportion of income spent

Availability of Substitutes

The demand for a good is elastic if a substitute for it is easy to find. Soft drink containers can be made of either aluminum or plastic and it doesn't matter which, so the demand for aluminum is elastic.

The demand for a good is inelastic if a substitute for it is hard to find. Oil has poor substitutes (imagine a coal-fueled car), so the demand for oil is inelastic.

Three main factors influence the ability to find a substitute for a good: whether the good is a luxury or a necessity, how narrowly it is defined, and the amount of time available to find a substitute for it.

■ FIGURE 5.1

The Range of Price Elasticities of Demand

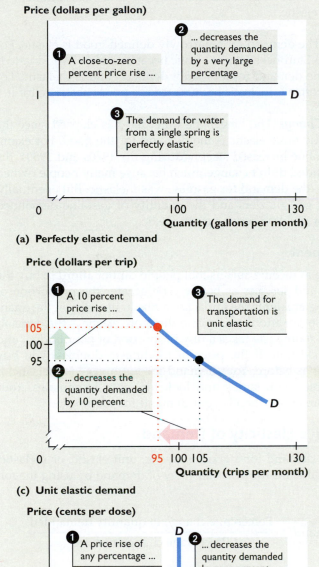

Price (dollars per gallon)

① A close-to-zero percent price rise ...

② ... decreases the quantity demanded by a very large percentage

③ The demand for water from a single spring is perfectly elastic

D

0 .... 100 130
Quantity (gallons per month)

(a) Perfectly elastic demand

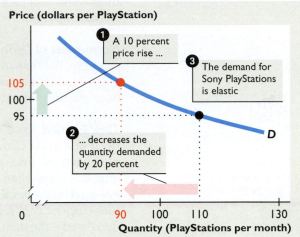

Price (dollars per PlayStation)

① A 10 percent price rise ...

③ The demand for Sony PlayStations is elastic

105
100
95

② ... decreases the quantity demanded by 20 percent

D

0 ...... 90 100 110 130
Quantity (PlayStations per month)

(b) Elastic demand

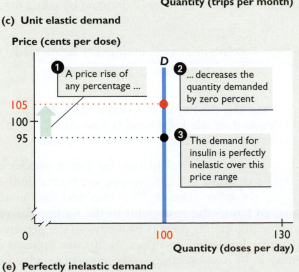

Price (dollars per trip)

① A 10 percent price rise ...

③ The demand for transportation is unit elastic

105
100
95

② ... decreases the quantity demanded by 10 percent

D

0 ..... 95 100 105 130
Quantity (trips per month)

(c) Unit elastic demand

Price (cents per pack)

110
100

① A 20 percent price rise ...

③ The demand for chewing gum is inelastic

90

② ... decreases the quantity demanded by 10 percent

D

0 ..... 95 100 105 130
Quantity (packs of gum per month)

(d) Inelastic demand

Price (cents per dose)

D

① A price rise of any percentage ...

② ... decreases the quantity demanded by zero percent

105
100
95

③ The demand for insulin is perfectly inelastic over this price range

0 .... 100 130
Quantity (doses per day)

(e) Perfectly inelastic demand

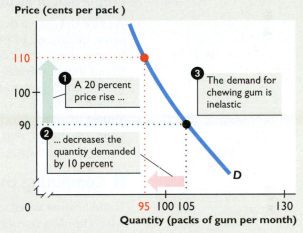

① A price rise brings ② a decrease in the quantity demanded. The relationship between the percentage change in the quantity demanded and the percentage change in price determines ③ the price elasticity of demand, which ranges from perfectly elastic (part a) to perfectly inelastic (part e).

Luxury Versus Necessity We call goods such as food and housing *necessities* and goods such as exotic vacations *luxuries*. A necessity has poor substitutes—you must eat—so the demand for a necessity is inelastic. A luxury has many substitutes—you don't absolutely have to go to the Galapagos Islands this summer—so the demand for a luxury is elastic.

Narrowness of Definition The demand for a narrowly defined good is elastic. For example, the demand for a Starbucks latte is elastic because a New World latte is a good substitute for it. The demand for a broadly defined good is inelastic. For example, the demand for coffee is inelastic because tea is a poor substitute for it.

Time Elapsed Since Price Change The longer the time that has elapsed since the price of a good changed, the more elastic is the demand for the good. For example, when the price of gasoline increased steeply during the 1970s and 1980s, the quantity of gasoline demanded didn't change much because many people owned gas-guzzling automobiles—the demand for gasoline was inelastic. But eventually, fuel-efficient cars replaced gas guzzlers and the quantity of gasoline demanded decreased—the demand for gasoline became more elastic.

Proportion of Income Spent

A price rise, like a decrease in income, means that people cannot afford to buy the same quantities of goods and services as before. The greater the proportion of income spent on a good, the greater is the impact of a rise in its price on the quantity of that good that people can afford to buy and the more elastic is the demand for the good. For example, toothpaste takes a tiny proportion of your budget and housing takes a large proportion. If the price of toothpaste doubles, you buy almost as much toothpaste as before. Your demand for toothpaste is inelastic. If your apartment rent doubles, you shriek and look for more roommates. Your demand for housing is more elastic than is your demand for toothpaste.

■ Computing the Price Elasticity of Demand

To determine whether the demand for a good is elastic, unit elastic, or inelastic, we compute a numerical value for the price elasticity of demand by using the following formula:

$$\text{Price elasticity of demand} = \frac{\text{Percentage change in quantity demanded}}{\text{Percentage change in price}}.$$

- If the price elasticity of demand is greater than 1, demand is elastic.
- If the price elasticity of demand equals 1, demand is unit elastic.
- If the price elasticity of demand is less than 1, demand is inelastic.

Figure 5.2 illustrates and summarizes the calculation for the Starbucks latte example. Initially, the price is $3 a cup and 15 cups an hour are demanded—the initial point in the figure. Then the price rises to $5 a cup and the quantity demanded decreases to 5 cups an hour—the new point in the figure. The price rises by $2 a cup and the average (midpoint) price is $4 a cup, so the percentage change in price is 50. The quantity demanded decreases by 10 cups an hour and the average (midpoint) quantity is 10 cups an hour, so the percentage change in quantity demanded is 100.

FIGURE 5.2

Price Elasticity of Demand Calculation

MyEconLab Animation

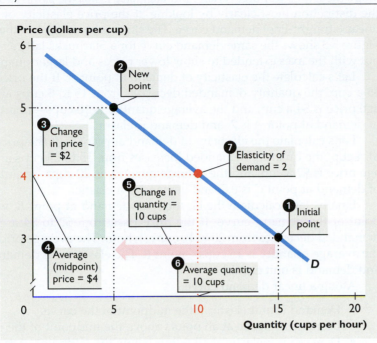

❶ At the initial point, the price is $3 a cup and the quantity demanded is 15 cups an hour.

❷ At the new point, the price is $5 a cup and the quantity demanded is 5 cups an hour.

❸ The change in price is $2 and ❹ the average price is $4, so the percentage change in price equals ($2 ÷ $4) × 100, which is 50 percent.

❺ The change in the quantity demanded is 10 cups and ❻ the average quantity demanded is 10 cups, so the percentage change in quantity demanded equals (10 cups ÷ 10 cups) × 100, which is 100 percent.

❼ The price elasticity of demand equals 100 percent ÷ 50 percent, which is 2.

Using the above formula, you can see that the price elasticity of demand for a Starbucks latte is

$$\text{Price elasticity of demand} = \frac{100 \text{ percent}}{50 \text{ percent}} = 2.$$

The price elasticity of demand is 2 at the midpoint between the initial price and the new price on the demand curve. Over this price range, the demand for a Starbucks latte is elastic.

Interpreting the Price Elasticity of Demand Number

The number we've just calculated for a Starbucks latte is only an example. We don't have real data on the price and quantity. But suppose we did have real data and we discovered that the price elasticity of demand for a Starbucks latte is 2. What does this number tell us?

It tells us three main things:

1. The demand for Starbucks latte is elastic. Being elastic, the good has plenty of convenient substitutes (such as other brands of latte) and takes only a small proportion of buyers' incomes.

2. Starbucks must be careful not to charge too high a price for its latte. Pushing the price up brings in more revenue per cup but wipes out a lot of potential business.

3. The flip side of the second point: Even a slightly lower price could create a lot of potential business and end up bringing in more revenue.

■ Elasticity Along a Linear Demand Curve

Slope measures responsiveness. But elasticity is *not* the same as *slope*. You can see the distinction most clearly by looking at the price elasticity of demand along a linear (straight-line) demand curve. The slope is constant, but the elasticity varies. Figure 5.3 shows the same demand curve for a Starbucks latte as that in Figure 5.2 but with the axes extended to show lower prices and larger quantities demanded.

Let's calculate the elasticity of demand at point *A*. If the price rises from $3 to $5 a cup, the quantity demanded decreases from 15 to 5 cups an hour. The average price is $4 a cup, and the average quantity is 10 cups—point *A*. The elasticity of demand at point *A* is 2, and demand is elastic.

Let's calculate the elasticity of demand at point *C*. If the price falls from $3 to $1 a cup, the quantity demanded increases from 15 to 25 cups an hour. The average price is $2 a cup, and the average quantity is 20 cups—point *C*. The elasticity of demand at point *C* is 0.5, and demand is inelastic.

Finally, let's calculate the elasticity of demand at point *B*, which is the midpoint of the demand curve. If the price rises from $2 to $4 a cup, the quantity demanded decreases from 20 to 10 cups an hour. The average price is $3 a cup, and the average quantity is 15 cups—point *B*. The elasticity of demand at point *B* is 1, and demand is unit elastic.

Along a linear demand curve,

• Demand is unit elastic at the midpoint of the curve.
• Demand is elastic at all points above the midpoint of the curve.
• Demand is inelastic at all points below the midpoint of the curve.

■ **FIGURE 5.3**

Elasticity Along a Linear Demand Curve   MyEconLab Animation

On a linear demand curve, the slope is constant but the elasticity decreases as the price falls and the quantity demanded increases.

❶ At point *A*, demand is elastic.

❷ At point *B*, which is the midpoint of the demand curve, demand is unit elastic.

❸ At point *C*, demand is inelastic.

Demand is elastic at all points above the midpoint of the demand curve and inelastic at all points below the midpoint of the demand curve.

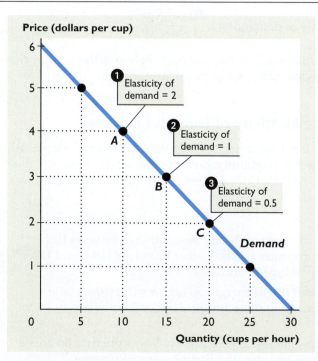

EYE on the GLOBAL ECONOMY
Price Elasticities of Demand

A rich American student is casual about her food. It costs only a few dollars a day, and she's going to have her burger, even at double the price. But a poor Tanzanian boy takes his food with deadly seriousness. He has a tough time getting, preparing, and even defending his food. A rise in the price of food means that he must cut back and eat even less.

The figure shows the percentage of income spent on food and the price elasticity of demand for food in ten countries. The larger the proportion of income spent on food, the larger is the price elasticity of demand for food.

As the low-income countries become richer, the proportion of income they spend on food will decrease and their demand for food will become more inelastic. Consequently, the world's demand for food will become more inelastic.

Harvests fluctuate and bring fluctuations in the price of food. And as the world demand for food becomes

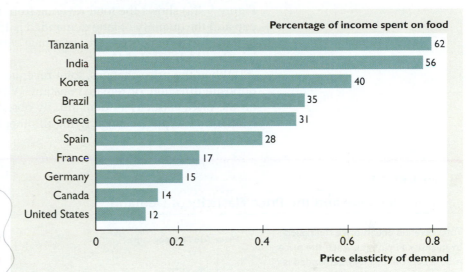

more and more inelastic, the fluctuations in the prices of food items will become larger.

The table shows a few real-world price elasticities of demand. The numbers in the table range from 1.52 for metals to 0.12 for food. Metals have good substitutes, such as plastics, while food has virtually no substitutes. As we move down the list of items, they have

fewer good substitutes and are more likely to be regarded as necessities.

Some Price Elasticities of Demand

Good or Service	Elasticity
Elastic Demand	
Metals	1.52
Electrical engineering products	1.39
Mechanical engineering products	1.30
Furniture	1.26
Motor vehicles	1.14
Instrument engineering products	1.10
Professional services	1.09
Transportation services	1.03
Inelastic Demand	
Gas, electricity, and water	0.92
Oil	0.91
Chemicals	0.89
Beverages (all types)	0.78
Clothing	0.64
Tobacco	0.61
Banking and insurance services	0.56
Housing services	0.55
Agricultural and fish products	0.42
Books, magazines, and newspapers	0.34
Food	0.12

SOURCES OF DATA: See page C1.

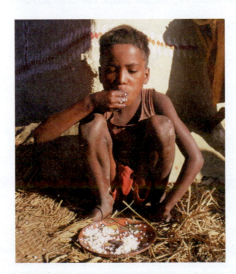

■ Total Revenue and the Price Elasticity of Demand

Total revenue

The amount spent on a good and received by its seller and equals the price of the good multiplied by the quantity sold.

Total revenue is the amount spent on a good and received by its sellers and equals the price of the good multiplied by the quantity of the good sold. For example, suppose that the price of a Starbucks latte is $3 and that 15 cups an hour are sold. Then total revenue is $3 a cup multiplied by 15 cups an hour, which equals $45 an hour.

We can use the demand curve for Starbucks latte to illustrate total revenue. Figure 5.4(a) shows the total revenue from the sale of latte when the price is $3 a cup and the quantity of latte demanded is 15 cups an hour. Total revenue is shown by the blue rectangle, the area of which equals $3, its height, multiplied by 15, its length, which equals $45.

When the price changes, total revenue can change in the same direction, the opposite direction, or remain constant. Which of these outcomes occurs depends on the price elasticity of demand. By observing the change in total revenue that results from a price change (with all other influences on the quantity remaining

■ **FIGURE 5.4**

Total Revenue and the Price Elasticity of Demand

MyEconLab Animation

Total revenue equals price multiplied by quantity. In part (a), when the price is $3 a cup, the quantity demanded is 15 cups an hour and total revenue equals $45 an hour. When the price rises to $5 a cup, the quantity demanded decreases to 5 cups an hour and total revenue decreases to $25 an hour. Demand is elastic.

In part (b), when the price is $50 a book, the quantity demanded is 5 million books a year and total revenue equals $250 million a year. When the price rises to $75 a book, the quantity demanded decreases to 4 million books a year and total revenue increases to $300 million a year. Demand is inelastic.

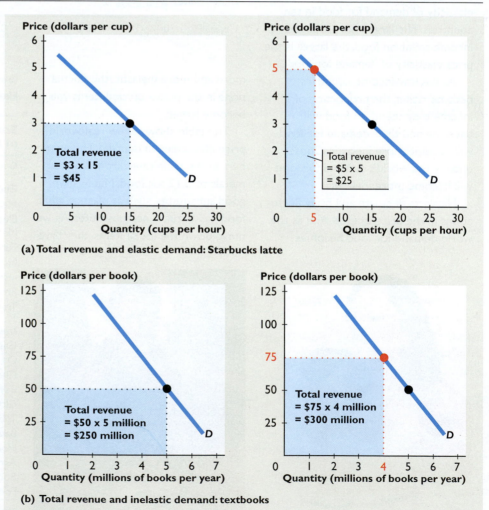

(a) Total revenue and elastic demand: Starbucks latte

(b) Total revenue and inelastic demand: textbooks

unchanged), we can estimate the price elasticity of demand. This method of estimating the price elasticity of demand is called the **total revenue test**.

If demand is elastic, a given percentage rise in price brings a larger percentage decrease in the quantity demanded, so total revenue—price multiplied by quantity—decreases. Figure 5.4(a) shows this outcome. When the price of a latte is $3, the quantity demanded is 15 cups an hour and total revenue is $45 ($3 × 15). If the price of a latte rises to $5, the quantity demanded decreases to 5 cups an hour and total revenue *decreases* to $25 ($5 × 5).

If demand is inelastic, a given percentage rise in price brings a smaller percentage decrease in the quantity demanded, so total revenue increases. Figure 5.4(b) shows this outcome. When the price of a textbook is $50, the quantity demanded is 5 million textbooks a year and total revenue is $250 million ($50 × 5 million). If the price of a textbook rises to $75, the quantity demanded decreases to 4 million textbooks a year and total revenue *increases* to $300 million ($75 × 4 million).

The relationship between the price elasticity of demand and total revenue is

- If price and total revenue change in opposite directions, demand is elastic.
- If a price change leaves total revenue unchanged, demand is unit elastic.
- If price and total revenue change in the same direction, demand is inelastic.

Total revenue test
A method of estimating the price elasticity of demand by observing the change in total revenue that results from a price change (with all other influences on the quantity sold remaining unchanged).

EYE on the PRICE OF GAS
What Do You Do When the Price of Gasoline Rises?

If you are like most people, you complain when the price of gasoline rises, but you don't cut back very much on your gas purchases.

University of London economists Phil Goodwin, Joyce Dargay, and Mark Hanly studied the effects of a hike in the price of gasoline on the quantity of gasoline demanded and on the volume of road traffic.

By using data for the United States and a large number of other countries, they estimated that a 10 percent rise in the price of gasoline decreases the quantity of gasoline used by 2.5 percent within one year and by 6 percent after five years.

Price Elasticity of Demand

We can translate these numbers into price elasticities of demand for gasoline.

The short-run (up to one year) price elasticity of demand is 2.5 percent divided by 10 percent, which equals 0.25. The long-run (after five years) price elasticity of demand is 6 percent divided by 10 percent, which equals 0.6. Because these price elasticities are less than one, the demand for gasoline is inelastic.

When the price of gasoline rises, the quantity of gasoline demanded decreases but the amount spent on gasoline increases.

The effect of a rise in the price of gasoline on the volume of traffic is smaller than on the quantity of gasoline used.

A 10-percent rise in the price of gasoline decreases the volume of traffic by only 1 percent within one year and by 3 percent after five years.

How can the volume of traffic fall by less than the quantity of gasoline used? The answer is by switching to smaller, more fuel-efficient vehicles.

The price elasticity of demand for gasoline is low—the demand for gasoline is inelastic—because gasoline has poor substitutes, but it does have a substitute—a smaller vehicle.

■ Applications of the Price Elasticity of Demand

Does a frost in Florida bring a massive or a modest rise in the price of oranges? And does a smaller orange crop mean bad news or good news for orange growers? Knowledge of the price elasticity of demand for oranges enables us to answer these questions.

Orange Prices and Total Revenue

Economists have estimated the price elasticity of demand for agricultural products to be about 0.4—an inelastic demand. If this number applies to the demand for oranges, then

$$\text{Price elasticity of demand} = 0.4 = \frac{\text{Percentage change in quantity demanded}}{\text{Percentage change in price}}.$$

A Florida frost is bad news for buyers of orange juice and for growers who lose their crops, but good news for growers who escape the frost.

If supply changes and demand doesn't, the percentage change in the quantity demanded equals the percentage change in the equilibrium quantity. So if a frost in Florida decreases the orange harvest and decreases the equilibrium quantity of oranges by 1 percent, the price of oranges will rise by 2.5 percent. The percentage change in the quantity demanded (1 percent) divided by the percentage change in price (2.5 percent) equals the price elasticity of demand (0.4).

So the answer to the first question is that when the frost strikes, the price of oranges will rise by a larger percentage than the percentage decrease in the quantity of oranges. But what happens to the total revenue of the orange growers?

The answer is again provided by knowledge of the price elasticity of demand. Because the price rises by a larger percentage than the percentage decrease in quantity, total revenue increases. A frost is bad news for consumers and those growers who lose their crops, but good news for growers who escape the frost.

Addiction and Elasticity

We can gain important insights that might help to design potentially effective policies for dealing with addiction to drugs, whether legal (such as tobacco and alcohol) or illegal (such as crack cocaine or heroin). Nonusers' demand for addictive substances is elastic. A moderately higher price leads to a substantially smaller number of people trying a drug and so exposing themselves to the possibility of becoming addicted to it. But the existing users' demand for addictive substances is inelastic. Even a substantial price rise brings only a modest decrease in the quantity demanded.

Cracking down on imports of illegal drugs limits supply, which leads to a large price increase. But it also increases the expenditure on drugs by addicts and increases the amount of crime that finances addiction.

These facts about the price elasticity of demand mean that high taxes on cigarettes and alcohol limit the number of young people who become habitual users of these products, but high taxes have only a modest effect on the quantities consumed by established users.

Similarly, effective policing of imports of an illegal drug that limits its supply leads to a large price rise and a substantial decrease in the number of new users but only a small decrease in the quantity consumed by addicts. Expenditure on the drug by addicts increases. Further, because many drug addicts finance their purchases with crime, the amount of theft and burglary increases.

Because the price elasticity of demand for drugs is low for addicts, any successful policy to decrease drug use will be one that focuses on the demand for drugs and attempts to change preferences through rehabilitation programs.

CHECKPOINT 5.1

Define the price elasticity of demand, and explain the factors that influence it and how to calculate it.

MyEconLab
You can work these problems in Study Plan 5.1 and get instant feedback.

Practice Problems

When the price of a good increased by 10 percent, the quantity demanded of it decreased by 2 percent.

1. Is the demand for this good elastic, unit elastic, or inelastic?

2. Does this good have close substitutes or poor substitutes? Is this good more likely to be a necessity or a luxury and to be narrowly or broadly defined? Why?

3. Calculate the price elasticity of demand for this good; explain how the total revenue from the sale of the good has changed; and explain which of the following goods this good is most likely to be: orange juice, bread, toothpaste, theater tickets, clothing, blue jeans, or Super Bowl tickets.

In the News

Music giant chops price to combat downloads

In 2003, when music downloading first took off, Universal Music slashed the price of a CD from $21 to $15. The company said that it expected the price cut to boost the quantity of CDs sold by 30 percent, other things remaining the same.

Source: *Globe and Mail*, September 4, 2003

What was Universal Music's estimate of the price elasticity of demand for CDs? Was the demand estimated to be elastic or inelastic?

Solutions to Practice Problems

1. The demand for a good is *inelastic* if the percentage decrease in the quantity demanded is less than the percentage increase in its price. In this example, a 10 percent price rise brings a 2 percent decrease in the quantity demanded, so demand is inelastic.

2. Because the good has an inelastic demand, it most likely has poor substitutes, is a necessity rather than a luxury, and is broadly defined.

3. Price elasticity of demand = Percentage change in the quantity demanded ÷ Percentage change in price. In this example, the price elasticity of demand is 2 percent divided by 10 percent, or 0.2. An elasticity less than 1 means that demand is inelastic. When demand is inelastic, a price rise increases total revenue. This good is most likely a necessity (bread), or has poor substitutes (toothpaste), or is broadly defined (clothing).

Solution to In the News

Price elasticity of demand = Percentage change in the quantity demanded ÷ Percentage change in price. The percentage change in the price equals [($21 − $15)/($18)] × 100, which is 33.3 percent. The percentage change in the quantity is 30 percent. So Universal Music's estimate of the price elasticity of demand for CDs was 30 percent ÷ 33.3 percent, or 0.9. Because the percentage change in the quantity is less than the percentage change in the price, demand is estimated to be inelastic, which is what an elasticity of 0.9 means.

You know that when demand increases, the equilibrium price rises and the equilibrium quantity increases. But does the price rise by a large amount and the quantity increase by a little? Or does the price barely rise and the quantity increase by a large amount? To answer this question, we need to know the price elasticity of supply.

Price elasticity of supply
A measure of the responsiveness of the quantity supplied of a good to a change in its price when all other influences on sellers' plans remain the same.

The **price elasticity of supply** is a measure of the responsiveness of the quantity supplied of a good to a change in its price when all other influences on sellers' plans remain the same. We determine the price elasticity of supply by comparing the percentage change in the quantity supplied with the percentage change in price.

■ Elastic and Inelastic Supply

The supply of a good might be

- Elastic
- Unit elastic
- Inelastic

Perfectly elastic supply
When the quantity supplied changes by a very large percentage in response to an almost zero percentage change in price.

Elastic supply
When the percentage change in the quantity supplied exceeds the percentage change in price.

Unit elastic supply
When the percentage change in the quantity supplied equals the percentage change in price.

Inelastic supply
When the percentage change in the quantity supplied is less than the percentage change in price.

Perfectly inelastic supply
When the percentage change in the quantity supplied is zero for any percentage change in the price.

Figure 5.5 illustrates the range of supply elasticities. Figure 5.5(a) shows the extreme case of a **perfectly elastic supply**—an almost zero percentage change in price brings a very large percentage change in the quantity supplied. Figure 5.5 (b) shows an **elastic supply**—the percentage change in the quantity supplied exceeds the percentage change in price. Figure 5.5(c) shows a **unit elastic supply**—the percentage change in the quantity supplied equals the percentage change in price. Figure 5.5(d) shows an **inelastic supply**—the percentage change in the quantity supplied is less than the percentage change in price. And Figure 5.5(e) shows the extreme case of a **perfectly inelastic supply**—the percentage change in the quantity supplied is zero when the price changes.

■ Influences on the Price Elasticity of Supply

What makes the supply of some things elastic and the supply of others inelastic? The two main influences on the price elasticity of supply are

- Production possibilities
- Storage possibilities

Production Possibilities

Some goods can be produced at a constant (or very gently rising) opportunity cost. These goods have an elastic supply. The silicon in your computer chips is an example of such a good. Silicon is extracted from sand at a tiny and almost constant opportunity cost, so the supply of silicon is perfectly elastic.

Some goods can be produced in only a fixed quantity. These goods have a perfectly inelastic supply. A beachfront home in Malibu can be built only on a unique beachfront lot, so the supply of these homes is perfectly inelastic.

Hotel rooms in New York City can't easily be used as office accommodation and office space cannot easily be converted into hotel rooms, so the supply of hotel rooms in New York City is inelastic. Paper and printing presses can be used to produce textbooks or magazines, and the supplies of these goods are elastic.

FIGURE 5.5

The Range of Price Elasticities of Supply

MyEconLab Animation

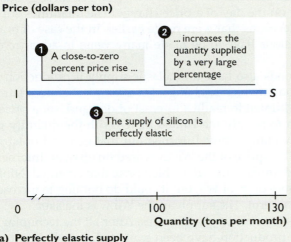

(a) Perfectly elastic supply

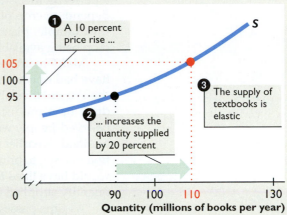

(b) Elastic supply

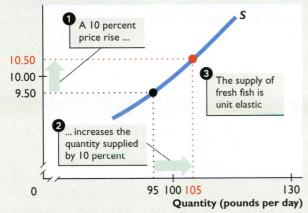

(c) Unit elastic supply

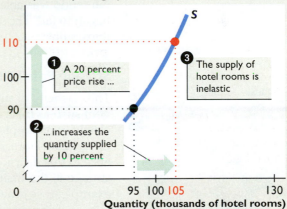

(d) Inelastic supply

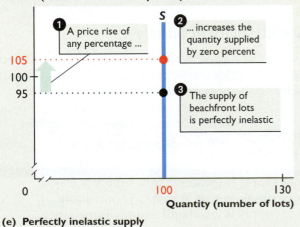

(e) Perfectly inelastic supply

❶ A price rise brings ❷ an increase in the quantity supplied. The relationship between the percentage change in the quantity supplied and the percentage change in price determines ❸ the price elasticity of supply, which ranges from perfectly elastic (part a) to perfectly inelastic (part e).

Time Elapsed Since Price Change As time passes after a price change, it becomes easier to change production plans and supply becomes more elastic. For some items—fruits and vegetables are examples—it is difficult or perhaps impossible to change the quantity supplied immediately after a price change. These goods have a perfectly inelastic supply on the day of a price change. The quantities supplied depend on crop-planting decisions that were made earlier. In the case of oranges, for example, planting decisions have to be made many years in advance of the crop being available.

Many manufactured goods also have an inelastic supply if production plans have had only a short period in which to change. For example, before it launched the Wii in November 2006, Nintendo made a forecast of demand, set a price, and drew up a production plan to supply the United States with the quantity that it believed people would be willing to buy. It turned out that demand outstripped Nintendo's earlier forecast. The price of the Wii increased on eBay, an Internet auction market, to bring market equilibrium. At the high price that emerged, Nintendo would have liked to ship more units of Wii, but it could do nothing to increase the quantity supplied in the near term. The supply of the Wii was inelastic.

As time passes, the elasticity of supply increases. After all the technologically possible ways of adjusting production have been exploited, supply is extremely elastic—perhaps perfectly elastic—for most manufactured items. In 2007, Nintendo was able to step up the production rate of the Wii and the price on eBay began to fall. The supply of Wii had become more elastic as production continued to expand.

Storage Possibilities

The elasticity of supply of a good that cannot be stored (for example, a perishable item such as fresh strawberries) depends only on production possibilities. But the elasticity of supply of a good that can be stored depends on the decision to keep the good in storage or offer it for sale. A small price change can make a big difference to this decision, so the supply of a storable good is highly elastic. The cost of storage is the main influence on the elasticity of supply of a storable good. For example, rose growers in Colombia, anticipating a surge in demand on Valentine's Day in February, hold back supplies in late January and early February and increase their inventories of roses. They then release roses from inventory for Valentine's Day.

Fresh strawberries must be sold before they deteriorate, so their supply is inelastic.

■ Computing the Price Elasticity of Supply

To determine whether the supply of a good is elastic, unit elastic, or inelastic, we compute a numerical value for the price elasticity of supply in a way similar to that used to calculate the price elasticity of demand. We use the formula:

$$\text{Price elasticity of supply} = \frac{\text{Percentage change in quantity supplied}}{\text{Percentage change in price}}.$$

- If the price elasticity of supply is greater than 1, supply is elastic.
- If the price elasticity of supply equals 1, supply is unit elastic.
- If the price elasticity of supply is less than 1, supply is inelastic.

Let's calculate the price elasticity of supply of roses. Suppose that in a normal month, the price of roses is $40 a bouquet and 6 million bouquets are supplied. And suppose that in February, the price rises to $80 a bouquet and the quantity supplied increases to 24 million bouquets. Figure 5.6 illustrates the supply of roses and summarizes the calculation. The figure shows the initial point at $40 a bouquet and the new point at $80 a bouquet. The price increases by $40 a bouquet and the average, or midpoint, price is $60 a bouquet, so the percentage change in the price is 66.67 percent. The quantity supplied increases by 18 million bouquets and the average, or midpoint, quantity is 15 million bouquets, so the percentage change in the quantity supplied is 120 percent.

Using the above formula, you can see that the price elasticity of supply of roses is

$$\text{Price elasticity of supply} = \frac{120 \text{ percent}}{66.67 \text{ percent}} = 1.8.$$

The price elasticity of supply is 1.8 at the midpoint between the initial point and the new point on the supply curve. In this example, over this price range, the supply of roses is elastic.

FIGURE 5.6

Price Elasticity of Supply Calculation

MyEconLab Animation

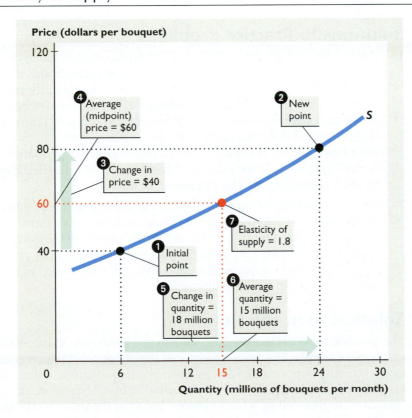

❶ At the initial point, the price is $40 a bouquet and the quantity supplied is 6 million bouquets a month.

❷ At the new point, the price is $80 a bouquet and the quantity supplied is 24 million bouquets a month.

❸ The change in price is $40, and ❹ the average price is $60, so the percentage change in price equals ($40 ÷ $60) × 100, which is 66.67 percent.

❺ The change in the quantity supplied is 18 million bouquets and ❻ the average quantity supplied is 15 million bouquets, so the percentage change in quantity supplied is (18 million ÷ 15 million) × 100, which is 120 percent.

❼ The price elasticity of supply equals 120 percent ÷ 66.6 percent, which is 1.8.

CHECKPOINT 5.2

Define the price elasticity of supply, and explain the factors that influence it and how to calculate it.

Practice Problems

A 10 percent increase in the price of a good increased the quantity supplied of the good by 1 percent after one month and by 25 percent after one year.

1. Is the supply of this good elastic, unit elastic, or inelastic? Is this good likely to be produced using factors of production that are easily obtained? What is the price elasticity of supply of this good?

2. What is the price elasticity of supply after one year? Has the supply of this good become more elastic or less elastic? Why?

In the News

Weak coal prices hit China's third-largest coal miner

The chairman of Yanzhou Coal Mining, Wang Xin, reported that the demand for coal has fallen by 11.9 percent to 7.92 million tons from 8.99 million tons a year earlier, despite the price falling by 10.6 percent.

Source: Dow Jones, April 27, 2009

Calculate the price elasticity of supply of coal. Is the supply of coal elastic or inelastic?

Solutions to Practice Problems

1. The supply of a good is *inelastic* if the percentage increase in the quantity supplied is less than the percentage increase in price. In this example, a 10 percent price rise brings a 1 percent increase in the quantity supplied, so supply is inelastic. Because the quantity supplied increases by such a small percentage after one month, the factors of production that are used to produce this good are more likely to be difficult to obtain.

    The price elasticity of supply = Percentage change in the quantity supplied ÷ Percentage change in the price. In this example, the price elasticity of supply equals 1 percent divided by 10 percent, or 0.1.

2. The price elasticity of supply = Percentage change in the quantity supplied ÷ Percentage change in the price. After one year, the price elasticity of supply is 25 percent divided by 10 percent, or 2.5. The supply of the good has become more elastic over the year since the price rise. Possibly other producers have gradually started producing the good and with the passage of time more factors of production can be reallocated.

Solution to In the News

The demand for coal decreased, so we can use these data to calculate the price elasticity of supply. The price elasticity of supply equals the percentage change in the quantity supplied divided by the percentage change in the price. The price elasticity of supply equals 11.9 percent divided by 10.6 percent, or 1.12. The quantity supplied fell by a larger percentage than the price, so the supply of coal is elastic, which is what a price elasticity of supply of 1.12 means.

5.3   CROSS ELASTICITY AND INCOME ELASTICITY

Domino's Pizza in Chula Vista has a problem. Burger King has just cut its prices. Domino's manager, Pat, knows that pizzas and burgers are substitutes. He also knows that when the price of a substitute for pizza falls, the demand for pizza decreases. But by how much will the quantity of pizza bought decrease if Pat maintains his current price?

Pat also knows that pizza and soda are complements. He knows that if the price of a complement of pizza falls, the demand for pizza increases. So he wonders whether he might keep his customers by cutting the price he charges for soda. But he wants to know by how much he must cut the price of soda to keep selling the same quantity of pizza with cheaper burgers all around him.

To answer these questions, Pat needs to calculate the cross elasticity of demand. Let's examine this elasticity measure.

■ Cross Elasticity of Demand

The **cross elasticity of demand** is a measure of the responsiveness of the demand for a good to a change in the price of a substitute or complement when other things remain the same. It is calculated by using the formula:

$$\text{Cross elasticity of demand} = \frac{\text{Percentage change in quantity demanded of a good}}{\text{Percentage change in price of one of its substitutes or complements}}.$$

Cross elasticity of demand
A measure of the responsiveness of the demand for a good to a change in the price of a substitute or complement when other things remain the same.

Suppose that when the price of a burger falls by 10 percent, the quantity of pizza demanded decreases by 5 percent.* The cross elasticity of demand for pizza with respect to the price of a burger is

$$\text{Cross elasticity of demand} = \frac{-5 \text{ percent}}{-10 \text{ percent}} = 0.5.$$

The cross elasticity of demand for a substitute is positive. A *fall* in the price of a substitute brings a *decrease* in the quantity demanded of the good. The quantity demanded of a good and the price of one of its substitutes change in the *same* direction.

Suppose that when the price of soda falls by 10 percent, the quantity of pizza demanded increases by 2 percent. The cross elasticity of demand for pizza with respect to the price of soda is

$$\text{Cross elasticity of demand} = \frac{+2 \text{ percent}}{-10 \text{ percent}} = -0.2.$$

The cross elasticity of demand for a complement is negative. A *fall* in the price of a complement brings an *increase* in the quantity demanded of the good. The quantity demanded of a good and the price of one of its complements change in *opposite* directions.

---

*As before, these percentage changes are calculated by using the midpoint method.

■ **FIGURE 5.7**

Cross Elasticity of Demand

① A burger is a *substitute* for pizza. When the price of a burger falls, the demand curve for pizza shifts leftward from D_0 to D_1. At the price of $10 a pizza, people plan to buy fewer pizzas. The cross elasticity of the demand for pizza with respect to the price of a burger is *positive*.

② Soda is a *complement* of pizza. When the price of soda falls, the demand for pizza increases and the demand curve for pizza shifts rightward from D_0 to D_2. At the price of $10 a pizza, people plan to buy more pizzas. The cross elasticity of the demand for pizza with respect to the price of soda is *negative*.

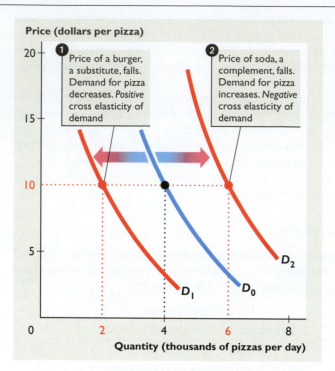

Figure 5.7 illustrates these two cross elasticities of demand for pizza. With the price of a pizza constant at $10, when the price of a burger falls, the demand for pizza decreases and the demand curve for pizza shifts leftward from D_0 to D_1. When the price of soda falls, the demand for pizza increases and the demand curve for pizza shifts rightward from D_0 to D_2. The magnitude of the cross elasticity determines how far the demand curve shifts.

■ **Income Elasticity of Demand**

The U.S. and global economies are expanding, and people are enjoying rising incomes. This increasing prosperity brings an increasing demand for most types of goods. But by how much will the demand for different items increase? Will the demand for some items increase so rapidly that we spend an increasing percentage of our incomes on them? And will the demand for some items decrease?

Income elasticity of demand
A measure of the responsiveness of the demand for a good to a change in income when other things remain the same.

The answer depends on the income elasticity of demand. The **income elasticity of demand** is a measure of the responsiveness of the demand for a good to a change in income when other things remain the same. It is calculated by using the following formula:

$$\text{Income elasticity of demand} = \frac{\text{Percentage change in quantity demanded}}{\text{Percentage change in income}}.$$

The income elasticity of demand falls into three ranges:

- Greater than 1 (normal good, income elastic)
- Between zero and 1 (normal good, income inelastic)
- Less than zero (inferior good)

As our incomes increase: items that have

- An income elastic demand take an increasing share of income
- An income inelastic demand take a decreasing share of income
- A negative income elasticity of demand take an absolutely smaller amount of income.

You can make some strong predictions about how the world will change over the coming years by knowing the income elasticities of demand of different goods and services. The table provides a sampling of numbers.

These estimated income elasticities of demand tell us that we can expect air travel—both domestic and international—to become hugely more important; increasing share of our incomes will be spent on watching movies, eating out in restaurants, using public transporation and getting haircuts. Two other prominent items not shown in the table, items for which demand is income elastic, are health care and education. As our incomes grow, we can expect education and health care to take increasing shares of our incomes.

As our incomes grow, we'll spend a decreasing percentage on clothing, phone calls, and food. The income elasticity of demand for food is less than one, even for the poorest people. So we can predict a continuation of the trends of the past—shrinking agriculture and manufacturing, and expanding services.

Table 5.1

Some Income Elasticities of Demand

Good or Service	Elasticity
Income Elastic	
Airline travel	5.82
Movies	3.41
Foreign travel	3.08
Electricity	1.94
Restaurant meals	1.61
Local buses and trains	1.38
Haircuts	1.36
Income Inelastic	
Tobacco	0.86
Alcoholic beverages	0.62
Clothing	0.51
Newspapers	0.38
Telephone	0.32
Food	0.14

SOURCES OF DATA: See page C1.

EYE on YOUR LIFE
Your Price Elasticities of Demand

Pay close attention the next time the price of something that you buy rises. Did you spend more, the same, or less on this item?

Your expenditure on a good is equal to the price of the good multiplied by the quantity that you buy.

But recall that a seller's total revenue is equal to the price of the good multiplied by the quantity sold.

Because the buyer's expenditure on a good is equal to the seller's total revenue, the total revenue test that the seller uses to estimate the price elasticity of demand for the good sold can also be used by a buyer.

You can determine whether your demand for a good is elastic, unit elas-tic, or inelastic by noting what happens to your total expenditure on the good when its price changes.

When the price of a good rises, your demand for that good is

- *Elastic* if your expenditure on it decreases.
- *Unit elastic* if your expenditure on it remains constant.
- *Inelastic* if your expenditure on it increases.

Think about why your demand for a good might be elastic, unit elastic, or inelastic by checking back to the list of influences on the price elasticity of demand on page 116.

Most likely, as we noted in the chapter opener, when the price of gasoline rises, you use almost as much as you did at the lower price. Gasoline has poor substitutes and your demand for gasoline is inelastic.

What do you do if the price of using your cell phone falls? Do you spend less on your cell phone, as you would if your demand for cell phone service is inelastic? Or do you spend more on your cell phone, which would indicate an elastic demand for cell phone service?

What about your iPod and iTunes? Is your demand for these items elastic or inelastic? And is your demand for textbooks elastic or inelastic? You can estimate all these elasticities.

CHECKPOINT 5.3

Define the cross elasticity of demand and the income elasticity of demand, and explain the factors that influence them.

Practice Problems

1. The quantity demanded of good *A* increases by 5 percent when the price of good *B* rises by 10 percent and other things remain the same. Are goods *A* and *B* complements or substitutes? Describe how the demand for good *A* changes and calculate the cross elasticity of demand.

2. When income rises by 5 percent and other things remain the same, the quantity demanded of good *C* increases by 1 percent. Is good *C* a normal good or an inferior good? Describe how the demand for good *C* changes and calculate the income elasticity of demand for good *C*.

In the News

Rising incomes make China the world's largest luxury goods market

China is estimated to become the world's largest luxury goods market over the next decade, boosted by rising incomes and a transition from saving to spending culture.

Source: ibtimes.com, February 2, 2011

Are luxury goods normal goods or just not necessities? Explain your answer.

Solutions to Practice Problems

1. Goods *A* and *B* are substitutes because when the price of good *B* rises, the quantity demanded of good *A* increases. People switch from good *B* to good *A*. The demand for good *A* increases (Figure 1).
    Cross elasticity of demand = Percentage change in the quantity demanded of good *A* ÷ Percentage increase in the price of good *B*.
    Cross elasticity of demand = 5 ÷ 10, or 0.5.

2. Good *C* is a normal good; as income rises, the quantity demanded increases. The demand for good *C* increases (Figure 2).
    Income elasticity of demand = Percentage change in the quantity demanded of good *C* ÷ Percentage increase in income.
    Income elasticity of demand = 1 ÷ 5, or 0.2.

Solution to In the News

To know whether a good is a normal good, we need to calculate the income elasticity of demand. A normal good is a good that has a positive income elasticity of demand. The source of the increase in the sales of luxury goods is rising incomes and people spending their past savings. As people spend more, the quantity of luxury goods bought increases, so the income elasticity of demand for luxury goods is positive. Luxury goods are normal goods.

FIGURE 1

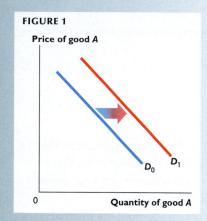

Price of good A / Quantity of good A / D_0 / D_1

FIGURE 2

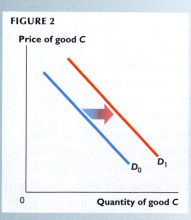

Price of good C / Quantity of good C / D_0 / D_1

CHAPTER SUMMARY

Key Points

1 Define the price elasticity of demand, and explain the factors that influence it and how to calculate it.

- The demand for a good is elastic if, when its price changes, the percentage change in the quantity demanded exceeds the percentage change in price.
- The demand for a good is inelastic if, when its price changes, the percentage change in the quantity demanded is less than the percentage change in price.
- The price elasticity of demand for a good depends on how easy it is to find substitutes for the good and on the proportion of income spent on it.
- Price elasticity of demand equals the percentage change in the quantity demanded divided by the percentage change in price.
- If demand is elastic, a rise in price leads to a decrease in total revenue. If demand is unit elastic, a rise in price leaves total revenue unchanged. And if demand is inelastic, a rise in price leads to an increase in total revenue.

2 Define the price elasticity of supply, and explain the factors that influence it and how to calculate it.

- The supply of a good is elastic if, when its price changes, the percentage change in the quantity supplied exceeds the percentage change in price.
- The supply of a good is inelastic if, when its price changes, the percentage change in the quantity supplied is less than the percentage change in price.
- The main influences on the price elasticity of supply are the flexibility of production possibilities and storage possibilities.

3 Define the cross elasticity of demand and the income elasticity of demand, and explain the factors that influence them.

- Cross elasticity of demand shows how the demand for a good changes when the price of one of its substitutes or complements changes.
- Cross elasticity is positive for substitutes and negative for complements.
- Income elasticity of demand shows how the demand for a good changes when income changes. For a normal good, the income elasticity of demand is positive. For an inferior good, the income elasticity of demand is negative.

Key Terms

Cross elasticity of demand, 129
Elastic demand, 114
Elastic supply, 124
Income elasticity of demand, 130
Inelastic demand, 114
Inelastic supply, 124

Perfectly elastic demand, 114
Perfectly elastic supply, 124
Perfectly inelastic demand, 114
Perfectly inelastic supply, 124
Price elasticity of demand, 112
Price elasticity of supply, 124

Total revenue, 120
Total revenue test, 121
Unit elastic demand, 114
Unit elastic supply, 124

CHAPTER CHECKPOINT

Study Plan Problems and Applications

When the price of home heating oil increased by 20 percent, the quantity demanded decreased by 2 percent and the quantity of wool sweaters demanded increased by 10 percent. Use this information to work Problems **1** and **2**.

1. Use the total revenue test to determine whether the demand for home heating oil is elastic or inelastic.

2. If the price of a wool sweater did not change, calculate the cross elasticity of demand for wool sweaters with respect to the price of home heating oil. Are home heating oil and wool sweaters substitutes or complements? Why?

3. Figure 1 shows the demand for movie tickets. Is the demand for movie tickets elastic or inelastic over the price range $7 to $9 a ticket? If the price falls from $9 to $7 a ticket, explain how the total revenue from the sale of movie tickets will change. Calculate the price elasticity of demand for movie tickets when the price is $8 a ticket.

4. The price elasticity of demand for Pete's chocolate chip cookies is 1.5. Pete wants to increase his total revenue. Would you recommend that Pete raise or lower his price of cookies? Explain your answer.

Use the following information to work Problems **5** and **6**.

The price of a plane ride rises by 10 percent. The price elasticity of demand for plane rides is 0.5 and the price elasticity of demand for train rides is 0.2. The cross elasticity of demand for train rides with respect to the price of a plane ride is 0.4.

5. Calculate the percentage changes in the quantity demanded of plane rides and train rides.

6. Given the rise in the price of a plane ride, what percentage change in the price of a train ride will leave the quantity demanded of train rides unchanged?

7. A survey found that when incomes increased by 10 percent, the following changes in quantities demanded occurred: spring water up by 5 percent; sports drinks down by 2 percent; cruises up by 15 percent. Which demand is income elastic? Which is income inelastic? Which are normal goods?

Use the following information to work Problems **8** and **9**.

Record U.S. corn crop, up 24%, is forecast

The USDA reported that world corn production will be 9.9 percent greater than last year's, while U.S. corn production will be 24 percent larger. The price of corn is expected to be 46 percent higher than last year's price.

Source: *Bloomberg News*, August 11, 2007

8. Calculate the U.S. price elasticity of supply of corn. Is this supply elastic?

9. Calculate the world price elasticity of supply of corn.

10. In May 2011, higher food prices forced consumers to cut spending.

Source: CNN Money, June 4, 2011

Is the demand for food elastic or inelastic? Explain your answer.

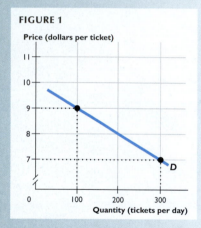

FIGURE 1

Price (dollars per ticket)

Instructor Assignable Problems and Applications

Your instructor can assign these problems as homework, a quiz, or a test in MyEconLab.

 Use the following information to work Problems **1** and **2**.

Why the tepid response to higher gasoline prices?

Most studies report that when U.S. gas prices rise by 10 percent, the quantity purchased falls by 1 to 2 percent. In September 2005, the retail gasoline price was $2.90 a gallon, about $1.00 higher than in September 2004, but purchases of gasoline fell by only 3.5 percent.

Source: *The New York Times*, October 13, 2005

1. Calculate the price elasticity of demand for gasoline implied by what most studies have found.

2. Compare the elasticity implied by the data for the period from September 2004 to September 2005 with that implied by most studies. What might explain the difference?

3. When heavy rain ruined the banana crop in Central America, the price of bananas rose from $1 a pound to $2 a pound. Banana growers sold fewer bananas, but their total revenue remained unchanged. By how much did the quantity of bananas demanded change? Is the demand for bananas from Central America elastic, unit elastic, or inelastic?

4. The income elasticity of demand for haircuts is 1.5, and the income elasticity of demand for food is 0.14. You take a weekend job, and the income you have to spend on food and haircuts doubles. If the prices of food and haircuts remain the same, will you double your expenditure on haircuts and double your expenditure on food? Explain why or why not.

5. Drought cuts the quantity of wheat grown by 2 percent. If the price elasticity of demand for wheat is 0.5, by how much will the price of wheat rise? If pasta makers estimate that this change in the price of wheat will increase the price of pasta by 25 percent and decrease the quantity demanded of pasta by 8 percent, what is the pasta makers' estimate of the price elasticity of demand for pasta? If pasta sauce makers estimate that, with the change in the price of pasta, the quantity of pasta sauce demanded will decrease by 5 percent, what is the pasta sauce makers' estimate of the cross elasticity of demand for pasta sauce with respect to the price of pasta?

6. "In a market in which demand is price inelastic, producers can gouge consumers and the government must set high standards of conduct for producers to ensure that consumers gets a fair deal." Do you agree or disagree with each part of this statement? Explain how you might go about testing the parts of the statement that are positive and lay bare the normative parts.

Use the following information to work Problems **7** and **8**.

Almonds galore!

The quantity of almonds harvested in 2008–2009 was expected to increase by 22 percent, while total receipts of growers was expected to increase by 17 percent.

Source: Almond Board of California

7. Was the price of almonds expected to rise or fall? Did a change in the supply of or demand for almonds bring about this expected change in the price?

8. If the price of almonds changed as a result of a change in the supply of almonds, is the demand for almonds elastic or inelastic? Explain your answer.

Multiple Choice Quiz

1. When the price of ice cream rises from $3 to $5 a scoop, the quantity of ice cream bought decreases by 10 percent. The price elasticity of demand for ice cream is _____.

   A. 5
   B. 0.2
   C. 50
   D. 2.5

2. In Pioneer Ville, the price elasticity of demand for bus rides is 0.5. When the price of a bus ticket rises by 5 percent, _____.

   A. the demand for bus rides increases by 10 percent
   B. the quantity of bus rides demanded increases by 2.5 percent
   C. the demand for bus rides decreases by 2.5 percent
   D. the quantity of bus rides demanded decreases by 2.5 percent

3. The price elasticity of demand for a good is 0.2. A 10 percent rise in the price will _____ the total revenue from sales of the good.

   A. decrease
   B. increase
   C. decrease the quantity sold with no change in
   D. not change

4. If the price of a good falls and expenditure on the good rises, the demand for the good is _____.

   A. elastic
   B. perfectly elastic
   C. inelastic
   D. unit elastic

5. When the price of a good rises from $5 to $7 a unit, the quantity supplied increases from 110 to 130 units a day. The price elasticity of supply is _____. The supply of the good is _____.

   A. 60; elastic
   B. 10; elastic
   C. 0.5; inelastic
   D. 2; inelastic

6. The cross elasticity of demand for good A with respect to good B is 0.2. A 10 percent change in the price of good B will lead to a ____ percent change in the quantity of good A demanded. Goods A and B are _____.

   A. 2; substitutes
   B. 0.5; complements
   C. −2; complements
   D. −0.5; substitutes

7. A 2 percent increase in income increases the quantity demanded of a good by 1 percent. The income elasticity of demand for this good is _____. The good is a _____ good.

   A. 2; normal
   B. −2; inferior
   C. 1/2; normal
   D. 2; inferior

Should price gouging be illegal?

Efficiency and Fairness of Markets

6

When you have completed your study of this chapter, you will be able to

1 Describe the alternative methods of allocating scarce resources and define and explain the features of an efficient allocation.

2 Distinguish between value and price and define consumer surplus.

3 Distinguish between cost and price and define producer surplus.

4 Evaluate the efficiency of the alternative methods of allocating resources.

5 Explain the main ideas about fairness and evaluate the fairness of the alternative methods of allocating scarce resources.

6.1   ALLOCATION METHODS AND EFFICIENCY

Because resources are scarce, they must be allocated somehow among their competing uses. Doing nothing and leaving the allocation to chance is one method of allocation. The goal of this chapter is to evaluate the ability of markets to allocate resources efficiently and fairly—to allocate them in the social interest.

But trading in markets is only one of several methods of allocating resources. To know whether the market does a good job, we need to compare it with its alternatives. We also need to know what is meant by an efficient and fair allocation.

Economists have much more to say about efficiency than about fairness, so efficiency is the main focus of this chapter. We leave the difficult issue of fairness until the final section. We begin by describing the alternative ways in which resources might be allocated. Then we explain the characteristics of an efficient allocation.

■ Resource Allocation Methods

Resources might be allocated by using any one or some combination of the following methods:

- Market price
- Command
- Majority rule
- Contest
- First-come, first-served
- Sharing equally
- Lottery
- Personal characteristics
- Force

Let's see how each method works and look at an example of each.

Market Price

When a market price allocates a scarce resource, the people who get the resource are those who are willing and able to pay the market price. People who don't value the resource as highly as the market price leave it for others to buy and use.

Most of the scarce resources that you supply get allocated by market price. For example, you sell your labor services in a market, and you buy most of what you consume in markets.

Two kinds of people decide not to pay the market price: those who can afford to pay but choose not to buy and those who are too poor and simply can't afford to pay.

For many goods and services, distinguishing between those who choose not to buy and those who can't afford to pay doesn't matter. For a few items, that distinction does matter. For example, some poor people can't afford to pay school fees and doctor's fees. The inability of poor people to buy items that most people consider to be essential is not handled well by the market price method and is usually dealt with by one of the other allocation methods.

But for most goods and services, the market turns out to do a good job. We'll examine just how good a job it does later in this chapter.

Market price allocates resources to those who are willing and able to pay.

Command

A **command system** allocates resources by the order (command) of someone in authority. Many resources get allocated by command. In the U.S. economy, the command system is used extensively inside firms and government bureaus. For example, if you have a job, it is most likely that someone tells you what to do. Your labor time is allocated to specific tasks by a command.

Sometimes, a command system allocates the resources of an entire economy. The former Soviet Union is an example. North Korea and Cuba are the only remaining command economies.

A command system works well in organizations in which the lines of authority and responsibility are clear and it is easy to monitor the activities being performed. But a command system works badly when applied to an entire economy. The range of activities to be monitored is just too large, and it is easy for people to fool those in authority. The system works so badly in North Korea that it fails even to deliver an adequate supply of food.

Majority Rule

Majority rule allocates resources in the way that a majority of voters choose. Societies use majority rule for some of their biggest decisions. For example, majority rule decides the tax rates that end up allocating scarce resources between private use and public use. And majority rule decides how tax dollars are allocated among competing uses such as national defense and health care for the aged.

Having 200 million people vote on every line in a nation's budget would be extremely costly, so instead of direct majority rule, the United States (and most other countries) use the system of representative government. Majority rule determines who will represent the people, and majority rule among the representatives decides the detailed allocation of scarce resources.

Majority rule works well when the decisions being made affect large numbers of people and self-interest must be suppressed to use resources most effectively.

Contest

A contest allocates resources to a winner (or a group of winners). The most obvious contests are sporting events. Maria Sharapova and Serena Williams do battle on a tennis court, and the winner gets twice as much in prize money as the loser.

But contests are much more general than those in a sports arena, though we don't call them contests in ordinary speech. For example, Bill Gates won a big contest to provide the world's personal computer operating system, and Natalie Portman won a type of contest to rise to the top of the movie-acting business.

Contests do a good job when the efforts of the "players" are hard to monitor and reward directly. By dangling the opportunity to win a big prize, people are motivated to work hard and try to be the "winner." Even though only a few people end up with a big prize, many people work harder in the process of trying to win and so total production is much greater than it would be without the contest.

First-Come, First-Served

A first-come, first-served method allocates resources to those who are first in line. Most national parks allocate campsites in this way. Airlines use first-come, first-served to allocate standby seats at the departure gate. A freeway is an everyday example of first-come, first-served. This scarce transportation resource gets allo-

Command system
A system that allocates resources by the order of someone in authority.

A command allocates resources by the order of someone in authority.

Voting allocates resources in the way that the majority wants.

A contest allocates resources to the winner, in sport and business.

First-come, first-served allocates resources to the first in line.

cated to the first to arrive at the on-ramp. If too many vehicles enter the freeway, the speed slows and people, in effect, wait in line for a bit of the "freeway" to become free!

First-come, first-served works best when, as in the above examples, a scarce resource can serve just one user at a time in a sequence. By serving the user who arrives first, this method minimizes the time spent waiting in line for the resource to become free.

Sharing Equally

When a resource is shared equally, everyone gets the same amount of it. You perhaps use this method to share dessert at a restaurant. People sometimes jointly own a vacation apartment and share its use equally.

To make equal shares work, people must agree on how to use the resource and must make an arrangement to implement the agreement. Sharing equally can work for small groups who share a set of common goals and ideals.

Lottery

Lotteries allocate resources to those who pick the winning number, draw the lucky cards, or come up lucky on some other gaming system. State lotteries and casinos reallocate millions of dollars worth of goods and services every year.

But lotteries are far more widespread than state jackpots and roulette wheels in casinos. They are used in a variety of situations to allocate scarce resources. For example, some marathon organizers use lotteries to determine who gets to participate and some airports use them to allocate landing slots to airlines.

Lotteries work well when there is no effective way to distinguish among potential users of a scarce resource.

Personal Characteristics

When resources are allocated on the basis of personal characteristics, people with the "right" characteristics get the resources. Some of the resources that matter most to you are allocated in this way. The people you like are the ones you spend the most time with. You try to avoid having to spend time with people you don't like. People choose marriage partners on the basis of personal characteristics. The use of personal characteristics to allocate resources is regarded as completely natural and acceptable.

But this method also gets used in unacceptable ways. Allocating the best jobs to white, Anglo-Saxon males and discriminating against minorities and women is an example.

Force

Force plays a crucial role, for both good and ill, in allocating scarce resources. Let's start with the ill.

War, the use of military force by one nation against another, has played an enormous role historically in allocating resources. The economic supremacy of European settlers in the Americas and Australia owes much to the use of this method.

Theft, the taking of the property of others without their consent, also plays a large role. Both large-scale organized crime and small-scale petty crime collectively allocate billions of dollars worth of resources annually. A large amount of

Sharing allocates resources by mutual agreement.

A lottery allocates resources to the one who draws the winning number.

Personal characteristics allocate resources based on whom we like.

Force protects the rule of law and facilitates economic activity.

theft today is conducted by using sophisticated electronic methods that move resources from banks and thousands of innocent people.

But force plays a crucial positive role in allocating resources. It provides an effective method for the state to transfer wealth from the rich to the poor and the legal framework in which voluntary exchange in markets takes place.

Most income and wealth redistribution in modern societies occurs through a taxation and benefits system that is enforced by the power of the state. We vote for taxes and benefits—a majority vote allocation—but we use the power of the state to ensure that everyone complies with the rules and pays their allotted share.

A legal system is the foundation on which our market economy functions. Without courts to enforce contracts, it would be difficult to do business. But the courts could not enforce contracts without the ability to apply force if necessary. The state provides the ultimate force that enables the courts to do their work.

More broadly, the force of the state is essential to uphold the principle of the *rule of law*. This principle is the bedrock of civilized economic (and social and political) life. With the rule of law upheld, people can go about their daily economic lives with the assurance that their property will be protected—that they can sue for violations of their property (and be sued if they violate the property of others).

Free from the burden of protecting their property and confident in the knowledge that those with whom they trade will honor their agreements, people can get on with focusing on the activity at which they have a comparative advantage and trading for mutual gain.

In the next sections of this chapter, we're going to see how a market achieves an efficient use of resources, examine obstacles to efficiency, and see how sometimes, an alternative method might improve on the market. But first we need to be clear about the meaning of efficiency. What are the characteristics of an efficient allocation of resources?

■ Using Resources Efficiently

In everyday language, *efficiency* means getting the most out of something. An efficient automobile is one that gets the best possible gas mileage; an efficient furnace is one that uses as little fuel as possible to deliver its heat. In economics, efficiency means getting the most out of the entire economy.

Efficiency and the *PPF*

The **production possibilities frontier** (*PPF*) is the boundary between the combinations of goods and services that can be produced and those that cannot be produced given the available factors of production and state of technology (p. 60). Production is efficient when the economy is *on* its *PPF* (Chapter 3, pp. 62–63). Production at a point *inside* the *PPF* is *inefficient*.

Allocative efficiency is achieved when the quantities of goods and services produced are those that people *value most highly*. To put it another way, resources are allocated efficiently when we cannot produce more of one thing without giving up something else *that people value more highly*. If we can give up some units of one good to get more of something that is *valued more highly*, we haven't achieved the most valued point on the *PPF*.

The *PPF* tells us what it is *possible* to produce but it doesn't tell us about the *value* of what we produce. To find the *highest-valued* point on the *PPF*, we need some information about value. *Marginal benefit* provides that information.

Production possibilities frontier
The boundary between the combinations of goods and services that can be produced and the combinations that cannot be produced, given the available factors of production and the state of technology.

Allocative efficiency
A situation in which the quantities of goods and services produced are those that people *value most highly*—it is not possible to produce more of a good or service without giving up some of another good that people *value more highly*.

Marginal Benefit

Marginal benefit is the benefit that people receive from consuming *one more unit* of a good or service. People's *preferences* determine marginal benefit and we can measure the marginal benefit from a good or service by what people *are willing to* give up to get *one more* unit of it.

The more we have of any good or service, the smaller is our marginal benefit from it—*the principle of decreasing marginal benefit*. Think about your own marginal benefit from pizza. You really enjoy the first slice. A second slice is fine, too, but not quite as satisfying as the first one. But eat three, four, five, six, and more slices, and each additional slice is less enjoyable than the previous one. You get diminishing marginal benefit from pizza. The more pizza you have, the less of some other good or service you are willing to give up to get one more slice.

Figure 6.1 illustrates the economy's marginal benefit schedule and marginal benefit curve for pizza. The schedule and curve show the same information. In the schedule and on the curve, the quantity of other goods that people *are willing to give up* to get one more pizza *decreases* as the quantity of pizza available *increases*.

Marginal Cost

To achieve allocative efficiency, we must compare the marginal benefit from pizza with its marginal cost. *Marginal cost* is the opportunity cost of producing one more unit of a good or service (see p. 10) and is measured by the slope of the production possibilities frontier (see pp. 66–67). The marginal cost of a good increases as the quantity produced of that good increases.

■ **FIGURE 6.1**

Marginal Benefit from Pizza

The table and the graph show the marginal benefit from pizza.

Possibility *A* and point *A* tell us that if 2,000 pizzas a day are produced, people are willing to give up 15 units of other goods for a pizza. Each point *A*, *B*, and *C* in the graph represents the possibility in the table identified by the same letter.

The line passing through these points is the marginal benefit curve. The marginal benefit from pizza decreases as the quantity of pizza available increases.

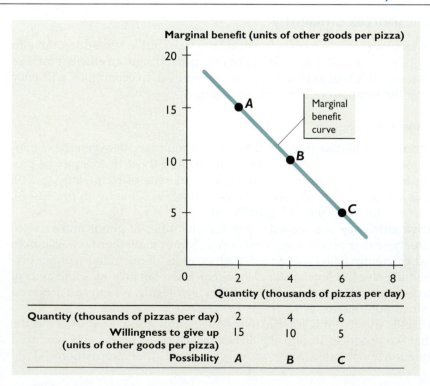

Quantity (thousands of pizzas per day)	2	4	6
Willingness to give up (units of other goods per pizza)	15	10	5
Possibility	A	B	C

Figure 6.2 illustrates the economy's marginal cost schedule and marginal cost curve. In the schedule and along the curve, which show the same information, the quantity of other goods that people *must give up* to get one more pizza *increases* as the quantity of pizza produced *increases*.

We can now use the concepts of marginal benefit and marginal cost to discover the efficient quantity of pizza to produce.

Efficient Allocation

The efficient allocation is the highest-valued allocation. To find this allocation, we compare marginal benefit and marginal cost.

If the marginal benefit from pizza exceeds its marginal cost, we're producing too little pizza (and too many units of other goods). If we increase the quantity of pizza produced, we incur a cost but receive a larger benefit from the additional pizza. Our allocation of resources becomes more efficient.

If the marginal cost of pizza exceeds its marginal benefit, we're producing too much pizza (and too little of other goods). Now if we decrease the quantity of pizza produced, we receive a smaller benefit from pizza but save an even greater cost of pizza. Again, our allocation of resources becomes more efficient.

Only when the marginal benefit and marginal cost of pizza are equal are we allocating resources efficiently. Figure 6.3 on the next page illustrates this efficient allocation and provides a graphical summary of the above description of allocative efficiency.

■ FIGURE 6.2

Marginal Cost of Pizza

MyEconLab Animation

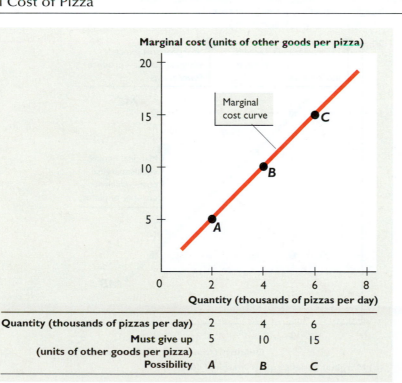

Quantity (thousands of pizzas per day)	2	4	6
Must give up (units of other goods per pizza)	5	10	15
Possibility	*A*	*B*	*C*

The table and the graph show the marginal cost of a pizza. Marginal cost is the opportunity cost of producing one more unit. It is derived from the *PPF* and is measured by the slope of the *PPF*.

Points *A*, *B*, and *C* in the graph represent the possibilities in the table. The marginal cost curve shows that the marginal cost of a pizza increases as the quantity of pizza produced increases.

■ FIGURE 6.3

The Efficient Quantity of Pizza

MyEconLab Animation

Production efficiency occurs at all points on the *PPF*, but *allocative efficiency* occurs at only one point on the *PPF*.

❶ When 2,000 pizzas are produced in part (a), the marginal benefit from pizza exceeds its marginal cost in part (b). Too few pizzas are being produced. If more pizzas and less of other goods are produced, the value of production increases and resources are used more efficiently.

❷ When 6,000 pizzas are produced in part (a), the marginal cost of a pizza exceeds its marginal benefit in part (b). Too many pizzas are being produced. If fewer pizzas and more of other goods are produced, the value of production increases and resources are used more efficiently.

❸ When 4,000 pizzas a day are produced in part (a), the marginal cost of a pizza equals its marginal benefit in part (b). The efficient quantity of pizzas is being produced. It is not possible to get greater value from the economy's scarce resources. If one less pizza and more other goods are produced, the value of the lost pizza exceeds the value of the additional other goods, so total value falls. And if one more pizza and less other goods are produced, the value of the gained pizza is less than the value of the lost other goods, so again total value falls.

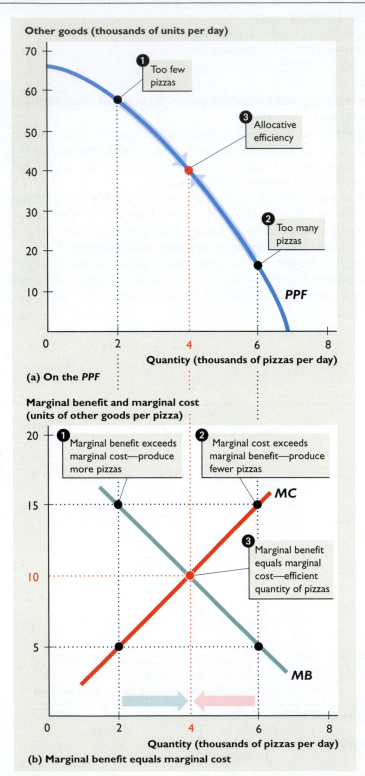

(a) On the *PPF*

(b) Marginal benefit equals marginal cost

CHECKPOINT 6.1

Describe the alternative methods of allocating scarce resources and define and explain the features of an efficient allocation.

MyEconLab
You can work these problems in Study Plan 6.1 and get instant feedback.

Practice Problems

1. Which method is used to allocate the following scarce resources?
   • Campus parking space between student areas and faculty areas
   • A spot in a restricted student parking area
   • Textbooks
   • Host city for the Olympic Games

Use Figure 1, which shows a nation's *PPF,* and Table 1, which shows its marginal benefit and marginal cost schedules, to work Problems **2** and **3**.

2. What is the marginal benefit from bananas when 1 pound of bananas is grown? What is the marginal cost of growing 1 pound of bananas?

3. On Figure 1, mark two points: Point *A* at which production is efficient but too much coffee is produced for allocative efficiency; and point *B,* the point of allocative efficiency.

In the News

AC/DC's "Black Ice" tour breaks records down under
The 40,000 tickets for the March 6 gig sold out in seven minutes—a record. Many people who camped out overnight missed getting a ticket.

Source: *WAToday,* May 25, 2009

What method was used to allocate AC/DC concert tickets? Was it efficient?

Solutions to Practice Problems

1. Campus parking is allocated by command. The spot in a restricted student parking area is allocated by first-come, first-served. Textbooks are allocated by market price. The Olympic Games' host city is allocated by contest.

2. The marginal benefit from 1 pound of bananas is 3 pounds of coffee. Marginal benefit is the amount of coffee that the nation is *willing to give up* to get *one additional* pound of bananas. The marginal cost of growing 1 pound of bananas is 1 pound of coffee. Marginal cost is the amount of coffee that the nation *must give up* to get *one additional* pound of bananas.

3. Point *A* on Figure 2 shows production efficiency (on the *PPF*) but not allocative efficiency because from Table 1 marginal benefit from bananas exceeds the marginal cost—too few bananas are produced. Point *B* is the point of allocative efficiency: It is on the *PPF* and marginal benefit equals marginal cost.

Solution to In the News

The concert organizer used first-come, first-served to allocate tickets. The allocation was efficient if the concert-goer's willingness to pay (the ticket price plus the opportunity cost of time spent in the line), which is also the marginal benefit, equaled the organizer's marginal cost of providing one more seat.

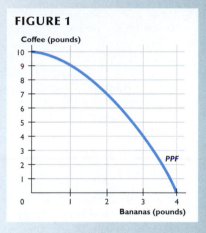

FIGURE 1

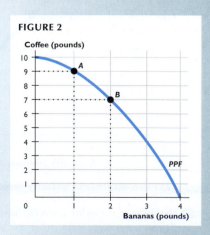

FIGURE 2

TABLE 1 MARGINAL BENEFIT AND MARGINAL COST

Bananas (pounds)	Willing to give up (pounds of coffee per pound of bananas)	Must give up
1	3	1
2	2	2
3	1	3

6.2 VALUE, PRICE, AND CONSUMER SURPLUS

To investigate whether a market is efficient, we need to understand the connection between demand and marginal benefit and between supply and marginal cost.

■ Demand and Marginal Benefit

In everyday life, when we talk about "getting value for money," we're distinguishing between *value* and *price*. Value is what we get, and price is what we pay. In economics, the everyday idea of value is *marginal benefit,* which we measure as the maximum price that people are willing to pay for another unit of the good or service. The demand curve tells us this price. In Figure 6.4(a), the demand curve shows the quantity demanded at a given price—when the price is $10 a pizza, the quantity demanded is 10,000 pizzas a day. In Figure 6.4(b), the demand curve shows the maximum price that people are willing to pay when there is a given quantity—when 10,000 pizzas a day are available, the most that people are willing to pay for the 10,000th pizza is $10. The marginal benefit from the 10,000th pizza is $10.

> A demand curve is a marginal benefit curve. The demand curve for pizza tells us the dollars' worth of other goods and services that people are willing to forgo to consume one more pizza.

■ **FIGURE 6.4**

Demand, Willingness to Pay, and Marginal Benefit   MyEconLab Animation

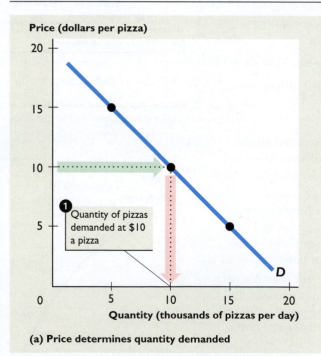

(a) Price determines quantity demanded

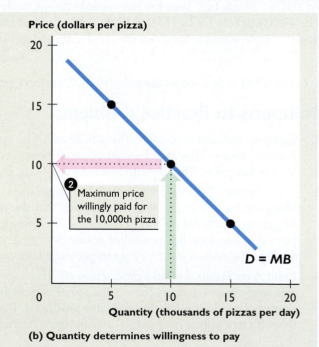

(b) Quantity determines willingness to pay

❶ The demand curve for pizza, *D*, shows the quantity of pizza demanded at each price, other things remaining the same. At $10 a pizza, the quantity demanded is 10,000 pizzas a day.

❷ The demand curve shows the maximum price willingly paid (marginal benefit) for a given quantity. If 10,000 pizzas are available, the maximum price willingly paid for the 10,000th pizza is $10. The demand curve is also the marginal benefit curve *MB.*

■ Consumer Surplus

We don't always have to pay as much as we're willing to pay. When people buy something for less than it is worth to them, they receive a consumer surplus. **Consumer surplus** is the excess of marginal benefit from a good over the price paid for it, summed over the quantity consumed.

Figure 6.5 illustrates consumer surplus. The demand curve for pizza tells us the quantity of pizza that people plan to buy at each price and the marginal benefit from pizza at each quantity. If the price of a pizza is $10, people buy 10,000 pizzas a day. Expenditure on pizza is $100,000, which is shown by the area of the blue rectangle.

To calculate consumer surplus, we must find the consumer surplus on each pizza and add these consumer surpluses together. For the 10,000th pizza, marginal benefit equals $10 and people pay $10, so the consumer surplus on this pizza is zero. For the 5,000th pizza (highlighted in the figure), marginal benefit is $15. So on this pizza, consumer surplus is $15 minus $10, which is $5. For the first pizza, marginal benefit is almost $20, so on this pizza, consumer surplus is almost $10.

Consumer surplus—the sum of the consumer surpluses on the 10,000 pizzas that people buy—is $50,000 a day, which is shown by the area of the green triangle. (The base of the triangle is 10,000 pizzas a day and its height is $10, so its area is (10,000 × $10) ÷ 2 = $50,000.)

The total benefit is the amount paid, $100,000 (blue rectangle), plus consumer surplus, $50,000 (green triangle), and is $150,000. Consumer surplus is the total benefit minus the amount paid, or net benefit to consumers.

Consumer surplus
The marginal benefit from a good or service in excess of the price paid for it, summed over the quantity consumed.

■ FIGURE 6.5

Demand and Consumer Surplus

MyEconLab Animation

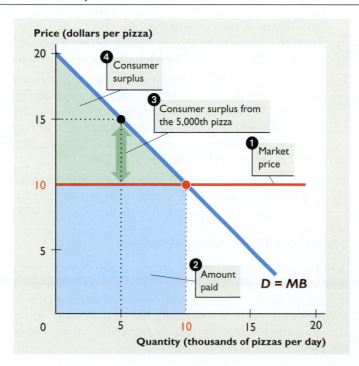

❶ The market price of a pizza is $10.

❷ At the market price, people buy 10,000 pizzas a day and spend $100,000 on pizza—the blue rectangle.

❸ The demand curve tells us that people are willing to pay $15 for the 5,000th pizza, so consumer surplus on the 5,000th pizza is $5.

❹ Consumer surplus from the 10,000 pizzas that people buy is $50,000—the area of the green triangle.

The total benefit from pizza is the $100,000 that people pay plus the $50,000 consumer surplus they receive, or $150,000.

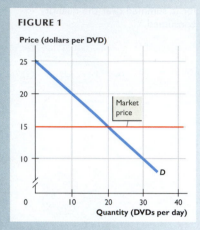

FIGURE 1

CHECKPOINT 6.2

Distinguish between value and price and define consumer surplus.

Practice Problems

Figure 1 shows the demand curve for DVDs and the market price of a DVD.

1. What is the willingness to pay for the 20th DVD? Calculate the value of the 10th DVD and the consumer surplus on the 10th DVD.

2. What is the quantity of DVDs bought? Calculate the consumer surplus, the amount spent on DVDs, and the total benefit from the DVDs bought.

3. If the price of a DVD rises to $20, what is the change in consumer surplus?

In the News

Airfares stacked against consumers

The airlines change prices from day to day. For example, the fare on one Delta flight from New York to Los Angeles jumped from $755 to $1,143 from a Friday to Saturday in April, then fell to $718 on Sunday.

Source: boston.com, June 22, 2011

Jodi planned a trip from New York to Los Angeles and was equally happy to travel on Friday, Saturday, or Sunday. The Saturday price was the most she was willing to pay. On which day do you predict she travelled and how much consumer surplus did she receive?

Solutions to Practice Problems

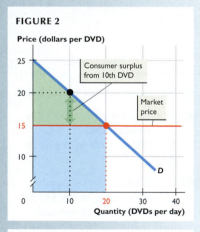

FIGURE 2

1. The willingness to pay for the 20th DVD is the price on the demand curve at 20 DVDs, which is $15 (Figure 2). The value of the 10th DVD is its marginal benefit which is also the maximum price that someone is willing to pay for it. In Figure 2, the value of the 10th DVD is $20. The consumer surplus on the 10th DVD is its marginal benefit minus the price paid for the DVD, which is $20 − $15 = $5 (the length of the green arrow in Figure 2).

2. The quantity of DVDs bought is 20 a day, and the consumer surplus is ($25 − $15) × 20 ÷ 2 = $100 (the green triangle in Figure 2). The amount spent on DVDs is the price multiplied by the quantity bought, which is $15 × 20 = $300 (the area of the blue rectangle in Figure 2). The total benefit from DVDs is the amount spent on DVDs plus the consumer surplus from DVDs, which is $300 + $100 = $400.

FIGURE 3

3. If the price rises to $20, the quantity bought decreases to 10 a day. Consumer surplus decreases to ($25 − $20) × 10 ÷ 2 = $25 (the area of the green triangle in Figure 3). Consumer surplus decreases by $75 (from $100 to $25).

Solution to In the News

Being equally happy to travel on any of the three days means that Jodi's marginal benefit from the trip was the same on each day. Because Saturday's price of $1,143 was the most she was willing to pay, that is her marginal benefit. Being rational, Jodi would travel on the day with the lowest price, Sunday, and pay a fare of $718. Her consumer surplus would be her marginal benefit of $1,143 minus the price she paid, $718, which equals $425.

6.3 COST, PRICE, AND PRODUCER SURPLUS

You are now going to learn about cost, price, and producer surplus, which parallels what you've learned about value, price, and consumer surplus.

■ Supply and Marginal Cost

Just as buyers distinguish between *value* and *price,* so sellers distinguish between *cost* and *price.* Cost is what a seller must give up to produce the good, and price is what a seller receives when the good is sold. The cost of producing one more unit of a good or service is its *marginal cost.* It is just worth producing one more unit of a good or service if the price for which it can be sold equals marginal cost. The supply curve tells us this price. In Figure 6.6(a), the supply curve shows the quantity supplied at a given price—when the price of a pizza is $10, the quantity supplied is 10,000 pizzas a day. In Figure 6.6(b), the supply curve shows the minimum price that producers must receive to supply a given quantity—to supply 10,000 pizzas a day, producers must be able to get at least $10 for the 10,000th pizza. The marginal cost of the 10,000th pizza is $10. So:

A supply curve is a marginal cost curve. The supply curve of pizza tells us the dollars' worth of other goods and services that people must forgo if firms produce one more pizza.

■ FIGURE 6.6

Supply, Minimum Supply Price, and Marginal Cost

MyEconLab Animation

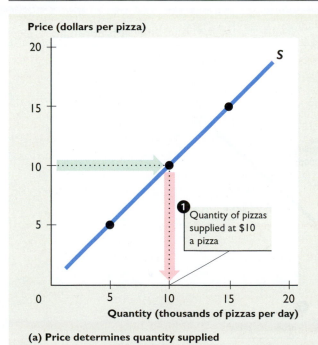

(a) Price determines quantity supplied

❶ The supply curve of pizza, *S,* shows the quantity of pizza supplied at each price, other things remaining the same. At $10 a pizza, the quantity supplied is 10,000 pizzas a day.

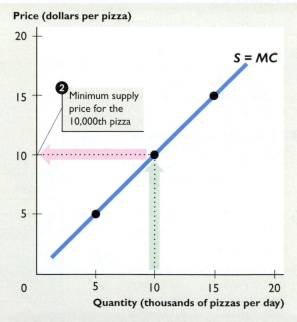

(b) Quantity determines minimum supply price

❷ The supply curve shows the minimum price that firms must be offered to supply a given quantity. The minimum supply price equals marginal cost, which for the 10,000th pizza is $10. The supply curve is also the marginal cost curve *MC.*

■ Producer Surplus

Producer surplus
The price of a good in excess of the marginal cost of producing it, summed over the quantity produced.

When the price exceeds marginal cost, the firm obtains a producer surplus. **Producer surplus** is the excess of the price of a good over the marginal cost of producing it, summed over the quantity produced.

Figure 6.7 illustrates the producer surplus for pizza producers. The supply curve of pizza tells us the quantity of pizza that producers plan to sell at each price. The supply curve also tells us the marginal cost of pizza at each quantity produced. If the price of a pizza is $10, producers plan to sell 10,000 pizzas a day. The total revenue from pizza is $100,000 per day.

To calculate producer surplus, we must find the producer surplus on each pizza and add these surpluses together. For the 10,000th pizza, marginal cost equals $10 and producers receive $10, so the producer surplus on this pizza is zero. For the 5,000th pizza (highlighted in the figure), marginal cost is $6. So on this pizza, producer surplus is $10 minus $6, which is $4. For the first pizza, marginal cost is $2, so on this pizza, producer surplus is $10 minus $2, which is $8.

Producer surplus—the sum of the producer surpluses on the 10,000 pizzas that firms produce—is $40,000 a day, which is shown by the area of the blue triangle. The base of the triangle is 10,000 pizzas a day and its height is $8, so its area is (10,000 × $8) ÷ 2 = $40,000.

The total cost of producing pizza is the amount received from selling it, $100,000, minus the producer surplus, $40,000 (blue triangle), and is $60,000 (the red area). Producer surplus is the total amount received minus the total cost, or net benefit to producers.

■ **FIGURE 6.7**

Supply and Producer Surplus

MyEconLab Animation

❶ The market price of a pizza is $10. At this price, producers plan to sell 10,000 pizzas a day and receive a total revenue of $100,000 a day.

❷ The supply curve shows that the marginal cost of the 5,000th pizza a day is $6, so producers receive a producer surplus of $4 on the 5,000th pizza.

❸ Producer surplus from the 10,000 pizzas sold is $40,000 a day—the area of the blue triangle.

❹ The cost of producing 10,000 pizzas a day is the red area beneath the marginal cost curve. It equals total revenue of $100,000 minus producer surplus of $40,000 and is $60,000 a day.

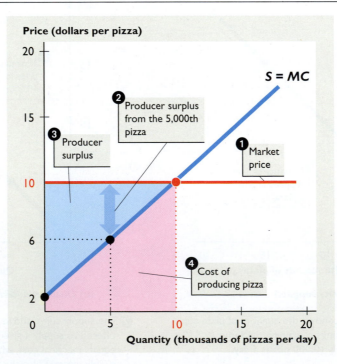

CHECKPOINT 6.3

Distinguish between cost and price and define producer surplus.

Practice Problems

Figure 1 shows the supply curve of DVDs and the market price of a DVD.

1. What is the minimum supply price of the 20th DVD? Calculate the marginal cost of the 10th DVD and the producer surplus on the 10th DVD.
2. What is the quantity of DVDs sold? Calculate the producer surplus, the total revenue from the DVDs sold, and the cost of producing the DVDs sold.
3. If the price of a DVD falls to $10, what is the change in producer surplus?

In the News

Is Australia's ski season headed for a wipeout?

The Australian dollar has soared 26% against the U.S. dollar since last June, making those foreign lift tickets cheaper than those in Australia, and travel agents report a jump in interest in travel to North American ski destinations like Vail and Aspen.

Source: The Wall Street Journal, June 6, 2011

As Australians switch from skiing in Australia and flock to Vail and Aspen, how will the Australian ski operators' producer surplus change? How will the Vail and Aspen ski operators' producer surplus change?

Solutions to Practice Problems

1. The minimum supply price of the 20th DVD is the marginal cost of the 20th DVD, which is $15 (Figure 2). The marginal cost of the 10th DVD is equal to the minimum supply price for the 10th DVD, which is $10. The producer surplus on the 10th DVD is its market price minus the marginal cost of producing it, which is $15 − $10 = $5 (the blue arrow in Figure 2).
2. The quantity sold is 20 a day. Producer surplus equals ($15 − $5) × 20 ÷ 2, which is $100 (the area of the blue triangle in Figure 2). The total revenue is price multiplied by quantity sold. Total revenue is $15 × 20 = $300. The cost of producing DVDs equals total revenue minus producer surplus, which is $300 − $100 = $200 (the red area in Figure 2).
3. The quantity sold decreases to 10 a day. The producer surplus decreases to ($10 − $5) × 10 ÷ 2 = $25 (the area of the blue triangle in Figure 3). The change in producer surplus is a decrease of $75 (from $100 down to $25).

Solution to In the News

Producer surplus is the excess of the price of a good over the marginal cost of producing it, summed over the quantity produced.

In Australia, the demand for ski tickets decreases, the price and quantity of tickets sold decreases, and Australian ski operators' producer surplus decreases.

In Vail and Aspen, the demand for ski tickets increases, the price and quantity of tickets sold increases, and ski operators' producer surplus increases.

MyEconLab

You can work these problems in Study Plan 6.3 and get instant feedback.

FIGURE 1

FIGURE 2

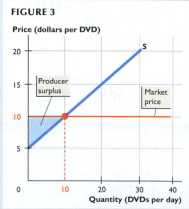

FIGURE 3

6.4 ARE MARKETS EFFICIENT?

Figure 6.8 shows the market for pizza. The demand curve is *D,* the supply curve is *S,* the equilibrium price is $10 a pizza, and the equilibrium quantity is 10,000 pizzas a day. The market forces that you studied in Chapter 4 (pp. 99–100) pull the pizza market to its equilibrium and coordinate the plans of buyers and sellers. But does this competitive equilibrium deliver the efficient quantity of pizza?

If the equilibrium is efficient, it does more than coordinate plans. It coordinates them in the best possible way. Resources are used to produce the quantity of pizza that people value most highly. It is not possible to produce more pizza without giving up some of another good or service that is valued more highly. And if a smaller quantity of pizza is produced, resources are used to produce some other good that is not valued as highly as the pizza that is forgone.

■ Marginal Benefit Equals Marginal Cost

To check whether the equilibrium in Figure 6.8 is efficient, recall the interpretation of the demand curve as a marginal benefit curve and the supply curve as a marginal cost curve. The demand curve tells us the marginal benefit from pizza. The supply curve tells us the marginal cost of pizza. Where the demand curve and the supply curve intersect, marginal benefit equals marginal cost.

■ FIGURE 6.8

An Efficient Market for Pizza

MyEconLab Animation

❶ Market equilibrium occurs at a price of $10 a pizza and a quantity of 10,000 pizzas a day.

❷ The supply curve is also the marginal cost curve.

❸ The demand curve is also the marginal benefit curve.

Because at the market equilibrium, marginal benefit equals marginal cost, the ❹ efficient quantity of pizza is produced. The sum of the ❺ consumer surplus and ❻ producer surplus is maximized.

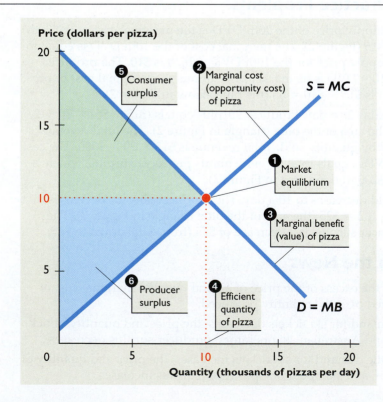

This condition—marginal benefit equals marginal cost—is the condition that delivers an efficient use of resources. Because a competitive equilibrium allocates resources to the activities that create the greatest possible value, it is efficient.

■ Total Surplus Is Maximized

Another way of checking that the equilibrium is efficient is to look at the total surplus that it generates. **Total surplus** is the sum of producer surplus and consumer surplus. A price above the equilibrium might increase producer surplus, but it would decrease consumer surplus by more. And a price below the equilibrium price might increase consumer surplus, but it would decrease producer surplus by more. The competitive equilibrium price maximizes total surplus.

Total surplus
The sum of producer surplus and consumer surplus.

In Figure 6.8, if production is less than 10,000 pizzas a day, someone is willing to buy a pizza for more than it costs to produce. Buyers and sellers will gain if production increases. If production exceeds 10,000 pizzas a day, it costs more to produce a pizza than anyone is willing to pay for it. Buyers and sellers will gain if production decreases. Only when 10,000 pizzas a day are produced is there no unexploited gain from changing the quantity of pizza produced, and total surplus is maximized.

Buyers and sellers each attempt to do the best they can for themselves—they pursue their self-interest. No one plans for an efficient outcome for society as a whole. No one worries about the social interest. Buyers seek the lowest possible price, and sellers seek the highest possible price. But as buyers and sellers pursue their self-interest, this astonishing outcome occurs: The social interest is served.

■ The Invisible Hand

Writing in his *Wealth of Nations* in 1776, Adam Smith was the first to suggest that competitive markets send resources to the uses in which they have the highest value. Smith believed that each participant in a competitive market is "led by an invisible hand to promote an end [the efficient use of resources] which was no part of his intention."

You can see the effects of the invisible hand at work every day. Your campus bookstore is stuffed with texts at the start of each term. It has the quantities that it predicts students will buy. The coffee shop has the variety and quantities of drinks and snacks that people plan to buy. Your local clothing store has the sweatpants and socks and other items that you plan to buy. Truckloads of textbooks, coffee and cookies, and sweatpants and socks roll along our highways and bring these items to where you and your friends want to buy them. Firms that don't know you anticipate your wants and work hard to help you satisfy them.

No government organizes all this production, and no government auditor monitors producers to ensure that they serve the social interest. The allocation of scarce resources is not planned. It happens because prices adjust to make buying plans and selling plans compatible, and it happens in a way that sends resources to the uses in which they have the highest value.

Adam Smith explained why all this amazing activity occurs. "It is not from the benevolence of the butcher, the brewer, or the baker that we expect our dinner," he wrote, "but from their regard to their own interest."

Publishing companies, coffee growers, garment manufacturers, and a host of other producers are led by their regard for *their* own interest to serve *your* interest.

EYE on the U.S. ECONOMY
The Invisible Hand and e-Commerce

You can see the influence of the invisible hand at work in the cartoon and in today's information economy.

The cold drinks vendor has both cold drinks and shade. He has an opportunity cost and a minimum supply price of each item. The park bench reader has a marginal benefit from a cold drink and from shade. The transaction that occurs tells us that for shade, the reader's marginal benefit exceeds the vendor's marginal cost but for a cold drink, the vendor's marginal cost exceeds the reader's marginal benefit. The transaction creates consumer surplus and producer surplus. The vendor obtains a producer surplus from selling the shade for more than its opportunity cost, and the reader obtains a consumer surplus from buying the shade for less than its marginal benefit. In the third frame of the cartoon, both the consumer and the producer are better off than they were in the first frame. The umbrella has moved to its highest-valued use.

The market economy relentlessly performs the activity illustrated in the cartoon to achieve an efficient allocation of resources. New technologies have cut the cost of using the Internet and during the past few years, hundreds of Web sites have been established that are dedicated to facilitating trade in all types of goods, services, and factors of production.

The electronic auction site eBay (http://www.ebay.com/), has brought a huge increase in consumer surplus and producer surplus, and helps to achieve ever greater allocative efficiency.

© The New Yorker Collection 1985
Mike Twohy from cartoonbank.com. All Rights Reserved.

Market Failure

Markets do not always achieve an efficient outcome. We call a situation in which a market delivers an inefficient outcome one of **market failure**. Market failure can occur because either too little of an item is produced—underproduction—or too much is produced—overproduction.

Underproduction

In Figure 6.9(a), the quantity of pizza produced is 5,000 a day. At this quantity, consumers are willing to pay $15 for a pizza that costs only $6 to produce. The quantity produced is inefficient—there is underproduction.

A **deadweight loss**, which is the decrease in total surplus that results from an inefficient underproduction or overproduction, measures the scale of the inefficiency. The area of the gray triangle in Figure 6.9(a) measures the deadweight loss.

Overproduction

In Figure 6.9(b), the quantity of pizza produced is 15,000 a day. At this quantity, consumers are willing to pay only $5 for a pizza that costs $14 to produce. By producing the 15,000th pizza, $9 is lost. Again, the gray triangle shows the deadweight loss. The total surplus is smaller than its maximum by the amount of the deadweight loss. The deadweight loss is borne by the entire society. It is not a loss for the producer and a gain for the consumers. It is a *social* loss.

Market failure
A situation in which the market delivers an inefficient outcome.

Deadweight loss
The decrease in total surplus that results from an inefficient underproduction or overproduction.

FIGURE 6.9

Inefficient Outcomes

MyEconLab Animation

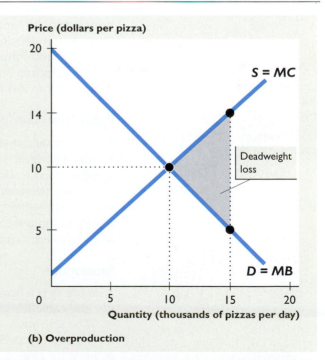

(a) Underproduction

(b) Overproduction

If production is restricted to 5,000 pizzas a day, a deadweight loss (the gray triangle) arises. Total surplus is reduced by the area of the deadweight loss triangle. Underproduction is inefficient.

If production increases to 15,000 pizzas, a deadweight loss arises. Total surplus is reduced by the area of the deadweight loss triangle. Overproduction is inefficient.

■ Sources of Market Failure

Obstacles to efficiency that bring market failure and create deadweight losses are

- Price and quantity regulations
- Taxes and subsidies
- Externalities
- Public goods and common resources
- Monopoly
- High transactions costs

Price and Quantity Regulations

Price regulations that put a cap on the rent a landlord is permitted to charge and laws that require employers to pay a minimum wage sometimes block the price adjustments that balance the quantity demanded and the quantity supplied and lead to underproduction. *Quantity regulations* that limit the amount that a farm is permitted to produce also lead to underproduction.

Taxes and Subsidies

Taxes increase the prices paid by buyers and lower the prices received by sellers. So taxes decrease the quantity produced and lead to underproduction. *Subsidies,* which are payments by the government to producers, decrease the prices paid by buyers and increase the prices received by sellers. So subsidies increase the quantity produced and lead to overproduction.

Externalities

An *externality* is a cost or a benefit that affects someone other than the seller and the buyer of a good. An electric utility creates an *external cost* by burning coal that brings acid rain and crop damage. The utility doesn't consider the cost of pollution when it decides how much power to produce. The result is overproduction.

A condominium owner would provide an *external benefit* if she installed a smoke detector. But she doesn't consider her neighbor's marginal benefit and decides not to install a smoke detector. The result is underproduction.

Public Goods and Common Resources

A *public good* benefits everyone and no one can be excluded from its benefits. National defense is an example. It is in everyone's self-interest to avoid paying for a public good (called the *free-rider problem*), which leads to its underproduction.

A *common resource* is owned by no one but used by everyone. Atlantic salmon is an example. It is in everyone's self-interest to ignore the costs of their own use of a common resource that fall on others (called the *tragedy of the commons*), which leads to overproduction.

Monopoly

A *monopoly* is a firm that is the sole provider of a good or service. Local water supply and cable television are supplied by firms that are monopolies.

The self-interest of a monopoly is to maximize its profit. Because the monopoly has no competitors, it can set the price to achieve its self-interested goal. To achieve its goal, a monopoly produces too little and charges too high a price, which leads to underproduction.

High Transactions Costs

Stroll around a shopping mall and observe the retail markets in which you participate. You'll see that these markets employ enormous quantities of scarce labor and capital resources. It is costly to operate any market. Economists call the opportunity costs of making trades in a market **transactions costs.**

Transactions costs
The opportunity costs of making trades in a market.

To use market prices as the allocators of scarce resources, it must be worth bearing the opportunity cost of establishing a market. Some markets are just too costly to operate. For example, when you want to play tennis on your local "free" court, you don't pay a market price for your slot on the court. You hang around until the court becomes vacant, and you "pay" with your waiting time.

When transactions costs are high, the market might underproduce.

■ Alternatives to the Market

When a market is inefficient, can one of the alternative non-market methods that we described at the beginning of this chapter do a better job? Sometimes it can.

Table 6.1 summarizes the sources of market failure and the possible remedies. Often, majority rule might be used, but majority rule has its own shortcomings. A group that pursues the self-interest of its members can become the majority. For example, price and quantity regulations that create deadweight loss are almost always the result of a self-interested group becoming the majority and imposing costs on the minority. Also, with majority rule, votes must be translated into actions by bureaucrats who have their own agendas.

Managers in firms issue commands and avoid the transactions costs that they would incur if they went to a market every time they needed a job done. First-come, first-served saves a lot of hassle in waiting lines. These lines could have markets in which people trade their place in the line—but someone would have to enforce the agreements. Can you imagine the hassle at a busy Starbucks if you had to buy your spot at the head of the line?

There is no one mechanism for allocating resources efficiently. But markets bypassed by command systems inside firms and supplemented by majority rule and first-come, first-served do an amazingly good job.

■ **Table 6.1**

Market Failure and Some Possible Remedies

Reason for market failure	Possible remedy
1. Price and quantity regulations	Remove regulation by majority rule
2. Taxes and subsidies	Minimize deadweight loss by majority rule
3. Externalities	Minimize deadweight loss by majority rule
4. Public goods	Allocate by majority rule
5. Common resources	Allocate by majority rule
6. Monopoly	Regulate by majority rule
7. High transactions costs	Command or first-come, first-served

CHECKPOINT 6.4

Evaluate the efficiency of the alternative methods of allocating resources.

Practice Problems

Figure 1 shows the market for paper.

1. At the market equilibrium, what are consumer surplus, producer surplus, and total surplus? Is the market for paper efficient? Why or why not?

2. Lobbyists for a group of news magazines persuade the government to pass a law that requires producers to sell 50 tons of paper a day. Is the market for paper efficient? Why or why not? Shade the deadweight loss on the figure.

3. An environmental lobbying group persuades the government to pass a law that limits the quantity of paper that producers sell to 20 tons a day. Is the market for paper efficient? If not, what is the deadweight loss?

In the News

Senate votes to end ethanol subsidies
The Senate has voted to end the $6 billion a year in subsidies paid to the ethanol industry for the past three decades. Refiners would lose the 45-cent-a-gallon subsidy, and the tax on imported ethanol would be eliminated.

Source: USA Today, June 16, 2011

Describe the efficiency of the market for ethanol with the $6 billion subsidies in place. If the subsidies and taxes are eliminated, explain how the efficiency of the market for ethanol would change.

Solutions to Practice Problems

1. Market equilibrium is 40 tons a day at a price of $3 a ton (Figure 2). Consumer surplus = ($9 − $3) × 40 ÷ 2 = $120 (the area of the green triangle in Figure 2). Producer surplus is ($3 − $1) × 40 ÷ 2, which equals $40 (the area of the blue triangle in Figure 2). Total surplus is the sum of consumer surplus and producer surplus, which is $160.
   The market is efficient because marginal benefit (on the demand curve) equals marginal cost (on the supply curve) and total surplus (consumer surplus plus producer surplus) is maximized.

2. The market is inefficient because marginal cost exceeds marginal benefit. Deadweight loss is the area of the gray triangle 1 in Figure 3.

3. This market is now inefficient because marginal benefit exceeds marginal cost. The deadweight loss is the area of the gray triangle 2 in Figure 3.

Solution to In the News

Subsidies to producers increase the supply of the good, which decreases the market price. The price received by producers equals the market price plus the subsidy per gallon, which results in overproduction and inefficiency. A deadweight loss arises. By eliminating the subsidies and taxes, overproduction will decrease. The market for ethanol will be more efficient, and the deadweight loss will decrease.

FIGURE 1

Price (dollars per ton)

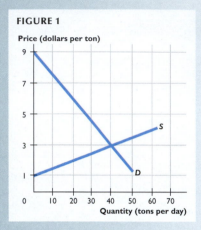

FIGURE 2

Price (dollars per ton)

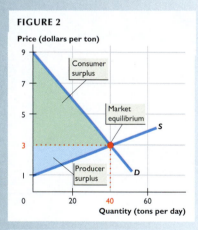

FIGURE 3

Price (dollars per ton)

6.5 ARE MARKETS FAIR?

Following a severe winter storm or hurricane, the prices of many essential items jump. Is it fair that disaster victims should be hit with higher prices? Many low-skilled people work for a wage that is below what most would regard as a living wage. Is that fair? How do we decide whether something is fair or unfair?

Economists have a clear definition of efficiency but they do not have a similarly clear definition of fairness. Also, ideas about fairness are not exclusively economic ideas. They involve the study of ethics.

To study ideas about fairness, think of economic life as a game—a serious game—that has *rules* and a *result*. Two broad and generally conflicting approaches to fairness are

- It's not fair if the *rules* aren't fair.
- It's not fair if the *result* isn't fair.

■ It's Not Fair If the *Rules* Aren't Fair

Harvard philosopher Robert Nozick argued for the fair rules view in a book entitled *Anarchy, State, and Utopia*, published in 1974. Nozick argued that fairness requires two rules:

- The state must establish and protect private property rights.
- Goods and services and the services of factors of production may be transferred from one person to another only by voluntary exchange with everyone free to engage in such exchange.

The first rule says that everything that is valuable—all scarce resources and goods—must be owned by individuals and that the state must protect private property rights. The second rule says that the only way a person can acquire something is to buy it in voluntary trade.

If these rules are followed, says Nozick, the outcome is fair. It doesn't matter how unequally the economic pie is shared provided that the people who bake it supply their services voluntarily in exchange for the share of the pie offered in compensation. Opportunity is equal but the result might be unequal. This fair rules approach is consistent with allocative efficiency.

■ It's Not Fair If the *Result* Isn't Fair

Most people think that the fair rules approach leads to too much inequality—to an unfair result: For example, that it is unfair for a bank president to earn millions of dollars a year while a bank teller earns only thousands of dollars a year.

But what is "too unequal"? Is it fair for some people to receive twice as much as others but not ten times as much or a hundred times as much? Or is all that matters that the poorest people shouldn't be "too poor"?

There is no easy answer to these questions. Generally, greater equality is regarded as good but there is no measure of the most desirable shares.

The fair result approach conflicts with allocative efficiency and leads to what is called the **big tradeoff**—a tradeoff between efficiency and fairness that recognizes the cost of making income transfers.

The big tradeoff is based on the fact that income can be transferred to people with low incomes only by taxing people with high incomes. But taxing people's

Big tradeoff
A tradeoff between efficiency and fairness that recognizes the cost of making income transfers.

EYE on PRICE GOUGING
Should Price Gouging Be Illegal?

Price gouging is the practice of selling an essential item for a much higher price than normal, and usually occurs following a natural disaster. In Florida and Texas, where hurricanes happen all too often, price gouging is illegal.

Whether price gouging *should* be illegal depends on the view of fairness employed and on the facts about whether the buyers or the sellers are the poorer group.

The standard view of economists is that price gouging should *not* be illegal and that it is the expected and *efficient* response to a change in demand.

After a hurricane, the demand for items such as generators, pumps, lamps, gasoline, and camp stoves increases and the prices of these items rise in a natural response to the change in demand.

The figure illustrates the market for camp stoves. The supply of stoves is the curve S, and in normal times, the demand for stoves is D_0. The price is $20 per stove and the equilibrium quantity is 5 stoves per day.

Following a hurricane that results in a lengthy power failure, the demand for camp stoves increases to D_1. Provided there is no price gouging law, the equilibrium price of a stove jumps to $40 and the equilibrium quantity increases to 7 stoves per day.

This outcome is efficient because the marginal cost of a stove (on the supply curve) equals the marginal benefit from a stove (on the demand curve).

If a strict price gouging law requires the price after the hurricane to be the *same* as the price before the hurricane,

the price of a stove is stuck at $20.

At this price, the quantity of stoves supplied remains at 5 per day and a deadweight loss shown by the gray triangle arises. The price gouging law is inefficient, and the price rise is efficient.

Whether a doubling of the price is *fair* depends on the idea of fairness used. On the *fair rules* view, the price rise is fair. Trade is voluntary and both the buyer and the seller are better off. On the *fair outcome* view, the price rise might be considered unfair if the buyers are poor and the sellers are rich. But if the buyers are rich and the sellers are poor, the price rise would be considered fair even on the fair result view.

After Hurricane Katrina, John Shepperson bought 19 generators, loaded them into a rented U-Haul vehicle, and drove the 600 miles from his home in Kentucky to a place in Mississippi that had no power. He offered his generators to eager buyers for twice the price he had paid for them. But before he could complete a sale, the Mississippi police swooped in on him. They confiscated his generators and put him in jail for four days. His crime: price gouging.

Was it efficient to stop Mr. Shepperson from selling his generators? Was it fair either to him or his deprived customers?

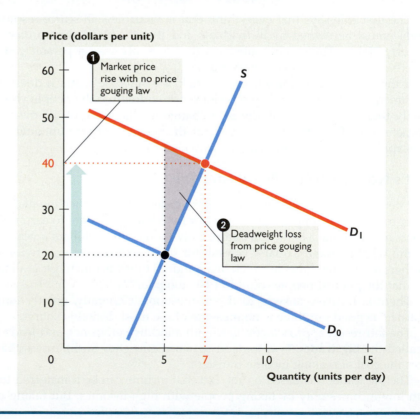

EYE on YOUR LIFE
Allocation Methods, Efficiency, and Fairness

You live in the national economy, your state economy, your regional economy, and your own household economy. The many decisions you must make affect efficiency and fairness at all these levels. Think about your household economy.

Make a spreadsheet and on it identify all the factors of production that your household owns. Count all the person-hours available and any capi-

tal. Show how these resources are allocated.

By what methods are your household's scarce resources allocated? Identify those allocated by market price; by command; by first-come, first-served; and by equal shares. Are any resources allocated by majority vote?

Now the tough part: Are these resources allocated efficiently—is the

value of your household's resources maximized? Think about how you can check whether marginal benefit equals marginal cost for each of your household's activities.

And now an even tougher question: Are your household's resources allocated fairly? Think about the two ideas of fairness and how they apply in your household.

income from employment discourages work. It results in the quantity of labor being less than the efficient quantity. Taxing people's income from capital discourages saving. It results in the quantity of capital being less than the efficient quantity. With smaller quantities of both labor and capital, the quantity of goods and services produced is less than the efficient quantity. The economic pie shrinks.

Income redistribution creates a tradeoff between the size of the economic pie and the equality with which it is shared. The greater the scale of income redistribution through income taxes, the greater is the inefficiency—the smaller is the pie.

There is a second source of inefficiency: A dollar taken from a rich person does not end up as a dollar in the hands of a poorer person. Some of the dollar is spent on administration of the tax and transfer system, which includes the cost of accountants, auditors, and lawyers. These activities use skilled labor and capital resources that could otherwise be used to produce other goods and services that people value.

You can see that when all these costs are taken into account, transferring a dollar from a rich person does not give a dollar to a poor person. It is even possible that those with low incomes end up being worse off. For example, if a highly taxed entrepreneur decides to work less hard and shut down a business, low-income workers get fired and must seek other, perhaps even lower-paid, work.

■ Compromise

Most people, and probably most economists, have sympathy with the Nozick view but think it too extreme. They see a role for taxes and government income support schemes to transfer some income from the rich to the poor. Such transfers could be considered voluntary in the sense that they are decided by majority voting, and even those who vote against such transfers voluntarily participate in the political process.

Once we agree that using the tax system to make transfers from the rich to the poor is fair, we need to determine just what we mean by a fair tax. We'll look at this big question when we study the tax system in Chapter 8.

MyEconLab
You can work these problems in Study Plan 6.5 and get instant feedback.

CHECKPOINT 6.5

Explain the main ideas about fairness and evaluate the fairness of the alternative methods of allocating scarce resources.

Practice Problems

A winter storm cuts the power supply and isolates a small town in the mountains. The people rush to buy candles from the town store, which is the only source of candles. The store owner decides to ration the candles to one per family but to keep the price of a candle unchanged.

1. Who gets to use the candles? Who receives the consumer surplus and who receives the producer surplus on candles?

2. Is the allocation efficient? Is the allocation fair?

In the News

National parks to offer free-entry weekends
Interior Secretary Ken Salazar said he hoped American families would take the opportunity during these hard times to enjoy an affordable weekend vacation in our national parks. Most Americans live within an hour's drive of a national park.

Source: *Los Angeles Times*, June 3, 2009

Which families will be most likely to visit the national parks on the free weekends? Is the policy to waive the admission fair?

Solutions to Practice Problems

1. The people who buy candles from the town store are not necessarily the people who use the candles. A buyer from the town store can sell a candle and will do so if he or she can get a price that exceeds his or her marginal benefit. The people who value the candles most—who are willing to pay the most—will use the candles.
    Only the people who are willing to pay the most for candles receive the consumer surplus on candles, and the store owner receives the same producer surplus as normal. People who sell the candles they buy from the store receive additional producer surplus.

2. The allocation is efficient because the people who value the candles most use them. Two views of fairness: The rules view is that if the rule of one candle per family is followed and exchange is voluntary, then the outcome is fair. But the results view is that if the candles are allocated unequally, then the allocation is unfair.

Solution to In the News

Most of the families will be those who own a car and do not work on weekends. The idea of waiving the admission is to allow families to enjoy an affordable vacation in these hard times. If the families hit by the hard times are the ones that visit the national parks, then, in the fair result view, the policy is fair. But if families hit by the hard times are the ones who do not visit, then, in the fair result view, the policy is unfair. If the families who visit the national parks do so voluntarily, then, no matter which families visit, in the fair rules view, the policy is fair.

CHAPTER SUMMARY

Key Points

1 **Describe the alternative methods of allocating scarce resources and define and explain the features of an efficient allocation.**

- The methods of allocating scarce resources are market price; command; majority rule; contest; first-come, first-served; sharing equally; lottery; personal characteristics; and force.
- Allocative efficiency occurs when resources are used to create the greatest value, which means that marginal benefit equals marginal cost.

2 **Distinguish between value and price and define consumer surplus.**

- Marginal benefit is measured by the maximum price that consumers are willing to pay for another unit of a good or service.
- A demand curve is a marginal benefit curve.
- Value is what people are *willing to* pay; price is what they *must* pay.
- Consumer surplus equals the excess of marginal benefit over price, summed over the quantity consumed.

3 **Distinguish between cost and price and define producer surplus.**

- Marginal cost is measured by the minimum price producers must be offered to increase production by one unit.
- A supply curve is a marginal cost curve.
- Opportunity cost is what producers *must* pay; price is what they *receive*.
- Producer surplus equals the excess of price over marginal cost, summed over the quantity produced.

4 **Evaluate the efficiency of the alternative methods of allocating resources.**

- In a competitive equilibrium, marginal benefit equals marginal cost and resource allocation is efficient.
- Price and quantity regulations, taxes, subsidies, externalities, public goods, common resources, monopoly, and high transactions costs lead to market failure and create deadweight loss.

5 **Explain the main ideas about fairness and evaluate the fairness of the alternative methods of allocating scarce resources.**

- Ideas about fairness divide into two groups: fair *results* and fair *rules*.
- Fair rules require private property rights and voluntary exchange, and fair results require income transfers from the rich to the poor.

Key Terms

Allocative efficiency, 141
Big tradeoff, 159
Command system, 139
Consumer surplus, 147

Deadweight loss, 155
Market failure, 155
Producer surplus, 150

Production possibilities frontier, 141
Total surplus, 153
Transactions costs, 157

CHAPTER CHECKPOINT

Study Plan Problems and Applications

At McDonald's, no reservations are accepted; at Puck's at the St. Louis Art Museum, reservations are accepted; at the Bissell Mansion restaurant, reservations are essential. Use this information to answer Problems **1** to **3**.

1. Describe the method of allocating table resources in these three restaurants.

2. Why do you think restaurants have different reservation policies, and why might each restaurant be using an efficient allocation method?

3. Why don't all restaurants use the market price to allocate their tables?

Table 1 shows the demand and supply schedules for sandwiches. Use Table 1 to work Problems **4** to **7**.

4. Calculate the equilibrium price of a sandwich, the consumer surplus, and the producer surplus. What is the efficient quantity of sandwiches?

5. If the quantity demanded decreases by 100 sandwiches an hour at each price, what is the equilibrium price and what is the change in total surplus?

6. If the quantity supplied decreases by 100 sandwiches an hour at each price, what is the equilibrium price and what is the change in total surplus?

7. If Sandwiches To Go, Inc., buys all the sandwich producers and cuts production to 100 sandwiches an hour, what is the deadweight loss that is created? If Sandwiches To Go, Inc., rations sandwiches to two per person, by what view of fairness would the allocation be unfair?

Use the following information to work Problems **8** and **9**.

Table 2 shows the demand and supply schedules for sandbags before and during a major flood. During the flood, suppose that the government gave all families an equal quantity of sandbags. Resale of sandbags is not permitted.

8. How would total surplus and the price of a sandbag change?

9. Would the outcome be more efficient than if the government took no action? Explain.

10. The winner of the men's or women's tennis singles at the U.S. Open is paid twice as much as the runner-up, but it takes two players to have a singles final. Is this compensation arrangement efficient? Is it fair? Explain why it might illustrate the big tradeoff.

Use the following information to work Problems **11** and **12**.

eBay saves billions for bidders

On eBay, the bidder who places the highest bid wins the auction and pays only what the second highest bidder offered. Researchers Wolfgang Jank and Galit Shmueli reported that purchasers on eBay in 2003 paid $7 billion less than their winning bids. Because each bid shows the buyer's willingness to pay, the winner receives an estimated consumer surplus of $4 or more.

Source: *InformationWeek*, January 28, 2008

11. What method is used to allocate goods on eBay? How does an eBay auction influence consumer surplus from the good?

12. Does the seller receive a producer surplus? Are auctions on eBay efficient?

TABLE 1

Price (dollars per sandwich)	Quantity demanded	Quantity supplied
	(sandwiches per hour)	
0	400	0
1	350	50
2	300	100
3	250	150
4	200	200
5	150	250
6	100	300
7	50	350
8	0	400

TABLE 2

Price (dollars per bag)	Quantity demanded before flood	Quantity demanded during flood	Quantity supplied
	(thousands of bags)		
0	40	70	0
1	35	65	5
2	30	60	10
3	25	55	15
4	20	50	20
5	15	45	25
6	10	40	30
7	5	35	35
8	0	30	40

Instructor Assignable Problems and Applications

Your instructor can assign these problems as homework, a quiz, or a test in MyEconLab.

1. **Panic in paradise: Are high fares the new reality for Hawaii?**

   On March 31, 2008, Hawaii lost 15 percent of its air service as Aloha Airlines and the cheap-flight airline ATA suddenly shut down. Stranded travelers were offered flights to West coast cities at $1,000 one way. Within a month, the fare to west coast cities dropped to about $200 a round trip. Stranded travelers complained of price gouging.

   Source: *USA Today*, April 23, 2008

   Under what conditions would the $1,000 fare be considered "price gouging"? Under what conditions would the $1,000 fare be an example of the market price method of allocating scarce airline seats?

Table 1 shows the demand schedule for haircuts and the supply schedule of haircuts. Use Table 1 to work Problems **2** and **3**.

2. What is the quantity of haircuts bought, the value of a haircut, and the total surplus from haircuts?

3. Suppose that all salons agree to charge $40 a haircut. What is the change in consumer surplus, the change in producer surplus, and the deadweight loss created?

In California, farmers pay a lower price for water than do city residents. Use this information to work Problems **4** to **6**.

4. What is this method of allocation of water resources? Is this allocation of water efficient? Is this use of scarce water fair? Why or why not?

5. If farmers were charged the same price as city residents pay, how would the price of agricultural produce, the quantity of produce grown, consumer surplus, and producer surplus change?

6. If all water in California is sold for the market equilibrium price, would the allocation of water be more efficient? Why or why not?

Use the following information to work Problems **7** and **8**.

The world's largest tulip and flower market

Every day over 19 million tulips and flowers are auctioned at the Dutch market called "The Bloemenveiling." These Dutch auctions match buyers and sellers.

Source: Tulip-Bulbs.com

In a Dutch auction, the auctioneer announces the highest price. If no one offers to buy the flowers, the auctioneer lowers the price until a buyer is found.

7. What method is used to allocate flowers at the Bloemenveiling?

8. How does a Dutch flower auction influence consumer surplus and producer surplus? Are the flower auctions at the Bloemenveiling efficient?

9. **New Zealand's private forests**

   In the early 1990s, the government auctioned half the national forests, converting these forests from public ownership to private ownership. The government's decision was an incentive to get the owners to operate like farmers—that is, take care of the resource and to use it to make a profit.

   Source: *Reuters*, September 7, 2007

   Was the timber industry efficient before the auction and did logging companies operate in the social interest or self-interest? What effect has private ownership had on efficiency of the timber industry?

TABLE 1

Price (dollars per haircut)	Quantity demanded	supplied
	(haircuts per day)	
0	100	0
10	80	0
20	60	20
30	40	40
40	20	60
50	0	80

MyEconLab

You can work this quiz in
Chapter 6 Study Plan and get
instant feedback.

Multiple Choice Quiz

1. The method of allocation that most stores use during Thanksgiving sales is:

   A. a combination of market price and lottery
   B. first-come, first-served
   C. a combination of contest and command
   D. a combination of market price and first-come, first-served

2. All of the following statements are correct *except* _____.

   A. the value of an additional unit of the good equals the marginal benefit from the good
   B. marginal benefit is the excess of value over the price paid, summed over the quantity consumed
   C. the maximum price willingly paid for a unit of a good is the marginal benefit from it
   D. price is what we pay for a good but value is what we get from it

3. Choose the best statement.

   A. An increase in the demand for a good increases producer surplus.
   B. If producers decrease the supply of the good, their producer surplus will increase.
   C. Producer surplus equals the total revenue from selling the good.
   D. Producer surplus is the excess of the value of the good over the market price, summed over the quantity produced.

4. The market for a good is efficient if _____.

   A. the marginal cost of producing the good is minimized
   B. the marginal benefit from the good is maximized
   C. the consumer surplus is maximized
   D. the total surplus is maximized

5. When the marginal benefit from a good exceeds its marginal cost, _____.

   A. there is overproduction of the good
   B. a deadweight loss, which is the excess of marginal benefit over marginal cost, arises
   C. producer surplus decreases and consumer surplus increases
   D. total production increases and efficiency increases

6. Market failure arises if _____.

   A. there is overproduction of the good but not if there is underproduction
   B. the deadweight loss is zero
   C. producer surplus exceeds consumer surplus
   D. total surplus is not maximized

7. The allocation of resources is fair _____.

   A. in the rules view if everyone has equal opportunity
   B. in the results view if most resources are distributed to the poorest people
   C. in the rules view if owners of the resources are protected by property rights and all transfers of resources are voluntary
   D. in the results view if resources are transferred voluntarily so that everyone has the same quantity

Can the President repeal the laws of supply and demand?

Government Actions in Markets

7

When you have completed your study of this chapter, you will be able to

1 Explain how a price ceiling works and show how a rent ceiling creates a housing shortage, inefficiency, and unfairness.

2 Explain how a price floor works and show how the minimum wage creates unemployment, inefficiency, and unfairness.

3 Explain how a price support in the market for an agricultural product creates a surplus, inefficiency, and unfairness.

167

7.1 PRICE CEILINGS

Price ceiling or price cap
A government regulation that places an *upper* limit on the price at which a particular good, service, or factor of production may be traded.

A **price ceiling** (also called a **price cap**) is a government regulation that places an *upper* limit on the price at which a particular good, service, or factor of production may be traded. Trading at a higher price is illegal.

A price ceiling has been used in several markets, but the one that looms largest in everyone's budget is the housing market. The price of housing is the rent that people pay for a house or apartment. Demand and supply in the housing market determine the rent and the quantity of housing available.

Figure 7.1 illustrates the apartment rental market in Biloxi, Mississippi. The rent is $550 a month, and 4,000 apartments are rented.

Suppose that Biloxi apartment rents have increased by $100 a month in the past two years and that a Citizens' Action Group asks the mayor to roll rents back.

■ A Rent Ceiling

Rent ceiling
A regulation that makes it illegal to charge more than a specified rent for housing.

Responding to the demand, the mayor imposes a **rent ceiling**—a regulation that makes it illegal to charge more than a specified rent for housing.

The effect of a rent ceiling depends on whether it is imposed at a level above or below the equilibrium rent. In Figure 7.1, if the rent ceiling is set *above* $550 a month, nothing would change because people are already paying $550 a month.

But a rent ceiling that is set *below* the equilibrium rent has powerful effects on the market outcome. The reason is that the rent ceiling attempts to prevent the rent from rising high enough to regulate the quantities demanded and supplied. The law and the market are in conflict, and one (or both) of them must yield.

■ FIGURE 7.1

A Housing Market

MyEconLab Animation

The figure shows the demand curve, *D*, and the supply curve, *S*, for rental housing.

❶ The market is in equilibrium when the quantity demanded equals the quantity supplied.

❷ The equilibrium price (rent) is $550 a month.

❸ The equilibrium quantity is 4,000 units of housing.

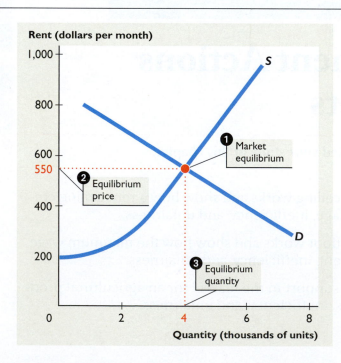

Figure 7.2 shows a rent ceiling that is set below the equilibrium rent at $400 a month. We've shaded the area *above* the rent ceiling because any rent in this region is illegal. The first effect of a rent ceiling is a housing shortage. At a rent of $400 a month, the quantity of housing supplied is 3,000 units and the quantity demanded is 6,000 units. So $400 a month, there is a shortage of 3,000 units of housing.

But the story does not end here. The 3,000 units of housing that owners are willing to make available must somehow be allocated among people who are seeking 6,000 units. This allocation might be achieved in two ways:

- A black market
- Increased search activity

A Black Market

A **black market** is an illegal market that operates alongside a government-regulated market. A rent ceiling sometimes creates a black market in housing as frustrated renters and landlords try to find ways of raising the rent above the legally imposed ceiling. Landlords want higher rents because they know that renters are willing to pay more for the existing quantity of housing. Renters are willing to pay more to jump to the front of the line.

Because raising the rent is illegal, landlords and renters use creative tricks to get around the law. One of these tricks is for a new tenant to pay a high price for worthless fittings—perhaps paying $2,000 for threadbare drapes. Another is for the tenant to pay a high price for new locks and keys—called "key money."

Figure 7.3 shows how high the black market rent might go in Biloxi. With strict enforcement of the rent ceiling, the quantity of housing available is 3,000

Black market
An illegal market that operates alongside a government-regulated market.

FIGURE 7.2

A Rent Ceiling Creates a Shortage

MyEconLab Animation

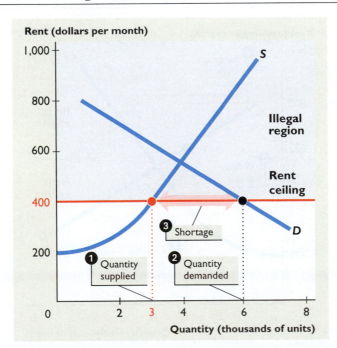

A rent ceiling is imposed below the equilibrium rent. In this example, the rent ceiling is $400 a month.

❶ The quantity of housing supplied decreases to 3,000 units.

❷ The quantity of housing demanded increases to 6,000 units.

❸ A shortage of 3,000 units arises.

units. But at this quantity, renters are willing to offer as much as $625 a month—the amount determined on the demand curve.

So a small number of landlords illegally offer housing for rents up to $625 a month. The black market rent might be at any level between the rent ceiling of $400 and the maximum that a renter is willing to pay of $625.

Increased Search Activity

Search activity
The time spent looking for someone with whom to do business.

The time spent looking for someone with whom to do business is called **search activity**. We spend some time in search activity almost every time we buy something, and especially when we buy a big item such as a car or a home. When a price ceiling creates a shortage of housing, search activity *increases*. In a rent-controlled housing market, frustrated would-be renters scan the newspapers. Keen apartment seekers race to be first on the scene when news of a possible apartment breaks.

The *opportunity cost* of a good is equal to its price *plus* the value of the search time spent finding the good. So the opportunity cost of housing is equal to the rent plus the value of the search time spent looking for an apartment. Search activity is costly. It uses time and other resources, such as telephones, automobiles, and gasoline that could have been used in other productive ways. In Figure 7.3, to find accommodation at $400 a month, someone who is willing to pay a rent of $625 a month would be willing to spend on search activity an amount that is equivalent to adding $225 a month to the rent ceiling.

A rent ceiling controls the rent portion of the cost of housing but not the search cost. So when the search cost is added to the rent, some people end up paying a higher opportunity cost for housing than they would if there were no rent ceiling.

■ FIGURE 7.3

A Rent Ceiling Creates a Black Market and Housing Search

MyEconLab Animation

With a rent ceiling of $400 a month,

❶ 3,000 units of housing are available.

❷ Someone is willing to pay $625 a month for the 3,000th unit of housing.

❸ Black market rent might be as high as $625 a month or search activity might be equivalent to adding $225 a month to the rent ceiling.

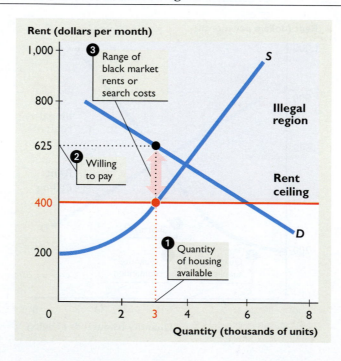

■ Are Rent Ceilings Efficient?

In a housing market with no rent ceiling, market forces determine the equilibrium rent. The quantity of housing demanded equals the quantity of housing supplied. In this situation, scarce housing resources are allocated efficiently because the marginal cost of housing equals the marginal benefit. Figure 7.4(a) shows this efficient outcome in the Biloxi apartment rental market. In this efficient market, total surplus—the sum of *consumer surplus* (the green area) and *producer surplus* (the blue area)—is maximized at the equilibrium rent and quantity of housing (see Chapter 6, p. 153).

Figure 7.4(b) shows that with a rent ceiling, the outcome is inefficient. Marginal benefit exceeds marginal cost. Producer surplus and consumer surplus shrink, and a deadweight loss (the gray area) arises. This loss is borne by the people who can't find housing and by landlords who can't offer housing at the lower rent ceiling.

But the total loss exceeds the deadweight loss. Resources get used in costly search activity or in evading the law in the black market. The value of these resources might be as large as the red rectangle. There is yet a further loss: the cost of enforcing the rent ceiling law. This loss, which is borne by taxpayers, is not visible in the figure.

■ **FIGURE 7.4**

The Inefficiency of a Rent Ceiling

MyEconLab Animation

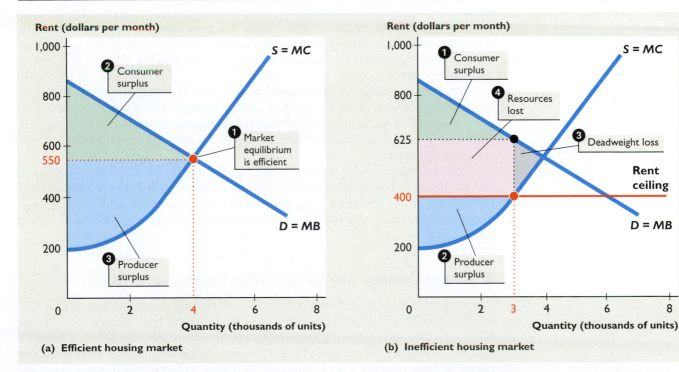

(a) Efficient housing market

(b) Inefficient housing market

❶ The market equilibrium is efficient with marginal benefit equal to marginal cost. Total surplus, the sum of ❷ consumer surplus (green area) and ❸ producer surplus (blue area), is maximized.

A rent ceiling is inefficient. ❶ Consumer surplus and ❷ producer surplus shrink, a ❸ deadweight loss arises, and ❹ resources are lost in search activity and evading the rent ceiling law.

With rent ceilings, landlords have no incentive to maintain buildings, and both the quality and quantity of housing supplied decrease.

Although a rent ceiling creates inefficiency, not everyone loses. The people who pay the rent ceiling get an increase in consumer surplus, and landlords who charge a black market rent get an increase in producer surplus.

The costs of a rent ceiling that we've just considered are only the initial costs. With the rent below the market equilibrium rent, landlords have no incentive to maintain their buildings. So over time, both the quality and quantity of housing supplied *decrease* and the loss arising from a rent ceiling increases.

The size of the loss from a rent ceiling depends on the elasticities of supply and demand. If supply is inelastic, a rent ceiling brings a small decrease in the quantity of housing supplied. And if demand is inelastic, a rent ceiling brings a small increase in the quantity of housing demanded. So the more inelastic the supply or the demand, the smaller is the shortage of housing and the smaller is the deadweight loss.

■ Are Rent Ceilings Fair?

We've seen that rent ceilings prevent scarce resources from being allocated efficiently—resources do not flow to their highest-valued use. But don't they ensure that scarce housing resources are allocated more fairly?

You learned in Chapter 6 (pp. 159–161) that fairness is a complex idea about which there are two broad views: fair *results* versus fair *rules.* Rent controls violate the fair rules view of fairness because they block voluntary exchange. But do they deliver a fair result? Do rent ceilings ensure that scarce housing goes to the poor people whose need is greatest?

Blocking rent adjustments that bring the quantity of housing demanded into equality with the quantity supplied doesn't end scarcity. So when the law prevents the rent from adjusting and blocks the price mechanism from allocating scarce housing, some other allocation mechanism must be used. If that mechanism were one that provided the housing to the poorest, then the allocation might be regarded as fair.

But the mechanisms that get used do not usually achieve such an outcome. First-come, first-served is one allocation mechanism. Discrimination based on race, ethnicity, or sex is another. Discrimination against young newcomers and in favor of old established families is yet another. None of these mechanisms delivers a fair outcome.

Rent ceilings in New York City provide examples of these mechanisms at work. The main beneficiaries of rent ceilings in New York City are families that have lived in the city for a long time—including some rich and famous ones. These families enjoy low rents while newcomers pay high rents for hard-to-find apartments.

■ If Rent Ceilings Are So Bad, Why Do We Have Them?

The economic case against rent ceilings is now widely accepted, so *new* rent ceiling laws are rare. But when governments try to repeal rent control laws, as the New York City government did in 1999, current renters lobby politicians to maintain the ceilings. Also, people who are prevented from finding housing would be happy if they got lucky and managed to find a rent-controlled apartment. For these reasons, there is plenty of political support for rent ceilings.

Apartment owners who oppose rent ceilings are a minority, so their views are not a powerful influence on politicians. Because more people support rent ceilings than oppose them, politicians are sometimes willing to support them too.

CHECKPOINT 7.1

Explain how a price ceiling works and show how a rent ceiling creates a housing shortage, inefficiency, and unfairness.

MyEconLab

You can work these problems in Study Plan 7.1 and get instant feedback.

Practice Problems

Figure 1 shows the rental market for apartments in Corsicana, Texas.

1. What is the rent and how many apartments are rented? If a rent ceiling of $900 a month is set, what is the rent and how many apartments are rented?

2. If the city government imposes a rent ceiling of $600 a month, what is the rent and how many apartments are rented? If a black market develops, how high could the black market rent be? Explain.

3. With a strictly enforced rent ceiling of $600 a month, is the housing market efficient? What is the deadweight loss? Is the housing market fair? Explain.

In the News

Rising oil prices worry U.S. finance chiefs

Tupperware's CFO says rising oil prices would cause the company to pay $15 million more for resin, which is based on oil, than it did a year ago. Resin prices are closely tied to the price of oil, which peaked at $114 a barrel in April.

Source: *The Wall Street Journal*, June 27, 2011

If the government puts a price cap on resin at today's price ($100 a barrel), explain why a shortage will occur. Which allocation method would most likely be used to distribute resin?

Solutions to Practice Problems

1. The equilibrium rent is $800 a month, and 3,000 apartments are rented. A rent ceiling of $900 a month is above the equilibrium rent, so the outcome is the market equilibrium rent of $800 a month with 3,000 apartments rented.

2. With the rent ceiling at $600 a month, the number of apartments rented is 1,000 and the rent is $600 a month (Figure 2). In a black market, some people are willing to rent an apartment for more than the rent ceiling. The highest rent that someone would offer is $1,200 a month. This rent equals someone's willingness to pay for the 1,000th apartment (Figure 2).

3. The housing market is not efficient. With 1,000 apartments rented, marginal benefit exceeds marginal cost and a deadweight loss arises (Figure 2). The deadweight loss equals to the area of the gray triangle, which is (1,200 − 600) × (3,000 − 1,000) ÷ 2. The deadweight loss is $600,000, The allocation of housing is less fair on both views of fairness: It blocks voluntary transactions and does not provide more housing to those most in need.

Solution to In the News

Resin is made from oil, so if the price of oil increases, then the cost of making resin increases, and the supply of resin decreases. The equilibrium price of resin rises. The higher equilibrium price will exceed the price cap of $100 a barrel, and there is a shortage of resin. Resin will most likely be allocated by first-come, first-served. Alternatively, the government could ration resin, in which case it would be allocated by command.

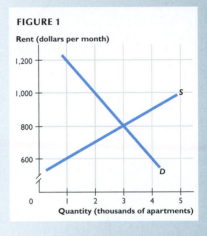

FIGURE 1

Rent (dollars per month)

Quantity (thousands of apartments)

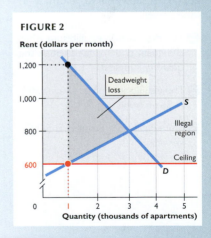

FIGURE 2

Rent (dollars per month)

Quantity (thousands of apartments)

7.2   PRICE FLOORS

Price floor
A government regulation that places a *lower* limit on the price at which a particular good, service, or factor of production may be traded.

A **price floor** is a government regulation that places a *lower* limit on the price at which a particular good, service, or factor of production may be traded. Trading at a lower price is illegal.

Price floors are used in many markets, but the one that looms largest is the labor market. The price of labor is the wage rate that people earn. Demand and supply in the labor market determine the wage rate and the quantity of labor employed.

Figure 7.5 illustrates the market for fast-food servers in Yuma, Arizona. In this market, the demand for labor curve is *D*. On this demand curve, at a wage rate of $10 an hour, the quantity of fast-food servers demanded is zero. If A&W, Burger King, Taco Bell, McDonald's, Wendy's, and the other fast-food places had to pay servers $10 an hour, they wouldn't hire any. They would replace servers with vending machines! But at wage rates below $10 an hour, they would hire servers. At a wage rate of $5 an hour, firms would hire 5,000 servers.

On the supply side of the market, no one is willing to work for $2 an hour. To attract servers, firms must pay more than $2 an hour.

Equilibrium in this market occurs at a wage rate of $5 an hour with 5,000 people employed as servers.

Suppose that the government thinks that no one should have to work for a wage rate as low as $5 an hour and decides that it wants to increase the wage rate. Can the government improve conditions for these workers by passing a minimum wage law? Let's find out.

■ **FIGURE 7.5**

A Market for Fast-Food Servers

MyEconLab Animation

The figure shows the demand curve, *D*, and the supply curve, *S*, for fast-food servers.

❶ The market is in equilibrium when the quantity demanded equals the quantity supplied.

❷ The equilibrium price (wage rate) is $5 an hour.

❸ The equilibrium quantity is 5,000 servers.

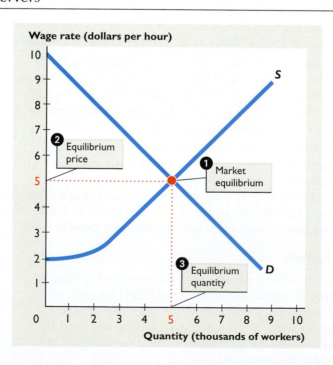

■ The Minimum Wage

A **minimum wage law** is a government regulation that makes hiring labor services for less than a specified wage illegal. Firms are free to pay a wage rate that exceeds the minimum wage but may not pay less than the minimum. A minimum wage is an example of a price floor.

The effect of a price floor depends on whether it is set below or above the equilibrium price. In Figure 7.5, the equilibrium wage rate is $5 an hour, and at this wage rate, firms hire 5,000 workers. If the government introduced a minimum wage below $5 an hour, nothing would change. The reason is that firms are already paying $5 an hour, and because this wage exceeds the minimum wage, the wage rate paid doesn't change. Firms continue to hire 5,000 workers.

But the aim of a minimum wage is to boost the incomes of low-wage earners. So in the markets for the lowest-paid workers, the minimum wage will exceed the equilibrium wage.

Suppose that the government introduces a minimum wage of $7 an hour. Figure 7.6 shows the effects of this law. Wage rates below $7 an hour are illegal, so we've shaded the illegal region *below* the minimum wage. Firms and workers are no longer permitted to operate at the equilibrium point in this market because it is in the illegal region. Market forces and political forces are in conflict.

The government can set a minimum wage, but it can't tell employers how many workers to hire. If firms must pay a wage rate of $7 an hour, they will hire only 3,000 workers. At the equilibrium wage rate of $5 an hour, firms hired 5,000 workers. So when the minimum wage is introduced, firms lay off 2,000 workers.

Minimum wage law

A government regulation that makes hiring labor services for less than a specified wage illegal.

■ FIGURE 7.6

A Minimum Wage Creates Unemployment

MyEconLab Animation

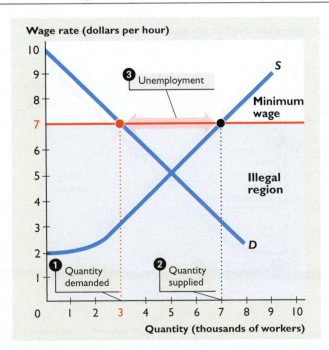

A minimum wage is introduced above the equilibrium wage rate. In this example, the minimum wage rate is $7 an hour.

❶ The quantity of labor demanded decreases to 3,000 workers.

❷ The quantity of labor supplied increases to 7,000 people.

❸ 4,000 people are unemployed.

But at a wage rate of $7 an hour, 2,000 people who didn't want to work for $5 an hour will now try to find work as servers. So at $7 an hour, the quantity supplied is 7,000 people. With 2,000 workers fired and another 2,000 looking for work at the higher wage rate, 4,000 people who would like to work as servers are unemployed.

The 3,000 jobs available must somehow be allocated among the 7,000 people who are willing to work as servers. How is this allocation achieved? The answer is by increased job-search activity and illegal hiring.

Increased Job-Search Activity

Finding a good job takes a great deal of time and other resources. With a minimum wage, more people are looking for jobs than the number of jobs available. Frustrated unemployed people spend time and other resources searching for hard-to-find jobs. In Figure 7.7, to find a job at $7 an hour, someone who is willing to work for $3 an hour (on the supply curve) would be willing to spend $4 an hour (the minimum wage rate of $7 an hour minus $3 an hour) on job-search activity. For a job that might last a year or more, this amount is large.

Illegal Hiring

With more people looking for work than the number of jobs available, some firms and workers might agree to do business at an illegal wage rate below the minimum wage in a black market. An illegal wage rate might be at any level between the minimum wage rate of $7 an hour and the lowest wage rate at which someone is willing to work, $3 an hour.

FIGURE 7.7

A Minimum Wage Creates Job Search and Illegal Hiring

MyEconLab Animation

The minimum wage rate is set at $7 an hour:

1 3,000 jobs are available.

2 The lowest wage rate for which someone is willing to work is $3 an hour. In a black market, illegal wage rates might be as low as $3 an hour.

3 The maximum that might be spent on job search is an amount equivalent to $4 an hour—the $7 they would receive if they found a job minus the $3 they are willing to work for.

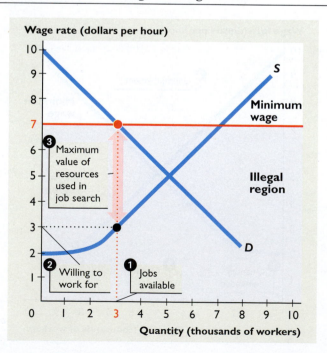

EYE on the U.S. ECONOMY
The Federal Minimum Wage

The *Fair Labor Standards Act* sets the federal minimum wage, but most states set their own minimum at a higher level than the federal minimum.

The figure shows the minimum wage since 1991 in terms of what it would buy at 2011 prices.

The minimum wage creates unemployment, but how much? Between 2007 and 2009, when the minimum wage increased by 38 percent (see figure), the employment of 16 to 19 year olds fell by 28 percent. Part of that increase most likely was caused by the rise in the minimum wage.

Most economists believe that a 10 percent rise in the minimum wage decreases teenage employment by between 1 and 3 percent.

David Card of the University of California at Berkeley and Alan Krueger of Princeton University have challenged this consensus view. They say that a rise in the minimum wage in California, New Jersey, and Texas *increased* the employment rate of low-income workers. They suggest three reasons why a rise in the wage rate might increase employment:

(1) Workers become more conscientious and productive.

(2) Workers are less likely to quit, so costly labor turnover is reduced.

(3) Managers make a firm's operations more efficient.

Most economists are skeptical about these ideas and say that if higher wages make workers more productive and reduce labor turnover, firms will freely pay workers a higher wage. They also argue that there are other explanations for the employment increase that Card and Krueger found.

Daniel Hamermesh of the University of Texas at Austin says that Card and Krueger got the timing wrong. Firms anticipated the wage rise and so cut employment before it occurred. Looking at employment changes after the minimum wage increased missed its main effect. Finis Welch of Texas A&M University and Kevin Murphy of the University of Chicago say that the employment effects that Card and Krueger found are caused by regional differences in economic growth, not by changes in the minimum wage.

Pizza delivery people gain from the minimum wage.

Also, looking only at employment misses the supply-side effect of the minimum wage. It brings an increase in the number of people who drop out of high school to look for work.

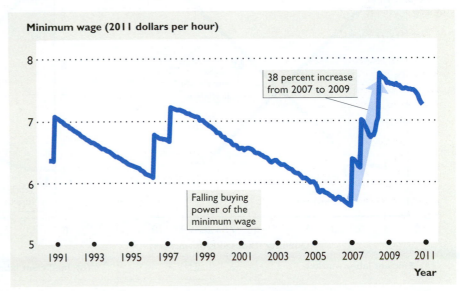

SOURCE OF DATA: Bureau of Labor Statistics.

◼ Is the Minimum Wage Efficient?

The efficient allocation of a factor of production is similar to that of a good or service, which you studied in Chapter 6. The demand for labor tells us about the marginal benefit of labor to the firms that hire it. Firms benefit because the labor they hire produces the goods or services that they sell. Firms are willing to pay a wage rate equal to the benefit they receive from an additional hour of labor. In Figure 7.8(a), the demand curve for labor tells us the marginal benefit that the firms in Yuma receive from hiring fast-food servers. The marginal benefit minus the wage rate is a surplus for the firms.

The supply of labor tells us about the marginal cost of working. To work, people must forgo leisure or working in the home, activities that they value. The wage rate received minus the marginal cost of working is a surplus for workers.

An efficient allocation of labor occurs when the marginal benefit to firms equals the marginal cost borne by workers. Such an allocation occurs in the labor market in Figure 7.8(a). Firms enjoy a surplus (the blue area), and workers enjoy a surplus (the green area). The sum of these surpluses is maximized.

Figure 7.8(b) shows the loss from a minimum wage. With a minimum wage of $7 an hour, 3,000 workers are hired. Marginal benefit exceeds marginal cost. The firms' surplus and workers' surplus shrink, and a deadweight loss (the gray area) arises. This loss falls on the firms that cut back employment and the people who can't find jobs at the higher wage rate.

◼ **FIGURE 7.8**

The Inefficiency of the Minimum Wage   MyEconLab Animation

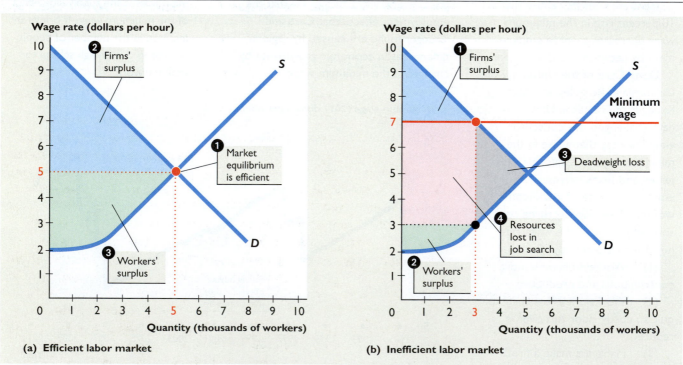

(a) **Efficient labor market**

(b) **Inefficient labor market**

❶ The market equilibrium is efficient with marginal benefit equal to marginal cost. The sum of ❷ the firms' surplus (blue area) and ❸ workers' surplus (green area) is maximized.

A minimum wage is inefficient. ❶ The firms' surplus and ❷ workers' surplus shrink, a ❸ deadweight loss arises, and ❹ resources are lost in job search.

But the total loss exceeds the deadweight loss. Resources get used in costly job-search activity as each unemployed person keeps looking for a job—writing letters, making phone calls, going to interviews, and so on. The value of these resources might be as large as the red rectangle.

■ Is the Minimum Wage Fair?

The minimum wage is unfair on both views of fairness: It delivers an unfair *result* and imposes unfair *rules*. The *result* is unfair because only those people who find jobs benefit. The unemployed end up worse off than they would be with no minimum wage. And those who get jobs were probably not the least well off. Personal characteristics, which means discrimination, allocates jobs and is another source of unfairness. The minimum wage imposes unfair *rules* because it blocks voluntary exchange. Firms are willing to hire more labor and people are willing to work more, but they are not permitted by the minimum wage law to do so.

■ If the Minimum Wage Is So Bad, Why Do We Have It?

Although the minimum wage is inefficient, not everyone loses from it. The people who find jobs at the minimum wage rate are better off. Other supporters of the minimum wage believe that the elasticities of demand and supply in the labor market are low, so not much unemployment results. Labor unions support the minimum wage because it puts upward pressure on all wage rates, including those of union workers. Nonunion labor is a substitute for union labor, so when the minimum wage rises, the demand for union labor increases.

EYE on PRICE REGULATION
Can the President Repeal the Laws of Supply and Demand?

The President has a powerful pen, but one that holds no magical powers. When the President signs a Bill or an Executive Order to bring in a new law or regulation, the outcome is not always exactly what was intended. A mismatch between intention and outcome is almost inevitable when a law or regulation seeks to block the laws of supply and demand.

You've seen the problems created by the federal minimum wage law, which leaves teenagers without jobs. There would also be problems at the other extreme of the labor market if the law tried to place a cap on executive pay.

In the spring of 2009, the "Cap Executive Officer Pay Act of 2009" was introduced in the Senate. The goal of the Act was to limit the compensation of executives and directors of firms receiving government handouts. The Act defined compensation broadly as all forms of cash receipts, property, and any perks. The cap envisaged was an annual compensation no greater than that of the President of the United States.

This Act never made it to the President's desk for his signature, but you can see some of the problems that would have risen if it had. Setting aside the difficult task of determining

the President's compensation (does it include the use of the White House and Air Force One?), placing a cap on executive pay would work like putting a ceiling on home rents that you've studied in this chapter. The quantity of executive services supplied would decrease and the most talented executives would seek jobs with the unregulated employers. The firms in the most difficulty—those receiving government funding—would face the added challenge of recruiting and keeping competent executives and directors. The deadweight loss from this action would be large. It is fortunate that the idea didn't have legs!

MyEconLab

You can work these problems in Study Plan 7.2 and get instant feedback.

FIGURE 1

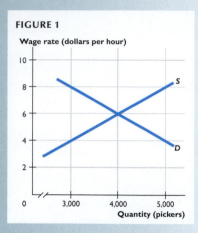

CHECKPOINT 7.2

Explain how a price floor works and show how the minimum wage creates unemployment, inefficiency, and unfairness.

Practice Problems

Figure 1 shows the market for tomato pickers in southern California.

1. What is the equilibrium wage rate and how many tomato pickers are employed? If California introduces a minimum wage of $4 an hour, how many tomato pickers are employed and how many are unemployed?

2. If California introduces a minimum wage of $8 an hour, how many tomato pickers are employed and how many are unemployed? What is the lowest wage that some workers might be able to earn if a black market develops?

3. Is the minimum wage of $8 an hour efficient? Who gains and who loses from the minimum wage of $8 an hour? Is it fair?

In the News

Hong Kong introduces a minimum wage

Hong Kong's first minimum wage is set at $HK28 an hour—$HK5 less than labor unions wanted, but $HK5 more than the employers had offered. About 315,000 people will be affected by the new wage.

Source: *The Economist*, January 11, 2011

What will be the effects of the minimum wage if the employers' offer is equal to the equilibrium wage? What will be the effects of the minimum wage if the labor unions' demand is equal to the equilibrium wage?

Solutions to Practice Problems

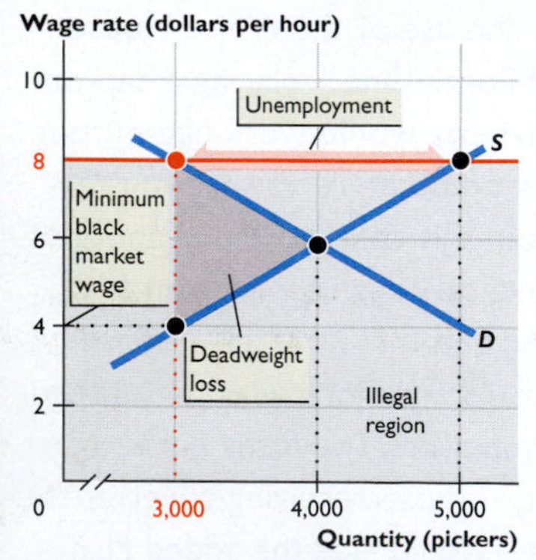

1. The equilibrium wage rate is $6 an hour, and 4,000 pickers are employed. The minimum wage of $4 an hour is below the equilibrium wage rate, so 4,000 tomato pickers are employed and no worker is unemployed.

2. The minimum wage of $8 an hour is above the equilibrium wage rate, so 3,000 pickers are employed (determined by the demand) and 5,000 people would like to work as pickers for $8 an hour (determined by the supply), so 2,000 are unemployed (Figure 2). If a black market developed, the lowest wage that someone might be able to earn would be $4 an hour (Figure 2).

3. The minimum wage of $8 an hour is not efficient because it creates a deadweight loss—the marginal benefit to growers exceeds the marginal cost to workers. Tomato pickers who find work at $8 an hour gain. Tomato growers and unemployed pickers lose. The minimum wage is unfair on both the fair rules and fair results views of fairness.

FIGURE 2

Wage rate (dollars per hour)

Solution to In the News

If the employers' offer of $HK23 an hour is the equilibrium wage rate, then the minimum wage exceeds the equilibrium wage and some of the 315,000 workers will become unemployed. If the union's demand of $HK33 an hour is the equilibrium wage rate, then the minimum wage is below the equilibrium wage and the minimum wage has no effect on the quantity of labor employed.

7.3 PRICE SUPPORTS IN AGRICULTURE

"The nation has got to eat," declared President George W. Bush when he asked Congress to spend $170 billion to support U.S. farmers. The United States is not alone among the advanced economies in spending billions of dollars each year on farm support. Governments in all the advanced economies do it, and none more than those of the European Union and Japan.

■ How Governments Intervene in Markets for Farm Products

The methods that governments use to support farms vary, but they almost always involve three elements:

- Isolate the domestic market from global competition
- Introduce a price floor
- Pay farmers a subsidy

Isolate the Domestic Market

A government can't regulate a market price without first isolating the domestic market from global competition. If the cost of production in the rest of the world is lower than that in the domestic economy and if foreign producers are free to sell in the domestic market, the forces of demand and supply drive the price down and swamp any efforts by the government to influence the price.

To isolate the domestic market, the government restricts imports from the rest of the world.

Introduce a Price Floor

A price floor in an agricultural market is called a **price support**, because the floor is maintained by a government guarantee to buy any surplus output at that price. You saw that a price floor in the labor market—a minimum wage—creates a surplus of labor that shows up as unemployment. A price support in an agricultural market also generates a surplus. At the support price, the quantity supplied exceeds the quantity demanded. What happens to the surplus makes the effects of a price support different from those of a minimum wage. The government buys the surplus.

Price support
A price floor in an agricultural market maintained by a government guarantee to buy any surplus output at that price.

Pay Farmers a Subsidy

A **subsidy** is a payment by the government to a producer to cover part of the cost of production. When the government buys the surplus produced by farmers, it provides them with a subsidy. Without the subsidy, farmers could not cover their costs because they would not be able to sell the surplus.

Let's see how a price support works.

Subsidy
A payment by the government to a producer to cover part of the cost of production.

■ Price Support: An Illustration

To see the effects of a price support, we'll look at the market for sugar beets. Both the United States and the European Union have price supports for sugar beets.

Figure 7.9 shows the market. This market is isolated from rest-of-world influences. The demand curve, D, tells us the quantities demanded at each price in the domestic economy only. And the supply curve, S, tells us the quantity supplied at each price by domestic farmers.

Free Market Reference Point

With no price support, the equilibrium price is $25 a ton and the equilibrium quantity is 25 million tons a year. The market is efficient only if the price in the rest of the world is also $25 a ton. If the price in the rest of the world is less than $25 a ton, it is efficient for the domestic farmers to produce less and for some sugar beets to be imported at the lower price (lower opportunity cost) available in the rest of the world. But if the price in the rest of the world exceeds $25 a ton, it is efficient for domestic farmers to increase production and export some sugar beets.

Price Support and Subsidy

Suppose the government introduces a price support and sets the support price at $35 a ton. To make the price support work, the government agrees to pay farmers $35 for every ton of sugar beets they produce and can't sell in the market.

The farmers produce the quantity shown by the market supply curve. At a price of $35 a ton, the quantity supplied is 30 million tons a year, so production increases to this amount.

Domestic users of sugar beets cut back their purchases. At $35 a ton, the quantity demanded is 20 million tons a year, and purchases decrease to this amount.

Because farmers produce a greater quantity than domestic users are willing to buy, something must be done with the surplus. If the farmers just dumped the surplus on the market, you can see what would happen. The price would fall to that at which consumers are willing to pay for the quantity produced.

To make the price support work, the government buys the surplus. In this example, the government buys 10 million tons for $35 a ton and provides a subsidy to the farmers of $350 million.

■ **FIGURE 7.9**

The Domestic Market for Sugar Beets

MyEconLab Animation

The market for sugar beets is isolated from global competition.

❶ With no intervention, the competitive equilibrium price is $25 a ton and the equilibrium quantity is 25 million tons a year.

❷ The government intervenes in this market and sets a support price at $35 a ton.

❸ The quantity produced increases to 30 million tons a year.

❹ The quantity bought by domestic users decreases to 20 million tons a year.

❺ The government buys the surplus of 10 million tons a year and pays farmers a subsidy of $350 million.

❻ A deadweight loss arises.

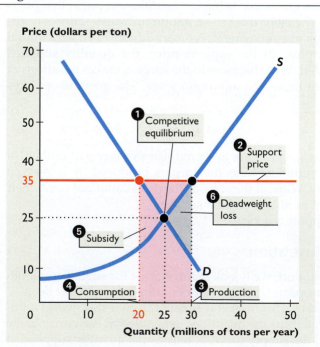

The price support increases farmers' total revenue. Without a subsidy, farmers would receive a total revenue of $625 million ($25 a ton multiplied by 25 million tons). With a subsidy, they receive a total revenue of $1,050 million ($35 a ton multiplied by 30 million tons).

The price support is inefficient because it creates a deadweight loss. Farmers gain but consumers, who are also the tax-payers who end up paying the subsidy, lose. And consumers' losses exceed the farmers' gains by the amount of the deadweight loss.

Effects on the Rest of the World

The rest of the world receives a double-whammy from price supports. First, import restrictions in advanced economies deny developing economies access to the food markets of the advanced economies. The result is lower prices and smaller farm production in the developing economies.

Second, the surplus produced in the advanced economies gets sold in the rest of the world. Both the price and the quantity produced in the rest of the world are depressed even further.

The subsidies received by U.S. farmers are paid not only by U.S. taxpayers and consumers but also by poor farmers in the developing economies.

We explore global markets in action in Chapter 9. There you will see other ways in which intervention in markets brings inefficiencies and redistributes the gains from trade.

EYE on YOUR LIFE
Price Ceilings and Price Floors

Price ceilings and price floors operate in many of the markets in which you trade, and they require you to take a stand as a citizen and voter.

Unless you live in New York City, you're not likely to live in a rent controlled house or apartment. Because economists have explained the unwanted effects of rent ceilings that you've learned about in this chapter, this type of market intervention is now rare.

But you run into a price ceiling almost every time you use a freeway.

The zero price for using a freeway is a type of price ceiling. The next time you're stuck in traffic and moving at a crawl, think about how a free market in road use would cut the congestion and allow you to zip along.

In Singapore, a transponder on your dashboard would be clocking up the dollars and cents as you drive around the city. The price varies with the time of day, the traffic density, and where in the city you are. As a result, you would never be stuck in slow-moving traffic.

You encounter a price floor in the labor market. Have you wanted a job and been willing and available to work, but unable to get hired? Would you have taken a job for a slightly lower wage if one had been available?

You also encounter price floors (price supports) in markets for food. You pay more for tomatoes, sugar, oranges, and many other food items than the minimum cost of producing them.

Develop your own policy position on price floors and price ceilings.

FIGURE 1

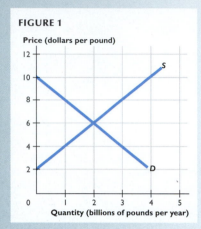

Price (dollars per pound)

Quantity (billions of pounds per year)

CHECKPOINT 7.3

Explain how a price support in the market for an agricultural product creates a surplus, inefficiency, and unfairness.

Practice Problems

Figure 1 shows the market for tomatoes.

1. What are the equilibrium price and quantity of tomatoes? Is the market for tomatoes efficient?

2. If the government introduces a price support at $8 per pound, what is the quantity of tomatoes produced, the quantity demanded, and the subsidy received by tomato farmers?

3. With a price support set at $8 per pound, is the market for tomatoes efficient? Who gains and who loses from the price support? What is the deadweight loss? Could the price support be regarded as being fair?

In the News

French farmers man the blockades in Brussels

Farmers want the dairy industry to guarantee a minimum (powdered) milk price of 300 euros a ton—against 210 euros a ton this month. Max Bottier, a dairy farmer in Normandy, said that he needs 300 euros a ton to break even.

Source: *The Times*, May 26, 2009

If a support price for milk is set at 300 euros a ton, how will the quantity of milk produced and the quantity bought by consumers change? Who buys the surplus? Will the European milk market be more or less efficient than it is today?

Solutions to Practice Problems

1. The equilibrium price is $6 a pound; the equilibrium quantity is 2 billion pounds. The market is efficient—marginal benefit equals marginal cost.

2. At a support price of $8 a pound, 3 billion pounds are produced and 1 billion pounds are demanded, so there is a surplus of 2 billion pounds (Figure 2). The subsidy is $8 per pound on 2 billion pounds, which is $16 billion.

3. The market is not efficient because at the quantity produced, the marginal benefit (on the demand curve) is less than the marginal cost (on the supply curve). Farmers gain. They produce more and receive a higher price on what they sell in the market as well as the government subsidy. Consumers/taxpayers lose. They pay more for tomatoes and pay taxes to fund the subsidy. The deadweight loss is $2 billion (the area of the gray triangle). The outcome is unfair on both views of fairness unless farmers are poorer than consumers, in which case it might be fair to boost farmers' incomes.

FIGURE 2

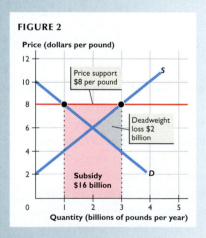

Price (dollars per pound)

Price support $8 per pound

Deadweight loss $2 billion

Subsidy $16 billion

Quantity (billions of pounds per year)

Solution to In the News

The market price of powdered milk is 210 euros a ton. A support price of 300 euros a ton will increase the quantity supplied, decrease the quantity demanded, and create a surplus of milk. To maintain the price at 300 euros a ton, the government will have to buy the surplus at the support price. The market will be less efficient because it creates a deadweight loss.

CHAPTER SUMMARY

Key Points

1 Explain how a price ceiling works and show how a rent ceiling creates a housing shortage, inefficiency, and unfairness.

- A price ceiling set above the equilibrium price has no effects.
- A price ceiling set below the equilibrium price creates a shortage and increased search activity or a black market.
- A price ceiling is inefficient and unfair.
- A rent ceiling is an example of a price ceiling.

2 Explain how a price floor works and show how the minimum wage creates unemployment, inefficiency, and unfairness.

- A price floor set below the equilibrium price has no effects.
- A price floor set above the equilibrium price creates a surplus and increased search activity or illegal trading.
- A price floor is inefficient and unfair.
- A minimum wage is an example of a price floor.

3 Explain how a price support in the market for an agricultural product creates a surplus, inefficiency, and unfairness.

- A price support increases the quantity produced, decreases the quantity consumed, and creates a surplus.
- To maintain the support price, the government buys the surplus and subsidizes the producer.
- A price support benefits the producer but costs the consumer/taxpayer more than the producer gains—it creates a deadweight loss.
- A price support is inefficient and is usually unfair.

Key Terms

Black market, 169
Minimum wage law, 175
Price cap, 168
Price ceiling, 168
Price floor, 174

Price support, 181
Rent ceiling, 168
Search activity, 170
Subsidy, 181

MyEconLab

You can work these problems in Chapter 7 Study Plan and get instant feedback.

TABLE 1

Rent (dollars per month)	Quantity demanded	Quantity supplied
	(rooms)	
500	2,500	2,000
550	2,250	2,000
600	2,000	2,000
650	1,750	2,000
700	1,500	2,000
750	1,250	2,000

TABLE 2

Wage rate (dollars per hour)	Quantity demanded	Quantity supplied
	(student workers)	
10.00	600	300
10.50	500	350
11.00	400	400
11.50	300	450
12.00	200	500
12.50	100	550

TABLE 3

Price (dollars per pound)	Quantity demanded	Quantity supplied
	(pounds per week)	
1.00	5,000	2,000
2.00	4,500	2,500
3.00	4,000	3,000
4.00	3,500	3,500
5.00	3,000	4,000
6.00	2,500	4,500

CHAPTER CHECKPOINT

Study Plan Problems and Applications

Table 1 shows the demand and supply schedules for on-campus housing. Use Table 1 to work Problems **1** to **3**.

1. If the college puts a rent ceiling on rooms of $650 a month, what is the rent, how many rooms are rented, and is the on-campus housing market efficient?

2. If the college puts a strictly enforced rent ceiling on rooms of $550 a month, what is the rent, how many rooms are rented, and is the on-campus housing market efficient? Explain why or why not.

3. Suppose that with a strictly enforced rent ceiling on rooms of $550 a month, a black market develops. How high could the black market rent be and would the on-campus housing market be fair? Explain your answer.

Use Table 2, which shows the demand and supply schedules for student workers at on-campus venues, to work Problems **4** to **6**.

4. If the college introduces a minimum wage of $10.50 an hour, how many students are employed at on-campus venues and how many are unemployed?

5. If the college introduces a strictly enforced minimum wage of $11.50 an hour, how many students are employed, how many are unemployed, and what is the lowest wage at which some students would be willing to work?

6. If the college introduces a strictly enforced minimum wage of $11.50 an hour, who gains and who loses from the minimum wage, and is the campus labor market efficient or fair?

Use Table 3, which shows the demand and supply schedules for mushrooms, to work Problems **7** and **8**.

7. Suppose that the government introduces a price support for mushrooms of $4 per pound. What are the quantity of mushrooms produced, the surplus of mushrooms, and the deadweight loss created?

8. Suppose that the government introduces a price support for mushrooms of $6 per pound. Who gains and who loses? What are the quantity of mushrooms produced, the surplus of mushrooms, and the deadweight loss?

Use the following news clip to work Problems **9** and **10**.

Coal shortage at China plants

The government of China has set price controls on coal and gasoline in an attempt to shield poor urban families and farmers from rising world energy prices. Chinese power plants have run short of coal, sales of luxury, gas-guzzling cars have increased, and gasoline consumption has risen. Oil refiners are incurring losses and plan to cut production.

Source: CNN, May 20, 2008

9. Are China's price controls price floors or price ceilings? Draw a graph to illustrate the shortages of coal and gasoline created by the price controls.

10. Explain how China's price controls have changed consumer surplus, producer surplus, total surplus, and the deadweight loss in the markets for coal and gasoline. Draw a graph to illustrate your answer.

Instructor Assignable Problems and Applications

Your instructor can assign these problems as homework, a quiz, or a test in MyEconLab.

1. Suppose that Congress caps executive pay at a level below the equilibrium.
    * Explain how the quantity of executives demanded, the quantity supplied, and executive pay will change, and explain why the outcome is inefficient.
    * Draw a graph of the market for corporate executives. On your graph, show the market equilibrium, the pay cap, the quantity of executives supplied and the quantity demanded at the pay cap, and the deadweight loss created. Also show the highest pay that an executive might be offered in a black market.

Use the following information to work Problems **2** to **4**.

Concerned about the political fallout from rising gas prices, suppose that the U.S. government imposes a price ceiling of $3.00 a gallon on gasoline.

2. Explain how the market for gasoline would react to this price ceiling if the oil-producing nations increased production and drove the equilibrium price of gasoline to $2.50 a gallon. Would the U.S. gasoline market be efficient?

3. Explain how the market for gasoline would react to this price ceiling if a global shortage of oil sent the equilibrium price of gasoline to $3.50 a gallon. Would the U.S. gasoline market be efficient?

4. Under what conditions would the price ceiling create lines at the pumps?

5. Suppose the government introduced a ceiling on lawyers' fees. How would the amount of work done by lawyers, the consumer surplus of people who hire lawyers, and the producer surplus of law firms change? Would this fee ceiling result in an efficient and fair use of resources? Why or why not?

Use the following information to work Problems **6** and **7**.

Australian unions lobbying for $21 wage rise for lowest paid
Australia's Fair Trade Commission (FTC) sets the minimum wage for the year. In 2008, the minimum wage was set at $544 a week. In the current negotiations, unions are lobbying for a $21 a week rise and businesses for a $8 a week rise.
Source: *Bloomberg*, March 23, 2009

Suppose that in 2009 the equilibrium wage turns out to be $560 a week.

6. If the FTC raises the minimum wage by $8 a week, what wage per week will low-skilled workers be paid? Will the outcome be efficient?

7. If the FTC raises the minimum wage by $21 a week, what wage per week will low-skilled workers be paid? Will the outcome be efficient?

Use the following information to work Problems **8** and **9**.

Crop prices erode farm subsidy program
High corn and soybean prices mean farmers are making the most money in their lives. The reason: Grain prices are far too high to trigger payouts under the U.S. primary farm-subsidy program's "price support" formula. The market has done what Congress couldn't do and that is "slash farm subsidies."
Source: *The Wall Street Journal*, July 25, 2011

8. Draw a graph to illustrate the soybean market when the soybean price was low. Show the quantity of soybeans produced, the subsidy farmers received, and the deadweight loss created.

9. In the market for corn with a price support, explain why the corn price has risen and ended up being too high to "trigger payouts."

Multiple Choice Quiz

1. A rent ceiling creates a _____ of housing if it _____ the equilibrium rent.

   A. surplus; is less than
   B. shortage; is less than
   C. surplus; exceeds
   D. shortage; exceeds

2. A price ceiling imposed below the equilibrium price _____.

   A. creates a black market in which the price might equal or exceed the equilibrium price
   B. creates a black market in which the price equals the price ceiling
   C. leads to increased search activity, which reduces the shortage of the good
   D. increases the demand for the good, which makes the shortage even larger

3. A price ceiling is _____ if it is set _____ the market equilibrium price.

   A. efficient and fair; below
   B. unfair but efficient; equal to
   C. efficient and unfair; above
   D. inefficient and unfair; below

4. A price floor influences the outcome of a market if it is _____.

   A. set below the equilibrium price
   B. set above the equilibrium price
   C. an incentive for buyers to increase demand for the good
   D. an incentive for sellers to decrease supply of the good

5. A minimum wage set above the market equilibrium wage rate _____.

   A. increases both employment and the quantity of labor supplied
   B. decreases unemployment and raises the wage rate of those employed
   C. raises the wage rate of those employed and increases the supply of jobs
   D. increases unemployment and decreases employment

6. A minimum wage is _____.

   A. efficient if the wage paid rises and more people look for jobs
   B. inefficient if workers' surplus decreases and firms' surplus increases
   C. inefficient if job search increases and total surplus decreases
   D. efficient if workers' surplus increases and firms' surplus decreases

7. A support price set above the equilibrium price _____.

   A. creates a shortage, increases farmers' total revenue, and is efficient
   B. creates a surplus, which the government buys and dumps on the rest of the world to keep the U.S. market price equal to the price support
   C. is inefficient because farmers' marginal cost exceeds U.S. consumers' marginal benefit
   D. is efficient because farmers' marginal cost equals U.S. consumers' marginal benefit

8. Choose the best statement.

   A. A subsidy to peanut growers lowers peanut growers' costs, lowers the market price of peanuts, and increases the demand for peanuts.
   B. A price support for peanut growers is a guaranteed price for peanuts, which increases the quantity of peanuts produced.
   C. A price support and a subsidy to peanut growers will make the peanut market more efficient if the support price is below the market price.
   D. For a support price set above the equilibrium price to increase peanut growers' incomes, they must also receive a subsidy.

Does Congress decide who pays the taxes?

Taxes

When you have completed your study of this chapter, you will be able to

1 Explain how taxes change prices and quantities, are shared by buyers and sellers, and create inefficiency.

2 Explain how income taxes and Social Security taxes change wage rates and employment, are shared by employers and workers, and create inefficiency.

3 Review ideas about the fairness of the tax system.

CHAPTER CHECKLIST

8.1 TAXES ON BUYERS AND SELLERS

Almost every time you buy something—a late-night order of chow mein, a plane ticket, a tank of gasoline—you pay a tax. On some items, you pay a sales tax that is added to the advertised price. On other items, you pay an excise tax—often at a high rate like the tax on gasoline—that is included in the advertised price.

But do you really pay these taxes? When a tax is added to the advertised price, isn't it obvious that *you* pay the tax? Isn't the price higher than it otherwise would be by an amount equal to the tax?

What about a tax that is buried in the price, such as that on gasoline? Who pays that tax? Does the seller just pass on the full amount of the tax to you, the buyer? Or does the seller pay the tax by taking a lower price and leaving the price you pay unchanged?

To answer these questions, let's suppose that TIFS, the Tax Illegal File Sharing lobby, has persuaded the government to collect a $10 tax on every new MP3 player and to use the tax revenue to compensate artists. But an argument is raging between those who claim that the buyer benefits from using the MP3 player and should pay the tax and those who claim that the seller profits and should pay the tax.

■ Tax Incidence

Tax incidence is the division of the burden of a tax between the buyer and the seller. We're going to find the incidence of a $10 tax on MP3 players with two different taxes: a tax on the buyer and a tax on the seller.

Figure 8.1 shows the market for MP3 players. With no tax, the equilibrium price is $100 and the equilibrium quantity is 5,000 players a week.

When a good is taxed, it has two prices: a price that excludes the tax and a price that includes the tax. Buyers respond only to the price that includes the tax, because that is the price they pay. Sellers respond only to the price that excludes the tax, because that is the price they receive. The tax is like a wedge between these two prices.

Figure 8.1(a) shows what happens if the government taxes the buyer. The tax doesn't change the buyer's willingness and ability to pay. The demand curve, *D*, tells us the *total* amount that buyers are willing and able to pay. Because buyers must pay $10 to the government on each item bought, the red curve *D − tax* tells us what the buyers are willing to pay to the sellers. The red curve, *D − tax*, lies $10 *below* the blue demand curve.

Market equilibrium occurs where the red *D − tax* curve intersects the supply curve, *S*. The buyer pays the equilibrium net-of-tax price $95 plus the $10 tax: $105. The seller receives the net-of-tax price $95. The government collects a tax revenue of $10 a player on 2,000 players, or $20,000 (shown by the purple rectangle).

Figure 8.1(b) shows what happens if the government taxes the seller. The tax acts like an increase in the suppliers' cost, so supply decreases and the supply curve shifts to the red curve labeled *S + tax*. This curve tells us what sellers are willing to accept, given that they must pay the government $10 on each item sold. The red curve, *S + tax*, lies $10 *above* the blue supply curve.

Market equilibrium occurs where the red *S + tax* curve intersects the demand curve, *D*. The buyer pays the equilibrium price $105. The seller receives the net-of-tax price $95. The government collects a tax revenue of $20,000.

In both cases, the buyer and the seller split the $10 tax and pay $5 each.

Does "tax free" really mean that the seller pays the tax?

Tax incidence
The division of the burden of a tax between the buyer and the seller.

FIGURE 8.1

A Tax on MP3 Players

MyEconLab Animation

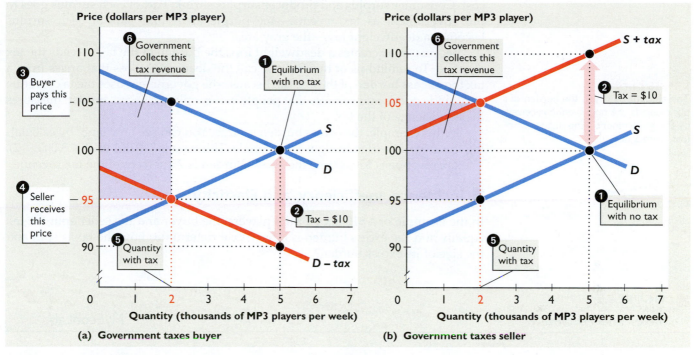

(a) Government taxes buyer

(b) Government taxes seller

❶ In both parts of the figure, with no tax, the price of an MP3 player is $100 and 5,000 players a week are bought.

❷ In part (a), a $10 tax on buyers of MP3 players shifts the demand curve down to D − tax and in part (b), a $10 tax on sellers of MP3 players shifts the supply curve up to S + tax.

In both parts of the figure:

❸ The price paid by the buyer rises to $105—an increase of $5;

❹ The price received by the seller falls to $95—a decrease of $5;

❺ The quantity decreases to 2,000 players a week; and

❻ The government collects tax revenue of $20,000 a week—the purple rectangle.

In both cases, the burden of the tax is split equally between the buyer and the seller—each pays $5 per player.

You can now see that the argument about making the buyer pay or the seller pay is futile. The buyer pays the same price, the seller receives the same price, and the government receives the same tax revenue on the same quantity regardless of whether the government taxes the buyer or the seller.

In this example, the buyer and the seller share the burden of the tax equally. But in most cases, the burden will be shared unequally and might even fall entirely on one side of the market. We'll explore what determines the incidence of a tax, but first, let's see how a tax creates inefficiency.

■ Taxes and Efficiency

You've seen that resources are used efficiently when marginal benefit equals marginal cost. You've also seen that a tax places a wedge between the price the buyer pays and the price the seller receives. But the buyer's price equals marginal benefit and the seller's price equals marginal cost. So a tax puts a wedge between marginal benefit and marginal cost. The equilibrium quantity is less than the efficient quantity, and a deadweight loss arises.

Figure 8.2 shows the inefficiency of a tax. We'll assume that the government taxes the seller. In part (a), with no tax, marginal benefit equals marginal cost and the market is efficient. In part (b), with a tax, marginal benefit exceeds marginal cost. Consumer surplus and producer surplus shrink. Part of each surplus goes to the government as tax revenue—the purple area—and part of each surplus becomes a deadweight loss—the gray area.

Because a tax creates a deadweight loss, the burden of the tax exceeds the tax revenue. To remind us of this fact, we call the deadweight loss that arises from a tax the **excess burden** of the tax. But because the government uses the tax revenue to provide goods and services that people value, only the excess burden measures the inefficiency of the tax.

In this example, the excess burden is large. You can see how large by calculating the area of the deadweight loss triangle. This area is $15,000 ($10 × 3,000 ÷ 2). The tax revenue is $20,000, so the excess burden is 75 percent of the tax revenue.

Excess burden

The amount by which the burden of a tax exceeds the tax revenue received by the government—the deadweight loss from a tax.

■ Incidence, Inefficiency, and Elasticity

In the example of a $10 tax on MP3 players, the buyer and the seller split the tax equally and the excess burden is large. What determines how the tax is split and the size of its excess burden?

■ **FIGURE 8.2**

Taxes and Efficiency

MyEconLab Animation

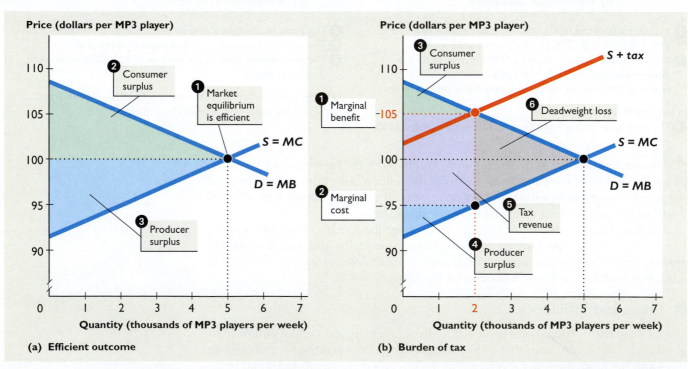

(a) Efficient outcome

(b) Burden of tax

❶ The market is efficient with marginal benefit equal to marginal cost. Total surplus—the sum of ❷ consumer surplus (green area) and ❸ producer surplus (blue area)—is at its maximum possible level.

A $10 tax drives a wedge between ❶ marginal benefit and ❷ marginal cost. ❸ Consumer surplus and ❹ producer surplus shrink by the amount of the ❺ tax revenue plus the ❻ deadweight loss. The deadweight loss is the excess burden of the tax.

The incidence of a tax and its excess burden depend on the elasticities of demand and supply in the following ways:

- For a given elasticity of supply, the more inelastic the demand for the good, the larger is the share of the tax paid by the buyer.
- For a given elasticity of demand, the more inelastic the supply of the good, the larger is the share of the tax paid by the seller.
- The excess burden is smaller, the more inelastic is demand *or* supply.

■ Incidence, Inefficiency, and the Elasticity of Demand

To see how the division of a tax between the buyer and the seller and the size of the excess burden depend on the elasticity of demand, we'll look at two extremes.

Perfectly Inelastic Demand: Buyer Pays and Efficient

Figure 8.3(a) shows the market for insulin, a vital daily medication of diabetics. Demand is perfectly inelastic at 100,000 doses a week, as shown by the vertical demand curve. With no tax, the price is $2 a dose. A 20¢ a dose tax raises the price to $2.20, but the quantity does not change. The tax leaves the price received by the seller unchanged but raises the price paid by the buyer by the entire tax. The outcome is efficient (there is no deadweight loss) because marginal benefit equals marginal cost.

Perfectly Elastic Demand: Seller Pays and Inefficient

Figure 8.3(b) shows the market for pink marker pens. Demand is perfectly elastic at $1 a pen, as shown by the horizontal demand curve. If pink pens are less expensive than other pens, everyone uses pink. If pink pens are more expensive than other pens, no one uses a pink pen. With no tax, the price of a pink pen is $1 and the quantity is 4,000 pens a week. A 10¢ a pen tax leaves the price at $1 a pen, but

■ FIGURE 8.3

Incidence, Inefficiency, and the Elasticity of Demand   MyEconLab Animation

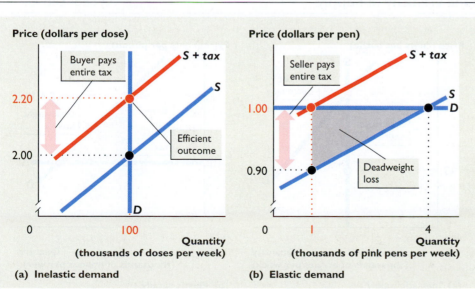

(a) Inelastic demand

(b) Elastic demand

In part (a), the demand for insulin is perfectly inelastic. A tax of 20¢ a dose raises the price by 20¢, and the buyer pays all the tax. But marginal benefit still equals marginal cost, so the outcome is efficient.

In part (b), the demand for pink marker pens is perfectly elastic. A tax of 10¢ a pen lowers the price received by the seller by 10¢, and the seller pays all the tax. Marginal benefit exceeds marginal cost, so the outcome is inefficient. The deadweight loss is the excess burden of the tax and measures its inefficiency.

the quantity decreases to 1,000 a week. The price paid by the buyer is unchanged and the seller pays the entire tax. The outcome is inefficient because marginal benefit exceeds marginal cost and a deadweight loss arises.

■ Incidence, Inefficiency, and the Elasticity of Supply

To see how the division of a tax between the buyer and the seller depends on the elasticity of supply, we'll again look at two extremes.

Perfectly Inelastic Supply: Seller Pays and Efficient

Figure 8.4(a) shows the market for spring water that flows at a constant rate that can't be controlled. Supply is perfectly inelastic at 100,000 bottles a week, as shown by the vertical supply curve. With no tax, the price is 50¢ a bottle and the 100,000 bottles that flow from the spring are bought. A tax of 5¢ a bottle leaves the quantity unchanged at 100,000 bottles a week. Buyers are willing to buy 100,000 bottles a week only if the price is 50¢ a bottle. The price remains at 50¢ a bottle, but the tax lowers the price received by the seller by 5¢ a bottle. The seller pays the entire tax.

Because marginal benefit equals marginal cost, there is no deadweight loss and the outcome is efficient.

Perfectly Elastic Supply: Buyer Pays and Inefficient

Figure 8.4(b) shows the market for sand from which computer-chip makers extract silicon. Supply of this sand is perfectly elastic at a price of 10¢ a pound as shown by the horizontal supply curve. With no tax, the price is 10¢ a pound and 5,000 pounds a week are bought. A 1¢ a pound sand tax raises the price to 11¢, and the quantity decreases to 3,000 pounds a week. The buyer pays the entire tax.

Because marginal benefit exceeds marginal cost, a deadweight loss arises and the outcome is inefficient.

■ **FIGURE 8.4**

Incidence, Inefficiency, and the Elasticity of Supply   MyEconLab Animation

In part (a), the supply of bottled spring water is perfectly inelastic. A tax of 5¢ a bottle lowers the price received by the seller by 5¢ a bottle, and the seller pays all the tax. Marginal benefit equals marginal cost, so the outcome is efficient.

In part (b), the supply of sand is perfectly elastic. A tax of 1¢ a pound increases the price by 1¢ a pound, and the buyer pays all the tax. Marginal benefit exceeds marginal cost, so the outcome is inefficient. The deadweight loss is the excess burden of the tax and measures its inefficiency.

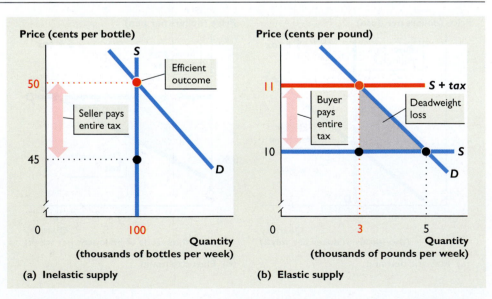

(a) Inelastic supply

(b) Elastic supply

CHECKPOINT 8.1

Explain how taxes change prices and quantities, are shared by buyers and sellers, and create inefficiency.

MyEconLab
You can work these problems in Study Plan 8.1 and get instant feedback.

Practice Problems

Figure 1 shows the market for basketballs in which basketballs are not taxed.

1. If buyers of basketballs are taxed $6 a ball, what price does the buyer pay and how many do they buy? What is the tax revenue collected?

2. If sellers of basketballs are taxed $6 a ball, what price does the seller receive and how many do they sell? What is the tax revenue collected?

3. If basketballs are taxed at $6 a ball, what is the excess burden of the tax? Is the demand for basketballs or the supply of basketballs more inelastic? Explain your answer.

In the News

Biggest U.S. tax hike on tobacco takes effect

The tax on cigarettes has risen from 39¢ to $1.01 a pack—an increase of 62¢ a pack. Before the tax hike, cigarettes were $5 a pack. In the past, a price increase of 10 percent cut cigarette consumption by 4 percent. With this new tax, at least 1 million of the 45 million smokers are expected to quit.
Source: USA Today, April 3, 2009

Is the demand for cigarettes elastic or inelastic? Will the price rise to $5.62 a pack? Who pays most of the tax increase—smokers or tobacco companies?

Solutions to Practice Problems

1. With a $6 tax on buyers, the demand curve shifts downward by $6 a ball as shown in Figure 2. The price that the buyer pays is $16 a basketball and 8 million basketballs a week are bought. The tax revenue is $6 × 8 million, which is $48 million a week (the purple rectangle in Figure 2).

2. With a $6 tax on sellers, the supply curve shifts upward by $6 a ball as shown in Figure 3. The price that the seller receives is $10 a basketball and 8 million basketballs a week are sold (Figure 3). The tax revenue is $6 × 8 million, which is $48 million a week (the purple rectangle in Figure 3).

3. The excess burden of the tax is $12 million. Excess burden equals the deadweight loss, the gray triangle, which is 4 million balls × $6 a ball ÷ 2. The $6 tax increases the price paid by buyers by $1 and lowers the price received by sellers by $5. Because the seller pays the larger share of the tax, the supply of basketballs is more inelastic than the demand for basketballs.

Solution to In the News

If a 10 percent price increase decreases consumption by 4 percent, the price elasticity of demand for cigarettes is 4/10, or 0.4. The demand for cigarettes is inelastic. With the demand inelastic, the 62¢ tax increase will not increase the price to $5.62. The price would rise to $5.62 only if the demand were perfectly inelastic. Buyers and sellers share the tax. Because demand is inelastic, buyers (smokers) will pay more of the 62¢ tax than the sellers (tobacco companies).

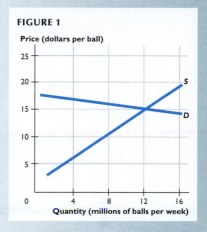
FIGURE 1

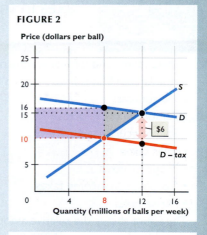
FIGURE 2

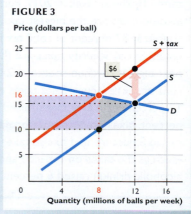
FIGURE 3

8.2 INCOME TAX AND SOCIAL SECURITY TAX

Income taxes are paid on personal incomes and corporate profits. In 2009, personal income taxes raised $1.25 trillion for the federal government and another $300 billion for state and local governments. Corporation income taxes raised $300 billion for the federal government and $50 billion for the state governments. We'll look first at the effects of personal income taxes, then at corporation income taxes, and finally at Social Security taxes.

■ The Personal Income Tax

Taxable income

Total income minus a personal exemption and a standard deduction (or other allowable deductions).

The amount of income tax that a person pays depends on her or his **taxable income**, which equals total income minus a *personal exemption* and a *standard deduction* (or other allowable deductions). For the federal income tax in 2011, the personal exemption was $3,650 and the standard deduction was $5,700 for a single person. So for a single person, taxable income equals total income minus $9,350.

The tax rate depends on the income level, and Figure 8.5 shows how the tax rate for a single person increases with income. The percentages in the table are

EYE on the U.S. ECONOMY
Taxes in the United States Today

Federal, state, and local governments in the United States have six main revenue sources:
• Personal income taxes
• Social Security taxes
• Sales taxes
• Property taxes
• Corporation income taxes
• Excise taxes
The figure shows the relative amounts raised by these taxes in 2011. Personal income taxes are the biggest tax source at 37 percent of total tax revenues. Social Security taxes are the next biggest revenue source at 24 percent of tax revenues. Sales taxes raised 13 percent; property taxes raised 12 percent, taxes on corporate profits raised 8 percent, and excise taxes (such as the taxes on tobacco and alcoholic drinks) raised 6 percent.

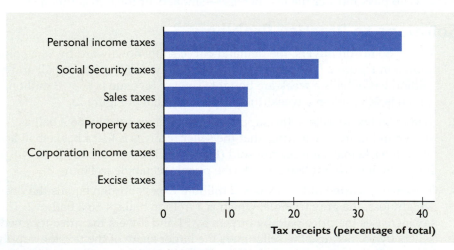

SOURCE OF DATA: *Economic Report of the President,* 2011.

Personal income taxes and Social Security taxes combine to create a high marginal tax rate on labor services that falls more on workers than on employers (see p. 198).

Taxes on corporate income mean that dividends on stocks get taxed twice, once as corporate income and once as personal income. These taxes fall mainly on firms rather than on the suppliers of capital and create a large deadweight loss (see p. 199).

■ **FIGURE 8.5**

U.S. Marginal Tax Rates and Average Tax Rates in 2011   MyEconLab Animation

Taxable income (dollars)	Marginal tax rate (percent)
$0 to $8,500	10
$8,501 to $34,500	15
$34,501 to $83,600	25
$83,601 to $174,400	28
$174,401 to $379,150	33
Over $379,150	35

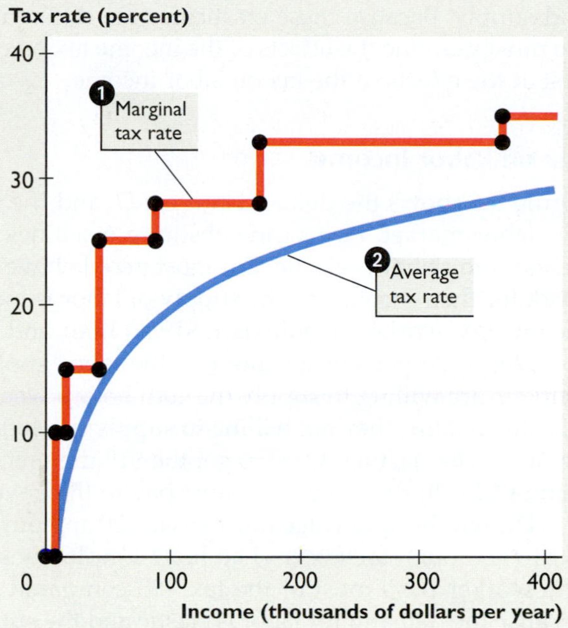

❶ The marginal tax rate increases with income. The table provides the data for 2011.

❷ The average tax rate increases with income, but the average rate is less than the marginal rate.

SOURCE OF DATA: Internal Revenue Service.

marginal tax rates. A **marginal tax rate** is the percentage of an additional dollar of income that is paid in tax. For example, if taxable income increases from $8,499 to $8,500, the tax paid on the additional dollar is 10¢ and the marginal tax rate is 10 percent. If taxable income increases from $379,150 to $379,151, the tax paid on the additional dollar is 35¢ and the marginal tax rate is 35 percent.

The **average tax rate** is the percentage of income that is paid in tax. The average tax rate is less than the marginal tax rate. For example, suppose a single person earns $50,000 in a year. Tax paid is zero on the first $9,350 plus $850 (10 percent) on the next $8,500 plus $3,900 (15 percent) on the next $26,000 plus $1,538 (25 percent) on the remaining $6,150. Total taxes equal $6,288, which is 12.6 percent of $50,000. The average tax rate is 12.6 percent.

If the average tax rate increases as income increases, the tax is a **progressive tax**. The personal income tax is a progressive tax. To see this feature of the income tax, calculate another average tax rate for someone whose income is $100,000 a year. Tax paid is zero on the first $9,350 plus $850 (10 percent) on the next $8,500 plus $3,900 (15 percent) on the next $26,000 plus $12,275 (25 percent) on the next $49,100 plus $1,974 (28 percent) on the remaining $7,050. Total taxes equal $18,999, which is 19.0 percent of $100,000. The average tax rate is 19.0 percent.

A progressive tax contrasts with a **proportional tax**, which has the same average tax rate at all income levels, and a **regressive tax**, which has a decreasing average tax rate as income increases.

Marginal tax rate
The percentage of an additional dollar of income that is paid in tax.

Average tax rate
The percentage of income that is paid in tax.

Progressive tax
A tax whose average rate increases as income increases.

Proportional tax
A tax whose average rate is constant at all income levels.

Regressive tax
A tax whose average rate decreases as income increases.

◼ The Effects of the Income Tax

Income tax is a tax on sellers of the services of labor, capital, and land. You know that the incidence and inefficiency of a tax depend on the elasticities of demand and supply. Because these elasticities are different for each factor of production, we must examine the effects of the income tax on each factor separately. Let's look first at the effects of the tax on labor income.

Tax on Labor Income

Figure 8.6 shows the demand curve, *LD,* and the supply curve, *LS,* in a competitive labor market. Firms can substitute machines for labor in many tasks, so the demand for labor is elastic. But most people have few good options other than to work for their income, so the supply of labor is inelastic. In this example, with no income tax, workers would earn $19 an hour and work 40 hours a week.

With a 20 percent income tax, the labor supply curve shifts to *LS + tax.* If workers are willing to supply the 40th hour a week for $19 with no tax, then with a 20 percent tax, they are willing to supply the 40th hour only if the wage is $23.75 an hour. That is, they want to get the $19 they received before plus $4.75 (20 percent of $23.75) that they now must pay to the government.

The equilibrium wage rate rises to $20 an hour, but the after-tax wage rate falls to $16 an hour—the tax is $4 an hour. Employment decreases to 35 hours a week. The worker pays most of the tax—$3 compared to the $1 the employer pays—because the demand for labor is elastic and the supply of labor is inelastic. The tax creates a deadweight loss shown by the gray triangle.

◼ **FIGURE 8.6**

A Tax on Labor Income

MyEconLab Animation

With no income tax, workers would earn $19 an hour and work 40 hours a week.

❶ Workers face a 20 percent marginal income tax rate. The income tax decreases the supply of labor, raises the wage rate, and lowers the after-tax wage rate. Because the demand for labor is elastic and the supply of labor is inelastic, the tax ❷ paid by the employer is less than that ❸ paid by the worker. The quantity of labor employed is less than the efficient quantity, so ❹ a deadweight loss arises.

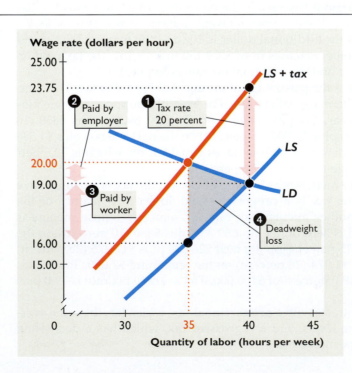

Tax on Capital Income

Capital income in the form of interest on bonds and bank deposits is taxed at the normal income tax rate. But capital income in the form of dividends on stocks is taxed twice. It is taxed as a dividend at 15 percent and it is taxed as corporate profit at the corporation income tax rate. (From 2008 to 2010, low-income earners will pay no tax on dividends.)

Figure 8.7 shows the demand curve, *KD*, and the supply curve, *KS*, in a competitive capital market. Because many tasks can be done by machines or labor, the demand for capital is elastic. Capital is internationally mobile, and its supply is highly elastic. In this example, firms can obtain all the capital they wish at an interest rate of 6 percent a year, so the supply of capital is perfectly elastic. With no capital income tax, firms use $40 billion worth of capital.

With a 40 percent tax on capital income, the supply curve shifts to *KS + tax*. Lenders want to receive an additional 4 percent interest to pay their capital income tax and are not willing to lend for less than 10 percent a year.

With the capital income tax, the quantity of capital decreases to $20 billion and the interest rate rises to 10 percent a year. Firms pay the entire capital income tax, and lenders receive the same after-tax interest rate as they receive in the absence of a capital income tax. The tax creates a deadweight loss shown by the gray triangle.

Tax on the Income from Land and Other Unique Resources

Each plot of land and reserve of mineral or other natural resource is unique, so its supply is perfectly inelastic. A fixed amount of the resource is supplied regardless of the rent offered for its use.

■ **FIGURE 8.7**

A Tax on Capital Income

MyEconLab Animation

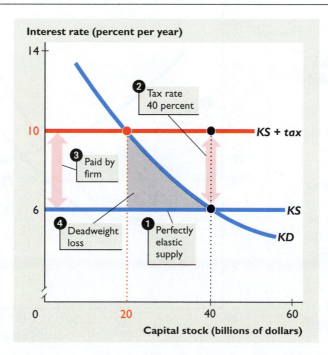

❶ The supply of capital is highly elastic (here perfectly elastic). With no tax on capital income, the interest rate is 6 percent a year and firms use $40 billion of capital.

With a ❷ 40 percent tax on income from capital, the supply curve becomes *KS + tax*. The interest rate rises to 10 percent a year, and ❸ firms pay the entire tax. The quantity of capital used is less than the efficient quantity, so ❹ a deadweight loss arises.

EYE on CONGRESS
Does Congress Decide Who Pays the Taxes?

Congress says that employers and workers pay the same Social Security tax contributions (7.65 percent each in 2011). But because the elasticity of demand for labor is much greater than the elasticity of supply of labor, workers end up paying most of the Social Security tax (see pp. 202–203).

Similarly, because the elasticity of demand for labor is greater than the elasticity of supply, the tax on wage income is paid mainly by workers. In contrast, the tax on capital income falls mainly on borrowers because the supply of capital is highly elastic.

But there is one thing that Congress can do to influence who pays a tax. It can pass a tax law (or tax rebate law) that doesn't impact the margin on which decisions turn. Recently, Congress passed such a law.

On February 17, 2009, the President signed the American Recovery and Reinvestment Act. Among the Act's many provisions is a "Making Work Pay" tax credit of $400 for a single worker and $800 for a couple.

A tax credit is a fixed reduction in the amount paid in personal income tax (in the current case, $400). For most people, a tax credit has no effect on their supply of labor. A worker gets the $400 tax credit regardless of how many hours he or she works. The tax credit doesn't influence the work-hours choice.

What influences the work-hours choice is the after-tax hourly wage rate, and that depends on the *marginal* income tax rate.

The figure illustrates the effects of a tax credit. The figure is similar to Figure 8.6 on p. 198. A 20 percent income tax rate shifts the labor supply curve from *LS* to *LS + tax*. With the demand for labor curve *LD*, the 20 percent tax raises the pre-tax wage rate by $1 to $20 per hour, lowers the after-tax wage rate by $3 to $16 per hour, and lowers the average workweek from 40 hours to 35 hours. With no tax rebate, the worker pays 75 percent of the tax and the employer pays 25 percent.

Suppose that Congress now passes an Act that gives workers a tax rebate of $30 a week. This rebate has no effect on the supply of labor because

Jacob Lew, with the President at the announcement of his appointment as Director of the Office of Management and Budget.

it isn't a rebate per hour worked. It is a fixed rebate amount independent of the hours worked. Workers now pay only 68 percent of the tax and employers pay 32 percent. Congress has worked around the elasticities!

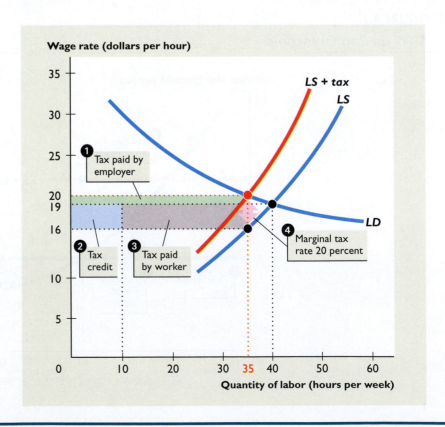

Figure 8.8(a) illustrates a tax on land income. In this example, a fixed 250 billion acres is supplied regardless of the rent. The equilibrium quantity of land is determined purely by supply and the equilibrium rent is determined by the demand for land. In this example, the equilibrium rent is $1,000 an acre.

When a 40 percent tax is imposed on rent income, landowners pay all of the tax. Their after-tax income falls to $600 an acre. This tax is efficient because the equilibrium quantity of land used is the same with the tax as without it. The tax generates no deadweight loss (excess burden) and is ideal from the perspective of efficiency.

The principle that applies to a tax on income from land also applies to the income from any unique resource that has a perfectly inelastic supply. Another example of such a resource is the talent of an outstanding movie star or television personality.

Figure 8.8(b) illustrates this case. Suppose that Angelina Jolie is willing to make an average of 3 movies per year. Her supply of services is perfectly inelastic at that quantity. Hollywood studios compete for her services, and the demand curve reflects their willingness to pay for them. The equilibrium price is $20 million per movie. If Angelina pays a 40 percent tax on this income, she receives an after-tax income of $12 million per movie. Angelina pays the entire tax. The price paid by the studios is unaffected by this tax, and Angelina makes the same number of movies with the tax as without it. This tax creates no deadweight loss (excess burden).

FIGURE 8.8

A Tax on Land and Other Unique Resource Income

MyEconLab Animation

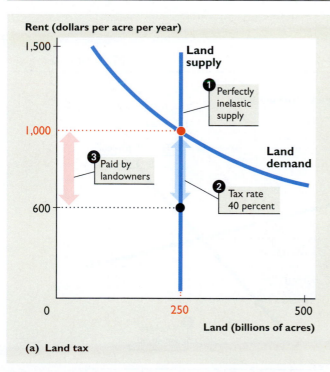

(a) Land tax

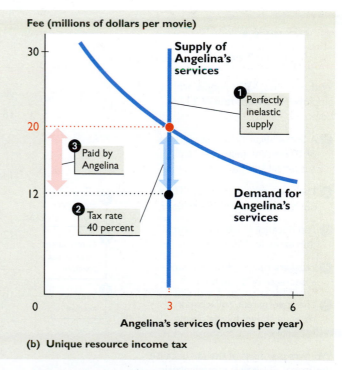

(b) Unique resource income tax

❶ In the markets for land and for the services of Angelina Jolie, supply is highly inelastic (here perfectly inelastic). With a ❷ 40 percent tax on income from these resources, the equilibrium quantity and the market price remain unchanged, and ❸ landowners and Angelina pay the entire tax. Because the quantity of the resource used is unchanged, the tax is efficient.

■ The Social Security Tax

Social Security is never far from the headlines. As the population gets older and more and more people begin to receive Social Security benefits, the cry to "fix Social Security" can only keep getting louder. The fundamental problem of ever-growing outlays must somehow be addressed.

One possible solution to the Social Security problem in the United States is to change the entitlements and cut the outlays. But this possibility is not popular and probably will not be the solution that is chosen. The other possibility is to increase the Social Security tax.

Currently, the law says that Social Security taxes fall equally on workers and employers. But does this outcome actually occur? If Congress decides to increase the Social Security tax, can Congress target employers and shield workers?

The Social Security tax is just like the other taxes you've studied in this chapter. Its incidence depends on the elasticities of demand and supply in the labor market and not on the wishes of Congress. Let's confirm this assertion by looking at two distinct arrangements: First, the tax is imposed only on workers, and second, the tax is imposed only on employers.

A Social Security Tax on Workers

Figure 8.9 shows the effects of a Social Security tax when the law says that workers must pay the entire tax. Without any taxes, the wage rate is $12 an hour and 4,000 people are employed. Now suppose that the government introduces a 20 percent Social Security tax on workers. If 4,000 people were willing to work for $12 an hour, this quantity of labor will now be supplied only if people can earn

■ FIGURE 8.9

A Social Security Tax on Workers

MyEconLab Animation

With no taxes, 4,000 people are employed at a wage rate of $12 an hour.

❶ A Social Security tax on workers of 20 percent shifts the supply curve to LS + tax.

❷ The wage rate rises to $12.50 an hour, an increase of 50¢ an hour.

❸ The quantity of labor employed decreases to 3,000 workers.

❹ Workers receive $10 an hour— a decrease of $2 an hour.

❺ The government collects tax revenue shown by the purple rectangle.

Workers pay most of the tax because the supply of labor is more inelastic than the demand for labor.

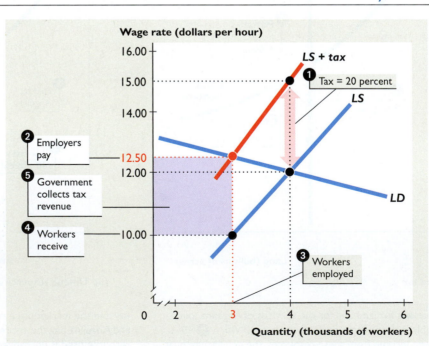

$12 an hour *after tax*. With a tax rate of 20 percent, the *pre-tax* wage rate will need to be $15 an hour to deliver an after-tax wage rate of $12 an hour. (Check that 20 percent of $15 is $3, so the wage rate *after* the tax is paid is $12.) The supply of labor curve shifts to the curve labeled *LS + tax*—a decrease in the supply of labor.

The wage rate rises to $12.50 an hour, and 3,000 workers are employed. Employees *receive* $12.50 an hour minus a 20 percent tax, which is $10 an hour. (Check that $2.50 equals 20 percent, or one fifth, of $12.50.)

So when the government puts a Social Security tax on workers, employers pay 50¢ an hour and workers pay $2 an hour. This division of the burden of the tax arises because the demand for labor is more elastic than the supply of labor.

A Social Security Tax on Employers

Figure 8.10 shows the effects of a Social Security tax on employers. As before, with no taxes, the equilibrium wage rate is $12 an hour and 4,000 people are employed. With a $2.50 an hour tax, firms are no longer willing to hire 4,000 people at a $12 an hour wage rate. Because firms must pay $2.50 an hour to the government, they will hire 4,000 people at a wage rate of $12 minus $2.50, which is $9.50 an hour.

The demand for labor decreases, and the demand curve shifts to *LD − tax*. The wage rate falls to $10 an hour, and 3,000 workers are employed. The total cost of labor to the firm is $12.50 an hour—the $10 an hour wage plus the $2.50 an hour tax.

The tax on employers delivers the same outcome as the tax on workers. Workers receive the same take-home wage, and firms pay the same total wage. Congress cannot decide who pays the Social Security tax. When the laws of Congress come into conflict with the laws of economics, economics wins. Congress can't repeal the laws of supply and demand!

FIGURE 8.10

A Social Security Tax on Employers   MyEconLab Animation

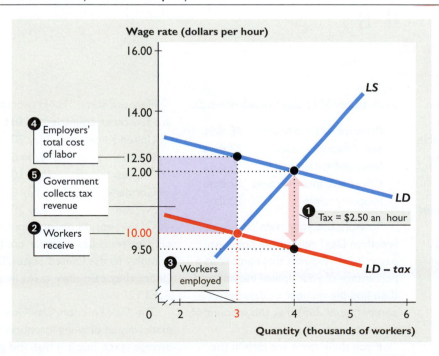

With no taxes, 4,000 people are employed at a wage rate of $12 an hour.

1 A tax on employers of $2.50 an hour shifts the demand curve leftward to *LD − tax*.

2 The wage rate falls to $10 an hour, a decrease of $2 an hour.

3 The quantity of labor employed decreases to 3,000 workers.

4 Employers' total cost of labor rises to $12.50 an hour—the wage rate of $10 an hour plus the $2.50 an hour tax.

5 The government collects tax revenue shown by the purple rectangle.

EYE on the PAST
The Origins and History of the U.S. Income Tax

1861 First federal income tax—3 percent on all incomes above $800 a year.

1872 Income tax was repealed. (Tariffs on imports provided government revenue.)

1895 Income tax reestablished, but the Supreme Court ruled it unconstitutional.

1913 The 16th Amendment to the Constitution made the federal income tax legal.

1913– 2011 Tax rates fluctuated. The top rate increased until 1920, decreased during the 1920s, and then increased until 1945 before decreasing in a number of steps to today's rate of 35 percent.

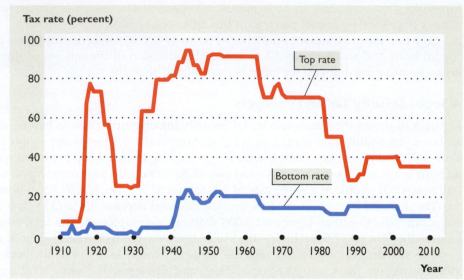

SOURCE OF DATA: Congressional Joint Committee on Taxation.

The bottom rate remained below 5 percent until the 1940s when it increased to 20 percent. In 1963 it decreased and since then, it has fluctuated between 10 percent and 15 percent.

EYE on YOUR LIFE
Tax Freedom Day

The Tax Foundation is an organization that seeks to promote a tax system that is as simple, transparent, and stable as possible, that minimizes excess burden, and that promotes trade and income growth.

Each year, to make the level of taxes as transparent as possible, the Tax Foundation calculates and publicizes "Tax Freedom Day"—the date by when an average U.S. citizen has worked long enough to pay the year's tax bill.

In 2011, "Tax Freedom Day" for Americans was April 12, the 102nd day of the year.

The 102 days Americans had to work to pay 2011 taxes break down as:

Personal income taxes	36 days
Social Security taxes	22 days
Sales and excise taxes	15 days
Corporate income taxes	12 days
Property taxes	12 days

To work out your own "Tax Freedom Day," record the taxes you pay in a year. Express this number as a percentage of your annual income and then find the number of days (as a percentage of 365) that this amount of tax represents.

If you think taxes are high in the United States, think again.

Here are some "Tax Freedom Days" in a few other countries in 2011:

United Kingdom	May 30
Canada	June 6
Belgium	June 10
Germany	July 8
Sweden	July 20

Of the world's major countries, only Australia has a similar tax freedom day to the United States. Down Under, they paid their taxes in 2011 by April 12.

The "Tax Freedom Day" is a dramatic way of drawing attention to high *average* taxes, but it is high *marginal* taxes that create inefficiency.

CHECKPOINT 8.2

MyEconLab
You can work these problems in Study Plan 8.2 and get instant feedback.

Explain how income taxes and Social Security taxes change wage rates and employment, are shared by employers and workers, and create inefficiency.

Practice Problems

1. Florida levies the following taxes: a 5.5 percent corporate income tax; a 6 percent sales tax; taxes of 4¢ a gallon on gasoline, 33.9¢ a pack on cigarettes, $0.48 a gallon on beer, and $2.25 a gallon on wine; and property taxes that vary across the counties and range from 1.4 percent to 2.0 percent of property values. Classify Florida's taxes into progressive, proportional, and regressive taxes.

2. Explain why Phil Mickelson pays his own Social Security tax and the PGA (the Professional Golf Association) pays none of it.

3. Is a tax on land rent or a tax on capital income more inefficient? Explain.

In the News

Illinois Governor proposes broad array of tax increases
Faced with a huge budget deficit, Illinois Governor Patrick Quinn has proposed a 50 percent increase in the personal income tax rate.
                              Source: *The Wall Street Journal*, March 20, 2009
Explain the effects of the tax hike on labor income. Will workers or employers pay most of the tax increase? How will the deadweight loss change?

Solutions to Practice Problems

1. If counties with the higher rates are those with high property values, then Florida's property taxes are progressive. The corporate income tax does not vary with income, so this tax is a proportional tax. Because saving increases with income, expenditure as a fraction of income decreases as income increases. The taxes on expenditure (sales tax, gasoline tax, cigarette tax, beer tax, and wine tax) are regressive taxes.

2. Phil Mickelson pays his Social Security tax and the PGA pays none of it because the supply of Phil Mickelson's services is (most likely) perfectly inelastic. The elasticities of demand and supply determine who pays the tax.

3. A tax on capital income is more inefficient than a tax on land rent. A tax on capital income has the larger effect on the quantity of factors of production employed than does a tax on land rent because the supply of land is perfectly inelastic, whereas the supply of capital is highly elastic. The larger the decrease in the quantity, the larger the deadweight loss created by the tax (the excess burden of the tax) and the more inefficient is the tax.

Solution to In the News

A tax on labor income will decrease the quantity of labor employed. The wage rate paid by employers will rise, the wage rate received by workers will fall, and the deadweight loss will increase. Because the demand for labor is elastic and the supply of labor is inelastic, most of the tax hike will be paid by the worker.

8.3   FAIRNESS AND THE BIG TRADEOFF

We've examined the incidence and the efficiency of different types of taxes. These topics have occupied most of this chapter because they are the issues about taxes that economics can address. But when political leaders debate tax issues, it is fairness, not just incidence and efficiency, that gets the most attention. Democrats complain that Republican tax cuts are unfair because they give the benefits of lower taxes to the rich. Republicans counter that because the rich pay most of the taxes, it is fair that they get most of the tax cuts. No easy answers are available to the questions about the fairness of taxes. Economists have proposed two conflicting principles of fairness to apply to a tax system:

- The benefits principle
- The ability-to-pay principle

■ The Benefits Principle

Benefits principle
The proposition that people should pay taxes equal to the benefits they receive from public goods and services.

The **benefits principle** is the proposition that people should pay taxes equal to the benefits they receive from public goods and services. This arrangement is fair because those who benefit most pay the most. The benefit principle makes tax payments and the consumption of government-provided services similar to private consumption expenditures. If taxes are based on the benefits principle, the people who enjoy the largest benefits pay the most for them.

To implement the benefits principle, it would be necessary to have an objective method of measuring each individual's marginal benefit from government-provided goods. In the absence of such a method, the principle can be used to justify a wide range of different taxes.

For example, the benefits principle can justify high fuel taxes to pay for public highways. Here, the argument would be that those who value the highways most are the people who use them most, and so they should pay most of the cost of providing them. Similarly, the benefits principle can justify high taxes on alcoholic beverages and tobacco products. Here, the argument would be that those who drink and smoke the most place the largest burden on public health-care services and so they should pay the greater part of the cost of those services.

The benefits principle can also be used to justify a progressive income tax. Here, the argument would be that the rich receive a disproportionately large share of the benefit from law and order and from living in a secure environment, so they should pay the largest share of providing these services.

■ The Ability-to-Pay Principle

Ability-to-pay principle
The proposition that people should pay taxes according to how easily they can bear the burden.

The **ability-to-pay principle** is the proposition that people should pay taxes according to how easily they can bear the burden. A rich person can more easily bear the burden of providing public goods than a poor person can, so the rich should pay higher taxes than the poor. The ability-to-pay principle involves comparing people along two dimensions: horizontally and vertically.

Horizontal Equity

Horizontal equity
The requirement that taxpayers with the same ability to pay should pay the same taxes.

If taxes are based on ability to pay, taxpayers with the same ability to pay should pay the same taxes, a situation called **horizontal equity.** While horizontal equity is easy to agree with in principle, it is difficult to implement in practice. If two people are identical in every respect, horizontal equity is easy to apply. But how do we compare people who are similar but not identical? The greatest difficulty arises in working out differences in ability to pay that arise from the state of a person's health and from a person's family responsibilities. The U.S. income tax has many special deductions and other rules that aim to achieve horizontal equity.

Vertical Equity

If horizontal comparisons are difficult, vertical comparisons are impossible. **Vertical equity** is the requirement that taxpayers with a greater ability to pay bear a greater share of the taxes. This proposition easily translates into the requirement that people with higher incomes should pay higher taxes. But it provides no help in determining how steeply taxes should increase as income increases. Should taxes be proportional to income? Should they be regressive? Should they be progressive? All of these arrangements have higher-income people paying higher taxes, so they all satisfy the basic idea of vertical equity. But most people have strong views that include the extent to which the rich should pay more.

You've seen that the U.S. tax code uses progressive income taxes—average tax rates that increase with income. Progressive taxes are justified as fair on the basis of the principle of vertical equity. But their use to achieve vertical equity produces a problem for the attainment of horizontal equity. The problem shows up most clearly in the U.S. tax code in its treatment of single people and married couples.

Vertical equity
The requirement that taxpayers with a greater ability to pay bear a greater share of the taxes.

■ The Marriage Tax Problem

Should a married couple (or two people living together) be treated as two individual taxpayers or as a single taxpayer? Until some changes were introduced in 2003, the U.S. tax code treated a married couple as a single taxpayer. This arrangement means that when a man and a woman get married, they stop paying income tax as two individuals and instead pay as one individual. To see the marriage tax problem, suppose the tax code (simpler than that in the United States) is as follows: no deductions or exemptions, incomes up to $20,000 a year bear no tax, and incomes in excess of $20,000 are taxed at 10 percent.

Now think about Al and Judy, two struggling young journalists, each of whom earns $20,000 a year and who get married. As single people, they paid no tax. Married, their income is $40,000, so they pay $2,000 a year in tax (10 percent of $20,000). Their marriage tax is $2,000 a year. (This example is *much* more severe than the marriage tax in the United States, but it serves to highlight the source of the problem.)

We could make a simple change to the tax law to overcome this problem for Al and Judy: Tax married couples as two single persons. That is what is done in most countries and what some economists say should be done in the United States. If we make this change in the tax law, Al and Judy pay no tax after their marriage just as before. We've solved the marriage tax problem.

Before we conclude that this small change to the tax code would clean up a source of unfairness, let's think about its effect on Denise and Frank. Frank is a painter whose work just doesn't sell. He has no income. Denise is a successful artist whose work is in steady demand and earns her $40,000 a year. As two single artists, Frank pays no tax and Denise pays $2,000 a year (10 percent of $20,000). If they marry, under the arrangement that taxes a married couple as a single taxpayer, they still pay $2,000 in tax.

A married couple or two individuals?

Now compare Frank and Denise with Al and Judy. If we tax married couples as a single taxpayer, both couples earn $40,000 a year and both pay income tax of $2,000 a year. But if we tax married couples as single persons, Frank and Denise pay $2,000 a year and Al and Judy pay nothing. So which is fair?

Horizontal equity requires Frank and Denise to be treated like Al and Judy. Taxing couples as a single taxpayer rather than taxing couples as single people achieves this outcome. But it taxes marriage, which seems unfair.

This problem arises from the progressive tax. It would not arise if taxes were proportional. Because horizontal equity conflicts with progressive taxes, some people say that only proportional taxes are fair.

■ The Big Tradeoff

Questions about the fairness of taxes conflict with efficiency questions and create the *big tradeoff* that you met in Chapter 6. The taxes that generate the greatest deadweight loss are those on the income from capital. But most capital is owned by a relatively small number of people who have the greatest ability to pay taxes. So there is a conflict between efficiency and fairness. We want a tax system that is efficient, in the sense that it raises the revenue that the government needs to provide public goods and services, but we want a tax system that shares the burden of providing these goods and services fairly. Our tax system is an evolving compromise that juggles these two goals.

MyEconLab

You can work these problems in Study Plan 8.3 and get instant feedback.

CHECKPOINT 8.3

Review ideas about the fairness of the tax system.

Practice Problem

1. In Hong Kong, the marginal income tax rates range from 2 percent to 20 percent. Does Hong Kong or the United States place greater weight on the ability-to-pay principle? Does Hong Kong or the United States place a greater weight on efficiency and a smaller weight on fairness?

In the News

Mayor Michael Nutter of Philadelphia is pushing the 2-cents-per-ounce tax on soda to help prevent cuts in the city's cash-strapped school system.
Source: *The Wall Street Journal*, June 14, 2011

Which principle of fairness will the mayor use to justify a tax on soda?

Solution to Practice Problem

1. Hong Kong's income tax rates are lower than those in the United States, so Hong Kong places a lower weight on the ability-to-pay principle. With lower income tax rates, Hong Kong places a greater weight on efficiency and a smaller weight on fairness.

Solution to In the News

The two principles of fairness are the benefits principle and the ability-to-pay principle. The mayor will justify the tax on the ability-to-pay principle and use the tax revenue raised to help finance the city's school system.

CHAPTER SUMMARY

Key Points

1 Explain how taxes change prices and quantities, are shared by buyers and sellers, and create inefficiency.

- Regardless of whether a tax is imposed on buyers or sellers, it has the same effects: The price paid by the buyer rises and the price received by the seller falls.

- A tax creates inefficiency by driving a wedge between marginal benefit and marginal cost and creating a deadweight loss.

- The less elastic the demand or the more elastic the supply, the greater is the price increase and the larger is the share of the tax paid by the buyer.

- If demand is perfectly elastic or supply is perfectly inelastic, the seller pays all the tax; if demand is perfectly inelastic or supply is perfectly elastic, the buyer pays all the tax.

- If demand or supply is perfectly inelastic, the tax creates no deadweight loss and is efficient.

2 Explain how income taxes and Social Security taxes change wage rates and employment, are shared by employers and workers, and create inefficiency.

- Taxes can be progressive (the average tax rate rises with income), proportional (the average tax rate is constant), or regressive (the average tax rate falls with income).

- The U.S. income tax is progressive.

- The shares of the income tax paid by firms and households depend on the elasticity of demand and the elasticity of supply of the factors of production.

- The elasticities of demand and supply, not Congress, determine who pays the income tax and who pays the Social Security tax.

- The more elastic is either the demand or supply of a factor of production, the greater is the excess burden of an income tax.

3 Review ideas about the fairness of the tax system.

- The two main principles of fairness of taxes—the benefits principle and the ability-to-pay principle—do not deliver universally accepted standards of fairness, and vertical equity and horizontal equity can come into conflict.

Key Terms

Ability-to-pay principle, 206
Average tax rate, 197
Benefits principle, 206
Excess burden, 192

Horizontal equity, 206
Marginal tax rate, 197
Progressive tax, 197
Proportional tax, 197

Regressive tax, 197
Taxable income, 196
Tax incidence, 190
Vertical equity, 207

MyEconLab

You can work these problems in Chapter 8 Study Plan and get instant feedback.

■:■ CHAPTER CHECKPOINT

Study Plan Problems and Applications

1. In Florida, sunscreen and sunglasses are vital items. If the tax on sellers of these items is doubled from 5.5 percent to 11 percent, who will pay most of the tax increase: the buyer or the seller? Will the tax increase halve the quantity of sunscreen and sunglasses bought?

2. Suppose that the government imposes a $2 a cup tax on coffee. What determines by how much Starbucks will raise its price? How will the quantity of coffee bought in coffee shops change? Will this tax raise much revenue?

Concerned about the political fallout from rising gas prices, the government cuts the tax on gasoline. Use this information to work Problems **3** and **4**.

3. Explain the effect of this tax cut on the price of gasoline and the quantity bought if, at the same time, the oil-producing nations increase production.

4. Explain the effect of this tax cut on the price of gasoline and the quantity bought if, at the same time, a global shortage of oil sends the price up.

Table 1 illustrates the market for Internet service. Use the information in Table 1 and a demand-supply graph to work Problems **5** and **6**.

5. What is the market price of Internet service? If the government taxes Internet service $15 a month, what price would the buyer of Internet service pay? What price would the seller of Internet service receive?

6. If the government taxes Internet service $15 a month, does the buyer or the seller pay more of the tax? What is the tax revenue? What is the excess burden of the tax? Is the tax proportional, progressive, or regressive?

Figure 1 illustrates the labor market in a country that does not tax labor income. Suppose that the government introduces a Social Security tax on workers of $2 per hour. Use this information to work Problems **7** and **8**.

7. How many workers are employed? What is the wage rate paid by employers and what is the workers' after-tax wage rate? How many workers are no longer employed?

8. If the government splits the Social Security tax equally between workers and employers, how many workers are employed? What is the wage rate paid by employers and what is the workers' after-tax wage rate?

9. In 2010, California legislators pledged to pass a soda tax in light of a new study linking soft drink consumption to obesity and related problems that cost California $41 billion a year in medical expenses. On the basis of what principle would this tax be fair?

10. **The downside of lower gas taxes**
    The federal gas tax is 18.4¢ a gallon and state gas taxes range from 20¢ to 40¢ a gallon. As motorists switch to more efficient cars, government gas tax revenue will fall. To raise revenue for infrastructure repairs, states are considering dropping the gas tax and introducing a mileage tax, perhaps 2.3¢ per mile.

    Source: CNNMoney, June 9, 2009

    How would a mileage tax differ from the gas tax in its effects on an owner of a gas guzzler and an owner of a fuel-efficient hybrid? Which tax would be fairer: the mileage tax or the gas tax?

TABLE 1

Price (dollars per month)	Quantity demanded	Quantity supplied
	(units per month)	
0	30	0
10	25	10
20	20	20
30	15	30
40	10	40
50	5	50
60	0	60

FIGURE 1

Wage rate (dollars per hour)

Instructor Assignable Problems and Applications

Use the following information to work Problems **1** and **2**.

In 2002, New York State raised the cigarette tax by 39¢ to $1.50 a pack. Then New York City raised the tax from 8¢ to $1.50 a pack. The total tax increased to $3 a pack, and the price of cigarettes rose to $7.50 a pack—the highest in the nation. The average income of smokers is less than that of non-smokers.

1. Draw a graph to show the effects of the $3 tax on the buyer's price, the seller's price, the quantity of cigarettes bought, the tax revenue, the consumer surplus, the producer surplus, and the excess burden of the tax. Does the buyer or seller pay more of the tax? Why?

2. Is this tax on cigarettes a progressive, regressive, or proportional tax?

Use the following information to work Problems **3** and **4**.

The supply of luxury boats is perfectly elastic, the demand for luxury boats is unit elastic, and with no tax on luxury boats, the price is $1 million and 240 luxury boats a week are bought. Now luxury boats are taxed at 20 percent.

3. What is the price that buyers pay? How is the tax split between the buyer and the seller? What is the government's tax revenue?

4. On a graph, show the excess burden of this tax. Is this tax efficient?

5. Figure 1 illustrates the market for chocolate bars. Suppose that the government levies a $1.50 tax on a chocolate bar. What is the change in the quantity of chocolate bars bought, who pays most of the tax, and what is the deadweight loss?

6. In an hour, a baker earns $10, a gas pump attendant earns $6, and a copy shop worker earns $7. Suppose that the government introduces an income tax of $1 an hour. Calculate the marginal tax rates for bakers, gas pump attendants, and copy shop workers. Is this tax progressive or regressive?

7. Larry earns $25,000 and pays $2,500 in tax, while Suzy earns $50,000 and pays $15,000 in tax. If Larry's income increases by $100, his tax increases by $12, but if Suzy's income increases by $100, her tax increases by $35. Calculate the average tax rate and marginal tax rate that Larry pays and that Suzy pays. Is this income tax fair? Explain.

8. A study of the Bush tax cuts of 2001 noted that the top 1 percent of income earners reaped the biggest benefits. What assumptions about the elasticities of demand and supply for high-wage labor and capital might be consistent with this assessment? What other facts about demand and supply and market outcomes would you need to know to verify this claim?

Use the following news clip to work Problems **9** and **10**.

Tax bites on travelers go deeper
Travelers complain about delayed flights, but they don't seem to be bothered by increased taxes on flights, car rentals, and hotel rooms. Taxes raise the average car rental bill 28 percent at airport locations. More municipalities are taxing airport rental customers to fund local venues, such as sports stadiums.
Source: *The New York Times*, April 10, 2007

9. Describe the effect of these municipal taxes on car rentals at airports. Who pays more of the tax: the renter or the car company?

10. Why do you think municipalities tax things that travelers buy as a way of raising the revenue to build local venues?

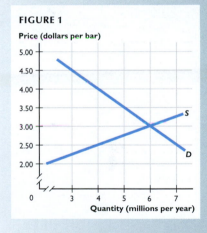

FIGURE 1

Price (dollars per bar)

Multiple Choice Quiz

1. If a tax of $1 a can is imposed on the buyers of sugary drinks, the demand for sugary drinks _____ and the price that buyers pay _____.

   A. doesn't change; doesn't change
   B. doesn't change; rises by $1 a can
   C. decreases; rises by more than $1 a can
   D. decreases; rises by less than $1 a can

2. A tax on candy will be paid by only _____.

   A. buyers if the supply of candy is perfectly elastic
   B. sellers if the demand for candy is perfectly inelastic
   C. buyers if the demand for candy is perfectly elastic
   D. sellers if the supply of candy is perfectly elastic

3. If the government imposes a new tax on plastic bags, _____.

   A. total surplus from bags shrinks by more than the amount of tax collected
   B. total surplus from bags shrinks by the amount of the tax revenue collected
   C. a deadweight loss arises equal to the amount of tax revenue collected
   D. the market for plastic bags remains efficient if the tax is fair

4. The demand for labor is more elastic than the supply of labor. An income tax _____ the wage rate paid by employers and _____.

   A. lowers; workers pay all the tax
   B. raises; workers pay most of the tax
   C. does not change; employers pay all the tax
   D. raises; employers pay most of the tax

5. The supply of low-skilled workers in China is perfectly elastic. In 2011, when China cut the tax on these workers' incomes from 5 percent to zero, _____.

   A. employers cut the wage rate but hired the same number of workers
   B. employers cut the wage rate and hired more workers
   C. employers didn't change the wage rate but hired more workers
   D. employers didn't change the wage rate and hired the same number of workers

6. The supply of land is perfectly inelastic so a tax on land rent is _____.

   A. efficient and the landowner pays all of the tax
   B. inefficient because the renter pays all of the tax
   C. inefficient if the tax is too high
   D. efficient and the renter pays all of the tax

7. The demand for labor is more elastic than the supply of labor. A Social Security tax imposed equally on workers and employers _____.

   A. raises the wage rate by more than the Social Security tax
   B. decreases employment and workers pay most of the tax
   C. increases the wage rate paid by employers by the amount of the tax
   D. is fair because workers and employers pay the same amount of tax

8. The _____ principle of fairness is the proposition that _____.

   A. benefit; people should pay taxes equal to the benefits they receive from the public goods bought with the tax revenue
   B. benefit; people should receive benefits equal to their ability to pay
   C. ability-to-pay; people should pay taxes equal to the benefits they receive
   D. ability-to-pay; people should receive benefits equal to their ability to pay

Who wins and who loses from globalization?

Global Markets in Action

9

When you have completed your study of this chapter, you will be able to

1 Explain how markets work with international trade.

2 Identify the gains from international trade and its winners and losers.

3 Explain the effects of international trade barriers.

4 Explain and evaluate arguments used to justify restricting international trade.

9.1 HOW GLOBAL MARKETS WORK

Imports
The goods and services that firms in one country buy from people and firms in other countries.

Exports
The goods and services that people and firms in one country sell to firms in other countries.

Because we trade with people in other countries, the goods and services that we buy and consume are not limited by what we produce. The goods and services that we buy from people and firms in other countries are our **imports**; the goods and services that we sell to firms in other countries are our **exports**.

■ International Trade Today

Global trade today is enormous. In 2009, global exports and imports (the two numbers are the same because what one country exports another imports) were about $15 trillion, which is 27 percent of the value of global production. The United States is the world's largest international trader and accounts for 10 percent of world exports and 15 percent of world imports. Germany and China, which rank 2 and 3 behind the United States, lag by a large margin.

In 2009, total U.S. exports were $1.5 trillion, which is about 11 percent of the value of U.S. production. Total U.S. imports were $1.9 trillion, which is about 13 percent of the value of total expenditure in the United States.

The United States trades both goods and services. In 2009, exports of services were $0.5 trillion (33 percent of total exports) and imports of services were $0.4 trillion (21 percent of total imports).

Our largest exports are services such as royalties, license fees, banking, business consulting, and other private services. Our largest exports of goods are chemicals and plastics and airplanes. Our largest imports are crude oil and automobiles. *Eye on the U.S. Economy* (p. 215) provides a bit more detail on our ten largest exports and imports.

■ What Drives International Trade?

Comparative advantage is the fundamental force that drives international trade. We defined comparative advantage in Chapter 3 (p. 74) as the ability of a person to perform an activity or produce a good or service at a lower opportunity cost than anyone else. This same idea applies to nations. We can define *national comparative advantage* as the ability of a *nation* to perform an activity or produce a good or service at a lower opportunity cost than *any other nation*.

The opportunity cost of producing a T-shirt is lower in China than in the United States, so China has a comparative advantage in producing T-shirts. The opportunity cost of producing an airplane is lower in the United States than in China, so the United States has a comparative advantage in producing airplanes.

You saw in Chapter 3 how Liz and Joe reaped gains from trade by specializing in the production of the good at which they have a comparative advantage and then trading. Both were better off. This same principle applies to trade among nations. Because China has a comparative advantage at producing T-shirts and the United States has a comparative advantage at producing airplanes, the people of both countries can gain from specialization and trade. China can buy airplanes from the United States at a lower opportunity cost than that at which it can produce them. And Americans can buy T-shirts from China for a lower opportunity cost than that at which U.S. firms can produce them. Also, through international trade, Chinese producers can get higher prices for their T-shirts and Boeing can sell airplanes for a higher price. Both countries gain from international trade.

Let's now illustrate the gains from trade that we've just described by studying demand and supply in the global markets for T-shirts and airplanes.

EYE on the U.S. ECONOMY
U.S. Exports and Imports

The blue bars in part (a) of the figure show the ten largest U.S. exports and the red bars in part (b) show the ten largest U.S. imports. The values are graphed as *net exports* and *net imports* because we both export and import items in most of the categories.

Five of our top ten exports are services—royalties and license fees (such as fees received by Hollywood movie producers on films shown abroad); financial services; business, profes-

sional, and technical services (such as the sale of advertising by Google to Adidas, a European sportswear maker); travel (such as the expenditure on a Florida vacation by a visitor from England); and education services (foreign students in our colleges and universities).

Automobiles and the fuel that runs them are our largest imports. We also import large quantities of clothing, furniture, TVs, DVD players, computers;

and industrial machinery and equipment. Insurance services also feature in our ten largest imports.

Although we import a large quantity of computers, we export many of the semiconductors (computer chips) inside those computers. The Intel chip in a Lenovo laptop built in China and imported into the United States is an example. This chip is made in the United States and exported to China.

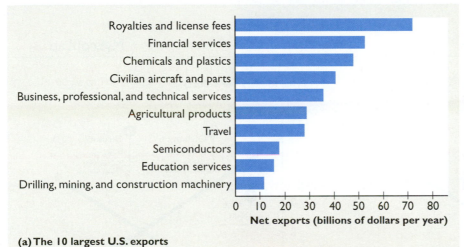

(a) The 10 largest U.S. exports

The United States exports airplanes …

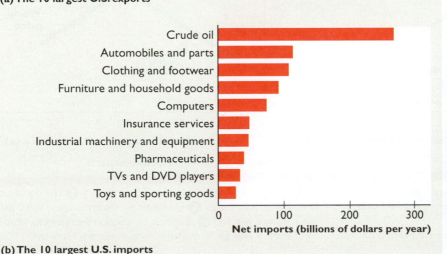

(b) The 10 largest U.S. imports

SOURCE OF DATA: Bureau of Economic Analysis.   *and imports crude oil.*

■ Why the United States Imports T-Shirts

Figure 9.1 illustrates the effects of international trade in T-shirts. The demand curve D_{US} and the supply curve S_{US} show the demand and supply in the U.S. domestic market only. The demand curve tells us the quantity of T-shirts that Americans are willing to buy at various prices. The supply curve tells us the quantity of T-shirts that U.S. garment makers are willing to sell at various prices.

Figure 9.1(a) shows what the U.S. T-shirt market would be like with no international trade. The price of a T-shirt would be $8 and 40 million T-shirts a year would be produced by U.S. garment makers and bought by U.S. consumers.

Figure 9.1(b) shows the market for T-shirts *with* international trade. Now the price of a T-shirt is determined in the world market, not the U.S. domestic market. The world price is *less than* $8 a T-shirt, which means that the rest of the world has a comparative advantage in producing T-shirts. The world price line shows the world price as $5 a T-shirt.

The U.S. demand curve, D_{US}, tells us that at $5 a T-shirt, Americans buy 60 million T-shirts a year. The U.S. supply curve, S_{US}, tells us that at $5 a T-shirt, U.S. garment makers produce 20 million T-shirts. To buy 60 million T-shirts when only 20 million are produced in the United States, we must import T-shirts from the rest of the world. The quantity of T-shirts imported is 40 million a year.

■ FIGURE 9.1

A Market with Imports

MyEconLab Animation

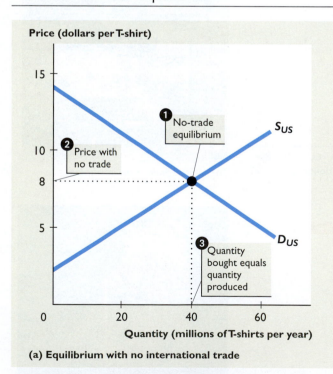

(a) Equilibrium with no international trade

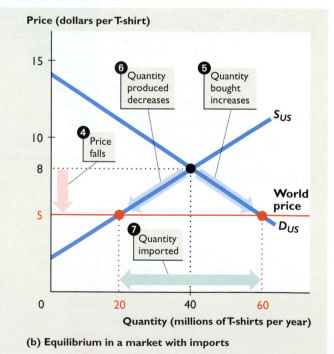

(b) Equilibrium in a market with imports

With no international trade, in part (a), ❶ domestic demand and domestic supply determine ❷ the equilibrium price at $8 a T-shirt and ❸ the quantity at 40 million T-shirts a year.

With international trade, in part (b), world demand and world supply determine the world price, which is $5 per T-shirt. ❹ The domestic price falls to $5 a T-shirt. ❺ Domestic purchases increase to 60 million T-shirts a year, and ❻ domestic production decreases to 20 million T-shirts a year. ❼ 40 million T-shirts a year are imported.

■ Why the United States Exports Airplanes

Figure 9.2 illustrates the effects of international trade in airplanes. The demand curve D_{US} and the supply curve S_{US} show the demand and supply in the U.S. domestic market only. The demand curve tells us the quantity of airplanes that U.S. airlines are willing to buy at various prices. The supply curve tells us the quantity of airplanes that U.S. aircraft makers are willing to sell at various prices.

Figure 9.2(a) shows what the U.S. airplane market would be like with no international trade. The price of an airplane would be $100 million and 400 airplanes a year would be produced by U.S. aircraft makers and bought by U.S. airlines.

Figure 9.2(b) shows the U.S. airplane market *with* international trade. Now the price of an airplane is determined in the world market, not the U.S. domestic market. The world price is *higher than* $100 million, which means that the United States has a comparative advantage in producing airplanes. The world price line shows the world price as $150 million.

The U.S. demand curve, D_{US}, tells us that at $150 million an airplane, U.S. airlines buy 200 airplanes a year. The U.S. supply curve, S_{US}, tells us that at $150 million an airplane, U.S. aircraft makers produce 700 airplanes a year. The quantity produced in the United States (700 a year) minus the quantity purchased by U.S. airlines (200 a year) is the quantity of U.S. exports, which is 500 airplanes a year.

■ FIGURE 9.2

A Market with Exports

MyEconLab Animation

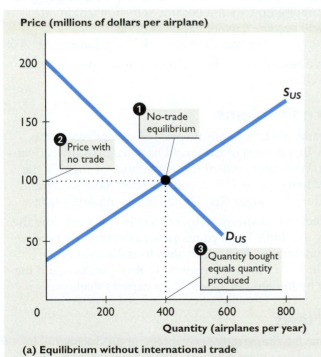

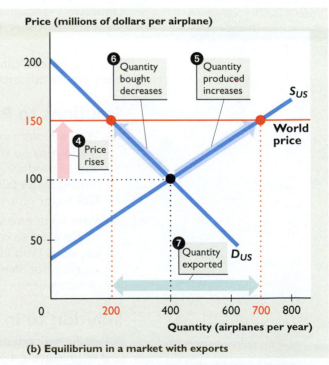

(a) Equilibrium without international trade

(b) Equilibrium in a market with exports

With no international trade, in part (a), ❶ domestic demand and domestic supply determine ❷ the equilibrium price at $100 million an airplane and ❸ the quantity at 400 airplanes a year. With international trade, in part (b), world demand and world sup-

ply determine the world price, which is $150 million an airplane. ❹ The domestic price rises. ❺ Domestic production increases to 700 airplanes a year, ❻ domestic purchases decrease to 200 airplanes a year, and ❼ 500 airplanes a year are exported.

CHECKPOINT 9.1

Explain how markets work with international trade.

Practice Problems

1. Suppose that the world price of sugar is 10 cents a pound, the United States does *not* trade internationally, and the U.S. equilibrium price of sugar is 20 cents a pound. The United States then begins to trade internationally.
   • How does the price of sugar in the United States change?
   • Do U.S. consumers buy more or less sugar?
   • Do U.S. sugar growers produce more or less sugar?
   • Does the United States export or import sugar?

2. Suppose that the world price of steel is $100 a ton, India does *not* trade internationally, and the equilibrium price of steel in India is $60 a ton. India then begins to trade internationally.
   • How does the price of steel in India change?
   • How does the quantity of steel produced in India change?
   • How does the quantity of steel bought by India change?
   • Does India export or import steel?

In the News

Underwater oil discovery to transform Brazil into a major exporter

The discovery of a huge oil field could make Brazil a large exporter of gasoline. Until two years ago Brazil imported oil; then it became self-sufficient in oil. With this discovery, Brazil will become a major exporter of oil.

Source: *The New York Times*, January 11, 2008

Describe Brazil's comparative advantage in producing oil, and explain why its comparative advantage has changed.

Solutions to Practice Problems

1. With no international trade, the U.S. domestic price of sugar exceeds the world price so we know that the rest of the world has a comparative advantage at producing sugar. With international trade, the price of sugar in the United States falls to the world price, U.S. consumers buy more sugar, and U.S. sugar growers produce less sugar. The United States imports sugar.

2. With no international trade, the domestic price of steel in India is below the world price so we know that India has a comparative advantage at producing steel. With international trade, the price of steel in India rises to the world price, steel mills in India increase the quantity they produce, and the quantity of steel bought by Indians decreases. India exports steel.

Solution to In the News

Before 2008, Brazil did not have a comparative advantage in producing oil. Its cost of producing a barrel of oil was higher than the world market price, so Brazil imported oil. With the discovery of the new oil field, the cost of producing a barrel of oil in Brazil will be below the world price. Now Brazil will have a comparative advantage in the production of oil. With this new comparative advantage, Brazil will become an exporter of oil.

9.2 WINNERS, LOSERS, AND NET GAINS FROM TRADE

You've seen how international trade lowers the price of an imported good and raises the price of an exported good. Buyers of imported goods benefit from lower prices, and sellers of exported goods benefit from higher prices. But some people complain about international competition: Not everyone gains. We're now going to see who wins and who loses from free international trade. You will then be able to understand who complains about international competition and why.

We'll also see why we never hear the consumers of imported goods complaining and why we never hear exporters complaining, except when they want greater access to foreign markets. And we'll see why we *do* hear complaints from producers about cheap foreign imports.

EYE on GLOBALIZATION
Who Wins and Who Loses from Globalization

Economists generally agree that the gains from globalization vastly outweigh the losses. But there are both winners and losers.

The U.S. consumer is a big winner. Globalization has brought iPods, Wii games, Nike shoes, and a wide range of other products to our shops at ever lower prices.

The Indian (and Chinese and other Asian) worker is another big winner. Globalization has brought a wider range of more interesting jobs and higher wages.

The U.S. (and European) textile workers and furniture makers are big losers. Their jobs have disappeared and many of them have struggled to find new jobs even when they've been willing to take a pay cut.

But one of the biggest losers is the African farmer. Blocked from global food markets by trade restrictions and subsidies in the United States and Europe, globalization is leaving much of Africa on the sidelines.

The U.S. consumer …

and Indian workers gain from globalization.

But some U.S. workers and …

African farmers lose.

■ Gains and Losses from Imports

We measure the gains and losses from imports by examining their effect on consumer surplus, producer surplus, and total surplus. The winners are those whose surplus increases and the losers are those whose surplus decreases.

Figure 9.3(a) shows what consumer surplus and producer surplus would be with no international trade. Domestic demand, D_{US}, and domestic supply, S_{US}, determine the price and quantity. The green area shows consumer surplus and the blue area shows producer surplus. Total surplus is the sum of consumer surplus and producer surplus.

Figure 9.3(b) shows how these surpluses change when the market opens to imports. The price falls to the world price. The quantity purchased increases to the quantity demanded at the world price, and consumer surplus expands to the larger green area $A + B + D$. The quantity produced decreases to the quantity supplied at the world price, and producer surplus shrinks to the smaller blue area C.

Part of the gain in consumer surplus, the area B, is a loss of producer surplus—a redistribution of total surplus. But the other part of the increase in consumer surplus, the area D, is a net gain. This increase in total surplus is the gain from imports and results from the lower price and increased purchases.

■ **FIGURE 9.3**

Gains and Losses in a Market with Imports   MyEconLab Animation

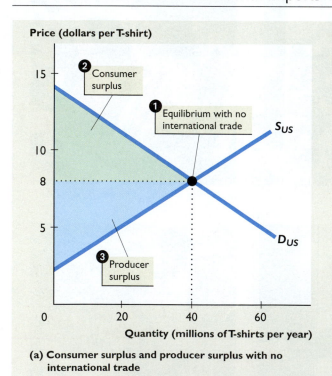

(a) Consumer surplus and producer surplus with no
    international trade

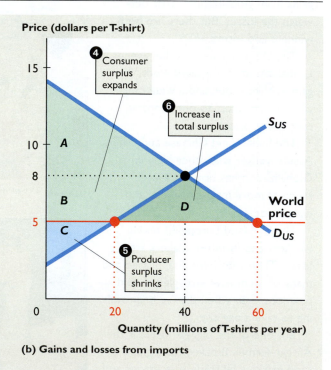

(b) Gains and losses from imports

With no international trade, ❶ equilibrium at the intersection of the domestic demand and domestic supply curves determines the price and quantity. ❷ The green area shows the consumer surplus and ❸ the blue area shows the producer surplus.

With international trade, the domestic price falls to the world price. ❹ Consumer surplus expands to the area $A + B + D$. Area B is a transfer of surplus from producers to consumers, and ❺ producer surplus shrinks to area C. ❻ Area D is an increase in total surplus.

■ Gains and Losses from Exports

We measure the gains and losses from exports just like we measured those from imports, by examining their effect on consumer surplus, producer surplus, and total surplus.

Figure 9.4(a) shows what the consumer surplus and producer surplus would be with no international trade. Domestic demand, D_{US}, and domestic supply, S_{US}, determine the price and quantity. The green area shows consumer surplus and the blue area shows producer surplus. The two surpluses sum to total surplus.

Figure 9.4(b) shows how the consumer surplus and producer surplus change when the good is exported. The price rises to the world price. The quantity bought decreases to the quantity demanded at the world price, and the consumer surplus shrinks to the green area A. The quantity produced increases to the quantity supplied at the world price, and the producer surplus expands from the blue area C to the larger blue area $B + C + D$.

Part of the gain of producer surplus, the area B, is a loss in consumer surplus—a redistribution of the total surplus. But the other part of the increase in producer surplus, the area D, is a net gain. This increase in total surplus is the gain from exports and results from the higher price and increased production.

■ FIGURE 9.4

Gains and Losses in a Market with Exports

MyEconLab Animation

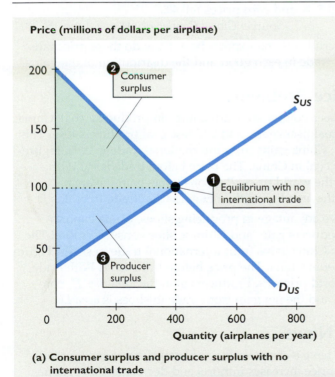

(a) Consumer surplus and producer surplus with no international trade

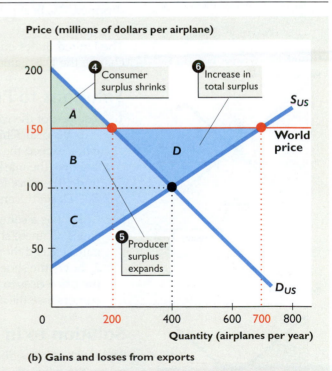

(b) Gains and losses from exports

With no international trade, ❶ equilibrium at the intersection of the domestic demand and domestic supply curves determines the price and quantity. ❷ The green area shows the consumer surplus and ❸ the blue area shows the producer surplus.

With international trade, the domestic price rises to the world price. ❹ Consumer surplus shrinks to the area A. ❺ Producer surplus expands to the area $B + C + D$. Area B is transferred from consumers to producers. ❻ Area D is an increase in total surplus.

CHECKPOINT 9.2

Identify the gains from international trade and its winners and losers.

Practice Problems

Before the 1980s, China did not trade internationally: It was self-sufficient in coal and shoes. Then China began to trade internationally. The world price of coal was less than China's domestic price and the world price of shoes was higher than its domestic price.

1. Does China import or export coal? Who, in China, gains and who loses from international trade in coal? Does China gain from this trade in coal? On a graph of the market for coal in China show the gains, losses, and net gain or loss from international trade in coal.

2. Does China import or export shoes? Who, in China, gains and who loses from international trade in shoes? Does China gain from this trade in shoes? On a graph of the market for shoes in China, show the gains, losses, and net gain or loss from international trade in shoes.

In the News

Commodities post big drop

World commodity prices have fallen in the past six weeks. Crude oil prices dropped 7%, beef prices fell 5 %, and corn prices fell 4%.

Source: *Global Commodity Watch*, June 15, 2011

The United States imports crude oil and exports beef. How do these price falls change the U.S. gains from trade in each good and the distribution of the gains?

Solutions to Practice Problems

1. The rest of the world has a comparative advantage in producing coal. China imports coal, Chinese coal users gain, and Chinese coal producers lose. The gains exceed the losses: China gains from international trade in coal. Figure 1 shows the market for coal in China. The price before trade is P_0. With trade, the price falls to the world price, P_1. Consumers gain the area $B + D$, producers lose the area B, and the net gain from trade in coal is D.

2. China has a comparative advantage in producing shoes. China exports shoes, Chinese shoe producers gain, and Chinese shoe consumers lose. The gains exceed the losses: China gains from international trade in shoes. Figure 2 shows the shoe market in China. The price before trade is P_0. With trade, the price rises to the world price, P_1. Producers gain the area $B + D$, consumers lose the area B, and the net gain from trade in shoes is area D.

Solution to In the News

The United States does not have a comparative advantage in producing crude oil, so the fall in the world price increases imports and decreases U.S. production. Consumer surplus increases, producer surplus decreases, but consumers gain more than producers lose. The United States has a comparative advantage in producing beef, so the fall in the world price decreases U.S. production. Producer surplus decreases, consumer surplus increases, but producers lose more than consumers gain.

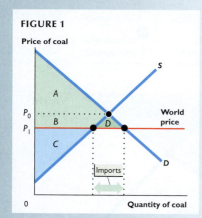

FIGURE 1

Price of coal

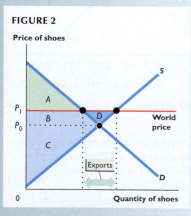

FIGURE 2

Price of shoes

9.3   INTERNATIONAL TRADE RESTRICTIONS

Governments use four sets of tools to influence international trade and protect domestic industries from foreign competition. They are

- Tariffs
- Import quotas
- Other import barriers
- Export subsidies

■ Tariffs

A **tariff** is a tax that is imposed on a good when it is imported. For example, the government of India imposes a 100 percent tariff on wine imported from California. When an Indian firm imports a $10 bottle of Californian wine, it pays the Indian government a $10 import duty.

The incentive for governments to impose tariffs is strong. First, they provide revenue to the government. Second, they enable the government to satisfy the self-interest of people who earn their incomes in import-competing industries. As you will see, tariffs and other restrictions on free international trade decrease the gains from trade and are not in the social interest. Let's see how.

Tariff
A tax imposed on a good when it is imported.

EYE on the PAST
The History of U.S. Tariffs

The figure shows the average tariff rate on U.S. imports since 1930. Tariffs peaked during the 1930s when Congress passed the Smoot-Hawley Act. With other nations, the United States signed the General Agreement on Tariffs and Trade (GATT) in 1947. In a series of rounds of negotiations, GATT achieved widespread tariff cuts for the United States and many other nations. Today, the World Trade Organization (WTO) continues the work of GATT and seeks to promote unrestricted trade among all nations.

The United States is a party to many trade agreements with individual countries or regions. These include the North American Free Trade Agreement (NAFTA) and the Central American Free Trade Agreement (CAFTA). These agreements have eliminated tariffs on most goods traded between the United States and the countries of Central and North America.

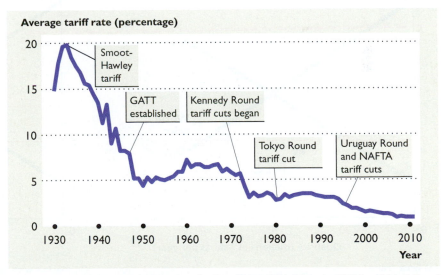

SOURCES OF DATA: The Budget for Fiscal Year 2006, Historical Tables, Table 2.5 and Bureau of Economic Analysis.

The Effects of a Tariff

To see the effects of a tariff, let's return to the example in which, with international free trade, the United States imports T-shirts. The T-shirts are imported and sold at the world price. Then, under pressure from U.S. garment makers, the U.S. government imposes a tariff on imported T-shirts. Buyers of T-shirts must now pay the world price plus the tariff. Several consequences follow in the market for T-shirts. Figure 9.5 illustrates these consequences.

Figure 9.5(a) is the same as Figure 9.1(b) and shows the situation with free international trade. The United States produces 20 million T-shirts and imports 40 million T-shirts a year at the world price of $5 a T-shirt.

Figure 9.5(b) shows what happens with a tariff, which is set at $2 per T-shirt. The following changes occur in the U.S. market for T-shirts:

- The price of a T-shirt in the United States rises by $2.
- The quantity of T-shirts bought in the United States decreases.
- The quantity of T-shirts produced in the United States increases.
- The quantity of T-shirts imported into the United States decreases.
- The U.S. government collects a tariff revenue.

FIGURE 9.5

The Effects of a Tariff

MyEconLab Animation

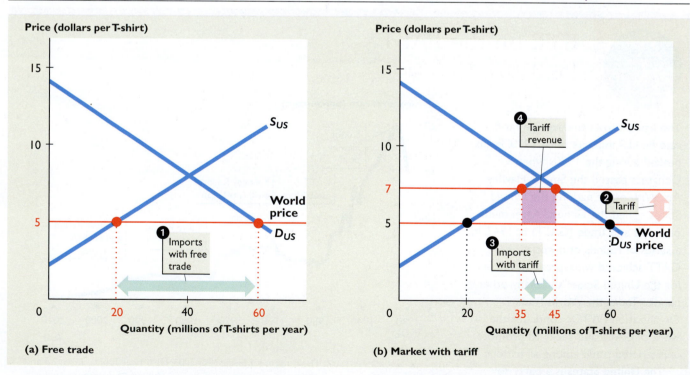

(a) Free trade

(b) Market with tariff

The world price of a T-shirt is $5. With free trade, in part (a), Americans buy 60 million T-shirts. The United States produces 20 million T-shirts and ❶ imports 40 million T-shirts.

❷ With a tariff of $2 per T-shirt in part (b), the domestic price rises

to $7 a T-shirt (the world price plus the tariff). Domestic production increases, purchases decrease, and ❸ the quantity imported decreases. ❹ The U.S. government collects tariff revenue of $2 on each T-shirt imported, which is shown by the purple rectangle.

Rise in Price of a T-Shirt To buy a T-shirt, Americans must pay the world price plus the tariff, so the price of a T-shirt rises by $2 to $7. Figure 9.5(b) shows the new domestic price line, which lies $2 above the world price line.

Decrease in Purchases The higher price of a T-shirt brings a decrease in the quantity demanded, which Figure 9.5(b) shows as a movement along the demand curve from 60 million T-shirts at $5 a T-shirt to 45 million T-shirts at $7 a T-shirt.

Increase in Domestic Production The higher price of a T-shirt stimulates domestic production, which Figure 9.5(b) shows as a movement along the supply curve from 20 million T-shirts at $5 a T-shirt to 35 million T-shirts at $7 a T-shirt.

Decrease in Imports T-shirt imports decrease by 30 million from 40 million to 10 million a year. Both the decrease in purchases and the increase in domestic production contribute to this decrease in imports.

Tariff Revenue The government's tariff revenue is $20 million—$2 per T-shirt on 10 million imported T-shirts—shown by the purple rectangle.

Winners, Losers, and the Social Loss from a Tariff

A tariff on an imported good creates winners and losers. When the U.S. government imposes a tariff on an imported good,

- U.S. producers of the good gain.
- U.S. consumers of the good lose.
- U.S. consumers lose more than U.S. producers gain.

U.S. Producers of the Good Gain Because the price of an imported T-shirt rises by the tariff, U.S. T-shirt producers are now able to sell their T-shirts for a higher price—the world price plus the tariff. As the price of a T-shirt rises, U.S. producers increase the quantity supplied. Because the marginal cost of producing a T-shirt in the United States is less than the higher price of all the T-shirts sold except for the marginal T-shirt, producer surplus increases. This increase in producer surplus is the gain to U.S. producers.

U.S. Consumers of the Good Lose Because the price of a T-shirt in the United States rises, the quantity of T-shirts demanded decreases. The combination of a higher price and smaller quantity bought decreases consumer surplus. This loss of consumer surplus represents the loss to U.S. consumers that arises from a tariff.

U.S. Consumers Lose More Than U.S. Producers Gain You've just seen that consumer surplus decreases and producer surplus increases, but which changes by more? Do consumers lose more than producers gain, or do producers gain more than consumers lose? Or is there just a straight transfer from consumers to producers? To answer these questions, we need to return to the demand and supply analysis of the market for T-shirts and compare the changes in consumer surplus and producer surplus.

Figure 9.6(a) is the same as Figure 9.3(b) and shows the consumer surplus and producer surplus with free international trade in T-shirts. The dark green area is the increase in total surplus that comes from free international trade. By comparing

■ FIGURE 9.6

The Winners and Losers from a Tariff

MyEconLab Animation

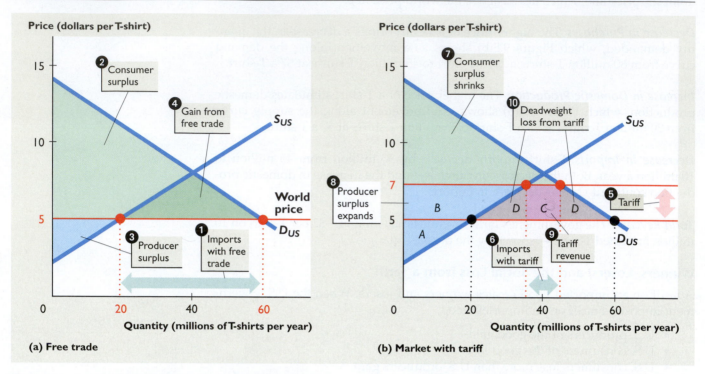

(a) Free trade

(b) Market with tariff

The world price of a T-shirt is $5. With free trade, ❶ the United States imports 40 million T-shirts. ❷ Consumer surplus, ❸ producer surplus, and ❹ the gains from free international trade are as large as possible. ❺ A tariff of $2 per T-shirt raises the price of a

T-shirt to $7. ❻ The quantity imported decreases. ❼ Consumer surplus shrinks by the areas B, C, and D. ❽ Producer surplus expands by area B. ❾ The government's tariff revenue is area C, and ❿ the tariff creates a deadweight loss equal to the areas D.

Figure 9.6(b) with Figure 9.6(a), you can see how a $2 tariff on imported T-shirts changes the surpluses. Producer surplus—the blue area—increases by the area labeled B. The increase in producer surplus is the gain by U.S. producers from the tariff. Consumer surplus—the green area—shrinks.

The decrease in consumer surplus divides into three parts. First, some of the consumer surplus is transferred to producers. The blue area B represents this loss of consumer surplus (and gain of producer surplus). Second, part of the consumer surplus is transferred to the government. The purple area C represents this loss of consumer surplus (and gain of government revenue). When the tariff revenue is spent, both consumers and producers receive some benefit, but there is no expectation that the buyers of T-shirts will receive the benefits of the expenditure of this tariff revenue from T-shirts. The tariff revenue is a loss to buyers of T-shirts.

The third part of the loss of consumer surplus is a transfer to no one: it is a *deadweight loss*. Consumers buy a smaller quantity at a higher price. The two gray areas labeled D represent this loss of consumer surplus. Total surplus decreases by this amount, which is the social loss from the tariff.

Let's now look at the second tool for restricting trade: quotas.

■ Import Quotas

An **import quota** is a quantitative restriction on the import of a good that limits the maximum quantity of a good that may be imported in a given period. The United States imposes import quotas on many items, including sugar, bananas, and textiles.

Quotas enable the government to satisfy the self-interest of people who earn their incomes in import-competing industries. You will see that like a tariff, a quota on imports decreases the gains from trade and is not in the social interest.

The Effects of an Import Quota

The effects of an import quota are similar to those of a tariff. The price rises, the quantity bought decreases, and the quantity produced in the United States increases. Figure 9.7 illustrates the effects.

Figure 9.7(a) shows the situation with free international trade. Figure 9.7(b) shows what happens with a quota that limits imports to 10 million T-shirts a year. The U.S. supply curve of T-shirts becomes the domestic supply curve, S_{US}, plus the quantity that the quota permits to be imported. So the U.S. supply curve becomes the curve labeled $S_{US} + quota$. The price of a T-shirt rises to $7, the

Import quota
A quantitative restriction on the import of a good that limits the maximum quantity of a good that may be imported in a given period.

■ **FIGURE 9.7**

The Effects of an Import Quota

MyEconLab Animation

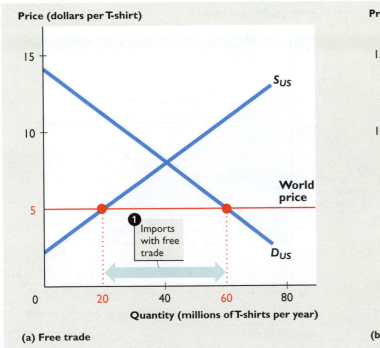

(a) Free trade

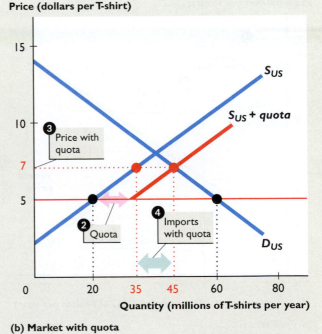

(b) Market with quota

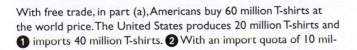

With free trade, in part (a), Americans buy 60 million T-shirts at the world price. The United States produces 20 million T-shirts and ❶ imports 40 million T-shirts. ❷ With an import quota of 10 mil-lion T-shirts, in part (b), the U.S. supply curve becomes $S_{US} + quota$. ❸ The price rises to $7 a T-shirt. Domestic production increases, purchases decrease, and ❹ the quantity imported decreases.

quantity of T-shirts bought in the United States decreases to 45 million a year, the quantity of T-shirts produced in the United States increases to 35 million a year, and the quantity of T-shirts imported into the United States decreases to the quota quantity of 10 million a year. All these effects of a quota are identical to the effects of a $2 per T-shirt tariff, as you can check in Figure 9.6(b).

Winners, Losers, and the Social Loss from an Import Quota

An import quota creates winners and losers that are similar to those of a tariff but with an interesting difference. When the government imposes an import quota,

- U.S. producers of the good gain.
- U.S. consumers of the good lose.
- Importers of the good gain.
- U.S. consumers lose more than U.S. producers and importers gain.

Figure 9.8 compares the gains from trade under free trade with those under a quota. Figure 9.8(a) shows the consumer surplus and producer surplus with free international trade in T-shirts. By comparing Figure 9.8(b) with Figure 9.8(a), you can see how an import quota of 10 million T-shirts changes the surpluses. Producer surplus—the blue area—increases by the area labeled *B*. The increase in

■ **FIGURE 9.8**

The Winners and Losers from an Import Quota

MyEconLab Animation

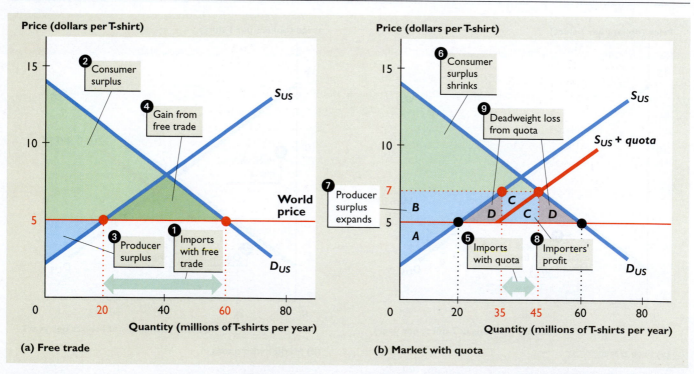

(a) Free trade

(b) Market with quota

The world price of a T-shirt is $5. With free trade, ❶ the United States imports 40 million T-shirts. ❷ Consumer surplus, ❸ producer surplus, and ❹ the gains from free trade are as large as possible. In part (b), an import quota raises the domestic price to $7 a

T-shirt. ❺ The quantity imported decreases. ❻ Consumer surplus shrinks by the areas *B*, *C*, and *D*. ❼ Producer surplus expands by area *B*. ❽ Importers' profit is the areas *C*, and ❾ the quota creates a deadweight loss equal to the areas *D*.

producer surplus is the gain by U.S. producers from the import quota. Consumer surplus—the green area—shrinks. This decrease is the loss to consumers from the import quota.

The decrease in consumer surplus divides into three parts. First, some of the consumer surplus is transferred to producers. The blue area *B* represents this loss of consumer surplus (and gain of producer surplus). Second, part of the consumer surplus is transferred to importers who buy T-shirts for $5 (the world price) and sell them for $7 (the domestic price). The blue areas *C* represent this loss of consumer surplus and profit for importers.

The third part of the loss of consumer surplus is a transfer to no one: it is a *deadweight loss*. Consumers buy a smaller quantity at a higher price. The two gray areas labeled *D* represent this loss of consumer surplus. Total surplus decreases by this amount, which is the social loss from the import quota.

You can now see the one difference between an import quota and a tariff. A tariff brings in revenue for the government while an import quota brings a profit for the importer. All the other effects are the same, provided the quota is set at the same level of imports that results from the tariff.

■ Other Import Barriers

Two sets of policies that influence imports are

- Health, safety, and regulation barriers
- Voluntary export restraints

Health, Safety, and Regulation Barriers

Thousands of detailed health, safety, and other regulations restrict international trade. For example, U.S. food imports are examined by the Food and Drug Administration to determine whether the food is "pure, wholesome, safe to eat, and produced under sanitary conditions." The discovery of BSE (mad cow disease) in just one U.S. cow in 2003 was enough to close down international trade in U.S. beef. The European Union bans imports of most genetically modified foods, such as U.S.-produced soybeans. Although regulations of the type we've just described are not designed to limit international trade, they have that effect.

Voluntary Export Restraints

A *voluntary export restraint* is like a quota allocated to a foreign exporter of the good. A voluntary export restraint decreases imports just like an import quota does, but the foreign exporter gets the profit from the gap between the domestic price and the world price.

■ Export Subsidies

A **subsidy** is a payment by the government to a producer. An *export subsidy* is a payment by the government to the producer of an exported good. The U.S. and European Union governments subsidize farm products. These subsidies stimulate the production and export of farm products, but they make it harder for producers in other countries, notably in Africa and Central and South America, to compete in global markets. Export subsidies bring gains to domestic producers, but they result in overproduction in the domestic economy and underproduction in the rest of the world and so create a deadweight loss (see Chapter 6, p. 155).

Subsidy
A payment by the government to a producer.

CHECKPOINT 9.3

Explain the effects of international trade barriers.

Practice Problems

Before 1995, the United States imposed tariffs on goods imported from Mexico and Mexico imposed tariffs on goods imported from the United States. In 1995, Mexico joined NAFTA. U.S. tariffs on imports from Mexico and Mexican tariffs on imports from the United States are gradually being removed.

1. Explain how the price that U.S. consumers pay for goods imported from Mexico and the quantity of U.S. imports from Mexico have changed. Who, in the United States, are the winners and losers from this free trade?

2. Explain how the quantity of U.S. exports to Mexico and the U.S. government's tariff revenue from trade with Mexico have changed.

3. Suppose that this year, tomato growers in Florida lobby the U.S. government to impose an import quota on Mexican tomatoes. Explain who, in the United States, would gain and who would lose from such a quota.

In the News

Indonesians bemoan Hollywood blockbuster blackout
Four months ago Indonesia imposed an import tariff on Hollywood movies. The tariff was meant "to protect local film makers." The major Hollywood studios responded by withdrawing their films from Indonesia.

Source: *The Jakarta Post*, July 6, 2011

Explain how this tariff influences the price of seeing a movie in Indonesia, the quantity of movies produced in Indonesia, and Indonesia's gains from trade with the United States. Who, in Indonesia, gains from the tariff and who loses?

Solutions to Practice Problems

1. The price that U.S. consumers pay for goods imported from Mexico has fallen and the quantity of U.S. imports from Mexico has increased. The winners are U.S. consumers of goods imported from Mexico and the losers are U.S. producers of goods imported from Mexico.

2. The quantity of U.S. exports to Mexico has increased and the U.S. government's tariff revenue from trade with Mexico has fallen.

3. With an import quota, the price of tomatoes in the United States would rise and the quantity bought would decrease. Consumer surplus would decrease. Growers would receive a higher price, produce a larger quantity, and producer surplus would increase. The U.S. total surplus in the tomato market would be redistributed from consumers to producers, but it would decrease.

Solution to In the News

The tariff raises the price of seeing a movie in Indonesia. The production of movies in Indonesia increases, and imports of Hollywood movies fall to zero. Indonesia's gains from trade with the United States decrease. With the higher price, consumer surplus decreases—consumers lose. Producer surplus increases—producers gain. The government collected zero tariff revenue.

9.4   THE CASE AGAINST PROTECTION

For as long as nations and international trade have existed, people have debated whether free international trade or protection from foreign competition is better for a country. The debate continues, but most economists believe that free trade promotes prosperity for all countries while protection reduces the potential gains from trade. We've seen the most powerful case for free trade: All countries benefit from their comparative advantage. But there is a broader range of issues in the free trade versus protection debate. Let's review these issues.

■ Three Traditional Arguments for Protection

Three traditional arguments for protection and restricting international trade are

- The national security argument
- The infant-industry argument
- The dumping argument

Let's look at each in turn.

The National Security Argument

The national security argument is that a country must protect industries that produce defense equipment and armaments and those on which the defense industries rely for their raw materials and other intermediate inputs. This argument for protection can be taken too far.

First, it is an argument for international isolation, for in a time of war, there is no industry that does not contribute to national defense. Second, if the case is made for boosting the output of a strategic industry—say aerospace—it is more efficient to achieve this outcome with a subsidy financed out of taxes than with a tariff or import quota. A subsidy would keep the industry operating at the scale that is judged appropriate, and free international trade would keep the prices faced by consumers at their world market levels.

The Infant-Industry Argument

The **infant-industry argument** is that it is necessary to protect a new industry to enable it to grow into a mature industry that can compete in world markets. The argument is based on an idea called *learning-by-doing*. By working repeatedly at a task, workers become better at that task and can increase the amount they produce in a given period.

There is nothing wrong with the idea of learning-by-doing. It is a powerful engine of human capital accumulation and economic growth. Learning-by-doing can change comparative advantage. If on-the-job experience lowers the opportunity cost of producing a good, a country might develop a comparative advantage in producing that good. Learning-by-doing does not justify protection.

It is in the self-interest of firms and workers who benefit from learning-by-doing to produce the efficient quantities. If the government protected these firms to boost their production, there would be an inefficient overproduction (just like the overproduction in Chapter 6, p. 156).

The historical evidence is against the protection of infant industries. Countries in East Asia that have not given such protection have performed well. Countries that have protected infant industries, as India once did, have performed poorly.

Infant-industry argument
The argument that it is necessary to protect a new industry to enable it to grow into a mature industry that can compete in world markets.

Dumping
When a foreign firm sells its exports at a lower price than its cost of production.

The Dumping Argument

Dumping occurs when a foreign firm sells its exports at a lower price than its cost of production. You might be wondering why a firm would ever want to sell any of its output at a price below the cost of production. Wouldn't such a firm be better off either selling nothing, or, if it could do so, raising its price to at least cover its costs? Two possible reasons why a firm might sell at a price below cost and therefore engage in dumping are

- Predatory pricing
- Subsidy

Predatory Pricing A firm that engages in *predatory pricing* sets its price below cost in the hope that it can drive its competitors out of the market. If a firm in one country tries to drive out competitors in another country, it will be *dumping* its product in the foreign market. The foreign firm sells its output at a price below its cost to drive domestic firms out of business. When the domestic firms have gone, the foreign firm takes advantage of its monopoly position and charges a higher price for its product. The higher price will attract new competitors, which makes it unlikely that this strategy will be profitable. For this reason, economists are skeptical that this type of dumping occurs.

Subsidy A *subsidy* is a payment by the government to a producer. A firm that receives a subsidy is able to sell profitably for a price below cost. Subsidies are very common in almost all countries. The United States and the European Union subsidize the production of many agricultural products and dump their surpluses on the world market. This action lowers the prices that farmers in developing nations receive and weakens the incentive to expand farming in poor countries. India and Europe have been suspected of dumping steel in the United States.

Whatever its source, dumping is illegal under the rules of the WTO, NAFTA, and CAFTA and is regarded as a justification for temporary tariffs. Consequently, anti-dumping tariffs have become important in today's world.

But there are powerful reasons to resist the dumping argument for protection. First, it is virtually impossible to detect dumping because it is hard to determine a firm's costs. As a result, the test for dumping is whether a firm's export price is below its domestic price. This test is a weak one because it can be rational for a firm to charge a lower price in markets in which the quantity demanded is highly sensitive to price and a higher price in a market in which demand is less price-sensitive.

Second, it is hard to think of a good that is produced by a single firm. Even if all the domestic firms were driven out of business in some industry, it would always be possible to find several and usually many alternative foreign sources of supply and to buy at prices determined in competitive markets.

Third, if a good or service were a truly global natural monopoly, the best way to deal with it would be by regulation—just as in the case of domestic monopolies. Such regulation would require international cooperation.

The three arguments for protection that we've just examined have an element of credibility. The counterarguments are in general stronger, so these arguments do not make the case for protection. They are not the only arguments that you might encounter. There are many others, four of which we'll now examine.

■ Four Newer Arguments for Protection

Four newer and commonly made arguments for restricting international trade are
that protection

- Saves jobs
- Allows us to compete with cheap foreign labor
- Brings diversity and stability
- Penalizes lax environmental standards

Saves Jobs

When Americans buy imported goods such as shoes from Brazil, U.S. workers
who produce shoes lose their jobs. With no earnings and poor prospects, these
workers become a drain on welfare and spend less, which creates a ripple effect of
further job losses. The proposed solution is to protect U.S. jobs by banning imports
of cheap foreign goods. The proposal is flawed for the following reasons.

First, free trade does cost some jobs, but it also creates other jobs. It brings about
a global rationalization of labor and allocates labor resources to their highest-valued
activities. Because of international trade in textiles, tens of thousands of workers in
the United States have lost jobs because textile mills and other factories have closed.
Tens of thousands of workers in other countries now have jobs because textile mills
have opened there. And tens of thousands of U.S. workers now have better-paying
jobs than as textile workers because other export industries have expanded and created more jobs than have been destroyed.

Second, imports create jobs. They create jobs for retailers that sell imported
goods and for firms that service those goods. They also create jobs by creating
incomes in the rest of the world, some of which are spent on imports of U.S.-made
goods and services.

Protection saves some particular jobs, but it does so at a high cost. For example, until 2005, textile jobs in the United States were protected by import quotas
imposed under an international agreement called the Multifiber Arrangement
(or MFA). The U.S. International Trade Commission (ITC) estimated that
because of import quotas, 72,000 jobs existed in textiles that would otherwise
disappear and annual clothing expenditure in the United States was $15.9 billion
($160 per family) higher than it would be with free trade. An implication of the
ITC estimate is that each textile job saved cost consumers $221,000 a year. The
end of the MFA led to the destruction of a large number of textile jobs in the
United States and Europe in 2005.

Allows Us to Compete with Cheap Foreign Labor

With the removal of protective tariffs in U.S. trade with Mexico, some people said
that jobs would be sucked into Mexico and that the United States would not be
able to compete with its southern neighbor. Let's see what's wrong with this view.

Labor costs depend on the wage rate and the quantity a worker produces. For
example, if a U.S. auto worker earns $30 an hour and produces 15 units of output
an hour, the average labor cost of a unit of output is $2. If a Mexican auto worker
earns $3 an hour and produces 1 unit of output an hour, the average labor cost of
a unit of output is $3. Other things remaining the same, the greater the output a
worker produces, the higher is the worker's wage rate. High-wage workers produce a large output. Low-wage workers produce a small output.

Although high-wage U.S. workers are more productive, on the average, than lower-wage Mexican workers, there are differences across industries. U.S. labor is relatively more productive in some activities than in others. For example, the productivity of U.S. workers in producing movies, financial services, and customized computer chips is relatively higher than their productivity in the production of metals and some standardized machine parts. The activities in which U.S. workers are relatively more productive than their Mexican counterparts are those in which the United States has a comparative advantage. By engaging in free trade, increasing our production and exports of the goods and services in which we have a comparative advantage, and decreasing our production and increasing our imports of the goods and services in which our trading partners have a comparative advantage, we can make ourselves and the citizens of other countries better off.

Brings Diversity and Stability

A diversified investment portfolio is less risky than one that has all of its eggs in one basket. The same is true for an economy's production. A diversified economy fluctuates less than an economy that produces only one or two goods.

Most economies, whether the rich, advanced United States, Japan, and Europe or the developing China and Brazil, have diversified production and do not have this type of stability problem. A few economies, such as Saudi Arabia, have a comparative advantage that leads to the specialized production of only one good. But even these economies can stabilize their income and consumption by investing in a wide range of production activities in other countries.

Penalizes Lax Environmental Standards

A new argument for protection is that many poorer countries, such as Mexico, do not have the same environmental standards that we have, and because they are willing to pollute and we are not, we cannot compete with them without tariffs. If these countries want free trade with the richer and "greener" countries, then they must raise their environmental standard.

This argument for trade restrictions is not entirely convincing. A poor country is less able than a rich one to devote resources to achieving high environmental standards. If free trade helps a poor country to become richer, then it will also help that country to develop the means to improve its environment. But there probably is a case for using the negotiation of free trade agreements such as NAFTA and CAFTA to hold member countries to higher environmental standards. There is an especially large payoff from using such bargaining to try to avoid irreversible damage to resources such as tropical rainforests.

So the four common arguments that we've just considered do not provide overwhelming support for protection. They all have flaws and leave the case for free international trade a strong one.

■ Why Is International Trade Restricted?

Why, despite all the arguments against protection, is international trade restricted? One reason that applies to developing nations is that the tariff is a convenient source of government revenue, but this reason does not apply to the United States where the government has access to income taxes and sales taxes.

Political support for international trade restrictions in the United States and most other developed countries arises from rent seeking. **Rent seeking** is lobbying and other political activity that seeks to capture the gains from trade. You've seen that free trade benefits consumers but shrinks the producer surplus of firms that compete in markets with imports.

The winners from free trade are the millions of consumers of low-cost imports, but the benefit per individual consumer is small. The losers from free trade are the producers of import-competing items. Compared to the millions of consumers, there are only a few thousand producers.

Now think about imposing a tariff on clothing. Millions of consumers will bear the cost in the form of a smaller consumer surplus and a few thousand garment makers and their employees will share the gain in producer surplus.

Because the gain from a tariff is large, producers have a strong incentive to incur the expense of lobbying *for* a tariff and *against* free trade. On the other hand, because each consumer's loss is small, consumers have little incentive to organize and incur the expense of lobbying *for* free trade. The gain from free trade for any one person is too small for that person to spend much time or money on a political organization to lobby for free trade. The loss from free trade will be seen as being so great by those bearing that loss that they will find it profitable to join a political organization to prevent free trade. Each group weighs benefits against costs and chooses the best action for themselves, but the anti-free-trade group will undertake more political lobbying than will the pro-free-trade group.

Rent seeking
Lobbying and other political activity that aims to capture the gains from trade.

EYE on YOUR LIFE
International Trade

International trade plays an extraordinarily large role in your life in three broad ways. It affects you as a

- Consumer
- Producer
- Voter

As a *consumer*, you benefit from the availability of a wide range of low-cost, high-quality goods and services that are produced in other countries.

Look closely at the labels on the items you buy. Where was your computer made? Where were your shirt and your shoes made? Where are the fruits and vegetables that you buy, especially in winter, grown?

The answers to all these questions are most likely Asia, Mexico, or South America. A few items were produced in Europe, Canada, and the United States.

As a *producer* (or as a potential producer if you don't yet have a job), you benefit from huge global markets for U.S. products. Your job prospects would be much dimmer if the firm for which you work didn't have global markets in which to sell its products.

People who work in the aircraft industry, for example, benefit from the huge global market for large passenger jets. Airlines from Canada to China are buying Boeing 777 aircraft as fast as they can be pushed out of the production line.

Even if you were to become a college professor, you would benefit from international trade in education services when your school admits foreign students.

As a *voter*, you have a big stake in the politics of free trade versus protection. As a buyer, your self-interest is hurt by tariffs and quotas on imported goods. Each time you buy a $20 sweater, you contribute $5 to the government in tariff revenue. But as a worker, your self-interest might be hurt by offshoring and by freer access to U.S. markets for foreign producers.

So as you decide how to vote, you must figure out what trade policy serves your self-interest and what best serves the social interest.

CHECKPOINT 9.4

Explain and evaluate arguments used to justify restricting international trade.

Practice Problems

1. Japan sets an import quota on rice. California rice growers would like to export more rice to Japan. What are Japan's arguments for restricting imports of Californian rice? Are these arguments correct? Who loses from this restriction in trade?

2. The United States has, from time to time, limited imports of steel from Europe. What argument has the United States used to justify this quota? Who wins from this restriction? Who loses?

3. The United States maintains an import quota on sugar. What is the argument for this import quota? Is this argument flawed? If so, explain why.

In the News

Indonesians bemoan Hollywood blockbuster blackout
The Indonesian import tariff on Hollywood movies was meant "to protect local film makers," but major Hollywood studios withdrew their films.

Source: *The Jakarta Post*, July 6, 2011

What argument is Indonesia using against free trade with the United States? What is wrong with Indonesia's argument?

Solutions to Practice Problems

1. The main arguments are that Japanese rice is a better quality rice and that the quota limits competition faced by Japanese farmers. The arguments are not correct. If Japanese consumers do not like the quality of Californian rice, they will not buy it. The quota does limit competition and the quota allows Japanese farmers to use their land less efficiently. The big losers are the Japanese consumers who pay about three times the U.S. price for rice.

2. The U.S. argument is that European producers dump steel on the U.S. market. With an import quota, U.S. steel producers will face less competition and U.S. jobs will be saved. Workers in the steel industry and owners of steel companies will win at the expense of U.S. buyers of steel.

3. The argument is that the import quota protects the jobs of U.S. workers. The argument is flawed because the United States does not have a comparative advantage in producing sugar and so an import quota allows the U.S. sugar industry to be inefficient. With free international trade in sugar, the U.S. sugar industry would exist but it would be much smaller and more efficient.

Solution to In the News

Indonesia is using the infant-industry argument: Protection is needed to allow its movie industry to mature and, through learning-by-doing, Indonesia will develop a comparative advantage in movie production. What's wrong with this argument is that protected industries generally perform poorly and the country does not develop the comparative advantage.

CHAPTER SUMMARY

Key Points

1 **Explain how markets work with international trade.**

- Comparative advantage drives international trade.
- When the world price of a good is lower than the price that balances domestic demand and supply, a country gains by decreasing production and importing the good.
- When the world price of a good is higher than the price that balances domestic demand and supply, a country gains by increasing production and exporting the good.

2 **Identify the gains from international trade and its winners and losers.**

- Compared to a no-trade situation, in a market with imports, consumer surplus is larger, producer surplus is smaller, and total surplus is larger with free international trade.
- Compared to a no-trade situation, in a market with exports, consumer surplus is smaller, producer surplus is larger, and total surplus is larger with free international trade.

3 **Explain the effects of international trade barriers.**

- Countries restrict international trade by imposing tariffs, import quotas, other import barriers, and export subsidies.
- Trade restrictions raise the domestic price of imported goods, lower the quantity imported, decrease consumer surplus, increase producer surplus, and create a deadweight loss.

4 **Explain and evaluate arguments used to justify restricting international trade.**

- The arguments that protection is necessary for national security, for infant industries, and to prevent dumping are weak.
- Arguments that protection saves jobs, allows us to compete with cheap foreign labor, makes the economy diversified and stable, and is needed to penalize lax environmental standards are flawed.
- Trade is restricted because protection brings small losses to a large number of people and large gains to a small number of people.

Key Terms

Dumping, 232

Exports, 214

Import quota, 227

Imports, 214

Infant-industry argument, 231

Rent seeking, 235

Subsidy, 229

Tariff, 223

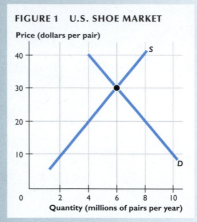

FIGURE 1   U.S. SHOE MARKET

Price (dollars per pair)

Quantity (millions of pairs per year)

FIGURE 2   BRAZIL'S SHOE MARKET

Price (dollars per pair)

Quantity (millions of pairs per year)

CHAPTER CHECKPOINT

Study Plan Problems and Applications

Use Figures 1 and 2 to work Problems **1** to **4**. Figure 1 shows the U.S. market for shoes and Figure 2 shows Brazil's market for shoes if there is no international trade in shoes between the United States and Brazil.

1. Which country has a comparative advantage in producing shoes? With international trade, explain which country would export shoes and how the price of shoes in the importing country and the quantity produced by the importing country would change. Explain which country gains from this trade.

2. The world price of a pair of shoes is $20. Explain how consumer surplus and producer surplus in the United States change as a result of international trade. On the graph, show the change in U.S. consumer surplus (label it *A*) and the change in U.S. producer surplus (label it *B*).

3. The world price of a pair of shoes is $20. Explain how consumer surplus and producer surplus in Brazil change as a result of international trade. Show the change in Brazil's consumer surplus (label it *C*) and the change in Brazil's producer surplus (label it *D*).

4. Who in the United States loses from free trade in shoes with Brazil? Explain why.

Use the following information to work Problems **5** to **7**.

5. The supply of roses in the United States is made up of U.S. grown roses and imported roses. Draw a graph to illustrate the U.S. rose market with free international trade. On your graph, mark the price of roses and the quantities of roses bought, produced, and imported into the United States.

6. Who in the United States loses from this trade in roses and would lobby for a restriction on the quantity of imported roses? If the U.S. government put a tariff on rose imports, show on your graph the U.S. consumer surplus that is redistributed to U.S. producers and also the government's tariff revenue.

7. Suppose that the U.S. government puts an import quota on roses. Show on your graph the consumer surplus that is redistributed to producers and importers and also the deadweight loss created by the import quota.

Use the following information to work Problems **8** to **10**.

U.S. expands China paper anti-dumping tariff
The U.S. Commerce Department has raised the tariff on glossy paper imports from China up to 99.65 percent, as a result of complaints by NewPage Corp. of Dayton, Ohio. Imports from China increased 166 percent from 2005 to 2006. This glossy paper is used in art books, high-end magazines, and textbooks.
                                        Source: *Reuters*, May 30, 2007

8. Explain who, in the United States, gains and who loses from this tariff on paper. How do you expect the prices of magazines and textbooks to change?

9. What is dumping? Who in the United States loses from China's dumping of glossy paper?

10. Explain what an anti-dumping tariff is. What argument might NewPage Corp. have used to persuade the U.S. Commerce Department to impose a 99.65 percent tariff?

Instructor Assignable Problems and Applications

Your instructor can assign these problems as homework, a quiz, or a test in MyEconLab.

Use the following information to work Problems **1** and **2**.

The future of U.S.–India relations

In May 2009, Secretary of State Hillary Clinton gave a major speech covering all the issues in U.S.–India relations. On economic and trade relations she noted that India maintains significant barriers to U.S. trade. The United States also maintains barriers against Indian imports such as textiles. Mrs. Clinton, President Obama, and Anand Sharma, the Indian Minister of Commerce and Industry, say they want to dismantle these trade barriers.

Source: www.state.gov

1. Explain who in the United States would gain and who might lose from dismantling trade barriers between the United States and India.

2. Draw a graph of the U.S. market for textiles and show how removing a tariff would change producer surplus, consumer surplus, and the deadweight loss from the tariff.

3. The United States exports wheat. Draw a graph to illustrate the U.S. wheat market if there is free international trade in wheat. On your graph, mark the price of wheat and the quantities bought, produced, and exported by the United States.

4. Suppose that the world price of sugar is 20 cents a pound, Brazil does not trade internationally, and the equilibrium price of sugar in Brazil is 10 cents a pound. Brazil then begins to trade internationally.
   • How does the price of sugar in Brazil change? Do Brazilians buy more or less sugar? Do Brazilian sugar growers produce more or less sugar?
   • Does Brazil export or import sugar and why?

5. The United States exports services and imports coffee. Why does the United States gain from exporting services and importing coffee? How do economists measure the net gain from this international trade?

Use Figure 1 and the following information to work Problems **6** to **8**.

Figure 1 shows the car market in Mexico when Mexico places no restriction on the quantity of cars imported. The world price of a car is $10,000.

6. If the government of Mexico introduces a $2,000 tariff on car imports, what will be the price of a car in Mexico, the quantity of cars produced in Mexico, the quantity imported into Mexico, and the government's tariff revenue?

7. If the government of Mexico introduces an import quota of 4 million cars a year, what will be the price of a car in Mexico, the quantity of cars produced in Mexico, and the quantity imported?

8. What argument might be used to encourage the government of Mexico to introduce a $2,000 tariff on car imports from the United States? Who will gain and who will lose as a result of Mexico's tariff?

9. In the 1950s, Ford and General Motors established a small car-producing industry in Australia and argued for a high tariff on car imports. The tariff has remained through the years. Until 2000, the tariff was 22.5 percent. What might have been Ford's and General Motors' argument for the high tariff? Is the tariff the best way to achieve the goals of the argument?

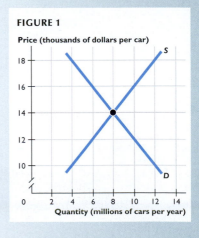

FIGURE 1

MyEconLab

You can work this quiz in Chapter 9 Study Plan and get instant feedback.

Multiple Choice Quiz

1. The fundamental force driving international trade is comparative _____.

    A. advantage: a country exports those goods that have high prices
    B. abundance: the country that produces more than it needs exports the good
    C. advantage: the country with the lower opportunity cost of production exports the good
    D. cost: a country trades with other countries that produce cheaper goods

2. A country will export wheat if, with no international trade, _____.

    A. it produces a surplus of wheat
    B. its opportunity cost of producing wheat is below the world price
    C. it's domestic price of wheat exceeds the world price
    D. other countries have a shortage of wheat

3. With free trade between the United States and Canada, the United States exports tomatoes and Canada exports maple syrup. U.S. consumers _____.

    A. of tomatoes gain and Canadian consumers of maple syrup lose
    B. of both tomatoes and maple syrup gain more than either producer
    C. of maple syrup gain more than U.S. producers of maple syrup lose
    D. of tomatoes gain more than U.S. producers of tomatoes lose

4. With free trade between China and the United States, the winners are _____ and the losers are _____.

    A. U.S. consumers of U.S. imports; U.S. producers of the U.S. import good
    B. China's consumers of China's imports; China's producers of its export good
    C. U.S. producers of the U.S. export good; U.S. consumers of U.S. imports
    D. China's consumers of China's export good; China's producers of its imported good

5. The U.S. tariff on paper ____ the U.S. price of paper, _____ U.S. production of paper and _____the U.S. gains from trade.

    A. raises; increases; increases
    B. doesn't change; increases; increases
    C. doesn't change; doesn't change; decreases
    D. raises; increases; decreases

6. If Korea imposes an import quota on U.S. oranges, losers include Korean _____ of oranges and U.S. _____ of oranges.

    A. consumers; consumers
    B. consumers; producers
    C. producers; consumers
    D. producers; producers

7. The people who support restricted international trade say that _____.

    A. protection saves jobs, in both the U.S. and foreign economies
    B. U.S. firms won't be able to compete with low-wage foreign labor if trade is free
    C. outsourcing sends jobs abroad, which brings diversification and makes our economy more stable
    D. protection is needed to enable U.S. firms to produce the things at which they have a comparative advantage

How can we limit climate change?

Externalities

When you have completed your study of this chapter, you will be able to

1 Explain why negative externalities lead to inefficient over-production and how property rights, pollution charges, and taxes can achieve a more efficient outcome.

2 Explain why positive externalities lead to inefficient underproduction and how public provision, subsidies, and vouchers can achieve a more efficient outcome.

EXTERNALITIES IN OUR DAILY LIVES

Externality
A cost or a benefit that arises from production and that falls on someone other than the producer; or a cost or benefit that arises from consumption and that falls on someone other than the consumer.

Negative externality
A production or consumption activity that creates an external cost.

Positive externality
A production or consumption activity that creates an external benefit.

An **externality** is a cost or a benefit that arises from production and that falls on someone other than the producer or a cost or a benefit that arises from consumption and that falls on someone other than the consumer. Before we embark on the two main tasks of this chapter, we're going to review the range of externalities, classify them, and give some everyday examples.

First, an externality can arise from either a production activity or a consumption activity. Second, it can be either a **negative externality**, which imposes an external cost, or a **positive externality**, which provides an external benefit. So there are four types of externalities:

- Negative production externalities
- Positive production externalities
- Negative consumption externalities
- Positive consumption externalities

■ Negative Production Externalities

When the U.S. Open tennis tournament is being played at Flushing Meadows, players, spectators, and television viewers around the world share a negative production externality that many New Yorkers experience every day: the noise of airplanes taking off from LaGuardia Airport. Aircraft noise imposes a large cost on millions of people who live under the flight paths to airports in every major city.

Logging and the clearing of forests are sources of another negative production externality. These activities destroy the habitat of wildlife and influence the amount of carbon dioxide in the atmosphere, which has a long-term effect on temperature. So these external costs are borne by everyone and by future generations.

Pollution, which we examine in more detail in the next section, is a major example of this type of externality.

■ Positive Production Externalities

To produce orange blossom honey, Honey Run Honey of Chico, California, locates beehives next to an orange orchard. The honeybees collect pollen and nectar from the orange blossoms to make the honey. At the same time, they transfer pollen

Negative production externality.

Positive production externality.

between the blossoms, which helps to fertilize the blossoms. Two positive production externalities are present in this example. Honey Run Honey gets a positive production externality from the owner of the orange orchard; and the orange grower gets a positive production externality from Honey Run.

■ Negative Consumption Externalities

Negative consumption externalities are a source of irritation for most of us. Smoking tobacco in a confined space creates fumes that many people find unpleasant and that pose a health risk. So smoking in restaurants and on airplanes generates a negative externality. To avoid this negative externality, many restaurants and all airlines ban smoking. But while a smoking ban avoids a negative consumption externality for most people, it imposes a negative external cost on smokers who would prefer to enjoy the consumption of tobacco while dining or taking a plane trip.

Noisy parties and outdoor rock concerts are other examples of negative consumption externalities. They are also examples of the fact that a simple ban on an activity is not a solution. Banning noisy parties avoids the external cost on sleep-seeking neighbors, but it results in the sleepers imposing an external cost on the fun-seeking partygoers.

Permitting dandelions to grow in lawns, not picking up leaves in the fall, allowing a dog to bark loudly or to foul a neighbor's lawn, and letting a cell phone ring in class are other examples of negative consumption externalities.

■ Positive Consumption Externalities

When you get a flu vaccination, you lower your risk of being infected. If you avoid the flu, your neighbor, who didn't get vaccinated, has a better chance of remaining healthy. Flu vaccinations generate positive consumption externalities.

When the owner of a historic building restores it, everyone who sees the building gets pleasure from it. Similarly, when someone erects a spectacular home—such as those built by Frank Lloyd Wright during the 1920s and 1930s—or other exciting building—such as the Chrysler and Empire State Buildings in New York or the Opera House in Sydney, Australia—an external consumption benefit flows to everyone who has an opportunity to view it.

Education, which we examine in more detail in this chapter, is a major example of this type of externality.

Negative consumption externality.

Positive consumption externality.

10.1 NEGATIVE EXTERNALITIES: POLLUTION

Pollution is an example of a *negative externality*. Both production and consumption activities create pollution. Here, we'll focus on pollution as a negative production externality. When a chemical factory dumps waste into a river, the people who live by the river and use it for fishing and boating bear the cost of the pollution. The chemical factory does not consider the cost of pollution when it decides the quantity of chemicals to produce. The factory's supply curve is based on its own costs, not on the costs that it inflicts on others. You're going to see that when external costs are present, we produce more output than the efficient quantity and we get more pollution than the efficient quantity.

Pollution and other environmental problems are not new. Preindustrial towns and cities in Europe had severe sewage disposal problems that created cholera epidemics and plagues that killed millions. Nor is the desire to find solutions to environmental problems new. The development in the fourteenth century of a pure water supply and the hygienic disposal of garbage and sewage are examples of early efforts to improve the quality of the environment.

Popular discussions about pollution focus on physical aspects of the environment, not on costs and benefits. A common assumption is that activities that damage the environment are wrong and must cease. An economic study of the environment emphasizes costs and benefits and economists talk about the efficient amount of pollution or environmental damage. This emphasis on costs and benefits does not mean that economists, as citizens, don't have the same goals as others and value a healthy environment. Nor does it mean that economists have the right answers and everyone else has the wrong ones. Rather, economics provides a set of tools and principles that help to clarify the issues.

The starting point for an economic analysis of the environment is the distinction between private costs and social costs.

■ Private Costs and Social Costs

A *private cost* of production is a cost that is borne by the producer of a good or service. *Marginal cost* is the cost of producing an *additional unit* of a good or service. So **marginal private cost** (*MC*) is the cost of producing an additional unit of a good or service that is borne by the producer of that good or service.

You've seen that an *external cost* is a cost of producing a good or service that is *not* borne by the producer but borne by other people. A **marginal external cost** is the cost of producing an additional unit of a good or service that falls on people other than the producer.

Marginal social cost (*MSC*) is the marginal cost incurred by the entire society—by the producer and by everyone else on whom the cost falls—and is the sum of marginal private cost and marginal external cost. That is,

$$MSC = MC + \text{Marginal external cost}.$$

We express costs in dollars, but we must always remember that a cost is an opportunity cost—the best thing we give up to get something. A marginal external cost is what someone other than the producer of a good or service must give up when the producer makes one more unit of the item. Something real that people value, such as a clean river or clean air, is given up.

Marginal private cost
The cost of producing an additional unit of a good or service that is borne by the producer of that good or service.

Marginal external cost
The cost of producing an additional unit of a good or service that falls on people other than the producer.

Marginal social cost
The marginal cost incurred by the entire society—by the producer and by everyone else on whom the cost falls. It is the sum of marginal private cost and marginal external cost.

Valuing an External Cost

Economists use market prices to put a dollar value on the cost of pollution. For example, suppose that there are two similar rivers, one polluted and the other clean. Five hundred identical homes are built along the side of each river. The homes on the clean river rent for $2,500 a month, and those on the polluted river rent for $1,500 a month. If the pollution is the only detectable difference between the two rivers and the two locations, the rent decrease of $1,000 per month is the cost of the pollution. For the 500 homes, the external cost is $500,000 a month.

External Cost and Output

Figure 10.1 shows an example of the relationship between output and cost in a chemical industry that pollutes. The marginal cost curve, *MC*, describes the private marginal cost borne by the firms that produce the chemical. Marginal cost increases as the quantity of the chemical produced increases. If the firms dump waste into a river, they impose an external cost that increases with the amount of the chemical produced. The marginal social cost curve, *MSC*, is the sum of marginal private cost and marginal external cost. For example, when firms produce 4,000 tons of chemical a month, marginal private cost is $100 a ton, marginal external cost is $125 a ton, and marginal social cost is $225 a ton.

In Figure 10.1, as the quantity of the chemical produced increases, the amount of pollution increases and the external cost of pollution increases. The quantity of the chemical produced and the pollution created depend on how the market for the chemical operates. First, we'll see what happens when the industry is free to pollute.

FIGURE 10.1

An External Cost

MyEconLab Animation

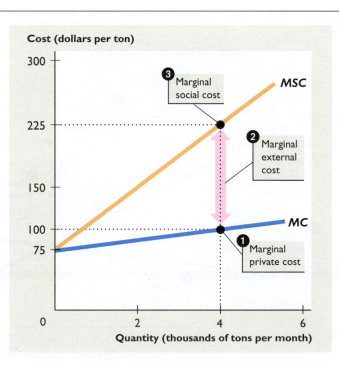

The *MC* curve shows the marginal private cost borne by the factories that produce a chemical. The *MSC* curve shows the sum of marginal private cost and marginal external cost.

When the quantity of chemical produced is 4,000 tons a month, ❶ marginal private cost is $100 a ton, ❷ marginal external cost is $125 a ton, and ❸ marginal social cost is $225 a ton.

■ Production and Pollution: How Much?

When an industry is unregulated, the amount of pollution it creates depends on the market equilibrium price and quantity of the good produced. Figure 10.2 illustrates the outcome in the market for a pollution-creating chemical.

The demand curve for the chemical is *D*. This curve also measures the marginal benefit, *MB*, to the buyers of the chemical (see Chapter 6, p. 146). The supply curve is *S*. This curve also measures the marginal private cost, *MC*, of the producers (see Chapter 6, p. 149). The supply curve is the marginal private cost curve because when firms make their production and supply decisions, they consider only the costs that they will bear. Market equilibrium occurs at a price of $100 a ton and a quantity of 4,000 tons of chemical a month.

This equilibrium is inefficient. You learned in Chapter 6 that the allocation of resources is efficient when marginal benefit equals marginal cost. But we must count all the costs—private and external—when we compare marginal benefit and marginal cost. With an external cost, the allocation is efficient when marginal benefit equals marginal *social* cost. This outcome occurs when the quantity of the chemical produced is 2,000 tons a month. The market equilibrium *overproduces* by 2,000 tons of chemical a month and creates a deadweight loss, the gray triangle.

Because the pollution creates a deadweight loss, reducing the amount of pollution and eliminating the deadweight loss brings potential gains for everyone. If some method can be found to achieve this outcome, everyone—the owners of the factories and the residents of the riverside homes—can gain. How can the people who live by the polluted river get the chemical factories to decrease their output of the chemical and create less pollution? Let's explore some solutions.

■ **FIGURE 10.2**

Inefficiency with an External Cost

MyEconLab Animation

The market supply curve is the marginal private cost curve, *S* = *MC*. The demand curve is the marginal benefit curve, *D* = *MB*. The marginal social cost curve is *MSC*.

❶ Market equilibrium at a price of $100 a ton and 4,000 tons of chemical a month is inefficient because ❷ marginal social cost exceeds ❸ marginal benefit.

❹ The efficient quantity of chemical is 2,000 tons a month where marginal benefit equals marginal social cost.

❺ The gray triangle shows the deadweight loss created by the pollution externality.

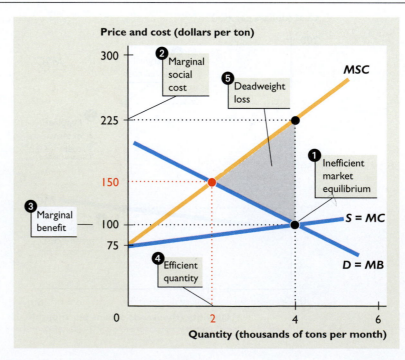

■ Property Rights

Sometimes it is possible to reduce the inefficiency arising from an externality by establishing a property right where one does not currently exist. **Property rights** are legally established titles to the ownership, use, and disposal of factors of production and goods and services that are enforceable in the courts.

Suppose that the chemical factories own the river and the 500 homes alongside it. The rent that people are willing to pay depends on the amount of pollution. Using the earlier example, suppose that people are willing to pay $2,500 a month to live alongside a pollution-free river but only $1,500 a month to live with the pollution created by 4,000 tons of chemical a month. If the factories produce this quantity of chemical, they forgo $1,000 a month for each home and a total of $500,000 a month.

Because they own the homes of the people who suffer from the pollution, the chemical factories are now confronted with the cost of their pollution decision. They might still decide to pollute, but if they do, they face the opportunity cost of their actions—forgone rent from the people who live by the river.

Figure 10.3 illustrates the outcome. With property rights in place, the marginal cost curve in Figure 10.2 no longer measures all the factories' costs of producing the chemical. It excludes the pollution cost that they must now bear. The former *MSC* curve now becomes the marginal private cost curve *MC*. The market supply curve is based on all the marginal costs and is the curve labeled *S = MC*.

Market equilibrium now occurs at a price of $150 a ton and a quantity of 2,000 tons a month. This outcome is efficient. The factories still produce some pollution, but it is the efficient quantity.

Property rights
Legally established titles to the ownership, use, and disposal of factors of production and goods and services that are enforceable in the courts.

■ **FIGURE 10.3**

Property Rights Achieve an Efficient Outcome

MyEconLab Animation

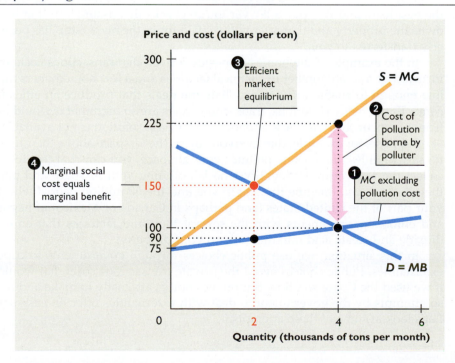

❶ With property rights, the marginal cost curve that excludes the cost of pollution shows only part of the producers' marginal cost.

The marginal private cost curve includes ❷ the cost of pollution, so the supply curve is *S = MC*.

❸ Market equilibrium is at a price of $150 a ton and a quantity of 2,000 tons of chemical a month and is efficient because ❹ marginal social cost equals marginal benefit.

■ The Coase Theorem

Does it matter how property rights are assigned? Does it matter whether the polluter or the victim of the pollution owns the resource that might be polluted? Until 1960, everyone—including economists who had thought long and hard about the problem—thought that it did matter. But in 1960, Ronald Coase had a remarkable insight, now called the Coase theorem.

The **Coase theorem** is the proposition that if property rights exist, only a small number of parties are involved, and transactions costs are low, then private transactions are efficient. There are no externalities because the transacting parties take all the costs and benefits into account. Furthermore, it doesn't matter who has the property right.

Application of the Coase Theorem

Let's apply the Coase theorem to the polluted river. In the example that we've just studied, the factories own both the river and the homes. Suppose that instead, the residents own both their homes and the river. Now the factories must pay a fee to the homeowners for the right to dump their waste. The greater the quantity of waste dumped into the river, the more the factories must pay. Again, the factories face the opportunity cost of the pollution they create. The quantity of chemical produced and the amount of waste dumped are the same, whoever owns the homes and the river. If the factories own them, they bear the cost of pollution because they receive a lower income from home rents. And if the residents own the homes and the river, the factories bear the cost of pollution because they must pay a fee to the homeowners. In both cases, the factories bear the cost of their pollution and dump the efficient amount of waste into the river.

The Coase solution works only when transactions costs are low. **Transactions costs** are the opportunity costs of conducting a transaction. For example, when you buy a house, you incur a series of transactions costs. You might pay a real estate agent to help you find the best place and a financial planner to help you get the best loan, and you pay a lawyer to run checks that assure you that the seller owns the property and that after you've paid for it, the ownership has been properly transferred to you.

In the example of the homes alongside a river, the transactions costs that are incurred by a small number of chemical factories and a few homeowners might be low enough to enable them to negotiate the deals that produce an efficient outcome. But in many situations, transactions costs are so high that it would be inefficient to incur them. In these situations, the Coase solution is not available.

Suppose, for example, that everyone owns the airspace above their homes up to, say, 10 miles. If someone pollutes your airspace, you can charge a fee. But to collect the fee, you must identify who is polluting your airspace and persuade them to pay you. Imagine the cost to you and the 50 million people who live in your part of the United States (and perhaps in Canada or Mexico) of negotiating and enforcing agreements with the several thousand factories that emit sulfur dioxide and create acid rain that falls on your property!

In this situation, we use public choices through governments to cope with externalities. Public choices avoid the private transactions costs that would arise if we used the Coase solution. But public choices are costly to make and monitor, so attempts by the government to deal with externalities offer no easy solution. Let's look at some of these attempts.

Coase theorem
The proposition that if property rights exist, only a small number of parties are involved, and transactions costs are low, then private transactions are efficient and the outcome is not affected by who is assigned the property right.

Transactions costs
The opportunity costs of conducting a transaction.

Government Actions in the Face of External Costs

The three main methods that governments use to cope with external costs are

- Pollution limits
- Pollution charges or taxes
- Marketable pollution permits (cap-and-trade)

Pollution Limits

A pollution limit seeks an efficient outcome by placing a quantity limit on a polluting activity. The 1990 Clean Air Act administered by the Environmental Protection Agency (EPA) employs this method and Figure 10.4 shows how it works. If the quantity produced is limited to the efficient quantity, the price rises so that marginal benefit equals marginal social cost. But because price exceeds marginal private cost, *MC*, a producer surplus arises.

Pollution limits are difficult to implement. The overall limit must be translated into a limit for each firm and compliance is costly to monitor. Also, because price exceeds marginal private cost, each firm has an incentive to increase its producer surplus by producing a quantity that exceeds the limit. The other two methods overcome some of these problems.

Pollution limits, charges or taxes, and cap-and-trade aim to curb greenhouse gas emissions.

Pollution Charges or Taxes

Pollution charges or pollution taxes seek an efficient outcome by making a polluter pay the marginal external cost of pollution. Pollution charges have been used only modestly in the United States, but are common in Europe.

FIGURE 10.4

A Pollution Limit

MyEconLab Animation

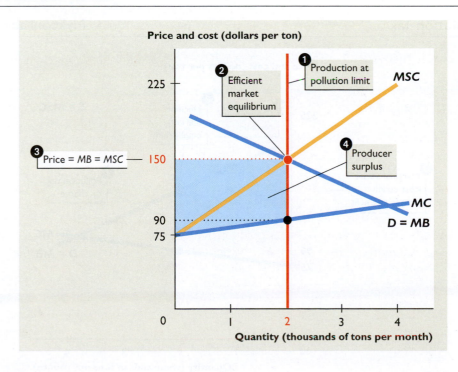

❶ A pollution limit is imposed that restricts production to the efficient quantity.

❷ The efficient market equilibrium is achieved.

❸ The market price is equal to marginal benefit, *MB*, and marginal social cost, *MSC*.

❹ Because the price exceeds marginal cost, producers get a producer surplus equal to the area of the blue rectangle.

Figure 10.5 illustrates the effects of a pollution charge or pollution tax. By charging or taxing the producer at a rate equal to marginal external cost, the marginal social cost curve becomes the market supply curve. The market price rises, the quantity produced decreases to the efficient quantity, and the government collects a tax or pollution charge revenue shown by the purple rectangle.

Marketable Pollution Permits (Cap-and-Trade)

Marketable pollution permits (also called cap-and-trade) seek an efficient outcome by assigning or selling pollution rights to individual producers who are then free to trade permits with each other. The 1990 Clean Air Act and the 1994 Regional Clean Air Incentives Market (RECLAIM) in the Los Angeles basin successfully use this method of dealing with air pollution. This approach is also the centerpiece of a proposed American Clean Energy and Security Act of 2009 (see p. 252).

If marginal external cost is assessed correctly, an efficient outcome is achieved with any of the methods. But governments cannot make an accurate determination of external costs. Also, more importantly, some producers have a lower marginal cost of avoiding pollution than others.

In practice, pollution limits and pollution charges and taxes end up failing to achieve an efficient outcome because they confront all producers with the same incentives to avoid pollution. Cap-and-trade overcomes this problem and is the most effective of the three methods. Cap-and-trade requires an accurate determination of the overall quantity of pollution that brings efficiency, but it provides the strongest available incentive to individual producers to find cost effective technologies that achieve the pollution targets.

FIGURE 10.5

A Pollution Charge or Pollution Tax   MyEconLab Animation

❶ A pollution charge or tax is imposed that is equal to the marginal external cost of pollution.

Because the pollution charge or tax equals the marginal external cost, the supply curve is the marginal social cost curve: S = MSC.

❷ Market equilibrium is efficient because ❸ marginal social cost equals marginal benefit.

❹ The government collects tax revenue equal to the area of the purple rectangle.

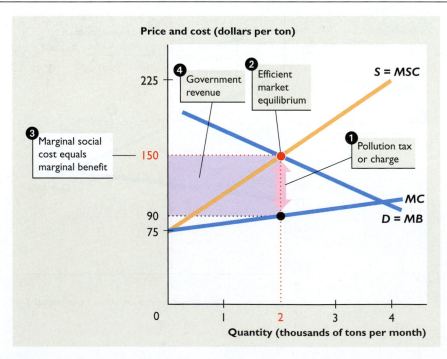

■ Switching to Clean Technologies

In explaining the effects of alternative ways of coping with negative externalities, we have focused on getting the efficient quantity of production of a polluting activity. There is another way of coping with negative externalities: change the technology from one that pollutes to one that is clean.

Most of the improvements in the quality of our air (described in *Eye on the U.S. Economy* below) have come from improved technologies rather than from producing less. These trend improvements in air quality have occurred despite increases in transportation and electricity production, two of the main polluters.

Confronted with the marginal external cost of their actions by any of the means we have described above, if the marginal cost of production using a clean technology is lower than the marginal *social* cost of using the polluting technology, producers will adopt the clean technology.

The switch to electric cars and trucks to avoid the pollution that comes from burning gasoline and diesel is already happening. But unless we produce the electricity used by these vehicles with a clean technology, we're not gaining much.

Whether the cost of producing electricity with clean technologies such as solar, wind, and tidal power is lower than the social cost of using natural gas, coal, and oil is hard to say and controversial. There is no agreed estimate of the marginal external cost of carbon emissions. There is no doubt that the external costs are present and possibly large. But we need precise measurement to determine the efficient mix of polluting and clean technologies.

EYE on the U.S. ECONOMY
U.S. Air Pollution Trends

Air quality in the United States has improved. The figure shows the trends since 1980 for the atmospheric concentrations of five main air pollutants monitored by the Environmental Protection Agency (EPA) and a sixth pollutant (suspended particulates) monitored since 1990.

By using a mix of regulation, pollution limits, economic incentives, and permit trading, the EPA has almost eliminated lead and has substantially decreased sulfur dioxide, carbon monoxide, nitrogen dioxide, and suspended particulates.

Ozone is harder to eliminate, but it has nonetheless fallen to 70 percent of its 1980 level.

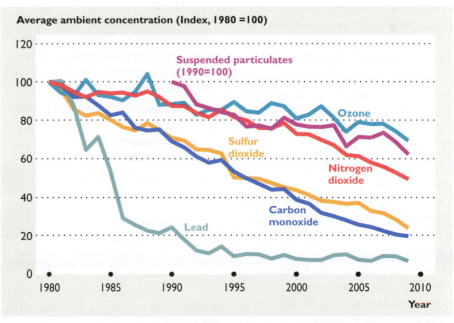

SOURCE OF DATA: Environmental Protection Agency, http://www.epa.gov/airtrends.

EYE on CLIMATE CHANGE
How Can We Limit Climate Change?

The average temperature of the Earth is rising and so is the atmospheric concentration of carbon dioxide, CO_2. The top figure shows these upward trends.

Scientists debate the contribution of human economic activity to the trends, but most believe it to be the source. Economists debate the costs and benefits of alternative ways of slowing CO_2 and other greenhouse gas (GHG) emissions, but most favor action.

Economists agree that lowering GHG emissions requires *incentives* to change.

One idea is to cap emissions and issue tradeable emissions permits, a system called *cap-and-trade*. Carbon emission permits are already priced on a global carbon trading market.

The idea also has backers in Congress. On May 15, 2009, Representative Henry Waxman introduced the American Clean Energy and Security Act of 2009, which would use a cap-and-trade scheme. With 2005 levels as the base, GHG emissions would be capped at 97 percent by 2012, 83 percent by 2020, 58 percent by 2030, and 17 percent by 2050.

The Congressional Budget Office estimates that in 2020, a permit to emit one ton of GHG would cost $28 and the cost of the scheme would be about $175 per household per year.

Another incentive might be a hike in the tax on gasoline. Americans pay a much lower gas tax than Europeans pay. The bottom figure shows the stark difference between the United States and the United Kingdom.

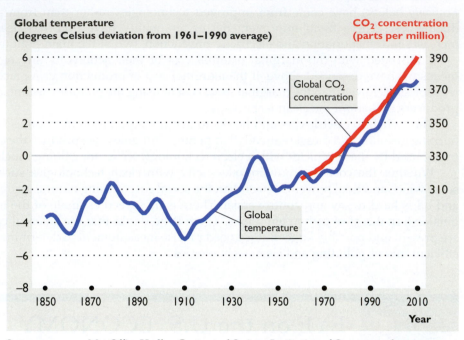

SOURCES OF DATA: Met Office Hadley Centre and Scripps Institution of Oceanography.

Why don't we have more aggressive caps and stronger incentives to encourage a larger reduction in GHG emissions? There are three reasons.

First, many people don't accept the scientific evidence that emissions produce global warming; second, the costs are certain and would be borne now, while the benefits would come many years in the future; and third, if current trends persist, by 2050, three quarters of carbon pollution will come not from the United States but from the developing economies.

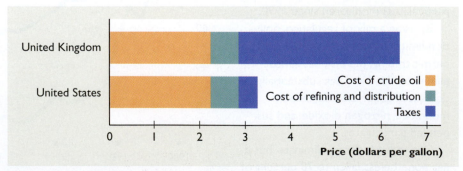

SOURCES OF DATA: Energy Information Administration, Automobile Association, and authors' assumptions.

CHECKPOINT 10.1

Explain why negative externalities lead to inefficient overproduction and how property rights, pollution charges, and taxes can achieve a more efficient outcome.

MyEconLab

You can work these problems in Study Plan 10.1 and get instant feedback.

Practice Problems

Figure 1 illustrates the unregulated market for a pesticide. When factories produce pesticide, they also create waste, which they dump into a lake on the edge of the town. The marginal external cost of the dumped waste is equal to the marginal private cost of producing the pesticide (that is, the marginal social cost of producing the pesticide is double the marginal private cost).

1. What is the quantity of pesticide produced if no one owns the lake and what is the efficient quantity of pesticide? What is the deadweight loss?

2. If the town owns the lake, what is the quantity of pesticide produced and how much does the town charge the factories to dump waste?

3. If the pesticide factories own the lake, how much pesticide is produced?

4. If no one owns the lake and the government levies a pollution tax, what is the tax per ton of pesticide that achieves the efficient outcome?

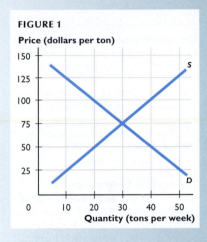

FIGURE 1

Price (dollars per ton)

In the News

New power-plant rule aids Northeast
A new Obama air pollution rule requires coal-fired power plants to reduce both smog and acid-rain causing pollutants. The coal industry says this rule is among the most expensive ever imposed by the EPA.
Source: *The Wall Street Journal*, July 7, 2011

Explain how a pollution limit will change the quantity of electricity produced. For whom would the pollution limit be expensive?

Solutions to Practice Problems

1. In Figure 2, production is 30 tons a week, the efficient quantity is 20 tons a week, and the deadweight loss is the area of the gray triangle.

2. The quantity of pesticide produced is the efficient quantity, 20 tons a week, and the town charge the factories $50 a ton of pesticide, which is the marginal external cost of the pollution produced by that quantity.

3. The factories produce the efficient quantity: 20 tons a week.

4. A pollution tax of $50 a ton paid by the factories achieves the efficient quantity of pesticide because the pollution tax equals the external cost.

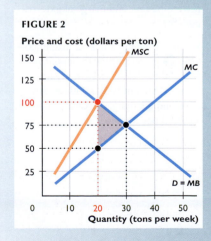

FIGURE 2

Price and cost (dollars per ton)

Solution to In the News

To reduce the amount of pollution, power plants must produce less. The quantity of electricity decreases and the price that consumers pay for electricity rises. The outcome is efficient if the quantity of electricity produced is that at which the marginal social cost of electricity equals its marginal benefit.

Education benefits the students who receive it, and the many other people with whom a well-educated person interacts. To study the economics of education, we must distinguish between its private benefits and its social benefits.

■ Private Benefits and Social Benefits

A *private benefit* is a benefit that the consumer of a good or service receives. The **marginal private benefit** (*MB*) is the benefit from an additional unit of a good or service that the consumer of that good or service receives.

An *external benefit* is a benefit from a good or service that someone other than the consumer receives. A **marginal external benefit** is the benefit from an additional unit of a good or service that people other than the consumer enjoy.

Marginal social benefit (*MSB*) is the marginal benefit enjoyed by society—by the consumers of a good or service (marginal private benefit) and by everyone else who benefits from it (the marginal external benefit). That is,

$$MSB = MB + \text{Marginal external benefit.}$$

Figure 10.6 illustrates these benefit concepts using as an example college education. (The same principles apply to all levels of education.) The marginal benefit curve, *MB*, describes the marginal private benefit—such as expanded job opportunities and higher incomes—enjoyed by college graduates. Marginal private benefit decreases as the quantity of education increases.

Marginal private benefit
The benefit from an additional unit of a good or service that the consumer of that good or service receives.

Marginal external benefit
The benefit from an additional unit of a good or service that people other than the consumer of that good or service enjoy.

Marginal social benefit
The marginal benefit enjoyed by society—by the consumer of a good or service and by everyone else who benefits from it. It is the sum of marginal private benefit and marginal external benefit.

■ **FIGURE 10.6**

An External Benefit

The *MB* curve shows the marginal private benefit enjoyed by the people who receive a college education. The *MSB* curve shows the sum of marginal private benefit and marginal external benefit.

When 15 million students attend college, ❶ marginal private benefit is $10,000 per student, ❷ marginal external benefit is $15,000 per student, and ❸ marginal social benefit is $25,000 per student.

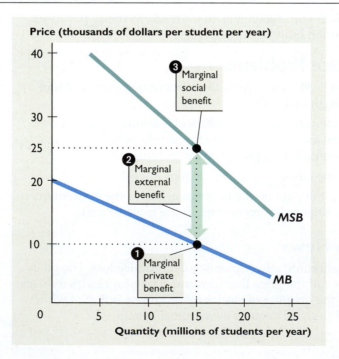

But college graduates generate external benefits. On the average, college graduates communicate more effectively with others and tend to be better citizens. Their crime rates are lower, and they are more tolerant of the views of others. A society with a large number of college graduates can support activities such as high-quality music, theater, and other organized social activities.

In the example in Figure 10.6, the marginal external benefit is $15,000 per student per year when 15 million students enroll in college. Marginal social benefit is the sum of marginal private benefit and marginal external benefit. For example, when 15 million students a year enroll in college, the marginal private benefit is $10,000 per student and the marginal external benefit is $15,000 per student, so the marginal social benefit is $25,000 per student.

The marginal social benefit curve, *MSB*, is the sum of marginal private benefit and marginal external benefit. It is steeper than the *MB* curve because marginal external benefit diminishes for the same reasons that *MB* diminishes.

When people make decisions about how much schooling to undertake, they consider only its private benefits and if education were provided by private schools that charged full-cost tuition, there would be too few college graduates.

Figure 10.7 shows the underproduction that would occur if all college education were left to the private market. The supply curve is the marginal cost curve of the private schools, $S = MC$. The demand curve is the marginal private benefit curve, $D = MB$. Market equilibrium is at a tuition of $15,000 per student per year and 7.5 million students per year. At this equilibrium, marginal social benefit is $38,000 per student, which exceeds marginal cost by $23,000. Too few students enroll in college. The efficient number is 15 million, where marginal social benefit equals marginal cost. The gray triangle shows the deadweight loss created by the underproduction.

■ **FIGURE 10.7**

Underproduction with an External Benefit

MyEconLab Animation

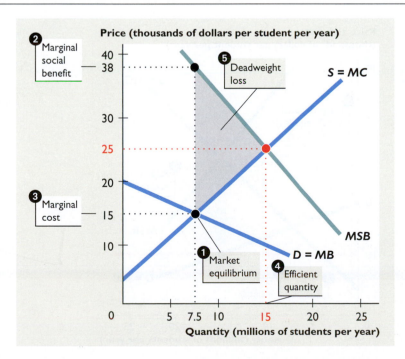

The market demand curve is the marginal private benefit curve, $D = MB$. The supply curve is the marginal cost curve, $S = MC$.

❶ Market equilibrium is at a tuition of $15,000 a year and 7.5 million students and is inefficient because ❷ marginal social benefit exceeds ❸ marginal cost.

❹ The marginal social benefit curve is *MSB*, so the efficient number of students is 15 million a year.

❺ The gray triangle shows the deadweight loss created because too few students enroll in college.

■ Government Actions in the Face of External Benefits

To get closer to producing the efficient quantity of a good or service that generates an external benefit, we make public choices through governments and modify the market outcome. To achieve a more efficient allocation of resources in the presence of external benefits, such as those that arise from education, governments can use three devices:

- Public provision
- Private subsidies
- Vouchers

Public Provision

Public provision is the production of a good or service by a public authority that receives most of its revenue from the government. Education services produced by the public universities, colleges, and schools are examples of public provision.

Figure 10.8 shows how public provision might overcome the underproduction that arises in Figure 10.7. Public provision cannot lower the cost of production, so marginal cost is the same as before. Marginal private benefit, marginal external benefit, and marginal social benefit are also the same as before.

The efficient quantity occurs where marginal social benefit equals marginal cost. In Figure 10.8, this quantity is 15 million students per year. Tuition is set to ensure that the efficient number of students enroll. That is, tuition is set at the level that equals the marginal private benefit at the efficient quantity. In Figure 10.8, tuition is $10,000 a year. The rest of the cost of the public university is borne by the taxpayers and, in this example, is $15,000 per student per year.

Public provision

The production of a good or service by a public authority that receives most of its revenue from the government.

■ **FIGURE 10.8**

Public Provision to Achieve an Efficient Outcome

MyEconLab Animation

❶ Marginal social benefit equals marginal cost with 15 million students enrolled in college, the ❷ efficient quantity.

❸ Tuition is set at $10,000 per year, and ❹ the taxpayers cover the remaining $15,000 of marginal cost per student.

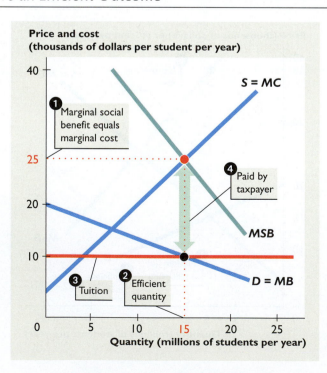

Private Subsidies

A **subsidy** is a payment by the government to a producer to cover part of the costs of production. By giving producers a subsidy, the government can induce private decision makers to consider external benefits when they make their choices.

Figure 10.9 shows how a subsidy to private colleges works. In the absence of a subsidy, the marginal cost curve is the market supply curve of private college education, $S = MC$. The marginal benefit is the demand curve, $D = MB$. In this example, the government provides a subsidy to colleges of $15,000 per student per year. We must subtract the subsidy from the marginal cost of education to find the colleges' supply curve. That curve is $S = MC - subsidy$ in the figure. The equilibrium tuition (market price) is $10,000 a year, and the equilibrium quantity is 15 million students. To educate 15 million students, colleges incur a marginal cost of $25,000 a year. The marginal social benefit is also $25,000 a year. So with marginal cost equal to marginal social benefit, the subsidy has achieved an efficient outcome. The tuition and the subsidy just cover the colleges' marginal cost.

Public Provision Versus Private Subsidy In the two methods we've just studied, the same number of students enroll and tuition is the same. So are these two methods of providing education services equally good? This question is difficult to resolve. The bureaucrats that operate public schools don't have as strong an incentive to minimize costs and maximize *quality* as those who run private schools. But for elementary and secondary education, *charter schools* (see p. 259) might be an efficient compromise between traditional public schools and subsidized private schools.

Subsidy

A payment by the government to a producer to cover part of the costs of production.

FIGURE 10.9

Private Subsidy to Achieve an Efficient Outcome

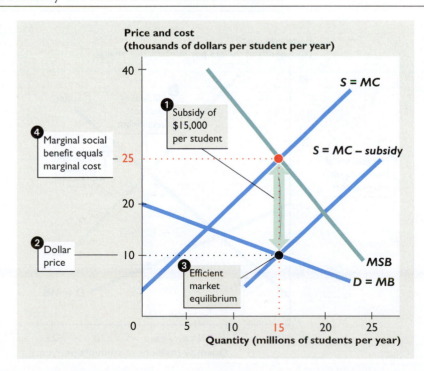

With a ❶ subsidy of $15,000 per student, the supply curve is $S = MC - subsidy$.

❷ The equilibrium price is $10,000.

❸ The market equilibrium is efficient with 15 million students enrolled in college because ❹ marginal social benefit equals marginal cost.

Voucher

A token that the government provides to households, which they can use to buy specified goods or services.

Vouchers

A **voucher** is a token that the government provides to households, which they can use to buy specified goods or services. Food stamps that the U.S. Department of Agriculture provides under a federal Food Stamp Program are examples of vouchers. Vouchers for college education could be provided to students. Let's see how they would work.

The government would provide each student with a voucher. Students would choose the school to attend and pay the tuition with dollars plus a voucher. Schools would exchange the vouchers they receive for dollars from the government. If the government set the value of a voucher equal to the marginal external benefit of a year of college at the efficient quantity, the outcome would be efficient.

Figure 10.10 illustrates an efficient voucher scheme in action. The government issues vouchers worth $15,000 per student per year. Each student pays $10,000 tuition and the government pays $15,000 per voucher, so the school collects $25,000 per student. The voucher scheme results in 15 million students attending college, the marginal cost of a student equals the marginal social benefit, and the outcome is efficient.

Do Vouchers Beat Public Provision and Subsidy? Vouchers provide public financial resources to the consumer rather than the producer. Economists generally believe that vouchers offer a more efficient outcome than public provision and subsidies because they combine the benefits of competition among private schools with the injection of the public funds needed to achieve an efficient level of output. Also, students and their parents can monitor school performance more effectively than the government can (see *Eye on the U.S. Economy* opposite.)

■ **FIGURE 10.10**

Vouchers Achieve an Efficient Outcome

MyEconLab Animation

With vouchers, buyers are willing to pay *MB* plus the value of the voucher.

❶ The government issues vouchers to each student valued at $15,000.

❷ The market equilibrium is efficient. With 15 million students enrolled in college, ❸ marginal social benefit equals marginal cost.

❹ Each student pays tuition of $10,000 (the dollar price) and the school collects $15,000 (the value of the voucher) from the government.

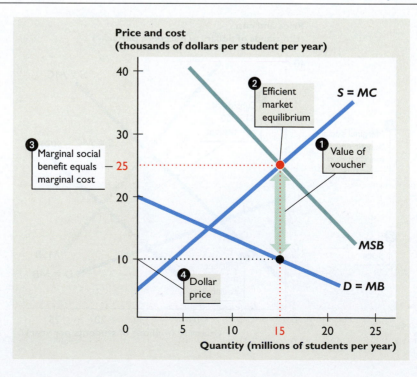

EYE on the U.S. ECONOMY
Education Quality: Charter Schools and Vouchers

The three methods of achieving efficient education have similar effects on the *quantity* of education but different effects on its *quality*. And quality has become a big issue with international league tables showing U.S. students performing worse on standardized math and science tests than those in more than 20 other countries. Here, we look at two ways of trying to improve the quality of U.S. education: charter schools and school vouchers.

Charter Schools

A *charter school* is a *public* school but one that is free to make its own education policy. Around 4,000 charter schools in 40 states are operating today and they teach more than 1 million students. When the demand for places in a charter school exceeds the supply, students are chosen by lottery.

How efficient are the charter schools?

School efficiency has two dimensions: cost per student and educational standard attained.

Charter schools perform well on both criteria. They cost less than public schools and they achieve more. Cost per student in New York charter schools is 18 percent less than regular public schools. And charter school students perform higher in math and reading than equivalent students who apply to but (randomly) don't get into a charter school.

Vouchers

School vouchers are much less used than charter schools and more controversial. But an increasing number of states, among them Wisconsin, Louisiana, Ohio, the District of Columbia, and New York, operate a

Stanford University professor Caroline Hoxby says: "Tell me your goals and I'll design you a voucher to achieve them."

school voucher program.

Studies of the effects of vouchers have generated more controversies than firm conclusions, but some economists are convinced that they offer the best solution.

EYE on YOUR LIFE
Externalities in Your Life

Think about the externalities, both negative and positive, that play a huge part in *your* life; and think about the incentives that attempt to align your self-interest with the social interest.

You respond to the gasoline tax by buying a little bit less gas than you otherwise would. As you saw in *Eye on Climate Change* (p. 252), this incentive is small compared to that in some other countries. With a bigger gas tax, such

as that in the United Kingdom, for example, you would find ways of getting by with a smaller quantity of gasoline and your actions and those of millions of others would make the traffic on our highways much lighter.

You are responding to the huge incentive of subsidized tuition by being in school. Without subsidized college education, fewer people would attend college and university and with fewer

college graduates, the benefits we all receive from living in a well-educated society would be smaller.

Think about your attitude as a citizen–voter to these two externalities. Should the gas tax be higher to discourage the use of the automobile? Should tuition be even lower to encourage even more people to enroll in school? Or have we got these incentives just right in the social interest?

CHECKPOINT 10.2

Explain why positive externalities lead to inefficient underproduction and how public provision, subsidies, and vouchers can achieve a more efficient outcome.

Practice Problems

Figure 1 shows the marginal private benefit from college education. The marginal cost of a college education is a constant $6,000 a year. The marginal external benefit from a college education is a constant $4,000 per student per year.

1. What is the efficient number of students? If colleges are private (no government involvement), how many people enroll, what is the tuition, and what is the deadweight loss?

2. If the government provides public colleges, what is the tuition that will achieve the efficient number of students? How much must taxpayers pay?

3. If the government subsidizes private colleges, what subsidy will achieve the efficient number of college students?

4. If the government offers students vouchers, what value of the voucher will achieve the efficient number of students?

In the News

Tuition hikes should frighten students

Despite the hard times, families will not be deprived of access to federal student loans. The real danger is a hike in tuition. Often in past recessions, states have cut funding for colleges and tuition has skyrocketed. The Cato Institute says a better policy would be for the states to maintain the subsidies to colleges.

Source: Michael Dannenberg, *USA Today*, October 22, 2008

If government cuts the subsidy to colleges, why will tuition rise and the number of students enrolled decrease? Why does the Cato Institute say that it's a better policy for government to maintain the subsidy?

Solutions to Practice Problems

1. In Figure 2, the efficient number of students is 50,000 a year. With no government involvement, enrollment is 30,000 students a year and tuition is $6,000 a year. The gray triangle shows the deadweight loss.

2. To enroll the efficient 50,000 students, public colleges would charge $2,000 per student and taxpayers would pay $4,000 per student (Figure 2).

3. A subsidy of $4,000 per student (equal to marginal external benefit).

4. The value of the voucher will be $4,000. Enrollment will be 50,000 if the tuition is $2,000. The private college tuition is $6,000, so to get 50,000 students to enroll, the value of the voucher will have to be $4,000.

Solution to In the News

A cut in the subsidy will increase the college's marginal cost. Tuition will rise and the number of students will decrease—a movement up along the demand curve. The Cato Institute says maintaining the subsidy is a better policy because it avoids the deadweight loss of a cut in the number of students.

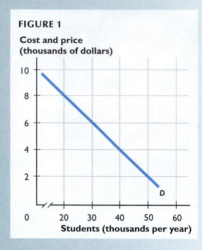

FIGURE 1

Cost and price
(thousands of dollars)

Students (thousands per year)

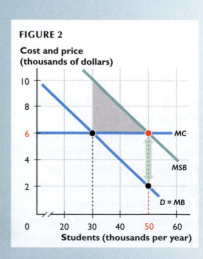

FIGURE 2

Cost and price
(thousands of dollars)

Students (thousands per year)

CHAPTER SUMMARY

Key Points

1 **Explain why negative externalities lead to inefficient overproduction and how property rights, pollution charges, and taxes can achieve a more efficient outcome.**

- External costs are costs of production that fall on people other than the producer of a good or service. Marginal social cost equals marginal private cost plus marginal external cost.

- Producers take account only of marginal private cost and produce more than the efficient quantity when there is a marginal external cost.

- Sometimes it is possible to overcome a negative externality by assigning a property right.

- When property rights cannot be assigned, governments might overcome a negative externality by using pollution limits, pollution charges or taxes, or marketable permits (cap-and-trade).

2 **Explain why positive externalities lead to inefficient underproduction and how public provision, subsidies, and vouchers can achieve a more efficient outcome.**

- External benefits are benefits that are received by people other than the consumer of a good or service. Marginal social benefit equals marginal private benefit plus marginal external benefit.

- External benefits from education arise because better-educated people are better citizens, commit fewer crimes, and support social activities.

- Vouchers or subsidies to private schools or the provision of public education below cost can achieve a more efficient provision of education.

Key Terms

Coase theorem, 248
Externality, 242
Marginal external benefit, 254
Marginal external cost, 244
Marginal private benefit, 254
Marginal private cost, 244
Marginal social benefit, 254
Marginal social cost, 244

Negative externality, 242
Positive externality, 242
Property rights, 247
Public provision, 256
Subsidy, 257
Transactions costs, 248
Voucher, 258

TABLE 1	DEMAND FOR ELECTRICITY
Price (cents per kilowatt)	Quantity demanded (kilowatts per day)
4	500
8	400
12	300
16	200
20	100
24	0

TABLE 2   PRIVATE AND EXTERNAL COSTS

Quantity (kilowatts per day)	Marginal cost	Marginal external cost
	(cents per kilowatt)	
0	0	0
100	2	2
200	4	4
300	6	6
400	8	8
500	10	10

TABLE 3

Students (millions per year)	Marginal benefit (dollars per student per year)
1	5,000
2	3,000
3	2,000
4	1,500
5	1,200
6	1,000
7	800
8	500

CHAPTER CHECKPOINT

Study Plan Problems and Applications

Table 1 shows the demand schedule for electricity from a coal burning utility. Table 2 shows the utility's cost of producing electricity and the external cost of the pollution created. Use this information to work Problems **1** to **3**.

1. With no pollution control, calculate the quantity of electricity produced, the price of electricity, and the marginal external cost of the pollution generated.

2. With no pollution control, calculate the quantity of electricity produced, the marginal social cost of the electricity generated, and the deadweight loss.

3. If the government levies a pollution tax such that the utility generates the efficient quantity of electricity, calculate the quantity of electricity generated, the price of electricity, the size of the pollution tax, and the tax revenue.

Use the following information to work Problems **4** and **5**.

Tom and Larry must spend a day working together. Tom likes to smoke cigars and the price of a cigar is $2. Larry likes a smoke-free environment.

4. If Tom's marginal benefit from a cigar a day is $20 and Larry's marginal benefit from a smoke-free environment is $25 a day, what is the outcome if they meet at Tom's home? What is the outcome if they meet at Larry's home?

5. If Tom's marginal benefit from a cigar a day is $25 and Larry's marginal benefit from a smoke-free environment is $20 a day, what is the outcome if they meet at Tom's home? What is the outcome if they meet at Larry's home?

Use Table 3 and the following information to work Problems **6** to **8**.

The marginal cost of educating a college student is $5,000 a year. Table 3 shows the marginal benefit schedule from a college education. The marginal external benefit from a college education is a constant $2,000 per student per year. There are no public colleges.

6. With no government involvement in college education, how many students enroll, what is the tuition, and what is the deadweight loss created?

7. If the government subsidizes colleges and sets the subsidy so that the efficient number of students enroll, what is the subsidy per student, how many students enroll, and what is the cost to taxpayers?

8. If the government offers vouchers to students, what is the value of the voucher that will encourage the efficient number of students to enroll?

9. Global solutions for local gridlock
The Toronto Board of Trade has warned that gridlock already costs the region $6 billion a year, with average commute times of 80 minutes, among the highest in North America. By 2031, that situation is going to get worse, adding an additional 27 minutes to the daily grind. Civic leaders are looking at the options: road tolls, a regional gas tax, and parking levies.
Source: *Toronto Star*, June 24, 2011

With road tolls, a regional gas tax, and parking levies would Toronto streets become less congested? If the new charges cut commute times, would the Toronto road system be more efficient? Explain your answers.

Instructor Assignable Problems and Applications

Your instructor can assign these problems as homework, a quiz, or a test in MyEconLab.

1. The price of gasoline in Europe is about three times that in the United States, mainly because the European gas tax is higher than the U.S. gas tax. In light of the principles you've learned in this chapter, what is the case for increasing the gas tax in the United States to the European level and what is the case against an increase in the gas tax to the European level?

2. **Polar ice cap shrinks further and thins**
   With global warming of the planet, the polar ice cap is shrinking. As the Arctic Sea expands more underwater mineral resources will be accessible. Countries are staking out territorial claims to parts of the polar region.
   Source: *The Wall Street Journal*, April 7, 2009

   Explain how ownership of these mineral resources will influence the amount of damage done to the Arctic Sea and its wildlife.

Use the following information to work Problems **3** and **4**.

Plans to curtail use of plastic bags, but not much action
Plastic bags have been blamed for street litter, ocean pollution, and carbon emissions produced by manufacturing and shipping them. Last summer, Seattle approved a 20-cents charge on plastic shopping bags, which was intended to reduce pollution by encouraging reusable bags.
Source: *The New York Times*, February 23, 2009

3. Explain how Seattle's 20-cents charge will change the use of plastic bags and how the deadweight loss created by plastic bags will change.

4. Explain why a complete ban on plastic bags would be inefficient.

Use the following information to work Problems **5** to **7**.

The marginal cost of educating a college student online is $3,000 a year. Table 1 shows the marginal private benefit schedule from a college education. The marginal external benefit is 50 percent of the marginal private benefit.

5. With no government involvement in college education, how many students enroll and what is the tuition? Calculate the deadweight loss created.

6. If the government subsidizes colleges so that the efficient number of students will enroll, what is the cost to taxpayers?

7. If the government offers vouchers to students and values them so that the efficient number of students will enroll, what is the value of the voucher?

8. **U.S. environmentalists back EU emission plan**
   The European Union has introduced a new law, which requires any airline operating to or from an EU airport after January 1 to participate in the EU cap-and-trade system. Under the EU plan, 15 percent of pollution credits for airlines will be auctioned off and the other 85 percent of credits are being given without charge.
   Source: *The Wall Street Journal*, June 30, 2011

   Explain the conditions under which a cap-and-trade system would reduce the amount of airline emissions to the efficient quantity.

TABLE 1

Students (millions per year)	Marginal private benefit (dollars per student per year)
1	6,000
2	5,000
3	4,000
4	3,000
5	2,000
6	1,000

MyEconLab

You can work this quiz in Chapter 10 Study Plan and get instant feedback.

Multiple Choice Quiz

1. Electricity has a negative production externality because _____ .

   A. its marginal benefit decreases as more of it is consumed
   B. the marginal private cost of producing it increases as more of it is produced
   C. the marginal social cost of producing it exceeds the marginal private cost of producing it
   D. a marginal external cost lowers the marginal benefit from consuming it

2. A steel making plant pollutes the air and water so _____ .

   A. the marginal social cost of producing steel exceeds the marginal private cost by the amount of the marginal external cost
   B. the marginal social cost of producing steel is less than the marginal private cost by the amount of the marginal external cost
   C. the marginal private cost of producing steel equals the marginal external cost plus the marginal social cost
   D. the marginal private cost of producing steel minus the marginal social cost equals the marginal external cost

3. An unregulated chemical factory that pollutes a river results in _____ and _____ .

   A. overproduction; a price that exceeds the marginal benefit from the good
   B. underproduction; a price that equals the marginal benefit from the good
   C. the efficient quantity produced; a marginal benefit equal to the marginal social cost
   D. an inefficient quantity produced; a marginal benefit below the marginal social cost

4. Steel production creates pollution. If a tax is imposed on steel production equal to the marginal external cost of the pollution it creates, _____.

   A. steel producers will cut pollution to zero
   B. the deadweight loss created by steel producers will be cut to zero
   C. the market price of steel will rise by the amount of the tax
   D. steel producers will continue to produce the inefficient quantity of steel

5. A good or service with a positive externality is one which _____.

   A. everyone wants to have access to
   B. is produced in the social interest
   C. the marginal social benefit exceeds the marginal private benefit
   D. the marginal external benefit exceeds the marginal private benefit

6. Because education generates a positive externality, _____.

   A. everyone who wants a college education should get one
   B. graduates' marginal benefit exceeds the society's value of the education
   C. the quantity of education undertaken will achieve the social interest if it is free
   D. subsidies to colleges or vouchers to students are means of achieving the efficient number of graduates

Should America build a high-speed rail network like Europe's?

Public Goods and Common Resources

When you have completed your study of this chapter, you will be able to

1 Distinguish among private goods, public goods, and common resources.

2 Explain the free-rider problem and how public provision might help to overcome it and deliver an efficient quantity of public goods.

3 Explain the tragedy of the commons and review its possible solutions.

11

What's the difference between the services provided by a city police department and those provided by Brink's, a private security firm that loads ATMs for banks? What's the difference between fish in the Pacific Ocean and fish on East Point Seafood Company's Seattle fish farm? What's the difference between a live Taylor Swift concert and a concert on network television? What's the difference between education and fast food? Each pair differs in many ways, but key is the extent to which people can be *excluded* from consuming them and the extent to which one person's consumption *rivals* the consumption of others.

■ Excludable

Excludable

A good, service, or resource is excludable if it is possible to prevent someone from enjoying its benefits.

A good, service, or resource is **excludable** if it is possible to prevent someone from enjoying its benefits. Brink's security services, East Point Seafood's fish, and Taylor Swift concerts are examples. You must pay to consume them.

A good, service, or resource is **nonexcludable** if it is impossible (or extremely costly) to prevent someone from benefiting from it. The services of the city police department, fish in the Pacific Ocean, and a concert on network television are examples. When a police cruiser slows the traffic on a highway to the speed limit, it lowers the risk of an accident to all the road users. It can't exclude some road users from the lower risk. Anyone with a boat can try to catch the fish in the ocean. Anyone with television can watch a network broadcast.

Nonexcludable

A good, service, or resource is nonexcludable if it is impossible (or extremely costly) to prevent someone from enjoying its benefits.

■ Rival

Rival

A good, service, or resource is rival if its use by one person decreases the quantity available for someone else.

A good, service, or resource is **rival** if its use by one person decreases the quantity available for someone else. Brink's security might work for two banks, but one truck can't deliver cash to two banks at the same time. A fish, whether in the ocean or on a fish farm, can be consumed only once. One seat at a concert can hold only one person at a time. These items are rival.

A good, service, or resource is **nonrival** if its use by one person does not decrease the quantity available for someone else. The services of the city police department and a concert on network television are nonrival. The arrival of one more person in a neighborhood doesn't lower the level of police protection enjoyed by the community. When one additional person switches on the TV, no other viewer is affected.

Nonrival

A good, service, or resource is nonrival if its use by one person does not decrease the quantity available for someone else.

■ A Fourfold Classification

Figure 11.1 classifies goods, services, and resources into four types using the two criteria that we've just considered.

Private Goods

Private good

A good or service that can be consumed by only one person at a time and only by the person who has bought it or owns it.

A good or service that is both rival and excludable (top left of Figure 11.1) is a **private good**: It can be consumed by only one person at a time and only by the person who has bought it or owns it. The fish on East Point's farm are an example of a private good. One person's consumption of a fish rivals others, and everyone except the person who bought a fish is excluded from consuming it.

Public Goods

A good or service that is both nonrival and nonexcludable (bottom right of Figure 11.1) is a **public good**: It can be consumed simultaneously by everyone, and no one can be excluded from enjoying its benefits. A flood-control levee is an example of a public good. Everyone who lives in a protected floodplain enjoys the benefits, and no one can be excluded from receiving those benefits. The system of law and order provided by the courts and the body of laws is another example.

Common Resources

A resource that is rival and nonexcludable (top right of Figure 11.1) is a **common resource**: A unit of it can be used only once, but no one can be prevented from using what is available. Ocean fish and the Earth's atmosphere are examples of common resources. Ocean fish are rival because a fish taken by one person is not available for anyone else, and they are nonexcludable because it is difficult to prevent people from catching them. The Earth's atmosphere is rival because oxygen used by one person is not available for anyone else, and it is nonexcludable because we can't prevent people from breathing!

Natural Monopoly Goods

A good that is nonrival but excludable (bottom left of Figure 11.1) is a good produced by a *natural monopoly*. We define natural monopoly in Chapter 15, p. 376. A natural monopoly is a firm that can produce at a lower cost than two or more firms can. Examples are the Internet, cable television, and a bridge or tunnel. One more user doesn't decrease the enjoyment of the other users, and people can be excluded with user codes, scramblers, and tollgates.

Public good
A good or service that can be consumed simultaneously by everyone and from which no one can be excluded.

Common resource
A resource that can be used only once, but no one can be prevented from using what is available.

FIGURE 11.1
Fourfold Classification of Goods

MyEconLab Animation

	Excludable	Nonexcludable
Rival	**Private goods** Food and drink, Car, House	**Common resources** Fish in ocean, Atmosphere, National parks
Nonrival	**Natural monopoly goods** Internet, Cable television, Bridge or tunnel	**Public goods** National defense, The law, Flood-control levees

Goods that are rival and excludable are private goods (top left).

Goods that are nonrival and nonexcludable are public goods (bottom right).

Goods and resources that are rival but nonexcludable are common resources (top right).

Goods that are nonrival but excludable are goods produced by a natural monopoly (bottom left).

SOURCE OF DATA: Adapted from and inspired by E. S. Savas, *Privatizing the Public Sector,* Chatham House Publishers, Inc., Chatham, NJ, 1982, p. 34.

EYE on the PAST
Is a Lighthouse a Public Good?

A lighthouse looks like a public good: *nonexcludable* and *nonrival*. But in the eighteenth century, lighthouses in England were built and operated by private companies that earned profits by charging tolls on ships docking at nearby ports. A ship that refused to pay the lighthouse toll was excluded from using the port. So even the services of a lighthouse, when it is near a port, are excludable! Such a lighthouse is an example of a natural monopoly good and not a public good.

CHECKPOINT 11.1

Distinguish among private goods, public goods, and common resources.

Practice Problems

1. Classify the following services for computer owners with an Internet connection as rival, nonrival, excludable, or nonexcludable:
   - eBay
   - A mouse
   - A Twitter page
   - MyEconLab Web site

2. Classify each of the following items as a public good, a private good, a natural monopoly good, or a common resource:
   - Fire protection
   - A seat at the final match of the U.S. Open (tennis)
   - A pay-per-view movie on television
   - The Mississippi River

Solutions to Practice Problems

1. eBay is nonrival and nonexcludable. A mouse is rival and excludable. Twitter is nonrival and you can choose to make your page excludable or nonexcludable. MyEconLab is nonrival and excludable.

2. Fire protection is nonrival and nonexcludable, so it is a public good. A seat at the final match of the U.S. Open is rival and excludable, so it is a private good. A pay-per-view movie is nonrival and excludable, so it is a natural monopoly good. The Mississippi River is rival and nonexcludable, so it is a common resource.

11.2   PUBLIC GOODS AND THE FREE-RIDER PROBLEM

Why does the U.S. government provide our national defense and district court system? Why do the state governments provide flood-control levees? Why do our city governments provide fire and police services? Why don't we buy our national defense from North Pole Protection, Inc., a private firm that competes for our dollars in the marketplace in the same way that McDonald's does? Why don't private engineering firms provide levees? Why don't we buy our policing and fire services from Brink's and other private firms? The answer is that all of these goods are public goods—goods that are nonexcludable and nonrival—and such goods create a free-rider problem.

■ The Free-Rider Problem

A **free rider** is a person who enjoys the benefits from a good or service without paying for it. Because everyone consumes the same quantity of a public good and no one can be excluded from enjoying its benefits, no one has an incentive to pay for it. Everyone has an incentive to free ride. The *free-rider problem* is that the private market, left on its own, would provide too small a quantity of a public good. To produce the efficient quantity, government action is required.

To see how a private market would provide too little of a public good and how government might provide the efficient quantity, we need to consider the marginal benefit from a public good and its marginal cost. The marginal benefit from a public good is a bit different from that of a private good, so we'll begin on the benefit side of the calculation.

Free rider
A person who enjoys the benefits of a good or service without paying for it.

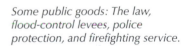

Some public goods: The law, flood-control levees, police protection, and firefighting service.

■ The Marginal Benefit from a Public Good

To learn about the marginal benefit from a public good, think about a concrete example. Lisa and Max share a common parking area that has no security lighting. Both of them would like some lights, but how many? What is the value or benefit from just one light, from adding a second, and perhaps from adding a third light? To answer this question, we must somehow combine the value of lights to both Lisa and Max and find the marginal benefit from different quantities of lights—the marginal benefit curve of lights.

For a private good, the marginal benefit curve is the market demand curve. Everyone pays the same market price for a private good, and each person chooses the quantity to buy at that price. In contrast, for a public good, everyone consumes the same quantity, but each person puts a different private value on that quantity. So how are we to find the equivalent of the demand curve for a public good? Figure 11.2 answers this question and illustrates the calculation of marginal benefit from a public good. It also shows the marginal social benefit curve.

Lisa and Max know their own marginal benefit from different levels of security lighting. The tables in parts (a) and (b) of Figure 11.2 show these marginal benefits. The curves MB_L and MB_M are Lisa's and Max's marginal benefit curves. Each person's marginal benefit from a public good diminishes as the quantity of the good increases—just as it does for a private good. For Lisa, the marginal benefit from the first light is $80, and from the second it is $60. By the time 5 lights are installed, Lisa's marginal benefit is zero. For Max, the marginal benefit from the first light is $50, and from the second it is $40. By the time 5 lights are installed, Max perceives only $10 worth of marginal benefit.

The table in part (c) of Figure 11.2 shows the marginal benefit for the entire economy. We obtain this curve by summing the individual marginal benefits at each quantity. For example, with 3 lights, the marginal benefit is $70 ($40 for Lisa plus $30 for Max) and with 4 lights, the marginal benefit is $40 ($20 for Lisa plus $20 for Max). The curve MSB is the marginal social benefit curve.

Because we find the marginal benefit from a public good by summing the marginal benefits of all individuals at each *quantity*, we find the MSB curve by summing the individual marginal benefit curves *vertically*. In contrast, to obtain the MB curve for a private good—which is also the market demand curve—we sum the quantities demanded by all individuals at each *price*—we sum the individual demand curves *horizontally* (see Chapter 4, p. 87).

Notice that the MSB curve for a public good is both a marginal private benefit curve and a marginal social benefit curve. A public good doesn't have external benefits (see p. 267). Because everyone can consume an equal quantity of a public good, everyone benefits from it. The MSB curve includes all the benefits.

The principle that we've learned in this example of security lights for Lisa and Max applies to a public good such as national defense in our economy with its millions of people. The marginal social benefit of national defense is the sum of the marginal benefits of all the people in the economy.

■ The Marginal Cost of a Public Good

The marginal cost of a public good is determined in exactly the same way as that of a private good. The principle of *increasing marginal cost* that you learned in Chapter 6 applies to the marginal cost of a public good. So the marginal cost curve of a public good slopes upward. A public good does not create an externality, so the marginal cost is also the marginal social cost.

FIGURE 11.2

Marginal Benefit of a Public Good

MyEconLab Animation

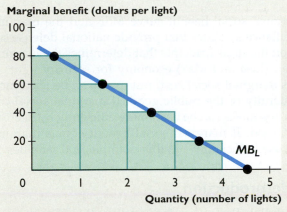

(a) Lisa's marginal benefit

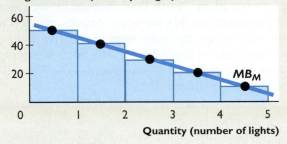

(b) Max's marginal benefit

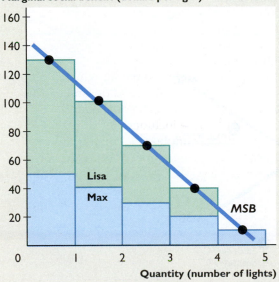

(c) Economy's marginal social benefit

The marginal benefit curves for a public good are MB_L for Lisa and MB_M for Max. The marginal benefit from the public good for the economy is the sum of the marginal benefits of all individuals at each quantity. The marginal social benefit curve for the economy is MSB.

Quantity of lights	0	1	2	3	4	5
Lisa's MB (dollars per light)		80	60	40	20	0

Quantity of lights	0	1	2	3	4	5
Max's MB (dollars per light)		50	40	30	20	10

Quantity of lights	0	1	2	3	4	5
Lisa's MB (dollars per light)		80	60	40	20	0
Max's MB (dollars per light)		50	40	30	20	10
Economy's MSB (dollars per light)		130	100	70	40	10

■ The Efficient Quantity of a Public Good

To determine the efficient quantity, we use the same principles that you learned in Chapter 6: We find the quantity at which marginal social benefit equals marginal social cost.

Figure 11.3 shows the marginal social benefit curve *MSB* and the marginal social cost curve *MSC* of surveillance satellites that provide national defense services. The *MSB* curve is based on the same principle that determines the marginal social benefit of the two-person (Lisa and Max) economy for security lights. If marginal social benefit exceeds marginal social cost, resources can be used more efficiently by increasing the quantity of the public good. If marginal social cost exceeds marginal social benefit, resources can be used more efficiently by decreasing the quantity of the public good. If marginal social benefit equals marginal social cost, resources are being used efficiently—in this example, 200 satellites.

■ Private Provision: Underproduction

Could a private firm—say, North Pole Protection, Inc.—deliver the efficient quantity of satellites? Most likely, it couldn't because no one would have an incentive to pay his or her share of the cost of the satellites. Everyone would reason as follows: "The number of satellites provided by North Pole Protection, Inc., is not affected by my decision to pay my share or not. My own private consumption will be greater if I free ride. If I do not pay, I enjoy the same level of security and I can buy more private goods. So I will free ride on the public good." Such reasoning is the free-rider problem. If everyone reasons the same way, North Pole Protection, Inc., has no revenue and so provides no satellites.

■ FIGURE 11.3

The Efficient Quantity and Private Underproduction of a Public Good

MyEconLab Animation

❶ With fewer than 200 satellites, marginal social benefit *MSB* exceeds marginal social cost *MSC*. An increase in the quantity will make resource use more efficient.

❷ With more than 200 satellites, marginal social cost exceeds marginal social benefit. A decrease in the quantity will make resource use more efficient.

❸ With 200 satellites, marginal social benefit *MSB* equals marginal social cost *MSC*. Resources are used efficiently.

❹ The efficient quantity is 200 satellites.

❺ Private provision leads to underproduction—in the extreme, to zero production.

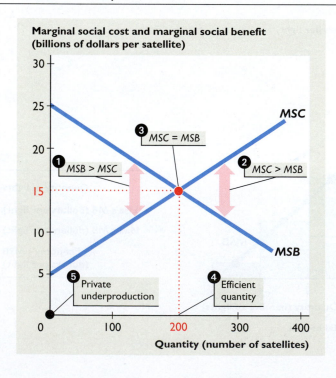

■ Public Provision: Efficient Production

The political process might be efficient or inefficient. We look first at an efficient outcome. There are two political parties, the Hawks and the Doves, which agree on all issues except for the quantity of defense satellites. The Hawks want 300 satellites, and the Doves want 100 satellites. Both parties want to get elected, so they run a voter survey and discover the *MSB* curve of Figure 11.4. They also consult with satellite producers to establish the marginal cost schedule. The parties then do a "what-if" analysis. If the Hawks propose 300 satellites and the Doves propose 100 satellites, the voters will be equally unhappy with both parties. Compared to the efficient quantity, the Doves want an underprovision of 100 satellites and the Hawks want an overprovision of 100 satellites. The deadweight losses are equal, and the election would be too close to call.

Contemplating this outcome, the Hawks realize that they are too hawkish to get elected. They figure that if they scale back to 250 satellites, they will win the election if the Doves propose 100 satellites. The Doves reason in a similar way and figure that if they increase the number of satellites to 150, they can win the election if the Hawks propose 300 satellites. Each party knows how the other is reasoning, and they realize that their party must provide 200 satellites, or it will lose the election. So both parties propose 200 satellites. The voters are indifferent between the parties, and each party receives 50 percent of the vote.

FIGURE 11.4

An Efficient Political Outcome

MyEconLab Animation

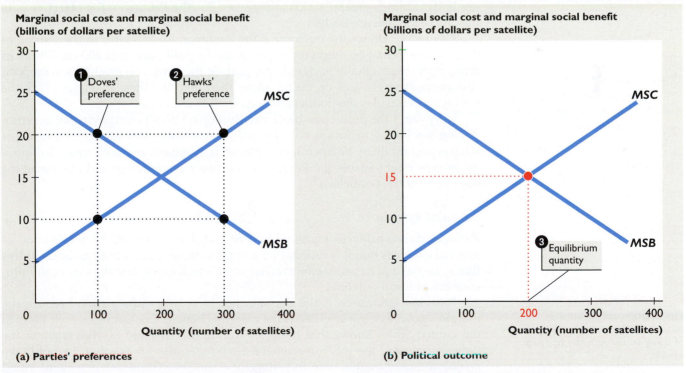

(a) Parties' preferences

(b) Political outcome

❶ The Doves would like to provide 100 satellites. ❷ The Hawks would like to provide 300 satellites.

❸ The political outcome is 200 satellites: Unless each party proposes 200 satellites, the other party can win an election.

Regardless of which party wins the election, 200 satellites are provided, and this quantity is efficient. In this example, competition in the political marketplace results in the efficient provision of a public good.

For this outcome to occur, voters must be well informed, evaluate the alternatives, and vote in the election. Political parties must be well informed about voter preferences. As you will see, we can't expect to achieve this outcome.

The Principle of Minimum Differentiation

Principle of minimum differentiation
The tendency for competitors to make themselves identical to appeal to the maximum number of clients or voters.

In the example that we've just studied, the two parties propose identical policies. This tendency toward identical policies is an example of the **principle of minimum differentiation**: To appeal to the maximum number of clients or voters, competitors tend to make themselves identical. This principle not only describes the behavior of political parties but also explains why fast-food restaurants cluster in the same block and even why new car models have similar features. If McDonald's opens a restaurant in a new location, it is more likely that Burger King will open next door to McDonald's rather than a mile down the road. If Chrysler designs a new back-up camera or a hands-free phone system, most likely Ford will too.

■ Public Provision: Overproduction

If competition between two political parties is to deliver the efficient quantity of satellites, the Defense Department—the Pentagon—must cooperate and help to achieve this outcome.

Objective of Bureaucrats

A bureau head seeks to maximize her or his department's budget because a bigger budget brings greater status and power. For the Pentagon, the objective is to maximize the defense budget.

Figure 11.5 shows the outcome if the Pentagon is successful in the pursuit of its goal. The Pentagon might try to persuade the politicians that 200 satellites cost more than the originally budgeted amount; or the Pentagon might press its position more strongly and argue for more than 200 satellites. In Figure 11.5, the Pentagon persuades the politicians to go for 300 satellites.

Why don't the politicians block the Pentagon? Won't overpaying or overproducing satellites cost future votes? It will if voters are well informed and know what is best for them. Voters might not be well informed, and well-informed interest groups might enable the Pentagon to achieve its objective and overcome the objections of the politicians.

Rational Ignorance

Rational choice balances marginal benefit and marginal cost. An implication of rational choice is that it is rational for a voter to be ignorant about an issue unless that issue has a perceptible effect on the voter's well-being and the voter can influence the political outcome.

Rational ignorance
The decision not to acquire information because the marginal cost of doing so exceeds the marginal benefit.

Rational ignorance is the decision not to acquire information because the marginal cost of doing so exceeds the marginal benefit. For example, each voter in the United States knows that he or she can make virtually no difference to the defense policy of the U.S. government. Each voter also knows that it would take an enormous amount of time and effort to become even moderately well informed about alternative defense technologies. So voters remain relatively uninformed

FIGURE 11.5

Inefficient Bureaucratic Overproduction

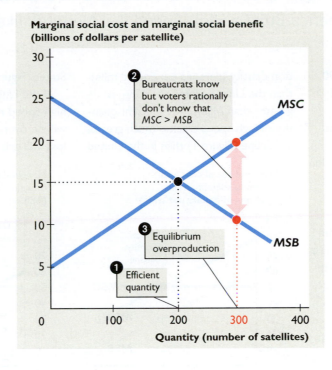

1 The efficient quantity is 200 satellites with marginal social benefit *MSB* equal to marginal social cost *MSC*.

2 Bureaucrats are well-informed and voters are rationally ignorant, so bureaucrats are able to increase production (and their budget) to a level at which marginal social cost *MSC* exceeds marginal social benefit *MSB*.

3 With 300 satellites, marginal social cost exceeds marginal social benefit and inefficient overproduction occurs.

about the technicalities of defense issues. (Although we are using defense policy as an example, the same principle applies to all aspects of government economic activity.)

All voters benefit from national defense, but not all voters produce national defense—only a small number work in the defense industry. Voters who own or work for firms that produce satellites have a direct personal interest in defense because it affects their incomes. These voters have an incentive to become well informed about defense issues and to lobby politicians to further their own interests. In collaboration with the defense bureaucracy, these voters exert a larger influence on public policy than do the relatively uninformed voters who only benefit from this public good.

■ Why Government Is Large and Growing

Government is large and it grows faster than the rest of the economy to take an ever larger share of production. Why?

Voter preferences for public goods drive the growth of government. The demand for national and personal security and the demand for other public services are *income elastic*. As incomes increase, the demand for these services increases by a larger percentage than the increase in income.

Inefficient bureaucratic overprovision of public goods and services might make government too big and too costly. There is no easy fix for this problem. Our ever-growing demand for education and health-care services contribute to the large and growing scale of government.

EYE on the U.S. INFRASTRUCTURE
Should America Build a High-Speed Rail Network like Europe's?

Train travel in Europe is fast: The 190 miles from Paris to Brussels takes 1 hour and 20 minutes. The 220 miles from Boston to New York City takes 3 hours and 40 minutes.

President Obama says that by 2036, he wants 80 percent of Americans to be able to go places by train as fast as Europeans can.

Why is the United States lagging in high-speed rail transportation? Is there underprovision or do we have the efficient amount of high-speed rail transportation?

The marginal social cost of high-speed rail track (*MSC* in the figures) is about $50 million a mile.

The marginal social benefit of high-speed rail (*MSB* in the figures) depends on the size and density of the population. Europe has a much higher popula-

tion density (persons per square mile) than the United States, so MSB_{EU} is greater than MSB_{US}. The efficient quantity of high-speed track is much greater in Europe (Figure 1) than in the United

States (Figure 2).

If the United States installs as much high-speed rail track as Europe has, it will be overprovided and a deadweight loss will arise.

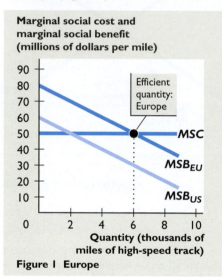

Marginal social cost and marginal social benefit (millions of dollars per mile)

Efficient quantity: Europe

MSC

MSB_{EU}

MSB_{US}

Quantity (thousands of miles of high-speed track)

Figure 1 Europe

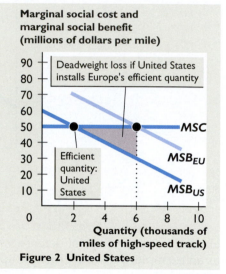

Marginal social cost and marginal social benefit (millions of dollars per mile)

Deadweight loss if United States installs Europe's efficient quantity

MSC

Efficient quantity: United States

MSB_{EU}

MSB_{US}

Quantity (thousands of miles of high-speed track)

Figure 2 United States

EYE on YOUR LIFE
A Student's Free-Rider Problem

MP3 music files are nonrival because they can be duplicated at the click of a mouse. Files can be created at zero opportunity cost. A music file is nonexcludable because it is costly to exclude anyone who wants to make an illegal copy of a file.

Because music files are nonrival and effectively nonexcludable, they create a free-rider problem.

If everyone obtained their music by copying the files of their friends, you

can see that it would not take long for the provision of songs to dry up. Only amateur performers who record for fun would be left in the business.

We tackle this free-rider problem by using the copyright laws that restrict the legal right to copy music files. The problem is that making something illegal isn't effective if it is difficult to detect and punish the illegal acts.

Another solution might be to put a tax on MP3 players and distribute the

revenue to performers and recording companies, but this approach doesn't provide an incentive to limit illegal file sharing. Once the player tax has been paid, it has no effect on how it is used.

The best solution currently available is for the courts to enforce property rights and for the recording companies to pursue illegal file sharers and hit them with large penalties. But the cost of enforcing these property rights is high.

CHECKPOINT 11.2

Explain the free-rider problem and how public provision might help to overcome it and deliver an efficient quantity of public goods.

MyEconLab
You can work these problems in Study Plan 11.2 and get instant feedback.

Practice Problems

1. For each of the following goods, explain whether there is a free-rider problem. If there is no such problem, how is it avoided?
   - Fire protection
   - A July 4th fireworks display
   - Interstate 80 in rural Wyoming

Use Table 1, which provides data about a mosquito control program, to work Problems **2** and **3**.

2. What quantity of spraying would a private control program provide? What is the efficient quantity of spraying? In a single-issue election on the quantity of spraying, what quantity would the winner of the election provide?

3. Suppose that the government sets up a Department of Mosquito Control and appoints a bureaucrat to run it. Would the department most likely underprovide, overprovide, or provide the efficient quantity of spraying?

TABLE 1

Quantity (square miles sprayed per day)	Marginal social cost	Marginal social benefit
	(dollars per day)	
0	0	6,000
1	1,000	5,000
2	2,000	4,000
3	3,000	3,000
4	4,000	2,000
5	5,000	1,000

In the News

Vaccination dodgers

Doctors struggle to eradicate polio worldwide, but one of their biggest problems is persuading parents to vaccinate their children. The discovery of the vaccine has eliminated polio from Europe and the law requires everyone to be vaccinated. People who refuse to be vaccinated are "free riders."

Source: USA Today, March 12, 2008

Explain why someone who has not opted out on medical or religious grounds and refuses to be vaccinated is a "free rider."

Solutions to Practice Problems

1. Fire protection is a public good; a July 4th fireworks display is a public good. In both cases, the free-rider problem is avoided by public provision and financing through taxes. Interstate 80 in rural Wyoming is a public good. The public good creates a free-rider problem that is avoided because governments collect various taxes via the tax on gas and the vehicle registration fee.

2. A private program would provide zero spraying because the free-rider problem would prevail. The efficient quantity is 3 square miles a day—the quantity at which the marginal social benefit equals the marginal social cost. The winner will provide the efficient quantity: 3 square miles sprayed a day.

3. The Department of Mosquito Control would most likely overprovide because the bureau would try to maximize its budget.

Solution to In the News

Polio is a serious disease that causes much suffering. If everyone in a neighborhood except one person gets vaccinated, then the unvaccinated person benefits from all the neighbors' vaccinations. The unvaccinated person is a free rider.

11.3   COMMON RESOURCES

Tragedy of the commons
The overuse of a common resource that arises when its users have no incentive to conserve it and use it sustainably.

Overgrazing the pastures around a village in Middle Ages England, and over-fishing the cod stocks of the North Atlantic Ocean during the recent past are tragedies of the commons. The **tragedy of the commons** is the overuse of a common resource that arises when its users have no incentive to conserve it and use it sustainably.

To study the tragedy of the commons and its possible remedies, we'll focus on the recent and current tragedy—overfishing and depleting the stock of Atlantic cod. We begin by thinking about the sustainable use of a renewable resource.

■ Sustainable Use of a Renewable Resource

A renewable natural resource is one that replenishes itself by the birth and growth of new members of the population. Fish, trees, and the fertile soil are all examples of this type of resource.

Focusing on fish, the sustainable catch is the quantity that can be caught year after year without depleting the stock. This quantity depends on the stock and in the interesting way illustrated in Figure 11.6.

If the stock of fish is small, the quantity of new fish born is also small, so the sustainable catch is small. If the fish stock is large, many fish are born, but they must compete with each other for food, so only a small number survive to reproduce and to grow large enough to catch.

EYE on the PAST
The Commons of England's Middle Ages

The term "the tragedy of the commons" comes from fourteenth century England, where areas of rough grassland surrounded villages. The commons were open to all and were used for grazing cows and sheep owned by the villagers.

Because the commons were open to everyone, no one had an incentive to ensure that the land was not over-grazed. The result was an overgrazing situation similar to that of overfishing in some of today's oceans.

During the sixteenth century, when the price of wool increased, England became a wool exporter to the world. Sheep farming became

profitable and sheep owners needed better control of the land they used, so the com-mons were gradually

enclosed and privatized. Overgrazing ended, and land use became more efficient.

FIGURE 11.6

Sustainable Catch

MyEconLab Animation

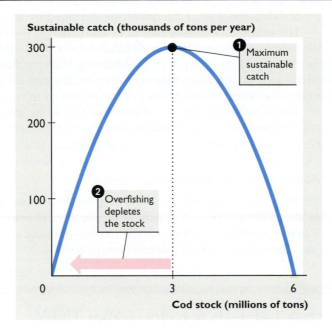

As the stock of fish increases (on the x-axis), the sustainable catch (on the y-axis) increases to a ❶ maximum sustainable catch. With a larger fish stock, the more the fish must compete for food and the sustainable catch decreases.

If for any fish stock, the catch exceeds the sustainable catch, ❷ overfishing occurs, which depletes the stock. Overfishing decreases the maximum sustainable catch.

Between a small and a large stock is a quantity of fish stock that maximizes the sustainable catch. In the example in Figure 11.6, this fish stock is 3 million tons and the sustainable catch is 300,000 tons a year. The maximum sustainable catch arises from a balancing of the birth of new fish from the stock and the availability of food to sustain the fish population.

If the quantity of fish caught equals the sustainable catch, the fish stock remains constant and is available for future generations of fishers in the same quantity that is available today. If the quantity caught is *less than* the sustainable catch, the fish stock grows; and if the quantity caught exceeds the sustainable catch, the fish stock shrinks—overfishing depletes the stock.

◼ The Overuse of a Common Resource

Why might overfishing occur? The answer is that fishers face only their own private cost and don't face the cost they impose on others—external cost. The *social* cost of fishing combines the *private* cost and *external* cost. Let's examine the costs of catching fish to see how the presence of external cost brings overfishing.

Private Cost, External Cost, and Social Cost

You can think of the *marginal private cost* of catching fish as the additional cost incurred by keeping a boat and crew at sea for long enough to increase the catch by one ton. Keeping a fishing boat at sea for an additional hour eventually runs into *diminishing marginal returns*. As the crew gets tired, storage facilities get overfull, and the boat's speed is cut to conserve fuel, the catch per hour decreases. The cost of keeping the boat at sea for an additional hour is constant, so the marginal cost of catching fish increases as the quantity caught increases.

The pursuit of self-interest results in overfishing.

The marginal private cost of catching fish determines an individual fisher's supply of fish. A profit-maximizing fisher is willing to supply the quantity at which the market price of fish covers the marginal private cost. The market supply of fish is the sum of the quantities supplied by individual fishers.

The marginal external cost of catching fish is the cost per additional ton that one fisher's catch imposes on all other fishers. This additional cost arises because one fisher's catch decreases the remaining stock, which makes it harder for other fishers to find and catch fish. So the more any one fisher catches, the longer each other fisher must spend at sea per ton of fish caught.

The marginal social cost of catching fish is the marginal private cost plus the marginal external cost. Both of its components increase as the quantity caught increases, so marginal social cost also increases with the quantity of fish caught.

Marginal Social Benefit and Demand

The marginal social benefit from fish is the price that consumers are willing to pay for an additional pound of fish. Marginal social benefit decreases as the quantity of fish consumed increases, so the market demand curve, which is also the marginal social benefit curve, slopes downward.

EYE on the GLOBAL ECONOMY
The North Atlantic Cod Tragedy of the Commons

Before 1970, Atlantic cod was abundant. It had been fished for many centuries and was a major food source for the first European settlers in North America. In 1812, there were more than 1,600 fishing boats in the waters off New England and Newfoundland, Canada. At that time, cod were huge fish, weighing in at more than 220 pounds and measuring up to 6 feet in length.

Fish were caught using lines and productivity was low. But low productivity limited the catch and enabled cod to be caught sustainably over hundreds of years.

The situation changed dramatically during the 1960s with the introduction of high-efficiency nets (called trawls, seines, and gill nets), sonar technology to find fish concentrations, and large ships with efficient processing and

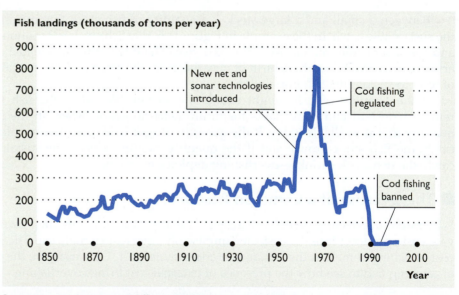

SOURCE OF DATA FOR GRAPH: Millennium Ecosystem Assessment.
SOURCE OF INFORMATION: Codfishes —Atlantic cod and its fishery, http://science.jrank.org/

storage facilities. These technological advances brought soaring cod harvests. In less than a decade, cod landings increased from less than 300,000 tons a year to 800,000 tons.

This volume of cod could not be taken without a serious collapse in the stock and in 1992, a total ban on cod fishing in the North Atlantic stabilized the population but at a very low level.

Overfishing Equilibrium

Figure 11.7 illustrates overfishing and how it arises. The market demand curve for fish is the marginal social benefit curve, *MSB*. The market supply curve is the marginal private cost curve, *MC*. Market equilibrium occurs at the intersection point of these two curves. The equilibrium quantity is 800,000 tons per year and the equilibrium price is $10 per pound.

At this market equilibrium, overfishing is running down the fish stock. Figure 11.7 illustrates why overfishing occurs. At the market equilibrium quantity, marginal social benefit (and willingness to pay) is $10 per pound, but the marginal social cost exceeds this amount. The marginal external cost is the cost of running down the fish stock.

Efficient Equilibrium and Deadweight Loss

What is the efficient use of a common resource? It is the use of the resource that makes the marginal social benefit from the resource equal to the marginal social cost of using it.

In Figure 11.7, the efficient quantity of fish is 300,000 tons per year—the quantity that makes marginal social cost (on the *MSC* curve) equal to marginal social benefit (on the *MSB* curve). At this quantity, the marginal catch of each individual fisher costs society what people are willing to pay for it.

Deadweight loss measures the cost of overfishing. The gray triangle in Figure 11.7 illustrates this loss. It is the marginal social cost minus the marginal social benefit from all the fish caught in excess of the efficient quantity.

FIGURE 11.7
Why Overfishing Occurs

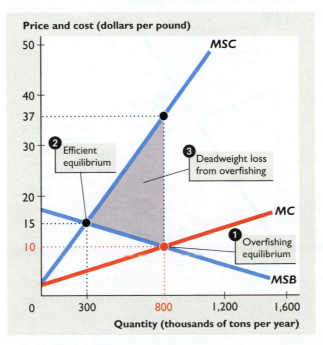

The market supply curve is the marginal private cost curve, *MC*, and the market demand curve is the marginal social benefit curve *MSB*.

1 Market overfishing equilibrium occurs at a quantity of 800,000 tons and a price of $10 a pound.

2 The marginal social cost curve is *MSC* and the efficient equilibrium is at a quantity of 300,000 tons a year.

3 The equilibrium quantity exceeds the efficient quantity and overfishing brings a deadweight loss.

■ Using the Commons Efficiently

It is easier to define the conditions under which a common resource is used efficiently than to deliver those conditions. To use a common resource efficiently, it is necessary to design an incentive mechanism that confronts the users of the resource with the marginal social consequences of their actions. The same principles apply to common resources as those that you met in Chapter 10 when you studied the external cost of pollution.

The three main methods that might be used to achieve the efficient use of a common resource are

- Property rights
- Production quotas
- Individual transferable quotas (ITQs)

Property Rights

A common resource that no one owns and that anyone is free to use contrasts with *private property*, which is a resource that someone owns and has an incentive to use in the way that maximizes its value. The resource is used efficiently. One way of overcoming the tragedy of the commons is to convert a common resource to private property. With private property rights, the owner of the resource faces the same conditions as society faces. It doesn't matter who owns the resource. The users of the resource that someone owns are confronted with the opportunity cost of using it. If the user is the owner, the opportunity cost of using it is forgone rental income. If the resource is used by someone who leases it from its owner, the opportunity cost of using it is the rent paid to the owner.

■ **FIGURE 11.8**

Property Rights Achieve the Efficient Use of a Common Resource   MyEconLab Animation

With property rights assigned to the fish stock, fishers pay the owner of the fish stock for permission to fish and face the marginal social cost of their decisions.

❶ The marginal cost curve, which is also the market supply curve, includes all the costs of fishing, so it is also the marginal social cost curve, $S = MC = MSC$.

❷ The market equilibrium occurs at the intersection of MSC and MSB and the resource use is efficient.

❸ The quantity caught, 300,000 tons, is the efficient quantity.

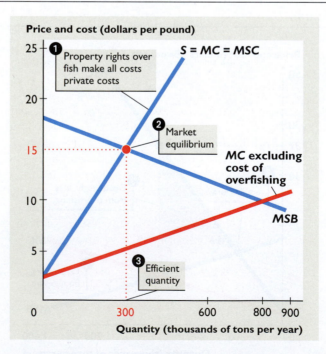

Figure 11.8 illustrates the efficient outcome when private property rights over a resource are established and enforced. The marginal private cost curve, MC, and the market supply curve, S, are the same as the marginal social cost curve, MSC: the curve labeled S = MC = MSC in the figure. The demand curve is the marginal social benefit curve, MSB in the figure. The market price and equilibrium quantity are determined by supply and demand at $15 per pound and an annual catch of 300,000 tons. Price equals marginal social benefit and marginal social cost, so the quantity produced is the efficient quantity.

The private property solution to the tragedy of the commons is available in some cases. It was the solution to the original tragedy of the commons in England's Middle Ages. It is also a solution that has been used to prevent overuse of the airwaves that carry cell-phone services. The right to use this space (called the frequency spectrum) has been auctioned by governments to the highest bidders. The owner of each part of the spectrum is the only one permitted to use it (or to license someone else to use it).

But assigning private property rights is not always feasible and it isn't a practical solution to the problem of overfishing. The cost of policing millions of square miles of ocean would be far greater than the benefit arising from it. Also, there would be international disputes about which country had the right to enforce property rights. Further, in some cases and the ocean fish stock is one of them, people have an emotional objection to assigning private property rights. Critics of private property rights say it is immoral for someone to own a resource that they regard as public. In the absence of property rights, some form of government intervention is used, one of which is a production quota.

Production Quotas

A *production quota* is an upper limit to the quantity of a good that may be produced in a specified period. The quota is allocated to individual producers, so each producer has its own quota.

Figure 11.9 shows a production quota that achieves an efficient outcome. The quota limits the catch (production) to 300,000 tons, the efficient quantity at which marginal social benefit, MSB, equals marginal social cost, MSC. If everyone catches their own quota, the outcome is efficient. But implementing a production quota has two problems.

First, it is in every fisher's self-interest to catch more fish than the quantity permitted under the quota. The reason is that the market price exceeds marginal private cost, so by catching more fish, a fisher gets a higher income. If enough fishers break the quota, overfishing occurs and the tragedy of the commons remains.

Second, marginal cost is not, in general, the same for all producers—as we're assuming here. Some producers have a comparative advantage in using a resource. Efficiency requires that the quota be allocated to the producers with the lowest marginal cost. But the government department that allocates quotas does not have information about the marginal cost of individual producers. Even if the government tried to get this information, producers would have an incentive to lie about their costs, so as to get a bigger quota.

A production quota can work, but only if the activities of every producer can be monitored and all producers have the same marginal cost. Where producers are difficult or very costly to monitor or where marginal cost varies across producers, a production quota cannot achieve an efficient outcome.

■ **FIGURE 11.9**

A Production Quota to Use a Common Resource Efficiently   MyEconLab Animation

❶ A production quota is set at the efficient quantity and each fisher is assigned a share of the quota.

❷ The market equilibrium is efficient, but the price, $15 a pound, exceeds the fishers' marginal cost, $5 a pound, so;

❸ fishers earn a profit on the marginal catch and;

❹ have an incentive to break the quota and overfish.

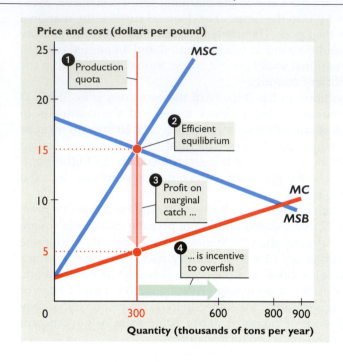

Individual Transferable Quotas

Where producers are difficult to monitor or where marginal cost varies across producers, a more sophisticated quota system, called an individual transferable quota, can be effective. An **individual transferable quota (ITQ)** is a production limit assigned to an individual who is then free to transfer (sell) the quota to someone else. A market in ITQs emerges and ITQs are traded at their market price.

The market price of an ITQ is the highest price that someone is willing to pay for one. That price is marginal social benefit minus marginal cost. The price of an ITQ will rise to this level because fishers who don't have a quota would be willing to pay this amount to get one.

A fisher with an ITQ could sell it for the market price, so by not selling the ITQ the fisher incurs an opportunity cost. The marginal cost of fishing, which now includes the opportunity cost of the ITQ, equals the marginal social benefit from the efficient quantity.

Figure 11.10 illustrates how ITQs work. Each fisher receives an allocation of ITQs and the total catch permitted by the ITQs is 300,000 tons per year. Fishers trade ITQs: Those with low marginal cost buy ITQs from those with high marginal cost, and the market price of an ITQ settles at $10 per pound of fish. The marginal private cost of fishing now becomes the original marginal private cost, *MC*, plus the price of the ITQ. The marginal private cost curve shifts upward from *MC* to *MC + price of ITQ* and each fisher is confronted with the marginal social cost of fishing.

Now no one has an incentive to cheat and exceed the quota because to do so would send marginal cost above the market price and result in a loss on the marginal catch. The outcome is efficient.

Individual transferable quota (ITQ)

A production limit assigned to an individual who is then free to transfer (sell) the quota to someone else.

FIGURE 11.10

An ITQ to Use a Common Resource Efficiently   MyEconLab Animation

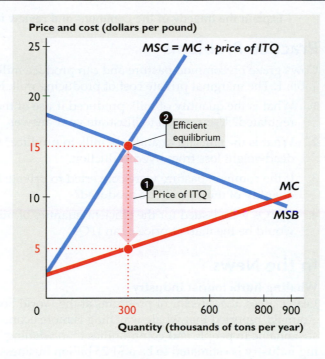

ITQs are issued such that the quantity of fish caught equals the efficient quantity.

❶ The market price of an ITQ equals the marginal external cost of fishing and confronts fishers with the marginal social cost of their decisions.

❷ The market equilibrium is efficient with 300,000 tons a year caught at the marginal social cost and market price of $15 a pound.

EYE on the GLOBAL ECONOMY
ITQs Work

Economists agree that ITQs offer an effective tool for achieving an efficient use of the stock of ocean fish.

Iceland, the Netherlands, and Canada were the first countries to adopt ITQs in the late 1970s. New Zealand was the first country to adopt them as a national policy in 1986.

Today, 28 fisheries in the United States and 150 major fisheries and 100 smaller fisheries around the world, representing 10 percent of the world's marine life harvest, is managed by ITQs.

Marine biologists and economists agree that ITQs prevent fish stocks from collapsing and restore fisheries in critical decline.

Studies based on large data sets of more than 10,000 fisheries and over more than half a century have shown that without ITQs, there would be a major collapse of the global fish stock, but that with ITQs, a fish crisis has been averted.

One study found that ITQs even reverse a trend decline and turn it around to a trend recovery.

Fisheries that are managed with ITQs are half as likely to collapse as those that are not.

ITQs help maintain fish stocks, but they also reduce the size of the fishing industry. This consequence of ITQs puts them against the self-interest of fishers.

In all countries, the fishing industry opposes restrictions on its activities, but in the countries that pioneered ITQs, the opposition was not strong enough to block them.

In the United States the opposition to ITQs was so strong that the fishing industry persuaded Congress to outlaw them. In 1996, Congress passed the Sustainable Fishing Act that put a moratorium on ITQs that lasted until 2004. Since then, many U.S. fisheries have been managed by ITQs and have begun to see their benefits. ITQs are a success story.

MyEconLab

You can work these problems in Study Plan 11.3 and get instant feedback.

TABLE 1

Quantity of milk (gallons per day)	Marginal external cost	Marginal social benefit
	(dollars per gallon)	
0	0	15
20	2	12
40	4	9
60	6	6
80	8	3
100	10	0

FIGURE 1

Price and cost (dollars per gallon)

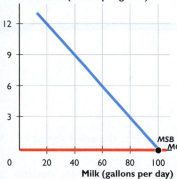

FIGURE 2

Price and cost (dollars per gallon)

CHECKPOINT 11.3

Explain the tragedy of the commons and review its possible solutions.

Practice Problems

Cows graze on common pasture and can produce milk in the amounts shown in Table 1. The marginal private cost of producing milk is zero.

1. What is the quantity of milk produced if use of the common pasture is not regulated? Use a graph to illustrate your answer.

2. What is the efficient quantity of milk to produce? On a graph show the deadweight loss from overproduction.

3. If the common pasture were converted to private land and fenced off, what quantity of milk would be produced?

4. If ITQs were issued for the efficient quantity of milk production, what would be the market price of an ITQ?

In the News

Whaling hurts tourist industry

Leah Garces, the director of programs at the World Society for the Protection of Animals, reported that whale watching is more economically significant and sustainable to people and communities than whaling. The global whale-watching industry is estimated to be a $1.25 billion business enjoyed by over 10 million people in more than 90 countries each year.

Source: BBC, June 2, 2009

Describe the tradeoff facing communities that live near whaling areas. How might a thriving whale-watching industry avoid the tragedy of the commons?

Solutions to Practice Problems

1. The quantity of milk produced is 100 gallons a day—the quantity at which the marginal private cost equals the marginal social benefit. See Figure 1.

2. The efficient quantity of milk is 60 gallons a day—the quantity at which the marginal social cost equals the marginal social benefit. Marginal social cost equals marginal private cost plus marginal external cost. The gray area in Figure 2 shows the deadweight loss from overproduction.

3. If the common pasture were converted to private land and fenced off, the quantity of milk produced would be the efficient quantity—60 gallons a day.

4. The market price of an ITQ would be $6 a gallon, which equals the marginal external cost at the efficient quantity of milk.

Solution to In the News

Communities in a whaling area face a tradeoff between whale hunting and developing a whale-watching business. With a thriving whale-watching industry, these communities will have an incentive to protect the whales and not overuse the natural resource.

CHAPTER SUMMARY

Key Points

1 Distinguish among private goods, public goods, and common resources.

- A private good is a good or service that is rival and excludable.
- A public good is a good or service that is nonrival and nonexcludable.
- A common resource is a resource that is rival but nonexcludable.

2 Explain the free-rider problem and how public provision might help to overcome it and deliver an efficient quantity of public goods.

- A public good creates a free-rider problem—no one has a private incentive to pay her or his share of the cost of providing a public good.
- The efficient level of provision of a public good is that at which marginal social benefit equals marginal social cost.
- Competition between political parties, each of which tries to appeal to the maximum number of voters, can lead to the efficient scale of provision of a public good and to both parties proposing the same policies—the principle of minimum differentiation.
- Bureaucrats try to maximize their budgets, and if voters are rationally ignorant, they might vote to support taxes that provide public goods in quantities that exceed the efficient quantity.

3 Explain the tragedy of the commons and review its possible solutions.

- Common resources create the tragedy of the commons—no one has a private incentive to conserve the resource and use it at an efficient rate.
- A common resource is used to the point at which the marginal private cost equals the marginal social benefit.
- The efficient use of a common resource is the point at which marginal social benefit equals marginal social cost.
- A common resource might be used efficiently by creating a private property right, setting a quota, or issuing individual transferable quotas.

Key Terms

CHAPTER CHECKPOINT

Study Plan Problems and Applications

Use the following list of items to work Problems **1** and **2**.

- New Year's Eve celebrations in Times Square, New York
- A city's sewer system
- New York subway system
- A skateboard
- Cable TV
- Niagara Falls

1. Classify each of the items in the list as a private good, a public good, a common resource, or a natural monopoly good. Explain each classification.

2. For each public good in the list, is there a free-rider problem? If not, how is the free-rider problem avoided?

3. Table 1 sets out Wendy's, Sara's, and Tom's total benefit from a public good. If Wendy, Sara, and Tom are the only people in the society and the government provided 3 units of the public good, calculate the marginal social benefit.

Use Figure 1 to work Problems **4** and **5**. It shows the marginal social benefit and marginal social cost of a waste disposal system in a city of 1 million people.

4. What is the efficient capacity of the waste disposal system and how much would each person have to pay in taxes if the city installed the efficient capacity?

5. If voters are well informed about the costs and benefits of the waste disposal system, what capacity will voters choose? If voters are rationally ignorant, will bureaucrats install the efficient capacity? Explain your answer.

Use Figure 2, which shows the market for North Atlantic tuna, to work Problems **6** to **8**.

6. a. What is the quantity of tuna that fishers catch and the price of tuna? Is there overfishing? Explain why or why not.
   b. If the stock of tuna is used efficiently, what would be the price of fish?

7. a. With a quota of 40 tons a month for the tuna fishing industry, what is the equilibrium price of tuna and the quantity of tuna that fishers catch?
   b. Is the equilibrium an overfishing equilibrium?

8. If the government issues ITQs to individual fishers that limit the total catch to the efficient quantity, what is the market price of an ITQ?

9. **Lawmakers set to allow speedier Arctic drilling**
The U.S. government will allow Arctic drilling that would speed the development of oil and gas reserves off the Alaskan coast. Environmentalists say that the area should not be drilled because there is wildlife in the area.
   Source: CNNMoney, June 21, 2011

Are the oil and gas reserves public goods, private goods, or common resources? When an oil company receives a permit to develop a particular oil reserve, is that oil reserve a public good or a private good? Will the oil company produce an inefficient quantity or the efficient quantity? Explain.

TABLE 1

Units of pubic good	Total benefit		
	Wendy	Sara	Tom
0	0	0	0
1	20	10	30
2	40	15	50
3	60	20	60
4	80	25	65
5	100	30	67

FIGURE 1

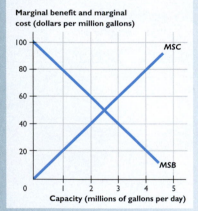

Marginal benefit and marginal cost (dollars per million gallons)

Capacity (millions of gallons per day)

FIGURE 2

Price and cost (dollars per ton)

Quantity (tons per month)

Instructor Assignable Problems and Applications

Your instructor can assign these problems as homework, a quiz, or a test in MyEconLab.

1. a. What type of good is a high-speed rail network?
    b. Why might it be provided by government rather than privately?
    c. Can you think of parts of the United States that have a similar population density to Europe where high-speed rail might be efficient?
    d. What information would be needed to determine the efficient amount of high-speed rail in the United States?

Use Table 1, which provides data about a dandelion control program, to work Problems **2** and **3**.

2. What quantity of spraying would a private control program provide? What is the efficient quantity of spraying?

3. Two political parties, the Conservers and the Eradicators, fight an election in which the only issue is the quantity of spraying to undertake. The Conservers want no spraying and the Eradicators want to spray 2.5 square miles a day. The voters are well-informed about the benefits and costs of the program. What is the outcome of the election?

4. If hikers and others were required to pay a fee to use the Appalachian Trail, would the use of this common resource be more efficient? Would it be even more efficient if the most popular spots such as Annapolis Rock had more highly priced access? Why do you think we don't see more market solutions to the tragedy of the commons?

Use the following information to answer Problems **5** to **7**.

A natural spring runs under land owned by ten people. Each person has the right to sink a well and can take water from the spring at a constant marginal cost of $5 a gallon. Table 2 sets out the marginal external cost and the marginal social benefit from the water.

5. Draw a graph to illustrate the market equilibrium. On your graph, show the efficient quantity of water taken.

6. If the government sets a production quota on the total amount of water such that the spring is used efficiently, what would that quota be?

7. If the government issues ITQs to land owners that limit the total amount of water taken to the efficient quantity, what is the market price of an ITQ?

8. **Ohio governor vetoes Ohio bill on Lake Erie water use**
    In 2008, the eight U.S. states and two Canadian provinces adjoining the lakes negotiated the Great Lakes Compact to prevent the region's water from being shipped or piped to arid regions. The compact also requires each state to regulate their own large-scale withdrawals from the lakes, their tributary streams, and underground sources. The Ohio bill that was vetoed would have allowed Ohio factories to pull more water out of Lake Erie.
    Source: *The Associated Press*, July 15, 2011

    Is water in the Great Lakes a public good, a private good, or a common resource? What do you think are the goals of the Great Lakes Compact? How might these goals be achieved?

TABLE 1

Quantity (square miles sprayed per day)	Marginal social cost	Marginal social benefit
	(dollars per day)	
0.5	0	600
1.0	100	500
1.5	200	400
2.0	300	300
2.5	400	200
3.0	500	100

TABLE 2

Quantity of water (gallons per day)	Marginal external cost	Marginal social benefit
	(dollars per gallon)	
10	1	10
20	2	9
30	3	8
40	4	7
50	5	6
60	6	5
70	7	4

Multiple Choice Quiz

1. A good is _____ if it is possible to prevent someone from enjoying its benefits and such a good might be a _____ good.

   A. rival; private
   B. excludable; public
   C. excludable; private
   D. nonexcludable; common resource

2. A free-rider problem arises if a good is _____.

   A. nonrival and nonexcludable
   B. nonrival and excludable
   C. rival and nonexcludable
   D. rival and excludable

3. The marginal social benefit of a public good is _____.

   A. the quantity demanded by all the people at a given price
   B. the amount that all the people are willing to pay for a given quantity
   C. the amount that all the people are willing to pay at a given quantity for one more unit
   D. the quantity demanded by all the people at a given marginal social cost

4. The efficient quantity of a public good is most likely to be delivered by _____.

   A. an election contest between two parties that want different quantities
   B. highly trained bureaucrats
   C. efficient private companies
   D. an individual transferable quota

5. A renewable common resource is used sustainably if _____.

   A. private benefits and public benefits are equal
   B. private benefits equal private costs
   C. the rate of renewal of the resource equals its rate of use
   D. the rate of use of the resource equals the social benefit from its use

6. Overfishing occurs if, at the quantity caught, _____.

   A. marginal social cost equals marginal private cost plus marginal external cost
   B. marginal social benefit equals the fishers' marginal private cost
   C. marginal social benefit equals marginal social cost
   D. marginal social benefit equals marginal private cost plus marginal external cost

7. All the following can achieve an efficient use of a common resource *except* _____.

   A. a production quota equal to the marginal external cost
   B. individual transferable quotas that total the efficient quantity
   C. assigning property rights to convert the common resource to private use
   D. individual transferable quotas that trade at marginal external cost

Used Car Center

How do you avoid buying
a lemon?

Markets with Private Information

12

**When you have completed your study of this chapter,
you will be able to**

1 Describe the lemons problem and explain how the used-car market
solves it.

2 Describe the asymmetric information problems in the insurance market and
explain how they are solved.

3 Explain the information problems and other economic problems in health-
care markets.

12.1 THE LEMONS PROBLEM AND ITS SOLUTION

In all the markets that you've studied so far, buyers and sellers are well informed about the features and the value of the item being traded. Buyers know the benefits they get and sellers know the costs they incur. The buyers' marginal benefit determines demand, the sellers' marginal cost determines supply, and demand and supply together determine the equilibrium price and quantity. And if none of the obstacles to efficiency described in Chapter 6 (see p. 156) are present, the market allocates resources efficiently.

In some markets, either the buyer or the seller has some relevant information to a transaction—**private information**—that the other lacks. One of these markets is the one for used cars. In this market, each seller has private information about the quality of the vehicle offered for sale. When you buy a used car, you hope it isn't a lemon, but until you have driven it for a month or two, you won't know for sure. But the person who sells you the car knows. When one side of a market has private information, we call the situation one of **asymmetric information**—a situation in which *either* the buyer *or* the seller has *private information*. How does a market with asymmetric information work? What determines the equilibrium price and quantity? Is the market efficient or inefficient?

These are the questions we'll now answer.

Private information
Information relevant to a transaction that is possessed by some market participants but not all.

Asymmetric information
A situation in which either the buyer or the seller has private information.

■ A Market for Used Cars with a Lemons Problem

When a person buys a used car, it might turn out to be a lemon. If the car *is* a lemon, it is worth less to the buyer than if it has no defects. Does the used-car market have different prices reflecting different qualities—a low price for a lemons and a higher price for a car without defects? It turns out that it does. But the market needs some help to do so and to overcome what is called the **lemons problem**—the problem that when it is not possible to distinguish reliable products from lemons, there are too many lemons—perhaps only lemons—and too few reliable products—perhaps none.

To see how the used-car market overcomes the lemons problem, we'll first look at a market that *does* have a lemons problem.

To explain the lemons problem as clearly as possible, we'll assume that there are only two kinds of cars: defective cars—*lemons*—and cars without defects, which we'll call *good cars*. Whether a car is a lemon is private information that is available only to the current owner. The buyer can't tell whether the car for sale is a lemon until after buying it, driving it for a few weeks, and learning as much about it as its current owner knows.

Lemons problem
The problem that when it is not possible to distinguish reliable products from lemons, there are too many lemons and too few reliable products.

George Akerlof of the University of California, Berkeley, and 2001 Nobel Laureate, was the first person to pose the lemons problem and the challenge that it presents for markets to allocate resources efficiently.

Buyers' Decisions and Demand

Even though the buyers of used cars don't know whether they are buying a good car or a lemon, the law of demand applies. The lower the price of a car, the greater is the quantity of cars demanded. But what determines demand and the willingness to pay is a bit different. To see why, let's think about the choice that a car buyer called Greg is about to make.

Greg wants to buy a used car and he would like to avoid buying a lemon. He knows that the value of a good car to him, his marginal benefit, is $20,000. But Greg has a low income, some spare time, and he knows how to fix a car, so he would be willing to buy a lemon if he could get it for an appropriately low price—a price equal to his marginal benefit from a lemon, which he says is $10,000.

Now think about Greg's dilemma. He has found a car priced at $15,990 (in the photo). He likes the look of the car, but is it a good one or a lemon? If the car is a good one, he gets a marginal benefit of, and would be willing to pay, $20,000. So buying the car for $15,990 gives him a consumer surplus of $4,110. But if the car is a lemon, his marginal benefit is only $10,000, so paying $15,990 for the car leaves him with a negative consumer surplus (a consumer deficit!) of $5,990.

Will Greg pay $15,990? The answer depends on the odds of avoiding a lemon and how Greg regards taking risks. Although he doesn't know the quality of the car, he knows what all his friends have told him about the cars they've bought from the same dealer. If all his friends bought good cars, he will be thinking that this car is most likely a good one too. In this case, he is willing to pay close to $20,000 and at $15,990, he would buy this car.

But if all Greg's friends bought lemons, he will be thinking that this car is most likely a lemon too. In this case, he is willing to pay only $10,000, so $15,990 is much more than what he would be willing to pay.

Other buyers are making decisions like Greg's and figuring out what they are willing to pay for a car of unknown quality. Some buyers are willing to pay more than Greg and some less. At higher prices, there are fewer buyers and at lower prices more buyers. The demand curve for used cars slopes downward.

Figure 12.1 illustrates the demand for used cars. If previous buyers say that they've never seen a lemon, buyers expect no lemons and the demand curve for used cars is D_G. If previous buyers say that they've never seen a good car, buyers expect only lemons and the demand curve is D_L. If previous buyers say that some cars were good ones and some were lemons, buyers expect to see some of each type of car and the demand curve will lie between D_G and D_L.

Is this car a good one with a marginal benefit of $20,000 and a consumer surplus of $4,110? Or is it a lemon with a marginal benefit of $10,000 and a consumer "deficit" of $5,990? Will Greg buy it?

FIGURE 12.1

The Demand for a Used Car of Unknown Quality

MyEconLab Animation

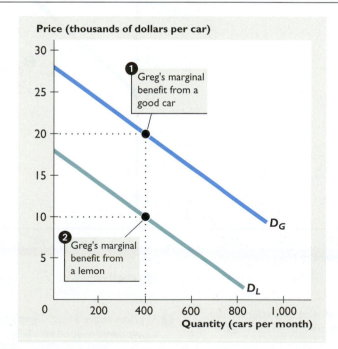

❶ If all Greg's friends bought good used cars, Greg might expect to buy a good one too and be willing to pay $20,000—his marginal benefit from a good car. The demand curve for good cars is D_G.

❷ If all Greg's friends bought lemons, Greg might expect to buy a lemon too and be willing to pay $10,000—his marginal benefit from a lemon. The demand curve for lemons is D_L.

The demand curve for used cars of unknown quality lies between D_L and D_G.

Sellers' Decisions and Supply

Now think about the sellers of used cars, who know the quality of their cars. There is nothing special about this supply: Sellers know their marginal cost, so they know the quantity they are willing to supply at a given price. The marginal cost of a lemon is less than that of a good car and over a range of low prices, only lemons are supplied. At higher prices, the quantity of lemons supplied falls off and good cars start to be supplied.

Figure 12.2 shows an example of what the supply curves might look like. In this example, lemons are offered for sale at prices up to $12,000 and at that price all the lemons available are supplied and good cars start to be offered for sale.

The Market Outcome

Demand and supply determine the price of a used car and the quantity traded, but the market doesn't work well. To explain, we'll focus on an extreme outcome in which only lemons get traded.

Suppose that buyers have learned from their friends that everyone who has bought a used car got a lemon. They assume that they, too, will get a lemon. Consequently, the demand for used cars is based on the willingness to pay for a lemon. The market demand is the demand for lemons, which delivers a low market price. At this low market price, good cars are worth more to their owners than

■ **FIGURE 12.2**

The Supply of Used Cars

MyEconLab Animation

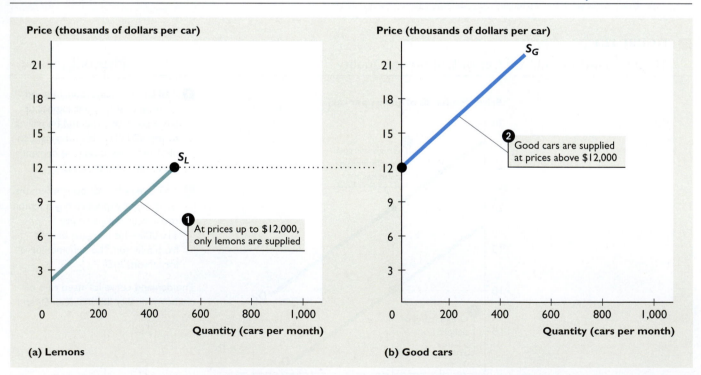

(a) Lemons

(b) Good cars

Suppliers of used cars know the quality of what they offer for sale.
❶ At prices below $12,000, only lemons are offered for sale and the supply curve of lemons is S_L.

❷ At prices above $12,000, good cars are offered for sale and the supply curve of good cars is S_G.

they would get from selling them, so no good cars are offered for sale: only lemons are available. So lemons are the only cars traded.

Figure 12.3 illustrates the used-car market that we've just described. The demand for used cars, D, is equal to the demand for lemons, D_L. The supply of used cars, S, is the supply of lemons up to $12,000 a car (the green segment of the supply curve) and the supply of lemons plus the supply of good cars at prices above $12,000 (the blue segment of the supply curve).

The equilibrium price is $10,000 per car and 400 lemons are traded each month.

Adverse Selection

This market suffers from adverse selection, a general problem that arises in markets with private information. **Adverse selection** is the tendency for people to enter into transactions that bring them benefits from their private information and impose costs on the uninformed party.

For example, Jackie hires salespeople and offers them a fixed wage contract. The only people Jackie attracts are lazy workers. Hardworking salespeople don't work for Jackie because they can earn more by working for someone who pays by results. Jackie's fixed-wage contract adversely selects those with private information—knowledge that they are lazy in this case—who use that knowledge to their own benefit and to impose costs on Jackie.

In the used-car market, the low price adversely selects lemons. The owners of lemons have a greater incentive to offer their cars for sale. In the extreme case (and in the above example), good cars disappear from the market. The owners of good cars have no incentive to offer them for sale. They hold on to their good cars because the market price is less than their marginal benefit.

Adverse selection
The tendency for people to enter into transactions that bring them benefits from their private information and impose costs on the uninformed party.

FIGURE 12.3

The Lemons Problem in a Used-Car Market

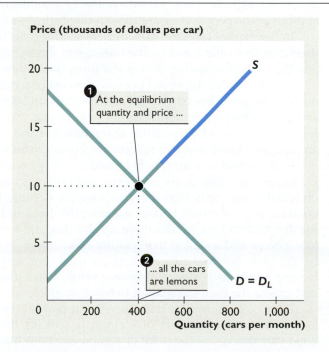

The demand for used cars is the demand for lemons, so the demand curve is $D = D_L$. The supply curve of used cars is S. The green portion of the curve is the supply of lemons and the blue portion adds the supply of good cars.

❶ The equilibrium price of a used car is $10,000.

❷ 400 used cars a month are traded and they are all lemons. At the equilibrium price, no good cars are offered for sale.

EYE on the MARKET FOR USED CARS
How Do You Avoid Buying a Lemon?

The used-car market in the United States might have a lemons problem, but it definitely works: It is a very active and successful market.

In 2008 (the latest year for which data are available), 50,000 used-car dealers sold 37 million cars at an average price of $8,000 per car.

This scale of operation contrasts with the market for new cars in which around 40 domestic and foreign producers sold 13 million cars at an average price of $26,500 per car.

The stock of cars on U.S. roads is 250 million, so with 37 million being traded, more than one car in seven changes hands each year.

What makes this market work and helps it overcome the lemons problem? The answer is dealers' warranties and third party inspection services.

By offering warranties, dealers *signal* that the cars they are selling are free from defects and, if a car should turn out to be a lemon, the dealer will bear the cost of fixing it.

■ A Used-Car Market with Dealers' Warranties

Signaling
When an informed person takes an action that sends information to uninformed persons.

How can used-car dealers convince buyers that a car isn't a lemon and that it is worth more than a lemon? The answer is: By giving a guarantee in the form of a warranty, the dealer *signals* which cars are good ones and which cars are lemons.

Signaling occurs when an informed person takes actions that send information to uninformed persons. The grades and degrees that a university awards students are signals. They inform potential (uninformed) employers about the abilities of the people they are considering hiring—see *Eye on Your Life* on p. 309.

In the market for used cars, dealers send signals by giving warranties on the used cars they offer for sale. The message in the signal is that the dealer agrees to pay the costs of repairing the car if it turns out to have a defect.

Buyers believe the signal because the cost of sending a false signal is high. A dealer who gives a warranty on a lemon ends up bearing a high cost of repairs—and gains a bad reputation. A dealer who gives a warranty only on good cars has few repair costs and a reputation that gets better and better. It pays dealers to send an accurate signal, and it is rational for buyers to believe the signal.

So a car with a warranty is a good car; a car without a warranty is a lemon. Buyers are now effectively as informed as sellers, so the demand for cars depends on whether the car is a good one or a lemon. Because the willingness to pay for a good car is greater than that for a lemon, the demand for good cars is greater than the demand for lemons. But there is still a demand for lemons from people with a low income and a skill at fixing faulty cars.

So there are now two markets for used cars: one for good cars and one for lemons and in each market there is a price. Warranties solve the lemons problem and enable the used-car market to function efficiently.

Figure 12.4 illustrates this outcome. In part (a) the demand for and supply of lemons determine the price of a lemon. In part (b), the demand for and supply of good cars determine the price of a good car. Both markets are efficient. The mar-

■ FIGURE 12.4

Warranties Make a Used-Car Market Efficient

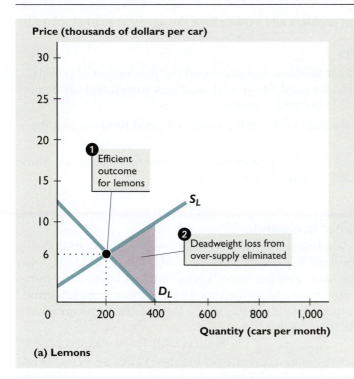

(a) Lemons

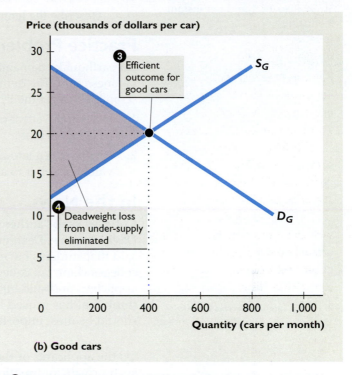

(b) Good cars

❶ The demand for and supply of lemons determine the equilibrium price and quantity of lemons and ❷ the deadweight loss from the over-supply of lemons (gray triangle) is eliminated.

❸ The demand for and supply of good cars determine the equilibrium price and quantity of good cars and ❹ the deadweight loss from the under-supply of good cars (gray triangle) is eliminated.

ginal cost of each quality of car equals its marginal benefit and the deadweight loss that arises with asymmetric information is eliminated.

Pooling Equilibrium and Separating Equilibrium

You've seen two outcomes in the market for used cars. Without warranties, there is only one message visible to the buyer: All cars look the same. So there is one price regardless of whether the car is a good car or a lemon. It is as if all the cars, good ones and lemons, are in one big pool. We call the outcome in a market when only one message is available and an uninformed person cannot determine quality a **pooling equilibrium**. In the example above, only lemons were traded. But in such a market it is possible that a few good cars will be traded, though not enough to make buyers believe they will be lucky enough to get one.

In a used-car market with warranties, there are two messages. Good cars have warranties, and lemons don't. So there are two car prices for the two types of cars. The information created by warranties *separates* good cars and lemons. So we call the outcome in a market when signaling provides full information to a previously uninformed person a **separating equilibrium**.

Notice that no government action is needed to get the used-car market to work well. Dealers' warranties, voluntarily provided, do the job. Nonetheless, consumer protection laws in most states include "lemon laws" and a federal "lemon law" specifies statutory remedies for used-car buyers in the event that a dealer fails to honor its warranty.

Pooling equilibrium
The outcome when only one message is available and an uninformed person cannot determine quality.

Separating equilibrium
The outcome when signaling provides full information to a previously uninformed person.

MyEconLab

You can work these problems in Study Plan 12.1 and get instant feedback.

 CHECKPOINT 12.1

Describe the lemons problem and explain how the used-car market solves it.

Practice Problems

An earthquake damaged car factories and decreased the production of popular Japanese cars. The demand for good late-model used cars soared and car dealers scrambled to get their hands on used vehicles.

1. Explain the effect of the eathquake on the price of a good used car and the price of a lemon.

2. If you have a late-model car that you know isn't a lemon, will you sell it privately or sell it to a dealer? Explain your answer.

In the News

Colleges seek "authenticity" in hopefuls

David Lesesne, Dean of Admissions at Sewanee, a Tennessee liberal arts college, said that students have become less authentic to themselves by trying to be what colleges want, but colleges have done the same. Schools are looking to draw more applicants and students are looking to gain acceptance. As those numbers grow I think that has caused both sides of the equation to lose a little focus on what should be most important: the match.

Source: *USA Today*, August 22, 2007

Do the applicants or the colleges have private information? Give an example of such private information. Does this market have an adverse selection problem?

Solutions to Practice Problems

1. The increase in demand for good used cars shifts the demand curve rightward and with no change in supply, the price of a good car rises. At the higher price, the *quantity supplied* of good cars increases. With a higher price for good cars, dealers have an incentive to fix problems with lemons and offer them for sale with a warranty as good cars, so the supply of lemons decreases (lemons and good cars are substitutes in production—see p. 95). The decrease in the supply of lemons raises their price.

2. If you sell your used car privately, you offer it without a warranty. Assuming the potential buyer doesn't know you, your car without a warranty would be perceived as a lemon. You would not be able to sell it for the price of the good car that it is. You would sell it to a dealer if he offered you more than the price of a lemon.

Solution to In the News

Colleges and students know the grades and test scores, so these are not private information. "Students have become less authentic to themselves" indicates that students try to present themselves as better than they are. The student's true self is private information. Schools try to draw more applicants by looking like comfortable, friendly, and relaxed places. The true quality of the school is the school's private information. With both schools and hopefuls having private information, adverse selection occurs in the market for college places and the best match isn't always achieved.

12.2 INFORMATION PROBLEMS IN INSURANCE MARKETS

Just as buyers and sellers gain from trading goods and services, so they can also gain by trading risk. But risk is a "bad," not a good. The good that is traded is *risk avoidance*. A buyer of risk avoidance can gain because the value of avoiding a risk is greater than the price that must be paid to others to get them to bear shares of it. And a seller of risk avoidance faces a lower cost of risk than the price that people are willing to pay to avoid it.

People trade risk in financial markets and insurance markets. Here, we'll focus on insurance markets.

■ Insurance Markets

You can see in *Eye on the U.S. Economy* below that insurance plays a huge role in our economic lives.

Insurance reduces the risk that each person faces by sharing or *pooling* the risks. When you buy insurance against the risk of an unwanted event, you pay an insurance company a *premium*. If the unwanted event occurs, the insurance company pays you the amount of the insured loss.

EYE on the U.S. ECONOMY
Insurance in the United States

We spend 12 percent of our income on insurance. That's more than we spend on cars or food. In addition, we buy Social Security and unemployment insurance through our taxes.

Auto insurance reduces the risk of financial loss in the event of an auto accident or theft. We spent $182 billion on this insurance in 2008 (see Figure).

Property and casualty insurance reduces the risk of financial loss in the event of an accident involving damage to property or persons. It includes workers' compensation and fire insurance. We spent $258 billion on this insurance in 2008.

Life insurance reduces the risk of financial loss in the event of death. Almost 80 percent of households in the United States have life insur-

ance, and the amount paid in premiums in 2008 was $475 billion.

Health insurance reduces the risk of financial loss in the event of illness.

It can provide funds to cover both lost earnings and the cost of medical care. We spent $783 billion on this type of insurance in 2008.

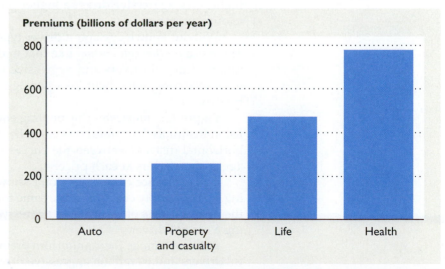

SOURCE OF DATA: U.S. Bureau of the Census, *Statistical Abstract of the United States: 2011*, Tables 131, 1220, and 1221.

Think about auto collision insurance. You know that there is a chance that you will be involved in an auto accident. The chance is small but always present. If you do have an accident and your car gets seriously damaged, you face the cost and inconvenience of getting it fixed. Worse, if you suffer serious personal injury, you also face a loss of income and the cost of medical care. For you, the cost of an auto accident is large and if you had to bear such cost, you'd like some help.

Because the chance that you will have a serious and costly auto accident is small, you can get that help by making a deal with an auto insurance company that is beneficial to both you and the insurer: You pay an annual premium to the insurance company and the company pays you a sum of money based on an agreed formula if you have an accident and incur a loss.

Insurance companies can get information from statistics on past accidents and costs that enable them to determine the premiums and payout conditions they can offer and still earn a profit. None of the company's policyholders knows whether they'll have an accident and the insurance company doesn't know *who* will have an accident, but it knows *how many* accidents there will be and what they will cost. An insurance company can *pool* the risks of a large population and enable everyone to share the costs.

People are happy to buy insurance at prices that enable insurance companies to make a profit because they are risk averse—they don't like risk—and by spreading the risk, insurance companies lower the risk for everyone.

But insurance companies do have a problem and it is a general problem that affects all types of insurance: Their customers have private information about their own behavior and its effects on the likelihood that they will make an insurance claim. There is asymmetric information in the insurance market.

■ Asymmetric Information in Insurance

Although asymmetric information is present in all types of insurance, we'll stick with auto collision insurance. Some drivers are careful and some are aggressive. A careful driver is less likely to have an accident than an aggressive driver. Each driver knows which type he or she is, but the insurance company doesn't know. Yet it would benefit the insurance company to know, for it could then charge the higher-risk aggressive driver a higher premium and the lower-risk careful driver a lower premium.

Without knowledge about driver types, all insured drivers get the same deal. There is a *pooling equilibrium* like that in the used-car market without dealer warranties. Careful drivers and aggressive drivers pay the same premium, but the insurance companies incur losses on aggressive drivers and make profits on careful drivers.

Figure 12.5 illustrates this pooling equilibrium outcome. The demand for collision insurance by careful drivers is D_C and the demand by all drivers is D. The horizontal distance between the curves D_C and D is the quantity demanded by aggressive drivers at each price.

The insurance companies don't know the driver type to which they are selling, so the supply curve, S, is the same for all drivers. It is based on an average of the marginal cost of insuring an aggressive driver and the marginal cost of insuring a careful driver.

In this example, the equilibrium premium is $1,000 a year and 60 million careful drivers and 60 million aggressive drivers are insured.

You're now going to see that this outcome is inefficient for two reasons: it creates moral hazard and adverse selection.

FIGURE 12.5

Inefficient Pooling Equilibrium in an Auto Insurance Market

MyEconLab Animation

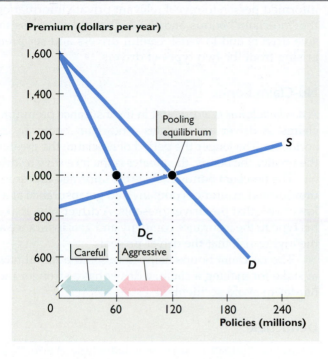

With no information on driver type, insurance companies offer all drivers the same deal. The insurance supply curve is S.

The demand curve D_C is the demand for auto insurance by careful drivers. The demand curve D is the demand for auto insurance by all drivers. The horizontal distance between the two demand curves is the quantity demanded by aggressive drivers at each premium level.

A pooling equilibrium occurs at the intersection of S and D at a premium of $1,000 a year with 120 million insured drivers divided equally between careful and aggressive.

In this equilibrium, moral hazard and adverse selection make insurance companies look for ways of separating the two driver types.

Moral Hazard

Moral hazard is the tendency for a person with private information to use it in ways that impose costs on an uninformed party with whom they have made an agreement.

Moral hazard arises in many settings. For example, big banks face moral hazard. They know they are too big for governments to let them fail so they make loans that are too risky. Insurance companies face moral hazard because an insured person is less likely than an uninsured person to behave in ways that avoid the insured loss. For example, fire insurance lessens the incentive to install smoke deterctors, fire alarms, and a sprinkler system.

In the case of auto insurance, a driver with full collision coverage has less incentive than a driver with little or no collision coverage to drive carefully. Once a person has bought insurance, her or his incentives change and the change adversely affects the interest of the insurance company.

Adverse Selection

Adverse selection arises because people at greater risk are more likely to buy insurance than those for whom a risk is very small. For example, a person with a family history of serious illness is more likely to buy health insurance than a person with a family history of good health. Similarly, an aggressive driver is more likely than a careful driver to take the fullest possible coverage. So more of the insured risks arise from the activities of the riskiest people.

Insurance companies have an incentive to find ways around the moral hazard and adverse selection problems. By doing so, they can lower premiums for low-risk people and raise premiums for high-risk people.

Moral hazard
The tendency for a person with private information to use it in ways that impose costs on an uninformed party with whom they have made an agreement.

Screening
When an uninformed person creates an incentive for an informed person to reveal relevant private information.

■ Screening in Insurance Markets

Screening occurs when an uninformed person creates an incentive for an informed person to reveal relevant private information. Insurance companies use the "no-claim" bonus and the deductible as *screens* to separate high-risk aggressive drivers and low-risk careful drivers and set premiums in line with the risk arising from the two types of drivers.

No-Claim Bonus

A *no-claim bonus* is a discount in the insurance premium for drivers who don't make claims. A driver accumulates a no-claim bonus by driving safely and avoiding accidents. The longer the period of no-claim, the greater is the no-claim bonus. And the greater the bonus, the greater is the incentive to drive carefully.

The no-claim bonus enables the informed driver to reveal her or his type to the uninformed insurance company and get insurance at a lower price, in line with the lower risk that the driver presents. A driver who makes claims also reveals her or his type to the insurance company and gets insurance at a higher price, in line with the higher risk that the driver presents.

The no-claim bonus helps to lessen the moral hazard problem. With a bonus at stake for making a claim, a driver has a stronger incentive to be careful and try harder to avoid accidents.

Deductible

Insurance companies also use a deductible. A *deductible* is the amount of a loss that the insured person agrees to bear personally. The larger the deductible, the lower is the premium, and the decrease in the premium is more than proportionate to the increase in the deductible. By offering insurance with full coverage—no deductible—on terms that are attractive only to aggressive high-risk drivers and by offering coverage with a deductible on more favorable terms that are attractive to careful low-risk drivers, insurance companies can do profitable business with everyone. Aggressive high-risk drivers choose policies with a low deductible and a high premium; careful low-risk drivers choose policies with a high deductible and a low premium.

The size of the deductible chosen reveals to the insurance company whether the driver is aggressive or careful.

■ Separating Equilibrium with Screening

With screening that indicates driver types, insurance companies can supply insurance on different terms to the different groups. With only two groups, aggressive and careful, it can offer premiums at two different levels: A higher premium for aggressive drivers and a lower premium for careful drivers. The higher premium is an incentive for aggressive drivers to behave as if they were careful, so the number of aggressive drivers decreases and the number of careful drivers increases. The outcome is a separating equilibrium.

Figure 12.6 illustrates this outcome and contrasts it with the pooling equilibrium that arises without screening.

Figure 12.6(a) shows the situation for careful drivers and 12.6(b) for aggressive drivers. We're assuming that the two groups are of equal size in the sense that they have identical demand curves, D_C and D_A (as before in Figure 12.5). But as you're about to see, the two groups don't end up of equal size when they have responded to the incentives they face.

FIGURE 12.6

Two Outcomes in Auto Insurance Compared

MyEconLab Animation

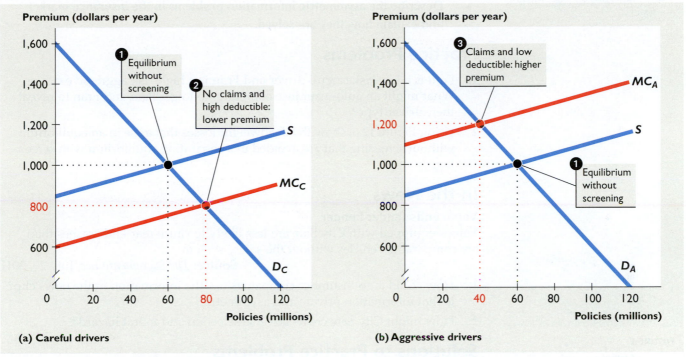

(a) Careful drivers

(b) Aggressive drivers

Careful drivers in part (a) have demand curve D_C and aggressive drivers in part (b) have demand curve D_A. With no screening, the supply curve of insurance is S in both parts.

1 Without screening the equilibrium premium is $1,000 and 60 million drivers are careful and 60 million are aggressive.

With screening, the supply curve of insurance to careful drivers in part (a) is MC_C and the supply curve of insurance to aggressive drivers in part (b) is MC_A.

In part (a) **2** equilibrium occurs at a premium of $800 and 80 million drivers reveal that they are careful.

In part (b) **3** equilibrium occurs at a premium of $1,200 and 40 million drivers reveal that they are aggressive.

In a separating equilibrium, 20 million drivers switch from being aggressive to being careful.

Without screening provided by a no-claim bonus and deductible, insurance companies offer the same supply of insurance to all drivers. The equilibrium without screening is the same as in Figure 12.5: Everyone pays $1,000 a year and there are 60 million of each type of driver.

With screening, the insurance companies base their supply to each group on the marginal cost (MC) of serving them. For careful drivers in part (a), the supply curve is MC_C. The equilibrium insurance premium is $800 a year and the number of drivers who are, or who behave as if they are, careful increases to 80 million. Without screening, the market *under*provides insurance to this group and is inefficient. With screening, the market is efficient.

For the aggressive drivers in part (b), the marginal cost of serving them is MC_A and this marginal cost determines the supply to this group. The equilibrium insurance premium is $1,200 a year and the number of drivers who remain aggressive decreases to 40 million. Without screening, the market *over*provides insurance to this group and is inefficient. Again, with screening, the market is efficient.

You've now seen two examples of markets with asymmetric information in which the creative signaling and screening overcomes what would be a market failure and achieves an efficient outcome.

CHECKPOINT 12.2

Describe the asymmetric information problems in the insurance market and explain how they are solved.

Practice Problems

1. Pam is a low-risk careful driver and Fran is a high-risk aggressive driver. What might an auto-insurance company do to get Pam and Fran to reveal their driver type?

2. Using Figure 12.6, show the deadweight losses that arise in an equilibrium without screening that are avoided in a separating equilibrium with screening.

In the News

Volvo ends fender bender
Volvos equipped with City Safe are less likely to cause rear-end crashes than are comparable vehicles without the safety system.

Source: *The Sacramento Bee*, July 29, 2011

1. How could auto-insurance companies use the information in the news clip? Is that information private and asymmetric?

2. How might City Safe create adverse selection and moral hazard?

Solutions to Practice Problems

1. The insurance company will offer policies with deductibles that enable drivers to reveal their private information. Pam reveals that she is a low-risk driver by taking a high deductible and low premium. Fran reveals that she is a high-risk driver by taking a low deductible and high premium.

2. For low-risk careful drivers, by taking a high deductible and low premium, 80 million get insurance for $800 a year compared to 60 million paying $1,000 a year without screening. The gray triangle in Figure 1 shows the deadweight loss avoided with screening from underprovision without screening.

   For high-risk aggressive drivers, by taking a low deductible and high premium, 40 million get insurance for $1,200 a year compared to 60 million paying $1,000 a year without screening. The gray triangle in Figure 2 shows the deadweight loss avoided with screening from overprovision without screening.

Solutions to In the News

1. The insurance companies know whether a car is a Volvo with the City Safe system and can use this information to separate the market by known risk differences. But this information is not private and not asymmetric.

2. Adverse selection: Drivers who know their driving style brings a high collision risk are more likely to buy a Volvo with City Safe. Moral hazard: Having bought a Volvo with City Safe, driving carelessly is less dangerous so some drivers become more careless.

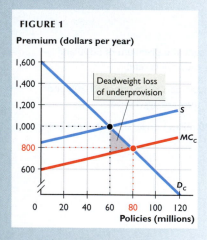

FIGURE 1

Premium (dollars per year)

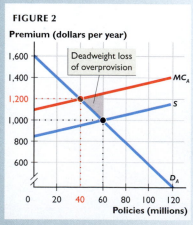

FIGURE 2

Premium (dollars per year)

12.3 HEALTH-CARE MARKETS

We're going to look at the health-care markets of the United States from an economic perspective. What are the economic problems these markets face? How do our health-care arrangements deal with these problems? How do other countries deal with the same problems? Does U.S. health care need reform?

■ Economic Problems in Health-Care Markets

Health care is two distinct products: health insurance—insurance that pays health-care bills—and health-care services—the services of physicians, specialists, nurses, other health-care professionals, and hospitals.

Left to competitive market forces with no government intervention both health insurance and health-care services would be underprovided for three economic reasons:

- Asymmetric information
- Missing insurance market
- Public-health externalities

Asymmetric Information

Asymmetric information, which brings adverse selection and moral hazard, is present in both markets. In the insurance market, the buyers have private information and in the care market the sellers have private information.

Adverse Selection and Moral Hazard in Health Insurance Some people exercise, eat healthy diets, watch their weight, and rarely get sick. Others are couch potatoes who don't exercise, eat high-fat and high-sugar diets, are overweight, and not only get sick more often but also are at long-term risk for diabetes and heart disease.

Information about whether a person has a healthy or unhealthy lifestyle is private information not available to the insurance companies.

Adverse selection arises because some of the healthiest people choose to be uninsured, at least during their younger years. *Moral hazard* arises because once insured, a person has less incentive to adopt a healthy lifestyle and some will yield to the temptation to drift into unhealthy habits.

Faced with a lack of information about individual lifestyle choices, health-insurance providers (like auto-insurance suppliers) offer lower premiums with high deductibles so that buyers can *reveal* information about their lifestyle. The fittest and healthiest choose a high deductible and low premium and the least fit and unhealthiest choose a low deductible and high premium. The market finds a *separating equilibrium.*

Moral Hazard in Health-Care Services High-quality providers of health-care services diagnose and prescribe treatments reliably and at the lowest possible cost. Low-quality providers make diagnosis errors and over-prescribe expensive drugs and other treatments. But the information about the quality and reliability of the health-care provider is private. The buyers (patients and insurance companies) don't know the quality of the providers. In this regard, the market for health-care services is like the market for used cars.

Moral hazard arises that increases the cost of health-care services. Providers have an incentive to play safe and overtreat a patient. Neither the patient nor the insurance company has information with which to prevent this inefficiency.

Health Maintenance Organizations partly address this moral hazard problem. By working with a limited number of service providers, an insurance company can monitor the quality of the service and control costs. But even with this arrangement, the service provider has more information than the insurer so the problem is lessened but not completely overcome.

■ Missing Insurance Market

Many people can't get private health insurance because they are too old or too sick or too disabled. Others with pre-existing conditions can get insurance but only with exclusions of the very health problems they are most likely to encounter. These are the people who have the greatest wants for health care but the least ability to get it without some alternative to the free market.

The missing insurance market is one that is blind to a person's known health risks. This market can be provided only with government intervention.

The U.S. health-care system deals with this problem by government provision of health insurance. Medicare pays the hospital costs and subsidizes the treatment costs of the aged (over 65) and some of the long-term disabled. Medicaid pays the health-care costs of those living in poverty and with long-term health-care needs.

These government programs provide health insurance for 88 million people but miss an estimated 46 million (see *Eye on the U.S. Economy* below). The total expenditure on them is driven by patient demand, not by decisions of Congress. As the population gets older and advances in medical technology keep people alive longer with expensive treatments, the cost of these programs grows.

EYE on the U.S. ECONOMY
Health Care in the United States: A Snapshot

Expenditure on health care takes more than 16 percent of U.S. incomes. A bit more than a half of this expenditure is private—spending on health-care insurance and out-of-pocket payments for health-care services. The rest is financed by taxes—spending by federal and state governments on Medicare and Medicaid.

Figure 1 shows the distribution of the health-care dollar across these types of expenditure.

Of the 301 million people in the United States, 167 million have private health insurance.

More than one half of all employed people—about 70 million—buy health insurance through their employer.

Tax breaks are available on health insurance payments, the largest being for the self-employed who can deduct the entire payment.

About 75 million people limit their health-care cost by using a Health Maintenance Organization (HMO).

The federal and state Medicare and Medicaid programs cover 88 million people.

An estimated 46 million have no health-care insurance, and a further 25 million are reckoned to be underinsured—have some insurance but not enough for a big emergency.

Some of the uninsured are healthy and *choose* not to insure. Others can't afford insurance and don't qualify for

Medicare or Medicaid.

Per person covered, government programs are more costly than private insurance because they serve the aged, the disabled, and the chronically sick.

Figure 2 shows expenditure per person. With 88 million people covered by Medicare and Medicaid at a total cost of $831 billion, governments spend $9,443 per person per year on these two programs.

The cost of private insurance per person covered is 50 percent of the cost of the government programs at $4,690 per person per year.

Out-of-pocket expenditure, which includes spending by the uninsured, is $1,304 per person per year.

■ Public-Health Externalities

The control of infectious diseases is a *public good* (see Chapter 11, p. 267). So public sanitation systems, which general public health relies upon, is provided by governments to avoid a *free rider problem* (see Chapter 11, p. 269).

Vaccination against an infectious disease is a *private good*, but one with a *positive externality* (see Chapter 10, p. 242 and 254–259). People who get a flu shot protect not only themselves but everyone with whom they come into contact. The marginal social benefit of flu shots exceeds the marginal private benefit.

The efficient quantity of flu shots exceeds the quantity that an unregulated market would provide. This feature of health care is a further reason why it is efficient to subsidize the care of the aged and those in poverty.

You've seen three economic reasons why health care isn't an ordinary good that we can expect the unregulated market to provide efficiently. You've also seen that U.S. health care is provided by a mixture of private and public insurance. How do the U.S. health-care markets compare with those in other countries?

■ Health-Care Systems in Other Countries

Every major country except the United States has a comprehensive national health-care system. Every person is insured under a government-funded national insurance program. Health-care services are provided by private clinics, hospitals, physicians, and specialists but they are paid for by governments.

Government expenditure on health care is financed by specific health insurance taxes and by general income taxes.

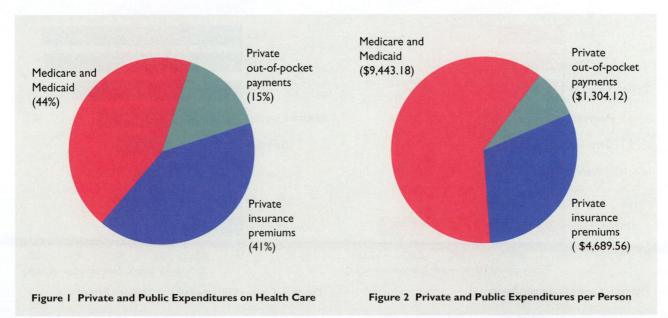

Figure 1 Private and Public Expenditures on Health Care

Figure 2 Private and Public Expenditures per Person

Source of data: U.S. Bureau of the Census, *Statistical Abstract of the United States: 2011*, Tables 131, 140, 142, and 145.

Resources in the public health-care system are allocated by physicians, specialists, and hospitals and are based on urgency of need, which results in patients often being placed on lengthy waiting lists.

No one is permitted to opt out of the national health service but in most countries, everyone *is* permitted to buy private insurance and private health care. In these countries, what is called a "two-tier" system sometimes emerges in which the rich buy private insurance and get higher-quality care and the poor get their health care from a lower-quality state system.

In a few countries, there is no private option. It is illegal to open a private clinic and sell private insurance that covers basic care provided by the state system. The idea of this restriction is to avoid the "two-tier" outcome.

EYE on the GLOBAL ECONOMY
Health-Care Expenditures and Health Outcomes

The best health care in America is the best in the world. But access to the best is not universally available and the inequality in access to health care in the United States is greater than in other similarly rich nations.

Figures 1 and 2 below compare the United States with seven other rich countries on health-care expenditures and a health-care efficiency index.

The expenditure data in Figure 1 are average dollars spent on health care per person in each country.

The efficiency data in Figure 2 are based on life expectancy, health inequality, and the fairness of financing health care.

The comparisons in the figures make U.S. health care look the most costly and least efficient among these

countries. But the comparison ignores international trade in health-care services. Tens of thousands of Canadians and people from other countries come to the United States to get high-quality health care. Expenditure on these foreigners raises U.S expenditure in Figure 1 and the greater healthiness of these foreigners raises the efficiency indexes of other countries in Figure 2.

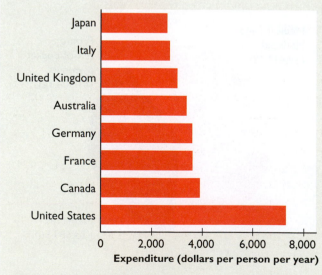

Figure 1 Expenditure per Person

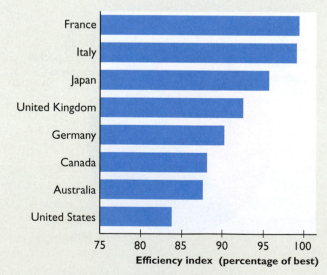

Figure 2 Overall Efficiency of Health-Care System

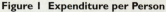
SOURCES OF DATA: OECD and the World Health Organization.

The comprehensive national health systems limit choice and impose long waiting times. But they do contain costs and they do so without, apparently, compromising the overall quality of health outcomes. *Eye on the Global Economy* on p. 308 provides some details.

■ A Reform Idea

The Medicare and Medicaid programs are in effect an open-ended commitment of public funds to the health care of the aged and those too poor to buy private health care. Health care in the United States faces two problems: Too many people are uninsured and health care costs too much. These problems are going to get worse if nothing major is done to reverse a trend.

The Obama Affordable Care Act addresses the first of these problems by requiring everyone to be insured and by creating a new Pre-Existing Condition Insurance Plan, financed partly by the government. But the Act does little to address the problem of overexpenditure, and this problem is extremely serious. It is so serious that without massive change, the present open-ended health-care programs will bankrupt the United States.

A solution to both the problem of coverage and access and the problem of over-expenditure has been suggested by Laurence Kotlikoff, an economics professor at Boston University. His proposal uses health-care *vouchers* to ensure universal coverage and a cap on total expenditure. Everyone would get a voucher and those with higher expected health-care costs would get a bigger voucher. Health-care vouchers would work like the education vouchers that we explain in Chapter 10 (see pp. 258–259). They would provide the cost discipline of the European and Canadian systems with the choice that is so important and valued by Americans.

Professor Laurence J. Kotlikoff of Boston University; author of The Healthcare Fix *and creator of Medicare Part C for All.*

EYE on YOUR LIFE
Signaling Your Ability

You've seen how used-car dealers signal with warranties. You, too, send signals.

You know how smart you are and how hard you're willing to work. But this information is private. It is known to you but not to your potential employers.

How can you signal your ability to potential employers? The answer is by your choice of education.

Michael Spence, an economist at Stanford University and joint winner of the 2001 Nobel Prize with George Akerlof and Joseph Stiglitz, explained how education choices send signals.

Think of people as having just two possible levels of ability: either high or low. Each person knows her or his own ability, but potential employers don't have this information.

People send signals to potential employers by their choice of education. For a low-ability person, the opportunity cost of a university education is high—not just the tuition and cost of books, but the cost in time and effort to get passing grades.

For a high-ability person, the opportunity cost of a college or university education is lower. For those peo-

ple, good grades take hard work but they can be attained with reasonable effort. So only people with high ability choose a college or university education.

Employers know each person's education (and grades), so they can offer a high wage for high ability and a low wage for low ability. There is a separating equilibrium in the market for workers of differing ability.

Even if your education contributed nothing to improve ability, it would still signal your ability.

MyEconLab
You can work these problems in Study Plan 12.3 and get instant feedback.

 # CHECKPOINT 12.3

Explain the information problems and other economic problems in health-care markets.

Practice Problems

1. Describe the asymmetric information problem in the market for health-care services and explain how the problem is dealt with.

2. What are the sources of inefficiency in the U.S. health-insurance market?

In the News

Your family's health-care costs: $19,393
The average health-care costs of American families who are insured through their jobs is $19,393, up 7.3 percent or $1,319 from last year. Of this increase, workers' out-of-pocket costs rose 9.2 percent. Payroll deductions for insurance coverage rose 9.3 percent. Employers have increasingly been offering health plans with larger deductibles to control their own costs and to force workers to use medical care more selectively.

Source: CNNMoney, May 11, 2011

1. How do larger deductibles help employers to control their own costs?
2. How do larger deductibles change the incentives that people face?
3. How do larger deductibles chosen by employers influence the distribution of health-care costs?

Solutions to Practice Problems

1. In the market for health-care services, the suppliers are physicians, specialists, other health-care professionals, and hospitals. The demanders are patients and the insurance companies that pay most of the patients' bills. Asymmetric information arises because medical workers have private information about a patient's condition, the treatments available, and the cost-effectiveness of the treatment they prescribe. They face moral hazard. HMOs with insurance companies selecting and monitoring service providers lessen the moral hazard.

2. The sources of inefficiency in the U.S. market for health insurance are pre-existing conditions and other serious health risks that are uninsurable, and underprovision, with 46 million Americans having no health insurance and millions more being underinsured.

Solutions to In the News

1. Larger deductibles lower the premiums and so lower employers' costs.
2. Larger deductibles strengthen the incentives for: (1) Healthy families to buy health-care insurance; (2) People not to visit the doctor with minor health problems; (3) People with unhealthy lifestyles to try to reform.
3. Larger deductibles chosen by employers lower their own share of health-care costs and increase the out-of-pocket costs of their insured employees.

CHAPTER SUMMARY

Key Points

1 **Describe the lemons problem and explain how the used-car market solves it.**

- In some markets, one side of a market has private information—asymmetric information.
- In the market for used cars, the seller knows and the buyer doesn't know if a car is a lemon.
- Adverse selection results in a pooling equilibrium with too many lemons and too few good cars being traded.
- Dealers' warranties act as signals and enable the market to achieve a separating equilibrium that is efficient.

2 **Describe the asymmetric information problems in the insurance market and explain how they are solved.**

- In insurance markets, buyers are better informed than sellers about the risk being insured.
- Without screening, too few low-risk people would be insured.
- Moral hazard arises in insurance: An insured person has less incentive than an uninsured person to avoid the insured loss.
- The no-claim bonus and deductible reveal risk and enable insurance markets to reach an efficient separating equilibrium.

3 **Explain the information problems and other economic problems in health-care markets.**

- Three economic problems in health-care markets are (1) asymmetric information, (2) missing insurance markets, and (3) public-health externalities.
- Adverse selection results in some of the healthiest choosing not to insure.
- Suppliers of health-care services have private information and buyers cannot monitor and control the quality and cost of service.
- The HMO controls costs by using a limited number of health-care providers and monitoring them.
- The market underprovides health care because it excludes those with the greatest health problems and has external benefits.
- Other countries have comprehensive national health-care systems with lower cost but limited choice. Health-care vouchers could cut cost, increase coverage, and retain choice.

Key Terms

Adverse selection, 295
Asymmetric information, 292
Lemons problem, 292

Moral hazard, 301
Pooling equilibrium, 297
Private information, 292

Screening, 302
Separating equilibrium, 297
Signaling, 296

CHAPTER CHECKPOINT

Study Plan Problems and Applications

1. Judy knows that her car is a lemon and offers it for sale. If the used-car market is working efficiently, will buyers know whether her car is a lemon? Why or why not?

2. Some car dealers offer used cars for sale with warranties and some offer them without warranties. Describe the equilibrium in the market for used cars. Is the market efficient?

3. **G.M. recalls 6,800 pickups for inaccurate shift-lever reading**
   General Motors is recalling 6,800 pickups from the 2011 model year because a defective clip could allow the automatic transmission's selector to appear to be in Park when it was not. A worker at the assembly plant discovered the problem.

   Source: *The New York Times*, July 1, 2011

   Did G.M. sell 6,800 lemons to people who bought the pickups? If G.M. did, what was the private information that it had that buyers did not know? If G.M. didn't, explain why not.

Use the following information to work Problems **4** and **5**.

Mary is an 18-year-old student, who recently bought a used car. Mary is looking to buy car insurance. Insurance companies compete for her business.

4. Is there a moral hazard problem in a transaction between Mary and an insurance company? Explain why or why not?

5. Is there an adverse selection problem in a transaction between Mary and an insurance company? Explain why or why not?

6. If you have private information that you are a more aggressive driver than your driving record indicates, would you buy collision insurance? If the insurance company offers you a large deductible or a no-claim bonus are you likely to take the offer? Why or why not?

Use the following information to work Problems **7** to **9**.

President Obama campaigned on a health-care reform plan that did not include mandatory health insurance. Hillary Clinton wanted mandatory health insurance with no opting out. In 2009, the President said he would support making health insurance mandatory with the cost covered by employers, but those who could not afford to pay and small businesses would be exempt.

7. If health insurance is optional, would healthy people be more likely or less likely to buy insurance?

8. What obstacles to efficiency does optional health insurance create?

9. U.S. health care per person costs twice that of other rich countries. Does the United States overprovide? Do other countries underprovide? What economic concepts do you need to answer? What data might be relevant?

10. Describe the situation if health care is delivered using the same methods that deliver basic education to all Americans. How would the health-care system you've described compare with that in the United States today? How would it compare to that in Canada?

Instructor Assignable Problems and Applications

Your instructor can assign these problems as homework, a quiz, or a test in MyEconLab.

1. Describe the used-car market in the United States. How many used cars get traded per year and at what average price? How does the market enable buyers to avoid a lemon? What role, if any, do governments play in the used-car market?

2. Zaneb is a high-school teacher and is well known in her community for her honesty, integrity, and sense of social responsibility. She is shopping for a used car. She plans to borrow the money to pay for it from her local bank and she plans to buy auto insurance from her local insurance company. What asymmetric information problems is Zaneb likley to enounter and what arrangements are likely to help cope with those problems? Explain your answers.

3. Suppose that there are two national football leagues: The Time League and The Bonus for Win League. The players have private information about their effort. In The Time League, players receive a fixed wage based on the time they spend practicing and playing matches. In The Bonus for Win League, the players are paid one wage for a loss, a higher wage for a tie, and the highest wage of all for a win. Describe the moral hazard and adverse selection problems in these two leagues. Which league best addresses these problems?

4. **Phillies hamstrung by no-trade clause**
Phillies general manager Pat Gillick, who previously built winners in Toronto, Baltimore, and Seattle, is no fan of blanket no-trade clauses. Gillick is so averse to giving out complete no-trade provisions that he says it could be a "deal breaker" when the Phillies negotiate with big free agents this winter.

Source: ESPN.com, November 8, 2000

Provide an example of private information that a baseball player who wants a no-trade clause possesses. Does a baseball player with a no-trade clause present a moral hazard to his baseball team? Does a baseball player with a no-trade clause present adverse selection problems to his baseball team?

5. What are the key economic problems in providing an efficient quantity and distribution of health-care insurance and service? Explain how the U.S. health-care system addresses these problems.

6. What are HMOs and what information problems do they help to deal with?

7. What are the problems that Medicare and Medicaid address and what problems do they cause?

8. What is the cost of health care in the United States compared to that in Canada and major European countries? Do health outcomes correlate with health-care costs? Can you think of explanations for the facts you've just provided?

9. What is Laurence Kotlikoff's proposal for fixing health care in the United States? Draw a graph to illustrate how his proposal would work and show whether it could be efficient.

MyEconLab

You can work this quiz in Chapter 12 Study Plan and get instant feedback.

Multiple Choice Quiz

1. A market with asymmetric information is one in which _____.

   A. sellers offer a product for sale at a low price and buyers are pleased to get a bargain
   B. sellers know how reliable the product is and they share that information with buyers
   C. only the buyers or the sellers have information about the quality of the product
   D. buyers are willing to pay less for the product than the seller is offering it for sale

2. The lemons problem does not arise in markets in which _____.

   A. buyers can separate reliable products and defective products
   B. sellers offer more defective products than reliable products for sale
   C. there is a shortage of lemons
   D. sellers have private information

3. In the market for used cars with no warranties, _____ lemons are bought and the equilibrium is a _____ equilibrium.

   A. too few; separating
   B. too many; separating
   C. only; pooling
   D. no; pooling

4. In a used-car market in which dealers offer cars with warranties, _____.

   A. there is private information
   B. a separating equilibrium does not occur
   C. a lemons problem does not arise
   D. the market is inefficient

5. Moral hazard arises in the insurance market because _____.

   A. buyers of insurance have private information that they can use
   B. insurance companies can offer a range of premiums to buyers
   C. buyers can opt to take a deductible or a no-claim bonus
   D. insurance companies can match premiums to customer risk

6. The private market delivers *too little* health care because _____.

   A. insurance companies cannot avoid the problems of moral hazard and adverse selection
   B. too many young healthy people buy insurance
   C. insurance companies cannot monitor health-care providers
   D. pre-existing health conditions are too costly to insure

7. The health-care system in the United States costs per person _____ what it costs in other rich countries and U.S. health outcomes rank _____.

   A. double; lower
   B. half; higher
   C. double; higher
   D. half; lower

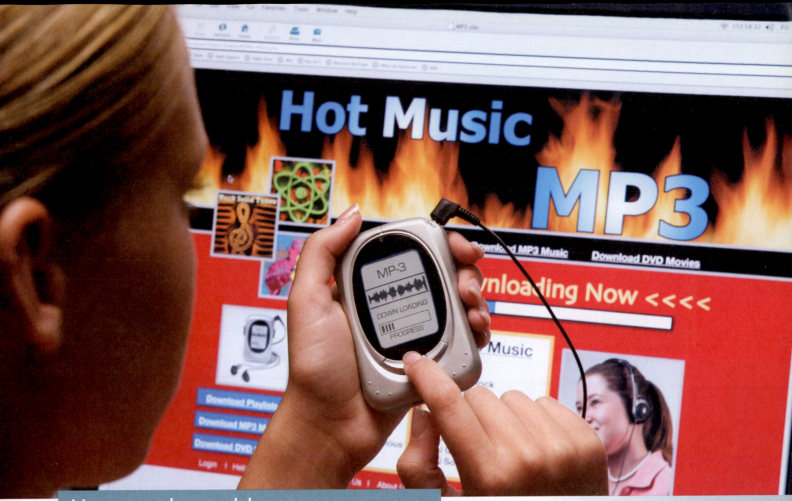

How much would you
pay for a song?

Consumer Choice and Demand

13

When you have completed your study of this chapter, you will be able to

CHAPTER CHECKLIST

1 Calculate and graph a budget line that shows the limits to a person's consumption possibilities.

2 Explain marginal utility theory and use it to derive a consumer's demand curve.

3 Use marginal utility theory to explain the paradox of value: why water is vital but cheap while diamonds are relatively useless but expensive.

13.1 CONSUMPTION POSSIBILITIES

We begin our study of consumption choices by learning about the limits to what a person can afford to buy. Consumption choices are limited by income and prices. We summarize these influences on buying plans in a budget line. We'll study the buying plans of a student like you whom we'll call Tina.

■ The Budget Line

Budget line

A line that describes the limits to consumption possibilities and that depends on a consumer's budget and the prices of goods and services.

A **budget line** describes the limits to consumption possibilities. Tina has already committed most of her income to renting an apartment, buying textbooks, paying her campus meal plan, and saving a few dollars each month. Having made these decisions, Tina has a remaining budget of $4 a day, which she spends on two goods: bottled water and chewing gum. The price of water is $1 a bottle, and the price of gum is 50¢ a pack. If Tina spends all of her available budget, she reaches the limits of her consumption of bottled water and gum.

Figure 13.1 illustrates Tina's budget line. Rows *A* through *E* in the table show five possible ways of spending $4 on these two goods. If Tina spends all of her $4 on gum, she can buy 8 packs a day. In this case, she has nothing available to spend on bottled water. Row *A* shows this possibility. At the other extreme, if Tina spends her entire $4 on bottled water, she can buy 4 bottles a day and no gum. Row *E* shows this possibility. Rows *B*, *C*, and *D* show three other possible combinations that Tina can afford.

■ **FIGURE 13.1**

Consumption Possibilities   MyEconLab Animation

Tina's budget line shows the boundary between what she can and cannot afford. The rows of the table list Tina's affordable combinations of bottled water and chewing gum when her budget is $4 a day, the price of water is $1 a bottle, and the price of chewing gum is 50¢ a pack. For example, row *A* tells us that Tina exhausts her $4 budget when she buys 8 packs of gum and no water.

The figure graphs Tina's budget line. Points *A* through *E* on the graph represent the rows of the table.

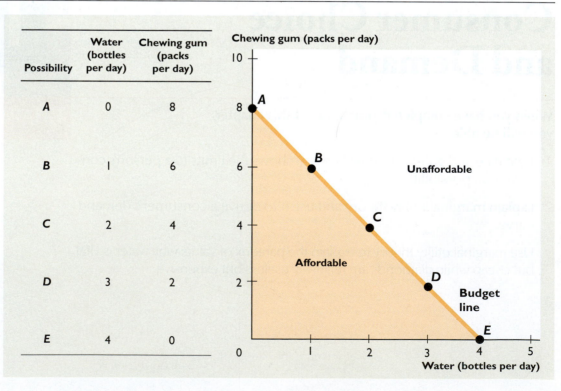

Possibility	Water (bottles per day)	Chewing gum (packs per day)
A	0	8
B	1	6
C	2	4
D	3	2
E	4	0

Points *A* through *E* in Figure 13.1 graph the possibilities in the table. The line passing through these points is Tina's budget line, which marks the boundary between what she can and cannot afford. She can afford any combination on the budget line and inside it (in the orange area). She cannot afford any combination outside the budget line (in the white area).

The budget line in Figure 13.1 is similar to the *production possibilities frontier*, or *PPF*, in Chapter 3 (pp. 60–61). Both curves show a limit to what is feasible. The *PPF* is a technological limit, so it changes only when technology changes. The budget line depends on the consumer's budget and on prices, so it changes when the budget or prices change.

■ A Change in the Budget

Figure 13.2 shows the effect of a change in Tina's budget on her consumption possibilities. When Tina's budget increases, her consumption possibilities expand, and her budget line shifts outward. When her budget decreases, her consumption possibilities shrink and her budget line shifts inward.

On the initial budget line (the same as in Figure 13.1), Tina's budget is $4. On a day when Tina loses her wallet with $2 in it, she has only $2 to spend. Her new budget line in Figure 13.2 shows how much she can consume with a budget of $2. She can buy any of the combinations on the $2 budget line.

On a day when Tina sells an old CD for $2, she has $6 available and her budget line shifts rightward. She can now buy any of the combinations on the $6 budget line.

■ **FIGURE 13.2**

Changes in a Consumer's Budget

MyEconLab Animation

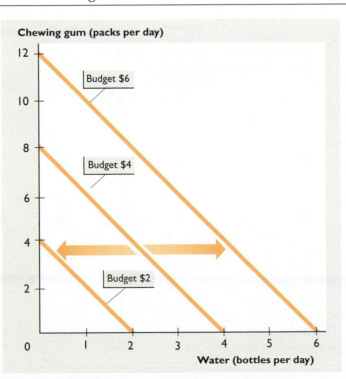

A decrease in the budget shifts the budget line leftward, and an increase in the budget shifts the budget line rightward.

■ Changes in Prices

If the price of one good rises when the prices of other goods and the budget remain the same, consumption possibilities shrink. If the price of one good falls when the prices of other goods and the budget remain the same, consumption possibilities expand. To see these changes in consumption possibilities, let's see what happens to Tina's budget line when the price of a bottle of water changes.

A Fall in the Price of Water

Figure 13.3 shows the effect on Tina's budget line of a fall in the price of a bottle of water from $1 to 50¢ when the price of gum and her budget remain unchanged. If Tina spends all of her budget on bottled water, she can now afford 8 bottles a day. Her consumption possibilities have expanded. Because the price of gum is unchanged, if she spends all her budget on gum, she can still afford only 8 packs of gum a day. Her budget line has rotated outward.

A Rise in the Price of Water

Figure 13.4 shows the effect on Tina's budget line of a rise in the price of a bottle of water from $1 to $2 when the price of gum and her budget remain unchanged. If Tina spends all of her budget on bottled water, she can now afford only 2 bottles a day. Tina's consumption possibilities have shrunk. Again, because the price of gum is unchanged, if Tina spends all her budget on gum, she can still afford only 8 packs of gum a day. Her budget line has rotated inward.

Lower prices in a sale expand consumption possibilities.

■ **FIGURE 13.3**

A Fall in the Price of Water

MyEconLab Animation

When the price of water falls from $1 a bottle to 50¢ a bottle, the budget line rotates outward and becomes less steep.

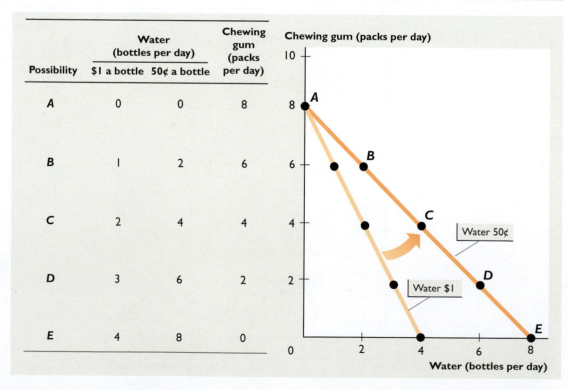

Possibility	Water (bottles per day) $1 a bottle	Water (bottles per day) 50¢ a bottle	Chewing gum (packs per day)
A	0	0	8
B	1	2	6
C	2	4	4
D	3	6	2
E	4	8	0

Prices and the Slope of the Budget Line

Notice that when the price of bottled water changes and the price of gum remains unchanged, the slope of the budget line changes. In Figure 13.3, when the price of bottled water falls, the budget line becomes less steep. In Figure 13.4, when the price of a bottle of water rises, the budget line becomes steeper.

Recall that "slope equals rise over run." The rise is an *increase* in the quantity of gum, and the run is a *decrease* in the quantity of bottled water. The slope of the budget line is negative, which means that there is a tradeoff between the two goods. Along the budget line, consuming more of one good implies consuming less of the other good. The slope of the budget line is an *opportunity cost*. It tells us what the consumer must give up to get one more unit of a good.

Let's calculate the slopes of the three budget lines in Figures 13.3 and 13.4:

- When the price of water is $1 a bottle, the slope of the budget line is 8 packs of gum divided by 4 bottles of water, which equals 2 packs of gum per bottle.
- When the price of water is 50¢ a bottle, the slope of the budget line is 8 packs of gum divided by 8 bottles of water, which equals 1 pack of gum per bottle.
- When the price of water is $2 a bottle, the slope of the budget line is 8 packs of gum divided by 2 bottles of water, which equals 4 packs of gum per bottle.

FIGURE 13.4

A Rise in the Price of Water

MyEconLab Animation

Possibility	Water (bottles per day) $2 a bottle	Water (bottles per day) $1 a bottle	Chewing gum (packs per day)
A	0	0	8
		1	6
B	1	2	4
		3	2
C	2	4	0

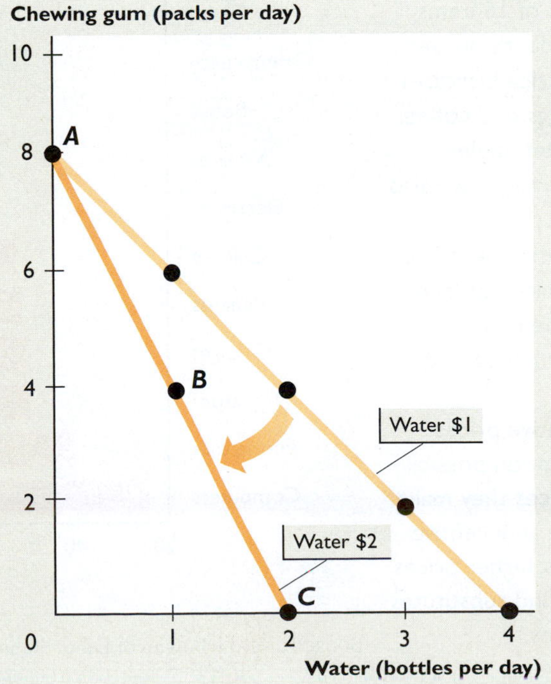

When the price of water rises from $1 a bottle to $2 a bottle, the budget line rotates inward and becomes steeper.

Think about what these slopes mean as opportunity costs. When the price of water is $1 a bottle and the price of gum is 50¢ a pack, it costs 2 packs of gum to buy a bottle of water. When the price of water is 50¢ a bottle and the price of gum is 50¢ a pack, it costs 1 pack of gum to buy a bottle of water. And when the price of water is $2 a bottle and the price of gum is 50¢ a pack, it costs 4 packs of gum to buy a bottle of water.

Another name for an opportunity cost is a relative price. A **relative price** is the price of one good in terms of another good. If the price of gum is 50¢ a pack and the price of water is $1 a bottle, the relative price of water is 2 packs of gum per bottle. It is calculated as the price of water divided by the price of gum ($1 a bottle ÷ 50¢ a pack = 2 packs per bottle).

When the price of the good plotted on the *x*-axis falls, other things remaining the same, the budget line becomes less steep, and the opportunity cost and relative price of the good on the *x*-axis fall.

Relative price
The price of one good in terms of another good—an opportunity cost. It equals the price of one good divided by the price of another good.

EYE on the U.S. ECONOMY
Relative Prices on the Move

Over a number of years, relative prices change a great deal. Some of the most dramatic changes have occurred in high-technology products such as computers. Many other relative prices have changed and many have fallen.

The figure shows the price changes between 2001 and 2011 of 16 items that feature in most student's budgets.

The largest relative price increases are those of gasoline, eggs, and coffee. The relative prices of beef, apples, bread, airfares, and electricity have also increased.

The largest relative price decrease is that of a computer, which has fallen by almost 20 percent. The relative prices of phone calls, tomatoes, and oranges have also fallen.

These changes in relative prices change people's consumption possibilities and change the choices they make.

Lower prices provide an incentive to buy greater quantities; higher prices provide an incentive to find substitutes and buy smaller quantities.

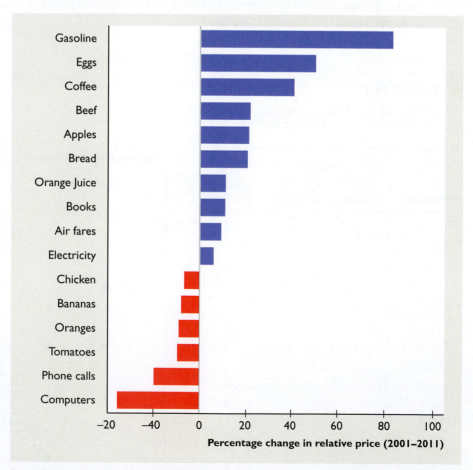

SOURCE OF DATA: Bureau of Labor Statistics.

CHECKPOINT 13.1

Calculate and graph a budget line that shows the limits to a person's consumption possibilities.

MyEconLab
You can work these problems in Study Plan 13.1 and get instant feedback.

Practice Problems

Jerry's burger and magazine budget is $12 a week. The price of a burger is $2, and the price of a magazine is $4.

1. List the combinations of burgers and magazines that Jerry can afford.

2. What is the relative price of a magazine? Explain your answer.

3. Draw a graph of Jerry's budget line with the quantity of magazines plotted on the x-axis. Describe how his budget line changes if, other things remaining the same, the following changes occur one at a time:
   - The price of a magazine falls.
   - Jerry's budget for burgers and magazines increases.

In the News

Paying for gas forces painful sacrifices
With the average gas price hitting $3.70 a gallon, many people cut back on other things, such as meals-to-go at the grocery store and shopping.
Source: CNNMoney, May 4, 2011

Consider Robyn who buys only two goods: gasoline and meals-to-go. As the gas price rises, describe the change in her consumption possibilities, the relative price of a meal-to-go, and her budget in terms of meals-to-go.

Solutions to Practice Problems

1. Jerry can afford 3 magazines and no burgers; 2 magazines and 2 burgers; 1 magazine and 4 burgers; no magazines and 6 burgers.

2. The relative price of a magazine is the number of burgers that Jerry must forgo to get 1 magazine, which equals the price of a magazine divided by the price of a burger, or 2 burgers per magazine.

3. The budget line is a straight line from 6 burgers on the y-axis to 3 magazines on the x-axis (Figure 1). With a lower price of a magazine, Jerry can buy more magazines. His budget line rotates outward (Figure 2). With a bigger budget, Jerry can buy more of both goods. His budget line shifts outward (Figure 3).

Solution to In the News

A higher gas price shrinks Robyn's consumption possibilities—her budget line rotates inward. The relative price of a meal-to-go is the price of a meal-to-go divided by the gas price. A higher gas price lowers the relative price of a meal-to-go. Robyn's budget in terms of meals-to-go is the number of meals-to-go that she can buy. A higher gas price does not change her budget in terms of meals-to-go.

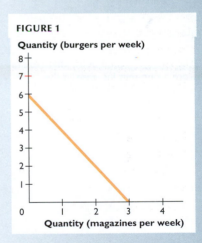

FIGURE 1
Quantity (burgers per week)

Quantity (magazines per week)

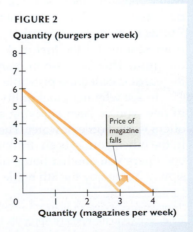

FIGURE 2
Quantity (burgers per week)

Price of magazine falls

Quantity (magazines per week)

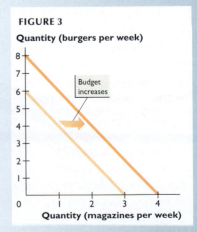

FIGURE 3
Quantity (burgers per week)

Budget increases

Quantity (magazines per week)

Utility
The benefit or satisfaction that a person gets from the consumption of a good or service.

The budget line tells us about consumption *possibilities*, but it doesn't tell us a person's consumption *choice*. Choices depend on *possibilities* and *preferences*. To describe preferences, economists use the concept of utility.* **Utility** is the benefit or satisfaction that a person gets from the consumption of a good or service. To understand how we use utility to explain people's choices, we distinguish between two concepts:

- Total utility
- Marginal utility

■ Total Utility

Total utility
The total benefit that a person gets from the consumption of a good or service. Total utility generally increases as the quantity consumed of a good increases.

Total utility is the total benefit that a person gets from the consumption of a good or service. Total utility depends on the quantity of the good consumed *in a given period*—more consumption generally gives more total utility. Table 13.1 shows Tina's total utility from bottled water and chewing gum. If she consumes no bottled water and no gum, she gets no utility. If she consumes 1 bottle of water a day, she gets 15 units of utility. If she consumes 1 pack of gum a day, it provides her with 32 units of utility. As Tina increases the quantity of bottled water or the packs of gum she consumes, her total utility increases.

■ Marginal Utility

Marginal utility
The change in total utility that results from a one-unit increase in the quantity of a good consumed.

Marginal utility is the change in total utility that results from a one-unit increase in the quantity of a good consumed. Table 13.1 shows the calculation of Tina's marginal utility from bottled water and chewing gum. Let's find Tina's marginal utility from a 3rd bottle of water a day (highlighted in the table). Her total utility from 3 bottles is 36 units, and her total utility from 2 bottles is 27 units. So for Tina, the marginal utility from drinking a 3rd bottle of water each day is

$$\text{Marginal utility of 3rd bottle} = 36\,\text{units} - 27\,\text{units} = 9\,\text{units}.$$

In the table, marginal utility appears midway between the quantities because the *change* in consumption produces the *marginal* utility. The table displays the marginal utility from each quantity of water and gum consumed.

Notice that Tina's marginal utility decreases as her daily consumption of water and gum increases. For example, her marginal utility from bottled water decreases from 15 units for the first bottle per day to 12 units from the second and 9 units from the third. Similarly, her marginal utility from chewing gum decreases from 32 units for the first pack per day to 16 units for the second and 8 units for the third. This decrease in marginal utility as the quantity of a good consumed increases is called the principle of **diminishing marginal utility.**

Diminishing marginal utility
The general tendency for marginal utility to decrease as the quantity of a good consumed increases.

To see why marginal utility diminishes, think about the following situations: In one, you've been studying all day and have had nothing to drink. Someone offers you a bottle of water. The marginal utility you get from that water is large. In the other, you've been drinking all day and you've drunk 7 bottles. Now someone offers you another bottle of water, and you say thanks very much and sip it slowly. You enjoy the 8th bottle of the day, but the marginal utility from it is tiny.

---

*Economists also use an alternative method of describing preferences called *indifference curves*, which are described in the optional appendix to this chapter.

TABLE 13.1

Tina's Total Utility and Marginal Utility

Bottled water			Chewing gum		
Quantity (bottles per day)	Total utility	Marginal utility	Quantity (packs per day)	Total utility	Marginal utility
0	0		0	0	
		15			32
1	15		1	32	
		12			16
2	27		2	48	
		9			8
3	36		3	56	
		6			6
4	42		4	62	
		5			4
5	47		5	66	
		4			2
6	51		6	68	
		3			1
7	54		7	69	
		2			0
8	56		8	69	

The table shows Tina's total utility and marginal utility from bottled water and chewing gum. Marginal utility is the change in total utility when the quantity consumed increases by one unit. When Tina's consumption of bottled water increases from 2 bottles a day to 3 bottles a day, her total utility from bottled water increases from 27 units to 36 units. So Tina's marginal utility of the 3rd bottle a day is 9 units. Total utility increases and marginal utility diminishes as the quantity consumed increases.

Similarly, suppose you've been unable to buy a pack of gum for more than a day. A friend offers you a pack. Relief! You chew and receive a lot of utility. On another day, you've chewed until your jaws ache and have gone through 7 packs. You're offered an 8th, and this time you say thanks very much but I'll pass on that one. The 8th pack of gum would bring you no marginal utility.

EYE on the PAST
Jeremy Bentham, William Stanley Jevons, and the Birth of Utility

The concept of utility was revolutionary when Jeremy Bentham (1748–1832) proposed it in the early 1800s. He used the idea to advance his then radical support for free education, free medical care, and social security. It was another fifty years before William Stanley Jevons (1835–1882) developed the concept of *marginal* utility and used it to predict people's consumption choices. For the first time, economists could distinguish between cost and value and a basic theory of demand was born.

Jeremy Bentham

William Stanley Jevons

■ Graphing Tina's Utility Schedules

We illustrate a consumer's preferences with a total utility curve and a marginal utility curve like those in Figure 13.5. Part (a) shows that as Tina drinks more bottled water, her total utility from water increases. It also shows that total utility increases at a decreasing rate—diminishing marginal utility. Part (b) graphs Tina's marginal utility. The steps in part (a) are placed side by side in part (b). The curve that passes through the midpoints of the bars in part (b) is Tina's marginal utility curve.

The numbers in Table 13.1 and the graphs in Figure 13.5 describe Tina's preferences and, along with her budget line, enable us to predict the choices that she makes. That is our next task.

■ Maximizing Total Utility

The consumer's goal is to allocate the available budget in the way that maximizes total utility. The consumer achieves this goal by choosing the affordable combination of goods at which the *sum* of the utilities obtained from all goods consumed is as large as possible.

Utility-maximizing rule
The rule that leads to the greatest total utility from all the goods and services consumed. The rule is
1. Allocate the entire available budget.
2. Make the marginal utility per dollar equal for all goods.

We can find a consumer's best budget allocation by using a two-step **utility-maximizing rule:**

1. Allocate the entire available budget.
2. Make the marginal utility per dollar equal for all goods.

Allocate the Available Budget

If a consumer can buy more of one good without buying less of another good, utility can be increased. When utility is maximized, it isn't possible to buy more of one good without decreasing the quantity of another good. In this situation, the consumer has allocated the entire available budget.

With a budget of $4, the price of water $1 per bottle, and the price of gum 50¢ a pack, Tina allocates her budget to bottled water and gum at a point *on* her budget line in Figure 13.1 (p. 316). If she was at a point *inside* her budget line, she could buy more water or more gum without giving up any of the other good and she would not be maximizing utility.

Equalize the Marginal Utility Per Dollar

Marginal utility per dollar
The marginal utility from a good relative to the price paid for the good.

The second step to maximizing utility is to find the affordable combination that makes the marginal utility per dollar equal for both goods. The **marginal utility per dollar** is the marginal utility from a good relative to the price of the good.

Calculating the Marginal Utility per Dollar The marginal utility per dollar equals the marginal utility from a good divided by the price of the good. For example, if Tina buys 2 packs of gum, her marginal utility from gum is 16 units. At a price of 50¢ a pack, her marginal utility *per dollar* from gum is 16 units divided by 50¢, which equals 32 units of utility per dollar.

Tina's Utility-Maximizing Choice If Tina spends $1 more on water and $1 less on gum, her total utility from water increases and her total utility from gum decreases. What happens to her total utility from both goods depends on the marginal utility per dollar for each good.

FIGURE 13.5

Total Utility and Marginal Utility

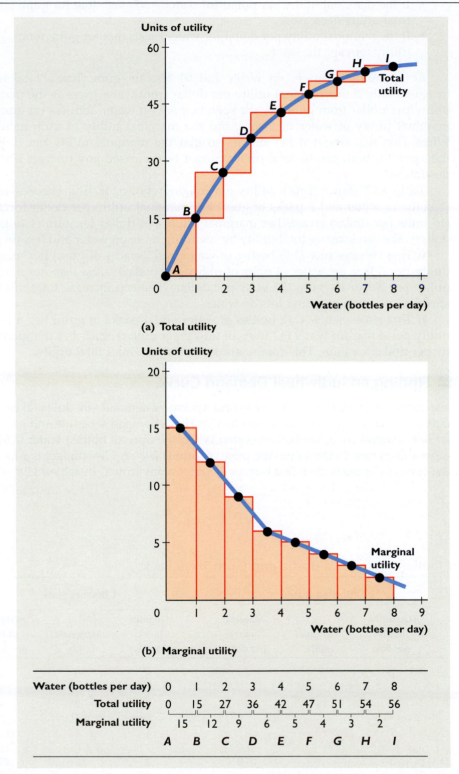

(a) Total utility

(b) Marginal utility

Part (a) graphs Tina's total utility from bottled water. It also shows the extra total utility she gains from each additional bottle of water—her marginal utility—as the steps along the total utility curve.

Part (b) shows how Tina's marginal utility from bottled water diminishes by placing the bars shown in part (a) side by side as a series of declining steps.

Water (bottles per day)	0	1	2	3	4	5	6	7	8
Total utility	0	15	27	36	42	47	51	54	56
Marginal utility		15	12	9	6	5	4	3	2
	A	B	C	D	E	F	G	H	I

- If the marginal utility per dollar for water *exceeds* that for gum, total utility increases.
- If the marginal utility per dollar for water *is less than* that for gum, total utility decreases.
- If the marginal utility per dollar for water *equals* that for gum, total utility remains the same.

By spending $1 more on water and $1 less on gum, Tina's total utility increases only if the marginal utility per dollar from water exceeds the marginal utility per dollar from gum. As she spends more on water and less on gum, the marginal utility of water decreases and the marginal utility of gum increases. When Tina has allocated her dollars so that the marginal utility per dollar is the same for both goods, total utility cannot be increased any further: Utility is maximized.

Table 13.2 shows Tina's utility-maximizing choice. If Tina chooses row *B* (1 bottle of water and 6 packs of gum) her marginal utility per dollar for water (15 units per dollar) *exceeds* her marginal utility per dollar for gum (4 units per dollar). She can increase total utility by spending more on water and less on gum.

If Tina chooses row *D* (3 bottles of water and 2 packs of gum) her marginal utility per dollar for water (9 units of utility per dollar) *is less than* her marginal utility per dollar for gum (32 units per dollar). She can increase total utility by spending more on gum and less on water.

If Tina chooses row *C* (2 bottles of water and 4 packs of gum) her marginal utility per dollar for water (12 units of utility per dollar) *equals* her marginal utility per dollar for gum. This combination maximizes Tina's total utility.

Which one has the highest marginal utility per dollar?

■ Finding an Individual Demand Curve

We can use marginal utility theory to find a person's demand schedule and demand curve. In fact, we've just found one entry in Tina's demand schedule and one point on her demand curve for bottled water: When the price of bottled water is $1 and other things remain the same (the price of gum is 50¢ and her budget is $4 a day), the quantity of water that Tina buys is 2 bottles a day (row *C* in Table 13.2).

■ **TABLE 13.2**

Tina's Marginal Utilities per Dollar: Water $1 a Bottle and Gum 50¢ a Pack

The rows of the table show Tina's marginal utility per dollar from water and gum for the affordable combinations when the price of water is $1 a bottle, the price of gum is 50¢ a pack, and her budget is $4. By equalizing the marginal utilities per dollar from water and gum, Tina maximizes her total utility. Her utility-maximizing choice is to buy 2 bottles of water and 4 packs of gum.

	Bottled water			Chewing gum		
	Quantity (bottles per day)	Marginal utility	Marginal utility per dollar	Quantity (packs per day)	Marginal utility	Marginal utility per dollar
A	0			8	0	0
				7	1	2
B	1	15	15	6	2	4
				5	4	8
C	2	12	12	4	6	12
				3	8	16
D	3	9	9	2	16	32
				1	32	64

■ **TABLE 13.3**

Tina's Marginal Utilities per Dollar: Water 50¢ a Bottle and Gum 50¢ a Pack

	Bottled water			Chewing gum		
	Quantity (bottles per day)	Marginal utility	Marginal utility per dollar	Quantity (packs per day)	Marginal utility	Marginal utility per dollar
D	3	9	18	5	4	8
E	4	6	12	4	6	12
F	5	5	10	3	8	16

The rows of the table show Tina's marginal utility per dollar from water and gum for the affordable combinations when the price of water is 50¢ a bottle, the price of gum is 50¢ a pack, and her budget is $4. By equalizing the marginal utilities per dollar from water and gum, Tina maximizes her total utility. Her utility-maximizing choice is to buy 4 bottles of water and 4 packs of gum.

To find another point on Tina's demand curve for bottled water, let's see what Tina buys when the price of water falls to 50¢ a bottle. If Tina continued to buy 2 bottles of water and 4 packs of gum, her marginal utility per dollar for water would increase from 12 to 24 and be twice the marginal utility per dollar for gum (row C in Table 13.2). Also, Tina would spend only $3, so she would have another $1 available.

Row E of Table 13.3 shows Tina's new utility-maximizing choice, and this choice is a second point on her demand curve for bottled water: When the price of bottled water is 50¢ (other things remaining the same), Tina buys 4 bottles of water a day. Figure 13.6 shows Tina's demand curve that we've just derived.

■ **FIGURE 13.6**

Tina's Demand for Bottled Water

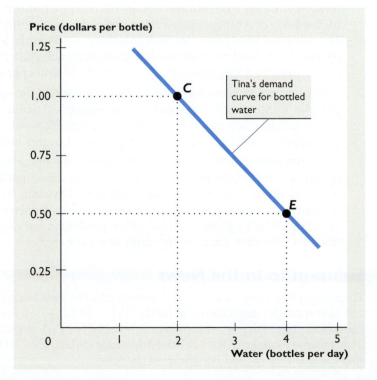

When the price of water is $1 a bottle (and her budget is $4 and the price of a pack of gum is 50¢), Tina buys 2 bottles of water and 4 packs of gum a day. She is at point C on her demand curve for water.

When the price of water falls to 50¢ a bottle and other things remain the same, Tina buys 4 bottles of water and 4 packs of gum a day and moves to point E on her demand curve for bottled water.

CHECKPOINT 13.2

Explain marginal utility theory and use it to derive a consumer's demand curve.

Practice Problems

TABLE 1

Burgers		Magazines	
Quantity per week	Total utility	Quantity per week	Total utility
0	0	0	0
1	14	1	100
2	24	2	120
3	32	3	134
4	38	4	144

Table 1 shows Jerry's total utility from burgers and magazines. The price of a burger is $2, the price of a magazine is $4, and Jerry has $12 a week to spend.

1. Calculate Jerry's marginal utility and marginal utility per dollar from burgers when he buys 4 burgers a week. Calculate Jerry's marginal utility per dollar from magazines when he buys 1 magazine a week.

2. If Jerry buys 4 burgers and 1 magazine a week, does he maximize his total utility? To maximize total utility will he buy more or fewer burgers? Explain.

3. What quantities of burgers and magazines maximize Jerry's utility?

In the News

Pricier bread and cereal. Coming soon?
Surging wheat and corn prices could hit the items in your grocery basket soon.
Source: CNN Money, May 19, 2011

How does the rise in the price of food change the budget line and the quantity of food that Americans buy?

Solutions to Practice Problems

1. The marginal utility from the 4th burger equals the total utility from 4 burgers minus the total utility from 3 burgers, which is 6 units. Jerry's marginal utility per dollar from burgers equals his marginal utility of 6 units divided by the price of a burger, $2, which equals 3 units of utility per dollar.
   The marginal utility from the first magazine is 100 units. Jerry's marginal utility per dollar from magazines equals his marginal utility, 100 units, divided by the price of a magazine, $4, which equals 25 units per dollar.

2. If Jerry buys 4 burgers for $8 and 1 magazine for $4, he spends his $12 budget. His marginal utility per dollar from burgers (3, solution **1**) is less than his marginal utility per dollar from magazines (25, solution **1**), so Jerry does *not* maximize total utility. He must buy fewer burgers and more magazines.

3. Jerry maximizes utility if he buys 2 burgers and 2 magazines a week. He spends $4 on burgers and $8 on magazines, which equals his $12 budget. His marginal utility from burgers ($24 - 14$) is 10. Dividing 10 by $2 gives 5 units of utility per dollar. His marginal utility from magazines ($120 - 100$) is 10. Dividing 20 by $4 gives 5 units of utility per dollar. Jerry's marginal utility per dollar is 5 for each good, so his utility is maximized.

Solution to In the News

The budget line rotates inward. Consumers allocate their budget between food (F) and non-food (N) items such that $(MU_F/P_F) = (MU_N/P_N)$. As the price of food rises, (MU_F/P_F) falls. So with $(MU_F/P_F) < (MU_N/P_N)$, consumers will reallocate their income to make (MU_F/P_F) rise and equal (MU_N/P_N). To make (MU_F/P_F) rise, the quantity of food bought must decrease.

13.3 EFFICIENCY, PRICE, AND VALUE

Marginal utility theory helps us to deepen our understanding of the concept of efficiency and to see more clearly the distinction between *value* and *price*. Let's see how.

■ Consumer Efficiency

When Tina allocates her limited budget to maximize her total utility, she is using her resources efficiently. Any other allocation of her budget would leave her able to attain a higher level of total utility.

But when Tina has allocated her budget to maximize her total utility, she is *on* her demand curve for each good. A demand curve describes the quantity demanded at each price *when total utility is maximized*. When we studied efficiency in Chapter 6, we learned that a demand curve is also a willingness-to-pay curve. It tells us a consumer's *marginal benefit*—the benefit from consuming an additional unit of a good. You can now give the idea of marginal benefit a deeper meaning.

> **Marginal benefit is the maximum price a consumer is willing to pay for an extra unit of a good or service when total utility is maximized.**

■ The Paradox of Value

For centuries, philosophers were puzzled by the paradox of value. Water is more valuable than a diamond because water is essential to life itself. Yet water is much cheaper than a diamond. Why? Adam Smith tried to solve this paradox, but it was not until marginal utility theory had been developed that anyone could give a satisfactory answer.

You can solve this puzzle by distinguishing between *total* utility and *marginal* utility. Total utility tells us about relative value; marginal utility tells us about relative price. The total utility from water is enormous, but remember, the more we consume of something, the smaller is its marginal utility. We use so much water that its marginal utility—the benefit we get from one more glass of water—diminishes to a small value. Diamonds, on the other hand, have a small total utility relative to water, but because we buy few diamonds, they have a large marginal utility. When a household has maximized its total utility, it has allocated its budget so that the marginal utility per dollar is equal for all goods. Diamonds have a high price and a high marginal utility. Water has a low price and a low marginal utility. When the high marginal utility of diamonds is divided by the high price of a diamond, the result is a marginal utility per dollar that equals the low marginal utility of water divided by the low price of water. The marginal utility per dollar is the same for diamonds as for water.

Consumer Surplus

Consumer surplus measures value in excess of the amount paid. In Figure 13.7, the demand for and supply of water in part (a) determine the price of water P_W and the quantity of water consumed Q_W. The demand for and supply of diamonds in part (b) determine the price of a diamond P_D and the quantity of diamonds Q_D. Water is cheap but provides a large consumer surplus, while diamonds are expensive but provide a small consumer surplus.

■ FIGURE 13.7

The Paradox of Value

MyEconLab Animation

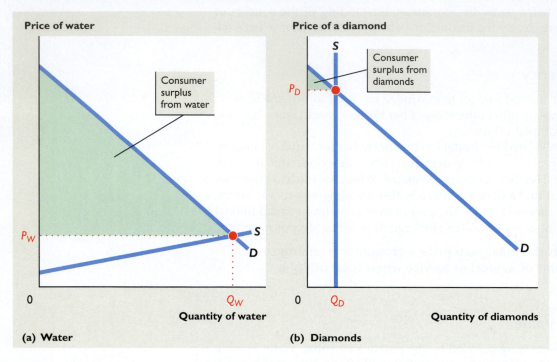

(a) Water

(b) Diamonds

Part (a) shows the demand for water, D, and the supply of water, S. Demand and supply determine the price of water at P_W and the quantity at Q_W. The consumer surplus from water is the large green triangle.

Part (b) shows the demand for diamonds, D, and the supply of diamonds, S. Demand and supply determine the price of a diamond at P_D and the quantity at Q_D. The consumer surplus from diamonds is the small green triangle.

Water is valuable—has a large consumer surplus—but cheap. Diamonds are less valuable than water—have a smaller consumer surplus—but are expensive.

EYE on SONG DOWNLOADS
How Much Would You Pay for a Song?

You might say that you're willing to pay only 99¢ for a song, but that's not the answer of the average consumer. And it is probably not really your answer either. It is also not what the answer would have been just a few years ago.

We can work out what people are willing to pay for a song by finding the demand curve for songs and then finding the consumer surplus.

To find the demand curve, we need to look at the prices and quantities in the market for songs.

In 2010 (the most recent year for which we have the numbers) Americans spent $7 billion on all forms of recorded music, down from $14 billion in 2000. But the combined quantity of discs and downloads bought *increased* from 1 billion in 2000 to 1.5 billion in 2010 and the average price of a unit of recorded music fell from $14 to $3.75.

The average price fell because the mix of formats changed dramatically. In 2001, we bought 900 million CDs; in 2010, we bought only 225 million CDs

and downloaded 1.3 billion music files. Figure 1 shows the longer history of the changing formats of recorded music.

The music that we buy isn't just one good—it is several different goods. We'll distinguish singles from albums and focus on the demand for singles.

In 2001, we bought 106 million singles and paid $4.95 on the average for each one. In 2010, we downloaded 1,160 million singles files and paid an average price of $1.20 each.

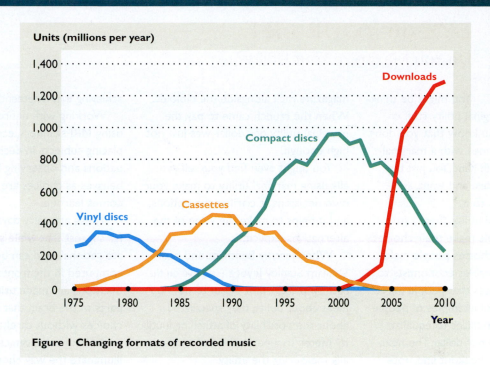

Figure 1 Changing formats of recorded music

The market for singles downloads has created a consumer surplus.

Figure 2 shows the demand curve in the market for singles. One point on the demand curve is the 2001 price and quantity—106 million singles were bought at an average price of $4.95. Another point on the demand curve is that for 2010—1,160 million singles downloaded at $1.20 each.

If the demand curve has not shifted and is linear (assumed here), we can calculate the change in consumer surplus generated by the fall in price and increase in quantity demanded. The green area is this change in consumer surplus. That increase in consumer surplus is $1.976 billion or $1.70 per single.

The increase in consumer surplus of $1.70 per song is an estimate of how much more the average buyer would be willing to pay for a song on average.

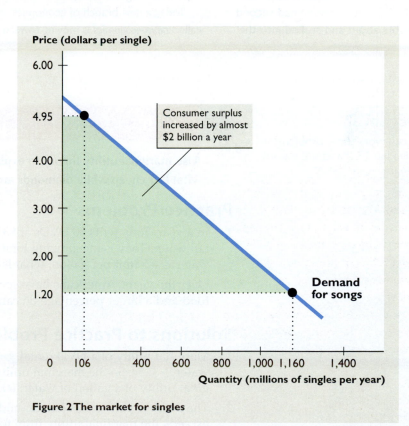

Figure 2 The market for singles

EYE on YOUR LIFE
Do You Maximize Your Utility?

You might be thinking that this marginal utility stuff is pretty unreal! You know that you don't go around the shops with a marginal utility calculator in hand. You just buy what you can afford and want, and that's all there is to it.

Well, marginal utility theory isn't about how people make their choices. It's about what choices people make. It's a tool that enables economists to explain the choices that people make.

You see lots of examples of people juggling their purchases to equalize marginal utilities per dollar. The next time you're in a checkout line, note the items that someone had second thoughts about and stuffed into the

magazine rack alongside the tabloids. When the crunch came to pay, the marginal utility per dollar was just not high enough.

You might even find yourself actually using marginal utility to make your own decisions. It clarifies the options, and it helps to make the value of the alternatives explicit.

When Jeremy Bentham, and later William Stanley Jevons (see *Eye on the Past* on p. 323), first began to develop ideas about utility, they speculated about the possibility of attaching a utility meter to a person's head and actually measuring the utility.

Today, a new branch of economics called *neuroeconomics* is moving toward

achieving that nineteenth-century dream.

Working with neuroscientists and using MRI scanners, economists are placing subjects in decision-making situations and observing how the brain behaves as choices are made and outcomes learned.

These are early days but results so far suggest that while some decisions are rational (and can be seen to be computed in the frontal cortex), other decisions are made using primitive parts of the brain that make snap choices without careful calculation.

As neuroeconomics advances, it will illuminate the way choices are made and might improve our ability to predict the choices that people make.

CHECKPOINT 13.3

Use marginal utility theory to explain the paradox of value: why water is vital but cheap while diamonds are relatively useless but expensive.

Practice Problems

1. In a year, Tony rents 50 DVDs at $3 each and pays $50 for 10,000 gallons of tap water. Tony is maximizing total utility. If Tony's marginal utility from water is 0.5 unit per gallon, what is his marginal utility from a DVD rental?

2. Over the years, Americans have spent a smaller percentage of income on food and a larger percentage on cars. Explain the paradox of value.

Solutions to Practice Problems

1. Marginal utility of a DVD rental ÷ $3 = Marginal utility of a gallon of water ÷ 0.5¢. So the marginal utility of a DVD rental is 600 times the marginal utility of a gallon of water: 600 × 0.5 or 300 units.

2. The average person has one car and the marginal utility from driving the car exceeds the marginal utility from food. While food is cheap and cars are expensive, consumers allocate their income to make the marginal utility per dollar equal for food and cars. There is no paradox of value.

CHAPTER SUMMARY

Key Points

1 Calculate and graph a budget line that shows the limits to a person's consumption possibilities.

- Consumption possibilities are constrained by the budget and prices. Some combinations of goods are affordable, and some are not affordable.
- The budget line is the boundary between what a person can and cannot afford with a given budget and given prices.
- The slope of the budget line determines the relative price of the good measured on the *x*-axis in terms of the good measured on the *y*-axis.
- A change in one price changes the slope of the budget line. A change in the budget shifts the budget line but does not change its slope.

2 Explain marginal utility theory and use it to derive a consumer's demand curve.

- Consumption possibilities and preferences determine consumption choices.
- Total utility is maximized when the entire budget is spent and marginal utility per dollar is equal for all goods.
- If the marginal utility per dollar from good *A* exceeds that from good *B*, total utility increases if the quantity purchased of good *A* increases and the quantity purchased of good *B* decreases.
- Marginal utility theory implies the law of demand. That is, other things remaining the same, the higher the price of a good, the smaller is the quantity demanded of that good.

3 Use marginal utility theory to explain the paradox of value: why water is vital but cheap while diamonds are relatively useless but expensive.

- When consumers maximize total utility, they use resources efficiently.
- Marginal utility theory resolves the paradox of value.
- When we talk loosely about value, we are thinking of *total* utility or consumer surplus, but price is related to *marginal* utility.
- Water, which we consume in large amounts, has a high total utility and a large consumer surplus but a low price and low marginal utility.
- Diamonds, which we consume in small amounts, have a low total utility and a small consumer surplus but a high price and a high marginal utility.

Key Terms

Budget line, 316
Diminishing marginal utility, 322
Marginal utility, 322

Marginal utility per dollar, 324
Relative price, 320
Total utility, 322

Utility, 322
Utility-maximizing rule, 324

CHAPTER CHECKPOINT

Study Plan Problems and Applications

Amy has $12 a week to spend on coffee and soda. The price of coffee is $2 a cup, and soda is $1 a can. Use this information to work Problems **1** and **2**.

1. Draw a graph of Amy's budget line. Can Amy buy 7 cans of soda and 2 cups of coffee a week? Can she buy 7 cups of coffee and 2 cans of soda a week? What is the relative price of a cup of coffee?

2. Suppose that the price of soda remains at $1 a can but the price of coffee rises to $3 a cup. Draw Amy's new budget line. If she buys 6 cans of soda, what is the maximum number of cups of coffee she can buy in a week? Has the relative price of coffee changed?

Use Table 1, which shows Ben's utility, to work Problems **3** and **4**.

3. Calculate the values of *A*, *B*, *C*, and *D* in the table. Does the principle of diminishing marginal utility apply to Ben's consumption of orange juice? Why or why not?

4. Would Ben ever want to buy more than one carton of orange juice a day or no orange juice? Explain your answer.

5. Every day, Josie buys 2 cups of coffee and 1 sandwich for lunch. The price of coffee is $2 a cup and the price of a sandwich is $5. Josie's choice of lunch maximizes her total utility, and she spends only $9 on lunch. Compare Josie's marginal utility from coffee with her marginal utility from the sandwich.

6. Susie spends $28 a week on sundaes and magazines. The price of a sundae is $4 and the price of a magazine is $4. Table 2 shows Susie's marginal utility from sundaes and magazines. How many sundaes does she buy? If the price of a sundae doubles to $8 and other things remain the same, how many sundaes will she buy? What are two points on her demand curve for sundaes?

7. In a week, Erin buys 1 six-pack of soda and sees 2 movies when a movie ticket is $10, soda is $5 a six-pack, and she has $25 to spend. If her budget increases and she has $50 to spend on soda and movies, what is the change in the relative price of a movie ticket? How do the marginal utility per dollar from movies and the marginal utility per dollar from soda change?

8. **Gas prices send surge of travelers to mass transit**
As the gas price shot up to $4 a gallon, more commuters switched from cars to trains and buses. In New York and Boston, public transit ridership is up 5 percent or more so far this year.
Source: *The New York Times*, May 10, 2008

Explain the effect of a rise in the price of gasoline on a commuter's budget line and the quantities of gasoline and public transit services purchased.

9. **Compared to other liquids, gasoline is cheap**
In 2008, when gasoline hit $4 a gallon, motorists complained, but they didn't complain about $1.59 for a 20-oz Gatorade and $18 for 16 ml of HP ink.
Source: *The New York Times*, May 27, 2008

The prices per gallon are $10.17 for Gatorade and $4,294.58 for printer ink. How can the paradox of value be used to explain why the fluids listed in the news clip might be less valuable than gasoline, yet far more expensive?

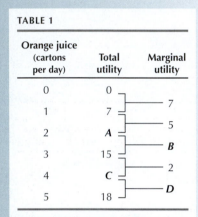

TABLE 1

Orange juice (cartons per day)	Total utility	Marginal utility
0	0	
1	7	7
2	A	5
3	15	B
4	C	2
5	18	D

TABLE 2

Sundaes		Magazines	
Quantity per week	Marginal utility	Quantity per week	Marginal utility
1	60	1	40
2	56	2	32
3	50	3	28
4	42	4	25
5	32	5	23
6	20	6	22

Instructor Assignable Problems and Applications

Your instructor can assign these problems as homework, a quiz, or a test in MyEconLab.

1. In 2007, Americans downloaded 800 million singles at 99¢ each and 40 million albums at $10 each. They also bought 3 million singles on a disc at $4.75 each and 500 million albums on discs at $15. What does marginal utility theory tell you about the ratio of the marginal utility from singles on discs to the marginal utility from singles downloads? What does it tell you about the ratio of the marginal utility from albums on discs to the marginal utility from album downloads?

2. Tim buys 2 pizzas and sees 1 movie a week when he has $16 to spend, a movie ticket is $8, and the price of a pizza is $4. What is the relative price of a movie ticket? If the price of a movie ticket falls to $4, how will Tim's consumption possibilities change? Explain.

3. Jim spends all his income on apartment rent, food, clothing, and vacations. He gets a pay raise from $3,000 a month to $4,000 a month. At the same time, airfares and other vacation-related expenses increase by 50 percent. How has Jim's budget in terms of airfares and other vacation-related expenses changed? Is Jim better off or worse off in his new situation?

Use Table 1, which shows Martha's total utility from cake and pasta, to work Problems **4** to **6**.

4. When Martha buys 3 cakes and 2 dishes of pasta a week, what is her total utility and her marginal utility from the third cake? If the price of a cake is $4, what is her marginal utility per dollar from cake?

5. When the price of a cake is $4, the price of pasta is $8 a dish, and Martha has $24 a week to spend, she buys 2 cakes and 2 dishes of pasta. Does she maximize her total utility? Explain your answer.

6. When the price of a cake is $4, Martha has $24 to spend, and the price of pasta falls from $8 to $4 a dish, what quantities of cake and pasta does Martha buy? What are two points on Martha's demand curve for pasta?

Use the following information to work Problems **7** and **8**.

Table 2 shows the marginal utility that Ali gets from smoothies and movies. Ali has $30 a week to spend. The price of a movie ticket is $6, and the price of a smoothie is $3.

7. If Ali buys 4 smoothies a week and sees 3 movies, does he spend all $30? What is his utility from smoothies and his utility from movies? Does he maximize his utility? If not, which good must he buy more of?

8. When Ali allocates his budget so as to maximize his utility, what does he buy and what is the marginal utility per dollar?

Use the following information to work Problems **9** and **10**.

In the land of free flight

As the time it takes to get through airports has increased, other means of travel have begun to look more attractive. Amtrak now competes comfortably with the airlines on its Boston–New York–Washington express rail service.

Source: *The Economist*, June 14, 2007

9. For a trip from Boston to Washington, compare the opportunity costs of taking Amtrak and United Airlines.

10. Compare the marginal utility per dollar from train travel and from air travel.

TABLE 1

Cake		Pasta	
Quantity per week	Total utility	Dishes per week	Total utility
0	0	0	0
1	10	1	20
2	18	2	36
3	25	3	48
4	31	4	56
5	36	5	60
6	40	6	60

TABLE 2

Quantity per week	Marginal utility from	
	smoothies	movies
1	7	30
2	6	24
3	5	18
4	4	12
5	3	6
6	2	0

Multiple Choice Quiz

1. A consumer's consumption possibilities depend on all of the following items *except* _____.

   A. the prices of the goods that the consumer wants to buy
   B. the consumer's budget
   C. the quantities of the goods that the consumer can afford
   D. the consumer's preferences

2. Jane's budget line _____.

   A. shifts outward with no change in its slope if her budget increases and prices don't change
   B. rotates inward if the prices of both goods double and her budget doesn't change
   C. shifts inward with no change in its slope if the price of one good rises and her budget doesn't change
   D. rotates outward if her budget increases and prices don't change

3. Total utility _____ and marginal utility _____ as more of a good is consumed.

   A. increases; increases
   B. diminishes; diminishes
   C. increases; diminishes
   D. diminishes; increases

4. Tom will maximize his total utility if he buys the quantities of pasta and milk at which _____.

   A. the marginal utility from pasta equals the marginal utility from milk
   B. he spends all of his budget and marginal utility from each good is equal
   C. the marginal utility from the more expensive good is less than the marginal utility from the cheaper good
   D. he spends all his budget and the marginal utility per dollar for pasta and milk are equal

5. Sara buys bread and bananas and is maximizing her total utility. If the price of bananas rises, Sara will maximize her total utility by _____.

   A. increasing her budget so that she can buy the same quantities
   B. buying more bananas and less bread
   C. buying fewer bananas and possibly more bread
   D. buying less bread and possibly more bananas

6. When Joe's budget increases, he will spend the increase in his budget on _____.

   A. normal goods
   B. inferior goods
   C. more of all the goods he usually buys
   D. essential goods

7. The paradox of value arises when people _____.

   A. prefer to buy cheap goods rather than expensive goods
   B. spend more on expensive useless goods than on cheap useful goods
   C. buy so much of a useful good that its price falls
   D. get the same marginal utility per dollar from cheap useful goods and useless expensive goods

APPENDIX: INDIFFERENCE CURVES

You are going to discover a neat idea—that of drawing a map of a person's preferences. A preference map is based on the intuitively appealing assumption that people can sort all the possible combinations of goods into three groups: preferred, not preferred, and indifferent. To make this idea concrete, let's ask Tina to tell us how she ranks combinations of bottled water and chewing gum.

■ An Indifference Curve

Figure A13.1(a) shows part of Tina's answer. She tells us that she currently consumes 2 bottles of water and 4 packs of gum a day at point C. She then lists all the combinations of bottled water and chewing gum that she says are as acceptable to her as her current consumption. When we plot these combinations of water and gum, we get the green curve. This curve is the key element in a map of preferences and is called an indifference curve.

An **indifference curve** is a line that shows combinations of goods among which a consumer is *indifferent*. The indifference curve in Figure A13.1(a) tells us that Tina is just as happy to consume 2 bottles of water and 4 packs of gum a day at point C as to consume the combination of water and gum at any other point along the indifference curve. Tina also says that she prefers all the combinations of bottled water and gum above the indifference curve—the yellow area—to those on the indifference curve. These combinations contain more water, more gum, or

Indifference curve
A line that shows combinations of goods among which a consumer is *indifferent*.

■ **FIGURE A13.1**

A Preference Map   MyEconLab Animation

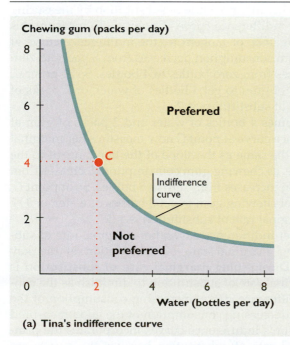

(a) Tina's indifference curve

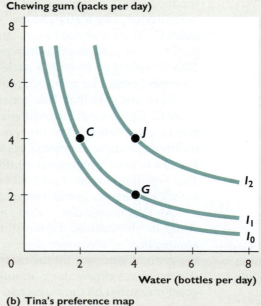

(b) Tina's preference map

In part (a), Tina consumes 2 bottles of water and 4 packs of chewing gum a day at point C. She is indifferent between all the points on the green indifference curve. She prefers any point above the indifference curve (yellow area) to any point on it, and she prefers any point on the indifference curve to any point below it (gray area).

Part (b) shows three indifference curves of Tina's preference map. She prefers point J to point C or G, so she prefers any point on I_2 to any point on I_1.

more of both. She also prefers any combination on the indifference curve to any combination in the gray area below the indifference curve. These combinations contain less water, less gum, or less of both.

The indifference curve in Figure A13.1(a) is just one of a whole family of such curves. This indifference curve appears again in Figure A13.1(b) labeled I_1. The curves labeled I_0 and I_2 are two other indifference curves. Tina prefers any point on indifference curve I_2 such as point J, to any point on indifference curve I_1, such as points C or G. She prefers any point on I_1 to any point on I_0. We refer to I_2 as being a higher indifference curve than I_1 and to I_1 as being higher than I_0.

A preference map is a series of indifference curves that resemble the contour lines on a map. By looking at the shape of the contour lines on a map, we can draw conclusions about the terrain. Similarly, by looking at the shape of the indifference curves, we can draw conclusions about a person's preferences.

■ Marginal Rate of Substitution

Marginal rate of substitution

The rate at which a person will give up good y (the good measured on the y-axis) to get more of good x (the good measured on the x-axis) and at the same time remain on the same indifference curve.

The concept of the marginal rate of substitution is the key to "reading" a preference map. The **marginal rate of substitution** (*MRS*) is the rate at which a person will give up good y (the good measured on the y-axis) to get more of good x (the good measured on the x-axis) and at the same time remain indifferent (remain on the same indifference curve). The marginal rate of substitution is measured by the magnitude of the slope of an indifference curve.

If the indifference curve is *steep*, the marginal rate of substitution is *high*. The person is willing to give up a large quantity of good y to get a small quantity of good x while remaining indifferent. If the indifference curve is *flat*, the marginal rate of substitution is *low*. The person is willing to give up only a small amount of good y to get a large amount of good x to remain indifferent.

Figure A13.2 shows you how to calculate the marginal rate of substitution. Suppose that Tina consumes 2 bottles of water and 4 packs of gum at point C on indifference curve I_1. We calculate her marginal rate of substitution by measuring the magnitude of the slope of the indifference curve at point C. To measure this magnitude, place a straight line against, or tangent to, the indifference curve at point C. Along that red line, as gum consumption decreases from 8 packs to zero packs, water consumption increases from zero bottles to 4 bottles. So at point C, Tina is willing to give up 8 packs of gum to get 4 bottles of water, or 2 packs of gum per bottle. Her marginal rate of substitution is 2.

Now suppose that Tina consumes 4 bottles of water and 2 packs of gum at point G. The slope of the indifference curve at point G now measures her marginal rate of substitution. That slope is the same as the slope of the line tangent to the indifference curve at point G. Here, as chewing gum consumption decreases from 4 packs to zero, water consumption increases from zero to 8 bottles. So at point G, Tina is willing to give up 4 packs of chewing gum to get 8 bottles of water, or 1/2 a pack of gum per bottle. Her marginal rate of substitution is 1/2.

Diminishing marginal rate of substitution

The general tendency for the marginal rate of substitution to decrease as the consumer moves down along the indifference curve, increasing consumption of the good measured on the x-axis and decreasing consumption of the good measured on the y-axis.

As Tina moves down along her indifference curve, her marginal rate of substitution diminishes. Diminishing marginal rate of substitution is the key assumption of consumer theory. **Diminishing marginal rate of substitution** is the general tendency for the marginal rate of substitution to diminish as the consumer moves down along an indifference curve, increasing consumption of the good measured on the x-axis and decreasing consumption of the good measured on the y-axis. The shape of a person's indifference curves incorporates the principle of the diminishing marginal rate of substitution because the curves are bowed toward the origin.

FIGURE A13.2

The Marginal Rate of Substitution   MyEconLab Animation

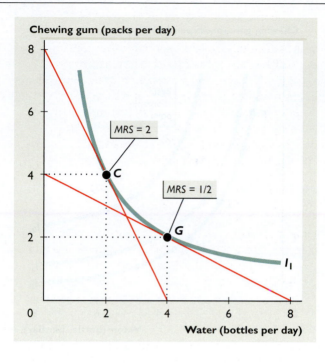

The magnitude of the slope of an indifference curve is called the marginal rate of substitution (*MRS*).

The red line at point *C* tells us that Tina is willing to give up 8 packs of gum to get 4 bottles of water. Her marginal rate of substitution at point *C* is 8 divided by 4, which equals 2.

The red line at point *G* tells us that Tina is willing to give up 4 packs of gum to get 8 bottles of water. Her marginal rate of substitution at point *G* is 4 divided by 8, which equals 1/2.

■ Consumer Equilibrium

The consumer's goal is to buy the affordable quantities of goods that make her or him as well off as possible. The indifference curves describe the consumer's preferences, and they tell us that the higher the indifference curve, the better off is the consumer. So the consumer's goal can be restated as: to allocate his or her budget in such a way as to get onto the highest attainable indifference curve.

The consumer's budget and the prices of the goods limit the consumer's choices. The budget line illustrated in Figure 13.1 (p. 316) summarizes the limits on the consumer's choice. We combine the indifference curves of Figure A13.1(b) with the budget line of Figure 13.1 to work out the consumer's choice and find the consumer equilibrium.

Figure A13.3 shows Tina's budget line from Figure 13.1 and her indifference curves from Figure A13.1(b). Tina's best affordable point is 2 bottles of water and 4 packs of gum—at point C. Here, Tina

- Is on her budget line.
- Is on her highest attainable indifference curve.
- Has a marginal rate of substitution between water and gum equal to the relative price of water and gum.

For every point inside the budget line, such as point *L*, there are points *on* the budget line that Tina prefers. For example, she prefers any point on the budget line between *F* and *H* to point *L*. So she chooses a point on the budget line.

Consumer Equilibrium

Tina's best affordable point is *C*. At that point, she is on her budget line and also on the highest attainable indifference curve.

At a point such as *H*, Tina is willing to give up more bottled water in exchange for chewing gum than she has to. She can move to point *L*, which is just as good as point *H*, and have some unspent budget. She can spend that budget and move to *C*, a point that she prefers to point *L*.

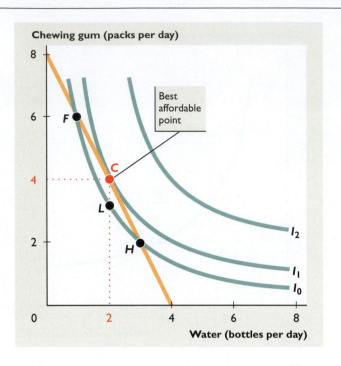

Checked out at the best affordable point.

Every point on the budget line lies on an indifference curve. For example, point *F* lies on the indifference curve I_0. At point *F*, Tina's marginal rate of substitution (the magnitude of the slope of the indifference curve I_0) is greater than the relative price (the magnitude of the slope of the budget line). Tina is willing to give up more chewing gum to get an additional bottle of water than the budget line says she must. So she moves along her budget line from *F* toward *C*. As she does so, she passes through a number of indifference curves (not shown in the figure) located between indifference curves I_0 and I_1. All of these indifference curves are higher than I_0 so Tina prefers any point on them to point *F*. When Tina gets to point *C*, she is on the highest attainable indifference curve. If she keeps moving along the budget line, she starts to encounter indifference curves that are lower than I_1. So Tina chooses point *C*—her best affordable point.

At the chosen point, the marginal rate of substitution (the magnitude of the slope of the indifference curve) equals the relative price (the magnitude of the slope of the budget line).

We can now use this model of consumer choice to predict the effect of a change in the price of water on the quantity of water demanded. That is, we can use this model to generate the demand curve for bottled water.

■ Deriving the Demand Curve

To derive Tina's demand curve for bottled water, we change the price of water, shift the budget line, and work out the new best affordable point. Figure A13.4(a) shows the change in the budget line and the change in consumer equilibrium when the price of water falls from $1 a bottle to 50¢ a bottle.

Initially, when the price of water is $1 a bottle, Tina consumes at point *C* in part (a). When the price of a bottle of water falls from $1 to 50¢, her budget line rotates outward and she can now get onto a higher indifference curve. Her best affordable point is now point *K*. Tina increases the quantity of water she buys from 2 to 4 bottles a day. She continues to buy 4 packs of gum a day.

Figure A13.4(b) shows Tina's demand curve for bottled water. When the price of water is $1 a bottle, she buys 2 bottles a day, at point *A*. When the price of water falls to 50¢ a bottle, she buys 4 bottles a day, at point *B*. Tina's demand curve traces out her best affordable quantity of water as the price of a bottle of water varies.

■ **FIGURE A13.4**

Deriving Tina's Demand Curve

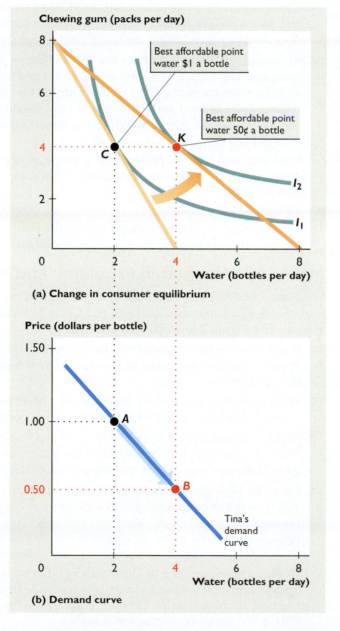

(a) Change in consumer equilibrium

(b) Demand curve

In part (a), when the price of water is $1 a bottle, Tina consumes at point *C*. When the price of water falls from $1 to 50¢ a bottle, she consumes at point *K*.

In part (b), when the price of water is $1 a bottle, Tina is at point *A*. When the price of water falls from $1 to 50¢ a bottle, Tina moves along her demand curve for bottled water from point *A* to point *B*.

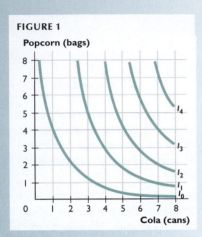

FIGURE 1
Popcorn (bags)

APPENDIX CHECKPOINT

Study Plan Problems and Applications

Each week Sara has $12 to spend on popcorn and cola. The price of popcorn is
$3 a bag, and the price of cola is $3 a can. Figure 1 illustrates Sara's preferences.
Use Figure 1 to work Problems **1** to **3**.

1. What is the relative price of cola and what is the opportunity cost of a can of
cola? Draw a graph of Sara's budget line with cola on the *x*-axis.

2. What quantities of popcorn and cola does Sara buy and what is her marginal rate of substitution of popcorn for cola at her consumption point?

3. Suppose that the price of cola falls to $1.50 a can and the price of popcorn
and Sara's budget remain unchanged. What quantities of popcorn and cola
does Sara buy now? What are two points on Sara's demand curve for cola?

4. In most states, there is no sales tax on food. Some people say that a consumption tax, a tax that is paid on all goods and services, would be better. If
all sales taxes are replaced by a consumption tax, what would happen to the
relative price of food and haircuts and how would you change your purchases of food and haircuts? Which tax would you prefer?

5. **Coffee king Starbucks raises its prices**
Starbucks will raise its prices by an average of 9¢ per beverage to cover its
increasing costs. Will rising prices cause Starbucks fans to cut back on their
java habits?
Source: *USA Today*, July 25, 2007
Draw a graph to illustrate the change in the budget line and the change in
the best affordable point for a consumer who buys fewer lattes a week.

Instructor Assignable Problems and Applications

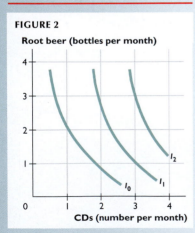

FIGURE 2
Root beer (bottles per month)

Marc has a budget of $20 a month to spend on root beer and CDs. The price of
root beer is $5 a bottle, and the price of a CD is $10. Figure 2 illustrates his preferences. Use Figure 2 to work Problems **1** to **3**.

1. What is the relative price of root beer in terms of CDs and what is the
opportunity cost of a bottle of root beer? Draw a graph of Marc's budget line
with CDs on the *x*-axis.

2. What quantities of root beer and CDs does Marc buy? What is his marginal
rate of substitution of CDs for root beer at the point at which he consumes?

3. Suppose that the price of a CD falls to $5 and the price of root beer and
Marc's budget remain unchanged. What quantities of root beer and CDs
does Marc now buy? What are two points on Marc's demand curve for CDs?

4. **Don't let high gas prices stall your summer plans**
With gas prices edging toward $4 a gallon, some would-be road warriors are
reassessing their plans for Memorial Day weekend. With gas prices already
up 25% since 2010, many are planning to stay fewer nights in roadside hotels.
Source: *USA Today*, May 8, 2011
Draw a preference map to illustrate a holiday traveler's preferences. Draw a
budget line for gasoline and nights in roadside hotels in 2010 and identify
the best affordable point. On your graph show the best affordable point in
2011 when the price of gasoline is higher.

Which store has the lower costs:
Wal-Mart or 7-Eleven?

Production and Cost

14

**When you have completed your study of this chapter,
you will be able to**

1 Explain and distinguish between the economic and accounting measures of a firm's cost of production and profit.

2 Explain the relationship between a firm's output and labor employed in the short run.

3 Explain the relationship between a firm's output and costs in the short run.

4 Derive and explain a firm's long-run average cost curve.

14.1   ECONOMIC COST AND PROFIT

The 20 million firms in the United States differ in size and in what they produce, but they all perform the same basic economic function: They hire factors of production and organize them to produce and sell goods and services. To understand the behavior of a firm, we need to know its goals.

■ The Firm's Goal

If you asked a group of entrepreneurs what they are trying to achieve, you would get many different answers. Some would talk about making a high-quality product, others about business growth, others about market share, and others about job satisfaction of the work force. All of these goals might be pursued, but they are not the fundamental goal. They are a means to a deeper goal.

The firm's goal is to *maximize profit*. A firm that does not seek to maximize profit is either eliminated or bought by firms that *do* seek to achieve that goal. To calculate a firm's profit, we must determine its total revenue and total cost. Economists have a special way of defining and measuring cost and profit, which we'll explain and illustrate by looking at Sam's Smoothies, a firm that is owned and operated by Samantha.

■ Accounting Cost and Profit

In 2011, Sam's Smoothies' total revenue from the sale of smoothies was $150,000. The firm paid $20,000 for fruit, yogurt, and honey; $22,000 in wages for the labor it hired; and $3,000 in interest to the bank. These expenses totaled $45,000.

Sam's accountant said that the depreciation of the firm's blenders, refrigerators, and shop during 2011 was $10,000. Depreciation is the fall in the value of the firm's capital, and accountants calculate it by using the Internal Revenue Service's rules, which are based on standards set by the Financial Accounting Standards Board. So the accountant reported Sam's Smoothies' total cost for 2011 as $55,000 and the firm's profit as $95,000—$150,000 of total revenue minus $55,000 of total costs.

Sam's accountant measures cost and profit to ensure that the firm pays the correct amount of income tax and to show the bank how Sam's has used its bank loan. Economists have a different purpose: to predict the decisions that a firm makes to maximize its profit. These decisions respond to *opportunity cost* and *economic profit*.

■ Opportunity Cost

To produce its output, a firm employs factors of production: land, labor, capital, and entrepreneurship. Another firm could have used these same resources to produce other goods or services. In Chapter 3 (pp. 66–67), resources can be used to produce either cell phones or DVDs, so the opportunity cost of producing a cell phone is the number of DVDs forgone. Pilots who fly passengers for Southwest Airlines can't at the same time fly freight for FedEx. Construction workers who are building an office high-rise can't simultaneously build apartments. A communications satellite operating at peak capacity can carry television signals or e-mail messages but not both at the same time. A journalist writing for the *New York Times* can't at the same time create Web news reports for CNN. And Samantha can't simultaneously run her smoothies business and a flower shop.

The highest-valued alternative forgone is the opportunity cost of a firm's production. From the viewpoint of the firm, this opportunity cost is the amount that the firm must pay the owners of the factors of production it employs to attract them from their best alternative use. So a firm's opportunity cost of production is the cost of the factors of production it employs.

To determine these costs, let's return to Sam's and look at the opportunity cost of producing smoothies.

Explicit Costs and Implicit Costs

The amount that a firm pays to attract resources from their best alternative use is either an explicit cost or an implicit cost. A cost paid in money is an **explicit cost.** Because the amount spent could have been spent on something else, an explicit cost is an opportunity cost. The wages that Samantha pays labor, the interest she pays the bank, and her expenditure on fruit, yogurt, and honey are explicit costs.

A firm incurs an **implicit cost** when it uses a factor of production but does not make a direct money payment for its use. The two categories of implicit cost are economic depreciation and the cost of the resources of the firm's owner.

Economic depreciation is the opportunity cost of the firm using capital that it owns. It is measured as the change in the *market value* of capital—the market price of the capital at the beginning of the period minus its market price at the end of the period. Suppose that Samantha could have sold her blenders, refrigerators, and shop on December 31, 2010, for $250,000. If she can sell the same capital on December 31, 2011, for $246,000, her economic depreciation during 2011 is $4,000. This is the opportunity cost of using her capital during 2011, not the $10,000 depreciation calculated by Sam's accountant.

Interest is another cost of capital. When the firm's owner provides the funds used to buy capital, the opportunity cost of those funds is the interest income forgone by not using them in the best alternative way. If Sam loaned her firm funds that could have earned her $1,000 in interest, this amount is an implicit cost of producing smoothies.

When a firm's owner supplies labor, the opportunity cost of the owner's time spent working for the firm is the wage income forgone by not working in the best alternative job. For example, instead of working at her next best job that pays $34,000 a year, Sam supplies labor to her smoothies business. This implicit cost of $34,000 is part of the opportunity cost of producing smoothies.

Finally, a firm's owner often supplies entrepreneurship, the factor of production that organizes the business and bears the risk of running it. The return to entrepreneurship is **normal profit.** Normal profit is part of a firm's opportunity cost because it is the cost of a forgone alternative—running another firm. Instead of running Sam's Smoothies, Sam could earn $16,000 a year running a flower shop. This amount is an implicit cost of production at Sam's Smoothies.

■ Economic Profit

A firm's **economic profit** equals total revenue minus total cost. Total revenue is the amount received from the sale of the product. It is the price of the output multiplied by the quantity sold. Total cost is the sum of the explicit costs and implicit costs and is the opportunity cost of production.

Explicit cost
A cost paid in money.

Implicit cost
An opportunity cost incurred by a firm when it uses a factor of production for which it does not make a direct money payment.

Economic depreciation
An opportunity cost of a firm using capital that it owns—measured as the change in the *market value* of capital over a given period.

Normal profit
The return to entrepreneurship. Normal profit is part of a firm's opportunity cost because it is the cost of not running another firm.

Economic profit
A firm's total revenue minus total cost.

TABLE 14.1

Economic Accounting

Item		
Total Revenue		$150,000
Explicit Costs		
Cost of fruit, yogurt, and honey	$20,000	
Wages	$22,000	
Interest	$3,000	
Implicit Costs		
Samantha's forgone wages	$34,000	
Samantha's forgone interest	$1,000	
Economic depreciation	$4,000	
Normal profit	$16,000	
Opportunity Cost		$100,000
Economic Profit		$50,000

Because one of the firm's implicit costs is *normal profit*, the return to the entrepreneur equals normal profit plus economic profit. If a firm incurs an economic loss, the entrepreneur receives less than normal profit.

Table 14.1 summarizes the economic cost concepts, and Figure 14.1 compares the economic view and the accounting view of cost and profit. Sam's total revenue (price multiplied by quantity sold) is $150,000; the opportunity cost of the resources that Sam uses is $100,000; and Sam's economic profit is $50,000.

FIGURE 14.1

Two Views of Cost and Profit

MyEconLab Animation

Both economists and accountants measure a firm's total revenue the same way. It equals the price multiplied by the quantity sold of each item. Economists measure economic profit as total revenue minus opportunity cost. Opportunity cost includes explicit costs and implicit costs. Normal profit is an implicit cost. Accountants measure profit as total revenue minus explicit costs—costs paid in money—and depreciation.

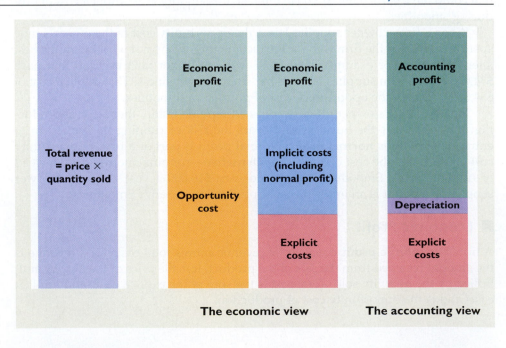

CHECKPOINT 14.1

Explain and distinguish between the economic and accounting measures of a firm's cost of production and profit.

MyEconLab
You can work these problems in Study Plan 14.1 and get instant feedback.

Practice Problems

Lee, a programmer, earned $35,000 in 2010, but in 2011, he began to manufacture body boards. After one year, he submitted the following data to his accountant.

- He stopped renting out his cottage for $3,500 a year and used it as his factory. The market value of the cottage increased from $70,000 to $71,000.
- He spent $50,000 on materials, phone, utilities, etc.
- He leased machines for $10,000 a year.
- He paid $15,000 in wages.
- He used $10,000 from his savings account, which pays 5 percent a year interest.
- He borrowed $40,000 at 10 percent a year from the bank.
- He sold $160,000 worth of body boards.
- Normal profit is $25,000 a year.

1. Calculate Lee's explicit costs, implicit costs, and economic profit.
2. Lee's accountant recorded the depreciation on Lee's cottage during 2011 as $7,000. What did the accountant say Lee's profit or loss was?

In the News

What does it cost to make 100 pairs of running shoes?

An Asian manufacturer of running shoes pays its workers $275 to make 100 pairs an hour. Workers use company-owned equipment that costs in forgone interest and economic depreciation $300 an hour. Materials cost $900.

Source: washpost.com

Which costs are explicit costs? Which are implicit costs? With total revenue from the sale of 100 pairs of shoes of $1,650, calculate economic profit.

Solutions to Practice Problems

1. Lee's explicit costs are costs paid with money: $50,000 on materials, phone, utilities, etc; $10,000 on leased machines; $15,000 in wages; and $4,000 in bank interest. These items total $79,000. Lee's implicit costs are $35,000 in forgone wages; $3,500 in forgone rent; $1,000 increase in the value of his cottage is economic depreciation of –$1,000; $500 in forgone interest; and $25,000 in normal profit. These items total $63,000. Economic profit equals total revenue ($160,000) minus total cost ($79,000 + $63,000), which equals $142,000. So economic profit is $160,000 − $142,000, or $18,000.
2. The accountant measures Lee's profit as total revenue minus explicit costs minus depreciation: $160,000 − $79,000 − $7,000, or $74,000.

Solution to In the News

Explicit costs are wages ($275) and materials ($900). Implicit costs are the forgone interest and economic depreciation ($300). Economic profit equals total revenue ($1,650) minus total cost ($1,475), which is $175.

SHORT RUN AND LONG RUN

The main goal of this chapter is to explore the influences on a firm's costs. The key influence on cost is the quantity of output that the firm produces per period. The greater the output rate, the higher is the total cost of production. But the effect of a change in production on cost depends on how soon the firm wants to act. A firm that plans to change its output rate tomorrow has fewer options than a firm that plans ahead and intends to change its production six months from now.

To study the relationship between a firm's output decision and its costs, we distinguish between two decision time frames:

• The short run
• The long run

The Short Run: Fixed Plant

Short run
The time frame in which the quantities of some resources are fixed. In the short run, a firm can usually change the quantity of labor it uses but not its technology and quantity of capital.

The **short run** is the time frame in which the quantities of some resources are fixed. For most firms, the fixed resources are the firm's technology and capital—its equipment and buildings. The management organization is also fixed in the short run. The fixed resources that a firm uses are its *fixed factors of production* and the resources that it can vary are its *variable factors of production*. The collection of fixed resources is the firm's *plant*. So in the short run, a firm's plant is fixed.

Sam's Smoothies' plant is its blenders, refrigerators, and shop. Sam's cannot change these inputs in the short run. An electric power utility can't change the number of generators it uses in the short run. An airport can't change the number of runways, terminal buildings, and traffic control facilities in the short run.

To increase output in the short run, a firm must increase the quantity of variable factors it uses. Labor is usually the variable factor of production. To produce more smoothies, Sam must hire more labor. Similarly, to increase the production of electricity, a utility must hire more engineers and run its generators for longer hours. To increase the volume of traffic it handles, an airport must hire more check-in clerks, cargo handlers, and air-traffic controllers.

Short-run decisions are easily reversed. A firm can increase or decrease output in the short run by increasing or decreasing the number of labor hours it hires.

The Long Run: Variable Plant

Long run
The time frame in which the quantities of *all* resources can be varied.

The **long run** is the time frame in which the quantities of *all* resources can be varied. That is, the long run is a period in which the firm can change its *plant*.

To increase output in the long run, a firm can increase the size of its plant. Sam's Smoothies can install more blenders and refrigerators and increase the size of its shop. An electric power utility can install more generators. And an airport can build more runways, terminals, and traffic-control facilities.

Long-run decisions are not easily reversed. Once a firm buys a new plant, its resale value is usually much less than the amount the firm paid for it. The fall in value is economic depreciation. It is called a *sunk cost* to emphasize that it is irrelevant to the firm's decisions. Only the short-run cost of changing its labor inputs and the long-run cost of changing its plant size are relevant to a firm's decisions.

We're going to study costs in the short run and the long run. We begin with the short run and describe the limits to the firm's production possibilities.

14.2 SHORT-RUN PRODUCTION

To increase the output of a fixed plant, a firm must increase the quantity of labor it employs. We describe the relationship between output and the quantity of labor employed by using three related concepts:

- Total product
- Marginal product
- Average product

■ Total Product

Total product (*TP*) is the total quantity of a good produced in a given period. Total product is an output *rate*—the number of units produced per unit of time (for example, per hour, day, or week). Total product changes as the quantity of labor employed increases and we illustrate this relationship as a total product schedule and total product curve like those in Figure 14.2. The total product schedule (the table below the graph) lists the maximum quantities of smoothies per hour that Sam can produce with her existing plant at each quantity of labor. Points *A* through *H* on the *TP* curve correspond to the columns in the table.

Total product
The total quantity of a good produced in a given period.

■ FIGURE 14.2

Total Product Schedule and Total Product Curve

MyEconLab Animation

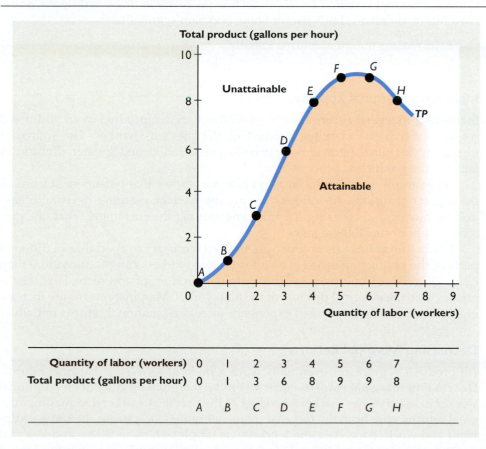

Quantity of labor (workers)	0	1	2	3	4	5	6	7
Total product (gallons per hour)	0	1	3	6	8	9	9	8
	A	B	C	D	E	F	G	H

The total product schedule shows how the quantity of smoothies that Sam's can produce changes as the quantity of labor employed changes. In column *C*, Sam's employs 2 workers and can produce 3 gallons of smoothies an hour.

The total product curve, *TP*, graphs the data in the table. Points *A* through *H* on the curve correspond to the columns of the table. The total product curve separates attainable outputs from unattainable outputs. Points below the *TP* curve are inefficient. Points on the *TP* curve are efficient.

Like the *production possibilities frontier* (see Chapter 3, p. 62), the total product curve separates attainable outputs from unattainable outputs. All the points that lie above the curve are unattainable. Points that lie below the curve, in the orange area, are attainable, but they are inefficient: They use more labor than is necessary to produce a given output. Only the points *on* the total product curve are efficient.

■ Marginal Product

Marginal product (*MP*) is the change in total product that results from a one-unit increase in the quantity of labor employed. It tells us the contribution to total product of adding one additional worker. When the quantity of labor increases by more than one worker, we calculate marginal product as

Marginal product = Change in total product ÷ Change in quanity of labor.

Figure 14.3 shows Sam's Smoothies' marginal product curve, *MP*, and its relationship with the total product curve. You can see that as the quantity of labor increases from 1 to 3 workers, marginal product increases. But as more than 3 workers are employed, marginal product decreases. When the seventh worker is employed, marginal product is negative.

Notice that the steeper the slope of the total product curve in part (a), the greater is marginal product in part (b). And when the total product curve turns downward in part (a), marginal product is negative in part (b).

The total product curve and marginal product curve in Figure 14.3 incorporate a feature that is shared by all production processes in firms as different as the Ford Motor Company, Jim's Barber Shop, and Sam's Smoothies:

* Increasing marginal returns initially
* Decreasing marginal returns eventually

Increasing Marginal Returns

Increasing marginal returns occur when the marginal product of an additional worker exceeds the marginal product of the previous worker. The source of increasing marginal returns is increased specialization and greater division of labor in the production process.

For example, if Samantha employs just one worker, that person must learn all the aspects of making smoothies: running the blender, cleaning it, fixing breakdowns, buying and checking the fruit, and serving the customers. That one person must perform all these tasks.

If Samantha hires a second person, the two workers can specialize in different parts of the production process. As a result, two workers can produce more than twice as much as one worker. The marginal product of the second worker is greater than the marginal product of the first worker. Marginal returns are increasing. Most production processes experience increasing marginal returns initially.

Decreasing Marginal Returns

All production processes eventually reach a point of *decreasing* marginal returns. **Decreasing marginal returns** occur when the marginal product of an additional worker is less than the marginal product of the previous worker. Decreasing marginal returns arise from the fact that more and more workers use the same equipment and work space. As more workers are employed, there is less and less that is productive for the additional worker to do. For example, if Samantha hires a

Marginal product
The change in total product that results from a one-unit increase in the quantity of labor employed.

Increasing marginal returns
When the marginal product of an additional worker exceeds the marginal product of the previous worker.

Decreasing marginal returns
When the marginal product of an additional worker is less than the marginal product of the previous worker.

FIGURE 14.3

Total Product and Marginal Product

MyEconLab Animation

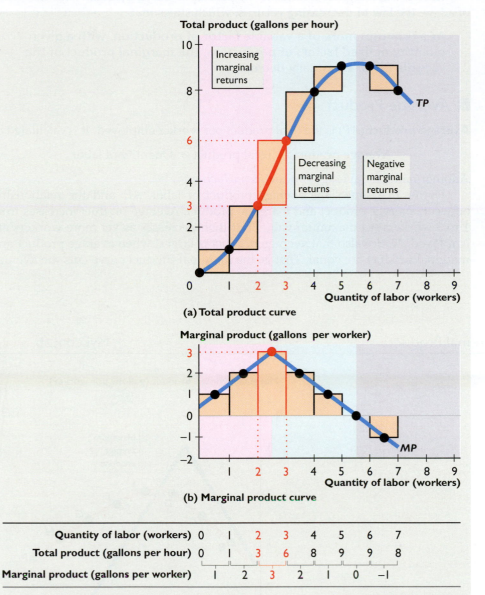

(a) Total product curve

(b) Marginal product curve

Quantity of labor (workers)	0	1	2	3	4	5	6	7
Total product (gallons per hour)	0	1	3	6	8	9	9	8
Marginal product (gallons per worker)		1	2	3	2	1	0	−1

The table calculates marginal product, and the orange bars illustrate it. When labor increases from 2 to 3 workers, total product increases from 3 gallons to 6 gallons of smoothies an hour. So marginal product is the orange bar whose height is 3 gallons (in both parts of the figure).

In part (b), marginal product is graphed midway between the labor inputs to emphasize that it is the result of *changing* inputs. Marginal product increases to a maximum (when 3 workers are employed in this example) and then declines—diminishing marginal product.

fourth worker, output increases but not by as much as it did when she hired the third worker. In this case, three workers exhaust all the possible gains from specialization and the division of labor. By hiring a fourth worker, Sam's produces more smoothies per hour, but the equipment is being operated closer to its limits. Sometimes the fourth worker has nothing to do because the machines are running without the need for further attention.

Hiring yet more workers continues to increase output but by successively smaller amounts until Samantha hires the sixth worker, at which point total product stops rising. Add a seventh worker, and the workplace is so congested that the workers get in each other's way and total product falls.

Decreasing marginal returns are so pervasive that they qualify for the status of a law: the **law of decreasing returns**, which states that

> **As a firm uses more of a variable factor of production, with a given quantity of fixed factors of production, the marginal product of the variable factor eventually decreases.**

■ Average Product

Average product (*AP*) is the total product per worker employed. It is calculated as

$$\text{Average product} = \text{Total product} \div \text{Quantity of labor.}$$

Another name for average product is *productivity*.

Figure 14.4 shows the average product of labor, *AP*, and the relationship between average product and marginal product. Average product increases from 1 to 3 workers (its maximum value) but then decreases as yet more workers are employed. Notice also that average product is largest when average product and marginal product are equal. That is, the marginal product curve cuts the average

Average product
Total product divided by the quantity of a factor of production. The average product of labor is total product divided by the quantity of labor employed.

■ **FIGURE 14.4**

Average Product and Marginal Product

MyEconLab Animation

The table calculates average product. For example, when the quantity of labor is 3 workers, total product is 6 gallons an hour, so average product is 6 gallons ÷ 3 workers = 2 gallons a worker.

The average product curve is *AP*. When marginal product exceeds average product, average product is increasing. When marginal product is less than average product, average product is decreasing.

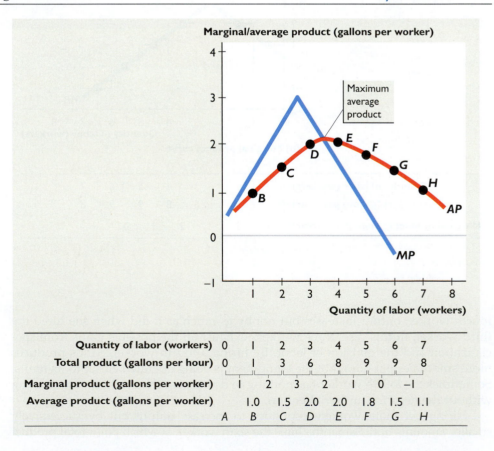

Quantity of labor (workers)	0	1	2	3	4	5	6	7
Total product (gallons per hour)	0	1	3	6	8	9	9	8
Marginal product (gallons per worker)		1	2	3	2	1	0	−1
Average product (gallons per worker)		1.0	1.5	2.0	2.0	1.8	1.5	1.1
	A	*B*	*C*	*D*	*E*	*F*	*G*	*H*

product curve at the point of maximum average product. For employment levels at which marginal product exceeds average product, the average product curve slopes upward and average product increases as more labor is employed. For employment levels at which marginal product is less than average product, the average product curve slopes downward and average product decreases as more labor is employed.

The relationship between average product and marginal product is a general feature of the relationship between the average value and the marginal value of any variable. *Eye on Your Life* looks at a familiar example.

EYE on YOUR LIFE
Your Average and Marginal Grades

Jen, a part-time student, takes one course each semester over five semesters. In the first semester, she takes calculus and her grade is a C (2). This grade is her marginal grade. It is also her average grade—her GPA.

In the next semester, Jen takes French and gets a B (3)—her new marginal grade. When the marginal value exceeds the average value, the average rises. Because Jen's marginal grade exceeds her average grade, the marginal grade pulls her average up. Her GPA rises to 2.5.

In the third semester, Jen takes economics and gets an A (4). Again her marginal grade exceeds her average, so the marginal grade pulls her average up. Jen's GPA is now 3—the average of 2, 3, and 4.

In the fourth semester, she takes history and gets a B (3). Now her marginal grade equals her average. When the marginal value equals the average value, the average doesn't change. So Jen's average remains at 3.

In the fifth semester, Jen takes English and gets a C (2). When the marginal value is below the average

value, the average falls. Because Jen's marginal grade, 2, is below her average of 3, the marginal grade pulls the average down. Her GPA falls.

This relationship between Jen's ❶ marginal grade and ❷ average grade is similar to the relationship between marginal product and average product.

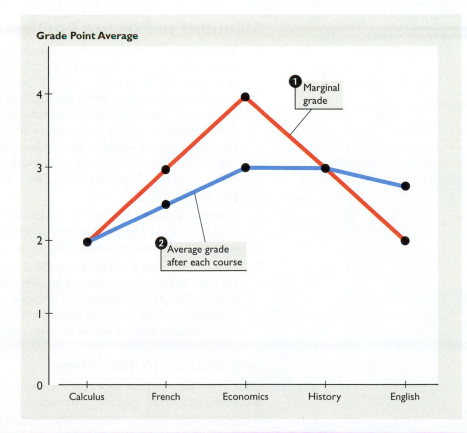

Grade Point Average

❶ Marginal grade

❷ Average grade after each course

(x-axis: Calculus, French, Economics, History, English)

MyEconLab

You can work these problems in Study Plan 14.2 and get instant feedback.

CHECKPOINT 14.2

Explain the relationship between a firm's output and labor employed in the short run.

Practice Problems

Tom leases a farmer's field and grows pineapples. Tom hires students to pick and pack the pineapples. Table 1 sets out Tom's total product schedule.

1. Calculate the marginal product of the third student and the average product of three students.

2. Over what range of numbers of students does marginal product increase?

3. When marginal product increases, is average product greater than, less than, or equal to marginal product?

In the News

Budget cuts bring layoffs to museums

The Detroit Institute of Arts cut its staff by 56 full-time and 7 part-time employees and canceled some of this year's planned exhibitions.

Source: The New York Times, February 25, 2009

As the number of workers decreased and some exhibitions were canceled, how did marginal product and average product of a worker change in the short run?

Solutions to Practice Problems

1. The marginal product of the third student is the change in total product that results from hiring the third student. When Tom hires 2 students, total product is 220 pineapples a day. When Tom hires 3 students, total product is 300 pineapples a day. Marginal product of the third student is the total product of 3 students minus the total product of 2 students, which is 300 pineapples – 220 pineapples or 80 pineapples a day.
Average product equals total product divided by the number of students. When Tom hires 3 students, total product is 300 pineapples a day, so average product is 300 pineapples a day ÷ 3 students, which equals 100 pineapples a day.

2. Marginal product of the first student is 100 pineapples a day, of the second student is 120 pineapples a day, and of the third is 80 pineapples a day. So marginal product increases when Tom hires the first and second students.

3. When Tom hires 1 student, marginal product is 100 pineapples and average product is 100 pineapples per student. When Tom hires 2 students, marginal product is 120 pineapples and average product is 110 pineapples per student. When Tom hires the second student, marginal product is increasing and average product is less than marginal product.

Solution to In the News

With a decrease in the number of exhibitions, output (number of visitors to the museum) might fall, but the percentage decrease in output is probably less than the percentage cut in labor services. Marginal product per worker increased and the increase in marginal product brought an increase in the average product.

TABLE 1

Labor (students)	Total product (pineapples per day)
0	0
1	100
2	220
3	300
4	360
5	400
6	420
7	430

14.3   SHORT-RUN COST

To produce more output (total product) in the short run, a firm must employ more labor, which means that it must increase its costs. We describe the relationship between output and cost using three cost concepts:

- Total cost
- Marginal cost
- Average cost

■ Total Cost

A firm's **total cost** (*TC*) is the cost of all the factors of production used by the firm. Total cost divides into two parts: total fixed cost and total variable cost. **Total fixed cost** (*TFC*) is the cost of a firm's fixed factors of production: land, capital, and entrepreneurship. In the short run, the quantities of these inputs don't change as output changes, so total fixed cost doesn't change as output changes. **Total variable cost** (*TVC*) is the cost of a firm's variable factor of production—labor. To change its output in the short run, a firm must change the quantity of labor it employs, so total variable cost changes as output changes.

Total cost is the sum of total fixed cost and total variable cost. That is,

$$TC = TFC + TVC.$$

Table 14.2 shows Sam's Smoothies' total costs. Sam's fixed costs are $10 an hour regardless of whether it operates or not—*TFC* is $10 an hour. To produce smoothies, Samantha hires labor, which costs $6 an hour. *TVC*, which increases as output increases, equals the number of workers per hour multiplied by $6. For example, to produce 6 gallons an hour, Samantha hires 3 workers, so *TVC* is $18 an hour. *TC* is the sum of *TFC* and *TVC*. So to produce 6 gallons an hour, *TC* is $28. Check the calculation in each row and note that to produce some quantities— 2 gallons an hour, for example—Sam hires a worker for only part of the hour.

Total cost
The cost of all the factors of production used by a firm.

Total fixed cost
The cost of the firm's fixed factors of production—the cost of land, capital, and entrepreneurship.

Total variable cost
The cost of the firm's variable factor of production—the cost of labor.

■ **TABLE 14.2**

Sam's Smoothies' Total Costs

Labor (workers per hour)	Output (gallons per hour)	Total fixed cost	Total variable cost	Total cost
		(dollars per hour)		
0	0	10	0	10.00
1.00	1	10	6.00	16.00
1.60	2	10	9.60	19.60
2.00	3	10	12.00	22.00
2.35	4	10	14.10	24.10
2.65	5	10	15.90	25.90
3.00	6	10	18.00	28.00
3.40	7	10	20.40	30.40
4.00	8	10	24.00	34.00
5.00	9	10	30.00	40.00

Sam's fixed factors of production are land, capital, and entrepreneurship. Total fixed cost is constant regardless of the quantity produced. Sam's variable factor of production is labor. Total variable cost is the cost of labor. Total cost is the sum of total fixed cost and total variable cost.

The highlighted row shows that to produce 6 gallons of smoothies, Sam's hires 3 workers. Total fixed cost is $10 an hour. Total variable cost is the cost of the 3 workers. At $6 an hour, 3 workers cost $18. Sam's total cost of producing 6 gallons an hour is $10 plus $18, which equals $28.

Figure 14.5 illustrates Sam's total cost curves. The green total fixed cost curve (*TFC*) is horizontal because total fixed cost does not change when output changes. It is a constant at $10 an hour. The purple total variable cost curve (*TVC*) and the blue total cost curve (*TC*) both slope upward because variable cost increases as output increases. The arrows highlight total fixed cost as the vertical distance between the *TVC* and *TC* curves.

Let's now look at Sam's Smoothies' marginal cost.

■ Marginal Cost

Marginal cost

The change in total cost that results from a one-unit increase in output.

In Figure 14.5, total variable cost and total cost increase at a decreasing rate at small levels of output and then begin to increase at an increasing rate as output increases. To understand these patterns in the changes in total cost, we need to use the concept of *marginal cost*.

A firm's **marginal cost** is the change in total cost that results from a one-unit increase in output. Table 14.3 calculates the marginal cost for Sam's Smoothies. When, for example, output increases from 5 gallons to 6 gallons an hour, total cost increases from $25.90 to $28. So the marginal cost of this gallon of smoothies is $2.10 ($28 – $25.90). Notice that marginal cost is located midway between the total costs to emphasize that it is the result of *changing* outputs

Marginal cost tells us how total cost changes as output changes. The final cost concept tells us what it costs, on average, to produce a unit of output. Let's now look at Sam's average costs.

■ **FIGURE 14.5**

Total Cost Curves at Sam's Smoothies

MyEconLab Animation

Total fixed cost (*TFC*) is constant—it graphs as a horizontal line—and total variable cost (*TVC*) increases as output increases. Total cost (*TC*) also increases as output increases. The vertical distance between the total cost curve and the total variable cost curve is total fixed cost, as illustrated by the two arrows.

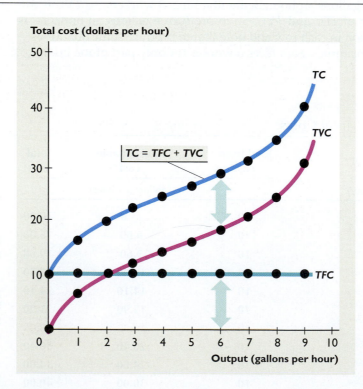

■ Average Cost

There are three average cost concepts:

- Average fixed cost
- Average variable cost
- Average total cost

Average fixed cost (*AFC*) is total fixed cost per unit of output. **Average variable cost** (*AVC*) is total variable cost per unit of output. **Average total cost** (*ATC*) is total cost per unit of output. The average cost concepts are calculated from the total cost concepts as follows:

$$TC = TFC + TVC.$$

Divide each total cost term by the quantity produced, *Q*, to give

$$\frac{TC}{Q} = \frac{TFC}{Q} + \frac{TVC}{Q}.$$

or

$$ATC = AFC + AVC.$$

Table 14.3 shows these average costs. For example, when output is 6 gallons an hour, average fixed cost is ($10 ÷ 6), which equals $1.67; average variable cost is ($18 ÷ 6), which equals $3.00; and average total cost is ($28 ÷ 6), which equals $4.67. Note that average total cost ($4.67) equals average fixed cost ($1.67) plus average variable cost ($3.00).

Average fixed cost
Total fixed cost per unit of output.

Average variable cost
Total variable cost per unit of output.

Average total cost
Total cost per unit of output, which equals average fixed cost plus average variable cost.

■ **TABLE 14.3**

Sam's Smoothies' Marginal Cost and Average Cost

Output (gallons per hour)	Total cost (dollars per hour)	Marginal cost (dollars per gallon)	Average fixed cost	Average variable cost	Average total cost
				(dollars per gallon)	
0	10.00		–	–	–
		6.00			
1	16.00		10.00	6.00	16.00
		3.60			
2	19.60		5.00	4.80	9.80
		2.40			
3	22.00		3.33	4.00	7.33
		2.10			
4	24.10		2.50	3.53	6.03
		1.80			
5	25.90		2.00	3.18	5.18
		2.10			
6	28.00		1.67	3.00	4.67
		2.40			
7	30.40		1.43	2.91	4.34
		3.60			
8	34.00		1.25	3.00	4.25
		6.00			
9	40.00		1.11	3.33	4.44

To produce 6 gallons of smoothies an hour, Sam's total cost is $28. Table 14.2 shows that this total cost is the sum of total fixed cost ($10) and total variable cost ($18).

Marginal cost is the increase in total cost that results from a one-unit increase in output. When Sam's increases output from 5 gallons to 6 gallons an hour, total cost increases from $25.90 to $28.00, an increase of $2.10 a gallon. The marginal cost of the sixth gallon an hour is $2.10. Marginal cost is located midway between the total costs to emphasize that it is the result of *changing* output.

When Sam's produces 6 gallons an hour, average fixed cost ($10 ÷ 6 gallons) is $1.67 a gallon; average variable cost ($18 ÷ 6 gallons) is $3.00 a gallon; average total cost ($28 ÷ 6 gallons) is $4.67 a gallon.

Figure 14.6 graphs the marginal cost and average cost data in Table 14.3. The red marginal cost curve (*MC*) is U-shaped because of the way in which marginal product changes. Recall that when Samantha hires a second or a third worker, marginal product increases and output increases to 6 gallons an hour (Figure 14.3 on p. 351). Over this output range, marginal cost decreases as output increases. When Samantha hires a fourth or more workers, marginal product decreases but output increases up to 9 gallons an hour (Figure 14.3). Over this output range, marginal cost increases as output increases.

The green average fixed cost curve (*AFC*) slopes downward. As output increases, the same constant total fixed cost is spread over a larger output. The blue average total cost curve (*ATC*) and the purple average variable cost curve (*AVC*) are U-shaped. The vertical distance between the average total cost and average variable cost curves is equal to average fixed cost—as indicated by the two arrows. That distance shrinks as output increases because average fixed cost decreases with increasing output.

The marginal cost curve intersects the average variable cost curve and the average total cost curve at their minimum points. That is, when marginal cost is less than average cost, average cost is decreasing; and when marginal cost exceeds average cost, average cost is increasing. This relationship holds for both the *ATC* curve and the *AVC* curve and is another example of the relationship you saw in Figure 14.4 for average product and marginal product.

■ **FIGURE 14.6**

Average Cost Curves and Marginal Cost Curve at Sam's Smoothies

MyEconLab Animation

Average fixed cost decreases as output increases. The average fixed cost curve (*AFC*) slopes downward. The average total cost curve (*ATC*) and average variable cost curve (*AVC*) are U-shaped. The vertical distance between these two curves is equal to average fixed cost, as illustrated by the two arrows.

Marginal cost is the change in total cost when output increases by one unit. The marginal cost curve (*MC*) is U-shaped and intersects the average variable cost curve and the average total cost curve at their minimum points.

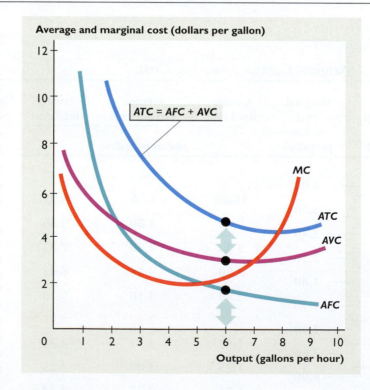

■ Why the Average Total Cost Curve Is U-Shaped

Average total cost, ATC, is the sum of average fixed cost, AFC, and average variable cost, AVC. So the shape of the ATC curve combines the shapes of the AFC and AVC curves. The U-shape of the average total cost curve arises from the influence of two opposing forces:

* Spreading total fixed cost over a larger output
* Decreasing marginal returns

When output increases, the firm spreads its total fixed costs over a larger output and its average fixed cost decreases—its average fixed cost curve slopes downward.

Decreasing marginal returns means that as output increases, ever larger amounts of labor are needed to produce an additional unit of output. So average variable cost eventually increases, and the AVC curve eventually slopes upward.

The shape of the average total cost curve combines these two effects. Initially, as output increases, both average fixed cost and average variable cost decrease, so average total cost decreases and the ATC curve slopes downward. But as output increases further and decreasing marginal returns set in, average variable cost begins to increase. Eventually, average variable cost increases more quickly than average fixed cost decreases, so average total cost increases and the ATC curve slopes upward.

All the short-run cost concepts that you've met are summarized in Table 14.4.

■ TABLE 14.4

A Compact Glossary of Costs

Term	Symbol	Definition	Equation
Fixed cost		The cost of a fixed factor of production that is independent of the quantity produced	
Variable cost		The cost of a variable factor of production that varies with the quantity produced	
Total fixed cost	TFC	Cost of the fixed factors of production	
Total variable cost	TVC	Cost of the variable factor of production	
Total cost	TC	Cost of all factors of production	$TC = TFC + TVC$
Marginal cost	MC	Change in total cost resulting from a one-unit increase in output (Q)	$MC = \Delta TC \div \Delta Q*$
Average fixed cost	AFC	Total fixed cost per unit of output	$AFC = TFC \div Q$
Average variable cost	AVC	Total variable cost per unit of output	$AVC = TVC \div Q$
Average total cost	ATC	Total cost per unit of output	$ATC = AFC + AVC$

*In this equation, the Greek letter delta (Δ) stands for "change in."

■ Cost Curves and Product Curves

A firm's cost curves and product curves are linked, and Figure 14.7 shows how. The upper graph shows the average product curve, AP, and the marginal product curve, MP. The lower graph shows the average variable cost curve, AVC, and the marginal cost curve, MC.

As labor increases up to 2.5 workers a day (upper graph), output increases to 4 units a day (lower graph). Marginal product and average product rise and marginal cost and average variable cost fall. At the point of maximum marginal product, marginal cost is at a minimum.

As labor increases to 3.5 workers a day (upper graph), output increases to 7 units a day (lower graph). Marginal product falls and marginal cost rises, but average product continues to rise and average variable cost continues to fall. At the point of maximum average product, average variable cost is at a minimum. As labor increases further, output increases. Average product diminishes and average variable cost increases.

■ Shifts in the Cost Curves

The position of a firm's short-run cost curves, in Figures 14.5 and 14.6, depends on two factors:

- Technology
- Prices of factors of production

Technology

A technological change that increases productivity shifts the total product curve upward. It also shifts the marginal product curve and the average product curve upward. With a better technology that increases productivity, the same factors of production can produce more output, so an advance in technology lowers the average and marginal costs and shifts the short-run cost curves downward.

For example, advances in robotic technology have increased productivity in the automobile industry. As a result, the product curves of Chrysler, Ford, and GM have shifted upward, and their average and marginal cost curves have shifted downward. But the relationships between their product curves and cost curves have not changed. The curves are still linked, as in Figure 14.7.

Often a technological advance results in a firm using more capital, a fixed factor of production, and less labor, a variable factor of production. For example, today telephone companies use computers to connect long-distance calls instead of the human operators they used in the 1980s. When a telephone company makes this change, total variable cost decreases and total cost decreases, but total fixed cost increases. This change in the mix of fixed cost and variable cost means that at small output levels, average total cost might increase, but at large output levels, average total cost decreases.

Prices of Factors of Production

An increase in the price of a factor of production increases costs and shifts the cost curves. But how the curves shift depends on which resource price changes. An increase in rent or some other component of *fixed* cost shifts the fixed cost curves (TFC and AFC) upward and shifts the total cost curve (TC) upward but leaves the variable cost curves (AVC and TVC) and the marginal cost curve (MC) unchanged.

FIGURE 14.7

Product Curves and Cost Curves

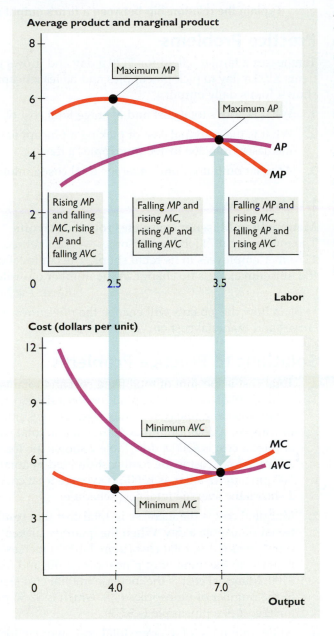

A firm's *MC* curve is linked to its *MP* curve. If, as the firm hires more labor up to 2.5 workers a day, the firm's marginal product rises, its marginal cost falls. If marginal product is at a maximum, marginal cost is at a minimum. If, as the firm hires more labor, its marginal product diminishes, its marginal cost rises.

A firm's *AVC* curve is linked to its *AP* curve. If, as the firm hires more labor up to 3.5 workers a day, its average product rises, its average variable cost falls. If average product is at a maximum, average variable cost is at a minimum. If as the firm hires more labor its average product diminishes, its average variable cost rises.

An increase in wage rates or some other component of *variable* cost shifts the variable cost curves (*TVC* and *AVC*) and the marginal cost curve (*MC*) upward but leaves the fixed cost curves (*AFC* and *TFC*) unchanged. So, for example, if the interest expense paid by a trucking company increases, the fixed cost of transportation services increases, but if the wage rate paid to truck drivers increases, the variable cost and marginal cost of transportation services increase.

CHECKPOINT 14.3

Explain the relationship between a firm's output and costs in the short run.

Practice Problems

Tom leases a farmer's field for $120 a day and grows pineapples. He pays students $100 a day to pick pineapples and he leases capital at $80 a day. Table 1 shows Tom's daily output.

1. What is Tom's total cost and average total cost of 300 pineapples a day?
2. What is the marginal cost of picking a pineapple when the quantity increases from 360 to 400 pineapples a day?
3. At what output is Tom's average total cost a minimum?

TABLE 1

Labor (students)	Output (pineapples per day)
0	0
1	100
2	220
3	300
4	360
5	400
6	420
7	430

In the News

Metropolitan Museum completes round of layoffs

The museum cut 74 jobs and 95 other workers retired. The museum also laid off 127 other employees in its retail shops. The cut in labor costs is $10 million, but the museum expects no change in the number of visitors.

Source: *The New York Times*, June 22, 2009

Explain how the job cuts will change the museum's short-run average cost curves and marginal cost curve.

Solutions to Practice Problems

TABLE 2

Labor	TP	TC	MC	ATC
0	0	200		–
			1.00	
1	100	300		3.00
			0.83	
2	220	400		1.82
			1.25	
3	300	500		1.67
			1.67	
4	360	600		1.67
			2.50	
5	400	700		1.75
			5.00	
6	420	800		1.90
			10.00	
7	430	900		2.09

1. Total cost is the sum of total fixed cost and total variable cost. Tom leases the field for $120 a day and capital for $80 a day, so Tom's total fixed cost is $200 a day. Total variable cost is the wages of the students. To produce 300 pineapples a day, Tom hires 3 students, so total variable cost is $300 a day and total cost is $500 a day. Table 2 shows the total cost (TC) schedule. Average total cost is the total cost divided by total product. The total cost of 300 pineapples a day is $500, so average total cost is $1.67 a pineapple. Table 2 shows the average total cost schedule.

2. Marginal cost is the increase in total cost that results from picking one additional pineapple a day. When the quantity picked increases from 360 to 400 pineapples a day, total cost (from Table 2) increases from $600 to $700. The increase in the number of pineapples is 40, and the increase in total cost is $100. Marginal cost is the increase in total cost ($100) divided by the increase in the number of pineapples (40), which is $2.50 per pineapple. So the marginal cost of a pineapple is $2.50.

3. At the minimum of average total cost, average total cost equals marginal cost. Minimum average total cost of a pineapple between 300 and 360 pineapples is $1.67. Table 2 shows that the marginal cost of increasing output from 300 to 360 pineapples a day is $1.67 a pineapple.

Solution to In the News

A cut in labor but no change in output increases marginal product of labor and decreases marginal cost. The MC, AVC, and ATC curves shift downward.

14.4 LONG-RUN COST

In the long run, a firm can vary both the quantity of labor and the quantity of capital. A small firm, such as Sam's Smoothies, can increase its plant size by moving into a larger building and installing more machines. A big firm such as General Motors can decrease its plant size by closing down some production lines.

We are now going to see how costs vary in the long run when a firm varies its plant—the quantity of capital it uses—along with the quantity of labor it uses.

The first thing that happens is that the distinction between fixed cost and variable cost disappears. All costs are variable in the long run.

■ Plant Size and Cost

When a firm changes its plant size, its cost of producing a given output changes. In Table 14.3 on p. 357 and Figure 14.6 on p. 358, the lowest average total cost that Samantha can achieve is $4.25 a gallon, which occurs when she produces 8 gallons of smoothies an hour. Samantha wonders what would happen to her average total cost if she increased the size of her plant by renting a bigger building and installing a larger number of blenders and refrigerators. Will the average total cost of producing a gallon of smoothies fall, rise, or remain the same?

Each of these three outcomes is possible, and they arise because when a firm changes the size of its plant, it might experience

- Economies of scale
- Diseconomies of scale
- Constant returns to scale

Economies of Scale

Economies of scale are features of a firm's technology that make average total cost *fall* as output increases. The main source of economies of scale is greater specialization of both labor and capital.

Specialization of Labor If Ford produced 100 cars a week, each production line worker would have to perform many different tasks. But if Ford produces 10,000 cars a week, each worker can specialize in a small number of tasks and become highly proficient at them. The result is that the average product of labor increases and the average total cost of producing a car falls.

Specialization also occurs off the production line. For example, a small firm usually does not have a specialist sales manager, personnel manager, and production manager. One person covers all these activities. But when a firm is large enough, specialists perform these activities. Average product increases, and the average total cost falls.

Specialization of Capital At a small output rate, firms often must employ general-purpose machines and tools. For example, with an output of a few gallons an hour, Sam's Smoothies uses regular blenders like the one in your kitchen. But if Sam's produces hundreds of gallons an hour, it uses commercial blenders that fill, empty, and clean themselves. The result is that the output rate is larger and the average total cost of producing a gallon of smoothies is lower.

Economies of scale
Features of a firm's technology that make average total cost *fall* as output increases.

Specialization of both labor and capital on an auto-assembly line.

Diseconomies of scale
Features of a firm's technology that make average total cost *rise* as output increases.

Diseconomies of Scale

Diseconomies of scale are features of a firm's technology that make average total cost *rise* as output increases. Diseconomies of scale arise from the difficulty of coordinating and controlling a large enterprise. The larger the firm, the greater is the cost of communicating both up and down the management hierarchy and among managers. Eventually, management complexity brings rising average total cost. Diseconomies of scale occur in all production processes but in some perhaps only at a very large output rate.

Constant Returns to Scale

Constant returns to scale
Features of a firm's technology that keep average total cost constant as output increases.

Constant returns to scale are features of a firm's technology that keep average total cost *constant* as output increases. Constant returns to scale occur when a firm is able to replicate its existing production facility including its management system. For example, Ford might double its production of Fusion cars by doubling its production facility for those cars. It can build an identical production line and hire an identical number of workers. With the two identical production lines, Ford produces exactly twice as many cars. The average total cost of producing a Fusion is identical in the two plants. Ford's average total cost remains constant as it increases production.

■ The Long-Run Average Cost Curve

Long-run average cost curve
A curve that shows the lowest average total cost at which it is possible to produce each output when the firm has had sufficient time to change both its plant size and labor employed.

The **long-run average cost curve** shows the lowest average total cost at which it is possible to produce each output when the firm has had sufficient time to change both its plant size and its labor force.

Figure 14.8 shows Sam's Smoothies' long-run average cost curve *LRAC*. This long-run average cost curve is derived from the short-run average total cost curves for different possible plant sizes.

With its current small plant, Sam's Smoothies operates on the average total cost curve ATC_1 in Figure 14.8. The other three average total cost curves are for

■ **FIGURE 14.8**

Long-Run Average Cost Curve

MyEconLab Animation

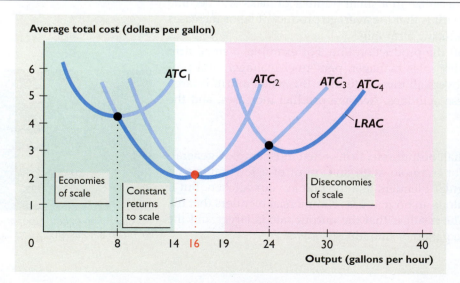

In the long run, Samantha can vary both the plant size and the quantity of labor she employs. The long-run average cost curve traces the lowest attainable average total cost of producing each output. The dark blue curve is the long-run average cost curve *LRAC*.

Sam's experiences economies of scale as output increases up to 14 gallons an hour, constant returns to scale for outputs between 14 gallons and 19 gallons an hour, and diseconomies of scale for outputs that exceed 19 gallons an hour.

successively bigger plants. In this example, for outputs up to 8 gallons an hour, the existing plant with average total cost curve ATC_1 produces smoothies at the lowest attainable average cost. For outputs between 8 and 16 gallons an hour, average total cost is lowest on ATC_2. For outputs between 16 and 24 gallons an hour, average total cost is lowest on ATC_3. And for outputs in excess of 24 gallons an hour, average total cost is lowest on ATC_4.

The segment of each of the four average total cost curves for which that plant has the lowest average total cost is highlighted in dark blue in Figure 14.8. The scallop-shaped curve made up of these four segments is Sam's Smoothies' long-run average cost curve.

Economies and Diseconomies of Scale

When economies of scale are present, the *LRAC* curve slopes downward. The *LRAC* curve in Figure 14.8 shows that Sam's Smoothies experiences economies of scale for output rates up to 14 gallons an hour. At output rates between 14 and 19 gallons an hour, the firm experiences constant returns to scale. And at output rates that exceed 19 gallons an hour, the firm experiences diseconomies of scale.

EYE on RETAILERS' COSTS
Which Store Has the Lower Costs: Wal-Mart or 7-Eleven?

Wal-Mart's "small" supercenters measure 99,000 square feet and serve an average of 30,000 customers a week. The average 7-Eleven store, most of which today are attached to gas stations, measures 2,000 square feet and serves 5,000 customers a week.

Which retailing technology has the lower operating cost? The answer depends on the scale of operation.

At a small number of customers per week, it costs less per customer to operate a store of 2,000 square feet than one of 99,000 square feet.

In the figure, the average total cost curve of operating a 7-Eleven store of 2,000 square feet is $ATC_{7-Eleven}$ and the average total cost curve of a store of 99,000 square feet is $ATC_{Wal-Mart}$. The dark blue curve is a retailer's long-run

average cost curve *LRAC*.

If the number of customers is Q a week, the average total cost per transaction is the same for both stores. For a store that serves more than Q customers a week, the least-cost method is the big store. For fewer than Q customers a week, the least-cost method is the small store. The least-cost store is not always the biggest.

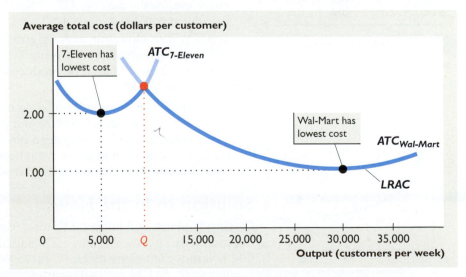

TABLE 1

Labor (students per day)	Output 1 field	Output 2 fields
	(pineapples per day)	
0	0	0
1	100	220
2	220	460
3	300	620
4	360	740
5	400	820
6	420	860
7	430	880

TABLE 2

TP (1 field)	ATC (1 field)	TP (2 fields)	ATC (2 fields)
100	3.00	220	2.27
220	1.82	460	1.30
300	1.67	620	1.13
360	1.67	740	1.08
400	1.75	820	1.10
420	1.90	860	1.16
430	2.09	880	1.25

FIGURE 1

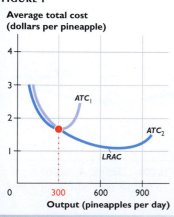

CHECKPOINT 14.4

Derive and explain a firm's long-run average cost curve.

Practice Problems

To grow pineapples, Tom leases 1 field for $120 a day and capital for $80 a day and hires students at $100 a day. Suppose that Tom now leases 2 fields for $240 a day and twice as much capital for $160 a day. Table 1 shows his outputs.

1. What is Tom's average total cost when he farms 2 fields and produces 220 pineapples a day?

2. Make a graph of Tom's average total cost curves using 1 field and 2 fields. Show on the graph Tom's long-run average cost curve. Over what output range will Tom use 1 field? 2 fields?

3. Does Tom experience constant returns to scale, economies of scale, or diseconomies of scale?

In the News

GM restructuring plan released

GM's restructuring plan will close 11 plants and reduce output at 3 others.
Source: boston.com, May 31, 2009

Explain the effects of the restructuring plan on GM's total fixed cost, total variable cost, short-run *ATC* curve, and *LRAC* curve.

Solutions to Practice Problems

1. Total cost equals fixed cost ($400 a day) plus $100 a day for each student. Tom can produce 220 pineapples with 2 fields and 1 student, so total cost is $500 a day. Average total cost is the total cost divided by output, which at 220 pineapples a day is $500 divided by 220, or $2.27. The "*ATC* (2 fields)" column of Table 2 shows Tom's average total cost schedule for 2 fields.

2. Figure 1 shows Tom's average total cost curve using 1 field as ATC_1. This curve graphs the data on *ATC* (1 field) and *TP* (1 field) in Table 2, which was calculated in Table 2 on p. 362. Using 2 fields, the average total cost curve is ATC_2. Tom's long-run average cost curve is the lower segments of the two *ATC* curves, highlighted in Figure 1. If Tom produces up to 300 pineapples a day, he will use 1 field. If he produces more than 300 pineapples a day, he will use 2 fields.

3. Tom experiences economies of scale up to an output of 740 pineapples a day because as he increases his plant and produces up to 740 pineapples a day, the average total cost of picking a pineapple decreases. (We don't have enough information to know what happens to Tom's average total cost if he uses three fields and three units of capital.)

Solution to In the News

Closing 11 plants will lower GM's total fixed cost; closing 11 plants and decreasing output at 3 plants will lower GM's total variable cost. With a smaller scale, GM will move left along its *LRAC* curve to the *ATC* curve associated with its smaller scale. As GM varies its output, it will move along that *ATC* curve.

CHAPTER SUMMARY

Key Points

1 Explain and distinguish between the economic and accounting measures of a firm's cost of production and profit.

- Firms seek to maximize economic profit, which is total revenue minus total cost.
- Total cost equals opportunity cost—the sum of explicit costs and implicit costs, which includes normal profit.

2 Explain the relationship between a firm's output and labor employed in the short run.

- In the short run, the firm can change the output it produces by changing only the quantity of labor it employs.
- A total product curve shows the limits to the output that the firm can produce with a given quantity of capital and different quantities of labor.
- As the quantity of labor increases, the marginal product of labor increases initially but eventually decreases—the law of decreasing returns.

3 Explain the relationship between a firm's output and costs in the short run.

- As total product increases, total fixed cost is constant, and total variable cost and total cost increase.
- As total product increases, average fixed cost decreases; average variable cost, average total cost, and marginal cost decrease at small outputs and increase at large outputs so their curves are U-shaped.

4 Derive and explain a firm's long-run average cost curve.

- In the long run, the firm can change the size of its plant.
- Long-run cost is the cost of production when all inputs have been adjusted to produce at the lowest attainable cost.
- The long-run average cost curve traces out the lowest attainable average total cost at each output when both the plant size and labor can be varied.
- The long-run average cost curve slopes downward with economies of scale and upward with diseconomies of scale.

Key Terms

Average fixed cost, 357
Average product, 352
Average total cost, 357
Average variable cost, 357
Constant returns to scale, 364
Decreasing marginal returns, 350
Diseconomies of scale, 364
Economic depreciation, 345

Economic profit, 345
Economies of scale, 363
Explicit cost, 345
Implicit cost, 345
Increasing marginal returns, 350
Law of decreasing returns, 352
Long run, 348
Long-run average cost curve, 364

Marginal cost, 356
Marginal product, 350
Normal profit, 345
Short run, 348
Total cost, 355
Total fixed cost, 355
Total product, 349
Total variable cost, 355

CHAPTER CHECKPOINT

Study Plan Problems and Applications

1. Joe runs a shoe shine stand at the airport. Joe has no skills, no job experience, and no alternative job. The return to entrepreneurship in the shoe shine business is $10,000 a year. Joe pays the airport rent of $2,000 a year, and his total revenue from shining shoes is $15,000 a year. He spent $1,000 on a chair, polish, and brushes and paid for these items using a loan that has an interest rate of 20 percent a year. At the end of one year, Joe was offered $500 for his business and all its equipment. Calculate Joe's annual explicit costs, implicit costs, and economic profit from his shoe shine business.

2. Len's body board factory rents equipment for shaping boards and hires students. Table 1 sets out Len's total product schedule. Construct Len's marginal product and average product schedules. Over what range of workers do marginal returns increase?

Use the following information to work Problems 3 to 6.

Len's body board factory pays $60 a day for equipment and $200 a day to each student it hires. Table 1 sets out Len's total product schedule.

3. Construct Len's total variable cost and total cost schedules. What does the difference between total cost and total variable cost at each output equal?

4. Construct the average fixed cost, average variable cost, and average total cost schedules and the marginal cost schedule.

5. At what output is Len's average total cost at a minimum? At what output is Len's average variable cost at a minimum?

6. Explain why the output at which average variable cost is at a minimum is smaller than the output at which average total cost is at a minimum.

7. Table 2 shows the costs incurred at Pete's peanut farm. Complete the table.

TABLE 1

Labor (workers per day)	Total product (body boards per day)
0	0
1	20
2	44
3	60
4	72

TABLE 2

L	TP	TVC	TC	AFC	AVC	ATC	MC
0	0	0	100				
1	10	35					
2	24	70					
3	38	105					
4	44	140					

8. **Gap will focus on smaller scale stores**
   Gap has too many 12,500 square feet stores. The target store size is 6,000 to 10,000 square feet, so Gap plans to combine previously separate stores. Some Gap Body, Gap Adult, and Gap Kids stores will be combined in one store.
   Source: CNN, June 10, 2008

   Thinking of a Gap store as a production plant, explain why Gap is reducing the size of its stores. Is Gap making a long-run decision or a short-run decision? Is Gap taking advantage of economies of scale?

Instructor Assignable Problems and Applications

Your instructor can assign these problems as homework, a quiz, or a test in MyEconLab.

1. If the *ATC* curves of a Wal-Mart store and a 7-Eleven store are like those in *Eye on Retailers' Costs* on p. 365, and if each type of store operates at its minimum *ATC*, which store has the lower total cost? How can you be sure? Which has the lower marginal cost? How can you be sure? Sketch each firm's marginal cost curve.

2. Sonya used to earn $25,000 a year selling real estate, but she now sells greeting cards. The return to entrepreneurship in the greeting cards industry is $14,000 a year. Over the year, Sonya bought $10,000 worth of cards from manufacturers and sold them for $58,000. Sonya rents a shop for $5,000 a year and spends $1,000 on utilities and office expenses. Sonya owns a cash register, which she bought for $2,000 with funds from her savings account. Her bank pays 3 percent a year on savings accounts. At the end of the year, Sonya was offered $1,600 for her cash register. Calculate Sonya's explicit costs, implicit costs, and economic profit.

Use the following information to work Problems **3** to **5**.

Yolanda runs a bullfrog farm. When she employs 1 person, she produces 1,000 bullfrogs a week. When she hires a second worker, her total product doubles. Her total product doubles again when she hires a third worker. When she hires a fourth worker, her total product increases but by only 1,000 bullfrogs. Yolanda pays $1,000 a week for equipment and $500 a week to each worker she hires.

3. Construct Yolanda's marginal product and average product schedules. Over what range of workers does marginal returns increase?

4. Construct Yolanda's total variable cost and total cost schedules. What is Yolanda's total fixed cost?

5. At what output is Yolanda's average total cost at a minimum?

6. Table 1 shows some of the costs incurred at Bill's Bakery. Calculate the values of *A, B, C, D*, and *E*. Show your work.

TABLE 1

L	TP	TVC	TC	AFC	AVC	ATC	MC
1	100	350	850	*C*	3.50	*D*	2.50
2	240	700	*B*	2.08	2.92	5.00	*E*
3	380	*A*	1,550	1.32	2.76	4.08	5.83
4	440	1,400	1,900	1.14	3.18	4.32	11.67
5	470	1,750	2,250	1.06	3.72	4.79	

7. **Grain prices go the way of the oil price**
   Rising crop prices have started to impact the price of breakfast for millions of Americans—cereal prices are rising.

   Source: *The Economist*, July 21, 2007

   Explain how the rising price of grain affects the average total cost and marginal cost of producing breakfast cereals.

Multiple Choice Quiz

1. A firm's cost of production equals _____.
    A. all the costs paid with money, called explicit costs
    B. the implicit costs of using all the firm's own resources
    C. all explicit costs and implicit costs, excluding normal profit
    D. the costs of all resources used by the firm whether bought in the market-place or owned by the firm

2. The average product of labor increases as output increases if _____.
    A. marginal product exceeds average product
    B. average product exceeds marginal product
    C. total product increases
    D. marginal product increases

3. Marginal returns start to decrease when more and more workers _____.
    A. have to share the same equipment and workspace
    B. produce less and less total output
    C. require jobs to be too specialized
    D. produce less and less average product

4. Average variable cost is at a minimum when _____.
    A. marginal cost equals average variable cost
    B. average total cost is at a minimum
    C. marginal cost exceeds average fixed cost
    D. average total cost exceeds average variable cost

5. An increase in the rent that a firm pays for its factory does not increase

    _____.
    A. total cost
    B. fixed cost
    C. marginal cost
    D. average fixed cost

6. An increase in the wage rate _____.
    A. shifts the average total cost curve and the marginal cost curve upward
    B. shifts the average fixed cost and average variable cost curve upward
    C. increases average variable cost but does not change marginal cost
    D. does not change average variable cost but increases average total cost

7. When average variable cost is at its minimum level, marginal product

    _____.
    A. equals average product
    B. exceeds average product
    C. is less than average product
    D. is at its maximum level

8. In the long run, with an increase in the plant size, _____.
    A. the short-run average total cost curve shifts downward
    B. the long-run average cost curve slopes downward
    C. the short-run average total cost curve shifts downward if economies of scale exist
    D. the average total cost of production rises

 15

Why did GM fail?

Perfect Competition

When you have completed your study of this chapter, you will be able to

1 Explain a perfectly competitive firm's profit-maximizing choices and derive its supply curve.

2 Explain how output, price, and profit are determined in the short run.

3 Explain how output, price, and profit are determined in the long run and explain why perfect competition is efficient.

MARKET TYPES

The four market types are

- Perfect competition
- Monopoly
- Monopolistic competition
- Oligopoly

■ Perfect Competition

Perfect competition
A market in which there are many firms, each selling an identical product; many buyers; no barriers to the entry of new firms into the industry; no advantage to established firms; and buyers and sellers are well informed about prices.

Perfect competition exists when

- Many firms sell an identical product to many buyers.
- There are no barriers to entry into (or exit from) the market.
- Established firms have no advantage over new firms.
- Sellers and buyers are well informed about prices.

These conditions that define perfect competition arise when the market demand for the product is large relative to the output of a single producer. This situation arises when economies of scale are absent so the efficient scale of each firm is small. But a large market and the absence of economies of scale are not sufficient to create perfect competition. In addition, each firm must produce a good or service that has no characteristics that are unique to that firm so that consumers don't care from which firm they buy. Firms in perfect competition all look the same to the buyer.

Wheat farming, fishing, wood pulping and paper milling, the manufacture of paper cups and plastic shopping bags, lawn service, dry cleaning, and the provision of laundry services are all examples of highly competitive industries.

■ Other Market Types

Monopoly
A market in which one firm sells a good or service that has no close substitutes and a barrier blocks the entry of new firms.

Monopoly arises when one firm sells a good or service that has no close substitutes and a barrier blocks the entry of new firms. In some places, the phone, gas, electricity, and water suppliers are local monopolies—monopolies that are restricted to a given location. For many years, a global firm called DeBeers had a near international monopoly in diamonds. Microsoft has a near monopoly in producing the operating system for a personal computer.

Monopolistic competition
A market in which a large number of firms compete by making similar but slightly different products.

Monopolistic competition arises when a large number of firms compete by making similar but slightly different products. Each firm is the sole producer of the particular version of the good in question. For example, in the market for running shoes, Nike, Reebok, Fila, Asics, New Balance, and many others make their own versions of the perfect shoe. The term "monopolistic competition" reminds us that each firm has a monopoly on a particular brand of shoe but the firms compete with each other.

Oligopoly
A market in which a small number of interdependent firms compete.

Oligopoly arises when a small number of *interdependent* firms compete. Airplane manufacture is an example of oligopoly. Oligopolies might produce almost identical products, such as Duracell and Energizer batteries; or they might produce differentiated products, such as the colas produced by Coke and Pepsi.

We study perfect competition in this chapter, monopoly in Chapter 16, monopolistic competition in Chapter 17, and oligopoly in Chapter 18.

15.1   A FIRM'S PROFIT-MAXIMIZING CHOICES

A firm's objective is to maximize *economic profit*, which is equal to *total revenue* minus the *total cost* of production. *Normal profit*, the return that the firm's entrepreneur can obtain on average, is part of the firm's cost.

In the short run, a firm achieves its objective by deciding the quantity to produce. This quantity influences the firm's total revenue, total cost, and economic profit. In the long run, a firm achieves its objective by deciding whether to enter or exit a market.

These are the key decisions that a firm in perfect competition makes. Such a firm does *not* choose the price at which to sell its output. The firm in perfect competition is a **price taker**—it cannot influence the price of its product.

Price taker
A firm that cannot influence the price of the good or service that it produces.

■ Price Taker

To see why a firm in perfect competition is a price taker, imagine that you are a wheat farmer in Kansas. You have a thousand acres under cultivation—which sounds like a lot. But then you go on a drive through Colorado, Oklahoma, Texas, and back up to Nebraska and the Dakotas. You find unbroken stretches of wheat covering millions of acres. And you know that there are similar vistas in Canada, Argentina, Australia, and Ukraine. Your thousand acres are a drop in the ocean. Nothing makes your wheat any better than any other farmer's, and all the buyers of wheat know the price they must pay. If the going price of wheat is $4 a bushel, you are stuck with that price. You can't get a higher price than $4, and you have no incentive to offer it for less than $4 because you can sell your entire output at that price.

The producers of most agricultural products are price takers. We'll illustrate perfect competition with another agriculture example: the market for maple syrup. The next time you pour syrup on your pancakes, think about the competitive market that gets this product from the sap of the maple tree to your table!

Dave's Maple Syrup is one of more than 11,000 similar firms in the maple syrup market of North America. Dave is a price taker. Like the Kansas wheat farmer, he can sell any quantity he chooses at the going price but none above that price. Dave faces a *perfectly elastic* demand. The demand for Dave's syrup is perfectly elastic because syrup from Don Harlow, Casper Sugar Shack, and all the other maple farms in North America are *perfect substitutes* for Dave's syrup.

We'll explore Dave's decisions and their implications for the way a competitive market works. We begin by defining some revenue concepts.

Wheat farmers and maple syrup farmers are price takers.

■ Revenue Concepts

In perfect competition, market demand and market supply determine the price. A firm's *total revenue* equals this given price multiplied by the quantity sold. A firm's **marginal revenue** is the change in total revenue that results from a one-unit increase in the quantity sold.

Marginal revenue
The change in total revenue that results from a one-unit increase in the quantity sold.

In perfect competition, marginal revenue equals price.

The reason is that the firm can sell any quantity it chooses at the going market price. So if the firm sells one more unit, it sells it for the market price and total revenue increases by that amount. This increase in total revenue is marginal revenue.

The table in Figure 15.1 illustrates the equality of marginal revenue and price. The price of syrup is $8 a can. Total revenue is equal to the price multiplied by the quantity sold. So if Dave sells 10 cans, his total revenue is 10 × $8 = $80. If the quantity sold increases from 10 cans to 11 cans, total revenue increases from $80 to $88, so marginal revenue is $8 a can, the same as the price.

Figure 15.1 illustrates price determination and revenue in the perfectly competitive market. Market demand and market supply in part (a) determine the market price. Dave is a price taker, so he sells his syrup for the market price. The demand curve for Dave's syrup is the horizontal line at the market price in part (b). Because price equals marginal revenue, the demand curve for Dave's syrup is Dave's marginal revenue curve (MR). The total revenue curve (TR), in part (c), shows the total revenue at each quantity sold. Because he sells each can for the market price, the total revenue curve is an upward-sloping straight line.

■ Profit-Maximizing Output

As output increases, total revenue increases, but total cost also increases. Because of *decreasing marginal returns* (see Chapter 14, pp. 350–352), total cost eventually increases faster than total revenue. There is one output level that maximizes economic profit, and a perfectly competitive firm chooses this output level.

■ **FIGURE 15.1**

Demand, Price, and Revenue in Perfect Competition

MyEconLab Animation

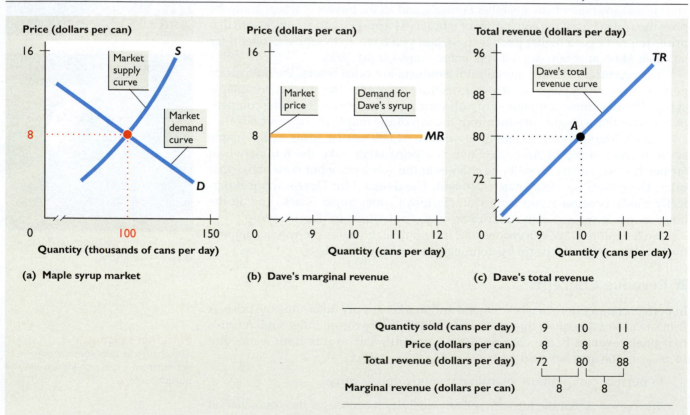

Quantity sold (cans per day)	9	10	11
Price (dollars per can)	8	8	8
Total revenue (dollars per day)	72	80	88
Marginal revenue (dollars per can)		8	8

Part (a) shows the market for maple syrup. The market price is $8 a can. The table calculates total revenue and marginal revenue.

Part (b) shows the demand curve for Dave's syrup, which is Dave's marginal revenue curve (MR).

Part (c) shows Dave's total revenue curve (TR). Point A corresponds to the second column of the table.

One way to find the profit-maximizing output is to use a firm's total revenue and total cost curves. Profit is maximized at the output level at which total revenue exceeds total cost by the largest amount. Figure 15.2 shows how to do this for Dave's Maple Syrup.

The table lists Dave's total revenue, total cost, and economic profit at different output levels. Figure 15.2 (a) shows the total revenue and total cost curves. These curves are graphs of the numbers shown in the first three columns of the table. The total revenue curve (*TR*) is the same as that in Figure 15.1(c). The total cost curve (*TC*) is similar to the one that you met in Chapter 14 (p. 356). Figure 15.2(b) is an economic profit curve.

Dave makes an economic profit on outputs between 4 and 13 cans a day. At outputs of fewer than 4 cans a day and more than 13 cans a day, he incurs an economic loss. Outputs of 4 cans and 13 cans are *break-even points*—points at which total cost equals total revenue and economic profit is zero.

The profit curve is at its highest when the vertical distance between the *TR* and *TC* curves is greatest. In this example, profit maximization occurs at an output of 10 cans a day. At this output, Dave's economic profit is $29 a day.

■ **FIGURE 15.2**

Total Revenue, Total Cost, and Economic Profit   MyEconLab Animation

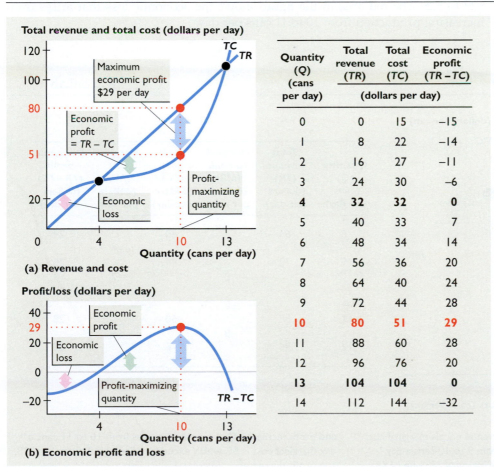

(a) Revenue and cost

(b) Economic profit and loss

Quantity (Q) (cans per day)	Total revenue (TR)	Total cost (TC)	Economic profit (TR – TC)
	(dollars per day)		
0	0	15	–15
1	8	22	–14
2	16	27	–11
3	24	30	–6
4	32	32	0
5	40	33	7
6	48	34	14
7	56	36	20
8	64	40	24
9	72	44	28
10	80	51	29
11	88	60	28
12	96	76	20
13	104	104	0
14	112	144	–32

In part (a), economic profit is the vertical distance between the total cost and total revenue curves. Dave's maximum economic profit is $29 a day ($80 − $51) when output is 10 cans a day.

In part (b), economic profit is the height of the profit curve.

■ Marginal Analysis and the Supply Decision

Another way to find the profit-maximizing output is to use *marginal analysis,* which compares marginal revenue, *MR,* with marginal cost, *MC.* As output increases, marginal revenue is constant but marginal cost eventually increases.

If marginal revenue exceeds marginal cost ($MR > MC$), then the revenue from selling one more unit exceeds the cost of producing that unit and an *increase* in output increases economic profit. If marginal revenue is less than marginal cost ($MR < MC$), then the revenue from selling one more unit is less than the cost of producing that unit and a *decrease* in output increases economic profit. If marginal revenue equals marginal cost ($MR = MC$), then the revenue from selling one more unit equals the cost incurred to produce that unit. Economic profit is maximized and either an increase or a decrease in output *decreases* economic profit. The rule $MR = MC$ is a prime example of marginal analysis.

Figure 15.3 illustrates these propositions. If Dave increases output from 9 cans to 10 cans a day, marginal revenue ($8) exceeds marginal cost ($7), so by producing the 10th can economic profit increases. The last column of the table shows that economic profit increases from $28 to $29. The blue area in the figure shows the increase in economic profit when production increases from 9 to 10 cans per day.

If Dave increases output from 10 cans to 11 cans a day, marginal revenue ($8) is less than marginal cost ($9), so by producing the 11th can, economic profit decreases. The last column of the table shows that economic profit decreases from $29 to $28. The red area in the figure shows the economic loss that arises from increasing production from 10 to 11 cans per day.

■ **FIGURE 15.3**

Profit-Maximizing Output

MyEconLab Animation

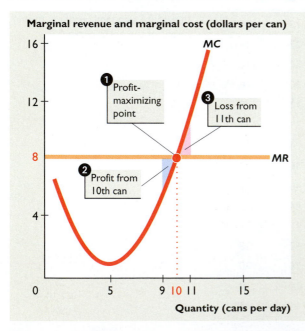

Quantity (Q) (cans per day)	Total revenue (TR) (dollars per day)	Marginal revenue (MR) (dollars per can)	Total cost (TC) (dollars per day)	Marginal cost (MC) (dollars per can)	Economic profit (TR − TC) (dollars per day)
8	64		40		24
		8		4	
9	72		44		28
		8		7	
10	80		51		29
		8		9	
11	88		60		28
		8		16	
12	96		76		20

❶ Profit is maximized when marginal revenue equals marginal cost at 10 cans a day. **❷** If output increases from 9 to 10 cans a day, marginal cost is $7, which is less than the marginal revenue of $8, and profit increases. **❸** If output increases from 10 to 11 cans a day, marginal cost is $9, which exceeds the marginal revenue of $8, and profit decreases.

Dave maximizes economic profit by producing 10 cans a day, the quantity at which marginal revenue equals marginal cost.

A firm's profit-maximizing output is its *quantity supplied*. Dave's *quantity supplied* at a price of $8 a can is 10 cans a day. If the price were higher than $8 a can, he would increase production. If the price were lower than $8 a can, he would decrease production. These profit-maximizing responses to different prices are the foundation of the law of supply:

Other things remaining the same, the higher the price of a good, the greater is the quantity supplied of that good.

■ Temporary Shutdown Decision

Sometimes, the price falls so low that a firm cannot cover its costs. What does the firm do in such a situation? The answer depends on whether the firm expects the low price to be permanent or temporary.

If a firm incurs an economic loss that it believes is permanent and sees no prospect of ending, the firm exits the market. We'll study this action later in this chapter when we look at the firm's decisions in the long run (pp. 386–392).

If a firm incurs an economic loss that it believes is temporary, it remains in the market, but it might temporarily shut down. To decide whether to produce or to shut down, the firm compares the loss it would incur in the two situations.

Loss When Shut Down

If the firm shuts down temporarily, it receives no revenue and incurs no variable costs. The firm still incurs fixed costs. So, if a firm shuts down, it incurs an economic loss equal to total fixed cost. This loss is the largest that a firm need incur.

Loss When Producing

A firm that produces an output receives revenue and incurs both fixed costs and variable costs. The firm incurs an economic loss equal to total fixed cost *plus* total variable cost *minus* total revenue. If total revenue exceeds total variable cost, the firm's economic loss is less than total fixed cost. But if total revenue is less than total variable cost, the firm's economic loss will exceed total fixed cost.

The Shutdown Point

If total revenue is less than total variable cost, a firm shuts down temporarily and limits its loss to an amount equal to total fixed cost. If total revenue just equals total variable cost, a firm is indifferent between producing and shutting down. This situation arises when price equals minimum average variable cost and the firm produces the quantity at which average variable cost is a minimum—called the **shutdown point.**

Figure 15.4 illustrates the firm's shutdown decision and the shutdown point that we've just described for Dave's maple syrup farm. Dave's average variable cost curve is *AVC* and his marginal cost curve is *MC*. Average variable cost has a minimum of $3 a can when output is 7 cans a day. The *MC* curve intersects the *AVC* curve at its minimum. (We explained this relationship between the marginal and average values of a variable in Chapter 14; see pp. 352–353 and pp. 356–358.) The figure shows the marginal revenue curve *MR* when the price is $3 a can, a *price equal to minimum average variable cost.*

Shutdown point
The point at which price equals minimum average variable cost and the quantity produced is that at which average variable cost is at its minimum.

■ **FIGURE 15.4**

The Shutdown Decision

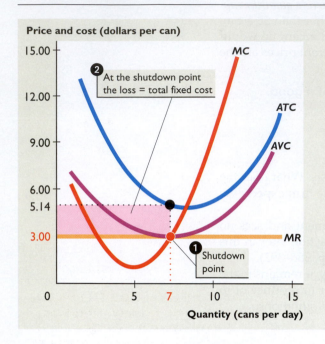

Quantity (Q) (cans per day)	Total revenue (TR)	Total variable cost (TVC)	Total fixed cost (TFC)	Total cost (TC)	Economic profit (TR − TC)
		(dollars per day)			
6	18	19	15	34	−16
7	21	21	15	36	−15
8	24	25	15	40	−16

❶ The shutdown point is at minimum average variable cost. At a price below minimum average variable cost, the firm shuts down and produces no output. At a price equal to minimum average variable cost, the firm is indifferent between shutting down and producing no output or producing the output at minimum average variable cost. Either way, ❷ the firm minimizes its economic loss and incurs a loss equal to total fixed cost.

If Dave produces at the shutdown point, he produces 7 cans a day and sells them for $3 a can. He incurs an economic loss equal to $2.14 a can and a total economic loss of $15 a day, which equals his total fixed cost. If Dave shuts down, he also incurs an economic loss equal to total fixed cost.

The table lists Dave's total revenue, total variable cost, total fixed cost, total cost, and economic profit at three output levels. The middle output, 7 cans a day, is that at which Dave's average variable cost is at its minimum—$3 a can. By examining the numbers in the table, you can see that when the price is $3 a can, Dave incurs a loss equal to total fixed cost by producing 7 cans a day.

■ **The Firm's Short-Run Supply Curve**

A perfectly competitive firm's short-run supply curve shows how the firm's profit-maximizing output varies as the price varies, other things remaining the same. This supply curve is based on the marginal analysis and shutdown decision that we've just explored.

Figure 15.5 derives Dave's supply curve. Part (a) shows the marginal cost and average variable cost curves, and part (b) shows the supply curve. There is a direct link between the marginal cost and average variable cost curves and the firm's supply curve. Let's see what that link is.

In Figure 15.5(a), if the price is above minimum average variable cost, Dave maximizes profit by producing the output at which marginal cost equals marginal revenue, which also equals price. We determine the quantity produced at each price from the marginal cost curve. At a price of $8 a can, the marginal revenue curve is MR_1 and Dave maximizes profit by producing 10 cans a day. If the price rises to $12 a can, the marginal revenue curve is MR_2 and Dave increases production to 11 cans a day.

If price equals minimum average variable cost, Dave maximizes profit (minimizes loss) by either producing the quantity at the shutdown point or shutting down and producing no output. But if the price is below minimum average variable cost, Dave shuts down and produces no output.

Figure 15.5(b) shows Dave's short-run supply curve. At prices that exceed minimum average variable cost, the supply curve is the same as the marginal cost curve. At prices below minimum average variable cost, Dave shuts down and produces nothing. His supply curve runs along the vertical axis. At a price of $3 a can, Dave is indifferent between shutting down and producing 7 cans a day at the shutdown point (T). Either way, he incurs a loss equal to total fixed cost.

So far, we have studied one firm in isolation. We have seen that the firm's profit-maximizing actions depend on the price, which the firm takes as given. In the next section, you'll learn how market supply is determined.

FIGURE 15.5

A Perfectly Competitive Firm's Supply Curve

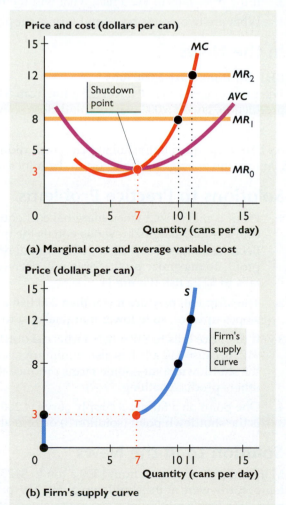

(a) Marginal cost and average variable cost

(b) Firm's supply curve

Part (a) shows that at $12 a can, Dave produces 11 cans a day; at $8 a can, he produces 10 cans a day; and at $3 a can, he produces either 7 cans a day or nothing. At any price below $3 a can, Dave produces nothing. The minimum average variable cost is the shutdown point.

Part (b) shows Dave's supply curve. At $3 a can, Dave is indifferent between producing the quantity at the shutdown point T and not producing. At all prices above $3 a can, Dave's supply curve is made up of the marginal cost curve, in part (a), *above* minimum average variable cost. At all prices below $3 a can, Dave produces nothing and his supply curve runs along the vertical axis.

CHECKPOINT 15.1

Explain a perfectly competitive firm's profit-maximizing choices and derive its supply curve.

Practice Problems

1. Sarah's Salmon Farm produced 1,000 fish last week. The marginal cost was $30 a fish, average variable cost was $20 a fish, and the market price was $25 a fish. Did Sarah maximize profit? If Sarah did not maximize profit and if nothing has changed will she increase or decrease the number of fish she produces to maximize her profit this week?

Use the following information to work Problems 2 to 4.

Trout farming is a perfectly competitive industry and all trout farms have the same cost curves. When the market price is $25 a fish, farms maximize profit by producing 200 fish a week. At this output, average total cost is $20 a fish, and average variable cost is $15 a fish. Minimum average variable cost is $12 a fish.

2. If the price falls to $20 a fish, will a farm produce 200 fish a week?

3. If the price falls to $12 a fish, what will the trout farmer do?

4. What are two points on a trout farm's supply curve?

In the News

BHP Billiton to axe 6,000 jobs
The price of coal has fallen to $125 a ton from $300 a ton. BHP Billiton will cut production, lay off 6,000 workers, and close some mines for six months.

Source: FT.com, January 21, 2009

As BHP responded to the fall in price, how did its marginal cost change? What is minimum average variable cost in the mines that closed?

Solutions to Practice Problems

1. Profit is maximized when marginal cost equals marginal revenue. In perfect competition, marginal revenue equals the market price and is $25 a fish. Because marginal cost exceeded marginal revenue, Sarah did not maximize profit. To maximize profit, Sarah will decrease her output until marginal cost falls to $25 a fish (Figure 1).

2. The farm will produce fewer than 200 fish a week. The marginal cost curve slopes upward, so to lower marginal cost to $20, the farm cuts production.

3. If the price falls to $12 a fish, farms cut output until marginal cost equals $12. Because $12 a fish is also minimum average variable cost, farms are at the shutdown point—some farms produce the profit-maximizing output and others produce nothing.

4. One point on a farmer's supply curve is 200 fish at $25 a fish. Another point is the shutdown point (solution 3) or zero at a price below $12 a fish.

Solution to In the News

Marginal cost decreased from $300 a ton to $125 a ton. The mines that closed temporarily were at the shutdown point. The price of $125 a ton is equal to or below the firm's minimum average variable cost.

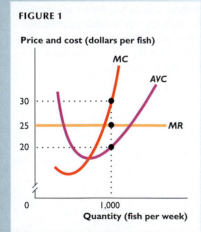

FIGURE 1

15.2   OUTPUT, PRICE, AND PROFIT IN THE SHORT RUN

Demand and supply determine the price and quantity in a perfectly competitive market. We first study short-run supply when the number of firms is fixed.

Market Supply in the Short Run

The market supply curve in the short run shows the quantity supplied at each price by a fixed number of firms. The quantity supplied at a given price is the sum of the quantities supplied by all firms at that price.

   Figure 15.6 shows the supply curve for the competitive syrup market. In this example, the market consists of 10,000 firms exactly like Dave's Maple Syrup. The table shows how the market supply schedule is constructed. The shutdown point occurs at a price of $3 a can. At prices below $3 a can, every firm in the market shuts down; the quantity supplied is zero. At a price of $3 a can, each firm is indifferent between shutting down and producing nothing or operating and producing 7 cans a day. The quantity supplied by each firm is *either* 0 or 7 cans, and the quantity supplied in the market is *between* 0 (all firms shut down) and 70,000 (all firms produce 7 cans a day each). At prices above $3 a can, we sum the quantities supplied by the 10,000 firms, so the quantity supplied in the market is 10,000 times the quantity supplied by one firm.

   At prices below $3 a can, the market supply curve runs along the price axis. Supply is perfectly inelastic. At $3 a can, the market supply curve is horizontal. Supply is perfectly elastic. Above $3 a can, the supply curve is upward sloping.

■ FIGURE 15.6

The Market Supply Curve   MyEconLab Animation

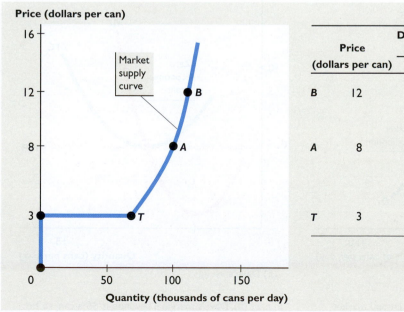

	Price	Dave's quantity supplied	Market quantity supplied
	(dollars per can)	(cans per day)	
B	12	11	110,000
A	8	10	100,000
T	3	0 or 7	0 to 70,000

A market with 10,000 identical firms has a supply schedule like that of an individual firm, but the quantity supplied is 10,000 times greater. Market supply is perfectly elastic at the price at which the shutdown point occurs.

■ Short-Run Equilibrium in Normal Times

Market demand and market supply determine the price and quantity bought and sold. Figure 15.7(a) shows a short-run equilibrium in the syrup market. The market supply curve S is the same as that in Figure 15.6.

If the demand curve D_1 shows market demand, the equilibrium price is $5 a can. Although market demand and market supply determine this price, each firm takes the price as given and produces its profit-maximizing output, which is 9 cans a day. Because the market has 10,000 firms, market output is 90,000 cans a day.

Figure 15.7(b) shows the situation that Dave faces. The price is $5 a can, so Dave's marginal revenue is constant at $5 a can. Dave maximizes profit by producing 9 cans a day.

Figure 15.7(b) also shows Dave's average total cost curve (ATC). Recall that average total cost is the cost per unit produced. It equals total cost divided by the quantity of output produced.

Here, when Dave produces 9 cans a day, his average total cost is $5 a can, exactly the same as the market price. So Dave sells syrup for exactly the same price as his average cost of production and economic profit is zero.

Making zero economic profit means that Dave earns normal profit from running his business.

The short-run equilibrium in which a firm makes zero economic profit is just one of three possible situations. A competitive market might also deliver a positive economic profit or an economic loss. Let's look at these other two cases.

■ FIGURE 15.7

Zero Economic Profit in the Short Run

MyEconLab Animation

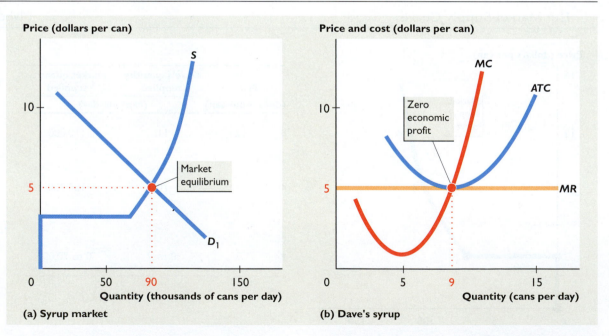

(a) Syrup market

(b) Dave's syrup

In part (a), with market demand curve D_1 and market supply curve S, the equilibrium market price is $5 a can.

In part (b), Dave's marginal revenue is $5 a can, so he produces 9 cans a day. At this quantity, price ($5) equals average total cost, so Dave makes zero economic profit.

■ Short-Run Equilibrium in Good Times

Market demand might be greater or less than D_1 in Figure 15.7 and the price might be higher or lower than $5 a can. Figure 15.8(a) shows another short-run equilibrium in the syrup market. The supply curve S is the same as that in Figure 15.6.

If the demand curve D_2 shows market demand, the equilibrium price is $8 a can. Although market demand and market supply determine this price, each firm takes the price as given and produces its profit-maximizing output, which is 10 cans a day. Because the market has 10,000 firms, market output is 100,000 cans a day.

Figure 15.8(b) shows the situation that Dave faces. The price is $8 a can, so Dave's marginal revenue is constant at $8 a can. Dave maximizes profit by producing 10 cans a day.

Figure 15.8(b) also shows Dave's average total cost curve (*ATC*). Recall that average total cost is the cost per unit produced. It equals total cost divided by the quantity of output produced. Here, when Dave produces 10 cans a day, his average total cost is $5.10 a can. So the price of $8 a can exceeds average total cost by $2.90 a can. This amount is Dave's economic profit per can.

If we multiply the economic profit per can of $2.90 by the number of cans, 10 a day, we arrive at Dave's economic profit, which is $29 a day.

The blue rectangle shows this economic profit. The height of that rectangle is the profit per can, $2.90, and the length is the quantity of cans, 10 a day, so the area of the rectangle (height × length) measures Dave's economic profit of $29 a day.

■ **FIGURE 15.8**

Positive Economic Profit in the Short Run

MyEconLab Animation

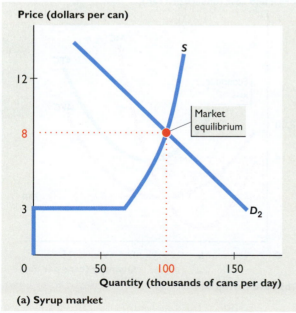

(a) Syrup market

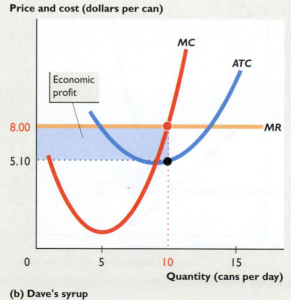

(b) Dave's syrup

In part (a), with market demand curve D_2 and market supply curve S, the equilibrium market price is $8 a can.

In part (b), marginal revenue is $8 a can. Dave produces 10 cans a day. Because price ($8) exceeds average total cost ($5.10), the firm makes a positive economic profit.

■ Short-Run Equilibrium in Bad Times

Figure 15.9 shows the syrup market in a loss-incurring situation. The market demand curve is now D_3. The market still has 10,000 firms and their costs are the same as before, so the market supply curve, S, is also the same as before.

With the demand and supply curves shown in Figure 15.9(a), the equilibrium price of syrup is $3 a can and the equilibrium quantity is 70,000 cans a day.

Figure 15.9(b) shows the situation that Dave faces. The price is $3 a can, so Dave's marginal revenue is constant at $3 a can. Dave maximizes profit by producing 7 cans a day.

Figure 15.9(b) also shows Dave's average total cost curve (*ATC*), and you can see that when Dave produces 7 cans a day, his average total cost is $5.14 a can. Now the price of $3 a can is less than average total cost by $2.14 a can. This amount is Dave's economic loss per can. If we multiply the economic loss per can of $2.14 by the number of cans, 7 a day, we arrive at Dave's economic loss, which is shown by the red rectangle.

Figure 15.9(b) also shows Dave's average variable cost (*AVC*) curve. Notice that Dave is operating at the shutdown point. Dave might equally well produce no output. Either way, his economic loss would be equal to his total fixed cost. If the price were a bit higher than $3, Dave would still incur an economic loss, but a smaller one. And if the price were lower than $3, Dave would shut down and incur an economic loss equal to total fixed cost.

■ **FIGURE 15.9**

Economic Loss in the Short Run

MyEconLab Animation

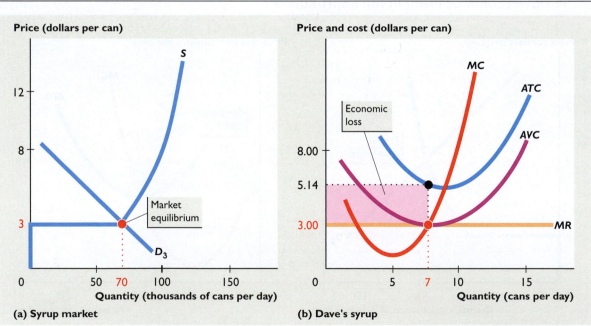

(a) Syrup market

(b) Dave's syrup

In part (a), with market demand curve D_3 and market supply curve S, the equilibrium market price is $3 a can.

In part (b), Dave's marginal revenue is $3 a can, so he produces 7 cans a day. At this quantity, price ($3) is less than average total cost ($5.14), so Dave incurs an economic loss shown by the red rectangle.

CHECKPOINT 15.2

Explain how output, price, and profit are determined in the short run.

Practice Problems

Tulip growing is perfectly competitive and all growers have the same costs. The market price is $25 a bunch, and each grower maximizes profit by producing 2,000 bunches a week. Average total cost is $20 a bunch, and average variable cost is $15 a bunch. Minimum average variable cost is $12 a bunch.

1. What is the economic profit that each grower is making in the short run?
2. What is the price at the grower's shutdown point?
3. What is each grower's economic profit at the shutdown point?

In the News

Corn hits record high price
Corn prices have surged 80 percent in the past year, driven up by a global rush for grains to feed people and livestock and to make biofuel.

Source: *USA Today*, June 26, 2008

Explain why the price of corn surged. Explain how marginal revenue, the marginal cost of producing corn, and the farm's economic profit changed.

Solutions to Practice Problems

1. The market price ($25) exceeds the average total cost ($20), so growers make an economic profit of $5 a bunch. Each grower produces 2,000 bunches a week, so a grower's economic profit is $10,000 a week. Figure 1 illustrates the situation. The grower's marginal revenue equals the market price ($25). The grower maximizes profit by producing 2,000 bunches, so at 2,000 bunches the marginal cost curve (*MC*) cuts the marginal revenue curve (*MR*). The average total cost of producing 2,000 bunches is $20, so the *ATC* curve passes through this point. Economic profit equals the area of the blue rectangle.

2. The price at which a grower will shut down temporarily is equal to minimum average variable cost—$12 a bunch (Figure 1).

3. At the shutdown point, the grower incurs an economic loss equal to total fixed cost. Figure 2 shows the data to calculate *TFC*. When 2,000 bunches a week are grown, *ATC* is $20 a bunch and *AVC* is $15 a bunch. *ATC* = *AFC* + *AVC*, so *AFC* is $5 a bunch. Total fixed cost equals $10,000 a week—*FTC* = *AFC* × *Q*, $5 a bunch × 2,000 bunches a week. At the shutdown point, the grower incurs an economic loss of $10,000 a week.

Solution to In the News

An increase in the market demand for corn increased the market price. The market is competitive, so the farm's marginal revenue (equal to market price) increased. To maximize profit (produce the quantity at which marginal revenue equals marginal cost), the farm increases the quantity produced and moves up along its *MC* curve. In the short run, economic profit increases.

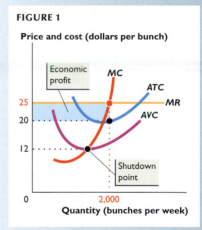

FIGURE 1

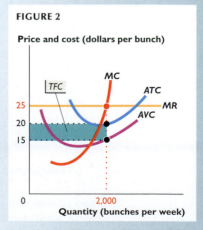

FIGURE 2

15.3 OUTPUT, PRICE, AND PROFIT IN THE LONG RUN

Competitive markets are in a constant state of change. Price, quantity, and economic profit fluctuate as demand and supply change. None of the three situations that we described on the previous pages—normal times, good times, or bad times—last forever in perfect competition. Market forces operate to compete away economic profits and eliminate economic losses to move the price toward the lowest possible price. That price equals minimum average total cost. In the long run, a firm in perfect competition produces at minimum average total cost and makes zero economic profit. (The firm's entrepreneur earns normal profit—part of the firm's total costs.)

Figure 15.10 illustrates a perfectly competitive market in long-run equilibrium and highlights the forces that bring the market to this situation. In Figure 15.10(a), the firm's average total cost curve is ATC, and the firm produces at the point of minimum average total cost—9 cans a day at an average total cost of $5 a can. If the price rises above or falls below $5 a can, market forces operate to move the price back toward $5 a can. The arrows pointing toward $5 represent these forces.

In Figure 15.10(b) the market demand curve is D. With this market demand, the price equals minimum average total cost only if the market supply curve is S. If supply is less than S (the supply curve is to the left of S), the price is above $5 a can; if supply exceeds S (the supply curve is to the right of S), the price is below $5 a can. Market forces operate to shift the supply curve back to S, and the arrows pointing toward S represent these forces.

■ **FIGURE 15.10**

Long-Run Equilibrium

MyEconLab Animation

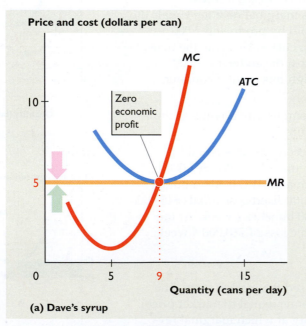

(a) Dave's syrup

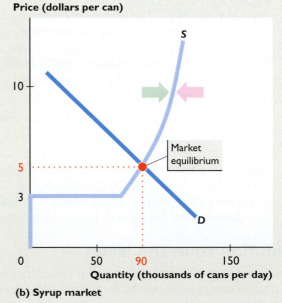

(b) Syrup market

In part (a), minimum average total cost is $5 a can. In long-run equilibrium, the price and marginal revenue are pulled to this level. The firm makes zero economic profit.

In part (b), if the price is above $5 a can, above minimum ATC in part (a), supply increases and the price falls. If the price is below $5, supply decreases and the price rises.

■ Entry and Exit

Entry and exit are the market forces that shift the supply curve and move the price to minimum average total cost in the long run. In the short run, firms might make a positive economic profit (as in Figure 15.8) or incur an economic loss (as in Figure 15.9). But in the long run, firms makes zero economic profit.

In the long run, firms respond to economic profit and economic loss by either entering or exiting a market. New firms enter a market in which the existing firms are making economic profits, and some existing firms exit a market in which firms are incurring economic losses. Temporary economic profit or temporary economic loss, like a win or loss at a casino, does not trigger entry and exit. But the prospect of persistent economic profit or economic loss does.

Entry and exit influence the market price, the quantity produced, and economic profit. The immediate effect of the decision to enter or exit a market is to shift the market supply curve. If more firms enter a market, supply increases and the market supply curve shifts rightward. If some firms exit a market, supply decreases and the market supply curve shifts leftward.

Let's see what happens when new firms enter a market.

The Effects of Entry

Figure 15.11 shows the effects of entry. Initially, the market is in long-run equilibrium. Demand is D_0, supply is S_0, the price is $5 a can, and the quantity is 90,000 cans a day. A surge in the popularity of syrup increases demand, and the demand curve shifts to D_1. The price rises to $8 a can, and firms in the syrup market increase output to 100,000 cans a day and make an economic profit.

Times are good for syrup producers like Dave, so other potential syrup producers want some of the action. New firms begin to enter the market. As they do

With the prospect of economic profit, a new business opens.

■ FIGURE 15.11

The Effects of Entry

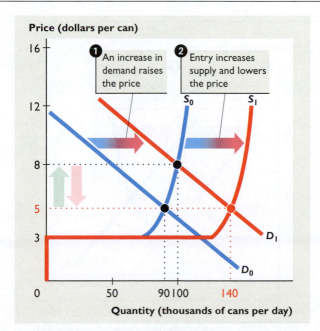

Price (dollars per can)

❶ An increase in demand raises the price

❷ Entry increases supply and lowers the price

Quantity (thousands of cans per day)

Starting in long-run equilibrium, ❶ demand increases and the market demand curve shifts from D_0 to D_1. The price rises from $5 to $8 a can.

Economic profit brings entry. ❷ As firms enter the market, the market supply curve shifts rightward, from S_0 to S_1. The equilibrium price falls from $8 to $5 a can, and the quantity produced increases from 100,000 to 140,000 cans a day.

so, supply increases and the market supply curve shifts rightward to S_1. With the greater market supply and unchanged market demand, the market price falls from $8 to $5 a can and the equilibrium quantity increases to 140,000 cans a day.

Market output increases, but because the price falls, Dave and the other producers decrease output. As the price falls, each firm's output gradually returns to its original level. Because the number of firms in the market increases, the market as a whole produces more.

As the price falls, each firm's economic profit decreases. When the price falls to $5 a can, economic profit disappears and each firm makes zero economic profit. The entry process stops, and the market is again in long-run equilibrium.

You have just discovered a key proposition:

> **Economic profit is an incentive for new firms to enter a market, but as they do so, the price falls and the economic profit of each existing firm decreases.**

■ The Effects of Exit

Figure 15.12 shows the effects of exit. Again we begin on demand curve D_0 and supply curve S_0 in long-run equilibrium. Now suppose that the development of a new high-nutrition, low-fat breakfast food decreases the demand for pancakes, and as a result, the demand for maple syrup decreases. The demand curve shifts from D_0 to D_2. Firms' costs are the same as before, so the market supply curve is S_0.

With demand at D_2 and supply at S_0, the price falls to $3 a can and 70,000 cans a day are produced. The firms in the syrup market incur economic losses.

Times are tough for syrup producers, and Dave must seriously think about leaving his dream business and finding some other way of making a living. But other producers are in the same situation as Dave, and some start to exit the market while Dave is still thinking through his options.

Economic loss brings exit.

■ **FIGURE 15.12**

The Effects of Exit

MyEconLab Animation

Starting in long-run equilibrium, ❶ demand decreases and the market demand curve shifts from D_0 to D_2. The price falls from $5 to $3 a can.

Economic loss brings exit. ❷ As firms exit the market, the market supply curve shifts leftward, from S_0 to S_2. The equilibrium price rises from $3 to $5 a can, and the quantity produced decreases from 70,000 to 50,000 cans a day.

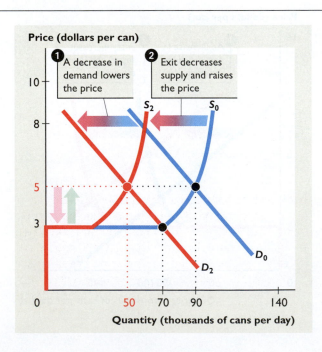

As firms exit, the market supply curve shifts leftward to S_2. With the decrease in market supply, output decreases from 70,000 to 50,000 cans and the market price rises from $3 to $5 a can.

As the price rises, Dave and each other firm that remains in the market move up along their supply curves and increase output. That is, for each firm that remains in the market, the profit-maximizing output *increases*. As the price rises and each firm sells more, economic loss decreases. When the price rises to $5 a can, each firm makes a zero economic profit. Dave earns normal profit (part of the firm's total cost) and he is happy that he can still make a living producing syrup.

You have just discovered a second key proposition:

Economic loss is an incentive for firms to exit a market, but as they do so, the price rises and the economic loss of each remaining firm decreases.

■ Change in Demand

Initially, a competitive market is in long-run equilibrium and the firms are making zero economic profit (and entrepreneurs are earning normal profit). Now market demand increases. The market price rises, firms increase production to keep marginal cost equal to price, and firms make an economic profit. The market is now in short-run equilibrium but not in long-run equilibrium.

Economic profit is an incentive for new firms to enter the market. As firms enter, market supply increases and the market price falls. With a lower price, firms decrease output to keep marginal cost equal to price.

Notice that as firms enter the market, market output increases, but each firm's output decreases. Eventually, enough firms enter to eliminate economic profit and the market returns to long-run equilibrium.

The key difference between the initial long-run equilibrium and the new long-run equilibrium is the number of firms. A permanent increase in demand increases the number of firms. Each firm produces the same output in the new long-run equilibrium as initially and makes zero economic profit. In the process of moving from the initial equilibrium to the new one, firms make economic profits.

The demand for airline travel in the world economy increased during the 1990s, and the deregulation of the airlines freed up firms to seek profit opportunities in this market. The result was a massive rate of entry of new airlines. The process of competition and change in the airline market were similar to what we have just studied.

A decrease in demand triggers a similar response, except in the opposite direction. The decrease in demand brings a lower price, economic loss, and exit. Exit decreases market supply, raises the price, and eliminates the economic loss.

■ Technological Change

Firms are constantly discovering lower-cost techniques of production. For example, the cost of producing a personal computer has fallen. So has the cost of producing an MP3 player and other electronic products. Most cost-saving production techniques can be implemented only by investing in a new plant. Consequently, it takes time for a technological advance to spread through an industry. Firms whose plants are on the verge of being replaced are quick to adopt the new technology, while firms whose plants have recently been replaced continue to operate with old technology until they can no longer cover their average variable cost. Once average variable cost cannot be covered, a firm scraps even a relatively new plant (embodying an old technology) in favor of a plant with a new technology.

New technology lowers cost, so as firms adopt a new technology, their cost curves shift downward. With lower costs, firms are willing to supply a given quantity at a lower price, or, equivalently, they are willing to supply a larger quantity at a given price. In other words, market supply increases, and the market supply curve shifts rightward. With a given demand, the quantity produced increases and the price falls.

Firms that adopt the new technology make an economic profit, so new-technology firms enter. Firms that stick with the old technology incur economic losses, so they either exit or switch to the new technology. As new-technology firms enter and old-technology firms exit, the price falls and the quantity produced increases. Eventually, the market arrives at a long-run equilibrium in

EYE on the AUTO INDUSTRY
Why Did GM Fail?

On June 1, 2009, General Motors filed for bankruptcy protection.

Old GM

GM Chief Executive Officer Fritz Henderson blames GM's failure on the expansion of global competitors who produce at lower costs.

GM's operating costs are both fixed plant costs and variable labor costs. The firm also has "legacy" costs: fixed costs of honoring its pension obligations to its retirees and its debt obligations to its bond holders.

In 2008, (in round numbers) GM produced 8 million vehicles, received a total revenue of $144 billion, had a total cost of $176 billion, and incurred an economic loss of $32 billion. To remain in business, the firm obtained loans from the U.S. and Canadian governments.

The figure shows the situation that old GM faced in 2008. The average price at which it could sell a vehicle

was $18,000. To maximize profit (minimize loss), GM sold 8 million vehicles. Average total cost at 8 million vehicles was $22,000, so the economic loss

was $4,000 per vehicle. With no prospect of turning this loss around, old GM had no alternative but to exit the industry.

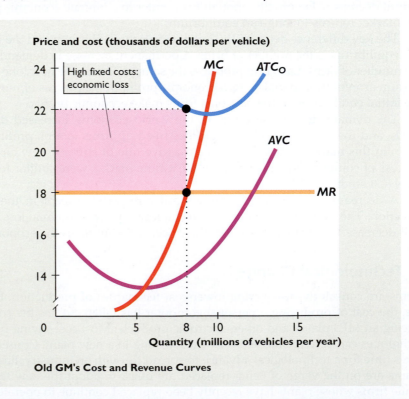

Old GM's Cost and Revenue Curves

which all the firms use the new technology and each firm makes zero economic profit.

Because competition eliminates economic profit in the long run, technological change brings only temporary gains to firms. But the lower prices and better products that technological advances bring are permanent gains for consumers.

The process that we've just described is one in which some firms experience economic profits and others experience economic losses—a period of dynamic change for a market. Some firms do well, and others do badly. Often, the process has a geographical dimension—the expanding new-technology firms bring prosperity to what was once the boondocks, and with old-technology firms going out of business, traditional industrial regions decline. Sometimes, the new-technology firms are in a foreign country, while the old-technology firms are in the domestic economy. The information revolution of the 1990s produced many examples of changes like these. Commercial banking (a competitive but less than perfectly

---

New GM

On the day old GM filed for bankruptcy, its executives started to talk about the new GM. The firm's "restructuring" Web site reported plans for cost savings and investment in new green technology vehicles.

Creating a new profitable GM is a complex and detailed task that will require creative thinking and action by its management team. But one feature of the restructuring is crucial: cutting the fixed legacy costs.

Restructuring GM won't change the market price of vehicles—the global market determines that price. Nor is the restructuring likely to have much effect on the marginal cost of producing a vehicle—technology and factor prices determine marginal cost.

Cutting fixed cost is the only point at which the new GM can have a major impact on its profitability.

The figure (right) shows the minimum that the new GM must do: It must cut fixed cost to shift its ATC curve downward from ATC_O to ATC_N.

GM can then maximize profit at the same quantity, 8 million vehicles a year, but operate with an average total cost equal to the price of a vehicle and so make zero economic profit.

A bigger cut in fixed cost would enable the new GM to make a positive economic profit. But in the long run as new firms enter the global market, economic profit will likely fall to zero.

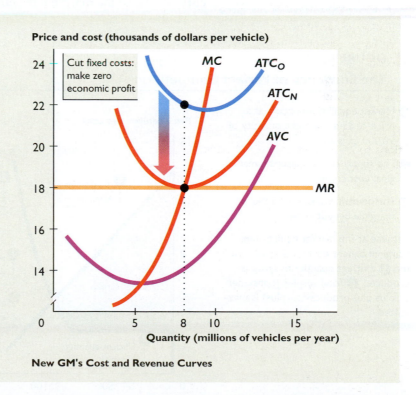

New GM's Cost and Revenue Curves

competitive industry), was traditionally concentrated in New York, San Francisco, and other large cities, but now flourishes in Charlotte, North Carolina, which has become the nation's number three commercial banking city. Television shows and movies, traditionally made in Los Angeles and New York, are now made in large numbers in Orlando and Toronto.

Technological advances are not confined to the information and entertainment markets. Food production has seen major technological change, and today, genetic engineering is fueling that change.

◼ Is Perfect Competition Efficient?

Perfect competition is efficient. To see why, first recall the conditions for an efficient allocation of resources. Resources are used efficiently when it is not possible to get more of one good without giving up something that is valued more highly. To achieve this outcome, marginal benefit must equal marginal cost. That is the outcome that perfect competition achieves.

We derive a firm's supply curve in perfect competition from its marginal cost curve. The supply curve is the marginal cost curve at all points above the minimum of average variable cost (the shutdown price). Because the market supply curve is found by summing the quantities supplied by all the firms at each price, the market supply curve is the entire market's marginal cost curve.

The demand curve is the marginal benefit curve. Because the supply curve and demand curve intersect at the equilibrium price, that price equals both marginal cost and marginal benefit.

Figure 15.13 illustrates the efficiency of perfect competition. We've labeled the demand curve $D = MB$ and the supply curve $S = MC$ to remind you that these curves are also the marginal benefit (MB) and marginal cost (MC) curves.

◼ **FIGURE 15.13**

The Efficiency of Perfect Competition

MyEconLab Animation

❶ Market equilibrium occurs at a price of $5 a can and a quantity of 90,000 cans a day.

❷ The supply curve is also the marginal cost curve.

❸ The demand curve is also the marginal benefit curve.

Because at the market equilibrium, marginal benefit equals marginal cost, the ❹ efficient quantity of syrup is produced. ❺ Total surplus (consumer surplus plus producer surplus) is maximized.

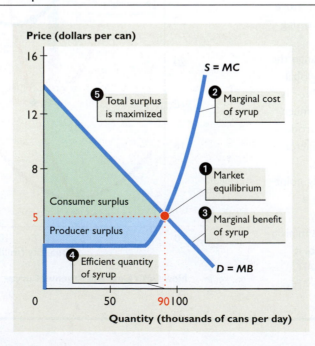

These curves intersect at the equilibrium price and quantity. The price equals marginal benefit and marginal cost, and the equilibrium quantity is efficient. The total surplus, which is the sum of consumer surplus and producer surplus, is maximized. Any departure from this outcome is inferior to it and brings an avoidable deadweight loss.

■ Is Perfect Competition Fair?

You studied the fairness of markets in Chapter 6 (pp. 159–161) and saw that there are two views of fairness: fair rules and fair results. The outcome is fair in the rules view if property rights are enforced and people acquire resources, goods, and services through voluntary exchange. The outcome is fair in the results view if the poorest aren't too poor and the richest aren't too rich, but there is no unique criterion for determining what is too poor or too rich.

In the short run, if a temporary shortage occurs in a competitive market, perhaps caused by bad weather or natural disaster, the price shoots upward. In such situations, some people might make large windfall gains and others, possibly a majority, might be confronted with high prices for essential items. In the fair results view, such a situation might be considered unfair.

But perfect competition in the long run seems to be fair on both views of fairness. It places no restrictions on anyone's actions, all trade is voluntary, consumers pay the lowest possible prices, and entrepreneurs earn only normal profit.

EYE on YOUR LIFE
The Perfect Competition that You Encounter

Many of the markets that you encounter every day are highly competitive and almost perfectly competitive. And while you don't run into perfect competition on a daily basis, you do have dealings in some perfectly competitive markets. Two of those markets are the Internet auctions organized by eBay and one of its subsidiaries, StubHub.

If you have a ticket for a game between the Giants and the Braves but can't use it, you can sell it on StubHub for the going market price (minus a commission). And if you're desperate to see the game but missed out on getting a ticket, you can buy

one for the going price (plus a commission) on the same Web site.

StubHub takes a commission and makes a profit. But competition between StubHub, TicketMaster, and other ticket brokers ensure that profits are competed away in the long run, with entrepreneurs earning normal profit.

Just about every good or service that you buy and take for granted, no matter where you buy it, is available because of the forces of competition. Your home, your food, your clothing, your books, your DVDs, your MP3 files, your computer, your bike, your car, . . . ; the list is endless. No one organizes all the magic that enables

you to buy this vast array of products. Competitive markets and entrepreneurs striving to make the largest possible profit make it happen.

When either demand or technology changes and makes the current allocation of resources the wrong one, the market swiftly and silently acts. It sends signals to entrepreneurs that bring entry and exit and a new and efficient use of scarce resources.

It is no exaggeration or hype to say that your entire life is influenced by and benefits immeasurably from the forces of competition. Adam Smith's invisible hand might be hidden from view, but it is enormously powerful.

CHECKPOINT 15.3

Explain how output, price, and profit are determined in the long run and explain why perfect competition is efficient.

Practice Problems

Tulip growing is a perfectly competitive industry, and all tulip growers have the same cost curves. The market price of tulips is $15 a bunch, and each grower maximizes profit by producing 1,500 bunches a week. The average total cost of producing tulips is $21 a bunch. Minimum average variable cost is $12 a bunch, and the minimum average total cost is $18 a bunch.

1. What is a tulip grower's economic profit in the short run and how does the number of tulip growers change in the long run?

2. In the long run, what is the price and the tulip grower's economic profit?

In the News

Cotton farmers face a formidable foe

The growing season has just begun and pigweed is spreading quickly, towering above the plants, and crowding out sunlight. This new breed of pigweed is resistant to herbicides. Scientists estimate that thousands of acres have already been plowed back, and that it could cost $20 an acre to fend off the weed.

Source: *USA Today*, July 18, 2008

How will the cost of growing cotton change? What effect will this weed have on the cotton market in the short run? How will the cotton market change in the long run?

Solutions to Practice Problems

1. The price is less than average total cost, so the tulip grower is incurring an economic loss in the short run. Because the price exceeds minimum average variable cost, the tulip grower continues to produce. The economic loss equals the loss per bunch ($21 minus $15) multiplied by the number of bunches (1,500), which equals $9,000 (Figure 1).

   Because tulip growers are incurring economic losses, some growers will exit in the long run. The number of tulip growers will decrease.

2. In the long run, the price will be such that economic profit is zero. That is, as growers exit, the price will rise until it equals minimum average total cost. The long-run price will be $18 a bunch (Figure 2).

   A tulip grower's economic profit in the long run will be zero because average total cost equals price (Figure 2).

Solution to In the News

To produce any cotton, farms will have to incur a cost of $20 an acre. This cost is a fixed cost, so the farm's marginal cost does not change. With acres of cotton already plowed back, the market supply of cotton will decrease in the short run and the market price will rise. To maximize profit, farms produce the quantity at which marginal revenue equals marginal cost. With a higher price and no change in marginal cost, farms with a crop will make positive economic profit. In the long run, farms will grow more cotton and the market price will fall until all farms are making zero economic profit.

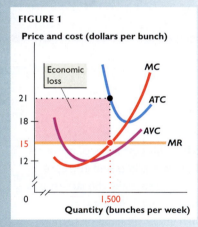

FIGURE 1

Price and cost (dollars per bunch)

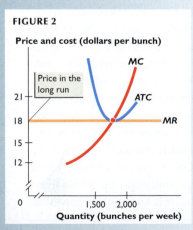

FIGURE 2

Price and cost (dollars per bunch)

CHAPTER SUMMARY

Key Points

1   Explain a perfectly competitive firm's profit-maximizing choices and derive its supply curve.

- A perfectly competitive firm is a price taker.
- Marginal revenue equals price.
- The firm produces the output at which price equals marginal cost.
- If price is less than minimum average variable cost, the firm temporarily shuts down.
- A firm's supply curve is the upward-sloping part of its marginal cost curve at all prices at or above minimum average variable cost (the shutdown point) and the vertical axis at all prices below minimum average variable cost.

2   Explain how output, price, and profit are determined in the short run.

- Market demand and market supply determine price.
- Firms choose the quantity to produce that maximizes profit, which is the quantity at which marginal cost equals price.
- In short-run equilibrium, a firm can make a positive economic profit, make zero economic profit, or incur an economic loss.

3   Explain how output, price, and profit are determined in the long run and explain why perfect competition is efficient.

- Economic profit induces entry, which increases market supply and lowers price and profit. Economic loss induces exit, which decreases market supply, raises price, and lowers the losses.
- In the long run, economic profit is zero and there is no entry or exit.
- An increase in demand increases the number of firms and increases the equilibrium quantity.
- An advance in technology that lowers the cost of producing a good increases market supply, lowers the price, and increases the quantity.
- Perfect competition is efficient because it makes marginal benefit equal marginal cost, and it is fair because trade is voluntary, consumers pay the lowest possible prices, and entrepreneurs earn normal profit.

Key Terms

Marginal revenue, 373
Monopolistic competition, 372
Monopoly, 372
Oligopoly, 372

Perfect competition, 372
Price taker, 373
Shutdown point, 377

CHAPTER CHECKPOINT

Study Plan Problems and Applications

1. In what type of market is each good or service in the following list sold? Explain your answers.

- Wheat
- Jeans
- Printer cartridges
- Toothpaste
- Gym membership in a town with one gym

2. Explain why in a perfectly competitive market, the firm is a price taker. Why can't the firm choose the price at which it sells its good?

3. Table 1 shows the demand schedule for Lin's Fortune Cookies. Calculate Lin's marginal revenue for each quantity demanded. Compare Lin's marginal revenue and price. In what type of market does Lin's Fortune Cookies operate?

Table 1 shows the demand schedule for Lin's Fortune Cookies. Table 2 shows some cost data for Lin's. Use this information to work Problems **4** to **7**. (Hint: Make a sketch of Lin's short-run cost curves.)

4. At a market price of $50 a batch, what quantity does Lin's produce and what is the firm's economic profit in the short run?

5. At a market price of $35.20 a batch, what quantity does Lin's produce and what is the firm's economic profit in the short run?

6. Create Lin's short-run supply schedule and make a graph of Lin's short-run supply curve. Explain why only part of Lin's short-run supply curve is the same as its marginal cost curve.

7. At a market price of $83 a batch, what quantity does Lin's produce and what is the firm's economic profit in the short run? Do firms enter or exit the market and what is Lin's economic profit in the long run?

Use the following information to work Problems **8** to **10**.

Maple-syrup makers strike gold

Sugaring season in Vermont is going full blast. Vermont, the biggest U.S. syrup producer, produces about 500,000 gallons a year. In 2007, maple syrup cost an average of $35 a gallon; this year, the price is $45 a gallon. Canada is usually a huge producer, but with a poor season it has seen a 30 percent drop in production. As consumers turn to natural and organic products and buy locally made food, demand for maple syrup has rocketed.

Source: *USA Today*, March 30, 2009

8. Draw a graph to describe the maple syrup market and the cost and revenue of one firm in 2007, assuming that all firms are making zero economic profit.

9. Starting with the industry in long-run equilibrium, explain how the drop in the Canadian supply, other things remaining the same, affects the maple syrup market and an individual producer in the short run.

10. Starting with the industry in long-run equilibrium, explain how the increase in the demand for maple syrup, other things remaining the same, affects the maple syrup market and an individual producer in the short run.

TABLE 1

Price (dollars per batch)	Quantity demanded (batches per day)
50	0
50	1
50	2
50	3
50	4
50	5
50	6

TABLE 2

Quantity (batches per day)	AFC	AVC	ATC	MC
		(dollars per batch)		
1	84.0	51.0	135	
				37
2	42.0	44.0	86	
				29
3	28.0	39.0	67	
				27
4	21.0	36.0	57	
				32
5	16.8	35.2	52	
				40
6	14.0	36.0	50	
				57
7	12.0	39.0	51	
				83
8	10.5	44.5	55	

Instructor Assignable Problems and Applications

Your instructor can assign these problems as homework, a quiz, or a test in MyEconLab.

1. Why did old GM file for bankruptcy?

2. How will the new GM overcome the problems of the old GM?

3. In what type of market is each of the following goods and services sold? Explain your answers.
   - Breakfast cereals
   - Cell phones
   - The only restaurant in a small town
   - Oranges
   - Cable TV in a town with one cable company

4. Suppose that the restaurant industry is perfectly competitive. Joe's Diner is always packed in the evening but rarely has a customer at lunchtime. Why doesn't Joe's Diner close—temporarily shut down—at lunchtime?

Use the following information to work Problems 5 to 7.

Figure 1 shows the short-run cost curves of a toy producer. The market has 1,000 identical producers and Table 1 shows the market demand schedule for toys.

5. At a market price of $21 a toy, what quantity does the firm produce in the short run and does the firm make a positive economic profit, a zero economic profit, or an economic loss?

6. At a market price of $12 a toy, how many toys does the firm produce and what is its economic profit in the short run? How will the number of firms in the market change in the long run?

7. At what market prices would the firm shut down temporarily? What is the market price of a toy in long-run equilibrium? How many firms will be in the toy market in the long run? Explain your answer.

Use the following information to work Problems 8 and 9.

California plans to crack down on the use of fumigants by growers of strawberries. The biggest burden will fall on Ventura County's growers, who produce about 90 percent of the nation's crop.

8. Draw graphs of the U.S. strawberry market in long-run equilibrium before the pollution crackdown: one of the U.S. market and one of a California grower. Now show the short-run effects of the pollution crackdown.

9. On the graph, show the long-run effects of the pollution crackdown.

Use the following information to work Problems 10 and 11.

Big drops in prices for crops make it tough down on the farm
Corn, soybean, and wheat prices have fallen roughly 50 percent from the historic highs of earlier this year. With better-than expected crop yields, world grain production will rise nearly 5 percent this year. Grain prices have also become more closely tied to oil prices because of the growing corn-based ethanol industry.

Source: *USA Today*, October 23, 2008

10. Why did grain prices fall in 2008? Draw a graph to show that short-run effect on an individual farmer's economic profit.

11. Explain the effect of the falling oil price on the market for ethanol. If the price of oil remains low for some years, what will be the long-run effects on the market for ethanol and the number of ethanol producers?

FIGURE 1

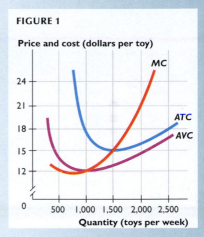

TABLE 1

Price (dollars per toy)	Quantity demanded (thousands of toys per week)
24	1,000
21	1,500
18	2,000
15	2,500
12	3,000

Multiple Choice Quiz

1. In perfect competition, all the following situations arise *except* _____.

   A. firms produce an identical good or service
   B. each firm chooses the price at which to sell the good it produces
   C. firms can sell any quantity they choose to produce at the market price
   D. buyers know each seller's price

2. A firm that is producing the quantity at which marginal cost exceeds both average total cost and the market price will increase its economic profit by _____.

   A. producing a larger quantity
   B. raising the price to equal marginal cost
   C. producing a smaller quantity
   D. producing the quantity that minimizes average total cost

3. A firm will shut down in the short run if at the profit-maximizing quantity, _____.

   A. total revenue is less than total cost
   B. marginal revenue is less than average fixed cost
   C. average total cost exceeds the market price
   D. marginal revenue is less than average variable cost

4. In the short run, the profit-maximizing firm will _____.

   A. break even if marginal revenue equals marginal cost
   B. make an economic profit if marginal cost is less than average total cost
   C. incur an economic loss if average fixed cost exceeds marginal revenue
   D. incur an economic loss if average total cost exceeds marginal revenue

5. A firm's short-run supply curve is the same as _____ if it produces the good.

   A. its marginal revenue curve
   B. the upward-sloping part of its marginal cost curve
   C. its marginal cost curve above minimum average variable cost
   D. its marginal cost curve above minimum average total cost

6. A permanent increase in demand _____ economic profit in the short run and some firms will ____ in the long run.

   A. does not change; exit the market
   B. increases; enter the market
   C. increases; raise their price
   D. does not change; advertise their good

7. Perfect competition is efficient because all the following conditions hold *except* _____.

   A. total product is maximized
   B. firms maximize profit and produce on their supply curves
   C. consumers get a real bargain and pay a price below the value of the good
   D. firms minimize their average total cost of producing the good

Are Microsoft's prices too high?

Monopoly

When you have completed your study of this chapter, you will be able to

1 Explain how monopoly arises and distinguish between single-price monopoly and price-discriminating monopoly.

2 Explain how a single-price monopoly determines its output and price.

3 Compare the performance of a single-price monopoly with that of perfect competition.

4 Explain how price discrimination increases profit.

5 Explain why natural monopoly is regulated and the effects of regulation.

16.1 MONOPOLY AND HOW IT ARISES

Monopoly
A market in which one firm sells a good or service that has no close substitutes and a barrier blocks the entry of new firms.

A **monopoly** is a market in which one firm sells a good or service that has no close substitutes and in which a barrier to entry prevents competition from new firms.

Markets for local telephone service, gas, electricity, and water are examples of local monopoly. GlaxoSmithKline has a monopoly on AZT, a drug that is used to treat AIDS. DeBeers, a South African firm, controls 80 percent of the world's production of raw diamonds—close to being a monopoly but not quite one.

The market for diamonds is close to being a monopoly.

■ How Monopoly Arises

Monopoly arises when there are

- No close substitutes
- A barrier to entry

No Close Substitutes

If a good has a close substitute, even though only one firm produces it, that firm effectively faces competition from the producers of substitutes. Water supplied by a local public utility is an example of a good that does not have close substitutes. While it does have a close substitute for drinking—bottled spring water—it has no effective substitutes for doing the laundry, taking a shower, or washing a car.

The availability of close substitutes isn't static. Technological change can create substitutes and weaken a monopoly. For example, the creation of courier services such as UPS and the development of the fax machine and e-mail provide close substitutes for the mail-carrying services provided by the U.S. Postal Service and have weakened its monopoly. Broadband fiber-optic phone lines and satellite dishes have weakened the monopoly of cable television companies.

The arrival of a new product can also create a monopoly. For example, the technologies of the information age have provided opportunities for Google and Microsoft to become near monopolies in their markets.

A Barrier to Entry

Barrier to entry
Any constraint that protects a firm from competitors.

Any constraint that protects a firm from the arrival of new competitors is a **barrier to entry.** There are three types of barrier to entry:

- Natural
- Ownership
- Legal

Natural monopoly
A monopoly that arises because one firm can meet the entire market demand at a lower average total cost than two or more firms could.

Natural Barrier to Entry A **natural monopoly** exists when the technology for producing a good or service enables one firm to meet the entire market demand at a lower average total cost than two or more firms could. One electric power distributor can meet the market demand for electricity at a lower cost than two or more firms could. Imagine two or more sets of wires running to your home so that you could choose your electric power supplier.

Figure 16.1 illustrates a natural monopoly in the distribution of electric power. Here, the demand curve for electric power is *D*, and the long-run average cost curve is *LRAC*. Economies of scale prevail over the entire length of this *LRAC* curve, indicated by the fact that the curve slopes downward. One firm can produce 4 million kilowatt-hours at 5¢ a kilowatt-hour. At this price, the quantity

FIGURE 16.1

Natural Monopoly

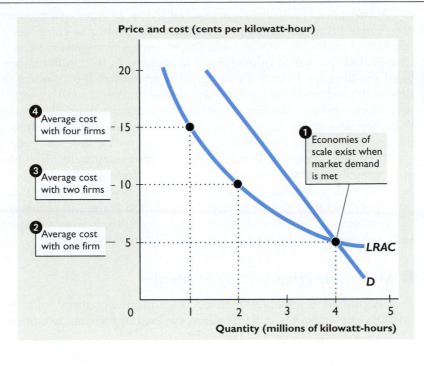

The demand curve for electric power is *D*, and the long-run average cost curve is *LRAC*.

1 Economies of scale exist over the entire *LRAC* curve.

One firm can distribute 4 million kilowatt-hours at a **2** cost of 5¢ a kilowatt-hour.

Two firms can distribute this same total output at a **3** cost of 10¢ a kilowatt-hour.

Four firms can distribute this same total output at a **4** cost of 15¢ a kilowatt-hour.

One firm can meet the market demand at a lower cost than two or more firms can, and the market is a natural monopoly.

demanded is 4 million kilowatt-hours. So if the price was 5¢ a kilowatt-hour, one firm could supply the entire market. If two or more firms shared the market, average total cost would be higher.

To see why the situation shown in Figure 16.1 creates a barrier to entry, think about what would happen if a second firm tried to enter the market. Such a firm would find it impossible to make a profit. If it produced less than the original firm, it would have to charge a higher price and it would have no customers. If it produced the same quantity as the original firm, the price would fall below average total cost for both firms and one of them would be forced out of business. There is room for only one firm in this market.

Ownership Barrier to Entry A monopoly can arise in a market in which competition and entry are restricted by the concentration of ownership of a natural resource. If DeBeers controlled 100 percent of the world's production of raw diamonds, it would be an example of this type of monopoly. There is no natural barrier to entry in diamonds. Even though the diamond is a relatively rare mineral, its sources of supply could have many owners who compete in a global competitive auction market. Only by buying control over all the world's diamonds would DeBeers be able to prevent entry and competition.

Legal Barrier to Entry A legal barrier to entry creates a legal monopoly. A **legal monopoly** is a market in which competition and entry are restricted by the granting of a public franchise, government license, patent, or copyright.

A *public franchise* is an exclusive right granted to a firm to supply a good or service, an example of which is the U.S. Postal Service's exclusive right to deliver

Legal monopoly
A market in which competition and entry are restricted by the granting of a public franchise, government license, patent, or copyright.

first-class mail. A *government license* controls entry into particular occupations, professions, and industries. An example is Michael's Texaco in Charleston, Rhode Island, which is the only firm in the area licensed to test for vehicle emissions.

A *patent* is an exclusive right granted to the inventor of a product or service. A *copyright* is an exclusive right granted to the author or composer of a literary, musical, dramatic, or artistic work. Patents and copyrights are valid for a limited time period that varies from country to country. In the United States, a patent is valid for 20 years. Patents are designed to encourage the *invention* of new products and production methods. They also stimulate *innovation*—the use of new inventions—by encouraging inventors to publicize their discoveries and offer them for use under license. Patents have stimulated innovations in areas as diverse as soybean seeds, pharmaceuticals, memory chips, and video games.

Most monopolies are regulated by government agencies. To understand why governments regulate monopolies and what effects regulations have, we need to know how an unregulated monopoly behaves. So we'll first study an unregulated monopoly and then look at monopoly regulation at the end of this chapter.

A monopoly sets its own price, but in doing so, it faces a market constraint. Let's see how the market limits a monopoly's pricing choices.

■ Monopoly Price-Setting Strategies

A monopoly faces a tradeoff between price and the quantity sold. To sell a larger quantity, the monopoly must set a lower price. But there are two price-setting possibilities that create different tradeoffs:

- Single price
- Price discrimination

Single Price

Single-price monopoly
A monopoly that must sell each unit of its output for the same price to all its customers.

A **single-price monopoly** is a firm that must sell each unit of its output for the same price to all its customers. DeBeers sells diamonds (of a given size and quality) for the same price to all its customers. DeBeers is a *single-price* monopoly because if it tried to sell at a higher price to some customers than to others, only the low-price customers would buy from DeBeers. The others would buy from DeBeers's low-price customers.

Price Discrimination

Price-discriminating monopoly
A monopoly that sells different units of a good or service for different prices not related to cost differences.

A **price-discriminating monopoly** is a firm that sells different units for different prices not related to cost differences. Many firms price discriminate. Airlines offer a dizzying array of different prices for the same trip. Pizza producers charge one price for a single pizza and almost give away a second one. Different customers might pay different prices (like airfares), or one customer might pay different prices for different quantities bought (like the bargain price for a second pizza).

When a firm price discriminates, it appears to be doing its customers a favor. In fact, it is charging each group of customers the highest price it can get them to pay and is increasing its profit.

Not all monopolies can price discriminate. The main obstacle to the practice of price discrimination is resale by the customers who buy for a low price. Because of resale possibilities, price discrimination is limited to monopolies that sell goods and services that cannot be resold.

CHECKPOINT 16.1

Explain how monopoly arises and distinguish between single-price monopoly and price-discriminating monopoly.

MyEconLab
You can work these problems in Study Plan 16.1 and get instant feedback.

Practice Problems

Use the information about the firms listed below to work Problems **1** and **2**.

  a Coca-Cola cuts its price below that of Pepsi-Cola to increase profit.
  b A single firm, protected by a barrier to entry, produces a personal service that has no close substitutes.
  c A barrier to entry exists, but the good has some close substitutes.
  d A museum offers discounts to students and seniors.
  e A firm can sell any quantity it chooses at the going price.
  f A firm experiences economies of scale even when it produces the quantity that meets the entire market demand.

1. Which of the six cases are monopolies or might give rise to monopoly?

2. Which are legal monopolies and which are natural monopolies? Can any of them price discriminate? If so, why?

In the News

Deal raises monopoly concerns
A deal between United Continental and Air Canada looks like an "effective merger" of all of their Canadian and U.S. operations. The deal would create a monopoly on 10 major high-demand, transborder routes and substantially reduce competition on nine others. Prices would be higher and choice restricted.
                                Source: CBC News, June 27, 2011

What type of monopoly would be created on the 10 major high-demand routes? With higher prices and restricted choice, what would be the barrier to entry?

Solutions to Practice Problems

1. Monopoly arises when a single firm produces a good or service that has no close substitutes and a barrier to entry exists. Monopoly arises in **b** and **f**. In **a**, there is more than one firm. In **c**, the good has close substitutes. In **d**, a monopoly might be able to price discriminate, but other types of firms (for example, pizza producers) price discriminate and they are not monopolies. In **e**, the demand for the firm's output is perfectly elastic and there is no limit to what it can sell. This firm operates in a perfectly competitive market.

2. Natural monopoly exists when one firm can meet the entire market demand at a lower price than two or more firms could: **f** is a natural monopoly, but **b** could be. Legal monopoly exists when the granting of a right creates a barrier to entry: **b** might be a legal monopoly. Because a personal service cannot be resold, **b** could price discriminate.

Solution to In the News

This deal would create a legal monopoly on 10 major high-demand, transborder routes. With higher prices, the monopoly might make positive economic profits, which would be an incentive for other airlines to offer service on these routes. The barrier would be the granting of landing slots and boarding gates.

16.2 SINGLE-PRICE MONOPOLY

To understand how a single-price monopoly makes its output and price decisions, we must first study the link between price and marginal revenue.

■ Price and Marginal Revenue

Because in a monopoly there is only one firm, the demand for the firm's output is the market demand. Let's look at Bobbie's Barbershop, the sole supplier of haircuts in Cairo, Nebraska. The table in Figure 16.2 shows the demand schedule for Bobbie's haircuts. For example, at $12, consumers demand 4 haircuts an hour (row *E*).

Total revenue is the price multiplied by the quantity sold. For example, in row *D*, Bobbie sells 3 haircuts at $14 each, so total revenue is $42. *Marginal revenue* is the change in total revenue resulting from a one-unit increase in the quantity sold. For example, if the price falls from $16 (row *C*) to $14 (row *D*), the quantity sold increases from 2 to 3 haircuts. Total revenue rises from $32 to $42, so the change in total revenue is $10. Because the quantity sold increases by 1 haircut, marginal revenue equals the change in total revenue and is $10. Marginal revenue is placed between the two rows to emphasize that marginal revenue relates to the *change* in the quantity sold.

Figure 16.2 shows the market demand curve and Bobbie's marginal revenue curve (*MR*) and also illustrates the calculation that we've just made. At each output, marginal revenue is less than price—the marginal revenue curve lies below the demand curve because a lower price is received on *all* units sold, not just on the marginal unit. For example, at a price of $16, Bobbie sells 2 haircuts (point *C*). If she lowers the price to $14 a haircut, she sells 3 haircuts and has a revenue gain

■ **FIGURE 16.2**

Demand and Marginal Revenue

MyEconLab Animation

The table shows the market demand schedule and Bobbie's total revenue and marginal revenue schedules.

If the price falls from $16 to $14, the quantity sold increases from 2 to 3 haircuts.

❶ Total revenue lost on 2 haircuts is $4; ❷ total revenue gained on 1 haircut is $14; and ❸ marginal revenue is $10.

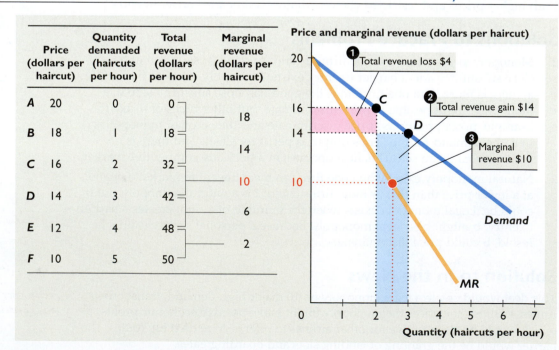

Price (dollars per haircut)	Quantity demanded (haircuts per hour)	Total revenue (dollars per hour)	Marginal revenue (dollars per haircut)
A 20	0	0	
			18
B 18	1	18	
			14
C 16	2	32	
			10
D 14	3	42	
			6
E 12	4	48	
			2
F 10	5	50	

of $14 on the third haircut. But she now receives only $14 a haircut on the first two—$2 a haircut less than before. So she loses $4 of revenue on the first 2 haircuts. To calculate marginal revenue, she must deduct this amount from the revenue gain of $14. So her marginal revenue is $10, which is less than the price.

Notice that the marginal revenue curve has *twice the slope* of the demand curve. When the price falls from $20 to $10, the quantity demanded increases from zero to 5 but the quantity on the *MR* curve increases from zero to 2.5.

■ Marginal Revenue and Elasticity

In Chapter 5 (pp. 120–121), you learned about the *total revenue test* for the price elasticity of demand. If a *fall* in price *increases* total revenue, demand is elastic; and if a *fall* in price *decreases* total revenue, demand is inelastic.

The total revenue test implies that when demand is elastic, marginal revenue is positive and when demand is inelastic, marginal revenue is negative. Figure 16.3 illustrates this relationship between elasticity and marginal revenue.

In part (a) as the price *falls* from $20 to $10, marginal revenue (shown by the blue bars) is *positive* and in part (b) total revenue *increases*, so demand is elastic. In part (a) as the price *falls* from $10 to zero, marginal revenue (the red bars) is *negative* and in part (b), total revenue *decreases*, so demand is *inelastic*. At a price of $10, total revenue is at a maximum, demand is unit elastic, and marginal revenue is zero.

■ **FIGURE 16.3**

Marginal Revenue and Elasticity

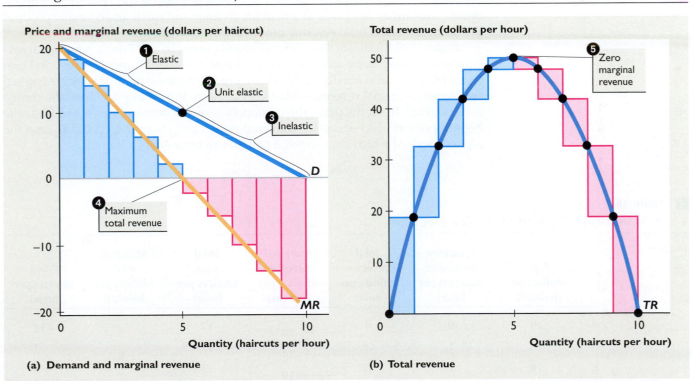

(a) Demand and marginal revenue

(b) Total revenue

As the price falls, if marginal revenue is positive (the blue bars), ❶ demand is elastic; if marginal revenue is zero, ❷ demand is unit elastic; if marginal revenue is negative (the red bars), ❸ demand is inelastic. At zero marginal revenue in part (a), ❹ total revenue is maximized. And at maximum total revenue in part (b), ❺ marginal revenue is zero.

The relationship between marginal revenue and elasticity implies that a monopoly never profitably produces along the inelastic range of its demand curve. If a monopoly did produce along the inelastic range of its demand curve, it could increase total revenue by raising its price and selling a smaller quantity. But by producing less, the firm's total cost would fall and the firm's profit would increase. Let's look at a monopoly's output and price decision.

■ Output and Price Decision

To determine the output level and price that maximize a monopoly's profit, we study the behavior of both revenue and costs as output varies.

Table 16.1 summarizes the information we need about Bobbie's revenue, costs, and economic profit. Economic profit, which equals total revenue minus total cost, is maximized at $12 an hour when Bobbie sells 3 haircuts an hour for $14 each. If she sold 2 haircuts for $16 each, her economic profit would be only $9. And if she sold 4 haircuts for $12 each, her economic profit would be only $8.

You can see why 3 haircuts is Bobbie's profit-maximizing output by looking at the marginal revenue and marginal cost. When Bobbie increases output from 2 to 3 haircuts, her marginal revenue is $10 and her marginal cost is $7. Profit increases by the difference, $3 an hour. If Bobbie increases output yet further, from 3 to 4 haircuts, her marginal revenue is $6 and her marginal cost is $10. In this case, marginal cost exceeds marginal revenue by $4, so profit decreases by $4 an hour.

Figure 16.4 illustrates the information contained in Table 16.1. Part (a) shows Bobbie's total revenue curve (TR) and her total cost curve (TC). It also shows Bobbie's economic profit as the vertical distance between the TR and TC curves. Bobbie maximizes her profit at 3 haircuts an hour and earns an economic profit of $12 an hour ($42 of total revenue minus $30 of total cost).

Figure 16.4 (b) shows the market demand curve (D) and Bobbie's marginal revenue curve (MR) along with her marginal cost curve (MC) and average total cost curve (ATC). Bobbie maximizes profit by producing the output at which marginal cost equals marginal revenue—3 haircuts an hour. But what price does she charge for a haircut? To set the price, the monopoly uses the demand curve and finds the highest price at which it can sell the profit-maximizing output. In Bobbie's case, the highest price at which she can sell 3 haircuts an hour is $14 a haircut.

■ **Table 16.1**

A Monopoly's Output and Price Decision

	Price (dollars per haircut)	Quantity demanded (haircuts per hour)	Total revenue (dollars per hour)	Marginal revenue (dollars per haircut)	Total cost (dollars per hour)	Marginal cost (dollars per haircut)	Profit (dollars per hour)
A	20	0	0		12		−12
				18		5	
B	18	1	18		17		1
				14		6	
C	16	2	32		23		9
				10		7	
D	14	3	42		30		12
				6		10	
E	12	4	48		40		8
				2		15	
F	10	5	50		55		−5

When Bobbie produces 3 haircuts an hour, her average total cost is $10 (read from the *ATC* curve at the quantity 3 haircuts) and her price is $14 (read from the *D* curve). Her profit per haircut is $4 ($14 minus $10). Bobbie's economic profit is shown by the blue rectangle, which equals the profit per haircut ($4) multiplied by the number of haircuts (3 an hour), for a total of $12 an hour.

A positive economic profit is an incentive for firms to enter a market. But barriers to entry prevent that from happening in a monopoly. So in a monopoly, the firm can make a positive economic profit and continue to do so indefinitely.

A monopoly charges a price that exceeds marginal cost, but does it always make an economic profit? The answer is no. Bobbie makes a positive economic profit in Figure 16.4. But suppose that Bobbie's landlord increases the rent she pays for her barbershop. If Bobbie pays an additional $12 an hour in shop rent, her fixed cost increases by that amount. Her marginal cost and marginal revenue don't change, so her profit-maximizing output remains at 3 haircuts an hour. Her profit decreases by the additional rent of $12 an hour to zero. If Bobbie pays more than an additional $12 an hour for rent, she incurs an economic loss. If this situation were permanent, Bobbie would go out of business. But monopoly entrepreneurs are creative, and Bobbie might find another shop at a lower rent.

FIGURE 16.4

A Monopoly's Profit-Maximizing Output and Price

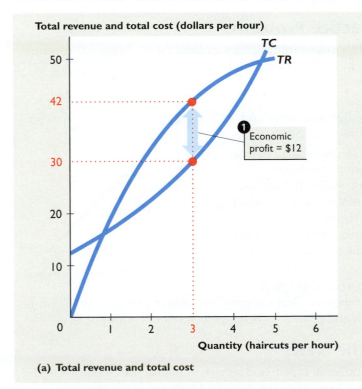

(a) Total revenue and total cost

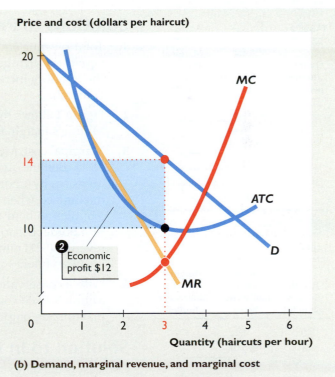

(b) Demand, marginal revenue, and marginal cost

In part (a), economic profit is maximized when total revenue (*TR*) minus total cost (*TC*) is greatest. ❶ Economic profit, the vertical distance between *TR* and *TC*, is $12 an hour at 3 haircuts an hour.

In part (b), economic profit is maximized when marginal cost (*MC*) equals marginal revenue (*MR*). The price is determined by the demand curve (*D*) and is $14. ❷ Economic profit, the blue rectangle, is $12—the profit per haircut ($4) multiplied by 3 haircuts.

MyEconLab

You can work these problems in Study Plan 16.2 and get instant feedback.

TABLE 1

Price (dollars per bottle)	Quantity (bottles per hour)	Total cost (dollars per hour)
10	0	1
9	1	2
8	2	4
7	3	7
6	4	12
5	5	18

TABLE 2

Quantity (bottles per hour)	Total revenue (dollars per hour)	Marginal revenue (dollars per bottle)
0	0	
		9
1	9	
		7
2	16	
		5
3	21	
		3
4	24	
		1
5	25	

TABLE 3

Quantity (bottles per hour)	Total cost (dollars per hour)	Marginal cost (dollars per bottle)
0	1	
		1
1	2	
		2
2	4	
		3
3	7	
		5
4	12	
		7
5	18	

CHECKPOINT 16.2

Explain how a single-price monopoly determines its output and price.

Practice Problems

Minnie's Mineral Springs is a single-price monopoly. Table 1 shows the demand schedule for Minnie's spring water (columns 1 and 2) and the firm's total cost schedule (columns 2 and 3).

1. Calculate Minnie's total revenue and marginal revenue schedules.
2. Draw the demand curve and Minnie's marginal revenue curve.
3. Calculate Minnie's profit-maximizing output, price, and economic profit.
4. If Minnie's is hit with a conservation tax of $14 an hour, what are Minnie's new profit-maximizing output, price, and economic profit?

In the News

Comcast offers faster home broadband in some U.S. cities
Comcast, the largest U.S. internet-service provider, introduced a new home-broadband package called Extreme 105, which can download files many times faster than most connections.

Source: CNN, April 14, 2011

How does Comcast determine the price of its broadband service?

Solutions to Practice Problems

1. Total revenue equals price multiplied by quantity sold. Marginal revenue equals the change in total revenue when the quantity increases by one unit (Table 2).

2. Figure 1 shows the demand curve and Minnie's marginal revenue curve.

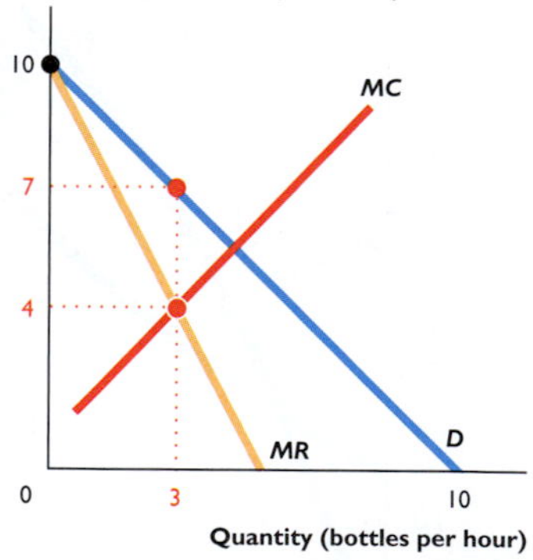

3. Marginal cost, MC, is the change in total cost when the quantity produced increases by 1 bottle (Table 3). Profit is maximized when $MR = MC$ by producing 3 bottles an hour (Figure 1). The price is $7 a bottle. Economic profit equals total revenue ($21) minus total cost ($7), which is $14 an hour.

4. With a conservation tax of $14 an hour, Minnie's fixed cost increases but marginal cost doesn't change, so the profit-maximizing output and price are unchanged. Economic profit is zero.

FIGURE 1

Price and cost (dollars per bottle)

Solution to In the News

Comcast is the only supplier of broadband service in many cities. Comcast undertakes a marketing survey to estimate the demand for its new faster service. Comcast knows its production costs, so to calculate its total costs it adds its marketing costs. Then Comcast calculates its profit-maximizing quantity of service. From its estimated demand for the service, Comcast calculates the highest price at which it expects it can sell the profit-maximizing quantity of the service.

16.3   MONOPOLY AND COMPETITION COMPARED

Imagine a market in which many small firms operate in perfect competition. Then suppose that a single firm buys out all these small firms and creates a monopoly. What happens in this market to the quantity produced, the price, and efficiency?

■ Output and Price

Figure 16.5 shows the market that we'll study. The market demand curve is D. Initially, with many small firms in the market, the market supply curve is S, which is the sum of the supply curves—and marginal cost curves—of the firms. The equilibrium price is P_C, which makes the quantity demanded equal the quantity supplied. The equilibrium quantity is Q_C. Each firm takes the price P_C and maximizes its profit by producing the output at which its own marginal cost equals the price.

A single firm now buys all the firms in this market. Consumers don't change, so the demand curve doesn't change. But the monopoly recognizes this demand curve as a constraint on its sales and knows that its marginal revenue curve is MR.

The market supply curve in perfect competition is the sum of the marginal cost curves of the firms in the industry. So the monopoly's marginal cost curve is the market supply curve of perfect competition—labeled $S = MC$. The monopoly maximizes profit by producing the quantity at which marginal revenue equals marginal cost, which is Q_M. This output is smaller than the competitive output, Q_C. The monopoly charges the price P_M, which is higher than P_C.

Compared to perfect competition, a single-price monopoly produces a smaller output and charges a higher price.

■ **FIGURE 16.5**

Monopoly's Smaller Output and Higher Price

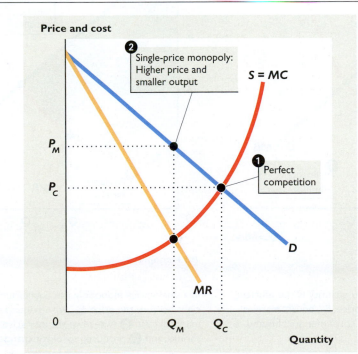

Price and cost

2 Single-price monopoly: Higher price and smaller output

$S = MC$

P_M

1 Perfect competition

P_C

D

MR

0   Q_M Q_C

Quantity

❶ A competitive industry produces the quantity Q_C at price P_C.

❷ A single-price monopoly produces the quantity Q_M at which marginal revenue equals marginal cost and sells that quantity for the price P_M. Compared to perfect competition, a single-price monopoly produces a smaller output and raises the price.

■ Is Monopoly Efficient?

You learned in Chapter 6 that resources are used efficiently when marginal benefit equals marginal cost. Figure 16.6(a) shows that perfect competition achieves this efficient use of resources. The demand curve ($D = MB$) shows the marginal benefit to consumers. The supply curve ($S = MC$) shows the marginal cost (opportunity cost) to producers. At the competitive equilibrium, the price is P_C and the quantity is Q_C. Marginal benefit equals marginal cost, and resource use is efficient. Total surplus (Chapter 6, p. 153), the sum of *consumer surplus,* the green triangle, and *producer surplus,* the blue area, is maximized.

Figure 16.6(b) shows that monopoly is inefficient. Monopoly output is Q_M and price is P_M. Price (marginal benefit) exceeds marginal cost and the underproduction creates a *deadweight loss* (Chapter 6, p. 155), which is shown by the gray area. Consumers lose partly by getting less of the good, shown by the gray triangle above P_C, and partly by paying more for the good. Consumer surplus shrinks to the smaller green triangle. Producers lose by selling less of the good, shown by the part of the gray area below P_C, but gain by selling their output for a higher price, shown by the dark blue rectangle. Producer surplus expands and is larger in monopoly than in perfect competition.

■ **FIGURE 16.6**

The Inefficiency of Monopoly   MyEconLab Animation

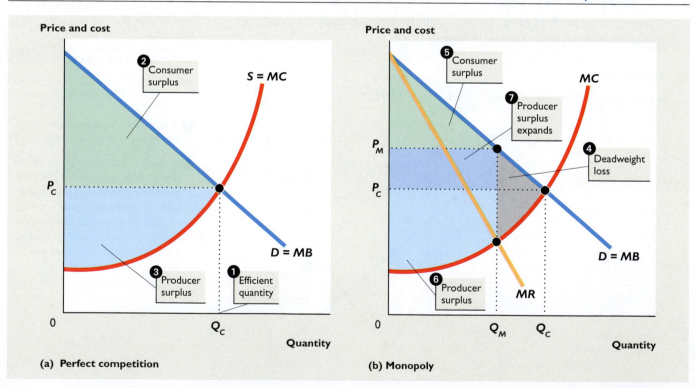

(a) Perfect competition

(b) Monopoly

In perfect competition, ❶ the equilibrium quantity is the efficient quantity, Q_C, because at that quantity the price, P_C, equals marginal benefit and marginal cost. The sum of ❷ consumer surplus and ❸ producer surplus is maximized.

In a single-price monopoly, the equilibrium quantity, Q_M, is inefficient because the price, P_M, which equals marginal benefit, exceeds marginal cost. ❹ A deadweight loss arises. ❺ Consumer surplus shrinks, and ❻ producer surplus expands by the area ❼.

■ Is Monopoly Fair?

Monopoly is inefficient because it creates a deadweight loss. But monopoly also *redistributes* consumer surplus. The producer gains, and the consumers lose.

Figure 16.6 shows this redistribution. The monopoly gets the difference between the higher price, P_M, and the competitive price, P_C, on the quantity sold, Q_M. So the dark blue rectangle shows the part of the consumer surplus taken by the monopoly. This portion of the loss of consumer surplus is not a loss to society. It is redistribution from consumers to the monopoly producer.

Are the gain for the monopoly and loss for consumers fair? You learned about two standards of fairness in Chapter 6: fair *results* and fair *rules*. Redistribution from the rich to the poor is consistent with the fair results view. So on this view of fairness, whether monopoly redistribution is fair or unfair depends on who is richer: the monopoly or the consumers of its product. It might be either. Whether the *rules* are fair depends on whether the monopoly has benefited from a protected position that is not available to anyone else. If everyone is free to acquire the monopoly, then the rules are fair. So monopoly is inefficient and it might be, but is not always, unfair.

The pursuit of monopoly profit leads to an additional costly activity that we'll now describe: rent seeking.

■ Rent Seeking

Rent seeking is the lobbying for special treatment from the government to create economic profit or to divert consumer surplus or producer surplus away from others. ("Rent" is a general term in economics that includes all forms of surplus such as consumer surplus, producer surplus, and economic profit.) Rent seeking does not always create a monopoly, but it always restricts competition and often creates a monopoly.

Rent seeking
The lobbying for special treatment from the government to create economic profit or to divert consumer surplus or producer surplus away from others.

Scarce resources can be used to produce the goods and services that people value or they can be used in rent seeking. Rent seeking is potentially profitable for the rent seeker but costly to society because it uses scarce resources purely to transfer wealth from one person or group to another person or group rather than to produce the things that people value.

To see why rent seeking occurs, think about the two ways in which a person might become the owner of a monopoly:

- Buy a monopoly.
- Create a monopoly by rent seeking.

Buy a Monopoly

A person might try to make a monopoly profit by buying a firm (or a right) that is protected by a barrier to entry. Buying a taxicab medallion in New York City is an example. The number of medallions is restricted, so their owners are protected from unlimited entry into the industry. A person who wants to operate a taxi must buy a medallion from someone who already has one.

But anyone is free to enter the bidding for a medallion. So competition among buyers drives the price up to the point at which they make only zero economic profit. For example, competition for the right to operate a taxi in New York City has led to a price of $600,000 for a taxi medallion, which is sufficiently high to eliminate economic profit for taxi operators and leave entrepreneurs with only normal profit.

■ Create a Monopoly by Rent Seeking

Because buying a monopoly means paying a price that soaks up the economic profit, creating a monopoly by rent seeking is an attractive alternative to buying one. Rent seeking is a political activity. It takes the form of lobbying and trying to influence the political process to get laws that create legal barriers to entry. Such influence might be sought by making campaign contributions in exchange for legislative support or by indirectly seeking to influence political outcomes through publicity in the media or by direct contact with politicians and bureaucrats. An example of a rent created in this way is the law that restricts the quantities of textiles that can be imported into the United States. Another is a law that limits the quantity of tomatoes that can be imported into the United States. These laws restrict competition, which decreases the quantity for sale and increases prices.

■ Rent-Seeking Equilibrium

Rent seeking is a competitive activity. If an economic profit is available, a rent seeker will try to get some of it. Competition among rent seekers pushes up the cost of rent seeking until it leaves the monopoly earning only a zero economic profit after paying the rent-seeking costs.

Figure 16.7 shows a rent-seeking equilibrium. The cost of rent seeking is a fixed cost that must be added to a monopoly's other costs. The average total cost curve, which includes the fixed cost of rent seeking, shifts upward until it just touches the demand curve. Consumer surplus is unaffected. But the deadweight loss of monopoly now includes the original deadweight loss plus the economic profit consumed by rent seeking, which the enlarged gray area shows.

■ **FIGURE 16.7**

Rent-Seeking Equilibrium

MyEconLab Animation

❶ Rent-seeking costs exhaust economic profit. The firm's rent-seeking costs are fixed costs. They increase total fixed cost and average total cost. The *ATC* curve shifts upward until, at the profit-maximizing price, the firm breaks even.

❷ Monopoly profit-maximization shrinks consumer surplus relative to its maximum level in perfect competition, but rent-seeking doesn't shrink consumer surplus any further.

❸ The deadweight loss increases.

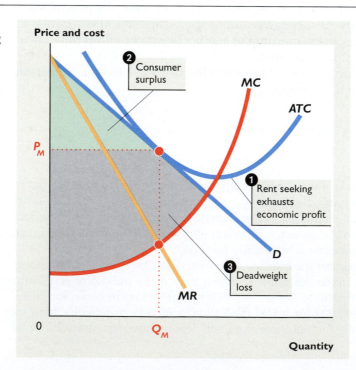

CHECKPOINT 16.3

MyEconLab
You can work these problems in
Study Plan 16.3 and get instant
feedback.

Compare the performance of a single-price monopoly with that
of perfect competition.

Practice Problems

Township is a small isolated community served by one newspaper that can
meet the market demand at a lower cost than two or more newspapers could.
The *Township Gazette* is the only source of news. Figure 1 shows the marginal
cost of printing the *Township Gazette* and the market demand for it. The *Township
Gazette* is a profit-maximizing, single-price monopoly.

1. How many copies of the *Township Gazette* are printed each day and what is
   the price of the *Township Gazette*?

2. What is the efficient number of copies of the *Township Gazette* and what is
   the price at which the efficient number of copies could be sold?

3. Is the number of copies printed the efficient quantity? Explain your answer.

4. On the graph, show the consumer surplus that is redistributed from consumers to the *Township Gazette* and the deadweight loss that arises because
   the *Township Gazette* is a monopoly.

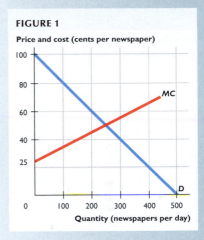

FIGURE 1

Price and cost (cents per newspaper)

In the News

Ticketmaster's near monopoly challenged as technology changes
In the 1990s, to see Michael Jordan or Garth Brooks live you had to buy the
ticket through Ticketmaster, or from a scalper. Today, Ticketmaster merged with
concert promoter Live Nation and now controls the sale of tickets to sports and
music events. Competitors have entered the market, and events tickets are now
sold through Internet auction markets.

How will the increased competition in the sale of tickets affect the service fee
component of the price and the efficiency of the market? Will scalpers survive?

Solutions to Practice Problems

1. The profit-maximizing quantity of the *Township Gazette* is 150 a day, where
   marginal revenue equals marginal cost. The price is 70¢ a copy (Figure 2).

2. The efficient quantity is 250 copies, where quantity demanded (marginal
   benefit) equals marginal cost and the price would be 50¢ a copy (Figure 2).

3. The number of copies printed is not efficient because the marginal benefit of
   the 150th copy (70¢) exceeds its marginal cost (40¢) (Figure 2).

4. In Figure 2, the blue rectangle ❶ shows the consumer surplus transferred
   from the consumers to the *Township Gazette* and the gray triangle ❷ shows
   the deadweight loss created.

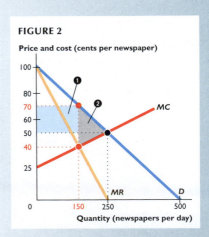

FIGURE 2

Price and cost (cents per newspaper)

Solution to In the News

The price you pay for an event ticket is the sum of the price of the event plus a
service fee. As a monopoly, Ticketmaster charges the profit-maximizing fee. The
monopoly has weakened and competition has increased, but sellers still charge
the profit-maximizing fee, although a lower fee. The ticket-selling market is more
efficient, but scalpers now compete with resale auctions and appear to survive.

Why does a hairdresser charge seniors $2 less than other customers?

Price discrimination—selling a good or service at a number of different prices—is widespread. You encounter it when you travel, go to the movies, get your hair cut, buy pizza, or visit an art museum. At first sight, it appears that price discrimination contradicts the assumption of profit maximization. Why would a movie operator allow children to see movies at half price? Why would a hairdresser charge students and senior citizens less? Aren't these firms losing profit by being nice to their customers?

Deeper investigation shows that far from lowering profit, price discriminators make a bigger profit than they would otherwise. So a monopoly has an incentive to find ways of discriminating and charging each buyer the highest possible price. Some people pay less with price discrimination, but others pay more.

Most price discriminators are *not* monopolies, but monopolies do price discriminate when they can. To be able to price discriminate, a firm must

- Identify and separate different types of buyers.
- Sell a product that cannot be resold.

Price discrimination is charging different prices for a single good or service because the willingness to pay varies across buyers. Not all price *differences* are price *discrimination*. Some goods that are similar but not identical have different prices because they have different production costs. For example, the cost of producing electricity depends on time of day. If an electric power company charges a higher price for consumption between 7:00 and 9:00 in the morning and between 4:00 and 7:00 in the evening than it does at other times of the day, the company is not price discriminating.

■ Price Discrimination and Consumer Surplus

The key idea behind price discrimination is to convert consumer surplus into economic profit. To extract every dollar of consumer surplus from every buyer, the monopoly would have to offer each individual customer a separate price schedule based on that customer's own willingness to pay. Such price discrimination cannot be carried out in practice because a firm does not have enough information about each consumer's demand curve. But firms try to extract as much consumer surplus as possible, and to do so, they discriminate in two broad ways:

- Among groups of buyers
- Among units of a good

Discriminating Among Groups of Buyers

To price discriminate among groups of buyers, the firm offers different prices to different types of buyers, based on things such as age, employment status, or some other easily distinguished characteristic. This type of price discrimination works when each group has a different average willingness to pay for the good or service.

For example, a face-to-face sales meeting with a customer might bring a large and profitable order. For salespeople and other business travelers, the marginal benefit from an airplane trip is large and the price that such a traveler will pay for a trip is high. In contrast, for a vacation traveler, any of several different trips or even no vacation trip are options. So for vacation travelers, the marginal benefit of a trip is small and the price that such a traveler will pay for a trip is low. Because business travelers are willing to pay more than vacation travelers are, it is possible for an airline to profit by price discriminating between these two groups.

Discriminating Among Units of a Good

To price discriminate among units of a good, the firm charges the same prices to all its customers but offers a lower price per unit for a larger number of units bought. When Pizza Hut charges $10 for one home-delivered pizza and $14 for two, it is using this type of price discrimination. In this example, the price of the second pizza is only $4.

Let's see how an airline exploits the differences in demand by business and vacation travelers and increases its profit by price discriminating.

■ Profiting by Price Discriminating

Global Air has a monopoly on an exotic route. Figure 16.8 shows the demand curve (D) for travel on this route and Global Air's marginal revenue curve (MR). It also shows Global Air's marginal cost (MC) and average total cost (ATC) curves.

Initially, Global is a single-price monopoly and maximizes its profit by producing 8,000 trips a year (the quantity at which MR equals MC). The price is $1,200 a trip. The average total cost of a trip is $600, so economic profit is $600 a trip. On 8,000 trips, Global's economic profit is $4.8 million a year, shown by the blue rectangle. Global's customers enjoy a consumer surplus shown by the green triangle.

■ FIGURE 16.8

A Single-Price Monopoly's Price and Economic Profit

MyEconLab Animation

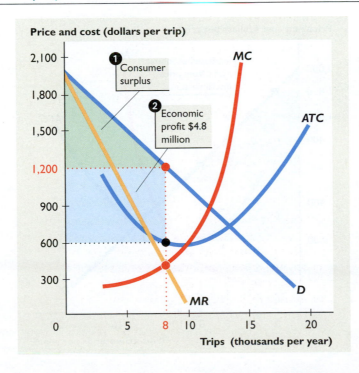

Global Air has a monopoly on an air route. The demand curve for travel on this route is D, and Global's marginal revenue curve is MR. Its marginal cost curve is MC, and its average total cost curve is ATC.

As a single-price monopoly, Global maximizes profit by selling 8,000 trips a year at $1,200 a trip.

❶ Global's customers enjoy a consumer surplus—the green triangle.

❷ Global's economic profit is $4.8 million a year—the blue rectangle.

Global is struck by the fact that many of its customers are business travelers, and Global suspects that they are willing to pay more than $1,200 a trip. So Global does some market research, which tells Global that some business travelers are willing to pay as much as $1,800 a trip. Also, these customers almost always make their travel plans at the last moment. Another group of business travelers is willing to pay $1,600. These customers know a week ahead when they will travel, and prefer a refundable ticket. Yet another group is willing to pay up to $1,400. These travelers know two weeks ahead when they will travel, and they are happy to buy a nonrefundable ticket.

So Global announces a new fare schedule: No restrictions, $1,800; 7-day advance purchase, refundable, $1,600; 14-day advance purchase, nonrefundable, $1,400; 14-day advance purchase, must stay at least 7 days, $1,200.

Figure 16.9 shows the outcome with this new fare structure and also shows why Global is pleased with its new fares. It sells 2,000 trips at each of its four prices. Global's economic profit increases by the area of the blue steps in the figure. Its economic profit is now its original $4.8 million a year plus an additional $2.4 million from its new higher fares. Consumer surplus has shrunk to the sum of the smaller green triangles.

■ Perfect Price Discrimination

Perfect price discrimination
Price discrimination that extracts the entire consumer surplus by charging the highest price that consumers are willing to pay for each unit.

But Global thinks that it can do even better. It plans to achieve **perfect price discrimination,** which extracts the entire consumer surplus by charging the highest price that consumers are willing to pay for each unit. To do so, Global must get creative and come up with a host of additional business fares ranging between $2,000 and $1,200, each one of which appeals to a small segment of the business market.

■ **FIGURE 16.9**

Price Discrimination

MyEconLab Animation

Global revises its fare structure. It now offers no restrictions at $1,800, 7-day advance purchase, refundable at $1,600, 14-day advance purchase, nonrefundable at $1,400, and 14-day advance purchase, must stay at least 7 days, at $1,200.

Global sells 2,000 units at each of its four new fares. Its economic profit increases by $2.4 million a year to $7.2 million a year, which is shown by the original blue rectangle plus the blue steps. Global's customers' consumer surplus shrinks to the sum of the green areas.

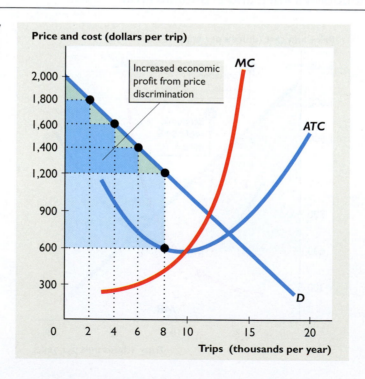

Once Global is discriminating finely between different customers and getting from each customer the maximum he or she is willing to pay, something special happens to marginal revenue. Recall that for the single-price monopoly, marginal revenue is less than price. The reason is that when the price is cut to sell a larger quantity, the price is lower on all units sold. But with perfect price discrimination, Global sells only the marginal seat at the lower price. All the other customers continue to buy for the highest price they are willing to pay. So for the perfect price discriminator, marginal revenue equals price and the demand curve becomes the marginal revenue curve.

With marginal revenue equal to price, Global can obtain yet greater profit by increasing output up to the point at which price (and marginal revenue) is equal to marginal cost.

So Global now seeks additional travelers who will not pay as much as $1,200 a trip but who will pay more than marginal cost. More creative pricing comes up with vacation specials and other fares that have combinations of advance reservation, minimum stay, and other restrictions that make these fares unattractive to Global's existing customers but attractive to a further group of travelers. With all these fares and specials, Global extracts the entire consumer surplus and maximizes economic profit.

Figure 16.10 shows the outcome with perfect price discrimination. The dozens of fares paid by the original travelers who are willing to pay between $1,200 and $2,000 have extracted the entire consumer surplus from this group and converted it into economic profit for Global. The new fares between $900 and $1,200 have attracted 3,000 additional travelers but have taken their entire consumer surplus also. Global is earning an economic profit of more than $9 million a year.

FIGURE 16.10

Perfect Price Discrimination

MyEconLab Animation

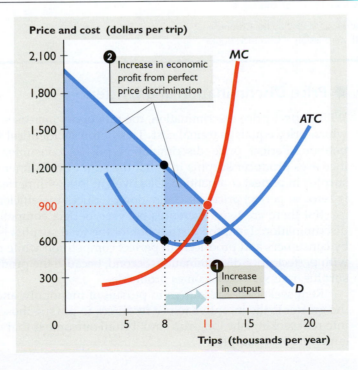

With perfect price discrimination, the demand curve becomes Global's marginal revenue curve. Economic profit is maximized when the lowest price equals marginal cost.

❶ Output increases to 11,000 passengers a year, and ❷ Global's economic profit increases to $9.35 million a year.

The normal coach fare from San Francisco to Washington, D.C., is $1,555, refundable and with no charge for a checked bag. With a checked baggage charge, a refundable ticket is $850 and a nonrefundable ticket is $271. On a typical flight, passengers might be paying as many as 20 different fares.

The airlines sort their customers according to their willingness to pay by offering a variety of options that attract price-sensitive leisure travelers but don't get bought by business travelers.

Despite the sophistication of the airlines' pricing schemes, almost 20 percent of seats fly empty. The marginal cost of filling an empty seat is close to zero, so a ticket sold at a few dollars would be profitable.

Low fares are now feasible, thanks to priceline.com and dozens of other online travel agents. Shopping around the airlines with bids from travelers, these agents broker thousands of tickets a day and obtain the lowest possible fares for their customers.

Would it bother you to hear how little I paid for this flight?

From William Hamilton, "Voodoo Economics," © 1992 by the Chronicle Publishing Company, p. 3. Reprinted with permission of Chronicle Books.

■ Price Discrimination and Efficiency

With perfect price discrimination, the monopoly increases output to the point at which price equals marginal cost. This output is identical to that of perfect competition. Perfect price discrimination pushes consumer surplus to zero but increases producer surplus to equal the sum of consumer surplus and producer surplus in perfect competition. Deadweight loss with perfect price discrimination is zero. So perfect price discrimination produces the efficient quantity.

But there are two differences between perfect competition and perfect price discrimination. First, the distribution of the total surplus is different. It is shared by consumers and producers in perfect competition while the producer gets it all with perfect price discrimination. Second, because the producer grabs all the total surplus, rent seeking becomes profitable.

Rent seekers use resources in pursuit of monopoly, and the bigger the rents, the greater is the incentive to use resources to pursue those rents. With free entry into rent seeking, the long-run equilibrium outcome is that rent seekers use up the entire producer surplus.

CHECKPOINT 16.4

Explain how price discrimination increases profit.

MyEconLab
You can work these problems in Study Plan 16.4 and get instant feedback.

Practice Problems

Village, a small isolated town, has one doctor. For a 30-minute consultation, the doctor charges a rich person twice as much as a poor person.

1. Does the doctor practice price discrimination? Is the doctor using resources efficiently? Does the doctor's pricing scheme redistribute consumer surplus? If so, explain how.

2. If the doctor decided to charge everyone the maximum price that he or she would be willing to pay, what would be the consumer surplus? Would the market for medical service in Village be efficient?

In the News

Feast on these great dining deals
Entrées at Patina in Los Angeles start at $40, but the four-course fixed menu is $59. And pair that with the waived corkage fee on Tuesdays. At Michael Mina, San Francisco, enjoy a three-course, prix-fixe lunch for $49 or pay up to $65 when ordering the same items individually at dinner.
Source: *USA Today*, July 29, 2011

Are Patina and Michael Mina price discriminating? Explain your answer.

Solutions to Practice Problems

1. The doctor practices price discrimination because rich people and poor people pay a different price for the same service: a 30-minute consultation. The doctor provides the profit-maximizing number of consultations and charges rich people more than poor people. As a monopoly, the total number of consultations is less than that at which marginal benefit equals the marginal cost of providing the medical service. Because marginal benefit does not equal marginal cost, the doctor is not using resources efficiently. With price discrimination, some consumer surplus is redistributed to the doctor as profit.

2. The doctor decides to practice perfect price discrimination. If successful, with perfect price discrimination, marginal revenue equals price. To maximize economic profit, the doctor increases the number of consultations to make the lowest price charged equal to the marginal cost of providing the service. The doctor takes the entire consumer surplus, so consumer surplus is zero.
   Marginal benefit equals price, so resources are being used efficiently.

Solution to In the News

A restaurant meal cannot be resold, so price discrimination is possible. Offering a four-course fixed menu at a lower price than the sum of the prices of the individual items is price discrimination. Diners who want fewer than four courses and want to be more selective about what they eat pay more. Waiving the corkage fee on Tuesdays is not price discrimination. Demand is lower on Tuesdays, so the profit-maximizing price is lower. Waiving the corkage fee is a way of price cutting without reprinting the menu.

16.5 MONOPOLY REGULATION

Natural monopoly presents a dilemma. With economies of scale, a natural monopoly produces at the lowest possible cost. But with market power, the monopoly has an incentive to raise the price above the competitive price and produce too little—to operate in the self-interest of the monopoly and not in the social interest.

Regulation—rules administered by a government agency to influence prices, quantities, entry, and other aspects of economic activity in a firm or industry—is a possible solution to this dilemma.

To implement regulation, the government establishes agencies to oversee and enforce the rules. For example, the Surface Transportation Board regulates prices on interstate railroads and some trucking and bus lines, and water and oil pipelines. By the 1970s, almost a quarter of the nation's output was produced by regulated industries (far more than just natural monopolies) and a process of deregulation began.

Deregulation is the process of removing regulation of prices, quantities, entry, and other aspects of economic activity in a firm or industry. During the past 30 years, deregulation has occurred in domestic air transportation, telephone service, interstate trucking, and banking and financial services. Cable TV was deregulated in 1984, re-regulated in 1992, and deregulated again in 1996.

Regulation is a *possible* solution to the dilemma presented by natural monopoly but not a sure bet solution. There are two theories about how regulation actually works: the *social interest theory* and the *capture theory*.

The **social interest theory** is that the political and regulatory process relentlessly seeks out inefficiency and introduces regulation that eliminates deadweight loss and allocates resources efficiently.

The **capture theory** is that the political and regulatory process gets captured by the regulated firm and ends up serving its self-interest, with maximum economic profit, underproduction, and deadweight loss. The regulator gets captured because the producer's gain is large and visible while each individual consumer's is small and invisible. No individual consumer has an incentive to oppose the regulation, but the producer has a big incentive to lobby for it.

Which theory of regulation best explains real-world regulations? Does regulation serve the social interest or the self-interest of monopoly producers?

◼ Efficient Regulation of a Natural Monopoly

A cable TV company is a *natural monopoly* (pp. 400–401)—it can supply the entire market at a lower price than two or more competing firms can. Cox Communications, based in Atlanta, supplies cable TV to households in 16 states. It has invested heavily in satellite receiving dishes, cables, and control equipment and so has large fixed costs. These fixed costs are part of the company's average total cost. Its average total cost decreases as the number of households served increases because the fixed cost is spread over a larger number of households. Unregulated, Cox Communications serves the number of households that maximizes profit. Like all single-price monopolies, the profit-maximizing quantity is less than the efficient quantity and underproduction results in a deadweight loss (see Figure 16.6, p. 410).

How can Cox be regulated to produce the efficient quantity of cable TV service? The answer is by being regulated to set its price equal to marginal cost, known as the **marginal cost pricing rule.** The quantity demanded at a price equal to marginal cost is the efficient quantity—the quantity at which marginal benefit equals marginal cost.

Figure 16.11 illustrates the marginal cost pricing rule. The demand curve for cable TV is *D*. Cox's marginal cost curve is *MC*. That marginal cost curve is (assumed to be) horizontal at $10 per household per month—that is, the cost of providing each additional household with a month of cable programming is $10. The efficient outcome occurs if the price is regulated at $10 per household per month with 8 million households served.

But there is a problem: Because average total cost exceeds marginal cost, a firm that follows the marginal cost pricing rule incurs an economic loss. So a cable TV company that is required to use a marginal cost pricing rule will not stay in business for long. How can the firm cover its costs and, at the same time, obey a marginal cost pricing rule?

One possibility is price discrimination (see pp. 414–418). Another possibility is to use a two-part price (called a *two-part tariff*). For example, local telephone companies charge consumers a monthly fee for being connected to the telephone system and then charge a price equal to marginal cost (zero) for each local call. A cable TV operator can charge a one-time connection fee that covers its fixed cost and then charge a monthly fee equal to marginal cost.

■ Second-Best Regulation of a Natural Monopoly

A natural monopoly cannot always be regulated to achieve an efficient outcome. Two possible ways of enabling a regulated monopoly to avoid an economic loss are

- Average cost pricing
- Government subsidy

■ **FIGURE 16.11**

Natural Monopoly: Marginal Cost Pricing

MyEconLab Animation

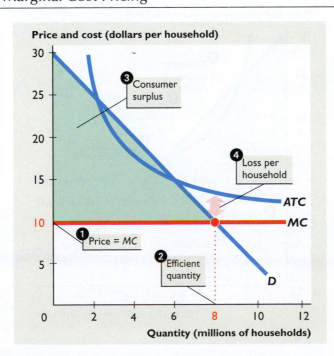

The market demand curve for cable TV is *D*. A cable TV operator's marginal cost *MC* is a constant $10 per household per month. Its fixed cost is large, and the average total cost curve, which includes average fixed cost, is *ATC*.

❶ Price is set equal to marginal cost at $10 a month.

At this price, ❷ the efficient quantity (8 million households) is served.

❸ Consumer surplus is maximized as shown by the green triangle.

❹ The firm incurs a loss on each household served, shown by the red arrow.

Average cost pricing rule
A rule that sets price equal to average total cost to enable a regulated firm to avoid economic loss.

Average Cost Pricing

The **average cost pricing rule** sets price equal to average total cost. With this rule the firm produces the quantity at which the average total cost curve cuts the demand curve. This rule results in the firm making zero economic profit—breaking even. But because for a natural monopoly average total cost exceeds marginal cost, the quantity produced is less than the efficient quantity and a deadweight loss arises. Figure 16.12 illustrates the average cost pricing rule. The price is $15 a month and 6 million households get cable TV. The gray triangle shows the deadweight loss.

Government Subsidy

A government subsidy is a direct payment to the firm equal to its economic loss. But to pay a subsidy, the government must raise the revenue by taxing some other activity. You saw in Chapter 8 that taxes themselves generate deadweight loss.

And the Second-Best Is...

Which is the better option, average cost pricing or marginal cost pricing with a government subsidy? The answer turns on the relative magnitudes of the two deadweight losses. Average cost pricing generates a deadweight loss in the market served by the natural monopoly. A subsidy generates deadweight losses in the markets for the items that are taxed to pay the subsidy. The smaller deadweight loss is the second-best solution to regulating a natural monopoly. Making this calculation in practice is too difficult and average cost pricing is generally preferred to a subsidy.

■ **FIGURE 16.12**

Natural Monopoly: Average Cost Pricing

MyEconLab Animation

1 Price is set equal to average total cost at $15 a month.

At this price, **2** the quantity served (6 million households) is less than the efficient quantity (8 million households).

3 Consumer surplus shrinks to the smaller green triangle.

4 A producer surplus enables the firm to pay its total fixed cost and break even.

5 A deadweight loss, shown by the gray triangle, arises.

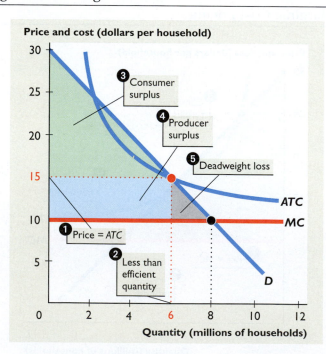

EYE on MICROSOFT
Are Microsoft's Prices Too High?

Microsoft's prices are too high in the sense that they exceed marginal cost and result in fewer copies of the Windows operating system and Office application than the efficient quantities.

Profit Maximization

The figure illustrates how Microsoft prices its products to maximize profit. The demand for copies of the Windows Vista operating system is D. The marginal revenue curve is MR. The marginal cost of an additional copy of Vista is very small and we assume it to be zero, with marginal cost curve MC.

Profit is maximized by producing the quantity at which marginal revenue equals marginal cost. In the figure, that quantity is 4 million copies of Vista per month. The price is $300 per copy and Microsoft receives a producer surplus shown by the blue rectangle.

Inefficiency

The efficient quantity is 8 million copies per month, where price and marginal benefit equal marginal cost. Because the actual quantity is smaller than the efficient quantity, a deadweight loss arises and the gray triangle shows its magnitude. The green triangle shows the consumer surplus.

Fixed Cost

The marginal cost of a copy of Windows Vista might be close to zero but the fixed cost of developing the software is large. Microsoft must at least earn enough revenue to pay these fixed costs.

Earning enough to pay the firm's fixed costs does not inevitably lead to inefficiency. Some firms with zero marginal cost and the market power to charge a high price do choose to provide the efficient quantity of their services at a zero price.

The Google Solution

Google is one such firm. The price of an Internet search on Google is zero. The quantity of searches is that at which the marginal benefit of a search equals zero marginal cost, so the quantity of searches is the efficient quantity.

Google earns revenue, and a very large revenue, by selling advertising that

more than pays its fixed operating costs.

Efficiency

Advertising on Google is more effective than a TV or poster advertisement because it is targeted at potential buyers of products based on the topics of their searches.

The Google solution delivers the efficient quantity of zero-marginal-cost Internet search activity.

The Google solution might also deliver the efficient quantity of advertising. It will do so if Google is able to achieve perfect price discrimination in the market for advertising.

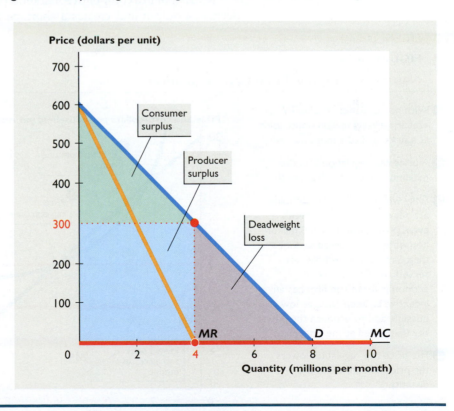

Implementing average cost pricing presents the regulator with a challenge because it is not possible to be sure of a firm's costs. So regulators use one of two practical rules:

- Rate of return regulation
- Price cap regulation

Rate of Return Regulation

Rate of return regulation
A regulation that sets the price at a level that enables a firm to earn a specified target rate of return on its capital.

Under **rate of return regulation,** the price is set at a level that enables the firm to earn a specified target rate of return on its capital. This type of regulation can end up serving the self-interest of the firm rather than the social interest. The firm's managers have an incentive to inflate costs by spending on items such as private jets, free baseball tickets (disguised as public relations expenses), and lavish entertainment. Managers also have an incentive to use more capital than the efficient amount. The *rate* of return on capital is regulated but not the *total* return on capital, and the greater the amount of capital, the greater is the total return.

Price Cap Regulation

Price cap regulation
A rule that specifies the highest price that a firm is permitted to set—a price ceiling.

For the reason that we've just examined, rate of return regulation is increasingly being replaced by price cap regulation. A **price cap regulation** is a price ceiling—a rule that specifies the highest price the firm is permitted to set. This type of regulation lowers the price and gives the firm an incentive to minimize its costs. But what happens to the quantity produced?

Recall that in a competitive market, a price ceiling set below the equilibrium price decreases output and creates a shortage (see Chapter 7, pp. 169–170). In contrast,

■ **FIGURE 16.13**

Natural Monopoly: Price Cap Regulation

MyEconLab Animation

❶ With no regulation, a cable TV operator serves 4 million households at a price of $20 a month.

❷ A price cap regulation sets the maximum price at $15 a month.

❸ Only when 6 million households are served can the firm break even. (When fewer than 6 million households are served or more than 6 million households are served, the firm incurs an economic loss.) The firm has an incentive to keep costs as low as possible and to produce the quantity demanded at the price cap.

❹ The price cap regulation lowers the price and increases the quantity.

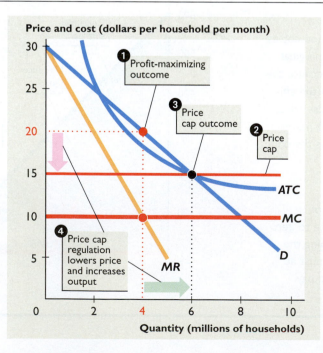

in natural monopoly a price ceiling increases output. The reason is that at the regulated price, the firm can sell any quantity it chooses up to the quantity demanded. So each additional unit sold brings in the same additional revenue: marginal revenue equals price. The regulated price exceeds marginal cost, so the profit-maximizing quantity becomes the quantity demanded at the price ceiling.

Figure 16.13 illustrates this outcome. Unregulated, a cable TV operator maximizes profit by serving 4 million households at a price of $20 a month. With a price cap set at $15 a month, the firm is permitted to sell any quantity it chooses at that price or at a lower price. The profit-maximizing quantity now increases to 6 million households. Serving fewer than 6 million households, the firm incurs a loss—average total cost exceeds the price cap. Serving more than 6 million households is possible but only by lowering the price along the demand curve. Again, average total cost exceeds price and the firm incurs a loss.

In Figure 16.13, the price cap delivers average cost pricing. In practice, the regulator might set the cap too high. For this reason, price cap regulation is often combined with **earnings sharing regulation**—a regulation that requires firms to make refunds to customers when profits rise above a target level.

Earnings sharing regulation
A regulation that requires firms to make refunds to customers when profits rise above a target level.

EYE on YOUR LIFE
Monopoly in Your Everyday Life

When Bill Gates decided to quit Harvard in 1975, he realized that PCs would need an operating system and applications programs to interact with the computer's hardware. He also knew that whoever owned the copyright on these programs would have a license to print money. And he wanted to be that person.

In less than 30 years, Bill Gates became the world's richest person. Such is the power of the right monopoly.

You, along with millions of other PC users, have willingly paid the monopoly price for Windows and Microsoft Office. Sure, the marginal cost of a copy of these programs is close to zero, so the quantity sold is way too few. There is a big deadweight loss.

Compared with the alternative of no Windows, you're better off. But are you better off than you would be if there were many alternatives to Windows competing for your attention? To answer this question, think about the applications—spreadsheets, word processing, and so on—that you need to make your computer useful. With lots of operating systems, what would happen to the cost of developing applications? Would you have more or less choice?

■ CHECKPOINT 16.5

Explain why natural monopoly is regulated and the effects of regulation.

Practice Problems

An unregulated natural monopoly bottles Elixir, a unique health product that has no substitutes. The monopoly's total fixed cost is $150,000, and its marginal cost is 10¢ a bottle. Figure 1 illustrates the demand for Elixir.

1. How many bottles of Elixir does the monopoly sell and what is the price of a bottle of Elixir? Is the monopoly's use of resources efficient?

2. Suppose that the government introduces a marginal cost pricing rule. What is the price of Elixir, the quantity sold, and the monopoly's economic profit?

3. Suppose that the government introduces an average cost pricing rule. What is the price of Elixir, the quantity sold, and the monopoly's economic profit?

In the News

Mexicans protest the plan to end the state oil monopoly
Protesters fight the plan to open Mexico's state oil monopoly to private investment. In Mexico, the government sets the price and taxes the monopoly's profit. The price in Mexico is $2.48 a gallon and in the United States is $3.37 a gallon.

Source: USA Today, April 13, 2008

Describe how the Mexican government regulates the domestic oil market.

Solutions to Practice Problems

1. The monopoly will produce 1 million bottles a year—the quantity at which marginal revenue equals marginal cost. The price is 30¢ a bottle—the highest price at which the monopoly can sell the 1 million bottles a year (Figure 2). The monopoly's use of resources is inefficient. If resource use were efficient, the monopoly would produce the quantity at which marginal benefit (price) equals marginal cost: 2 million bottles a year.

2. With a marginal cost pricing rule, the price is 10¢ a bottle and the monopoly produces 2 million bottles a year. The monopoly incurs an economic loss equal to its total fixed costs of $150,000 a year. The monopoly would need a subsidy from the government to keep it in business.

3. With an average cost pricing rule, the firm produces the quantity at which price equals average total cost. Average total cost equals average variable cost plus average fixed cost. Average variable cost equals marginal cost and is 10¢ a bottle. Average fixed cost is $150,000 divided by the quantity produced. For example, at 1 million bottles, average fixed cost is 15¢ and at 1.5 million bottles, average fixed cost is 10¢ a bottle. The average total cost of producing 1.5 million bottles is 20¢ a bottle and they can be sold for 20¢ a bottle. So the monopoly produces 1.5 million bottles a year and breaks even.

Solution to In the News

The price is not set equal to marginal cost (marginal cost pricing) because the oil company does not receive a subsidy. The price is not set equal to average total cost (average cost pricing) because the oil company does not break even. The government operates a price cap regulation and the company pays a profit tax.

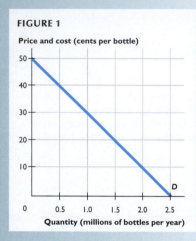

FIGURE 1

Price and cost (cents per bottle)

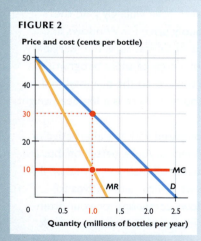

FIGURE 2

Price and cost (cents per bottle)

CHAPTER SUMMARY

Key Points

1 Explain how monopoly arises and distinguish between single-price monopoly and price-discriminating monopoly.

- In monopoly, a single producer of a good or service that has no close substitutes operates behind natural, ownership, or legal barriers to entry.
- A monopoly can price discriminate when there is no resale possibility.
- Where resale is possible, a firm charges a single price.

2 Explain how a single-price monopoly determines its output and price.

- The demand for a monopoly's output is the market demand, and a single-price monopoly's marginal revenue is less than price.
- A monopoly maximizes profit by producing the quantity at which marginal revenue equals marginal cost and by charging the maximum price that consumers are willing to pay for that quantity.

3 Compare the performance of a single-price monopoly with that of perfect competition.

- A single-price monopoly charges a higher price and produces a smaller quantity than does a perfectly competitive market and creates a deadweight loss.
- Monopoly imposes a loss on society that equals its deadweight loss plus the cost of the resources devoted to rent seeking.

4 Explain how price discrimination increases profit.

- Perfect price discrimination captures the entire consumer surplus. Prices are the highest that each consumer is willing to pay for each unit.
- With perfect price discrimination, the monopoly is efficient but rent seeking uses some or all of the producer surplus.

5 Explain why natural monopoly is regulated and the effects of regulation.

- Regulation might achieve an efficient use of resources or help the monopoly to maximize economic profit.
- A natural monopoly is efficient if its price equals marginal cost, but a second-best outcome is for price to equal average total cost.
- A price cap supported by earnings sharing regulation is the most effective practical method of regulating a natural monopoly.

Key Terms

CHAPTER CHECKPOINT

Study Plan Problems and Applications

1. Under what conditions does monopoly arise? Under what conditions can a monopoly price discriminate?

Use the following information to work Problems **2** to **4**.

Elixir Spring produces a unique and highly prized mineral water. The firm's total fixed cost is $5,000 a day, and its marginal cost is zero. Table 1 shows the demand schedule for Elixir water.

2. On a graph, show the demand curve for Elixir water and Elixir Spring's marginal revenue curve. What are Elixir's profit-maximizing price, output, and economic profit?

3. Compare Elixir's profit-maximizing price with the marginal cost of producing the profit-maximizing output. At the profit-maximizing price, is the demand for Elixir water inelastic or elastic?

4. Suppose that there are 1,000 springs, all able to produce this water at zero marginal cost and with zero fixed costs. Compare the equilibrium price and quantity produced with the price and quantity produced by Elixir water.

5. The Blue Rose Company is the only flower grower to have cracked the secret of making a blue rose. Figure 1 shows the demand for blue roses and the marginal cost of producing a blue rose. What is Blue Rose's profit-maximizing output? What price does it charge? Is the Blue Rose Company using its resources efficiently?

Hawaii Cable Television is a natural monopoly. Sketch a market demand curve and the firm's cost curves. Use your graph to work Problems **6** to **9**.

6. If Hawaii Cable is unregulated and maximizes profit, show in your graph the price, quantity, economic profit, consumer surplus, and deadweight loss.

7. If Hawaii Cable is unregulated and it gives householders a 50 percent discount for second and third connections, describe how its economic profit, consumer surplus, and deadweight loss would change.

8. If Hawaii Cable is regulated in the social interest, show in your graph the price, quantity, economic profit, consumer surplus, and deadweight loss.

9. If Hawaii Cable is subject to a price cap regulation that enables it to break even, show in your graph the price, quantity, economic profit, consumer surplus, and deadweight loss.

Use the following information to work Problems **10** and **11**.

FCC planning rules to open cable market
The Federal Communications Commission (FCC) will make it easier for independent programmers and rival video services to lease access to cable channels. The FCC will also limit the market share of a cable company to 30 percent.

Source: *The New York Times*, November 10, 2007

10. What barriers to entry exist in the cable television market? Are high cable prices evidence of monopoly power?

11. Draw a graph to illustrate the effects of the FCC's new regulations on the price, quantity, consumer surplus, producer surplus, and deadweight loss.

TABLE 1

Price (dollars per bottle)	Quantity (bottles per day)
10	0
8	2,000
6	4,000
4	6,000
2	8,000
0	10,000

FIGURE 1

Instructor Assignable Problems and Applications

Your instructor can assign these problems as homework, a quiz, or a test in **MyEconLab**.

Use the following information to work Problems **1** and **2**.

Microsoft: We're not gouging Europe on Windows 7 pricing

Regulators in the European Union have charged Microsoft with illegally tying Internet Explorer (IE) to Windows and mandated that a version of Windows be offered stripped of IE. A news report suggested that when Microsoft launches Windows 7, it will charge a higher price for the IE-stripped version than the price for a full version that includes IE. Microsoft denied this report but announced that it would offer the full version of Windows 7 at a lower upgrade price.

Source: computerworld.com

1. How does Microsoft set the price of Windows and would it be in the firm's self-interest to set a different price for a version stripped of IE?

2. Why might Microsoft offer the full version of Windows 7 to European customers at a lower upgrade price?

Use the following information to work Problems **3** and **4**.

Bobbie's Hair Care is a natural monopoly. Table 1 shows the demand schedule (the first two columns) and Bobbie's marginal cost schedule (the middle and third columns). Bobbie has done a survey and discovered that she has four types of customers each hour: one woman who is willing to pay $18, one senior who is willing to pay $16, one student who is willing to pay $14, and one boy who is willing to pay $12. Suppose that Bobbie's fixed costs are $20 an hour and Bobbie's price discriminates.

3. What is the price each type of customer is charged and how many haircuts an hour does Bobbie's sell? What is the increase in Bobbie's economic profit that results from price discrimination?

4. Who benefits from Bobbie's price discrimination? Is the quantity of haircuts efficient?

Use the following information to work Problems **5** to **10**.

Big Top is the only circus in the nation. Table 2 sets out the demand schedule for circus tickets and the cost schedule for producing the circus.

5. Calculate Big Top's profit-maximizing price, output, and economic profit if it charges a single price for all tickets.

6. When Big Top maximizes profit, what is the consumer surplus and producer surplus and is the circus efficient? Explain why or why not.

7. At the market equilibrium price, no children under 10 years old attend the circus. Big Top offers children under 10 a discount of 50 percent. How will this discount change the consumer surplus and producer surplus? Will Big Top be more efficient by offering the discount to children?

8. If Big Top is regulated to produce the efficient output, what is the quantity of tickets sold, what is the price of a ticket, and what would be the consumer surplus?

9. If Big Top is regulated to charge a price equal to average total cost, what is the quantity of tickets sold, the price of a ticket, and economic profit?

10. Draw a graph to illustrate the circus market if regulators set a price cap that enables Big Top to break even. Show the deadweight loss in your graph.

TABLE 1

Price (dollars per haircut)	Quantity (haircuts per hour)	Marginal cost (dollars per hour)
20	0	—
18	1	1
16	2	4
14	3	8
12	4	12
10	5	18

TABLE 2

Price (dollars per ticket)	Quantity (tickets per show)	Total cost (dollars per show)
20	0	1,000
18	100	1,600
16	200	2,200
14	300	2,800
12	400	3,400
10	500	4,000
8	600	4,600
6	700	5,200
4	800	5,800

Multiple Choice Quiz

1. A firm is a natural monopoly if _____.

A. it can produce the good at a price below its competitor's price
B. it can produce a larger quantity of the good than other firms could
C. the government grants it a public franchise or patent
D. it can satisfy the market demand at a lower average total cost than other firms can

2. A monopoly _____.

A. can choose its price and output and always has the option of price discriminating
B. is a price taker and by offering a range of discounts can price discriminate
C. that produces a good that cannot be resold might choose to price discriminate
D. book store that offers a discount on Tuesdays is price discriminating

3. A single-price monopoly maximizes profit by producing the quantity at which _____.

A. its total revenue will be as large as possible
B. marginal revenue equals marginal cost and setting the price equal to marginal revenue
C. marginal revenue equals marginal cost and setting the price equal to marginal cost
D. marginal revenue equals marginal cost and setting the price equal to the most people are willing to pay for that quantity

4. A monopoly sets its price such that demand for the good produced is _____ .

A. unit elastic
B. inelastic
C. elastic
D. either elastic or inelastic, but never unit elastic

5. A single-price monopoly is _____.

A. inefficient because it converts consumer surplus to producer surplus
B. inefficient because it produces too small an output and creates a dead-weight loss
C. efficient because buyers are paying a price equal to their willingness to pay
D. efficient because it is the only producer of the good

6. A monopoly that price discriminates _____.

A. benefits buyers because it offers the good at a variety of prices
B. gains because it converts consumer surplus to economic profit
C. uses resources more efficiently than would a competitive market
D. enables buyers to maximize their consumer surplus

7. Governments regulate natural monopoly by capping the price at _____.

A. marginal revenue and allowing the monopoly to maximize profit
B. marginal cost so that the monopoly is efficient and makes zero economic profit
C. average total cost, which allows the monopoly to be inefficient but make zero economic profit
D. the buyers' willingness to pay, which makes the monopoly operate efficiently

Monopolistic Competition

17

When you have completed your study of this chapter, you will be able to

1 Describe and identify monopolistic competition.

2 Explain how a firm in monopolistic competition determines its output and price in the short run and the long run.

3 Explain why advertising costs are high and why firms use brand names in monopolistic competition.

17.1 WHAT IS MONOPOLISTIC COMPETITION?

Most real-world markets lie between the extremes of perfect competition in Chapter 15 and monopoly in Chapter 16. Most firms possess some power to set their prices as monopolies do, and they face competition from the entry of new firms as the firms in perfect competition do. We call the markets in which such firms operate *monopolistic competition*. (Another market that lies between perfect competition and monopoly is *oligopoly*, which we study in Chapter 18.)

Monopolistic competition is a market structure in which

- A large number of firms compete.
- Each firm produces a differentiated product.
- Firms compete on price, product quality, and marketing.
- Firms are free to enter and exit.

■ Large Number of Firms

In monopolistic competition, as in perfect competition, the industry consists of a large number of firms. The presence of a large number of firms has three implications for the firms in the industry.

Small Market Share

Each firm supplies a small part of the market. Consequently, while each firm can influence the price of its own product, it has little power to influence the average market price.

No Market Dominance

Each firm must be sensitive to the average market price of the product, but it does not pay attention to any one individual competitor. Because all the firms are relatively small, no single firm can dictate market conditions, so no one firm's actions directly affect the actions of the other firms.

Collusion Impossible

Firms sometimes try to profit from illegal agreements—collusion—with other firms to fix prices and not undercut each other. Collusion is impossible when the market has a large number of firms, as it does in monopolistic competition.

■ Product Differentiation

Product differentiation is making a product that is slightly different from the products of competing firms. A differentiated product has close substitutes but it does not have perfect substitutes. Some people will pay more for one variety of the product, so when its price rises, the quantity demanded decreases but it does not (necessarily) decrease to zero. For example, Adidas, Asics, Diadora, Etonic, Fila, New Balance, Nike, Puma, and Reebok all make differentiated running shoes. Other things remaining the same, if the price of Adidas running shoes rises and the prices of the other shoes remain constant, Adidas sells fewer shoes.

■ Competing on Quality, Price, and Marketing

Product differentiation enables a firm to compete with other firms in three areas: quality, price, and marketing.

About 20 firms, each with a small market share, produce a wide variety of treadmills.

Product differentiation
Making a product that is slightly different from the products of competing firms.

Quality

The quality of a product is the physical attributes that make it different from the products of other firms. Quality includes design, reliability, the service provided to the buyer, and the buyer's ease of access to the product. Quality lies on a spectrum that runs from high to low. Go to the J.D. Power Consumer Center at jdpower.com, and you'll see the many dimensions on which this rating agency describes the quality of autos, boats, financial services, travel and accommodation services, telecommunication services, and new homes—all examples of products that have a large range of quality variety.

Price

Because of product differentiation, a firm in monopolistic competition faces a downward-sloping demand curve. So, like a monopoly, the firm can set both its price and its output. But there is a tradeoff between the product's quality and price. A firm that makes a high-quality product can charge a higher price than a firm that makes a low-quality product.

Marketing

Because of product differentiation, a firm in monopolistic competition must market its product. Marketing takes two main forms: advertising and packaging. A firm that produces a high-quality product wants to sell it for a suitably high price. To be able to do so, it must advertise and package its product in a way that convinces buyers that they are getting the higher quality for which they are paying. For example, drug companies advertise and package their brand-name drugs to persuade buyers that these items are superior to the lower-priced generic alternatives. Similarly, a low-quality producer uses advertising and packaging to persuade buyers that although the quality is low, the low price more than compensates for this fact.

■ Entry and Exit

In monopolistic competition, there are no barriers to entry. Consequently, a firm cannot make an economic profit in the long run. When firms make economic profits, new firms enter the industry. This entry lowers prices and eventually eliminates economic profits. When economic losses are incurred, some firms leave the industry. This exit increases prices and profits of the remaining firms and eventually eliminates the economic losses. In long-run equilibrium, firms neither enter nor leave the industry and the firms in the industry make zero economic profit.

■ Identifying Monopolistic Competition

Several factors must be considered to identify monopolistic competition and distinguish it from perfect competition on the one side and oligopoly and monopoly on the other side. One of these factors is the extent to which a market is dominated by a small number of firms. To measure this feature of markets, economists use two indexes called measures of concentration. These indexes are

- The four-firm concentration ratio
- The Herfindahl-Hirschman Index

The Four-Firm Concentration Ratio

Four-firm concentration ratio
The percentage of the total revenue in an industry accounted for by the four largest firms in the industry.

The **four-firm concentration ratio** is the percentage of the total revenue of the industry accounted for by the four largest firms in the industry. The range of the concentration ratio is from almost zero for perfect competition to 100 percent for monopoly. This ratio is the main measure used to assess market structure.

Table 17.1 shows two calculations of the four-firm concentration ratio: one for tire makers and one for printers. In this example, 14 firms produce tires. The four largest firms have 80 percent of the industry's total revenue, so the four-firm concentration ratio is 80 percent. In the printing industry, with 1,004 firms, the four largest firms have only 0.5 percent of the industry's total revenue, so the four-firm concentration ratio is 0.5 percent.

A low concentration ratio indicates a high degree of competition, and a high concentration ratio indicates an absence of competition. A monopoly has a concentration ratio of 100 percent—the largest (and only) firm has 100 percent of the total revenue. A four-firm concentration ratio that exceeds 60 percent is regarded as an indication of a market that is highly concentrated and dominated by a few firms—oligopoly. A ratio of less than 40 percent is regarded as an indication of a competitive market—monopolistic competition.

TABLE 17.1

Concentration Ratio Calculations

(a) Firms' total revenue

Tire makers		Printers	
Firm	(millions of dollars)	Firm	(millions of dollars)
Top, Inc.	200	Fran's	4
ABC, Inc.	250	Ned's	3
Big, Inc.	150	Tom's	2
XYZ, Inc.	100	Jill's	1
4 largest firms	700	4 largest firms	10
Other 10 firms	175	Other 1,000 firms	1,990
Industry	875	Industry	2,000

(b) Four-firm concentration ratios

Tire makers		Printers	
Total revenue of 4 largest firms	700	Total revenue of 4 largest firms	10
Industry's total revenue	875	Industry's total revenue	2,000

Four-firm concentration ratio

$$\frac{700}{875} \times 100 = 80 \text{ percent}$$

Four-firm concentration ratio

$$\frac{10}{2,000} \times 100 = 0.5 \text{ percent}$$

The Herfindahl-Hirschman Index

The **Herfindahl-Hirschman Index**—also called the HHI—is the square of the percentage market share of each firm summed over the 50 largest firms (or summed over all the firms if there are fewer than 50) in a market. For example, if there are four firms in a market and the market shares of the firms are 50 percent, 25 percent, 15 percent, and 10 percent, the Herfindahl-Hirschman Index is

$$\text{HHI} = 50^2 + 25^2 + 15^2 + 10^2 = 3{,}450.$$

In perfect competition, the HHI is small. For example, if each of the 50 largest firms in an industry has a market share of 0.1 percent, the HHI is $0.1^2 \times 50 = 0.5$. In a monopoly, the HHI is 10,000—the firm has 100 percent of the market: $100^2 = 10{,}000$.

The HHI became a popular measure of the degree of competition during the 1980s, when the Justice Department used it to classify markets. A market in which the HHI is less than 1,000 is regarded as being competitive and an example of monopolistic competition. A market in which the HHI lies between 1,000 and 1,800 is regarded as being moderately competitive. It probably is an example of monopolistic competition. But a market in which the HHI exceeds 1,800 is regarded as being uncompetitive. The Justice Department scrutinizes any merger of firms in a market in which the HHI exceeds 1,000 and is likely to challenge a merger if the HHI exceeds 1,800.

Concentration measures are a useful indicator of the degree of competition in a market, but they must be supplemented by other information to determine a market's structure. Table 17.2 summarizes the range of other information, along with the measures of concentration that determine which market structure describes a particular real-world market.

Herfindahl-Hirschman Index
The square of the percentage market share of each firm summed over the 50 largest firms (or summed over all the firms if there are fewer than 50) in a market.

■ **TABLE 17.2**

Market Structure

Characteristics	Perfect competition	Monopolistic competition	Oligopoly	Monopoly
Number of firms in industry	Many	Many	Few	One
Product	Identical	Differentiated	Identical or differentiated	No close substitutes or regulated
Barriers to entry	None	None	Moderate	High
Firm's control over price	None	Some	Considerable	Considerable
Concentration ratio	0	Low	High	100
HHI	Close to 0	Less than 1,800	More than 1,800	10,000
Examples	Wheat, corn	Food, clothing	Cereals	Local water supply

Limitations of Concentration Measures

The two main limitations of concentration measures alone as determinants of market structure are their failure to take proper account of

- The geographical scope of the market
- Barriers to entry and firm turnover

Geographical Scope of the Market Concentration measures take a national view of the market. Many goods are sold in a *national* market, but some are sold in a *regional* market and some in a *global* one. The ready-mix concrete industry consists of local markets. The four-firm concentration ratio for ready-mix concrete is 6.2, and the HHI is 26. These numbers suggest a market that is close to perfect competition. But there is a high degree of concentration in the ready-mix concrete industry in most cities, so this industry is not competitive despite its low measured concentration. The four-firm concentration ratio for automobiles is 87, and the HHI is 2,725. These numbers suggest a highly concentrated market. But competition from imports gives the auto market many of the features of monopolistic competition.

Barriers to Entry and Firm Turnover Concentration measures don't measure barriers to entry. Some industries are highly concentrated but have easy entry and an enormous amount of turnover of firms. For example, many small towns have few restaurants, but there are no restrictions on opening a restaurant and many firms attempt to do so.

A market with a high concentration ratio or HHI might nonetheless be competitive because low barriers to entry create *potential competition*. The few firms in a market face competition from many firms that can easily enter the market and will do so if economic profits are available.

EYE on the U.S. ECONOMY
Examples of Monopolistic Competition

These ten industries operate in monopolistic competition. They have a large number of firms, shown in parentheses after the industry's name. The red bars show the percentage of industry total revenue received by the 4 largest firms. The green bars show the percentage of industry total revenue received by the next 4 largest firms. The entire red, green, and blue bars show the percentage of industry total revenue received by the 20 largest firms. The Herfindahl-Hirschman Index is shown on the right.

SOURCE OF DATA: U.S. Census Bureau.

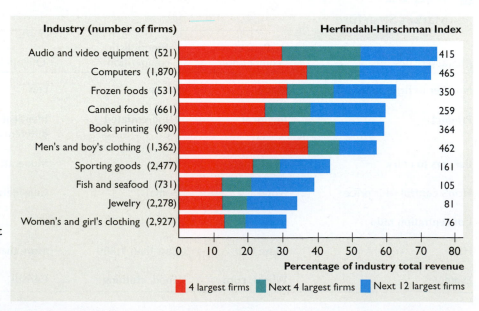

CHECKPOINT 17.1

Describe and identify monopolistic competition.

Practice Problems

Table 1 shows the total revenue of the 50 firms in the tattoo industry.

1. Calculate the four-firm concentration ratio and the HHI. What is the market structure of the tattoo industry?

2. What would the market structure of the tattoo industry be if each firm operated in a different city and the cities were spread across the nation?

3. What additional information would you need about the tattoo industry to be sure that it is an example of monopolistic competition?

4. Suppose that a new tattoo technology makes it easier for anyone to enter the tattoo market. How might the market structure change?

In the News

Is a prepaid phone plan right for you?
Cell-phone providers are offering no-contract plans. For example, T-Mobile's "flexpay" plans allow users to buy monthly service; Boost Mobile's no-contract plan has unlimited use; and Virgin Mobile's plan has unlimited calling for $49.99 a month. All providers are actively marketing their no-contract plans.
Source: *Wall Street Journal*, April 22, 2009

In what type of market are cell-phone plans sold? Explain your answer.

Solutions to Practice Problems

1. The four-firm concentration ratio is 46.6. The market shares of the four largest firms are 17.1, 12.4, 9.5, and 7.6.

   The HHI is 671.14. The market shares from largest to smallest are 17.1, 12.4, 9.5, 7.6, 1.9, and 0.8 percent. Square these numbers to get
   $292.41 + 153.76 + 90.25 + 57.76 + (3.61 \times 16) + (0.64 \times 30) = 671.14$.

   The four-firm concentration ratio and the HHI suggest that the tattoo industry is an example of monopolistic competition unless there are other reasons that would make the concentration measures unreliable guides.

2. If the 50 firms in the tattoo industry operate in different cities spread across the nation, each firm is effectively without competition. The market might be a series of monopolies.

3. The additional information needed is information about product differentiation; competition on price, quality, and marketing; and evidence of low barriers to the entry of new firms.

4. This new tattoo technology would most likely lead to the entry of more firms, greater product differentiation, and more competition.

Solution to In the News

The market structure is monopolistic competition. The number of cell-phone providers is large, and they offer differentiated services. No firm dominates the market and the firms compete on quality, price, and marketing. New cell-phone providers can enter the market with their own plan.

MyEconLab
You can work these problems in Study Plan 17.1 and get instant feedback.

TABLE 1

Firm	Total revenue (dollars)
Bright Spots	450
Freckles	325
Love Galore	250
Native Birds	200
Next 16 firms (each)	50
Next 30 firms (each)	20
Industry	**2,625**

17.2 OUTPUT AND PRICE DECISIONS

Think about the decisions that Tommy Hilfiger must make about Tommy jeans. First, the firm must decide on the design and quality of its jeans and on its marketing program. We'll suppose that Tommy Hilfiger has already made these decisions so that we can concentrate on the firm's output and pricing decision. But we'll study quality and marketing decisions in the next section.

Because Tommy Hilfiger has chosen the quality of its jeans and the amount of marketing activity, it faces given costs and market demand. How, with these costs and market demand for its jeans, does Tommy Hilfiger decide the *quantity* of jeans to produce and the *price* at which to sell them?

■ The Firm's Profit-Maximizing Decision

A firm in monopolistic competition makes its output and price decision just as a monopoly firm does. Tommy Hilfiger maximizes profit by producing the quantity at which marginal revenue equals marginal cost and by charging the highest price that buyers are willing to pay for this quantity.

Figure 17.1 illustrates this decision for Tommy jeans. The demand curve for Tommy jeans is *D*. The *MR* curve shows the marginal revenue curve associated with this demand curve and is derived just like the marginal revenue curve of a single-price monopoly in Chapter 16. The *ATC* curve shows the average total cost of producing Tommy jeans, and *MC* is the marginal cost curve. Profit is maximized by producing 125 pairs of jeans a day and selling them at a price of $75 a pair. When Tommy Hilfiger produces 125 pairs of jeans a day, average total cost is $25 a pair and economic profit is $6,250 a day ($50 a pair multiplied by 125 pairs a day). The blue rectangle shows Tommy Hilfiger's economic profit.

■ **FIGURE 17.1**

Output and Price in Monopolistic Competition

MyEconLab Animation

❶ Profit is maximized where marginal revenue equals marginal cost.

❷ The profit-maximizing quantity is 125 pairs of Tommy jeans a day.

❸ The profit-maximizing price is $75 a pair, which exceeds the average total cost of $25 a pair, so the firm makes an economic profit of $50 a pair.

❹ The blue rectangle illustrates economic profit and its area, which equals $6,250 a day ($50 a pair multiplied by 125 pairs), measures economic profit.

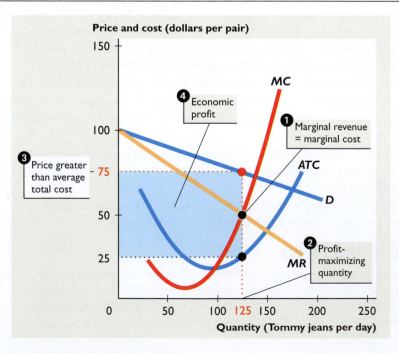

■ Profit Maximizing Might Be Loss Minimizing

Tommy Hilfiger in Figure 17.1 is making a healthy economic profit, but such an outcome is not inevitable. The demand for a firm's product might be too low for it to make an economic profit. Excite@Home was such a firm. Offering high-speed Internet service over the same cable that provides television, Excite@Home hoped to capture a large share of the Internet portal market in competition with AOL, MSN, and a host of other providers.

Figure 17.2 illustrates the situation facing Excite@Home in 2001. The demand curve for its portal service is *D*, the marginal revenue curve is *MR*, the average total cost curve is *ATC*, and the marginal cost curve is *MC*. Excite@Home maximizes profit—equivalently, it minimizes its loss—by producing the output at which marginal revenue equals marginal cost. In Figure 17.2, this output is 40,000 customers. Excite@Home charges the price that buyers are willing to pay for this quantity, which is determined by the demand curve and which is $40 a month. With 40,000 customers, Excite@Home's average total cost is $50 a customer, so Excite@Home incurs an economic loss of $400,000 a month ($10 a customer multiplied by 40,000 customers). The red rectangle shows the firm's economic loss.

The largest loss that a firm will incur is equal to total fixed cost. The reason is that if the profit-maximizing (loss-minimizing) price is less than average variable cost, the firm will shut down temporarily and produce nothing (just like a firm in perfect competition—see pp. 377–378).

So far, the firm in monopolistic competition looks like a single-price monopoly. It produces the quantity at which marginal revenue equals marginal cost and then charges the highest price that buyers are willing to pay for that quantity. The difference between monopoly and monopolistic competition lies in what happens when firms either make an economic profit or incur an economic loss.

■ FIGURE 17.2

Economic Loss in the Short Run

MyEconLab Animation

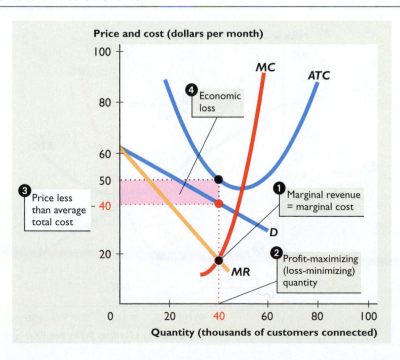

❶ Profit is maximized and loss is minimized where marginal revenue equals marginal cost.

❷ The loss-minimizing quantity is 40,000 customers connected.

❸ The price of $40 a month is less than average total cost of $50 a month, so the firm incurs an economic loss of $10 a customer.

❹ The red rectangle illustrates economic loss and its area, which equals $400,000 a month ($10 a customer multiplied by 40,000 customers), measures the economic loss.

■ Long Run: Zero Economic Profit

A firm like Excite@Home is not going to incur an economic loss for long. Eventually, it exits the market. So in the long run, no firm in the market will be incurring an economic loss. Also, there is no restriction on entry in monopolistic competition, so if firms in an industry are making economic profits, other firms have an incentive to enter that industry and each firm's economic profit falls. So in the long run, firms will enter until all firms are making zero economic profit.

Tommy Hilfiger is making an economic profit, which is an incentive for the Gap and Calvin Klein to start to make jeans similar to Tommy jeans. As they enter the jeans market, the demand for Tommy jeans decreases. At each point in time, the firm maximizes its profit by producing the quantity at which marginal revenue equals marginal cost and by charging the highest price that buyers are willing to pay for this quantity. But as demand decreases, marginal revenue decreases and the profit-maximizing quantity and price fall.

Figure 17.3 shows the long-run equilibrium. The demand curve for Tommy jeans and the marginal revenue curve have shifted leftward. The firm produces 75 pairs of jeans a day and sells them for $50 each. At this output level, average total cost is also $50 a pair. So Tommy Hilfiger is making zero economic profit on its jeans. When all the firms in the industry are making zero economic profit, there is no incentive for new firms to enter.

If demand is so low relative to costs that firms incur economic losses, exit will occur. As firms leave an industry, the demand for the products of the remaining firms increases and their demand curves shift rightward. The exit process ends when all the firms in the industry are making zero economic profit.

■ FIGURE 17.3

Output and Price in the Long Run

MyEconLab Animation

Economic profit encourages entry, which decreases the demand for each firm's product. Economic loss encourages exit, which increases the demand for each remaining firm's product.

When the demand curve touches the average total cost curve at the quantity at which marginal revenue equals marginal cost, the market is in long-run equilibrium.

❶ The output that maximizes profit is 75 pairs of Tommy jeans a day.

❷ The price, $50 a pair, equals average total cost.

❸ Economic profit is zero.

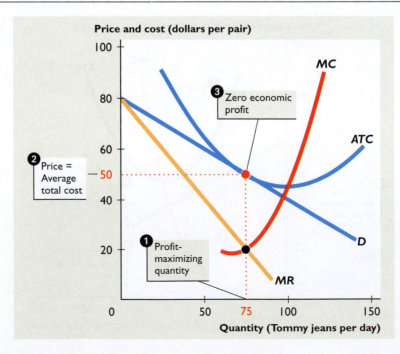

■ Monopolistic Competition and Perfect Competition

Figure 17.4 compares monopolistic competition and perfect competition in the long run and highlights two key differences: excess capacity and markup.

Excess Capacity

A firm's **efficient scale** is the quantity at which average total cost is a minimum—the quantity at the bottom of the U-shaped *ATC* curve. A firm's **excess capacity** is the amount by which its efficient scale exceeds the quantity that it produces. Figure 17.4(a) shows that in the long run Tommy Hilfiger has *excess capacity*. Because the demand curve for Tommy jeans is downward sloping, zero economic profit occurs where the *ATC* curve is downward sloping. A firm in perfect competition in the long run, Figure 17.4(b), has no excess capacity. Because its demand curve is horizontal, zero economic profit occurs at minimum average total cost.

Efficient scale
The quantity at which average total cost is a minimum.

Excess capacity
The amount by which the efficient scale exceeds the quantity that the firm produces.

Markup

A firm's **markup** is the amount by which its price exceeds its marginal cost. Figure 17.4(a) shows Tommy's markup. Figure 17.4(b) shows the zero markup of a firm in perfect competition. Buyers pay a higher price in monopolistic competition than in perfect competition and pay more than marginal cost.

Markup
The amount by which price exceeds marginal cost.

■ **FIGURE 17.4**

Excess Capacity and Markup in the Long Run

MyEconLab Animation

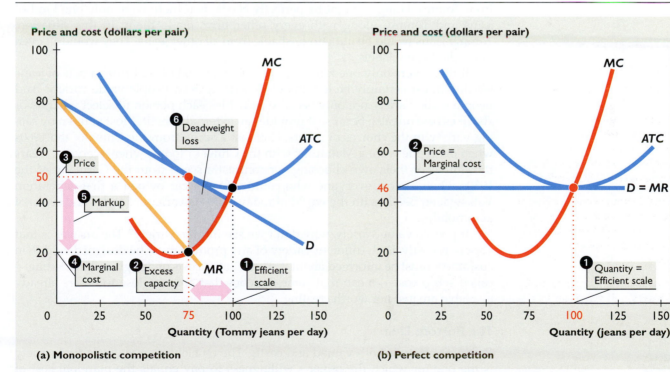

(a) Monopolistic competition

(b) Perfect competition

❶ The efficient scale (at minimum *ATC*) is 100 pairs a day. In the long run in monopolistic competition, the firm produces 75 jeans a day and has ❷ excess capacity. ❸ Price exceeds ❹ marginal cost by the amount of the ❺ markup and ❻ creates a deadweight loss.

In contrast, the firm in perfect competition has no excess capacity and no markup because the demand for the firm's output is perfectly elastic. ❶ The quantity produced equals the efficient scale and ❷ price equals marginal cost.

◼ Is Monopolistic Competition Efficient?

You've learned that resources are used efficiently when marginal benefit equals marginal cost. You've also learned that price measures marginal benefit. So if the price of a pair of Tommy jeans exceeds the marginal cost of producing them, the quantity of Tommy jeans produced is less than the efficient quantity. And you've just seen that in long-run equilibrium in monopolistic competition, price *does* exceed marginal cost.

Deadweight Loss

Because price exceeds marginal cost, monopolistic competition creates deadweight loss, just like monopoly. Figure 17.4(a) shows this deadweight loss. But is monopolistic competition less efficient than perfect competition?

Making the Relevant Comparison

Two economists meet in the street, and one asks the other, "How is your husband?" "Compared to what?" is the quick reply. This bit of economic wit illustrates a key point: Before we can make an effective comparison, we must check out the available alternatives.

The markup that drives a gap between price and marginal cost in monopolistic competition arises from product differentiation. Tommy jeans are not quite the same as jeans from Banana Republic, CK, Diesel, DKNY, Earl Jeans, Gap, Levi, Ralph Lauren, or any of the other dozens of producers of jeans, so the demand for Tommy jeans is not perfectly elastic. The only way in which the demand for jeans from Tommy Hilfiger might be perfectly elastic is if there were only one kind of jeans and Tommy, along with every other firm, made them. In this situation, Tommy jeans would be indistinguishable from all other jeans. They wouldn't even have identifying labels.

If there were only one kind of jeans, the marginal benefit from a pair of jeans would almost certainly be less than it is with variety. People value variety. And people value variety not only because it enables each person to select what he or she likes best but also because it provides an external benefit. Most of us enjoy seeing variety in the choices of others. Contrast a scene from the China of the 1960s when everyone wore a Mao tunic with the China of today, when everyone wears the clothes of their own choosing. Or contrast a scene from the Germany of the 1930s when almost everyone who could afford a car owned a first-generation Volkswagen Beetle with the world of today, with its variety of styles and types of automobiles.

If people value variety, why don't we see infinite variety? The answer is that variety is costly. Each different variety of any product must be designed, and then customers must be informed about it. These initial costs of design and marketing—called setup costs—mean that some varieties that are too close to others already available are just not worth creating.

The Bottom Line

Product variety is both valued and costly. The efficient degree of product variety is the one for which the buyer's willingness to pay equals the marginal cost of product variety. The loss that arises because the willingness to pay for one more unit of a given variety exceeds marginal cost is offset by a gain that arises from having more product variety. So compared to the alternative—complete product uniformity—monopolistic competition is efficient.

CHECKPOINT 17.2

Explain how a firm in monopolistic competition determines its output and price in the short run and the long run.

Practice Problems

Natti is a dot.com entrepreneur who has established a Web site at which people can design and buy awesome sunglasses. Natti pays $4,000 a month for her Web server and Internet connection. The sunglasses that her customers design are made to order by another firm, and Natti pays this firm $50 a pair. Natti has no other costs. Table 1 shows the demand schedule for Natti's sunglasses.

1. Calculate Natti's profit-maximizing output, price, and economic profit.

2. Do you expect other firms to enter the market and compete with Natti?

3. What happens to the demand for Natti's sunglasses in the long run? What happens to Natti's economic profit in the long run?

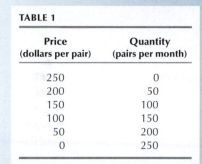

TABLE 1

Price (dollars per pair)	Quantity (pairs per month)
250	0
200	50
150	100
100	150
50	200
0	250

In the News

Condé Nast shuts down Portfolio
Condé Nast Publications launched its monthly business magazine *Portfolio* less than two years ago. In late 2008, Condé Nast cut its payroll and advertising budgets by an average of 5 percent. *Portfolio* was hit with the biggest cuts. Recently, Condé Nast shut down *Portfolio*.
Source: *The Wall Street Journal*, April 28, 2009
Explain the effects of the payroll and advertising budget cuts on Condé Nast's economic loss in the short run. Why did Condé Nast shut down *Portfolio*?

Solutions to Practice Problems

1. Marginal cost, *MC*, is $50 a pair—the price that Natti pays her supplier of sunglasses. To find marginal revenue, calculate the change in total revenue when the quantity increases by 1 pair of sunglasses. Figure 1 shows the demand curve, the marginal revenue curve, and the marginal cost curve. Profit is maximized when *MC = MR* and Natti sells 100 pairs a month. The price is $150, and average total cost, *ATC*, is $90—the sum of $50 marginal (and average variable) cost and $40 average fixed cost. Economic profit is $60 a pair on 100 pairs a month, so it is $6,000 a month.

2. Natti is making an economic profit, so firms have an incentive to enter the Web sunglasses market and will do so.

3. As firms enter the market, the demand for Natti's sunglasses decreases, the price of Natti's sunglasses falls, and Natti's economic profit decreases. In the long run, Natti's will make zero economic profit.

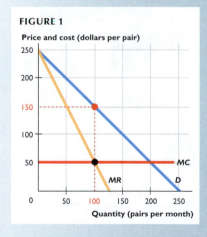

FIGURE 1

Solution to In the News

Payroll and advertising budgets are fixed costs, so a cut in these costs shifts the *ATC* and *MC* curves downward. With no change in the prices of the magazines, Condé Nast's economic loss decreased. Condé Nast shut down *Portfolio* because its loss from *Portfolio* exceeded its total fixed cost and the company expected the loss to continue in the coming year.

17.3 PRODUCT DEVELOPMENT AND MARKETING

When we studied a firm's output and price decisions, we supposed that the firm had already made its product quality and marketing decisions. We're now going to study these decisions and the impact they have on the firm's output, price, and economic profit.

■ Product Development

To enjoy economic profits, firms in monopolistic competition must be continually developing new products because whenever firms make economic profits, imitators emerge and set up business. So to maintain its economic profit, a firm must seek out new products that will provide it with a competitive edge, even if only temporarily. A firm that manages to introduce a new and differentiated product will temporarily face a less elastic demand and will be able to increase its price temporarily. The firm will make an economic profit. Eventually, new firms that make close substitutes for the innovative product will enter and compete away the economic profit. So to restore economic profit, the firm must again innovate.

Profit-Maximizing Product Development

The decision to develop a new product (or new version of a product) is based on the same type of profit-maximizing calculation that you've already studied. At a low level of product development, the marginal revenue from a better product exceeds the marginal cost. At a high level of product development, the marginal cost of a better product exceeds the marginal revenue. When the marginal cost of a better product equals the marginal revenue from a better product, the firm is doing the profit-maximizing amount of product development.

For example, when Electronic Arts released its latest version of Madden NFL, it was probably not the best game that Electronic Arts could have created. But it was a game with features whose marginal revenue—arising from consumers' willingness to pay—equaled the marginal cost of those features.

Efficiency and Product Development

Is product development an efficient activity? Does it benefit the consumer? There are two views about the answers to these questions. One view is that monopolistic competition brings to market many improved products that bring great benefits to the consumer. Clothing, kitchen and other household appliances, computers, computer programs, cars, and many other products keep getting better every year, and the consumer benefits from these improved products.

But many so-called improvements amount to little more than changing the appearance of a product or giving a different look to the packaging. In these cases, there is little objective benefit to the consumer.

But regardless of whether a product improvement is real or imagined, its value to the consumer is its marginal benefit, which equals the amount the consumer is willing to pay. In other words, the value of a product improvement is the increase in price that the consumer is willing to pay. The marginal benefit to the producer is marginal revenue, which in equilibrium equals marginal cost. Because price exceeds marginal cost in monopolistic competition, product improvement is not pushed to its efficient level.

A profit-maximizing game has features that users value at least as highly as the marginal cost of programming the features.

■ Marketing

Firms differentiate their products by designing and developing features that differ from those of their competitors' products. But firms also attempt to create a consumer perception of product differentiation even when actual differences are small. Advertising and packaging are the principal means firms use to achieve this end. An American Express card is a different product from a Visa card, but the actual differences are not the main ones that American Express emphasizes in its marketing. The deeper message is that if you use an American Express card, you can be like a celebrity or a high-profile successful person.

Marketing Expenditures

Firms incur huge costs to ensure that buyers appreciate and value the differences between their own products and those of their competitors. So a large proportion of the price that we pay covers the cost of selling a good, and this proportion is increasing. Advertising in newspapers and magazines and on radio, television, and the Internet is one type of selling cost, but it is not the only one. Selling costs include the cost of shopping malls that look like movie sets; glossy catalogs and brochures; and the salaries, airfares, and hotel bills of salespeople.

The total scale of advertising costs is hard to estimate, but some components can be measured. A survey conducted by a commercial agency found that about 15 percent of the price of liquor, 12 percent of the prices of movies and medical doctors, and about 10 percent of the price of beer cover advertising expenditures.

EYE on CELL PHONES
Which Cell Phone?

There is a lot of product differentiation in cell phones: Nokia makes 143 versions; Samsung makes 103; and Sony Ericsson makes 100. In the three months from April through June 2011, hundreds of new varieties of cell phones were announced by the top 20 firms in this market. Why is there so much variety in cell phones?

The answer is that preferences are diverse and the cost of matching the diversity of preference is low.

Think about the ways in which cell phones differ: just a few of them are their dimensions, weight, navigation tools, talk time, standby time, screen, camera features, audio features, memory, connectivity, processor speed, storage, and network capability.

Each one of these features comes in dozens of varieties. If we combine only 10 of these features, each having 6 varieties, there are 1 million different possible cell-phone designs.

Firms produce variety only when the marginal cost of doing so is less than the marginal benefit. The marginal cost of some cell-phone variety is not large. Adding a feature to a camera, making the memory a bit bigger, and using a more economical battery are all relatively low-cost adjustments that phone designers can make.

A new way of adding variety, at almost zero cost, brings product differentiation that makes each cell phone unique to the preferences of each individual. This new way is the cell-phone application, or app.

Apple has only two versions of the iPhone, but because of the large and growing number of program apps, each iPhone owner can load their phone with exactly the apps they want.

In long-run equilibrium, entry and innovation by each competitor will drive economic profit toward zero. Each cell-phone maker will offer a degree of product differentiation that equates the marginal cost of variety with its marginal revenue. But the pursuit of economic profit will spur ever more innovation and consumers will be confronted with ever wider choice.

For the U.S. economy as a whole, there are some 20,000 advertising agencies, which employ more than 200,000 people and have total revenue of $45 billion. But these numbers are only part of the total cost of advertising because many firms have their own internal advertising departments, the costs of which we can only guess.

Advertising expenditures and other selling costs affect firms' profits in two ways: They increase costs and they change demand. Let's look at these effects.

Selling Costs and Total Costs

Selling costs such as advertising expenditures increase the costs of a monopolistically competitive firm above those of a perfectly competitive firm or a monopoly. Advertising costs and other selling costs are fixed costs. They do not vary as total output varies. So, just like fixed production costs, advertising costs per unit of output decrease as production increases.

Figure 17.5 shows how selling costs and advertising expenditures change a firm's average total cost. The blue curve shows the average total cost of production. The red curve shows the firm's average total cost of production plus advertising. The height of the shaded area between the two curves shows the average fixed cost of advertising. The *total* cost of advertising is fixed. But the *average* cost of advertising decreases as output increases.

Figure 17.5 shows that if advertising increases the quantity sold by a large enough amount, it can lower average total cost. For example, if the quantity sold increases from 25 pairs of jeans a day with no advertising to 100 pairs of jeans a day with advertising, average total cost falls from $60 a pair to $40 a pair. The reason is that although the *total* fixed cost has increased, the greater fixed cost is spread over a greater output, so average total cost decreases.

■ **FIGURE 17.5**

Selling Costs and Total Costs

MyEconLab Animation

Selling costs such as the cost of advertising are fixed costs.

❶ When advertising costs are added to ❷ the average total cost of production, ❸ average total cost increases by more at small outputs than at large outputs.

❹ If advertising enables the quantity sold to increase from 25 pairs of jeans a day to 100 pairs a day, it *lowers* average total cost from $60 a pair to $40 a pair.

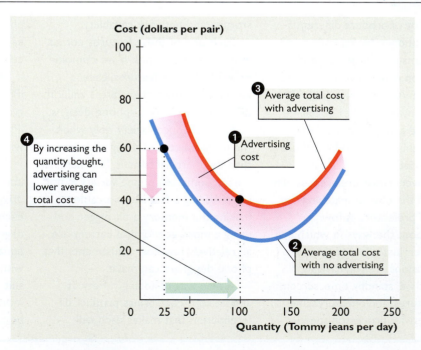

Selling Costs and Demand

Advertising and other selling efforts change the demand for a firm's product. But how? Does demand increase or does it decrease? The most natural answer is that advertising increases demand. By informing people about the quality of its products or by persuading people to switch from the products of other firms, a firm might expect to increase the demand for its own products.

But all firms in monopolistic competition advertise. And all seek to persuade customers that they have the best deal. If advertising enables a firm to survive, it might increase the number of firms in the market. And to the extent that it increases the number of firms, it decreases the demand for any one firm's products. With all firms advertising, the demand for any one firm's product might become more elastic. So advertising can end up not only lowering average total cost but also lowering the price and decreasing the markup.

Figure 17.6 illustrates this possible effect of advertising. In part (a), with no advertising, the demand for Tommy jeans is not very elastic. Profit is maximized at 75 pairs of jeans a day, and the markup is large. In part (b), advertising, which is a fixed cost, increases average total cost and shifts the average total cost curve upward from ATC_0 to ATC_1 but leaves the marginal cost curve unchanged at MC. Demand becomes much more elastic, the profit-maximizing quantity increases, and the markup shrinks.

■ FIGURE 17.6

Advertising and the Markup   MyEconLab Animation

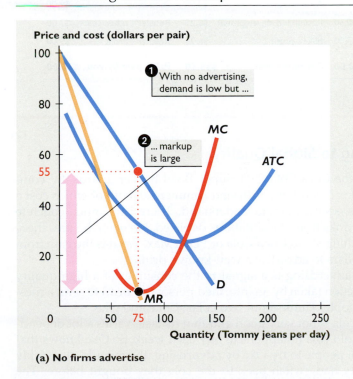

(a) No firms advertise

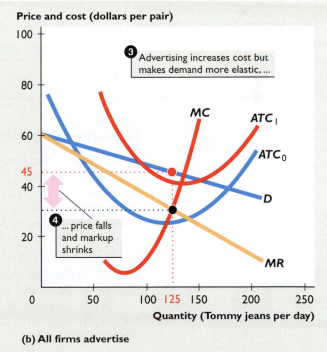

(b) All firms advertise

❶ With no firms advertising, demand is low and not very elastic, so the ❷ markup is large.

❸ Advertising shifts the average total cost curve upward from ATC_0 to ATC_1. If, with all firms advertising, demand becomes more elastic, ❹ the price falls and the markup shrinks.

EYE on YOUR LIFE
Some Selling Costs You Pay

When you buy a new pair of running shoes, you're buying materials that cost $9, paying the producer in Asia and the shipping company for production and transportation costs of $8, paying the U.S. government an import duty of $3, and paying advertisers, retailers, and others who provide sales and distribution services $50.

The table provides a breakdown of the cost of a pair of shoes. Notice the huge gap between the retailer's cost and the price that you pay. The retail markup is about 100 percent.

Running shoes are not unusual. Almost everything that you buy includes a selling cost component that exceeds one half of the total cost. Your clothing, food, electronic items, DVDs, magazines, and even your textbooks cost more to sell than they cost to produce.

| | Raw materials $9 | Production costs $8 | Import duty $3 | Selling costs $50 |

Manufacturer (Asia)		Nike (Beaverton, Oregon)		Retailer (your town)	
Materials	$9.00				
Cost of labor	$2.75	Cost of shoe to Nike	$20.00	Cost of shoe to retailer	$35.50
Cost of capital	$3.00	Sales, distribution, and administration	$5.00	Sales clerk's wages	$9.50
Profit	$1.75	Advertising	$4.00	Shop rent	$9.00
Shipping	$0.50	Research & development	$0.25	Retailer's other costs	$7.00
Import duty	$3.00	Nike's profit	$6.25	Retailer's profit	$9.00
Nike's cost	**$20.00**	**Retailer's cost**	**$35.50**	**Price paid by you**	**$70.00**

■ Using Advertising to Signal Quality

Some advertising, like the Coca-Cola 2011 Super Bowl border guards TV commercial and the Pepsi Max controlling girlfriend commercial, both of which cost a huge number of dollars, seems hard to understand. There isn't much concrete information about the drinks from the situations depicted. No one who sees these commercials learns anything about Coca-Cola or Pepsi Max. What is the gain from spending millions of dollars to advertise a well-known drink?

One answer is that advertising is a signal to the consumer of a high-quality product. A **signal** is an action taken by an informed person (or firm) to send a message to less-informed people. Think about two colas: Coke and Oke.

Oke knows that its cola is not very good and that its taste varies a lot depending on which cheap unsold cola it happens to buy each week. So Oke knows that while it could get a lot of people to try Oke by advertising, they would all quickly discover its poor quality and switch back to the cola they bought before. The amount that Oke spent on advertising would exceed the revenue that came in.

Coke, in contrast, knows that its product has a high-quality consistent taste and that once someone has tried it, there is a good chance that they'll never drink

Signal
An action taken by an informed person (or firm) to send a message to less-informed people.

anything but Coke. If Coke ran a costly advertising campaign, more people would try Coke and most would stick with it. The revenue earned would exceed the cost of the advertising campaign.

On the basis of this reasoning, Oke doesn't advertise but Coke does. And Coke spends a lot of money to make a big splash.

Cola drinkers who see Coke's splashy ads believe that the firm would not spend so much money advertising if its product were not truly good. So the cola drinker reasons that Coke is indeed a really good product. The flashy expensive ad has signaled that Coke is really good without saying anything about Coke.

Notice that if advertising is a signal, it doesn't need any specific product information. It just needs to be expensive and hard to miss. That's what a lot of advertising looks like. So the signaling theory of advertising predicts much of the advertising that we see.

■ Brand Names

Many firms create a brand name and spend a lot of money promoting it. Why? What benefit does a brand name bring to justify the sometimes high cost of establishing it? The basic answer is that a brand name provides consumers with information about the quality of a product and the producer with an incentive to achieve a high and consistent quality standard.

To see how a brand name helps the consumer, think about how you use brand names to get information about quality. You're on a road trip, and it is time to find a place to spend the night. You see roadside advertisements for Holiday Inn and Embassy Suites and for Joe's Motel and Annie's Driver's Stop. You know about Holiday Inn and Embassy Suites because you've stayed in them before. And you've seen their advertisements. You know what to expect from them. You have no information at all about Joe's and Annie's. They might be better than the lodging you do know about, but without that knowledge, you're not going to chance them. You use the brand name as information and stay at Holiday Inn.

This same story explains why a brand name provides an incentive to the producer to achieve high and consistent quality. Because no one would know whether they were offering a high standard of service, Joe's and Annie's have no incentive to do so. But equally, because everyone expects a given standard of service from Holiday Inn, a failure to meet a customer's expectation would almost surely lose that customer to a competitor. So Holiday Inn has a strong incentive to deliver what it promises in the advertising that creates its brand name.

■ Efficiency of Advertising and Brand Names

To the extent that advertising and brand names provide consumers with information about the precise nature of product differences and about product quality, they benefit the consumer and enable a better product choice to be made. But the opportunity cost of the additional information must be weighed against the gain to the consumer.

The final verdict on the efficiency of monopolistic competition is ambiguous. In some cases, the gains from extra product variety unquestionably offset the selling costs and the extra cost arising from excess capacity. The tremendous varieties of books and magazines, clothing, food, and drinks are examples of such gains. It is less easy to see the gains from being able to buy brand-name drugs that have a chemical composition identical to that of a generic alternative, but many people do willingly pay more for the brand-name alternative.

MyEconLab

You can work these problems in Study Plan 17.3 and get instant feedback.

CHECKPOINT 17.3

Explain why advertising costs are high and why firms use brand names in monopolistic competition.

Practice Problems

Bianca bakes delicious cookies. Her total fixed cost is $40 a day, and her average variable cost is $1 a bag. Few people know about Bianca's Cookies, and she maximizes her profit by selling 10 bags a day for $5 a bag. Bianca thinks that if she spends $50 a day on advertising, she will sell 25 bags a day for $5 a bag.

1. If Bianca's belief about the effect of advertising is correct, can she increase her economic profit by advertising?

2. If Bianca advertises, will her average total cost increase or decrease at the quantity produced?

3. If Bianca advertises, will she continue to sell her cookies for $5 a bag or will she raise her price or lower her price?

In the News

Purex tackles tough market, using new spin

Americans like to pour their own laundry detergent, but Dial plans to launch Purex Complete, a "3-in-1" laundry sheet embedded with detergent, fabric softener, and antistatic agents and in an easy to use container. Only about 50 percent of consumers currently use softener and antistatic agents (laundry additives). Dial will spend $50 million marketing Purex Complete.

Source: *The Wall Street Journal*, April 28, 2009

Why create a new laundry detergent when there are so many? What "new spin" would you stress in the marketing campaign?

Solutions to Practice Problems

1. With no advertising, Bianca's total revenue is $50 (10 bags at $5 a bag) and her total cost is $50 ($40 total fixed cost plus $10 total variable cost). Bianca's economic profit is zero. With $50 a day advertising expenditure, total revenue is $125 (25 bags at $5 a bag) and total cost is $115 ($90 total fixed cost plus $25 total variable cost). Bianca's economic profit with no price change is $10, so Bianca can increase her economic profit by advertising.

2. If Bianca advertises, her average total cost will decrease. With no advertising, her average total cost is $5 a bag ($50 ÷ 10). With advertising, her average total cost is $4.60 a bag ($115 ÷ 25).

3. We can't say if Bianca will sell her cookies for $5 a bag. Advertising changes the demand for her cookies. Although it increases fixed cost, marginal cost remains at $1 a bag. Bianca will sell the profit-maximizing quantity at the highest price she can charge for that quantity.

Solution to In the News

A new product is developed and launched if the marginal benefit from its development exceeds the marginal cost of its development. Because many consumers seem to find separate laundry additives inconvenient, the marketing campaign should target these people and stress the convenience feature.

CHAPTER SUMMARY

Key Points

1 Describe and identify monopolistic competition.

- Monopolistic competition is a market structure in which a large number of firms compete; each firm produces a product that is slightly different from the products of its competitors; firms compete on price, quality, and marketing; and new firms are free to enter the industry.

- Monopolistic competition is identified by a low degree of concentration measured by either the four-firm concentration ratio or the HHI.

2 Explain how a firm in monopolistic competition determines its output and price in the short run and the long run.

- The firm in monopolistic competition faces a downward-sloping demand curve and produces the quantity at which marginal revenue equals marginal cost.

- Entry and exit result in zero economic profit and excess capacity in long-run equilibrium.

3 Explain why advertising costs are high and why firms use brand names in monopolistic competition.

- Firms in monopolistic competition innovate and develop new products to maintain economic profit.

- Advertising expenditures increase total cost, but they might lower average total cost if the quantity sold increases by enough.

- Advertising expenditures might increase demand, but they might also increase competition and decrease the demand facing a firm.

- Whether monopolistic competition is inefficient depends on the value people place on product variety.

Key Terms

Efficient scale, 441
Excess capacity, 441
Four-firm concentration ratio, 434
Herfindahl-Hirschman Index, 435

Markup, 441
Product differentiation, 432
Signal, 448

CHAPTER CHECKPOINT

Study Plan Problems and Applications

1. Which of the following items are sold by firms in monopolistic competition? Explain your selections.
   - Cable television service
   - Wheat
   - Athletic shoes
   - Soda
   - Toothbrushes
   - Ready-mix concrete

2. The four-firm concentration ratio for audio equipment makers is 30 and for electric lamp makers is 89. The HHI for audio equipment makers is 415 and for electric lamp makers is 2,850. Which of these markets is an example of monopolistic competition?

Use Figure 1, which shows the demand curve, marginal revenue curve, and cost curves of Lite and Kool, Inc., a producer of running shoes in monopolistic competition, to work Problems 3 to 5.

3. In the short run, what quantity does Lite and Kool produce, what price does it charge, and does it make an economic profit?

4. In the short run, does Lite and Kool have excess capacity and what is its markup?

5. Do you expect firms to enter the running shoes market or exit from that market in the long run? Explain your answer.

Use Figure 2, which shows the demand curve, marginal revenue curve, and cost curves of Stiff Shirt, Inc., a producer of shirts in monopolistic competition, to work Problems 6 and 7.

6. In the short run, what is the quantity that Stiff Shirt produces, the price it charges, its economic profit, markup, and excess capacity?

7. In the long run, will new firms enter the shirt market or will firms exit from that market and will the price of a shirt rise or fall? Explain your answer.

8. Mike's, a firm in monopolistic competition, produces bikes. With no advertising, Mike's profit-maximizing output is 500 bikes a day and the price is $100 a bike. Now all firms begin to advertise. With advertising, Mike's maximizes profit by producing 1,000 bikes a day and charging $50 a bike. How does advertising change Mike's markup and excess capacity?

9. **Apple developing new iPad**
   Apple Inc. reported blowout earnings for the quarter ended June 25, due in part to the popularity of its iPad. The company sold 9.3 million units in the quarter, nearly triple what it sold a year earlier. Still, its next generation iPad is expected later in 2011.

   Source: *The Wall Street Journal*, August 19, 2011

   With Apple's iPad sales so strong, why would Apple Inc. be rushing to bring a more advanced iPad to the market? Explain how Apple's economic profit will likely change as competition in the iPad market intensifies.

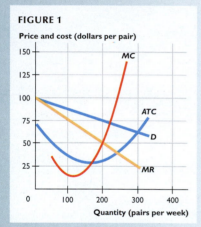

FIGURE 1

Price and cost (dollars per pair)

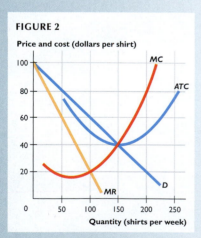

FIGURE 2

Price and cost (dollars per shirt)

Instructor Assignable Problems and Applications

Your instructor can assign these problems as homework, a quiz, or a test in MyEconLab

1. Washtenaw Dairy in Ann Arbor, Michigan, sells 63 flavors of Strohs Mooney's ice cream, and Ben and Jerry's Web site also lists 63 different flavors of ice cream. These numbers are similar to the varieties of cell phones sold by Samsung, Nokia, and Motorola. Toyota makes only 16 varieties of vehicles and Boeing makes 16 varieties of airplanes. Why is there more variety in cell phones and ice cream than in automobiles and airplanes?

2. The HHI for automobiles is 2,350, for sporting goods is 161, for batteries is 2,883, and for jewelry is 81. Which of these markets is an example of monopolistic competition?

Use Figure 1, which shows the demand curve, marginal revenue curve, and cost curves of La Bella Pizza, a firm in monopolistic competition, to work Problems **3** and **4**.

3. In the short run, what is the quantity that La Bella Pizza produces, the price it charges, its markup, and its excess capacity?

4. In the long run, how will the number of pizza producers change? What are the excess capacity and the deadweight loss created? Explain your answer.

Use the following information to work Problems **5** and **6**.

A new swing for female golfers
Callaway and Nike, two of the leading golf-equipment manufacturers, recently released new clubs designed for women. They are the hottest innovation in golf.
Source: *Time*, April 21, 2008

5. How are Callaway and Nike attempting to maintain economic profit? Draw a graph to illustrate Callaway's or Nike's short-run economic profit in the market for golf clubs for women.

6. Explain why the economic profit that Callaway and Nike make in this market is likely to be temporary. Draw a graph to illustrate their excess capacity in the long run.

7. Some people happily pay more for Coke or Pepsi than they are willing to pay for a nonbranded cola. And some people happily pay more for Tylenol than they are willing to pay for generic acetaminophen. How do brand names help consumers? How do brand names change the behavior of producers? Why would it not be efficient to make brand names illegal?

Use the following information to work Problems **8** and **9**.

Suppose that Tommy Hilfiger's marginal cost of a jacket is a constant $100 and at one of the firm's shops, total fixed cost is $2,000 a day. The profit-maximizing number of jackets sold in this shop is 20 a day. When the shops nearby start to advertise their jackets, this Tommy Hilfiger shop spends $2,000 a day advertising its jackets, and its profit-maximizing output jumps to 50 jackets a day.

8. What is this shop's average total cost of a jacket sold before it starts to advertise? What is its average total cost of a jacket with advertising?

9. Can you say what happens to Tommy's markup and its economic profit? Why or why not?

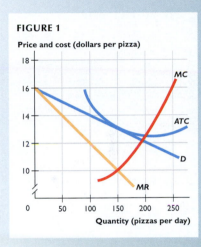

FIGURE 1

Price and cost (dollars per pizza)

MyEconLab
You can work this quiz in
Chapter 17 Study Plan and get
instant feedback.

Multiple Choice Quiz

1. Monopolistic competition differs from _____.

A. monopoly because firm's cannot set their own price
B. oligopoly because firms produce differentiated goods or services
C. perfect competition because the goods or services produced are differentiated
D. monopoly because the good produced by each firm has no close substitute

2. The four largest firms in a market have the following market shares of total revenue: 20 percent, 15 percent, 10 percent, and 5 percent. The _____ in this industry is _____.

A. four-firm concentration ratio; 50 percent
B. four-firm concentration ratio; 750 percent
C. Herfindahl-Hirschman Index; 50
D. Herfindahl-Hirschman Index; 2,500

3. A firm in monopolistic competition maximizes its profit by _____.

A. differentiating its good and producing the quantity at which price equals marginal revenue
B. producing the quantity at which marginal revenue equals marginal cost and then adding a markup
C. raising its price and producing so that it always has excess capacity
D. producing the quantity at which marginal cost equals marginal revenue and charging the highest price at which it can sell that quantity

4. A firm in monopolistic competition that is maximizing profit _____.

A. always makes a positive economic profit in the short run
B. never needs to shut down because its price always exceeds minimum average variable cost
C. might, in the short run, sell at a price that is less than average total cost
D. shuts down temporarily if it incurs a loss equal to total variable cost

5. In the long run, each firm in monopolistic competition _____.

A. makes zero economic profit
B. makes as much economic profit as it would if it was a monopoly
C. has the same markup and excess capacity as it would if the market was perfectly competitive
D. creates the same deadweight loss as it would if it was a monopoly

6. If one firm advertises and other firms in the market don't, then _____.

A. the demand for the advertised good becomes more elastic
B. the profit-maximizing quantity of the advertised good decreases because total fixed costs increase
C. the average cost of producing a small quantity of the advertised good rises but the average total cost of producing a large quantity might fall
D. the economic profit made from the advertised good increases

7. Each firm in monopolistic competition uses a brand name and advertising to achieve all of the following *except* to _____.

A. differentiate its good from its competitors' goods
B. signal quality and reliability of its good
C. signal its market share
D. influence the demand for its good

Is two too few?

Oligopoly

**When you have completed your study of this chapter,
you will be able to**

1 Describe and identify oligopoly and explain how it arises.

2 Explain the dilemma faced by firms in oligopoly.

3 Use game theory to explain how price and quantity are determined in oligopoly.

4 Describe the antitrust laws that regulate oligopoly.

18.1 WHAT IS OLIGOPOLY?

Oligopoly, like monopolistic competition, is a type of market that lies between perfect competition and monopoly. The firms in oligopoly might produce an identical product and compete only on price, or they might produce a differentiated product and compete on price, product quality, and marketing. The distinguishing features of oligopoly are that

- A small number of firms compete.
- Natural or legal barriers prevent the entry of new firms.

■ Small Number of Firms

In contrast to monopolistic competition and perfect competition, an oligopoly consists of a small number of firms. Each firm has a large share of the market, the firms are interdependent, and they face a temptation to collude.

Interdependence

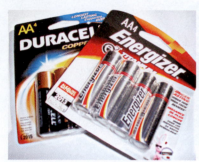

Energizer and Duracell dominate the market for batteries.

With a small number of firms in a market, each firm's actions influence the profits of the other firms. To see how, suppose you run one of the three gas stations in a small town. If you cut your price, your market share increases, and your profits might increase too. But the market share and profits of the other two firms fall. In this situation, the other firms will most likely cut their prices too. If they do cut their prices, your market share and profit take a tumble. So before deciding to cut your price, you must predict how the other firms will react and take into account the effects of those reactions on your own profit. Your profit depends on the actions of the other firms, and their profit depends on your actions. You and the other two firms are interdependent.

Temptation to Collude

Cartel
A group of firms acting together to limit output, raise price, and increase economic profit.

When a small number of firms share a market, they can increase their profits by forming a cartel and acting like a monopoly. A **cartel** is a group of firms acting together—colluding—to limit output, raise price, and increase economic profit. Cartels are illegal in the United States (and most other countries), although international cartels can operate legally (see *Eye on the Global Economy* on p. 463). But even when there is no formal cartel, firms might try to operate like a cartel.

For reasons that you'll discover in this chapter, cartels tend to be unstable and eventually break down.

■ Barriers to Entry

Either natural or legal barriers to entry can create oligopoly. You saw in Chapter 16 how economies of scale and demand form a natural barrier to entry that can create a *natural monopoly*. These same factors can also create a natural oligopoly.

Like natural monopoly, a natural oligopoly arises from the interaction of the market demand for a good or service and the extent of economies of scale in its production. Figure 18.1 illustrates two natural oligopolies.

Duopoly
A market with only two firms.

The demand curve, D (in both parts of the figure), shows the market demand for taxi rides in a town. If the average total cost curve of a taxi company is ATC_1 in part (a), the market is a natural **duopoly**—a market with only two firms. You

FIGURE 18.1

Natural Oligopoly

MyEconLab Animation

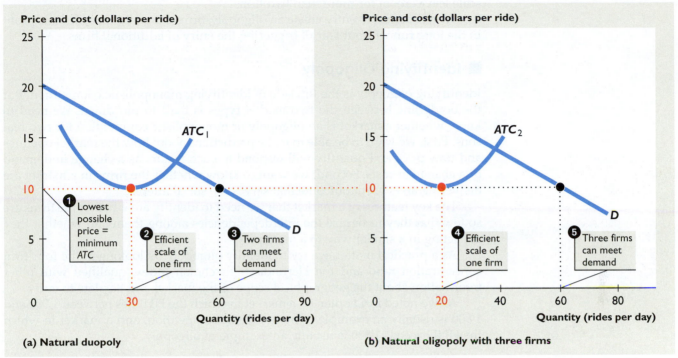

(a) Natural duopoly

(b) Natural oligopoly with three firms

❶ The lowest possible price is $10 a ride, which is the minimum average total cost. **❷** When a firm produces 30 rides a day, the efficient scale, **❸** two firms can satisfy the market demand. This natural oligopoly has two firms—a natural duopoly.

❹ When the efficient scale of one firm is 20 rides a day, **❺** three firms can satisfy the market demand at the lowest possible price. This natural oligopoly has three firms.

can probably see some examples of duopoly where you live. Some cities have only two suppliers of milk, two local newspapers, two taxi companies, two car rental firms, two copy centers, or two college bookstores.

Notice in part (a) that the efficient scale of one firm is 30 rides a day. The lowest price at which the firm would remain in business is $10 a ride. At that price, the quantity of rides demanded is 60 a day, the quantity that can be provided by just two firms. There is no room in this market for three firms. To sell more than 60 rides a day, the price would have to fall below $10 a ride. But then the firms would incur an economic loss, and one of them would exit. If there were only one firm, it would make an economic profit and a second firm would enter to take some of the business and economic profit.

If the average total cost curve of a taxi company is ATC_2 in part (b), the efficient scale of one firm is 20 rides a day. This market is large enough for three firms, but it is not large enough for a fourth firm. Economies of scale limit the market to three because each firm would incur an economic loss if there were four of them. And this market will not operate with two firms because with only two, economic profit would encourage the entry of a third firm.

A legal oligopoly arises when a legal barrier to entry protects the small number of firms in a market. A city might license two taxi firms or two bus companies, for example, even though the combination of market demand and economies of scale leaves room for more than two firms.

When barriers to entry create an oligopoly, firms can make an economic profit in the long run without fear of triggering the entry of additional firms.

■ Identifying Oligopoly

Identifying oligopoly is the flip side of identifying monopolistic competition. But the borderline between the two market types is hard to pin down. We need to know whether a market is an oligopoly or monopolistic competition for two reasons. First, we want to be able to make predictions about how the market operates and how price and quantity will respond to such factors as a change in demand or a change in costs. Second, we want to know whether the firms in a market are delivering an efficient outcome that serves the social interest.

The key features of a market that we need to identify are whether the firms are so few that they recognize the interdependencies among them and whether they are acting in a similar way to a monopoly.

As a practical matter, we try to identify oligopoly by looking at the four-firm concentration ratio and the Herfindahl-Hirschman Index, qualified with other information about the geographical scope of the market and barriers to entry.

As we noted in Chapter 17, a market in which the HHI lies between 1,000 and 1,800 is usually an example of monopolistic competition, and a market in which the HHI exceeds 1,800 is usually an example of oligopoly.

EYE on the U.S. ECONOMY
Examples of Oligopoly

You're familiar with some of the industries shown in the figure. You probably know, for example, that Kellogg's makes most of the breakfast cereals consumed in the United States. It is said that Kellogg's does more business before eight o'clock in the morning than most firms do all day!

You probably also know that Phillip Morris and RJ Reynolds make most of the cigarettes sold in the United States. You also know that you see Duracell, Energizer, and not much else when you go shopping for a battery. And the washing machine and dryer in your home were most likely made by General Electric, Maytag, or Whirlpool.

Some of the industries in the figure are less familiar, but you see a lot of their products without recognizing them. One of these industries is the manufacture of glass bottles and jars. When you buy anything that comes in glass, there's a good chance that the container was made in Toledo, Ohio, by Owens-Illinois, the world's largest glass packaging manufacturer.

There isn't much room for hesitation about identifying the first seven industries shown in the figure as oligopolies: They have a small number of firms, a high four-firm concentration ratio, and an HHI that exceeds 1,800.

All of these industries are ones in which the largest firms pay serious attention to each other and think hard about the impact of their decisions on their competitors and the repercussion they may themselves face from their competitors' reactions.

The last three industries in the figure are less easily classified. They might be considered borderline between oligopoly and monopolistic competition. The four-firm concentration ratio and HHI are high, but there are many firms in these industries. And while a few of the firms are very large, they face tough competition from the many others.

CHECKPOINT 18.1

Describe and identify oligopoly and explain how it arises.

Practice Problems

1. What are the distinguishing features of oligopoly?
2. Why are breakfast cereals made by firms in oligopoly? Why isn't there monopolistic competition in that industry?
3. *Business Week* reported that Energizer is gaining market share against competitor Duracell and its profit is rising despite the sharp rise in the price of zinc, a key battery ingredient. In what type of market are batteries sold? Explain your answer.

Solutions to Practice Problems

1. The distinguishing features of oligopoly are a small number of interdependent firms competing behind natural or legal barriers to entry.
2. Breakfast cereals are made by firms in oligopoly because economies of scale and the size of the market limit the number of firms that can make a profit.
3. The market for batteries is an oligopoly, and with two dominant firms, it is a duopoly. The number of firms is small, their actions are interdependent, and economies of scale and the market demand create a natural barrier to entry.

MyEconLab

You can work these problems in Study Plan 18.1 and get instant feedback.

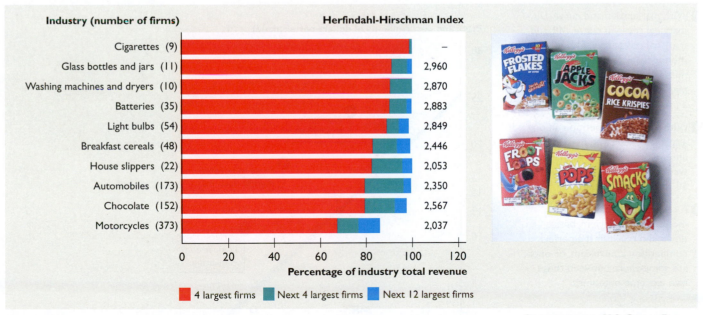

Industry (number of firms)	Herfindahl-Hirschman Index
Cigarettes (9)	–
Glass bottles and jars (11)	2,960
Washing machines and dryers (10)	2,870
Batteries (35)	2,883
Light bulbs (54)	2,849
Breakfast cereals (48)	2,446
House slippers (22)	2,053
Automobiles (173)	2,350
Chocolate (152)	2,567
Motorcycles (373)	2,037

Percentage of industry total revenue

■ 4 largest firms ■ Next 4 largest firms ■ Next 12 largest firms

SOURCE OF DATA: U.S. Census Bureau.

18.2 THE OLIGOPOLISTS' DILEMMA

Boeing and Airbus share the market for big passenger airplanes.

Oligopoly might operate like monopoly, like perfect competition, or somewhere between these two extremes. To see these alternative possible outcomes, we'll study duopoly in the market for airplanes. Airbus and Boeing are the only makers of large commercial jet aircraft. Suppose that they have identical costs. To keep the numbers simple, assume that total fixed cost is zero and that regardless of the rate of production, the marginal cost of an airplane is $1 million.

Figure 18.2 shows the market demand curve for airplanes. Airbus and Boeing share this market. The total quantity sold and the quantities sold by each firm depend on the price of an airplane.

■ Monopoly Outcome

If this industry had only one firm operating as a single-price monopoly, its marginal revenue curve would be the one shown in Figure 18.2. Marginal revenue equals marginal cost when 6 airplanes a week are produced and the price is $13 million an airplane. Total cost would be $6 million and total revenue would be $78 million, so economic profit would be $72 million a week.

■ **FIGURE 18.2**

A Market for Airplanes

MyEconLab Animation

❶ With market demand curve, *D*, marginal revenue curve, *MR*, and marginal cost curve, *MC*, a monopoly airplane maker maximizes profit by producing 6 airplanes a week and selling them at a price of $13 million an airplane.

❷ With perfect competition among airplane makers, the market equilibrium quantity is 12 airplanes a week and the equilibrium price is $1 million an airplane.

❸ A cartel might achieve the monopoly equilibrium, break down and result in the perfect competition equilibrium, or operate somewhere between these two extreme outcomes.

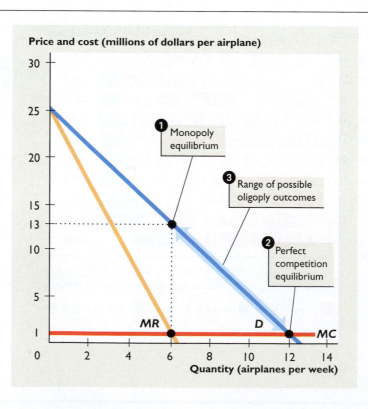

Cartel to Achieve Monopoly Outcome

Can the two firms achieve the monopoly outcome that we've just found and maximize their joint profit? They can attempt to do so by forming a cartel.

Suppose that Airbus and Boeing agreed to limit the total production of airplanes to 6 a week. The market demand curve tells us that the price would be $13 million per airplane and economic profit would be $72 million a week. Suppose that the two firms also agree to split the market evenly and each produce 3 airplanes a week. They would each make an economic profit of $36 million a week—see Table 18.1.

Would it be in the self-interest of Airbus and Boeing to stick to their agreement and limit production to 3 aircraft a week each?

To begin answering this question, notice that with the price of an airplane exceeding marginal cost, if one firm increased production, it would increase its profit. But if both firms increased output whenever price exceeded marginal cost, the end of the process would be the same as perfect competition.

■ Perfect Competition Outcome

You can see the perfect competition outcome in Figure 18.2. The equilibrium is where the market supply curve, which is the marginal cost curve, intersects the market demand curve. The quantity is 12 airplanes a week, and the price is the same as marginal cost—$1 million per airplane.

■ Other Possible Cartel Breakdowns

Because price exceeds marginal cost, a cartel is likely to break down. But a cartel might not unravel all the way to perfect competition. In *Eye on the Global Economy* on p. 463, you can see the brief history of a sometimes successful and sometimes unsuccessful cartel in the global market for oil. You can see why a cartel breaks down but not all the way to perfect competition by looking at some alternative outcomes in the airplane industry example.

Boeing Increases Output to 4 Airplanes a Week

Suppose that starting from a cartel that achieves the monopoly outcome, Boeing increases output by 1 airplane a week. Table 18.2 keeps track of the data. With Boeing producing 4 airplanes a week and Airbus producing 3 airplanes a week, total output is 7 airplanes a week. To sell 7 airplanes a week, the price must fall. The market demand curve in Figure 18.2 tells us that the quantity demanded is 7 airplanes a week when the price is $11 million an airplane.

Market total revenue would now be $77 million, total cost would be $7 million, and economic profit would fall to $70 million. But the distribution of this economic profit is now unequal. Boeing would gain, and Airbus would lose.

Boeing would now receive $44 million a week in total revenue, have a total cost of $4 million, and make an economic profit of $40 million. Airbus would receive $33 million a week in total revenue, incur a total cost of $3 million, and make an economic profit of $30 million.

So by increasing its output by 1 airplane a week, Boeing can increase its economic profit by $4 million and cause the economic profit of Airbus to fall by $6 million.

Because the two firms in this example are identical, we could rerun the above story with Airbus increasing production by 1 airplane a week and Boeing holding

TABLE 18.1   MONOPOLY OUTCOME

	Boeing	Airbus	Market total
Quantity (airplanes a week)	3	3	6
Price ($ million per airplane)	13	13	13
Total revenue ($ million)	39	39	78
Total cost ($ million)	3	3	6
Economic profit ($ million)	36	36	72

TABLE 18.2   BOEING INCREASES OUTPUT TO 4 AIRPLANES A WEEK

	Boeing	Airbus	Market total
Quantity (airplanes a week)	4	3	7
Price ($ million per airplane)	11	11	11
Total revenue ($ million)	44	33	77
Total cost ($ million)	4	3	7
Economic profit ($ million)	40	30	70

output at 3 a week. In this case, Airbus would make $40 million a week and Boeing would make $30 million a week.

Boeing is better off producing 4 airplanes a week if Airbus sticks with 3 a week. But is it in Airbus's interest to hold its output at 3 airplanes a week? To answer this question, we need to compare the economic profit Airbus makes if it maintains its output at 3 airplanes a week with the profit it makes if it produces 4 airplanes a week. How much economic profit does Airbus make if it produces 4 airplanes a week with Boeing also producing 4 airplanes a week?

Airbus Increases Output to 4 Airplanes a Week

With both firms producing 4 airplanes a week, total output is 8 airplanes a week. To sell 8 airplanes a week, the price must fall further. The market demand curve in Figure 18.2 tells us that the quantity demanded is 8 airplanes a week when the price is $9 million an airplane.

Table 18.3 keeps track of the data. Market total revenue would now be $72 million, total cost would be $8 million, and economic profit would fall to $64 million. With both firms producing the same output, the distribution of this economic profit is now equal.

Both firms would now receive $36 million a week in total revenue, have a total cost of $4 million, and make an economic profit of $32 million. For Airbus, this outcome is an improvement on the previous one by $2 million a week. For Boeing, this outcome is worse than the previous one by $8 million.

This outcome is better for Airbus, but would Boeing go along with it? You know that Boeing would be worse off if it decreased its output to 3 airplanes a week because it would get the outcome that Airbus has in Table 18.2—an economic profit of only $30 million a week. But would Boeing be better off if it increased output to 5 airplanes a week?

Boeing Increases Output to 5 Airplanes a Week

Suppose now that Airbus maintains its output at 4 airplanes a week and Boeing increases output to 5 a week. Table 18.4 keeps track of the data. Total output is now 9 airplanes a week. To sell this quantity, the price must fall to $7 million an airplane. Market total revenue is $63 million and total cost is $9 million, so economic profit for the two firms is $54 million. The distribution of this economic profit is again unequal. But now both firms would lose.

Boeing would now receive $35 million a week in total revenue, have a total cost of $5 million, and make an economic profit of $30 million—$2 million less than it would make if it maintained its output at 4 airplanes a week. Airbus would receive $28 million a week in total revenue, incur a total cost of $4 million, and make an economic profit of $24 million—$8 million less than before. So neither firm gains by increasing total output beyond 8 airplanes a week.

■ The Oligopoly Cartel Dilemma

With a cartel, both firms make the maximum available economic profit. If both increase production, both see their profit fall. If only one firm increases production, that firm makes a larger economic profit while the other makes a lower economic profit. So what will the firms do? We can speculate about what they will do, but to work out the answer, we need some game theory.

TABLE 18.3 AIRBUS INCREASES OUTPUT TO 4 AIRPLANES A WEEK

	Boeing	Airbus	Market total
Quantity (airplanes a week)	4	4	8
Price ($ million per airplane)	9	9	9
Total revenue ($ million)	36	36	72
Total cost ($ million)	4	4	8
Economic profit ($ million)	32	32	64

TABLE 18.4 BOEING INCREASES OUTPUT TO 5 AIRPLANES A WEEK

	Boeing	Airbus	Market total
Quantity (airplanes a week)	5	4	9
Price ($ million per airplane)	7	7	7
Total revenue ($ million)	35	28	63
Total cost ($ million)	5	4	9
Economic profit ($ million)	30	24	54

EYE on the GLOBAL ECONOMY
The OPEC Global Oil Cartel

The Organization of the Petroleum Exporting Countries (OPEC) is an international cartel of oil-producing nations. OPEC was created in Baghdad in 1960 by the governments of Iran, Iraq, Kuwait, Saudi Arabia, and Venezuela. Seven other nations, Qatar, Libya, United Arab Emirates, Algeria, Nigeria, Angola, and Ecuador are now members.

OPEC describes its objective as being "to co-ordinate and unify petroleum policies among member countries in order to secure fair and stable prices; . . . an efficient, economic, and regular supply of petroleum to consuming nations; and a fair return on capital to those investing in the industry." These words can be interpreted as being code for "restricting the production of oil to keep its price high."

During the 1960s, OPEC quietly built its organization and prepared the ground for its push to dominate the global oil market. Its first opportunity came in 1973 when, with an Arab-Israeli war raging, OPEC organized an embargo on oil shipments to the United States and Europe and the price of oil rose to four times its previous level. OPEC's second opportunity came with the Iranian revolution in 1979 when the price of oil more than doubled.

The figure shows both these price hikes. The price rose from about $8 a barrel in 1970 to more than $82 a barrel by 1980. (To compare prices over a number of years, we express them in terms of the value of the dollar in 2011.)

During the 1980s, many new sources of oil supply opened up and

OPEC ministers meeting at the organization's headquarters in Vienna

the OPEC cartel lost control of the global market. The cartel broke down, and the price of oil fell.

The price of oil remained remarkably stable during the 1990s, and the power of OPEC was countered by a large supply of oil from other sources.

From 2003 to 2008, the demand for oil grew dramatically in China and other Asian economies and OPEC again dominated the global market, restricted its production, and pushed the world price to a new high in 2008. But OPEC lost power again in the global recession of 2009.

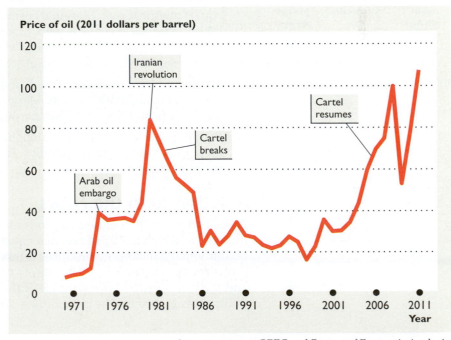

SOURCES OF DATA: OPEC and Bureau of Economic Analysis.

CHECKPOINT 18.2

Explain the dilemma faced by firms in oligopoly.

Practice Problems

Isolated Island has two natural gas wells, one owned by Tom and the other owned by Jerry. Each well has a valve that controls the flow of gas. The marginal cost of producing gas is zero. Table 1 gives the demand schedule for the gas.

1. If Tom and Jerry form a cartel and maximize their joint profit, what will be the price of gas and the quantity produced?

2. If Tom and Jerry are forced to sell at the perfectly competitive price, what will be the price of gas and the total quantity produced?

3. If Tom and Jerry compete as duopolists, what will be the price of gas?

In the News

Asian rice exporters to discuss cartel

Thailand, the world's largest rice exporter, proposed that the Asian rice exporters (Thailand, Cambodia, Laos, and Myanmar) form a cartel. The Philippines said it was a bad idea.

Source: CNN, May 6, 2008

Explain how an Asian profit-maximizing rice cartel would influence the global market for rice and the world price of rice. Is the Philippines correct?

Solutions to Practice Problems

1. If Tom and Jerry form a cartel and maximize their joint profit, they will charge the monopoly price. This price is the highest price the market will bear when together they produce the quantity at which marginal revenue equals marginal cost. Marginal cost is zero, so we need to find the price at which marginal revenue is zero. Marginal revenue is zero when total revenue is a maximum, which occurs when output is 6 units a day (Table 2) and price is $6 a unit (see the demand schedule in Table 1).

2. If Tom and Jerry are forced to sell at the perfectly competitive price, the price will equal marginal cost. Marginal cost is zero, so in this case, the price will be zero and the total quantity produced will be 12 units a day.

3. If Tom and Jerry compete as duopolists, they will increase production to more than the monopoly quantity. The price will fall, but they will not drive the price down to zero.

Solution to In the News

A rice cartel would operate as a profit-maximizing monopoly and produce the quantity at which marginal revenue equals marginal cost. The profit-maximizing quantity that a monopoly produces is less than the quantity that competitive rice growers currently produce. The supply of rice on the world market will decrease and the world price of rice will rise. If the cartel does not break down, then the Philippines is correct: The price of rice, a staple for the people of Asia, will rise.

TABLE 1

Price (dollars per unit)	Quantity demanded (units per day)
12	0
11	1
10	2
9	3
8	4
7	5
6	6
5	7
4	8
3	9
2	10
1	11
0	12

TABLE 2

Quantity (units per day)	Total revenue (dollars per day)	Marginal revenue (dollars per unit)
0	0	
		11
1	11	
		9
2	20	
		7
3	27	
		5
4	32	
		3
5	35	
		1
6	36	
		−1
7	35	
		−3
8	32	
		−5
9	27	
		−7
10	20	
		−9
11	11	
		−11
12	0	

18.3   GAME THEORY

Game theory is the tool that economists use to analyze *strategic behavior*—behavior that recognizes mutual interdependence and takes account of the expected behavior of others. John von Neumann invented game theory in 1937, and today it is a major research field in economics.

Game theory helps us to understand oligopoly and many other forms of economic, political, social, and even biological rivalries. We will begin our study of game theory and its application to the behavior of firms by thinking about familiar games that we play for fun.

Game theory
The tool that economists use to analyze *strategic behavior*—behavior that recognizes mutual interdependence and takes account of the expected behavior of others.

■ What Is a Game?

What is a game? At first thought, the question seems silly. After all, there are many different games. There are ball games and parlor games, games of chance and games of skill. But what is it about all these different activities that make them games? What do all these games have in common? All games share three features:

- Rules
- Strategies
- Payoffs

Let's see how these common features of games apply to a game called "the prisoners' dilemma." The **prisoners' dilemma** is a game between two prisoners that shows why it is hard to cooperate even when it would be beneficial to both players to do so. This game captures the essential feature of the duopolists' dilemma that we've just been studying. The prisoners' dilemma also provides a good illustration of how game theory works and how it generates predictions.

Prisoners' dilemma
A game between two prisoners that shows why it is hard to cooperate even when it would be beneficial to both players to do so.

■ The Prisoners' Dilemma

Art and Bob have been caught red-handed, stealing a car. During the district attorney's interviews with the prisoners, he begins to suspect that he has stumbled on the two people who committed a multimillion-dollar bank robbery some months earlier. But this is just a suspicion. The district attorney has no evidence on which he can convict them of the greater crime unless he can get them to confess. He makes the prisoners play a game with the following rules.

Rules

Each prisoner (player) is placed in a separate room and cannot communicate with the other player. Each is told that he is suspected of having carried out the bank robbery and that

- If both of them confess to the larger crime, each will receive a reduced sentence of 3 years for both crimes.
- If he alone confesses and his accomplice does not, he will receive an even shorter sentence of 1 year, while his accomplice will receive a 10-year sentence.
- If neither of them confesses to the larger crime, each will receive a 2-year sentence for car theft.

Strategies

All the possible actions of each player in a game.

Payoff matrix

A table that shows the payoffs for each player for every possible combination of actions by the players.

TABLE 18.5   PRISONERS' DILEMMA
PAYOFF MATRIX

Each square shows the payoffs for the two players, Art and Bob, for each possible pair of actions. In each square, the red triangle shows Art's payoff and the blue triangle shows Bob's. For example, if both confess, the payoffs are in the top left square.

Nash equilibrium

An equilibrium in which each player takes the best possible action given the action of the other player.

Strategies

In game theory, **strategies** are all the possible actions of each player. Art and Bob each have two possible strategies:

- Confess to the bank robbery.
- Deny having committed the bank robbery.

Payoffs

Because there are two players, each with two strategies, there are four possible outcomes:

- Both confess.
- Both deny.
- Art confesses and Bob denies.
- Bob confesses and Art denies.

Each prisoner can work out exactly what happens to him—his *payoff*—in each of these four situations. We can tabulate the four possible payoffs for each of the prisoners in what is called a payoff matrix for the game. A **payoff matrix** is a table that shows the payoffs for every possible action by each player given every possible action by the other player.

Table 18.5 shows a payoff matrix for Art and Bob. The squares show the payoffs for the two prisoners—the red triangle in each square shows Art's, and the blue triangle shows Bob's. If both prisoners confess (top left), each gets a prison term of 3 years. If Bob confesses but Art denies (top right), Art gets a 10-year sentence and Bob gets a 1-year sentence. If Art confesses and Bob denies (bottom left), Art gets a 1-year sentence and Bob gets a 10-year sentence. Finally, if both of them deny (bottom right), neither can be convicted of the bank robbery charge but both are sentenced for the car theft—a 2-year sentence.

Equilibrium

The equilibrium of a game occurs when each player takes the best possible action given the action of the other player. This equilibrium concept is called **Nash equilibrium.** It is so named because John Nash of Princeton University, who received the Nobel Prize for Economic Science in 1994, proposed it. (The same John Nash was portrayed by Russell Crowe in *A Beautiful Mind.*)

In the case of the prisoners' dilemma, equilibrium occurs when Art makes his best choice given Bob's choice and when Bob makes his best choice given Art's choice. Let's find the equilibrium.

First, look at the situation from Art's point of view. If Bob confesses, it pays Art to confess because in that case, he is sentenced to 3 years rather than 10 years. If Bob does not confess, it still pays Art to confess because in that case, he receives 1 year rather than 2 years. So no matter what Bob does, Art's best action is to confess.

Second, look at the situation from Bob's point of view. If Art confesses, it pays Bob to confess because in that case, he is sentenced to 3 years rather than 10 years. If Art does not confess, it still pays Bob to confess because in that case, he receives 1 year rather than 2 years. So no matter what Art does, Bob's best action is to confess.

Because each player's best action is to confess, each does confess, each gets a 3-year prison term, and the district attorney has solved the bank robbery. This is the equilibrium of the game.

Not the Best Outcome

The equilibrium of the prisoners' dilemma game is not the best outcome for the prisoners. Isn't there some way in which they can cooperate and get the smaller 2-year prison term? There is not, because the players cannot communicate with each other. Each player can put himself in the other player's place and can figure out what the other will do. The prisoners are in a dilemma. Each knows that he can serve only 2 years if he can trust the other to deny. But each also knows that it is not in the best interest of the other to deny. So each prisoner knows that he must confess, thereby delivering a bad outcome for both.

Let's now see how we can use the ideas we've just developed to understand the behavior of firms in oligopoly. We'll start by returning to the duopolists' dilemma.

■ The Duopolists' Dilemma

The dilemma of Airbus and Boeing is similar to that of Art and Bob. Each firm has two strategies. It can produce airplanes at the rate of

- 3 a week
- 4 a week

Because each firm has two strategies, there are four possible combinations of actions for the two firms:

- Both firms produce 3 a week (monopoly outcome).
- Both firms produce 4 a week.
- Airbus produces 3 a week and Boeing produces 4 a week.
- Boeing produces 3 a week and Airbus produces 4 a week.

■ The Payoff Matrix

Table 18.6 sets out the payoff matrix for this game. It is constructed in exactly the same way as the payoff matrix for the prisoners' dilemma in Table 18.5. The squares show the payoffs for Airbus and Boeing. In this case, the payoffs are economic profits. (In the case of the prisoners' dilemma, the payoffs were losses.)

The table shows that if both firms produce 4 a week (top left), each firm makes an economic profit of $32 million. If both firms produce 3 a week (bottom right), they make the monopoly profit, and each firm makes an economic profit of $36 million. The top right and bottom left squares show what happens if one firm produces 4 a week while the other produces 3 a week. The firm that increases production makes an economic profit of $40 million, and the one that keeps production at the monopoly quantity makes an economic profit of $30 million.

Equilibrium of the Duopolists' Dilemma

What do the firms do? To answer this question, we must find the equilibrium of the duopoly game.

TABLE 18.6   DUOPOLISTS' DILEMMA PAYOFF MATRIX

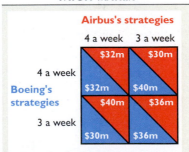

Each square shows the payoffs from a pair of actions. For example, if both firms produce 3 airplanes a week, the payoffs are recorded in the bottom right square. The red triangle shows Airbus's payoff, and the blue triangle shows Boeing's.

TABLE 18.7 THE NASH EQUILIBRIUM

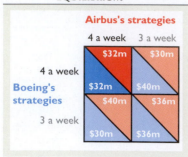

The Nash equilibrium is for each firm to produce 4 airplanes a week.

Using the information in Table 18.7, look at things from Airbus's point of view. Airbus reasons as follows: Suppose that Boeing produces 4 airplanes a week. If I, Airbus, produce 3 a week, I will make an economic profit of $30 million. If I also produce 4 a week, I will make an economic profit of $32 million. So I'm better off producing 4 airplanes a week. Airbus continues to reason: Now suppose Boeing produces 3 a week. If I produce 4 a week, I will make an economic profit of $40 million, and if I produce 3 a week, I will make an economic profit of $36 million. An economic profit of $40 million is better than an economic profit of $36 million, so I'm better off if I produce 4 airplanes a week. So regardless of whether Boeing produces 3 a week or 4 a week, it pays Airbus to produce 4 airplanes a week.

Because the two firms face identical situations, Boeing comes to the same conclusion as Airbus, so both firms produce 4 a week. The equilibrium of the duopoly game is that both firms produce 4 airplanes a week.

Collusion Is Profitable but Difficult to Achieve

In the duopolists' dilemma that you've just studied, Airbus and Boeing end up in a situation that is similar to that of the prisoners in the prisoners' dilemma game. They don't achieve the best joint outcome. Because each produces 4 airplanes a week, each makes an economic profit of $32 million a week.

If firms were able to collude, they would agree to limit their production to 3 airplanes a week each and they would each make the monopoly profit of $36 million a week.

The outcome of the duopolists' dilemma shows why it is difficult for firms to collude. Even if collusion were a legal activity, firms in duopoly would find it difficult to implement an agreement to restrict output. Like the players of the prisoners' dilemma game, the duopolists would reach a Nash equilibrium in which they produce more than the joint profit-maximizing quantity.

If two firms have difficulty maintaining a collusive agreement, oligopolies with more than two firms have an even harder time. The operation of OPEC (see *Eye on the Global Economy* on p. 463) illustrates this difficulty. To raise the price of oil, OPEC must limit global oil production. The members of this cartel meet from time to time and set a production limit for each member nation. Almost always, within a few months of a decision to restrict production, some (usually smaller) members of the cartel break their quotas, production increases, and the price sags below the cartel's desired target. The OPEC cartel plays an oligopoly dilemma game similar to the prisoners' dilemma. Only in 1973, 1979–1980, and 2005–2007 did OPEC manage to keep its members' production under control and raise the price of oil.

■ Advertising and Research Games in Oligopoly

Every month, Coke and Pepsi, Nike and Adidas, Procter & Gamble and Kimberly-Clark, Nokia and Motorola, and hundreds of other pairs of big firms locked in fierce competition spend millions of dollars on advertising campaigns and on research and development (R&D). They make decisions about whether to increase or cut the advertising budget or whether to undertake a large R&D effort aimed at lowering production costs or at making the product more reliable (usually, the more reliable a product, the more expensive it is to produce, but the more people are willing to pay for it). These choices can be analyzed as games. Let's look at some examples of these types of games.

Advertising Game

A key to success in the soft drink industry is to run huge advertising campaigns. These campaigns affect market share but are costly to run. Table 18.8 shows some hypothetical numbers for the advertising game that Pepsi and Coke play. Each firm has two strategies: Advertise or don't advertise. If neither firm advertises, they each make $50 million (bottom right of the payoff matrix). If each firm advertises, each firm's profit is lower by the amount spent on advertising (top left square of the payoff matrix). If Pepsi advertises but Coke does not, Pepsi gains and Coke loses (top right square of the payoff matrix). Finally, if Coke advertises and Pepsi does not, Coke gains and Pepsi loses (bottom left square).

Pepsi reasons as follows: Regardless of whether Coke advertises, we're better off advertising. Coke reasons similarly: Regardless of whether Pepsi advertises, we're better off advertising. Because advertising is the best strategy for both players, it is the Nash equilibrium. The outcome of this game is that both firms advertise and make less profit than they would if they could collude to achieve the cooperative outcome of no advertising.

Research and Development Game

A key to success in the disposable diaper industry is to design a product that people value highly relative to the cost of producing it. The firm that develops the most highly valued product and also develops the least-cost technology for producing it gains a competitive edge. It can undercut the rest of the market, increase its market share, and increase its economic profit. But it is costly to undertake the R&D that can ultimately result in an improved product and increased profit. So the cost of R&D must be deducted from the increased profit. If no firm does R&D, every firm can be better off, but if one firm initiates the R&D activity, all firms must follow.

Table 18.9 illustrates the dilemma (with hypothetical numbers) for the R&D game that Kimberly-Clark and Procter & Gamble play. Each firm has two strategies: Do R&D or do no R&D. If neither firm does R&D, Kimberly-Clark makes $30 million and Procter & Gamble makes $70 million (bottom right of the payoff matrix). If each firm does R&D, each firm's profit is lower by the amount spent on R&D (top left square of the payoff matrix). If Kimberly-Clark does R&D but Procter & Gamble does not, Kimberly-Clark gains and Procter & Gamble loses (top right square of the payoff matrix). Finally, if Procter & Gamble conducts R&D and Kimberly-Clark does not, Procter & Gamble gains and Kimberly-Clark loses (bottom left square).

Kimberly-Clark reasons as follows: Regardless of whether Procter & Gamble undertakes R&D, we're better off doing R&D. Procter & Gamble reasons similarly: Regardless of whether Kimberly-Clark does R&D, we're better off doing R&D.

Because R&D is the best strategy for both players, it is the Nash equilibrium. The outcome of this game is that both firms conduct R&D. They make less profit than they would if they could collude to achieve the cooperative outcome of no R&D.

The real-world situation has more players than Kimberly-Clark and Procter & Gamble. A large number of other firms strive to capture market share from Procter & Gamble and Kimberly-Clark. So the R&D effort by these two firms not only serves the purpose of maintaining shares in their own battle but also helps to keep barriers to entry high enough to preserve their joint market share.

TABLE 18.8 THE ADVERTISING GAME PAYOFF MATRIX

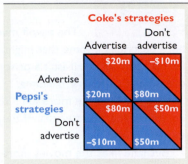

For each pair of strategies, the red triangle shows Coke's payoff, and the blue triangle shows Pepsi's. If both firms advertise, they make less than if neither firm advertises. But each firm is better off advertising if the other doesn't advertise. The Nash equilibrium for this prisoners' dilemma advertising game is for both firms to advertise.

TABLE 18.9 THE R&D GAME PAYOFF MATRIX

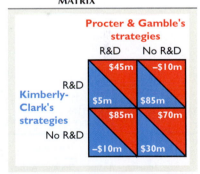

For each pair of strategies, the red triangle shows Procter & Gamble's payoff, and the blue triangle shows Kimberly-Clark's. If both firms do R&D, they make less than if neither firm undertakes R&D. But each firm is better off doing R&D if the other does no R&D. The Nash equilibrium for this prisoners' dilemma R&D game is for both firms to do R&D.

The payoff matrix here describes a game that might be familiar to you. But it isn't a prisoners' dilemma. It's a lovers' dilemma.

Jane and Jim have more fun if they do something together than if they do things alone.

But Jane likes the movies more than the ball game, and Jim likes the ball game more than the movies.

The payoff matrix describes how much they like the various outcomes (measured in units of utility).

What do they do?

By comparing the utility numbers for different strategies, you can figure out that Jim never goes to the movies alone and Jane never goes to the ball game alone.

You can also figure out that Jim doesn't go to the ball game alone and Jane doesn't go to the movies alone.

They always go out together. But do they go to the movies or the ball game?

The answer is that we can't tell. This game has no unique equilibrium. The payoffs tell you that Jane and Jim might go to either the game or the movies.

In a repeated game, they'll probably alternate between the two and might even toss a coin to decide which to go to on any given evening.

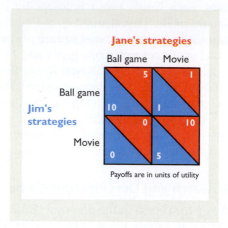

Payoffs are in units of utility

■ Repeated Games

The games that we've studied are played just once. In contrast, most real-world games get played repeatedly. This fact suggests that real-world duopolists might find some way of learning to cooperate so that they can enjoy a monopoly profit. If a game is played repeatedly, one player has the opportunity to penalize the other player for previous "bad" behavior. If Airbus produces 4 airplanes this week, perhaps Boeing will produce 4 next week. Before Airbus produces 4 this week, won't it take account of the possibility of Boeing producing 4 next week? What is the equilibrium of this more complicated dilemma game when it is repeated indefinitely?

The monopoly equilibrium might occur if each firm knows that the other will punish overproduction with overproduction, "tit for tat." Let's see why.

Table 18.10 keeps track of the numbers. Suppose that Boeing contemplates producing 4 airplanes in week 1. This move will bring it an economic profit of $40 million and will cut the economic profit of Airbus to $30 million. In week 2, Airbus will punish Boeing and produce 4 airplanes. But Boeing must go back to 3 airplanes to induce Airbus to cooperate again in week 3. So in week 2, Airbus makes an economic profit of $40 million, and Boeing makes an economic profit of $30 million. Adding up the profits over these two weeks of play, Boeing would have made $72 million by cooperating (2 × $36 million) compared with $70 million from producing 4 airplanes in week 1 and generating Airbus's tit-for-tat response.

What is true for Boeing is also true for Airbus. Because each firm makes a larger profit by sticking to the monopoly output, both firms do so and the monopoly price, quantity, and profit prevail.

In reality, whether a duopoly (or more generally an oligopoly) works like a one-play game or a repeated game depends primarily on the number of players and the ease of detecting and punishing overproduction. The larger the number of players, the harder it is to maintain the monopoly outcome.

TABLE 18.10 PAYOFFS WITH PUNISHMENT

Period of play	Cooperate		Overproduce	
	Boeing profit	Airbus profit	Boeing profit	Airbus profit
	(millions of dollars)			
1	36	36	40	30
2	36	36	30	40

EYE on the CHIPS DUOPOLY
Is Two Too Few?

The CPU in your computer or your game box—the brainpower of the machine—is made either by Intel Corporation or by Advanced Micro Devices, Inc. (AMD). Does competition between these duopolists achieve an efficient outcome—a win for the consumer—or just a win for one or both of the producers?

The answer is that Intel is the big winner. The pie chart shows that it dominates this market and the CPU prices graph shows that Intel's prices are generally higher than AMD's prices.

In the game that Intel and AMD play, the outcome is closer to monopoly than perfect competition. Producer surplus is maximized and consumer surplus is less than it would be in a competitive market. There is under-production and a deadweight loss.

SOURCES OF DATA: Intel, AMD, and sharkyextreme.com.

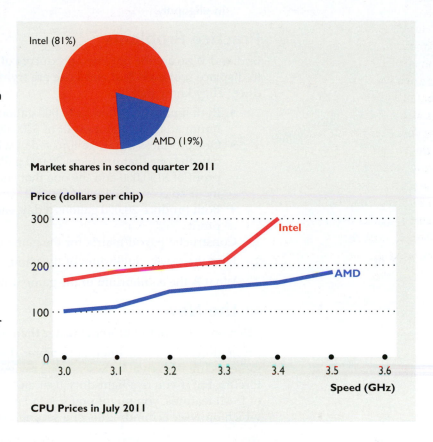

Market shares in second quarter 2011

CPU Prices in July 2011

■ Is Oligopoly Efficient?

The quantity produced of any good or service is the efficient quantity if the price (which measures marginal benefit) equals marginal cost. Does oligopoly produce efficient quantities of goods and services?

You've seen that if firms in oligopoly play a repeated prisoners' dilemma game, they can end up restricting output to the monopoly level and making the same economic profit as a monopoly would make. You've also seen that even when the firms don't cooperate, they don't necessarily drive the price down to marginal cost. So generally, oligopoly is not efficient. It suffers from the same source of inefficiency as monopoly.

Also, firms in oligopoly might end up operating at a higher average total cost than the lowest attainable cost because their advertising and research budgets are higher than the socially efficient level.

Because oligopoly creates inefficiency and firms in oligopoly have an incentive to try to behave like a monopoly, the United States has established antitrust laws that seek to reduce market power and move the oligopoly outcome closer to the efficient competitive outcome. In the next section, we study U.S. antitrust law.

471

CHECKPOINT 18.3

Use game theory to explain how price and quantity are determined in oligopoly.

Practice Problems

Bud and Wise are the only two producers of a New Age beer, which is designed to displace root beer. Bud and Wise are trying to work out the quantity to produce. They know that if:

- Both limit production to 10,000 gallons a day, they will make the maximum attainable joint profit of $200,000 a day—$100,000 a day each.
- One produces 20,000 gallons a day while the other produces 10,000 a day, the one that produces 20,000 gallons will make an economic profit of $150,000 and the one that sticks with 10,000 gallons will incur an economic loss of $50,000.
- Both produce 20,000 gallons a day, each will make zero economic profit.

1. Construct a payoff matrix for the game that Bud and Wise must play.
2. Find the Nash equilibrium of the game that Bud and Wise play.
3. What is the equilibrium of the game if Bud and Wise play it repeatedly?

In the News

Microsoft Internet Explorer is faster than Mozilla Firefox

Promotions of the new Internet Explorer IE8 say it is faster, more reliable, and more secure than rival browsers. One reviewer noted that IE8 is slower than Firefox, but if you're a light-duty user and attracted to the new IE's strong suite of fresh features, you might prefer it to Firefox. Another says the point isn't which browser is hundredths of a second faster, but other features.

Source: *USA Today*, March 23, 2009

What is the game that Microsoft and Mozilla have played in the past few years? How do you think the game will change in the coming years?

Solutions to Practice Problems

1. Table 1 shows the payoff matrix for the game that Bud and Wise must play.
2. The Nash equilibrium is for both to produce 20,000 gallons a day. To see why, notice that regardless of the quantity that Bud produces, Wise makes more profit by producing 20,000 gallons a day. The same is true for Bud. So Bud and Wise each produce 20,000 gallons a day.
3. If Bud and Wise play this game repeatedly, each produces 10,000 gallons a day and makes maximum economic profit. They can achieve this outcome by playing a tit-for-tat strategy.

Solution to In the News

They played a product development game: improving speed or adding features. The outcome is that both allocated development to increasing speed and as the reviewers imply their speeds are only hundredths of a second apart (basically the same). In the coming years, the development game will probably move away from speed and to additional features to maintain or expand market share.

TABLE 1

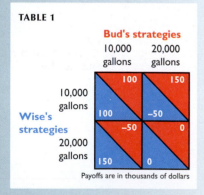

Payoffs are in thousands of dollars

18.4 ANTITRUST LAW

Antitrust law is the body of law that regulates oligopolies and prohibits them from becoming monopolies or behaving like monopolies.

■ The Antitrust Laws

Congress passed the first antitrust law, the Sherman Act, in 1890 in an atmosphere of outrage and disgust at the actions and practices of J. P. Morgan, John D. Rockefeller, and W. H. Vanderbilt—the so-called "robber barons."

A wave of mergers at the turn of the twentieth century produced stronger antitrust laws. The Clayton Act of 1914 supplemented the Sherman Act, and Congress created the Federal Trade Commission to enforce the antitrust laws.

Table 18.11 summarizes the two main provisions of the Sherman Act. Section 1 of the act is precise. Conspiring with others to restrict competition is illegal. But section 2 is general and imprecise. Just what is an "attempt to monopolize"? The Clayton Act and its two amendments, the Robinson-Patman Act of 1936 and Celler-Kefauver Act of 1950, which outlaw specific practices, answer this question. Table 18.11 describes these practices and summarizes the main provisions of these three acts.

■ Three Antitrust Policy Debates

Price fixing is *always* a violation of the antitrust law. If the Justice Department can prove the existence of price fixing, a defendant can offer no acceptable excuse. But other practices are more controversial and generate debate among antitrust lawyers and economists. We'll examine three of these practices:

- Resale price maintenance
- Predatory pricing
- Tying arrangements

Resale Price Maintenance

Most manufacturers sell their products to the final consumer indirectly through a wholesale and retail distribution system. **Resale price maintenance** occurs when a manufacturer agrees with a distributor on the price at which the product will be resold.

Resale price maintenance (also called vertical price fixing) *agreements* are illegal under the Sherman Act. But it isn't illegal for a manufacturer to refuse to supply a retailer who doesn't accept the manufacturer's guidance on what the price should be.

Attorneys general in 41 states alleged that Universal, Sony, Warner, Bertelsmann, and EMI kept CD prices artificially high between 1995 and 2000 with a practice called "minimum-advertised pricing." The companies denied the allegation but made a large payment to settle the case.

Does resale price maintenance create an inefficient or efficient use of resources? Economists can be found on both sides of this question.

Inefficient Resale Price Maintenance Resale price maintenance is inefficient if it enables dealers to charge the monopoly price. By setting and enforcing the resale price, the manufacturer might be able to achieve the monopoly price.

Antitrust law
A body of law that regulates oligopolies and prohibits them from becoming monopolies or behaving like monopolies.

Resale price maintenance
An agreement between a manufacturer and a distributor on the price at which a product will be resold.

■ **TABLE 18.11**

The Antitrust Laws: A Summary

The Sherman Act, 1890

Section 1:

Every contract, combination in the form of trust or otherwise, or conspiracy, in restraint of trade or commerce among the several States, or with foreign nations, is hereby declared to be illegal.

Section 2:

Every person who shall monopolize, or attempt to monopolize, or combine or conspire with any other person or persons, to monopolize any part of the trade or commerce among the several States, or with foreign nations, shall be deemed guilty of a felony.

Clayton Act, 1914

Robinson-Patman Act, 1936

Celler-Kefauver Act, 1950

These acts prohibit the following practices only if they substantially lessen competition or create monopoly:

1. Price discrimination.
2. Contracts that require other goods to be bought from the same firm (called tying arrangements).
3. Contracts that require a firm to buy all its requirements of a particular item from a single firm (called requirements contracts).
4. Contracts that prevent a firm from selling competing items (called exclusive dealing).
5. Contracts that prevent a buyer from reselling a product outside a specified area (called territorial confinement).
6. Acquiring a competitor's shares or assets.
7. Becoming a director of a competing firm.

Efficient Resale Price Maintenance Resale price maintenance might be efficient if it enables a manufacturer to induce dealers to provide the efficient standard of service. Suppose that SilkySkin wants shops to demonstrate the use of its new unbelievable moisturizing cream in an inviting space. With resale price maintenance, SilkySkin can offer all the retailers the same incentive and compensation. Without resale price maintenance, a discount drug store might offer SilkySkin products at a low price. Buyers would then have an incentive to visit a high-price shop and get the product demonstrated and then buy from the low-price shop. The low-price shop would be a free rider (like the consumer of a public good in Chapter 11, p. 269), and an inefficient level of service would be provided.

SilkySkin could pay a fee to retailers that provide good service and leave the resale price to be determined by the competitive forces of supply and demand. But it might be too costly for SilkySkin to monitor shops and ensure that they provided the desired level of service.

Predatory Pricing

Predatory pricing is setting a low price to drive competitors out of business with the intention of setting a monopoly price when the competition has gone. John D. Rockefeller's Standard Oil Company was the first to be accused of this practice in the 1890s, and it has been claimed often in antitrust cases since then. Predatory pricing is an attempt to create a monopoly and as such it is illegal under Section 2 of the Sherman Act.

It is easy to see that predatory pricing is an idea, not a reality. Economists are skeptical that predatory pricing occurs. They point out that a firm that cuts its price below the profit-maximizing level forgoes profit during the low-price period. Even if the firm succeeds in driving its competitors out of business, new competitors will enter when the firm raises its price above average total cost and makes an economic profit. So any potential gain from a monopoly position is temporary. A high and certain loss is a poor exchange for a temporary and uncertain gain. No case of predatory pricing has been definitively found.

Predatory pricing
Setting a low price to drive competitors out of business with the intention of setting a monopoly price when the competition has gone.

Tying Arrangements

A **tying arrangement** is an agreement to sell one product only if the buyer agrees to buy another, different product. With tying, the only way the buyer can get the one product is to buy the other product at the same time. Microsoft has been accused of tying Internet Explorer and Windows. Textbook publishers sometimes tie a Web site and a textbook and force students to buy both. (You can't buy the book you're now reading, new, without the Web site. But you can buy the Web site access without the book, so these products are not tied.)

Could publishers of textbooks make more money by tying a book and access to a Web site? The answer is sometimes but not always. Think about what you are willing to pay for a book and access to a Web site. To keep the numbers simple, suppose that you and other students are willing to pay $40 for a book and $10 for access to a Web site. The publisher can sell these items separately for these prices or bundled for $50. There is no gain to the publisher from bundling.

But now suppose that you and only half of the students are willing to pay $40 for a book and $10 for a Web site. And suppose that the other half of the students are willing to pay $40 for a Web site and $10 for a book. Now if the two items are sold separately, the publisher can charge $40 for the book and $40 for the Web site. Half the students buy the book but not the Web site, and the other half buy the Web site but not the book. But if the book and Web site are bundled for $50, everyone buys the bundle and the publisher makes an extra $10 per student. In this case, bundling has enabled the publisher to price discriminate.

There is no simple, clear-cut test of whether a firm is engaging in tying or whether, by doing so, it has increased its market power and profit and created inefficiency.

Tying arrangement
An agreement to sell one product only if the buyer agrees to buy another, different product.

■ Recent Antitrust Showcase: The United States Versus Microsoft

In 1998, the U.S. Department of Justice, along with a number of states, charged Microsoft, the world's largest producer of software for personal computers, with violations of both sections of the Sherman Act. A 78-day trial followed that pitched two prominent MIT economics professors against each other (Franklin Fisher for the government and Richard Schmalensee for Microsoft).

The Case Against Microsoft

The claims against Microsoft were that it

- Possessed monopoly power in the market for PC operating systems.
- Used *predatory pricing* and *tying arrangements* to achieve a monopoly in the market for Web browsers.
- Used other anticompetitive practices to strengthen its monopoly in these two markets.

It was claimed that with 80 percent of the market for PC operating systems, Microsoft had excessive monopoly power. This monopoly power arose from two barriers to entry: economies of scale and network economies. Microsoft's average total cost falls as production increases (economies of scale) because the fixed cost of developing an operating system like Windows is large while the marginal cost of producing one copy of Windows is small. Further, as the number of Windows users increases, the range of Windows applications expands (network economies), so a potential competitor would need to produce not only a competing operating system but also an entire range of supporting applications.

When Microsoft entered the Web browser market with its Internet Explorer (IE), it offered the browser for a zero price. This price was viewed as *predatory pricing*. Microsoft integrated IE with Windows so that anyone who uses this operating system would not need a separate browser such as Netscape Communicator. Microsoft's competitors claimed that this practice was an illegal *tying arrangement*.

Microsoft's Response

Microsoft challenged all these claims. It said that although Windows was the dominant operating system, it was vulnerable to competition from other operating systems such as Linux and Apple's Mac OS and that there was a permanent threat of competition from new entrants.

Microsoft claimed that integrating Internet Explorer with Windows provided a single, unified product of greater consumer value. Instead of tying, Microsoft said, the browser and operating system constituted a single product. It was like a refrigerator with a chilled water dispenser or an automobile with a stereo player.

The Outcome

The court agreed that Microsoft was in violation of the Sherman Act and ordered that it be broken into two firms: an operating systems producer and an applications producer. Microsoft successfully appealed this order. But in the final judgment, Microsoft was ordered to disclose details about how its operating system works to other software developers so that they could compete effectively against Microsoft. In the summer of 2002, Microsoft began to comply with this order.

■ Merger Rules

You've now seen how the antitrust laws can be used to prevent an oligopoly from becoming a monopoly or trying to behave like one. We end by examining another way of trying to gain monopoly power—two or more oligopoly firms merging to increase their ability to control the market price. Mergers are subject to rules that are designed to limit monopoly power from arising and we close our explanation of the antitrust laws by seeing how they are used to review and sometimes to block a merger.

Mergers are often in the headlines. United Airlines and Continental Airlines merged to firm United Continental in 2010. AT&T wants to take over T-Mobile to create one of the largest cell-phone operators. Firms can benefit from a merger in two ways: They can lower costs and they can increase market power. Lower costs are not a threat to the social interest but increased market power is. For this reason, the Federal Trade Commission (FTC) challenges proposed mergers that will substantially lessen competition and not bring lower costs.

To determine the effects of a merger on competitiveness, the FTC uses guidelines based on the Herfindahl-Hirschman Index (HHI), which is explained in Chapter 17 (p. 435). *Eye on the U.S. Economy*, below, describes the FTC guidelines and looks at a high-profile merger that was blocked by applying them.

EYE on the U.S. ECONOMY
No Soda Merger

The figure (part a) summarizes the Federal Trade Commission's (FTC) guidelines on mergers. In a market in which the Herfindahl-Hirschman Index (HHI) is less than 1,000, a proposed merger is not challenged. But if the HHI is above 1,000, the FTC considers a challenge. If the HHI is between 1,000 and 1,800, a merger is challenged if it would increase the HHI by 100 points. And if the HHI exceeds 1,800 the market is already so concentrated that a merger is challenged even if it increases the index by only 50 points.

In 1986, PepsiCo wanted to buy 7-Up and Coca-Cola wanted to buy Dr Pepper. But the market for soda is highly concentrated. Coca-Cola has a 39 percent share, PepsiCo has 28 percent, Dr Pepper is next with 7 percent, followed by 7-Up with 6 percent. One other producer, RJR, has a 5 percent market share. So the five largest firms in this market have an 85 percent market share. The Herfindahl-Hirschman index is more than 2,400.

With an HHI of this magnitude, a merger that increases the index by only 50 points is examined by the FTC.

Part (b) of the figure shows how the HHI would have changed with the mergers. A PepsiCo–7-Up merger would increase the index by more than 300 points, a Coca-Cola–Dr Pepper merger would increase it by more than 500 points, and both mergers together would increase the HHI by almost 800 points. The FTC decided to block these mergers.

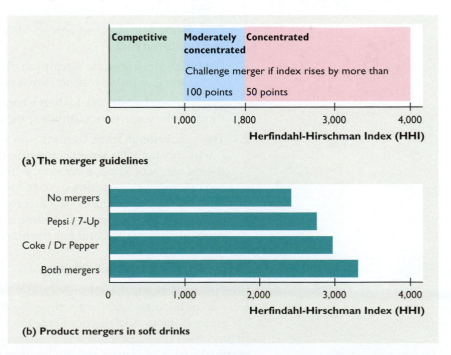

(a) The merger guidelines

(b) Product mergers in soft drinks

CHECKPOINT 18.4

Describe the antitrust laws that regulate oligopoly.

Practice Problems

1. Explain each of the following terms:
   - Attempt to monopolize
   - Price fixing
   - Predatory pricing
   - Tying arrangements
2. Since 1987, hundreds of hospital mergers have taken place and rarely has the U.S. Federal Trade Commission challenged a hospital merger. What can you infer about the structure of the market in hospital services?

In the News

Intel will find refuge in the courts

The European Union recently fined Intel $1.45 billion because it gave "loyalty discounts" to repeat customers, presumably increasing Intel's dominance in the microprocessor business—called predatory pricing in the United States.

Source: The Wall Street Journal, June 2, 2009

Did Intel practice predatory pricing? If every morning you pick up a coffee at Starbucks and it offers you a loyalty discount, is that predatory pricing?

Solutions to Practice Problems

1. An attempt to monopolize is an attempt by a company to drive out its competitors so that it can operate as a monopoly.

   Price fixing is making an agreement with competitors to set a specified price and not to vary it.

   Predatory pricing is the attempt to drive out competitors by charging a price that is too low for anyone to earn a profit.

   Tying arrangements exist when a company does not offer a buyer the opportunity to buy one item without at the same time buying another item.

2. The U.S. Federal Trade Commission will challenge a hospital merger only if it will substantially lessen competition. Such a situation will not arise if (1) the merger would not increase the likelihood of market power either because strong competitors exist or because the merging hospitals were sufficiently differentiated; (2) the merger would allow the hospitals to reduce cost; or (3) the merger would eliminate a hospital that otherwise would probably have failed and left the market.

Solution to In the News

Predatory pricing is the setting of a low price with the aim of driving competitors out of business and then setting the monopoly price when the competitors are gone. If the loyalty discount was intended to drive out AMD, Intel's competitor, then Intel's practice was predatory pricing. A loyalty discount at Starbucks isn't predatory pricing because the market for coffee is competitive. Driving out one coffee outlet will not create monopoly.

CHAPTER SUMMARY

Key Points

1 Describe and identify oligopoly and explain how it arises.

- Oligopoly is a market type in which a small number of interdependent firms compete behind a barrier to entry.
- Both natural (economies of scale and market demand) and legal barriers to entry create oligopoly.

2 Explain the dilemma faced by firms in oligopoly.

- If firms in oligopoly act together to restrict output, they make the same economic profit as a monopoly, but each firm can make a larger profit by increasing production.
- The oligopoly dilemma is whether to restrict or expand output.

3 Use game theory to explain how price and quantity are determined in oligopoly.

- In the prisoners' dilemma game, two players acting in their own interests harm their joint interest. Oligopoly is a prisoners' dilemma game.
- If firms cooperated, they could earn the monopoly profit, but in a one-play game, they overproduce and can drive the price and economic profit to the levels of perfect competition.
- Advertising and research and development create a prisoners' dilemma for firms in oligopoly.
- In a repeated game, a punishment strategy can lead to monopoly output, price, and economic profit.
- Oligopoly is usually inefficient because the price (marginal benefit) exceeds marginal cost and cost might not be the lowest attainable.

4 Describe the antitrust laws that regulate oligopoly.

- The Sherman Act (1890) and the Clayton Act (1914) make price-fixing agreements among firms illegal.
- Resale price maintenance might be efficient if it enables a producer to ensure the efficient level of service by distributors.
- Predatory pricing might bring temporary gains.
- Tying arrangements can facilitate price discrimination.
- The Federal Trade Commission examines and possibly blocks mergers if they would restrict competition too much.

Key Terms

Antitrust law, 473
Cartel, 456
Duopoly, 456
Game theory, 465
Nash equilibrium, 466
Payoff matrix, 466

Predatory pricing, 475
Prisoners' dilemma, 465
Resale price maintenance, 473
Strategies, 466
Tying arrangement, 475

CHAPTER CHECKPOINT

Study Plan Problems and Applications

Use the following information to work Problems **1** and **2**.

When the first automobiles were built in 1901, they were manufactured by skilled workers using hand tools. Later, in 1913, Henry Ford introduced the moving assembly line, which lowered costs and speeded production. Over the years, the production line has become ever more mechanized, and today robots have replaced people in many operations.

1. Sketch the average total cost curve and the demand curve for automobiles in 1901 and in 2012.

2. Describe the changing barriers to entry in the automobile industry and explain how the combination of market demand and economies of scale has changed the structure of the industry over the past 100 years.

Use the following information to work Problems **3** to **5**.

Isolated Island has two taxi companies, one owned by Ann and the other owned by Zack. Figure 1 shows the market demand curve for taxi rides, *D*, and the average total cost curve of one of the firms, *ATC*.

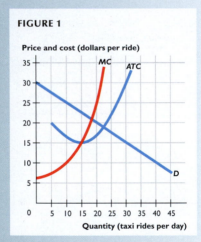

FIGURE 1

3. If Ann and Zack produce the same quantity of rides as would be produced in perfect competition, what are the quantity of rides, the price of a ride, and the economic profit of Ann and Zack? Would Ann and Zack have an incentive to collude and raise their price? Explain why or why not.

4. If Ann and Zack form a cartel and produce the same quantity of rides as would be produced in monopoly, what are the quantity of rides, the price of a ride, and the economic profit of Ann and Zack? Would Ann and Zack have an incentive to break the cartel agreement and cut their price? Explain why or why not.

5. Suppose that Ann and Zack have two strategies: collude, fix the monopoly price, and limit the number of rides or break the collusion, cut the price, and produce more rides. Create a payoff matrix for the game that Ann and Zack play, and find the Nash equilibrium for this game if it is played just once. Do the people of Isolated Island get the efficient quantity of taxi rides?

Use the following information to work Problems **6** and **7**.

Cola wars: What's your soft drink of choice?

Soft drink sales have fallen for six straight years as consumers switched to healthier alternatives such as juices, and cut back on spending in the recession. The two rivals have moved into bottled water, fruit juices, energy drinks, and sports drinks to try to maintain market share. Both companies saw decreased sales, but Pepsi had the greater loss. Overall, Coke product sales were down 0.5 percent while Pepsi saw a 2.6 percent decline.

Source: CBC News, March 18, 2011

6. Describe the strategies in the advertising and product development game that Coca-Cola and PepsiCo play. Why would you expect these strategies to *not* include cutting price?

7. With some assumed payoffs, create a payoff matrix for the game you've described in Problem 6. Find and explain the equilibrium outcome.

Instructor Assignable Problems and Applications

Your instructor can assign these problems as homework, a quiz, or a test in MyEconLab.

1. Intel and AMD have two pricing strategies: Set a high (monopoly) price or set a low (competitive) price. Suppose that if they both set a competitive price, economic profit for both is zero. If both set a monopoly price, Intel makes an economic profit of $860 million and AMD of $140 million. If Intel sets a low price and AMD sets a high price, Intel makes an economic profit of $100 million and AMD incurs an economic loss of $10 million; if Intel sets a high price and AMD sets a low price, Intel incurs an economic loss of $100 million and AMD makes an economic profit of $10 million.

    *   Create the payoff matrix for this game.
    *   What is the equilibrium of this game?
    *   Is the equilibrium efficient?
    *   Is this game a prisoners' dilemma?

Use the following information to work Problems **2** and **3**.

The United States claims that Canada subsidizes the production of softwood lumber and that imports of Canadian lumber damage the interests of U.S. producers. The United States has imposed a tariff on Canadian imports to counter the subsidy. Canada is thinking of retaliating by refusing to export water to California. Table 1 shows a payoff matrix for the game that the United States and Canada are playing.

2. What is the United States' best strategy? What is Canada's best strategy? What is the outcome of this game? Explain.

3. Is this game like a prisoners' dilemma or different in some crucial way? Explain. Which country would benefit more from a free trade agreement?

4. Agile Airlines is making $10 million a year economic profit on a route on which it has a monopoly. Wanabe Airlines is considering entering the market and operating on this route. Agile warns Wanabe to stay out and threatens to cut the price to the point at which Wanabe will make no profit if it enters. Wanabe does some research and determines that the payoff matrix for the game in which it is engaged with Agile is that shown in Table 2. Does Wanabe believe Agile's assertion? Does Wanabe enter or not? Explain.

Use this information to work Problems **5** and **6**.

21 airlines fined in price-fixing scheme

To date, 21 airlines have coughed up more than $1.7 billion in fines in one of the largest criminal antitrust investigations in U.S. history. To find a quick fix to avoid financial ruin, airlines came up with, according to federal prosecutors, a massive price-fixing scheme that artificially inflated international passenger and cargo fuel surcharges between 2000 and 2006. The scheme cost consumers hundreds of millions of dollars. The Justice Department called the case one of the largest antitrust settlements in U.S. history.

Source: Associated Press, March 5, 2011

5. Explain how the price-fixing scheme benefited the airlines and imposed costs on consumers.

6. Describe the price-fixing scheme as the equilibrium outcome of an oligopoly cartel game played by the airlines. Explain why the cartel survived.

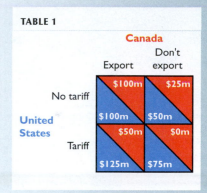

TABLE 1

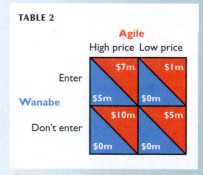

TABLE 2

MyEconLab

You can work this quiz in Chapter 18 Study Plan and get instant feedback.

Multiple Choice Quiz

1. Which of the following statements is *incorrect*. In oligopoly _____.

   A. barriers to entry prevent new firms entering
   B. each firm's profit is influenced by each other firms' advertising
   C. each firm's action is influenced by the actions and reactions of each other firm
   D. each firm is a price taker and the price is the monopoly profit-maximizing price

2. If firms in oligopoly form a cartel, it will likely break down because _____.

   A. firms cannot agree on how to share the economic profit
   B. the price set by the cartel is too low
   C. with price exceeding marginal cost, a firm might expand production to increase its profit
   D. firms realize that their allocation of resources is inefficient

3. The oligopoly dilemma is whether to _____.

   A. act together to restrict output and raise the price
   B. raise the price to the monopoly profit-maximizing price
   C. cheat on others in the cartel to take advantage of profit opportunities
   D. lower the price to the perfectly competitive price

4. In the prisoners' dilemma game, each player _____.

   A. consults the other player to determine his best action
   B. chooses the best outcome for the other player
   C. chooses the best outcome for himself
   D. chooses the best outcome for both players together

5. A Nash equilibrium _____.

   A. is the outcome that delivers maximum economic profit
   B. is the outcome in which each player takes the best action given the other player's action
   C. changes each time the game is played
   D. is the best possible outcome for the two players

6. In an advertising prisoners' dilemma game, _____.

   A. both firms will advertise and end up with lower profits than if neither advertises
   B. only one firm will advertise because the other firm sees the advertising expenditure as a waste
   C. the two firms agree on the total advertising budget and split it equally
   D. neither firm will advertise because both realize that it lowers profit

7. Each of the following practices violates U.S. antitrust law *except* _____.

   A. an agreement to sell one good only if the buyer purchases another good
   B. an agreement between the manufacturer and the seller to charge a given price for the good
   C. starting a price war with other sellers of a similar good
   D. cutting the price to increase market share to 100 percent, then raising the price.

Markets for Factors of Production

19

When you have completed your study of this chapter, you will be able to

1 Explain how the value of marginal product determines the demand for a factor of production.

2 Explain how wage rates and employment are determined and how labor unions influence labor markets.

3 Explain how capital and land rental rates and natural resource prices are determined.

THE ANATOMY OF FACTOR MARKETS

The four factors of production are

- Labor
- Capital
- Land (natural resources)
- Entrepreneurship

Factor markets
The markets in which the services of the factors of production are traded.

Factor prices
The prices of the services of the factors of production.

The *services* of labor, capital, and land are traded in **factor markets**, which determine their **factor prices**. Entrepreneurial services are not traded in markets and entrepreneurs receive the profit or bear the loss that results from their decisions. Let's take a brief look at the anatomy of the factor markets.

Markets for Labor Services

Labor services are the physical and mental work effort that people supply to produce goods and services. A *labor market* is a collection of people and firms who trade *labor services.* Some labor services are traded day by day, called casual labor. People who pick fruit and vegetables often just show up at a farm and take whatever work is available that day. But most labor services are traded on a contract, called a **job**. The price of labor services is a wage rate.

Job
A contract between a firm and a household to provide labor services.

Most labor markets have many buyers and sellers and are competitive. But in some labor markets a labor union organizes labor and introduces an element of monopoly into the market. We'll study both competitive labor markets and labor unions in this chapter.

Markets for Capital Services

Capital consists of the tools, instruments, machines, buildings, and other constructions that have been produced in the past and that businesses now use to produce goods and services. These physical objects are themselves goods—*capital goods*—and are traded in goods markets, just as bottled water and toothpaste are.

A market for *capital services* is a *rental market*—a market in which the services of capital are hired. An example of a market for capital services is the vehicle rental market in which Avis, Budget, Hertz, U-Haul, and many other firms offer automobiles and trucks for hire. The price of capital services is a rental rate.

Most capital services are not traded in a market. Instead, a firm buys capital equipment and uses it itself. But the services of the capital that a firm owns and operates itself have an *implicit* price that arises from depreciation and interest costs (see Chapter 14, p. 345). You can think of the price as the *implicit rental rate* of capital.

Markets for Land Services and Natural Resources

Land consists of all the gifts of nature—natural resources. The market for land as a factor of production is the market for the *services of land*—the *use* of land. The price of the services of land is a rental rate.

Nonrenewable natural resources
Natural resources that can be used only once and cannot be replaced once they have been used.

Most natural resources, such as farm land, can be used repeatedly. But a few natural resources are nonrenewable. **Nonrenewable natural resources** are resources that can be used only once and cannot be replaced once they have been used. Examples are oil, natural gas, and coal. The prices of natural resources are determined in global *commodity markets* and are called *commodity prices.*

19.1   THE DEMAND FOR A FACTOR OF PRODUCTION

We begin our study of factor markets by learning about the demand for factors of production, and we use labor as the example. The demand for a factor of production is a **derived demand**—it is derived from the demand for the goods and services that it is used to produce. You've seen, in Chapters 15 through 18, how a firm determines its profit-maximizing output. The quantities of factors of production demanded are a direct consequence of firms' output decisions. Firms hire the quantities of factors of production that maximize profit.

To decide the quantity of a factor of production to hire, a firm compares the cost of hiring an additional unit of the factor with its value to the firm. The cost of hiring an additional unit of a factor of production is the factor price. The value to the firm of hiring one more unit of a factor of production is called the factor's **value of marginal product,** which equals the price of a unit of output multiplied by the marginal product of the factor of production. To study the demand for a factor of production, we'll examine the demand for labor.

Derived demand
The demand for a factor of production, which is derived from the demand for the goods and services that it is used to produce.

Value of marginal product
The value to a firm of hiring one more unit of a factor of production, which equals the price of a unit of output multiplied by the marginal product of the factor of production.

■ Value of Marginal Product

Table 19.1 shows you how to calculate the value of the marginal product of labor at Max's Wash 'n' Wax car wash service. The first two columns show Max's *total product* schedule—the number of car washes per hour that each quantity of labor can produce. The third column shows the *marginal product* of labor—the change in total product that results from a one-unit increase in the quantity of labor employed. (See Chapter 14, pp. 349–353, for a refresher on product schedules.) Max can sell car washes at the going market price of $3 a wash. Given this information, we can calculate the value of marginal product (fourth column). It equals price multiplied by marginal product. For example, the marginal product of hiring the second worker is 4 car washes an hour. Each wash brings in $3, so the value of the marginal product of the second worker is $12 (4 washes at $3 each).

■ Table 19.1

Calculating the Value of Marginal Product

	Quantity of labor (workers)	Total product (car washes per hour)	Marginal product (washes per additional worker)	Value of marginal product (dollars per additional worker)
A	0	0		
			5	15
B	1	5		
			4	12
C	2	9		
			3	9
D	3	12		
			2	6
E	4	14		
			1	3
F	5	15		

The price of a car wash is $3. The value of the marginal product of labor equals the price of the product multiplied by marginal product of labor (column 3). The marginal product of the second worker is 4 washes, so the value of the marginal product of the second worker (in column 4) is $3 a wash multiplied by 4 washes, which is $12.

The Value of Marginal Product Curve

Figure 19.1 graphs the value of the marginal product of labor at Max's Wash 'n' Wax as the number of workers that Max hires changes. The blue bars that show the value of the marginal product of labor correspond to the numbers in Table 19.1. The curve labeled *VMP* is Max's value of marginal product curve.

■ A Firm's Demand for Labor

The value of the marginal product of labor and the wage rate determine the quantity of labor demanded by a firm. The value of the marginal product of labor tells us the additional revenue the firm earns by hiring one more worker. The wage rate tells us the additional cost the firm incurs by hiring one more worker.

Because the value of marginal product decreases as the quantity of labor employed increases, there is a simple rule for maximizing profit: Hire labor up to the point at which the value of marginal product equals the wage rate. If the value of marginal product of labor exceeds the wage rate, a firm can increase its profit by employing one more worker. If the wage rate exceeds the value of marginal product of labor, a firm can increase its profit by employing one less worker. But if the wage rate equals the value of the marginal product of labor, the firm cannot increase its profit by changing the number of workers it employs. The firm is making the maximum possible profit.

So the quantity of labor demanded by a firm is the quantity at which the wage rate equals the value of the marginal product of labor.

FIGURE 19.1

The Value of the Marginal Product at Max's Wash 'n' Wax

MyEconLab Animation

The blue bars show the value of the marginal product of the labor that Max hires based on the numbers in Table 19.1. The orange line is the firm's value of the marginal product of labor curve.

Quantity of labor (workers)	Value of marginal product (dollars per additional worker)
A 1	15
B 2	12
C 3	9
D 4	6
E 5	3

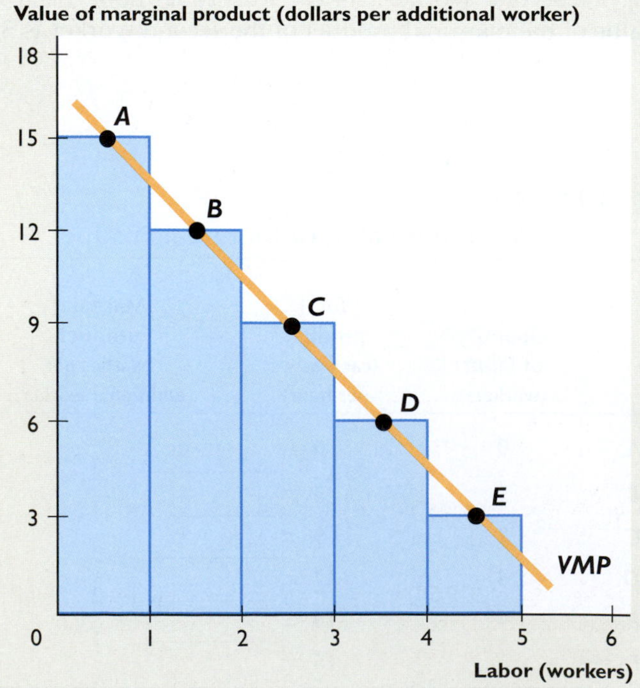

■ A Firm's Demand for Labor Curve

A firm's demand for labor curve is also its value of marginal product curve. If the wage rate falls and other things remain the same, a firm hires more workers. Figure 19.2 shows Max's value of marginal product curve in part (a) and demand for labor curve in part (b). The x-axis measures the number of workers hired in both parts. The y-axis measures the value of marginal product in part (a) and the wage rate—dollars per hour—in part (b).

Suppose the wage rate is $10.50 an hour. You can see in part (a) that if Max hires 1 worker, the value of the marginal product of labor is $15 an hour. Because this 1 worker costs Max only $10.50 an hour, he makes a profit of $4.50 an hour. If Max hires 2 workers, the value of the marginal product of the second worker is $12 an hour. So on this second worker, Max makes a profit of $1.50 an hour. Max's total profit per hour on the first two workers is $6 an hour—$4.50 on the first worker plus $1.50 on the second worker.

If Max hired 3 workers, his profit would fall. The third worker generates a value of marginal product of only $9 an hour but costs $10.50 an hour, so Max

■ FIGURE 19.2

The Demand for Labor at Max's Wash 'n' Wax

MyEconLab Animation

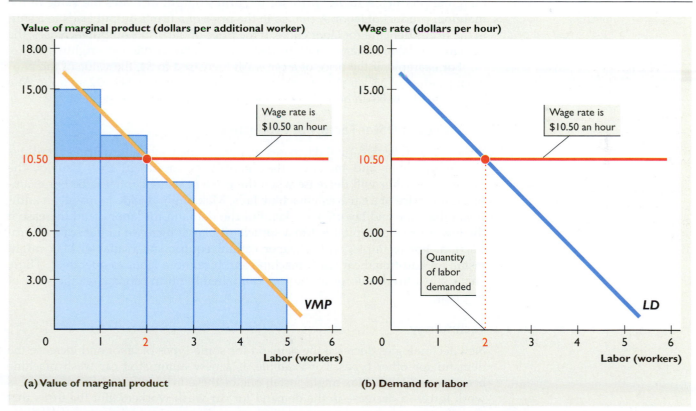

(a) Value of marginal product

(b) Demand for labor

At a wage rate of $10.50 an hour, Max makes a profit on the first 2 workers but would incur a loss on the third worker in part (a), so the quantity of labor demanded is 2 workers in part (b). Max's demand for labor curve in part (b) is the same as the value of

marginal product curve in part (a). The demand for labor curve slopes downward because the value of the marginal product of labor diminishes as the quantity of labor employed increases.

does not hire 3 workers. The quantity of labor demanded by Max when the wage rate is $10.50 an hour is 2 workers, which is a point on Max's demand for labor curve, *LD*, in Figure 19.2(b).

If the wage rate increased to $12.50 an hour, Max would decrease the quantity of labor demanded to 1 worker. If the wage rate decreased to $7.50 an hour, Max would increase the quantity of labor demanded to 3 workers.

A change in the wage rate brings a change in the quantity of labor demanded and a movement along the demand for labor curve. A change in any other influence on the firm's labor-hiring plans changes the demand for labor and shifts the demand for labor curve.

■ Changes in the Demand for Labor

The demand for labor depends on

- The price of the firm's output
- The prices of other factors of production
- Technology

The Price of the Firm's Output

The higher the price of a firm's output, the greater is its demand for labor. The price of output affects the demand for labor through its influence on the value of marginal product. A higher price for the firm's output increases the value of the marginal product of labor. A change in the price of a firm's output leads to a shift in the firm's demand for labor curve. If the price of the firm's output increases, the demand for labor increases and the demand for labor curve shifts rightward.

For example, if the price of a car wash increased to $4, the value of the marginal product of Max's third worker would increase from $9 to $12 an hour. At a wage rate of $10.50 an hour, Max would now hire 3 workers instead of 2.

The Prices of Other Factors of Production

If the price of using capital decreases relative to the wage rate, a firm substitutes capital for labor and increases the quantity of capital it uses. Usually, the demand for labor will decrease when the price of using capital falls. For example, if the price of a car wash machine falls, Max might decide to install an additional machine and lay off a worker. But the demand for labor could increase if the lower price of capital led to a sufficiently large increase in the scale of production. For example, with cheaper capital equipment available, Max might install an additional car wash machine and hire more labor to operate it. These factor substitutions occur in the *long run* when the firm can change the scale of its plant.

Technology

New technologies decrease the demand for some types of labor and increase the demand for other types. For example, if a new automated car wash machine becomes available, Max might install one of these machines and fire most of his work force—a decrease in the demand for car wash workers. But the firms that manufacture and service automatic car wash machines hire more labor—an increase in the demand for these types of labor. During the 1980s and 1990s, electronic telephone exchanges decreased the demand for telephone operators and increased the demand for computer programmers and electronics engineers.

CHECKPOINT 19.1

Explain how the value of marginal product determines the demand for a factor of production.

MyEconLab

You can work these problems in Study Plan 19.1 and get instant feedback.

Practice Problems

Kaiser's produces smoothies. The market for smoothies is perfectly competitive, and the price of a smoothie is $4. The labor market is competitive, and the wage rate is $40 a day. Table 1 shows Kaiser's total product schedule.

1. Calculate the marginal product and the value of the marginal product of the fourth worker.

2. How many workers will Kaiser's hire to maximize its profit? How many smoothies a day will Kaiser's produce?

3. If the price of a smoothie rises to $5, how many workers will Kaiser's hire?

4. Kaiser's installs a machine that increases the marginal product of labor by 50 percent. If the price of a smoothie remains at $4 and the wage rises to $48 a day, how many workers does Kaiser's hire?

TABLE 1

Workers	Smoothies per day
1	7
2	21
3	33
4	43
5	51
6	55

In the News

Where have America's jobs gone?

U.S. companies offer many reasons for their lack of robust hiring, including weak consumer spending. Over the past year, there has been an increase in manufacturing, transportation, and health-care jobs, but not in sectors related to homes and housing.

Source: *The Wall Street Journal*, July 12, 2011

Use the competitive goods and labor markets to explain why jobs in some sectors have grown but not in others.

Solutions to Practice Problems

1. The *MP* of the 4th worker equals the *TP* of 4 workers (43 smoothies) minus the *TP* of 3 workers (33 smoothies), which is 10 smoothies. The *VMP* of the 4th worker equals the *MP* of the 4th worker (10 smoothies) multiplied by the price of a smoothie ($4), which is $40 a day.

2. Kaiser's maximizes profit by hiring the number of workers that makes *VMP* equal to the wage rate ($40 a day). Kaiser's hires 4 workers. The marginal product of the 4th worker is 10 smoothies and the price of a smoothie is $4, so *VMP* is $40 a day. Kaiser's produces 43 smoothies a day.

3. Kaiser's maximizes profit by hiring 5 workers. The *MP* of the 5th worker is 8 smoothies and the price is $5, so *VMP* is $40 a day—equal to the wage rate.

4. When Kaiser's hires 5 workers, the *MP* of the 5th worker is 12 smoothies. The price of a smoothie is $4, so *VMP* is $48 a day— equal to the wage rate.

Solution to In the News

A profit-maximizing firm hires the quantity of labor at which the *VMP* of labor equals the market wage rate. *VMP* of labor equals *MP* multiplied by the price of the good. If the price of the good or *MP* increases, firms offer more jobs. If the price of the good or *MP* is unchanged, firm don't offer more jobs.

19.2 LABOR MARKETS

For most of us, a labor market is our only source of income. We work and earn a wage. What determines the amount of labor that we supply?

■ The Supply of Labor

People supply labor to earn an income. Many factors influence the quantity of labor that a person plans to provide, but a key factor is the wage rate.

To see how the wage rate influences the quantity of labor supplied, think about Larry's labor supply decision, which Figure 19.3 illustrates. Larry enjoys his leisure time, and he would be pleased if he didn't have to spend his evenings and weekends working at Max's Wash 'n' Wax. But Max pays him $10.50 an hour, and at that wage rate, Larry chooses to work 30 hours a week. The reason is that he is offered a wage rate that is high enough to make him regard this use of his time as the best available to him. If he were offered a lower wage rate, Larry would not be willing to give up so much leisure. If he were offered a higher wage rate, Larry would want to work even longer hours, but only up to a point. Offer Larry $25 an hour, and he would be willing to work a 40-hour week (and earn $1,000). With the goods and services that Larry can buy for $1,000, his priority would be a bit more leisure time if the wage rate increased further. If the wage rate increased above $25 an hour, Larry would cut back on his work hours and take more leisure. Larry's labor supply curve eventually bends backward.

■ **FIGURE 19.3**

An Individual's Labor Supply Curve

MyEconLab Animation

❶ At a wage rate of $10.50 an hour,

❷ Larry is willing to supply 30 hours a week of labor.

❸ Larry's quantity of labor supplied ❹ increases as the wage rate increases up to ❺ a maximum, and then further increases in the wage rate ❻ bring a decrease in the quantity of labor supplied. Larry's labor supply curve eventually bends backward.

	Wage rate (dollars per hour)	Quantity of labor (hours per week)
A	40.00	30
B	35.00	35
C	30.00	38
D	25.00	40
E	20.00	38
F	15.00	35
G	10.50	30
H	5.00	0

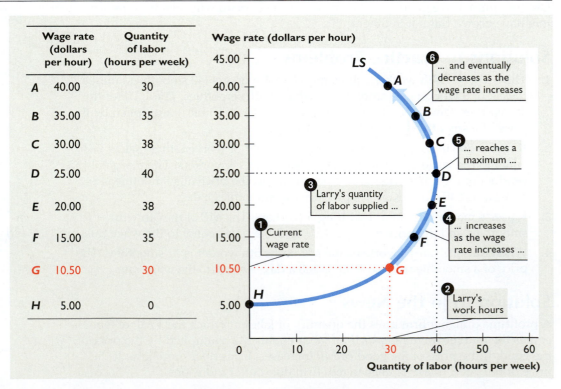

Market Supply Curve

Larry's supply curve shows the quantity of labor supplied by one person as that person's wage rate changes. Most people behave like Larry, but people have different wage rates at which they are willing to work and at which their labor supply curve bends backward. A market supply curve shows the quantity of labor supplied by all households in a particular job. It is found by adding together the quantities supplied by all households at each wage rate. Also, along a market supply curve, the wage rates available in other jobs remain the same. For example, along the supply curve of car wash workers, we hold constant the wage rates of car salespeople, mechanics, and all other types of labor.

Offer Larry more for car washing than for oil changing, and he will supply more of his labor to car washing. The market supply curve in a given job slopes upward like the one in Figure 19.4, which shows the market supply curve for car wash workers in a large city.

■ Influences on the Supply of Labor

The supply of labor changes when influences other than the wage rate change. The key factors that change the supply of labor are

- Adult population
- Preferences
- Time in school and training

■ **FIGURE 19.4**

The Supply of Car Wash Workers

MyEconLab Animation

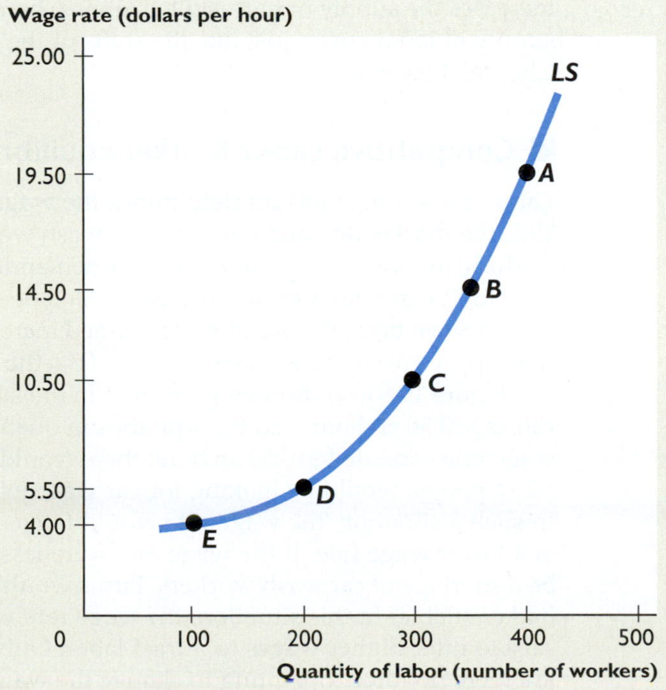

	Wage rate (dollars per hour)	Quantity of labor (workers)
A	19.50	400
B	14.50	350
C	10.50	300
D	5.50	200
E	4.00	100

The supply curve of car wash workers shows how the quantity of labor supplied changes when the wage rate changes, other things remaining the same. In a market for a specific type of labor, the quantity supplied increases as the wage rate increases, other things remaining the same.

Adult Population

An increase in the adult population, caused either by a birth rate that exceeds the death rate or by immigration, increases the supply of labor. Historically, the population of the United States has been strongly influenced by immigration.

Preferences

In 2011, 53 percent of women had jobs, up from 35 percent in 1959. In contrast, in 2011, 64 percent of men had jobs, down from 80 percent in 1959. Many factors contributed to these changes, which economists classify as *changes in preferences*. These changes occur slowly but accumulate to make a large difference in the supply of labor. The result has been a large increase in the supply of female labor and a decrease in the supply of male labor.

Time in School and Training

The more people who remain in school for full-time education and training, the smaller is the supply of low-skilled labor. Today in the United States, almost everyone completes high school and more than 50 percent of high-school graduates enroll in college or university. Although many students work part time, the supply of labor by students is less than it would be if they were full-time workers. So when more people pursue higher education, other things remaining the same, the supply of low-skilled labor decreases. But time spent in school and training converts low-skilled labor into high-skilled labor. The greater the proportion of people who receive a higher education, the greater is the supply of high-skilled labor.

When the amount of work that people want to do at a given wage rate changes, the supply of labor changes. An increase in the adult population or an increase in the percentage of women with jobs increases the supply of labor. An increase in college enrollment decreases the supply of low-skilled labor. Later, it increases the supply of high-skilled labor. Changes in the supply of labor shift the supply of labor curve, just like the shifts of the supply curves that you studied in Chapter 4 (p. 95).

■ Competitive Labor Market Equilibrium

Labor market equilibrium determines the wage rate and employment. In Figure 19.5, the market demand curve for car wash workers is *LD*. Here, if the wage rate is $10.50 an hour, the quantity of labor demanded is 300 workers. If the wage rate rises to $14 an hour, the quantity demanded decreases to 200. And if the wage rate falls to $9 an hour, the quantity demanded increases to 350. Figure 19.5 also shows the supply curve of car wash workers, *LS*—the same curve as in Figure 19.4.

Figure 19.5 also shows equilibrium in the labor market. The equilibrium wage rate is $10.50 an hour, and the equilibrium quantity is 300 car wash workers. If the wage rate exceeded $10.50 an hour, there would be a surplus of car wash workers. More people would be looking for car wash jobs than firms were willing to hire. In such a situation, the wage rate would fall as firms found it easy to hire people at a lower wage rate. If the wage rate were less than $10.50 an hour, there would be a shortage of car wash workers. Firms would not be able to fill all the jobs they had available. In this situation, the wage rate would rise as firms found it necessary to offer higher wages to attract labor. Only at a wage rate of $10.50 an hour are there no forces operating to change the wage rate.

EYE on the COACH
Why Is a Coach Worth $6 Million?

Nick Saban, head coach of the Alabama Crimson Tide, earns $6 million a year. University of Alabama full professors earn about $100,000 a year. Why does the University of Alabama pay its football coach the amount that it pays 60 professors?

Nick Saban is worth 60 professors because his value of marginal product (*VMP*) to the University of Alabama is 60 times that of a professor.

Few people have the talent and willingness to work hard and take the stress of being head coach of a top-flight college football team. Mr. Saban is one of these few people and possibly

the best of them. The consequence is that the supply of coaches like Nick Saban is small and inelastic.

To hire a top coach, the University of Alabama must pay the market price and that price is determined by the small supply and a high *VMP*.

The *VMP* of a football coach is high, much higher than that of a professor, because of the revenue that a successful football team generates. Some of that revenue comes directly from the game and includes the football gear and theme clothing licensed by the University. But most of the revenue comes from increased donations by

alumni and wealthy local and national patrons. The better the coach, the better is the team's performance and the greater is the revenue from these sources. Nick Saban brings in at least $6 million a year to the University of Alabama.

In contrast, a professor, even an outstanding one, generates a modest revenue for the University. He or she attracts a few students and obtains some research grant funds from the National Science Foundation or other private foundation. But the *VMP* of a professor is modest—around a 60th of the *VMP* of Nick Saban.

FIGURE 19.5
Labor Market Equilibrium

MyEconLab Animation

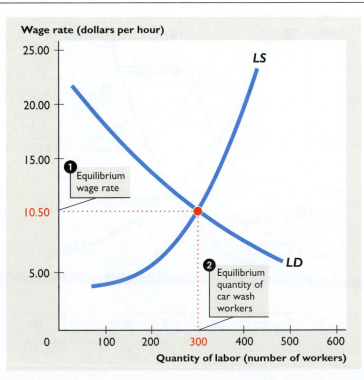

Labor market equilibrium determines the wage rate and employment. The wage rate adjusts to make the quantity of labor demanded equal the quantity of labor supplied.

❶ The equilibrium wage rate is $10.50 an hour.

❷ The equilibrium quantity of labor is 300 workers.

If the wage rate exceeds $10.50 an hour, the quantity supplied exceeds the quantity demanded and the wage rate falls.

If the wage rate is below $10.50 an hour, the quantity demanded exceeds the quantity supplied and the wage rate rises.

■ Labor Unions

Labor union
An organized group of workers that aims to increase wages and influence other job conditions of its members.

A **labor union** is an organized group of workers that aims to increase wages and influence other job conditions of its members. In some labor markets, labor unions have a powerful effect on the wage rate and employment. To see the effects of a labor union, let's see what happens if a union enters a competitive labor market.

A Union Enters a Competitive Labor Market

A labor union that enters a competitive labor market can try to restrict the supply of labor or it can try to increase the demand for labor. If the union restricts the supply of labor below its competitive level, the wage rate rises. If that is all the union is able to do, the wage rate rises, but the number of jobs decreases. There is a trade-off between the wage rate and the number of jobs.

Figure 19.6 illustrates a labor market before and after a union enters it. Before the union enters the market, the demand curve is LD_0, the supply curve is LS_0, the wage rate is $10.50 an hour, and 300 workers are employed.

When a labor union enters this market, it restricts the supply of labor and the supply of labor curve shifts leftward to LS_1. The wage rate rises to $15 an hour and employment decreases to 200 workers. The union simply picks its preferred position along the demand curve that defines the tradeoff it faces between employment and the wage rate.

Because restricting the supply of labor brings a higher wage rate at the cost of jobs, unions also try to increase the demand for labor.

■ FIGURE 19.6

A Competitive Labor Market and Unionized Labor Market Compared   **MyEconLab** Animation

❶ In a competitive labor market, the demand for labor is LD_0, the supply of labor is LS_0, the equilibrium wage rate is $10.50 an hour and the equilibrium quantity of labor is 300 workers.

❷ A labor union restricts the supply of labor and the supply of labor curve shifts leftward to LS_1.

❸ The wage rate rises to $15 an hour, but employment decreases to 200 workers—jobs are traded off for a higher wage rate.

❹ If the union action increases labor productivity and increases the demand for union labor, the demand for labor curve shifts rightward to LD_1.

❺ The wage rate rises further to $20 an hour and employment increases to 250 workers.

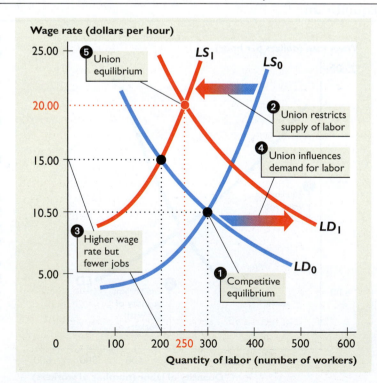

How Labor Unions Try to Increase the Demand for Labor

Labor unions try to increase the demand for the labor of their members by

- Increasing the value of marginal product of union members
- Supporting minimum wage laws
- Supporting immigration restrictions
- Supporting import restrictions

The value of marginal product of union members might be increased (and the demand for union labor increased) by union-organized and union-sponsored job training programs, by union-supported apprenticeship and other on-the-job training activities, and by professional certification.

A minimum wage law might increase the demand for union labor by increasing the cost of employing low-skilled nonunion labor. An increase in the wage rate of low-skilled labor leads to a decrease in the quantity demanded of low-skilled labor and to an increase in the demand for high-skilled union labor, a substitute for low-skilled labor.

Immigration increases the supply of labor. By supporting restrictive immigration laws, unions seek to decrease the supply of foreign workers and increase the demand for union labor.

By supporting import restrictions, labor unions try to increase the demand for the goods and services produced by unionized workers.

Figure 19.6 shows the effects of a labor union that is able to increase the demand for the labor of its members. The demand curve shifts rightward to LD_1, the wage rate rises to \$20 an hour, and employment increases to 250 workers.

Can Unions Restrict the Supply of Labor?

The union's ability to restrict the supply of labor is limited by how well it can prevent nonunion workers from offering their labor in the same market as union workers. The larger the fraction of the work force controlled by the union, the more effective the union can be in this regard.

It is difficult for unions to operate in markets where there is an abundant supply of willing nonunion workers. For example, the market for farm labor in southern California is very tough for a union to organize because of the steady flow of nonunion, often illegal, workers from Mexico. At the other extreme, unions in the construction industry can better control the supply of labor because they can influence the number of people who can obtain skills as electricians, plasterers, carpenters, and plumbers. Although not labor unions in a legal sense, the professional associations of dentists and physicians are well placed to restrict the supply of dentists and physicians. These groups control the number of qualified workers by controlling either the examinations that new entrants must pass or the entrance into professional degree programs.

The Scale of the Union-Nonunion Wage Gap

How much of a difference to wage rates do unions make? To answer this question, we must look at the wages of unionized and nonunionized workers who do similar work. The evidence suggests that after allowing for skill differences, the union-nonunion wage gap lies between 10 percent and 25 percent. For example, unionized airline pilots earn about 25 percent more than nonunion pilots with the same level of skill.

CHECKPOINT 19.2

Explain how wage rates and employment are determined and how labor unions influence labor markets.

Practice Problems

In Greenville, where fast-food outlets hire teenagers and seniors, the following events occur one at a time and other things remain the same. Explain the influence of each event on the market for fast-food workers.

1. Seniors flock to Greenville and make it their home.

2. Greenville becomes a major tourist center attracting thousands of additional visitors every day.

3. The price of fast food falls.

4. A labor union organizes fast-food workers and gets a law passed that raises the minimum age and lowers the maximum age at which a person can work in the fast-food industry.

In the News

VW exec knows of no talks to unionize Tennessee plant
Volkswagen opened the $1 billion plant in Chattanooga in May and hired its 2,000th employee there in July. Our hourly wage starts at $14.50 per hour, which is very competitive and we have great benefits.

Source: *The Wall Street Journal*, August 1, 2011

If this plant's workers join the union, explain how the wage rate will change.

Solutions to Practice Problems

1. An increase in the number of seniors increases the supply of fast-food labor. The supply curve shifts rightward from S_0 to S_2 (Figure 1). The wage rate falls, and the number of fast-food workers employed increases.

2. A boost in visitor numbers increases the demand for fast food, which in turn increases the demand for fast-food workers. The demand curve shifts rightward from D_0 to D_1 (Figure 2). The wage rate rises, and the number of fast-food workers employed increases.

3. A fall in the price of fast food decreases the demand for fast-food workers. The demand curve shifts leftward from D_0 to D_2 (Figure 2). The wage rate falls, and the number of fast-food workers employed decreases.

4. A rise in the minimum age and a fall in the maximum age at which a person can work in the fast-food industry decreases the supply of labor. The supply curve shifts leftward from S_0 to S_1 (Figure 1). The wage rate rises, and the number of fast-food workers employed decreases.

Solution to In the News

The union will try to raise the wage rate (or improve benefits). If the union can increase the value of marginal product of the workers, then the wage rate will rise. But if the union tries to increase the wage rate (or benefits) without an increase in the value of marginal product, the plant will cut the number of workers.

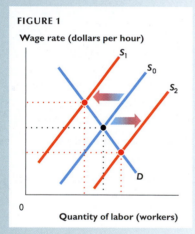

FIGURE 1

Wage rate (dollars per hour)

Quantity of labor (workers)

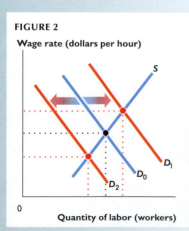

FIGURE 2

Wage rate (dollars per hour)

Quantity of labor (workers)

19.3 CAPITAL AND NATURAL RESOURCE MARKETS

The markets for capital and land can be understood by using the same basic ideas that you've seen when studying labor markets. But markets for nonrenewable natural resources are different. We'll now examine three groups of factor markets:

- Capital markets
- Land markets
- Nonrenewable natural resource markets

■ Capital Markets

The demand for capital is based on the *value of marginal product of capital*. Profit-maximizing firms hire capital services up to the point at which the value of marginal product of capital equals the *rental rate of capital*. The *lower* the rental rate, other things remaining the same, the *greater* is the quantity of capital *demanded*. The supply of capital responds in the opposite way to the rental rate. The *higher* the rental rate, other things remaining the same, the *greater* is the quantity of capital *supplied*. The equilibrium rental rate makes the quantity of capital demanded equal to the quantity supplied.

Figure 19.7 illustrates the market for the rental of tower cranes, capital used to construct high-rise buildings. With the demand curve *D* and supply curve *S*, the equilibrium rental rate is $1,000 per day and 100 tower cranes are rented.

■ **FIGURE 19.7**

A Market for Capital Services

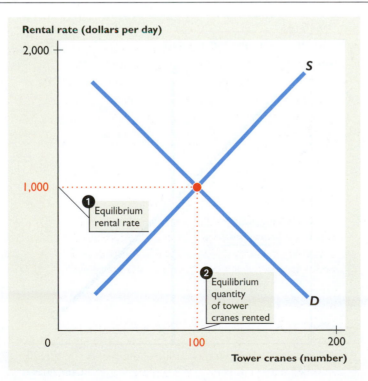

The demand curve for tower crane rentals is *D*, and the supply curve is *S*.

❶ The equilibrium rental rate is $1,000 per day.

❷ The equilibrium quantity of cranes rented is 100.

■ Land Markets

The demand for land, like the demand for labor and the demand for capital, is a derived demand and is based on the *value of marginal product of land*. Firms maximize profits by renting the quantity of land at which the value of marginal product of land equals the *rental rate of land*. The *lower* the rental rate, other things remaining the same, the *greater* is the quantity of land *demanded*.

But the supply of land is special: The quantity is fixed, so the quantity supplied cannot be changed by people's decisions. The supply of each particular block of land is *perfectly inelastic*.

The equilibrium land rental rate makes the quantity of land demanded equal to the quantity available. Figure 19.8 illustrates the market for a given parcel of land, a 10-acre block on Chicago's "Magnificent Mile." The quantity supplied is 10 acres regardless of the rent. The demand curve is *D* and the equilibrium rental rate is $1,000 an acre per day.

A change in the demand for land changes the equilibrium rental rate but leaves the quantity unchanged. The greater the demand, the higher is the rent—demand determines the rental rate. The rental rate for an acre of land in Manhattan is greater than that for an acre of farmland in Idaho because the value of marginal product and the demand for the land is greater in Manhattan than in Idaho. The price of a Big Mac at McDonald's on Fifth Avenue is higher than in downtown Boise, Idaho, but not because the rental rate on land in New York is higher. The rental rate on land is higher in New York because the greater demand for Big Macs (and most other things) in New York makes the demand for land greater in New York than in Boise.

■ **FIGURE 19.8**

A Market for Land

MyEconLab Animation

The demand curve for a 10-acre block of land is *D*, and the supply curve is *S*. Equilibrium occurs at a rental rate of $1,000 an acre per day.

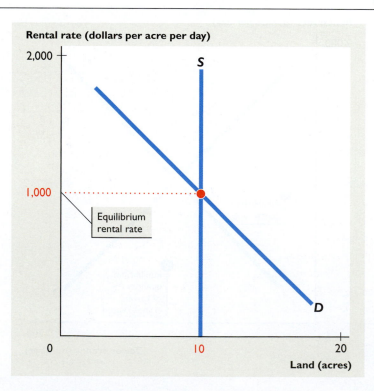

◼ Nonrenewable Natural Resource Markets

The nonrenewable natural resources are those that we use to produce energy. Burning one of these fuels converts it to energy and other by-products and the used resource cannot be re-used. The natural resources that we use to make metals are also nonrenewable, but they can be used again, at some cost, by recycling them.

The value of marginal product of oil, gas, and coal determine the demand for these nonrenewable natural resources. The demand side of the markets for these resources is just like the demand side of all factor markets.

It is the supply side of a nonrenewable natural resource market that is special.

The Quantity of a Nonrenewable Natural Resource

The *stock* of a nonrenewable natural resource is the quantity in existence at a given time. This quantity is fixed by nature and past use and is independent of the price of the resource. The *proven reserves* of a nonrenewable natural resource is the quantity that has been discovered and that can be accessed at prices close to the current price. This quantity increases over time because advances in technology enable ever less accessible sources to be discovered.

Both of these quantity concepts of a nonrenewable natural resource influence its price, but the influence is indirect. The direct influence on price is the rate at which the resource is supplied for use in production—the *supply of the resource*.

EYE on YOUR LIFE
Job Choice and Income Prospects

Your job choice will have a big impact on your income. To provide you with some guidance on this impact, the figure shows wage rates for 16 occupations (or groups of occupations) reported by the Bureau of Labor Statistics.

You can see that economists are highly paid but not the highest. John Maynard Keynes, one of the leading economists of the last century, expressed the hope that economists would one day be as useful as dentists. If wage rates measure usefulness, you can see that the average economist isn't as useful as the average dentist. Nor is a university teacher of economics as useful as a dentist!

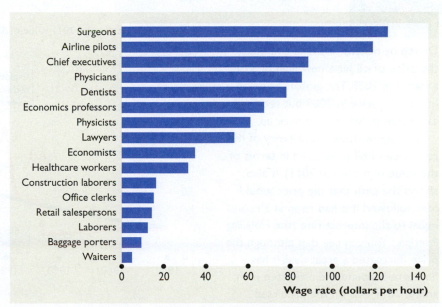

SOURCE OF DATA: National Compensation Survey, Bureau of Labor Statistics.

The Supply of a Nonrenewable Natural Resource

The owner of a nonrenewable natural resource is willing to supply any quantity for the right price. But what *is* the right price? It is the price that gives the same expected profit as holding the resource and selling it next year. This price is lower than the price expected next year by an amount determined by the interest rate.

To see why, think about the choices of Saudi Arabia, a country with a large inventory of oil. Saudi Arabia can sell oil right now and use the revenue to buy U.S. government bonds, or it can keep the oil in the ground and sell it next year.

If Saudi Arabia sells the oil and buys bonds, it earns the interest rate on the bonds. If it keeps its oil and sells it next year, it earns a profit equal to the price increase (or incurs a loss equal to the price decrease) between now and next year. If Saudi Arabia expects the percentage rise in the price of oil to exceed the interest rate it can earn on bonds, it will hold oil off the market. If it expects the percentage rise in the price of oil to be smaller than the interest rate it can earn on bonds, it will want to sell oil today.

Saudi Arabia will be equally happy to sell or hold oil at the price that makes next year's expected price higher than today's price by the same percentage as the interest rate. For example, if next year's expected price is $84 and the interest rate is 5 percent (0.05), Saudi Arabia will be willing to sell right now for $80 a barrel. It will sell none for less than $80 and will sell as much as possible at more than $80.

With the price expected to rise to $84 a barrel next year, Saudi Arabia is indifferent between selling oil now for $80 a barrel and not selling now but waiting until next year and selling it for $84 a barrel. Saudi Arabia expects to make the same return either way. So at $80 a barrel, Saudi Arabia will sell whatever quantity is demanded. Saudi Arabia's supply is *perfectly elastic* at $80 a barrel.

EYE on the GLOBAL ECONOMY
Oil and Metal Prices

Driven by booms in China and India, the price of oil hit a new high of $100 a barrel in 2008. The global recession halved the price in 2009 but renewed expansion in Asia sent it back up.

The figure shows the history of the real price of oil (measured in terms of the value of money in 2011). It also shows the path that the price would have followed if it had risen at a rate equal to the interest rate (the *Hotelling Principle*). You can see that although the price fluctuated a great deal, it has fluctuated around the predicted path and in 2011 was on the predicted path.

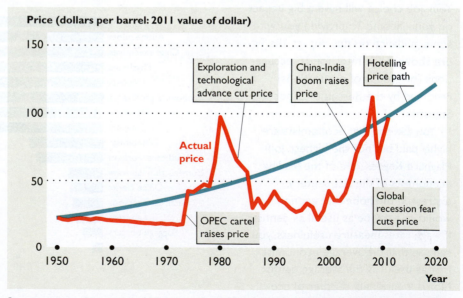

SOURCE OF DATA: International Monetary Fund, World Economic Outlook Database, April 2011.

Equilibrium in a Nonrenewable Natural Resource Market

In a nonrenewable natural resource market, the equilibrium price is the one that gives suppliers an expected profit equal to the interest rate. The equilibrium quantity is the quantity demanded at that price.

Over time, the equilibrium quantity of natural resources used changes as the demand for them changes. The price also changes over time, for two reasons.

First, expectations change. The forces that influence expectations are not well understood. The expected future price of a natural resource depends on the expected future rate of use and rate of discovery of new sources of supply. But one person's expectation about a future price also depends on guesses about other people's expectations. These guesses can change abruptly and become self-reinforcing. When the expected future price of a natural resource changes for whatever reason, its supply changes to reflect that expectation.

Second, suppliers of a natural resource expect the price to rise by the same percentage as the interest rate. If expectations are on the average correct and nothing happens to change expectations, the price *does* rise by the same percentage as the interest rate. The proposition that the price of a nonrenewable natural resource is expected to rise at a rate equal to the interest rate is called the *Hotelling Principle*. It was first realized by Harold Hotelling, an economist at Columbia University.

As *Eye on the Global Economy* below shows, actual prices do not follow the path predicted by the Hotelling Principle. The reason is that the future is unpredictable and expectations about future prices keep changing.

But the price of oil (and other energy resources) has increased, on the average, at a rate equal to the interest rate and may be expected to continue to do so.

The prices of metal ores (shown in the figure on this page) tell a very different story from the price of oil.

Back in 1980, ecologist Paul Ehrlich said that with rapid population growth, we would run out of natural resources. Arguing that human ingenuity would overcome pressure on resources, economist Julian Simon bet Ehrlich that the prices of five metals would fall during the 1980s.

The graph shows that Simon won the bet, and that metals prices continued to fall through 2002.

But they began to rise in 2003 and rose more steeply through the 2000s as demand from China and India grew.

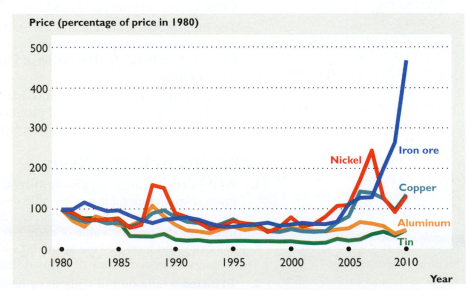

SOURCE OF DATA: International Monetary Fund, World Economic Outlook Database, April 2011.

CHECKPOINT 19.3

Explain how capital and land rental rates and natural resource prices are determined.

Practice Problems

LIST 1

- Beaches in Florida
- Lake Powell
- Empire State Building
- Silver mines in Arizona
- The Great Lakes
- National parks
- Redwood forests
- The Statue of Liberty

1. Which of the items in List 1 are nonrenewable natural resources, which are renewable natural resources, and which are not natural resources? Explain your answers.

2. In the market for a nonrenewable natural resource, explain what determines the equilibrium price and the equilibrium quantity.

In the News

Farmland more valuable than ever

The impact of higher oil prices is being felt on the farm in a number of ways. Feed grain prices and wheat prices have moved up significantly from a year ago. And at these higher prices land rents have gone up.

Source: *USA Today*, February 5, 2008

1. Explain how the growing demand for grain affects the market for farmland.

2. How might farmers meet the growing demand for farm products without having to use a greater quantity of land?

Solutions to Practice Problems

1. Natural resources include all the gifts of nature. A nonrenewable natural resource is one that once used cannot be used again. A renewable natural resource is one that can be used repeatedly.

   Nonrenewable natural resources include silver mines in Arizona.

   Renewable natural resources include beaches in Florida, Lake Powell, the Great Lakes, national parks, and redwood forests.

   The Empire State Building and the Statue of Liberty are national landmarks, but they are not natural resources. Labor and capital were used to build the Empire State Building. The Statue of Liberty was a gift from France and not a gift of nature.

2. In a nonrenewable natural resource market, the equilibrium price is the price that gives suppliers an expected profit equal to the interest rate. The equilibrium quantity is the quantity demanded at that price.

Solutions to In the News

1. As the demand for grain grows with no change in grain output, the price of grain rises. Farmland is a renewable resource—a factor of production. The demand for a factor of production is a derived demand, which is determined by the factor's value of marginal product (*VMP*). An increase in the price of grain increases the farmland's *VMP* and increases the demand for farmland. The rental rate of farmland rises.

2. To increase farm output without using more land, farms will have to become more productive. That is, they will have to use a better technology, which will increase the *MP* of land and increase the land's *VMP*.

CHAPTER SUMMARY

Key Points

1 **Explain how the value of marginal product determines the demand for a factor of production.**

- The demand for a factor of production is a derived demand—it is derived from the demand for the goods and services that the factor of production is used to produce.
- The quantity of a factor of production that is demanded depends on its price and the value of its marginal product, which equals the price of the product multiplied by marginal product.
- Changes in technology bring changes in the demand for labor.

2 **Explain how wage rates and employment are determined and how labor unions influence labor markets.**

- An individual's quantity of labor supplied is influenced by the wage rate: At low wage rates, the quantity of labor supplied increases as the wage rate rises; at high wage rates, the quantity of labor supplied *decreases* as the wage rate rises—the individual's supply of labor curve eventually bends backward.
- The quantity of labor supplied by all households increases as the wage rate rises—the market supply of labor curve is upward sloping.
- Wage rates are determined by demand and supply in labor markets.
- A labor union can raise the wage rate by restricting the supply of labor or by increasing the demand for labor.

3 **Explain how capital and land rental rates and natural resource prices are determined.**

- Capital and land rental rates are determined by demand and supply in capital and land markets; natural resource prices are determined by demand and supply in commodity markets.
- The demand for capital, land, and nonrenewable natural resources is determined by the value of their marginal products.
- The supply of land is perfectly inelastic and the demand for land determines the rental rate.
- The supply of a nonrenewable natural resource is perfectly elastic at a price that makes the expected price rise at a rate equal to the interest rate. Expectations fluctuate and so do natural resource prices.

Key Terms

Derived demand, 485
Factor markets, 484
Factor prices, 484
Job, 484

Labor union, 494
Nonrenewable natural
  resources, 484
Value of marginal product, 485

MyEconLab
You can work these problems in Chapter 19 Study Plan and get instant feedback.

CHAPTER CHECKPOINT

Study Plan Problems and Applications

1. A California asparagus farmer is maximizing profit. The price of asparagus is $2 a bunch, a farm worker's wage rate is $12 an hour, and the asparagus farm employs six workers. What is the marginal product of the sixth farm worker? If, when the price of asparagus rises to $3 a bunch, the farm hires eight workers, what is the marginal product of the eighth worker?

2. Through the 1990s, the percentage of high school students who decided to go to college increased. Draw a demand-supply graph to illustrate the effect of this increase on the market for college graduates. Explain its effect on the market for college professors.

3. If your college switched to online delivery of its courses, what changes do you predict would occur in the factor markets in the town where your college is located?

4. If soccer becomes more popular in the United States and basketball becomes less popular, is it true that professional basketball players will earn more than what they earn today? Use the laws of demand and supply in factor markets to explain your answer.

5. Suppose that Palm Island, the world's largest grower of coconuts, plans to build its first airport on 100 acres of productive farm land. Palm Islanders expected the world price of coconuts to rise by 200 percent next year and remain high for the next decade. Explain the influence of these events on Palm Island's labor market and land market.

6. Is it true that the opening of a new diamond mine in the Yukon in Canada will lower the world price of diamonds and lower the wage rate paid to diamond workers in South Africa? Use a graph to illustrate your answer.

Use the following information to work Problems **7** to **9**.

Robots on the farm
Commercial farms of the future may be staffed by robots that will identify, spray, and pick individual pieces of produce from plants, even when their targets are grapes, peppers, and apples that are as green as the leaves that surround them. Robots could also offer a timely supply of labor in many places, where there simply aren't enough itinerant workers available at the right times in the harvesting cycle.

Source: ABC News, April 17, 2011

7. Explain the effects of not enough itinerant workers at harvest time on the market for farm labor.

8. How will the use of robots change the value of marginal product of farm workers?

9. Explain how using robots will create better paying farm jobs.

Instructor Assignable Problems and Applications

Your instructor can assign these problems as homework, a quiz, or a test in MyEconLab.

1. Is the market for college football coaches competitive? If it is, why don't they all earn the same wage rate? Is the market for Nick Saban competitive? How is his compensation determined?

2. In the years after World War II, the birth rate increased and the so-called baby boom generation was created. That generation is now beginning to retire. Draw a demand-supply graph to illustrate the effects of this increase in the number of seniors on the market for medical services.

Use the following information to work Problems **3** and **4**.

A new coffee shop opens and to maximize profit it hires 5 workers at the competitive wage rate. The price of a cup of coffee is $4 and the value of marginal product of workers in the coffee shop is $12 an hour.

3. What is the marginal product of the coffee shop workers? How much does a coffee shop worker earn?

4. If the price of a cup of coffee rises from $4 to $5 and the coffee shop continues to hire workers at the competitive wage rate, explain how the value of marginal product and the number of workers hired will change.

5. "As more people buy Internet service, the price of Internet service will fall. The fall in the price of Internet service will lead to a fall in the wage rate paid to Web page designers." Is this statement true or false? Explain your answer.

6. Suppose that Bananaland is the world's largest grower of bananas. Bananaland plans to double its population in 3 years by hiring well-educated people from the United States. To increase the number of entrepreneurs, Bananaland encourages anyone with $1 million to immigrate. Explain the influence of these events on Bananaland's labor market and land market.

7. Hong Kong is much more densely populated than is the United States. Compare the rent on land in Hong Kong with that in Chicago. Can you explain why the percentage of commercial buildings that are new in downtown Chicago is less than that in Hong Kong?

Use the following information to work Problems **8** and **9**.

Unwinding in the capital of the Woodstock nation
In August 1969, in Bethel, N.Y., some 400,000 people swarmed to Max Yasgur's 600-acre farm for the Woodstock Music & Art Fair to hear rock acts like the Who and Jimi Hendrix. In 2007, with plenty of land available and only 100 miles from New York City, people built weekend homes. As a result of all the new development, Bethel has placed a temporary moratorium on subdivisions.
Source: The New York Times, September 21, 2007

8. Draw a graph to show the change in the land market from 1969 to 2007. Explain how the moratorium will influence the land market in 2008.

9. Draw a graph to show the Bethel labor market in 2007. Explain how the moratorium will influence the Bethel labor market in 2008.

MyEconLab

You can work this quiz in Chapter 19 Study Plan and get instant feedback.

Multiple Choice Quiz

1. A firm's demand for labor is determined by _____.

   A. the market wage rate
   B. the price of the good that the firm produces and the wage rate it pays
   C. the marginal product of labor and the market wage rate
   D. the price of the good that the firm produces and the marginal product of labor

2. The value of marginal product of labor increases if _____.

   A. more labor is hired
   B. more of the good is produced
   C. the market price of the good produced rises
   D. using a new technology reduces the demand for labor

3. An individual's supply of labor curve is _____.

   A. horizontal at the market wage rate
   B. upward sloping as the wage rate rises
   C. upward sloping at low wage rates but becomes downward sloping at high wage rates
   D. vertical at the standard number of hours a person works per day

4. In a competitive labor market for bakers, the equilibrium wage rate _____.

   A. rises if bakers become more productive
   B. falls if the supply of bakers decreases
   C. rises if the market price of bakery items falls
   D. rises if new technology makes it easier for anyone to be a baker

5. A union will _____ if it can _____.

   A. raise the wage rate of its members; decrease the marginal product of its union members
   B. raise the wage rate of its members; introduce minimum qualifications, which will restrict membership of the union
   C. increase the number of union jobs; restrict membership of the union
   D. increase the number of union jobs; increase the union wage rate

6. To maximize profit, a firm _____.

   A. uses the quantity of land at which the rental rate equals the value of marginal product of land
   B. balances the rental rate of capital against the wage rate of labor
   C. uses the quantity of capital at which the marginal revenue equals the value of marginal product of capital
   D. uses the quantity of capital at which the suppliers' expected profit equals the value of marginal product of capital

7. Which of the following statements about a nonrenewable natural resource market is *incorrect*?

   A. The demand for the resource is determined by its value of marginal product.
   B. The supply of the resource is perfectly elastic at the market price.
   C. The price of the resource is expected to rise over time at a rate equal to the interest rate.
   D. The supply of the resource is perfectly inelastic at the proven reserves.

Economic Inequality

20

When you have completed your study of this chapter, you will be able to

1 Describe the economic inequality in the United States.

2 Explain how economic inequality arises.

3 Explain how governments redistribute income and describe the effects of redistribution on economic inequality.

20.1   MEASURING ECONOMIC INEQUALITY

Market income

A household's wages, interest, rent, and profit earned in factor markets before paying income taxes.

Money income

Market income plus cash payments to households by the government.

To measure economic inequality, we look at the distributions of income and wealth. A household's *income* is the amount that it *receives in a given period*. A household's **market income** equals the wages, interest, rent, and profit that the household earns in factor markets before paying income taxes. The Census Bureau defines another income concept, **money income**, which equals *market income* plus cash payments to households by the government. We will use the *money income* concept to describe the distribution of income in the United States.

A household's *wealth* is the value of the things it *owns at a point in time*. Wealth is measured as the market value of a household's home, the stocks and bonds that it owns, and the money in its bank accounts minus its debts such as outstanding credit card balances.

To describe the *distribution of income*, imagine the population of the United States lined up from the lowest to the highest income earner. Now divide the line into five equal-sized groups, each with 20 percent of the population. These groups are called *quintiles*.

Next share out total money income among these groups so that the shares represent the U.S. income distribution. Table 20.1(a) lists the percentages received by each group.

Share out the pie of total wealth in a similar way. Table 20.1(b) shows the percentages owned by each of seven groups. The richest quintile has been broken down into smaller groups to show the wealth distribution inside the highest quintile.

■ **TABLE 20.1**

The Distributions of Money Income and Wealth in the United States

In part (a), the 20 percent of households with the lowest incomes receive 3.3 percent of total money income, while the 20 percent of households with the highest incomes receive 50.2 percent of total income.

In part (b), the poorest 40 percent of households own 0.2 percent of total wealth, while the richest 1 percent own 34.4 percent.

SOURCES OF DATA: Part (a) Current Population Reports, P60-239, *Income, Poverty, and Health Insurance Coverage in the United States: 2010*, U.S. Census Bureau, Washington, DC, 2011. Part (b) Edward N. Wolff, "Recent Trends in Household Wealth in the United States: Rising Debt and the Middle-Class Squeeze," www.levy.org/pubs/wp_502.pdf.

(a) Income distribution in 2010 (Median household income $49,445)

	Percentage of		Cumulative percentage of	
	Households	**Income**	**Households**	**Income**
A	**Lowest 20**	3.3	20	3.3
B	**Second 20**	8.5	40	11.8
C	**Third 20**	14.6	60	26.4
D	**Fourth 20**	23.4	80	49.8
E	**Highest 20**	50.2	100	100.0

(b) Wealth distribution in 2004 (Median household wealth $77,900)

	Percentage of		Cumulative percentage of	
	Households	**Wealth**	**Households**	**Wealth**
A'	**Lowest 40**	0.2	40	0.2
B'	**Next 20**	3.8	60	4.0
C'	**Next 20**	11.3	80	15.3
D'	**Next 10**	13.4	90	28.7
E'	**Next 5**	12.3	95	41.0
F'	**Next 4**	24.6	99	65.6
G'	**Highest 1**	34.4	100	100.0

Lorenz Curves

A **Lorenz curve** graphs the cumulative percentage of income (or wealth) on the *y*-axis against the cumulative percentage of households on the *x*-axis. Figure 20.1 shows the Lorenz curves for income and wealth in the United States. Graphing the cumulative percentage of income against the cumulative percentage of households makes the Lorenz curve for income and the points *A* to *D* on the graph correspond to the rows identified by those letters in the table. For example, row *B* and point *B* show that the 40 percent of households with the lowest incomes received 11.8 percent of total income—3.3 percent plus 8.5 percent from Table 20.1(a).

Graphing the cumulative percentage of wealth against the cumulative percentage of households makes the Lorenz curve for wealth and the points *A'* to *F'* on the graph correspond to the rows identified by those letters in the table of Figure 20.1. For example, row *C'* and point *C'* show that the poorest 80 percent of households owned 15.3 percent of total wealth—0.2 percent plus 3.8 percent plus 11.3 percent from Table 20.1(b).

If income (or wealth) were distributed equally, each 20 percent of households would receive 20 percent of total income (or own 20 percent of total wealth), and the Lorenz curve would be the straight line labeled "Line of equality." The Lorenz curves based on the actual distributions of income and wealth are always below the line of equality. The closer the Lorenz curve is to the line of equality, the more equal is the distribution. You can see that the Lorenz curve for wealth is much farther away from the line of equality than is the Lorenz curve for income. The distribution of wealth is much more unequal than the distribution of income.

Lorenz curve
A curve that graphs the cumulative percentage of income (or wealth) against the cumulative percentage of households.

FIGURE 20.1

Lorenz Curves for Income and Wealth in the United States

MyEconLab Animation

Cumulative percentage of		
Households	Income	Wealth
20	A 3.3	
40	B 11.8	A' 0.2
60	C 26.4	B' 4.0
80	D 49.8	C' 15.3
90		D' 28.7
95		E' 41.0
99		F' 65.6

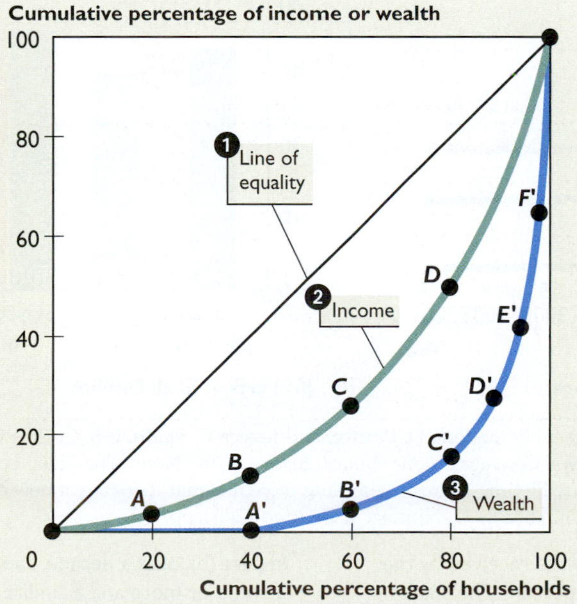

1 If income and wealth were distributed equally, the Lorenz curve would lie along the straight line labeled "Line of equality."

2 The income Lorenz curve shows the cumulative percentage of income graphed against the cumulative percentage of households. The 20 percent of households with the lowest incomes received 3.3 percent of total income, and the 80 percent of households with the lowest incomes received 49.8 percent.

3 The wealth Lorenz curve shows the cumulative percentage of wealth graphed against the cumulative percentage of households. The poorest 40 percent of households own 0.2 percent of total wealth, and 99 percent of households own 65.6 percent of total wealth. The richest 1 percent own 34.4 percent.

SOURCES OF DATA: See Table 20.1.

■ Inequality over Time

U.S. income inequality has increased. The highest incomes have increased faster than the lower incomes and the gap between the rich and the poor has widened.

Figure 20.2(a) shows this widening gap by looking at the income share of each quintile between 1970 and 2010. The data are based on *money income*. The figure shows that the share received by the highest quintile increased from 43 percent during the late 1960s to 50 percent in the 2000s. The percentage of total income received by each of the other quintiles decreased. The poorest quintile share fell from 4 percent to 3 percent; the second poorest quintile share fell from 11 percent to 9 percent; and the third (middle) quintile fell from 17 percent to 15 percent.

■ Economic Mobility

Economic mobility is the movement of a family up or down through the income distribution. If there were no economic mobility, a family would be stuck at a given point in the income distribution and be persistently poor, or rich, or somewhere in the middle. Also, in such a situation, the data on annual income distribution would be a good indicator of life-time inequality.

But if there is economic mobility, families move up or down through the income distribution and life-time inequality is not as severe as the inequality in the data for a single year. How much economic mobility is there?

FIGURE 20.2

Trends in the Distribution of Income and Economic Mobility   MyEconLab Animation

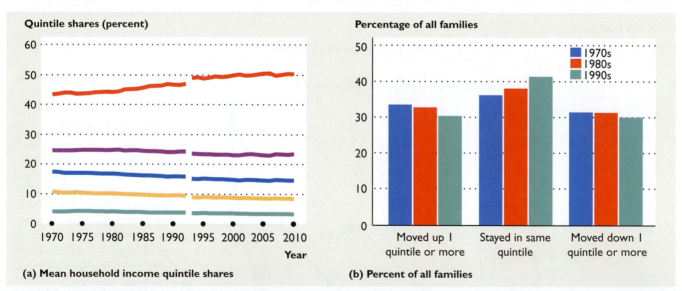

(a) Mean household income quintile shares   (b) Percent of all families

SOURCES OF DATA: Part (a) DeNavas-Walt, Carmen, Bernadette D. Proctor, and Jessica C. Smith, U.S. Census Bureau, Current Population Reports, P60-239, *Income, Poverty, and Health Insurance Coverage in the United States: 2010.* Note: The data collection method changed in 1993. Part (b) Katharine Bradbury and Jane Katz, "Are lifetime incomes becoming more unequal? Looking at new evidence on family income mobility," *Regional Review,* Federal Reserve Bank of Boston, Volume 12, Number 4, Quarter 4 2002, pp. 2–5.

In part (a), from 1970 to 2010 the income share received by the highest quintile rose from 43 percent to 50 percent. The shares received by the other quintiles fell. The lowest quintile share fell from 4 percent to 3 percent, the second lowest from 11 percent to 9 percent, and the middle from 17 percent to 15 percent.

In part (b), over a decade, about 30 percent of families move up a quintile or more and a similar percentage move down a quintile or more. Between 35 and 40 percent of families remain in the same quintile. Mobility through the quintiles has decreased over the 1980s and 1990s.

Katharine Bradbury and Jane Katz, economists at the Federal Reserve Bank of Boston, have provided an answer to this question and Figure 20.2(b) shows what they found. The figure shows the percentages of families that remained in the same quintile and that moved up or down by one quintile or more over a ten-year period.

About 30 percent of families move up by a quintile or more and a slightly smaller percentage move down by a quintile or more. Between 35 percent and 40 percent of families remain in the same quintile.

What is the source of economic mobility? Most of it arises from normal changes over a family's life cycle. Families experience income growth as their workers become more skilled and experienced. As a family continues to get older and its workers retire, its income falls. So if we look at three households that have identical *lifetime incomes*—that are *economically equal*—but one is young, one is middle-aged, and one is old, we will see a great deal of inequality. Inequality of annual incomes overstates the degree of lifetime inequality.

You've seen that income inequality is increasing, but is economic mobility also increasing? The data in Figure 20.2(b) answer this question, and they show a trend toward less economic mobility, not more. A decreasing percentage of families is moving either up or down a quintile or more and an increasing percentage of families is remaining in the same quintile. Why economic mobility has decreased remains a question for future research.

EYE on the GLOBAL ECONOMY
Global Inequality

There is much more income inequality in the global economy than in the United States. The Lorenz curves in this figure provide a comparative picture. You can see that the global Lorenz curve lies much farther from the line of equality than does the U.S. Lorenz curve.

Numbers that highlight the comparison are the percentages of families that get a half (50 percent) of the income. In the United States, the richest 20 percent of families get a half of the income and the remaining 80 percent share the other half. In the global economy the richest 10 percent of families get a half of the income and the remaining 90 percent share the other half.

Global incomes are rising and by some estimates, inequality is decreas-

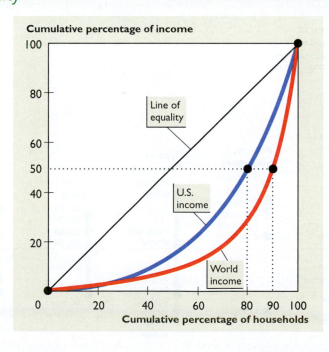

ing. But other estimates suggest that global inequality, like U.S. inequality, is

SOURCES OF DATA: U.S., see Figure 20.1. World, Branko Milanovic, "True World Income Distribution, 1988 and 1993: First Calculation Based on Household Surveys Alone," *Economic Journal*, 112, 2002.

increasing. Better data are needed to settle this issue.

EYE on INEQUALITY
Who Are the Rich and the Poor?

In the United States today (excluding the ultra rich sports and entertainment superstars and top corporate executives), the families with the highest incomes are likely to be college-educated Asian married couples between 45 and 54 years of age living together with two children somewhere in the West.

At the other extreme, the person with the lowest income is likely to be a black woman over 65 years of age who lives alone somewhere in the South and has fewer than nine years of elementary school education. Another low-income group are young women who have not completed high school, have a child (or children), and who live without a partner. These snapshot profiles are the extremes in the figure.

The figure illustrates the dominant importance of education in influencing income. Persons with a post-graduate professional degree (an MBA and a law degree are examples) or a doctorate degree earn, on average, five times the income of a person who has not completed high school.

Household size and type are the second largest influences on income. A married couple with two children have, on average, an income three times that of a single female household.

Age is almost as important as household size and type. People aged between 45 and 54 have incomes double those of people aged 65 and over and aged 15 to 24.

Race is another significant factor that influences income. Asian households earn, on average, double the income of Hispanic origin households.

Region of residence has a small influence on income, the Northeast having the highest incomes at almost 20 percent higher than those in the South.

Within these categories, there is enormous individual variation.

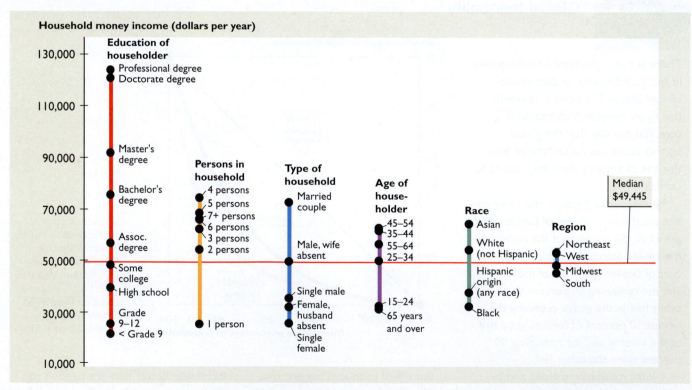

SOURCE OF DATA: Current Population Survey, HINC-01. Selected Characteristics of Households, by Total Money Income in 2009.

■ Poverty

Households with very low incomes are considered to be living in poverty. What is poverty? How do we measure it, how much poverty is there, and is the amount of poverty decreasing or increasing?

Poverty Defined and Measured

Poverty is a state in which a household's income is too low to be able to buy the quantities of food, shelter, and clothing that are deemed necessary.

The Census Bureau considers a household to be living in poverty if its income is less than a defined level that varies with household size and is updated each year to reflect changes in the cost of living. In 2010, the poverty level for a household with 2 adults and 2 children was an income of $22,113.

In 2010, 46 million Americans had incomes below the poverty level. Figure 20.3(a) shows the distribution of poverty by race in 2010. Almost one half (44 percent) of people living in poverty are white.

Poverty Incidence and Trends

To measure the *incidence* of poverty, we look at the poverty *rate*—the percentage of families living in poverty. In 2010, the poverty rate was 15.1 percent. Figure 20.3(b) shows the poverty rates and their trends for white, black, and Hispanic families from 1970 through 2010.

Poverty
A state in which a household's income is too low to be able to buy the quantities of food, shelter, and clothing that are deemed necessary.

■ FIGURE 20.3

Poverty Rates in the United States

MyEconLab Animation

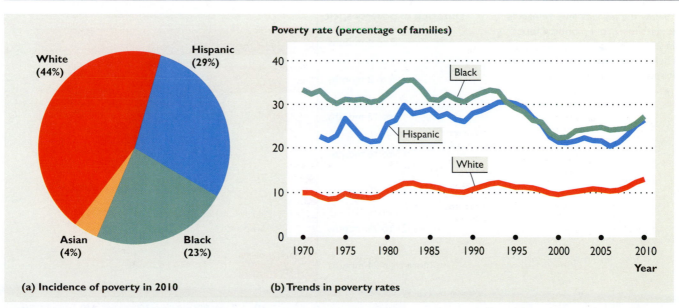

(a) Incidence of poverty in 2010

(b) Trends in poverty rates

SOURCE OF DATA: DeNavas-Walt, Carmen, Bernadette D. Proctor, and Jessica C. Smith, U.S. Census Bureau, Current Population Reports, P60–239, *Income, Poverty, and Health Insurance Coverage in the United States: 2010.*

White families account for 44 percent of the poor in part (a). But poverty *rates* for blacks and Hispanics are double those for whites in part (b). The poverty rate of black families fell during the 1980s and the 1990s. The poverty rate of Hispanics also fell during the 1990s, but it had previously increased. The poverty rates of all groups increased in 2009 and 2010.

For white families, the poverty rate has fluctuated around 10 percent. For black families, the poverty rate fell from 35 percent in 1983 to 24 percent in 2008 but the rate had increased to 27 percent by 2010. For Hispanic families, the poverty rate increased during the 1980s and then decreased during the 1990s. By 2006, the poverty rate for this group had fallen to a low of 20 percent. But during the years after 2006, the Hispanic poverty rate steadily increased and by 2010, it had reached 27 percent.

Poverty Duration

Another dimension of poverty is its duration. If a household is in poverty for a few months it faces serious hardship during those months, but it faces a less serious problem than it would if its poverty persisted for several months or, worse yet, for several years, or even generations.

Because the duration of poverty is an important additional indicator of the hardship that poverty brings, the Census Bureau provided measures of duration for the years 2001 to 2003. Figure 20.4 shows these data.

It turns out that almost 50 percent of poverty lasts for between 2 and 4 months. So for about a half of poor families, poverty is not persistent. But more than 20 percent of poverty lasts for more than a year, so a seriously large number of households experience chronic poverty.

In the next sections, we look at the sources of inequality and poverty and the policies that aim to redistribute income and lift the living standard of the poor.

■ **FIGURE 20.4**

The Duration of Poverty Spells in the United States

MyEconLab Animation

Almost 50 percent of the people who fall below the poverty level remain in that state for 2 to 4 months. More than 20 percent of the people who fall below the poverty level remain in that state for more than a year.

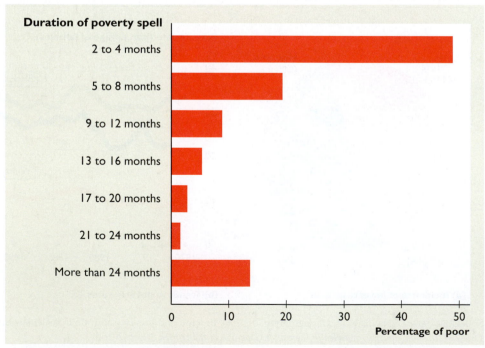

SOURCE OF DATA: U.S. Census Bureau, *Dynamics of Economic Well-Being: Poverty 2001–2003.*

CHECKPOINT 20.1

Describe the economic inequality in the United States.

MyEconLab

You can work these problems in Study Plan 20.1 and get instant feedback.

Practice Problems

Table 1 shows the distribution of money income in Canada and Table 20.1(a) on page 508 shows the distribution of money income in the United States.

1. Create a table that shows the cumulative percentages of households and income in Canada.

2. Draw the Lorenz curves for Canada and the United States. Compare the distribution of income in Canada with that in the United States. Which distribution is more unequal?

In the News

Minorities hit harder by economic issues
Plummeting home values, as well as home foreclosures, have had a big impact on the distribution of wealth because blacks and Hispanics have a much higher share of their wealth tied up in the value of their homes. Hispanics experienced the biggest loss of wealth because many bought homes in states where the real estate market had the steepest plunge in value.

Source: *USA Today*, August 5, 2011

Explain how the events described in the news clip changed the distribution of wealth. Which quintiles would experience an increase in their share of wealth?

Solutions to Practice Problems

1. Table 2 shows the cumulative percentages of Canadian households and income: The lowest 20 percent of households receive 4.8 percent of total income and the second lowest 20 percent receive 10.7 percent of total income, so the lowest 40 percent of households receive 15.5 percent of total income. The other rows of the table are calculated in a similar way.

2. A Lorenz curve plots the cumulative percentage of income against the cumulative percentage of households. The blue curve in Figure 1 plots the Canadian data in Table 2. The green curve is the U.S. Lorenz curve. The line of equality shows an equal distribution. The Canadian Lorenz curve lies closer to the line of equality than does the U.S. Lorenz curve, so the distribution of income in the United States is more unequal than that in Canada.

Solution to In the News

A household's wealth is the value of the things it owns at a point in time. Wealth is measured as the market value of a household's home, the stocks and bonds that it owns, and the money in its bank accounts minus its debts. Because most of the wealth of blacks and Hispanics is made up of their houses, as house prices fell and home foreclosures increased, the percentage of total wealth of the lowest quintiles fell and the percentage of total wealth held by wealthier quintiles increased. The distribution of wealth became more unequal.

TABLE 1   CANADIAN DATA

Households	Money income (percentage)
Lowest 20 percent	4.8
Second 20 percent	10.7
Third 20 percent	16.5
Fourth 20 percent	24.0
Highest 20 percent	44.0

TABLE 2

Cumulative percentage of	
Households	Income
20	4.8
40	15.5
60	32.0
80	56.0
100	100.0

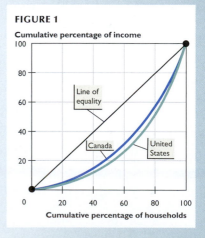

FIGURE 1

20.2 HOW ECONOMIC INEQUALITY ARISES

Economic inequality arises from a wide variety of factors. The five key ones that we'll examine here are

- Human capital
- Discrimination
- Financial and physical capital
- Entrepreneurial ability
- Personal and family characteristics

■ Human Capital

Human capital is the accumulated skill and knowledge of human beings. To see how human capital differences affect economic inequality, we'll study an economy with two levels of human capital, which we'll call *high-skilled labor* and *low-skilled labor.* Low-skilled labor might be law clerks, hospital orderlies, or bank tellers, and high-skilled labor might be attorneys, surgeons, or bank CEOs.

The Demand for High-Skilled and Low-Skilled Labor

High-skilled workers can perform tasks that low-skilled workers would perform badly or couldn't even perform at all. Imagine an untrained person doing surgery or piloting an airplane. High-skilled workers have a higher value of marginal product (*VMP*) than low-skilled workers do. As we learned in Chapter 19, a firm's demand for labor curve is derived from and is the same as the firm's value of marginal product of labor curve.

Figure 20.5(a) shows the demand curves for high-skilled and low-skilled labor. At any given employment level, firms are willing to pay a higher wage rate to a high-skilled worker than to a low-skilled worker. The gap between the two wage rates measures the value of marginal product of skill—for example, at an employment level of 2,000 hours, firms are willing to pay a high-skilled worker $25 an hour and a low-skilled worker only $10 an hour, a difference of $15 an hour. Thus the value of marginal product of skill is $15 an hour.

The Supply of High-Skilled and Low-Skilled Labor

A skill is costly to acquire and its opportunity cost includes expenditures, such as tuition, and lower earnings while the skill is being acquired. When a person goes to school full time, that cost is the total earnings forgone. When a person acquires a skill through on-the-job training, he or she earns a lower wage rate than someone who is doing a comparable job but not undergoing training. In this case, the cost of acquiring the skill is equal to the wage paid to a person not being trained minus the wage paid to a person being trained.

Because skills are costly to acquire, a high-skilled person is not willing to work for the same wage that a low-skilled person is willing to accept. The position of the supply curve of high-skilled workers reflects the cost of acquiring the skill. Figure 20.5(b) shows two supply curves: one of high-skilled workers and the other of low-skilled workers. The supply curve of high-skilled workers is S_H, and that of low-skilled workers is S_L.

The high-skilled worker's supply curve lies above the low-skilled worker's supply curve. The vertical distance between the two supply curves is the com-

FIGURE 20.5

Skill Differentials

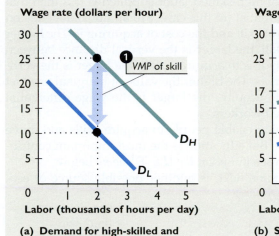

(a) Demand for high-skilled and
low-skilled labor

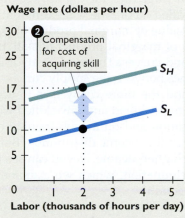

(b) Supply of high-skilled and
low-skilled labor

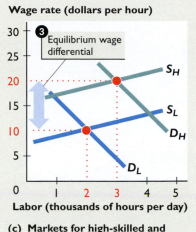

(c) Markets for high-skilled and
low-skilled labor

In part (a), D_L is the demand curve for low-skilled labor and D_H is the demand curve for high-skilled labor. **①** The vertical distance between these two curves is the value of marginal product of skill.

In part (b), S_L is the supply curve of low-skilled workers and S_H is the supply curve of high-skilled workers. **②** The vertical distance

between these two curves is the required compensation for the cost of acquiring a skill.

In part (c), in equilibrium, low-skilled workers earn a wage rate of $10 an hour and high-skilled workers earn a wage rate of $20 an hour. **③** The $10 wage differential is the equilibrium effect of acquiring skill.

pensation that high-skilled workers require for the cost of acquiring the skill. For example, suppose that the quantity of low-skilled labor supplied is 2,000 hours at a wage rate of $10 an hour. This wage rate compensates the low-skilled workers mainly for their time on the job. Consider next the supply of high-skilled workers. To induce high-skilled labor to supply 2,000 hours, firms must pay a wage rate of $17 an hour. This wage rate for high-skilled labor is higher than that for low-skilled labor because high-skilled labor must be compensated not only for the time on the job but also for the time and other costs of acquiring the skill.

Wage Rates of High-Skilled and Low-Skilled Labor

To work out the wage rates of high-skilled and low-skilled labor, we have to bring together the effects of skill on the demand for and supply of labor.

Figure 20.5(c) shows the demand curves and the supply curves for high-skilled and low-skilled labor. These curves are the same as those plotted in parts (a) and (b). Equilibrium occurs in the market for low-skilled labor where the supply and demand curves for low-skilled labor intersect. The equilibrium wage rate is $10 an hour, and the quantity of low-skilled labor employed is 2,000 hours. Equilibrium in the market for high-skilled workers occurs where the supply and demand curves for high-skilled workers intersect. The equilibrium wage rate is $20 an hour, and the quantity of high-skilled labor employed is 3,000 hours.

As you can see in Figure 20.5(c), the equilibrium wage rate of high-skilled labor is higher than that of low-skilled labor. There are two reasons why this occurs: First, high-skilled labor has a higher value of marginal product than does low-skilled labor, so at a given wage rate, the quantity of high-skilled labor demanded exceeds that of low-skilled labor. Second, skills are costly to acquire, so at a given wage rate, the quantity of high-skilled labor supplied is less than that of low-skilled labor. The wage differential (in this case, $10 an hour) depends on both the value of marginal product of skill and the cost of acquiring it. The higher the value of marginal product of skill, the larger is the vertical distance between the demand curves. The more costly it is to acquire a skill, the larger is the vertical distance between the supply curves. The higher the value of marginal product of skill and the more costly it is to acquire, the larger is the wage differential between high-skilled and low-skilled workers.

Education and on-the-job training enable people to acquire skills and move up through the income distribution. But education is the most important contributor to a higher income, as you can see in *Eye on the U.S. Economy* below.

Discrimination, which we examine next, is another possible source of economic inequality.

EYE on the U.S. ECONOMY
Does Education Pay?

The figure shows that there are large differences in earnings based on the degree of education.

Rates of return on high school and college education have been estimated to be in the range of 5 to 10 percent a year after allowing for inflation, which suggests that a college degree is a better investment than almost any other that a person can undertake.

Based on average income data, the gain from graduating from high school is $16,000 a year. But the gain from going to college or university and getting a bachelor's degree is greater and brings in an additional $43,000 a year.

Remaining at the university to complete a master's degree (usually one more year of study) brings in an extra $20,000 a year, and working for a professional degree increases income by another $54,000 a year.

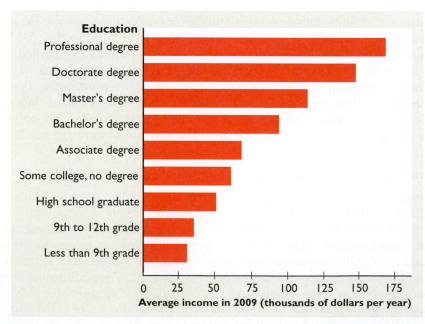

SOURCE OF DATA: Current Population Survey, HINC-01. Selected Characteristics of Households, by Total Money Income in 2009.

■ Discrimination

Persistent earnings differences exist between women and men and among the races. You can see them in *Eye on the U.S. Economy* below. Does discrimination contribute to these differences? It might, but economists can't isolate and measure the effect of discrimination, so we can't say by how much, or even whether, earnings differences arise from this source.

To see the difficulty in isolating the effects of discrimination, consider the market for investment advisors. Suppose that black women and white men are equally good at providing investment advice. If there is no race and sex discrimination, average wage rates are the same for both groups.

But if some people are willing to pay more for investment advice from a white man than they are willing to pay for the same advice from a black woman, the market-determined value of marginal product of black women is lower than that of white men, and the demand for investment advice from black women is lower than that from white men. The result is a lower equilibrium wage rate (and fewer high-paying jobs) for black women than for white men.

For discrimination to work in this way and bring *persistent* wage differences, people must be *persistently* willing to pay more than necessary for investment advice. People will begin to notice that they can get a better deal if they buy investment advice from black women. Substitution away from high-cost white men toward lower-cost black women will shift demand and eventually eliminate the wage difference.

EYE on the U.S. ECONOMY
Sex and Race Earnings Differences

The figure shows the earnings of different race and sex groups expressed as a percentage of the earnings of white men.

In 2010, white women earned, on average, 80 percent of what white men earned. Black men earned 73 percent, and black women earned 65 percent. Men and women of Hispanic origin earned only 70 percent and 60 percent, respectively, of white men's wages.

These earnings differentials have persisted over many years, and only those of women have begun to narrow in a significant way.

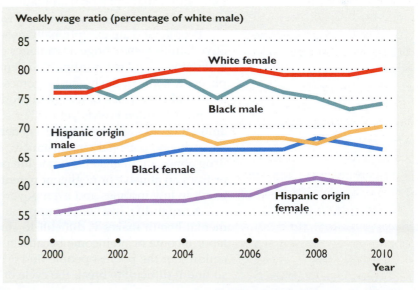

SOURCE OF DATA: Bureau of Labor Statistics.

■ Financial and Physical Capital

The people with the highest incomes are usually those who own large amounts of financial capital and physical capital. These people receive incomes in the form of interest and dividend payments and from capital gains—increases in the stock market value.

Families with a large amount of capital tend to become even more wealthy across generations for two reasons. First, they bequeath wealth to their children and second, rich people marry rich partners (on the average).

Saving, and the wealth accumulation that it brings, is not inevitably a source of increased inequality and can even be a source of increased equality. When a household saves to redistribute an uneven income over the life cycle, it enjoys more equal consumption. Also, if a lucky generation that has a high income saves a large amount and makes a bequest to a generation that is unlucky, this act of saving also decreases the degree of inequality.

■ Entrepreneurial Ability

Some of the most spectacularly rich people have benefited from unusual entrepreneurial talent. Household names such as Bill Gates (Microsoft), Sergey Brin and Larry Page (Google), and Mark Zuckerberg (Facebook) are examples of people who began life with modest amounts of wealth and modest incomes and through a combination of hard work, good luck, and outstanding entrepreneurship have become extremely rich.

But some very poor people, and some who fall below the poverty level, have also tried their hands at being entrepreneurs. We don't hear much about these people. They are not in the headlines. But they have put together a business plan, borrowed heavily, and through a combination of hard work, bad luck, and in some cases poor decisions have become extremely poor.

■ Personal and Family Characteristics

Each individual's personal and family characteristics play a crucial role, for either good or ill, in influencing economic well-being.

People who are exceptionally good looking and talented with stable and creative families enjoy huge advantages over the average person. Many movie stars, entertainers, and extraordinarily talented athletes are in this category. These people enjoy some of the highest incomes because their personal or family characteristics make the value of marginal product of their labor very large.

Success often breeds yet further success. A large income can generate a large amount of saving, which in turn generates yet more interest income.

Adverse personal circumstances, such as chronic physical or mental illness, drug abuse, or an unstable home life possibly arising from the absence of a parent or from an abusive or negligent parent, place a huge burden on many people and result in low incomes and even poverty.

A tough life, just like its opposite, can be self-reinforcing. Weak physical or mental health makes it difficult to study and obtain a skill and results in a low labor income or no income because a job is just too hard to hold down. And the children of the poorest people find it hard to get into college and university, and so find it difficult to break the cycle of poverty.

CHECKPOINT 20.2

Explain how economic inequality arises.

MyEconLab

You can work these problems in Study Plan 20.2 and get instant feedback.

Practice Problems

In the United States in 2010, 30 million people had full-time managerial and professional jobs that paid an average of $1,200 a week and 10 million people had full-time sales positions that paid an average of $600 a week.

1. Explain why managers and professionals are paid more than salespeople.

2. Explain why, despite the higher weekly wage, more people are employed as managers and professionals than as salespeople.

3. As more firms offer their goods and services for sale online, how does the market for salespeople change?

In the News

Trade schools boom with enrollees of all ages

Disappearing jobs have helped drive people to state-run trade schools. Patricia Parker, who is tired of getting laid off at factories decided to re-educate herself by taking a course in business system technology and getting a job at a medical office. Some are retraining as auto mechanics, a skill that won't be outsourced.

Source: *USA Today*, July 19, 2009

Why might people who previously worked in factories be going to trade school?

Solutions to Practice Problems

1. A typical manager or professional has incurred a higher cost of education and on-the-job training than has the typical salesperson. The supply curve of managers and professionals, S_H, lies above that of salespeople, S_L (Figure 1). With better education and on-the-job training, managers and professionals have more human capital and a higher value of marginal product than do salespeople. The demand curve for managers and professionals, D_H, is greater than the demand for salespeople, D_L. The figure shows why managers and professionals are paid more than salespeople.

2. Figure 1 shows that the demand and supply for each type of labor leads to a greater employment for managers and professionals than for salespeople.

3. As more people shop online, firms hire fewer salespeople. The demand for salespeople decreases and fewer people work in sales. How their wage rate changes depends on how the supply of salespeople changes.

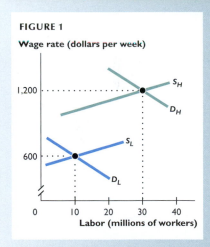

FIGURE 1

Solution to In the News

When factories close, the people who work in them lose some of their human capital. Patricia Parker and other people who previously worked in factories are going to trade school to invest in new human capital by obtaining skills that they believe will remain in demand as manufacturing jobs are lost when factories close and jobs are outsourced.

20.3 INCOME REDISTRIBUTION

We've described the distribution of income and wealth in the United States and examined the five main sources of economic inequality. Our task in this final section is to study the *redistribution* of income by government.

How do governments redistribute income? What is the scale of redistribution? Why do we vote for policies that redistribute income? What are the challenges in designing policies that achieve a fair and efficient distribution of income and reduction of poverty?

■ How Governments Redistribute Income

The three main ways in which governments in the United States redistribute income are

- Income taxes
- Income maintenance programs
- Subsidized services

Income Taxes

Income taxes may be progressive, regressive, or proportional (see Chapter 8, p. 197). A *progressive income tax* is one that taxes income at an average rate that increases with the level of income. A *regressive income tax* is one that taxes income at an average rate that decreases with the level of income. A *proportional income tax* (also called a *flat-rate income tax*) is one that taxes income at a constant rate, regardless of the level of income.

The federal government, most state governments, and some city governments impose income taxes. The detailed tax arrangements vary across the individual states, but the income tax system overall is progressive. The poorest working households receive money from the government through an earned income tax credit. The federal income tax rate starts at 10 percent of each additional dollar earned on the lowest taxed incomes and rises through 15 percent, 25 percent, 28 percent, 33 percent, and 35 percent of each additional dollar earned on successively higher incomes.

Income Maintenance Programs

Three main types of programs redistribute income by making direct payments (in cash, services, or vouchers) to people in the lower part of the income distribution. They are

- Social Security programs
- Unemployment compensation
- Welfare programs

Social Security Programs Social Security is a public insurance system paid for by compulsory payroll taxes on employers and employees. Social Security has two main components: Old Age, Survivors, Disability, and Health Insurance (OASDHI), which provides monthly cash payments to retired or disabled workers or their surviving spouses and children; and Medicare, which provides hospital and health insurance for the elderly and disabled. In 2011, Social Security supported 55 million people, who received average monthly checks of more than $1,000.

Unemployment Compensation To provide an income to unemployed workers, every state has established an unemployment compensation program. Under these programs, a tax is paid that is based on the income of each covered worker and such a worker receives a benefit when he or she becomes unemployed. The details of the benefits vary from state to state.

Welfare Programs The purpose of welfare programs is to provide incomes for people who do not qualify for Social Security or unemployment compensation. The programs are

1. Supplementary Security Income (SSI) program, which is designed to help the neediest elderly, disabled, and blind people

2. Temporary Assistance for Needy Families (TANF) program, which is designed to help families that have inadequate financial resources

3. Food Stamp program, which is designed to help the poorest households obtain a basic diet

4. Medicaid, which is designed to cover the costs of medical care for households that receive help under the SSI and TANF programs

Subsidized Services

A great deal of redistribution takes place in the United States through the provision of subsidized services—services provided by the government at prices far below the cost of production. The taxpayers who consume these goods and services receive a transfer in kind from the taxpayers who do not consume them. The two most important areas in which this form of redistribution takes place are education—both kindergarten through grade 12 and college and university—and health care. But neither necessarily redistributes from the rich to the poor.

In 2011–2012, a student enrolled at the University of California, Berkeley, who is not a resident of California paid a tuition of $37,400. This amount is probably close to the cost of providing a year's education at Berkeley. But a California resident paid tuition of only $14,460. So California households with a member enrolled at Berkeley received a benefit from the government of close to $23,000 a year. Many of these households have above-average incomes.

Government provision of health-care services has grown to equal the scale of private provision. Medicaid provides high-quality and high-cost health care to millions of people who earn too little to buy such services themselves. Medicaid redistributes from the rich to the poor. Medicare, which is available to all over 65 years of age, is not targeted at the poor.

■ The Scale of Income Redistribution

A household's income in the absence of government redistribution is its *market income*. We can measure the scale of income redistribution by calculating the percentage of market income paid in taxes minus the percentage received in benefits at each income level. The available data include redistribution through taxes and cash and noncash benefits to welfare recipients. The data do not include the value of subsidized services such as a college education, which might decrease the total scale of redistribution from the rich to the poor.

Figure 20.6 shows how government actions change the distribution of income. The figure shows two Lorenz curves and compares them with the line of equality.

Disposable income
Market income plus cash benefits paid by the government minus taxes.

The blue Lorenz curve describes the distribution of *market income*. The red Lorenz curve shows the distribution of **disposable income,** which is income after all taxes and benefits, including Medicaid and Medicare benefits. The Lorenz curve for *disposable income* is closer to the line of equality than that for *market income*, which tells us that the distribution of disposable income is more equal than the distribution of market income.

Figure 20.6(b) shows that redistribution increases the share received by the lowest three quintiles and decreases the share received by the highest two quintiles.

The sources of income at different income levels provide another measure of the scale of redistribution. The poorest quintile receives 80 percent of its income from the government. The second quintile receives 32 percent of its income from the government. In contrast, the richest quintile receives almost nothing from the government and receives a third of its income from capital—interest, dividends, and capital gains on financial assets.

FIGURE 20.6

The Scale of Income Redistribution

MyEconLab Animation

Taxes and income maintenance programs reduce the degree of inequality that the market generates. In part (a), the Lorenz curve moves closer to the line of equality.

Part (b) shows the redistribution in 2007. The quintile with the lowest incomes received net benefits that increased their share of total income by 3.5 percentage points. The quintile of total income with the highest incomes paid taxes that decreased their share of total income by 7.5 percentage points.

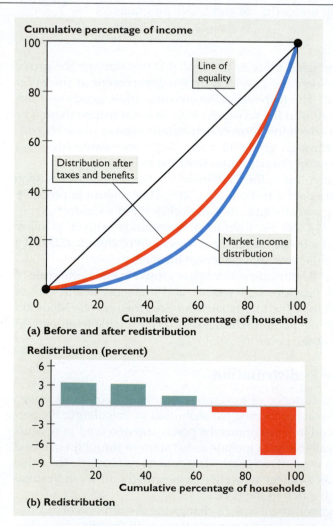

(a) Before and after redistribution

(b) Redistribution

SOURCE OF DATA: U.S. Census Bureau, Current Population Survey Annual Social and Economic Supplement.

■ Why We Redistribute Income

Why do we vote for government policies that redistribute income? Why don't we leave everyone to make voluntary contributions to charities that help the poor?

There are two ways of approaching these questions: normative and positive. The normative approach discusses why we *should* compel everyone to help the poor and looks for principles to guide the appropriate scale of redistribution. The positive approach seeks reasons why we *do* compel everyone to help the poor and tries to explain the actual scale of redistribution.

Normative Theories of Income Redistribution

Philosophy and politics, not economics, are the subjects that consider the normative theories of redistribution. Not surprisingly, there are several different points of view on whether income should be redistributed and, if so, on what scale.

Utilitarianism points to the ideal distribution being one of equality. But efficiency is also desirable. And greater equality can be achieved only at the cost of greater inefficiency—the *big tradeoff* (defined in Chapter 6, p. 159). The redistribution of income creates the big tradeoff because it uses scarce resources and weakens incentives, which decreases the total size of the economic pie to be shared.

A dollar collected from a rich person does not translate into a dollar received by a poor person. Some of it gets used up in the process of redistribution. Tax-collecting agencies such as the Internal Revenue Service and welfare-administering agencies (as well as tax accountants and lawyers) use skilled labor, computers, and other scarce resources to do their work. The bigger the scale of redistribution, the greater is the opportunity cost of administering it.

But the cost of collecting taxes and making welfare payments is a small part of the total cost of redistribution. A bigger cost arises from the inefficiency—*excess burden*—of taxes and benefits (see Chapter 8, p. 192). Greater equality can be achieved only by taxing productive activities such as work and saving. Taxing people's income from their work and saving lowers the after-tax income they receive. This lower income makes them work and save less, which in turn results in smaller output and less consumption not only for the rich who pay the taxes but also for the poor who receive the benefits.

Benefit recipients as well as taxpayers face weaker incentives. In fact, under the welfare arrangements that prevailed before the 1996 reforms, the weakest incentives to work were those faced by households that benefited from welfare. When a welfare recipient got a job, benefits were withdrawn and eligibility for programs such as Medicaid ended, so the household in effect paid a tax of more than 100 percent on its earnings. This arrangement locked poor households in a welfare trap.

Recognizing the tension between equality and efficiency, philosopher John Rawls proposed the principle that income should be redistributed to the point at which it maximizes the size of the slice of the economic pie received by the person with the smallest slice.

Libertarian philosophers such as Robert Nozick (see Chapter 6, p. 159) say that any redistribution is wrong because it violates the sanctity of private property and voluntary exchange.

Modern political parties stand in the center of the extremes that we've just described. Some favor a bit more redistribution than others, but the major political parties are broadly happy with the prevailing scale of redistribution.

Median voter theory
The theory that governments pursue policies that make the median voter as well off as possible.

Positive Theories of Income Redistribution

A good positive theory of income redistribution would explain why some countries have more redistribution than others and why redistribution has increased over the past 200 years. We don't have such a theory, but economists have proposed a promising idea called the median voter theory. The **median voter theory** is that the policies that governments pursue are those that make the median voter as well off as possible. If a proposal can be made that improves the well-being of the median voter, a political party that makes the proposal can improve its standing in an election.

The median voter theory arises from thinking about how a democratic political system such as that of the United States works. In this system, governments must propose policies that appeal to enough voters to get them elected. And in a majority voting system, the voter whose views carry the most weight is the one in the middle—the median voter.

The median voter wants income to be redistributed to the point at which her or his own after-tax income is as large as possible. Taxing the rich by too much would weaken their incentives to create businesses and jobs and lower the median voter's after-tax income. But taxing the rich by too little would leave some money on the table that could be transferred to the median voter.

The median voter might be concerned about the poor and want to reduce poverty. Unselfishly, the median voter might simply be concerned about the plight of the poor and want to help them. Self-interestedly, the median voter might believe that if there is too much poverty, there will be too much crime and some of it will touch her or his life.

If for either reason the median voter wants to help the poor, the political process will deliver a greater scale of redistribution to reflect this voter preference.

■ The Major Welfare Challenge

Among the poorest people in the United States (see p. 512) are young women who have not completed high school, have a child (or children), live without a partner, and are more likely to be black or Hispanic than white. These young women and their children present the major welfare challenge.

There are about 10 million single mothers, and a quarter of them receive no support from their children's fathers. The long-term solution to the problem of these women is education and job training—acquiring human capital. The short-term solution is welfare, but welfare must be designed in ways that strengthen the incentive to pursue the long-term solution. And a change in the U.S. welfare programs introduced during the 1990s pursues this approach.

The Current Approach: TANF

Passed in 1996, the Personal Responsibility and Work Opportunities Reconciliation Act created the Temporary Assistance for Needy Families (TANF) program. TANF is a block grant that is paid to the states, which administer payments to individuals. It is not an open-ended entitlement program. An adult member of a household receiving assistance must either work or perform community service, and there is a five-year limit for assistance.

These measures go a long way toward removing one of the most serious poverty problems while being sensitive to the potential inefficiency of welfare. But some economists want to go further and introduce a negative income tax.

Negative Income Tax

The negative income tax is not on the political agenda, but it is popular among economists, and it is the subject of several real-world experiments. A **negative income tax** provides every household with a guaranteed minimum annual income and taxes all earned income at a fixed rate. Suppose the guaranteed minimum annual income is $10,000 and the tax rate is 25 percent. A household with no earned income receives the $10,000 guaranteed minimum income from the government. This household "pays" income tax of *minus* $10,000, hence the name "negative income tax."

A household that earns $40,000 a year pays $10,000—25 percent of its earned income—to the government. But this household also receives from the government the $10,000 guaranteed minimum income, so it pays no net income tax. It has the break-even income. Households that earn between zero and $40,000 a year receive more from the government than they pay to the government. They "pay" a negative income tax.

A household that earns $60,000 a year pays $15,000—25 percent of its earned income—to the government. But this household receives from the government the $10,000 guaranteed minimum income, so it pays a net income tax of $5,000. All households that earn more than $40,000 a year pay more to the government than they receive from it. They pay a positive amount of income tax.

A negative income tax doesn't eliminate the excess burden of taxation, but it does improve the incentives to work and save at all levels of income.

Negative income tax
A tax and redistribution scheme that provides every household with a guaranteed minimum annual income and taxes all earned income at a fixed rate.

EYE on YOUR LIFE
What You Pay and Gain Through Redistribution

You are on both sides of the redistribution equation, but what's your bottom line? Are you a net receiver or a net payer? Try to figure out which.

Your Tax Payments

You might pay some income tax and you certainly pay sales taxes and taxes on gasoline and other items.

If you have a job, your payslip shows the amount of income tax you're paying.

You can calculate the sales taxes you pay by keeping track for a week every time you buy something.

You can work out how much gas and other taxes you pay by checking the scale of these taxes in your state at www.taxadmin.org.

Your Benefits

Now for the benefits. If you're receiving any direct cash payments such as unemployment benefits, these are easy to identify. But most likely, you don't receive any money from the government.

You do, though, receive the benefits of services provided by government. The biggest of these is most likely the cost of your education.

It costs much more than the tuition you're paying to provide your education. One estimate of the value of your education is the tuition paid by an out-of-state student minus the tuition paid by a state resident. Work out that number.

Now think about all the other benefits you receive from government. Try to estimate what all the government-provided services are worth to you.

Your Bottom Line

Now work out your bottom line—the benefits you receive minus the taxes you pay. Most likely, you have a net benefit, but that situation will change when you graduate. As your income rises, you will move to the other side of the redistribution equation.

TABLE 1 MARKET INCOME

Households	Income (millions of dollars per year)
Lowest 20 percent	5
Second 20 percent	10
Third 20 percent	18
Fourth 20 percent	28
Highest 20 percent	39

TABLE 2 TAXES AND BENEFITS

Households	Income tax (percent)	Benefits (millions of dollars)
Lowest 20 percent	0	10
Second 20 percent	10	8
Third 20 percent	18	3
Fourth 20 percent	28	0
Highest 20 percent	39	0

FIGURE 1

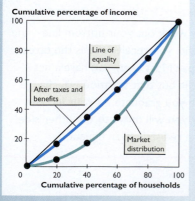

Cumulative percentage of income

CHECKPOINT 20.3

Explain how governments redistribute income and describe the effects of redistribution on economic inequality.

Practice Problems

Table 1 shows the distribution of market income in an economy and Table 2 shows how the government taxes and redistributes income.

1. Calculate the income shares of each quintile after tax and redistribution.
2. Draw this economy's Lorenz curves before and after taxes and benefits.

In the News

The 0% tax rate solution

In 2006, the lowest 40 percent of income earners received net payments equal to 3.6% of total income tax revenues. The third 20 percent of income earners pay 4.4% of total income tax revenues. That means the lowest 60 percent together pay less than 1% of income tax revenues.

Source: *The Wall Street Journal*, July 14, 2009

Would a policy that taxed the bottom 60 percent of income earners at a 0% tax rate and reduced redistribution by 1 percent of tax revenue have any merit?

Solutions to Practice Problems

1. Table 3 shows to obtain the income after tax and benefits, multiply each quintile's market income by the tax rate, subtract the taxes paid, and add the benefits received. Then calculate each quintile's share of total income.

TABLE 3

Households	Market income (millions of dollars)	Tax paid (millions of dollars)	Benefits received (millions of dollars)	Income after tax and benefits (millions of dollars)	Income after tax and benefits (percentage of total income)
Lowest 20 percent	5	0.0	10	15.0	16.0
Second 20 percent	10	1.0	8	17.0	18.1
Third 20 percent	18	3.2	3	17.8	19.0
Fourth 20 percent	28	7.8	0	20.2	21.5
Highest 20 percent	39	15.2	0	23.8	25.4

2. To draw the Lorenz curves, calculate the cumulative shares of total income. For example, before taxes and benefits, the lowest 20 percent have 5 percent and the lowest 40 percent have 15 percent (5 + 10). After taxes and benefits, the lowest 20 percent have 16 percent and the lowest 40 percent have 34.1 percent (16 + 18.1). Figure 1 plots the Lorenz curves.

Solution to In the News

The redistribution process uses resources. One dollar taken from a high income earner does not translate into one dollar for a low-income earner. Resources will be saved if 60 percent of workers don't have to file income tax. There will be a net social gain, which might be used to help the poor.

CHAPTER SUMMARY

Key Points

1 Describe the economic inequality in the United States.

- The distributions of income and wealth describe economic inequality.
- The 20 percent of households with the lowest incomes receive about 3 percent of total money income and the 1 percent of households with the highest wealth own about one third of total wealth.
- The distribution of income has become more unequal over the past few decades.
- During a decade, about 30 percent of families move up by a quintile or more and slightly fewer move down by a quintile or more.
- About 15 percent of Americans have incomes below the poverty level and for almost 20 percent, poverty lasts for more than one year.

2 Explain how economic inequality arises.

- Economic inequality arises from inequality of labor market outcomes, ownership of capital, entrepreneurial ability, and personal and family characteristics.
- In labor markets, skill differences result in earnings differences. Discrimination might also contribute to earnings differences.
- Inherited capital, unusual entrepreneurial talent, and personal or family good fortune or misfortune widen the gap between rich and poor.

3 Explain how governments redistribute income and describe the effects of redistribution on economic inequality.

- Governments redistribute income through progressive income taxes, income maintenance programs, and provision of subsidized services.
- Normative theories of redistribution recognize the tension between equality and efficiency—the big tradeoff—and seek principles to guide the political debate.
- The main positive theory of redistribution is the median voter theory.
- The negative income tax is a proposal for addressing the big tradeoff.

Key Terms

Disposable income, 524
Lorenz curve, 509
Market income, 508
Median voter theory, 526

Money income, 508
Negative income tax, 527
Poverty, 513

TABLE 1

Households	Money income (percentage)
Lowest 20 percent	8
Second 20 percent	13
Third 20 percent	18
Fourth 20 percent	23
Highest 20 percent	38

FIGURE 1

Wage rate (dollars per hour)

Labor (thousands of hours)

TABLE 2

Households	Market income (percentage)
Lowest 20 percent	5
Second 20 percent	9
Third 20 percent	20
Fourth 20 percent	30
Highest 20 percent	36

CHAPTER CHECKPOINT

Study Plan Problems and Applications

1. Table 1 shows the distribution of money income in Australia. Calculate the cumulative distribution of income for Australia and draw the Lorenz curve for Australian income. In which country is the income distribution more unequal: Australia or the United States?

2. **Rich-poor gap worries Chinese planners**

   In 1985, urban Chinese earned 1.9 times as much as people in the country-side, which is home to 60 percent of the population. By 2007, they earned 3.3 times as much according to the United Nations.

   Source: *The New York Times*, November 22, 2008

   Explain how the Lorenz curve in China changed between 1985 and 2007.

3. Figure 1 shows the market for low-skilled workers. With on-the-job training, low-skilled workers can become high-skilled workers. The value of marginal product of high-skilled workers at each employment level is twice the value of marginal product of low-skilled workers, but the cost of acquiring skill adds $2 an hour to the wage rate that will attract high-skilled labor. What is the equilibrium wage rate of low-skilled labor and the number of low-skilled workers employed? What is the equilibrium wage rate of high-skilled labor and the number of high-skilled workers employed?

4. Why do economists think that discrimination in the labor market is an unlikely explanation for the persistent inequality in earnings between women and men and among the races?

Use Table 2 and the following information to work Problems 5 to 7.

Suppose that the government redistributes income by taxing the 60 percent of households with the highest market incomes 10 percent, then distributing the tax collected as an equal benefit to the 40 percent with the lowest market income.

5. Calculate the distribution of income after taxes and benefits and draw the Lorenz curve (i) before taxes and benefits and (ii) after taxes and benefits.

6. If the cost of administering the redistribution scheme takes 50 percent of the taxes collected, what is the distribution of income after taxes and benefits?

7. If the people whose market incomes are taxed cut their work hours and their market incomes fall by 10 percent, what is the distribution of income after taxes and benefits?

8. **Wealth gap widens between whites and minorities**

   The median wealth of white U.S. households in 2009 was $113,149, compared with $6,325 for Hispanics and $5,677 for blacks. Those ratios, roughly 20 to 1 for blacks and 18 to 1 for Hispanics, far exceed the low mark of 7 to 1 for both groups reached in 1995, when economic growth lifted many low-income groups to the middle class.

   Source: Associated Press, July 26, 2011

   What does the data in the news clip tell us about the wealth Lorenz curve? During the period 1995 to 2009, describe how the distribution of wealth changed.

Instructor Assignable Problems and Applications

Your instructor can assign these problems as homework, a quiz, or a test in MyEconLab.

1. Education, household size, household type (marital status), age of householder, race, and region of residence all influence the degree of income inequality. Rank these influences in order of importance from most to least important.

2. Table 1 shows the income share for each household quintile and the cumulative shares. Provide the values for **A, B, C, D,** and **E**.

3. Table 2 shows the distribution of prize money among the top 20 professional golfers. Calculate the cumulative distribution of income of these golfers and draw the prize money Lorenz curve of these golfers. Which distribution is more unequal: the distribution of income of these golfers or that of the United States as a whole?

4. Suppose the cost of acquiring a skill increases and the value of marginal product of skill increases. Draw demand-supply graphs of the labor markets for high-skilled and low-skilled labor to explain what happens to the equilibrium wage rate of low-skilled labor, the equilibrium wage rate of high-skilled labor, and the number of high-skilled workers employed.

Use the following information to work Problems **5** and **6**.

In the United States in 2002, 130,000 aircraft mechanics and service technicians earned an average of $20 an hour whereas 30,000 elevator installers and repairers earned an average of $25 an hour. The skill and training for these two jobs are very similar.

5. Draw the demand and supply curves for these two types of labor. What feature of your graph accounts for the differences in the two wage rates and what feature accounts for the differences in the quantities employed of these two types of labor?

6. Suppose that a government law required both groups of workers to be paid $22.50 an hour. Draw a graph to illustrate what would happen to the quantities employed of the two types of labor.

7. **Income gap in New York is called nation's highest**
New York continues to have the highest income gap of any state. Experts claim that the income gap arises from the large number of poor unskilled immigrants. Mobility of these workers arises from a barrier to education.
Source: nytimes.com, January 27, 2006

Explain the effect of a large increase in foreign immigrants who are largely poor, unskilled workers on the market for low-skilled labor. Explain how better access to education would change New York's income gap.

8. **California progress**
In May, California voters rejected an increase in taxes to close a $26 billion budget gap. To generate more tax revenues, California will have to encourage new businesses and create jobs. With 50 percent of income tax revenues coming from the richest 1 percent of residents, the state needs lower rates. Income redistribution has gone too far.
Source: *The Wall Street Journal*, July 22, 2009

Does the median voter theory explain voters' rejection? If California lowers the highest tax rate to below the current 10.5 percent and cuts some free benefits, how might California's Lorenz curve change?

TABLE 1

Households	Income	
(quintile)	(%)	(cumulative %)
First	7.4	7.4
Second	13.2	A
Third	B	38.7
Fourth	25.0	C
Fifth	D	E

TABLE 2

Professional golfers	Income (percentage)
Lowest 20 percent	15
Second 20 percent	16
Third 20 percent	18
Fourth 20 percent	20
Highest 20 percent	31

Multiple Choice Quiz

1. A Lorenz curve plots the _____.

    A. trend in the cumulative percentage of income received by each quintile
       against trend in the number of households
    B. average income received by each quintile against the number of house-
       holds in the quintile
    C. percentage of total income received by each quintile against the percent-
       age of households in the quintile
    D. cumulative percentage of income against the cumulative percentage of
       households

2. Which of the following statements is correct?

    A. The closer the Lorenz curve is to the line of equality, the more unequal is
       the distribution of income.
    B. The farther the Lorenz curve is from the line of equality, the more
       unequal is the distribution of income.
    C. If the Lorenz curve crosses the line of equality the distribution of income
       is more unequal at high income levels than at low income levels.
    D. The Lorenz curve for wealth is closer to the line of equality than the
       Lorenz curve for income.

3. In recent years, as the gap between the rich and the poor has increased, the
   Lorenz curve has _____ .

    A. shifted away from the line of equality
    B. not changed, but there has been a movement down along it
    C. shifted closer to the line of equality
    D. not changed, but there has been a movement up along it

4. Of all the Americans who live in poverty, most are _____ families, while the
   highest poverty rate is among _____ families.

    A. black; Hispanic
    B. black; white
    C. white; black and Hispanic
    D. Hispanic; white

5. Economic inequality arises from all of the following *except* _____.

    A. inequality of human capital
    B. inequality of education attainment
    C. a shortage of high-skilled labor
    D. discrimination

6. Income redistribution in the United States results in the income share of the
   _____ rising and the income share of the _____ falling.

    A. lowest quintile; other four quintiles
    B. two lowest quintiles; other three quintiles
    C. three lowest quintiles; other two quintiles
    D. four lowest quintiles; highest quintile

7. When governments redistribute income, they _____.

    A. give every dollar collected in taxes to poor people
    B. are influenced by how people vote in elections
    C. improve economic efficiency
    D. set the tax and benefit rates that make everyone work and save more

Glossary

Ability-to-pay principle The proposition that people should pay taxes according to how easily they can bear the burden. (p. 206)

Absolute advantage When one person (or nation) is more productive than another—needs fewer inputs or takes less time to produce a good or perform a production task. (p. 73)

Adverse selection The tendency for people to enter into transactions that bring them benefits from their private information and impose costs on the uninformed party. (p. 295)

Allocative efficiency A situation in which the quantities of goods and services produced are those that people *value most highly*—it is not possible to produce more of a good or service without giving up some of another good that people *value more highly*. (p. 141)

Antitrust law A law that regulates oligopolies and prohibits them from becoming monopolies or behaving like monopolies. (p. 473)

Asymmetric information A situation in which either the buyer or the seller has private information. (p. 292)

Average cost pricing rule A rule that sets price equal to average total cost to enable a regulated firm to avoid economic loss. (p. 422)

Average fixed cost Total fixed cost per unit of output. (p. 357)

Average product Total product divided by the quantity of a factor of production. The average product of labor is total product divided by the quantity of labor employed. (p. 352)

Average tax rate The percentage of income that is paid in tax. (p. 197)

Average total cost Total cost per unit of output, which equals average fixed cost plus average variable cost. (p. 357)

Average variable cost Total variable cost per unit of output. (p. 357)

Barrier to entry Any constraint that protects a firm from competitors. (p. 400)

Benefit The benefit of something is the gain or pleasure that it brings. (p. 9)

Benefits principle The proposition that people should pay taxes equal to the benefits they receive from public goods and services. (p. 206)

Big tradeoff A tradeoff between efficiency and fairness that recognizes the cost of making income transfers. (p. 159)

Black market An illegal market that operates alongside a government- regulated market. (p. 169)

Budget line A line that describes the limits to consumption possibilities and that depends on a consumer's budget and the prices of goods and services. (p. 316)

Capital Tools, instruments, machines, buildings, and other items that have been produced in the past and that businesses now use to produce goods and services. (p. 35)

Capital goods Goods that are bought by businesses to increase their productive resources. (p. 32)

Capture theory The theory that the regulation serves the self-interest of the producer and results in maximum profit, underproduction, and deadweight loss. (p. 420)

Cartel A group of firms acting together to limit output, raise price, and increase economic profit. (p. 456)

Change in demand A change in the quantity that people plan to buy when any influence on buying plans other than the price of the good changes. (p. 88)

Change in the quantity demanded A change in the quantity of a good that people plan to buy that results from a change in the price of the good with all other influences on buying plans remaining the same. (p. 90)

Change in the quantity supplied A change in the quantity of a good that suppliers plan to sell that results from a change in the price of the good with all other influences on selling plans remaining the same. (p. 97)

Change in supply A change in the quantity that suppliers plan to sell when any influence on selling plans other than the price of the good changes. (p. 95)

Circular flow model A model of the economy that shows the circular flow of expenditures and incomes that result from decision makers' choices and the way those choices interact to determine what, how, and for whom goods and services are produced. (p. 46)

Coase theorem The proposition that if property rights exist, only a small number of parties are involved, and transactions costs are low, then private transactions are efficient and the outcome is not affected by who is assigned the property right. (p. 248)

Command system A system that allocates resources by the order of someone in authority. (p. 139)

Common resource A resource that can be used only once, but no one can be prevented from using what is available. (p. 267)

Comparative advantage The ability of a person to perform an activity or produce a good or service at a lower opportunity cost than anyone else. (p. 74)

Complement A good that is consumed with another good. (p. 88)

Complement in production A good that is produced along with another good. (p. 95)

Constant returns to scale Features of a firm's technology that keep average total cost constant as output increases. (p. 364)

Consumer surplus The marginal benefit from a good or service in excess of the price paid for it, summed over the quantity consumed. (p. 147)

Consumption goods and services Goods and services that are bought by individuals and used to provide personal enjoyment and contribute to a person's quality of life. (p. 32)

Correlation The tendency for the values of two variables to move together in a predictable and related way. (p. 12)

Cross elasticity of demand A measure of the responsiveness of the demand for a good to a change in the price of a substitute

or complement when other things remain the same. (p. 129)

Cross-section graph A graph that shows the values of an economic variable for different groups in a population at a point in time. (p. 22)

Deadweight loss The decrease in total surplus that results from an inefficient underproduction or overproduction. (p. 155)

Decreasing marginal returns When the marginal product of an additional worker is less than the marginal product of the previous worker. (p. 350)

Demand The relationship between the quantity demanded and the price of a good when all other influences on buying plans remain the same. (p. 85)

Demand curve A graph of the relationship between the quantity demanded of a good and its price when all the other influences on buying plans remain the same. (p. 86)

Demand schedule A list of the quantities demanded at each different price when all the other influences on buying plans remain the same. (p. 86)

Deregulation The process of removing the regulation of prices, quantities, entry, and other aspects of economic activity in a firm or industry. (p. 420)

Derived demand The demand for a factor of production, which is derived from the demand for the goods and services that it is used to produce. (p. 485)

Diminishing marginal rate of substitution The general tendency for the marginal rate of substitution to decrease as the consumer moves down along the indifference curve, increasing consumption of the good measured on the x-axis and decreasing consumption of the good measured on the y-axis. (p. 338)

Diminishing marginal utility The general tendency for marginal utility to decrease as the quantity of a good consumed increases.(p. 322)

Direct relationship A relationship between two variables that move in the same direction. (p. 24)

Diseconomies of scale Features of a firm's technology that make average total cost rise as output increases. (p. 364)

Disposable income Market income plus cash benefits paid by the government minus taxes. (p. 524)

Duopoly A market with only two firms. (p. 456)

Dumping When a foreign firm sells its exports at a lower price than its cost of production. (p. 232)

Earnings sharing regulation A regulation that requires firms to make refunds to customers when profits rise above a target level. (p. 425)

Economic depreciation An opportunity cost of a firm using capital that it owns—measured as the change in the *market value* of capital over a given period. (p. 345)

Economic growth The sustained expansion of production possibilities. (p. 71)

Economic model A description of some feature of the economic world that includes only those features assumed necessary to explain the observed facts. (p. 12)

Economic profit A firm's total revenue minus total cost. (p. 345)

Economics The social science that studies the choices that individuals, businesses, government, and entire societies make as they cope with *scarcity*, the *incentives* that influence those choices, and the arrangements that coordinate them. (p. 2)

Economies of scale Features of a firm's technology that make average total cost fall as output increases. (p. 363)

Efficient scale The quantity at which average total cost is a minimum. (p. 441)

Elastic demand When the percentage change in the quantity demanded exceeds the percentage change in price. (p. 114)

Elastic supply When the percentage change in the quantity supplied exceeds the percentage change in price. (p. 124)

Entrepreneurship The human resource that organizes labor, land, and capital to produce goods and services. (p. 36)

Equilibrium price The price at which the quantity demanded equals the quantity supplied. (p. 99)

Equilibrium quantity The quantity bought and sold at the equilibrium price. (p. 99)

Excess burden The amount by which the burden of a tax exceeds the tax revenue received by the government—the deadweight loss from a tax. (p. 192)

Excess capacity The amount by which the efficient scale exceeds the quantity that the firm produces. (p. 441)

Excludable A good, service, or resource is excludable if it is possible to prevent someone from enjoying its benefits. (p. 266)

Explicit cost A cost paid in money. (p. 345)

Export goods and services Goods and services that are produced in one country and sold in other countries. (p. 32)

Exports The goods and services that firms in one country sell to households and firms in other countries. (p. 214)

Externality A cost or a benefit that arises from production and

that falls on someone other than the producer; or a cost or benefit that arises from consumption and that falls on someone other than the consumer. (p. 242)

Factor markets Markets in which the services of factors of production are bought and sold. (pp. 46, 484)

Factor prices The prices of the services of the factors of production. The wage rate is the price of labor, the interest rate is the price of capital, and rent is the price of land. (p. 484)

Factors of production The productive resources that are used to produce goods and services—land, labor, capital, and entrepreneurship. (p. 34)

Firms The institutions that organize the production of goods and services. (p. 46)

Four-firm concentration ratio The percentage of the total revenue in an industry accounted for by the four largest firms in the industry. (p. 434)

Free rider A person who enjoys the benefits of a good or service without paying for it. (p. 269)

Game theory The tool that economists use to analyze *strategic behavior*—behavior that recognizes mutual interdependence and takes account of the expected behavior of others. (p. 465)

Goods and services The objects (goods) and the actions (services) that people value and produce to satisfy human wants. (p. 3)

Goods markets Markets in which goods and services are bought and sold. (p. 46)

Government goods and services Goods and services that are bought by governments. (p. 32)

Herfindahl-Hirschman Index The square of the percentage market

share of each firm summed over the 50 largest firms (or summed over all the firms if there are fewer than 50) in a market. (p. 435)

Horizontal equity The requirement that taxpayers with the same ability to pay should pay the same taxes. (p. 206)

Households Individuals or groups of people living together. (p. 46)

Human capital The knowledge and skill that people obtain from education, on-the-job training, and work experience. (p. 35)

Implicit cost An opportunity cost incurred by a firm when it uses a factor of production for which it does not make a direct money payment. (p. 345)

Import quota A quantitative restriction on the import of a good that limits the maximum quantity of a good that may be imported in a given period. (p. 227)

Imports The goods and services that households and firms in one country buy from firms in other countries. (p. 214)

Incentive A reward or a penalty—a "carrot" or a "stick"—that encourages or discourages an action. (p. 11)

Income elasticity of demand A measure of the responsiveness of the demand for a good to a change in income when other things remain the same. (p. 130)

Increasing marginal returns When the marginal product of an additional worker exceeds the marginal product of the previous worker. (p. 350)

Indifference curve A line that shows combinations of goods among which a consumer is *indifferent*. (p. 337)

Individual transferable quota (ITQ) A production limit that is assigned to an individual, who is free to transfer (sell) the quota to someone else. (p. 284)

Inelastic demand When the percentage change in the quantity demanded is less than the percentage change in price. (p. 114)

Inelastic supply When the percentage change in the quantity supplied is less than the percentage change in price. (p. 124)

Infant-industry argument The argument that it is necessary to protect a new industry to enable it to grow into a mature industry that can compete in world markets. (p. 231)

Inferior good A good for which demand decreases when income increases and demand increases when income decreases. (p. 89)

Interest Income paid for the use of capital. (p. 37)

Inverse relationship A relationship between two variables that move in opposite directions. (p. 25)

Job A contract between a firm and a household to provide labor services. (p. 484)

Labor The work time and work effort that people devote to producing goods and services. (p. 35)

Labor union An organized group of workers that aims to increase wages and influence other job conditions of its members. (p. 494)

Land The "gifts of nature," or *natural resources*, that we use to produce goods and services. (p. 34)

Law of decreasing returns As a firm uses more of a variable input, with a given quantity of fixed inputs, the marginal product of the variable input eventually decreases. (p. 352)

Law of demand Other things remaining the same, if the price of a good rises, the quantity

demanded of that good decreases; and if the price of a good falls, the quantity demanded of that good increases. (p. 85)

Law of market forces When there is a surplus, the price falls; when there is a shortage, the price rises. (p. 99)

Law of supply Other things remaining the same, if the price of a good rises, the quantity supplied of that good increases; and if the price of a good falls, the quantity supplied of that good decreases. (p. 92)

Legal monopoly A market in which competition and entry are restricted by the granting of a public franchise, government license, patent, or copyright. (p. 401)

Lemons problem The problem that when it is not possible to distinguish reliable products from lemons, there are too many lemons and too few reliable products. (p. 292)

Linear relationship A relationship that graphs as a straight line. (p. 24)

Long run The time frame in which the quantities of *all* resources can be varied. (p. 348)

Long-run average cost curve A curve that shows the lowest average total cost at which it is possible to produce each output when the firm has had sufficient time to change both its plant size and labor employed. (p. 364)

Lorenz curve A curve that graphs the cumulative percentage of income (or wealth) against the cumulative percentage of households. (p. 509)

Loss Income earned by an entrepreneur for running a business when that income is negative. (p. 37)

Macroeconomics The study of the aggregate (or total) effects on the national economy and the

global economy of the choices that individuals, businesses, and governments make. (p. 3)

Margin A choice on the margin is a choice that is made by comparing *all* the relevant alternatives systematically and incrementally. (p. 10)

Marginal benefit The benefit that arises from a one-unit increase in an activity. The marginal benefit of something is measured by what you *are willing to* give up to get *one additional* unit of it. (p. 10)

Marginal cost The opportunity cost that arises from a one-unit increase in an activity. The marginal cost of something is what you *must* give up to get one additional unit of it. (p. 10) The marginal cost of producing a good is the change in total cost that results from a one-unit increase in output. (p. 356)

Marginal cost pricing rule A rule that sets price equal to marginal cost to achieve an efficient output. (p. 420)

Marginal external benefit The benefit from an additional unit of a good or service that people other than the consumer of the good or service enjoy. (p. 254)

Marginal external cost The cost of producing an additional unit of a good or service that falls on people other than the producer. (p. 244)

Marginal private benefit The benefit from an additional unit of a good or service that the consumer of that good or service receives. (p. 254)

Marginal private cost The cost of producing an additional unit of a good or service that is borne by the producer of that good or service. (p. 244)

Marginal product The change in total product that results from a one-unit increase in the quantity of labor employed. (p. 350)

Marginal rate of substitution The rate at which a person will give up good *y* (the good measured on the *y*-axis) to get more of good *x* (the good measured on the *x*-axis) and at the same time remain on the same indifference curve. (p. 338)

Marginal revenue The change in total revenue that results from a one-unit increase in the quantity sold. (p. 373)

Marginal social benefit The marginal benefit enjoyed by society— by the consumer of a good or service and by everyone else who benefits from it. It is the sum of marginal private benefit and marginal external benefit. (p. 254)

Marginal social cost The marginal cost incurred by the entire society—by the producer and by everyone else on whom the cost falls. It is the sum of marginal private cost and marginal external cost. (p. 244)

Marginal tax rate The percentage of an additional dollar of income that is paid in tax. (p. 197)

Marginal utility The change in total utility that results from a one-unit increase in the quantity of a good consumed. (p. 322)

Marginal utility per dollar The marginal utility from a good relative to the price paid for the good. (p. 324)

Market Any arrangement that brings buyers and sellers together and enables them to get information and do business with each other. (p. 46)

Market demand The sum of the demands of all the buyers in a market. (p. 87)

Market equilibrium When the quantity demanded equals the quantity supplied—buyers' and sellers' plans are in balance. (p. 99)

Market failure A situation in which the market delivers an inefficient outcome. (p. 155)

Market income A household's wages, interest, rent, and profit earned in factor markets before paying income taxes. (p. 508)

Market supply The sum of the supplies of all the sellers in the market. (p. 94)

Markup The amount by which price exceeds marginal cost. (p. 441)

Median voter theory The theory that governments pursue policies that make the median voter as well off as possible. (p. 526)

Microeconomics The study of the choices that individuals and businesses make and the way these choices interact and are influenced by governments. (p. 2)

Minimum wage law A government regulation that makes hiring labor services for less than a specified wage illegal. (p. 175)

Money income Market income plus cash payments to households by the government. (p. 508)

Monopolistic competition A market in which a large number of firms compete by making similar but slightly different products. (p. 372)

Monopoly A market in which one firm sells a good or service that has no close substitutes and a barrier blocks the entry of new firms. (pp. 372, 400)

Moral hazard The tendency for a person with private information to use it in ways that impose costs on an uninformed party with whom they have made an agreement. (p. 301)

Nash equilibrium An equilibrium in which each player takes the best possible action given the action of the other player. (p. 466)

National debt The total amount that the federal government has borrowed to make expenditures that exceed tax revenue—to run a government budget deficit. (p. 50)

Natural monopoly A monopoly that arises because one firm can meet the entire market demand at a lower average total cost than two or more firms could. (p. 400)

Negative externality A production or consumption activity that creates an external cost. (p. 242)

Negative income tax A tax and redistribution scheme that provides every household with a guaranteed minimum annual income and taxes all earned income at a fixed rate. (p. 527)

Negative relationship A relationship between two variables that move in opposite directions. (p. 25)

Nonexcludable A good, service, or resource is nonexcludable if it is impossible (or extremely costly) to prevent someone from enjoying its benefits. (p. 266)

Nonrenewable natural resources Natural resources that can be used only once and that cannot be replaced once they have been used. (p. 484)

Nonrival A good, service, or resource is nonrival if its use by one person does not decrease the quantity available to someone else. (p. 266)

Normal good A good for which demand increases when income increases; demand decreases when income decreases. (p. 89)

Normal profit The return to entrepreneurship. Normal profit is part of a firm's opportunity cost because it is the cost of not running another firm. (p. 345)

Oligopoly A market in which a small number of interdependent firms compete. (p. 372)

Opportunity cost The opportunity cost of something is the best thing you *must* give up to get it. (p. 9)

Payoff matrix A table that shows the payoffs for each player for every possible combination of actions by the players. (p. 466)

Perfect competition A market in which there are many firms, each selling an identical product; many buyers; no barriers to the entry of new firms into the industry; no advantage to established firms; and buyers and sellers are well informed about prices. (p. 372)

Perfect price discrimination Price discrimination that extracts the entire consumer surplus by charging the highest price that consumers are willing to pay for each unit. (p. 416)

Perfectly elastic demand When the quantity demanded changes by a very large percentage in response to an almost zero percentage change in price. (p. 114)

Perfectly elastic supply When the quantity supplied changes by a very large percentage in response to an almost zero percentage change in price. (p. 124)

Perfectly inelastic demand When the percentage change in the quantity demanded is zero for any percentage change in the price. (p. 114)

Perfectly inelastic supply When the percentage change in the quantity supplied is zero for any percentage change in the price. (p. 124)

Pooling equilibrium The outcome when only one message is available and an uninformed person cannot determine quality. (p. 297)

Positive externality A production or consumption activity that creates an external benefit. (p. 242)

Positive relationship A relationship between two variables that move in the same direction. (p. 24)

Poverty A state in which a household's income is too low to be able to buy the quantities of food, shelter, and clothing that are deemed necessary. (p. 513)

Predatory pricing Setting a low price to drive competitors out of business with the intention of setting a monopoly price when the competition has gone. (p. 475)

Price cap A government regulation that places an upper limit on the price at which a particular good, service, or factor of production may be traded. (p. 168)

Price cap regulation A rule that specifies the highest price that a firm is permitted to set—a price ceiling. (p. 424)

Price ceiling A government regulation that places an *upper* limit on the price at which a particular good, service, or factor of production may be traded. (p. 168)

Price-discriminating monopoly A monopoly that sells different units of a good or service for different prices not related to cost differences. (p. 402)

Price elasticity of demand A measure of the responsiveness of the quantity demanded of a good to a change in its price when all other influences on buyers' plans remain the same. (p. 112)

Price elasticity of supply A measure of the responsiveness of the quantity supplied of a good changes to a change in its price when all other influences on sellers' plans remain the same. (p. 124)

Price floor A government regulation that places a *lower* limit on the price at which a particular good, service, or factor of production may be traded. (p. 174)

Price support A price floor in an agricultural market maintained by a government guarantee to buy any surplus output at that price. (p. 181)

Price taker A firm that cannot influence the price of the good or service that it produces. (p. 373)

Principle of minimum differentiation The tendency for competitors to make themselves identical to appeal to the maximum number of clients or voters. (p. 274)

Prisoners' dilemma A game between two prisoners that shows why it is hard to cooperate, even when it would be beneficial to both players to do so. (p. 465)

Private good A good or service that can be consumed by only one person at a time and only by the person who has bought it or owns it. (p. 266)

Private information Information relevant to a transaction that is possessed by some market participants but not all. (p. 292)

Producer surplus The price of a good in excess of the marginal cost of producing it, summed over the quantity produced. (p. 150)

Product differentiation Making a product that is slightly different from the products of competing firms. (p. 432)

Production efficiency A situation in which the economy is getting all that it can from its resources and cannot produce more of one good or service without producing less of something else. (p. 62)

Production possibilities frontier The boundary between the combinations of goods and services that can be produced and the combinations that cannot be produced, given the available factors of production and the state of technology. (pp. 60, 141)

Profit Income earned by an entrepreneur for running a business. (p. 37)

Progressive tax A tax whose average rate increases as income increases. (p. 197)

Property rights Legally established titles to the ownership, use, and disposal of factors of production and goods and services that are enforceable in the courts. (p. 247)

Proportional tax A tax whose average rate is constant at all income levels. (p. 197)

Public good A good or service that can be consumed simultaneously by everyone and from which no one can be excluded. (p. 267)

Public provision The production of a good or service by a public authority that receives most of its revenue from the government. (p. 256)

Quantity demanded The amount of any good, service, or resource that people are willing and able to buy during a specified period at a specified price. (p. 85)

Quantity supplied The amount of any good, service, or resource that people are willing and able to sell during a specified period at a specified price. (p. 92)

Rate of return regulation A regulation that sets the price at a level that enables a firm to earn a specified target rate of return on its capital. (p. 424)

Rational choice A choice that uses the available resources to best achieve the objective of the person making the choice. (p. 8)

Rational ignorance The decision not to acquire information because the marginal cost of doing so exceeds the marginal benefit. (p. 274)

Regressive tax A tax whose average rate decreases as income increases. (p. 197)

Regulation Rules administered by a government agency to influence prices, quantities, entry, and other aspects of economic activity in a firm or industry. (p. 420)

Relative price The price of one good in terms of another good—an opportunity cost. It equals the price of one good divided by the price of another good. (p. 320)

Rent Income paid for the use of land (p. 37)

Rent ceiling A regulation that makes it illegal to charge more than a specified rent for housing. (p. 168)

Rent seeking Lobbying and other political activity that aims to capture the gains from trade. The act of obtaining special treatment by the government to create economic profit or to divert consumer surplus or producer surplus away from others. (pp. 235, 411)

Resale price maintenance An agreement between a manufacturer and a distributor on the price at which a product will be resold. (p. 473)

Rival A good, service, or resource is rival if its use by one person decreases the quantity available to someone else. (p. 266)

Scarcity The condition that arises because wants exceed the ability of resources to satisfy them. (p. 2)

Scatter diagram A graph of the value of one variable against the value of another variable. (p. 22)

Screening When an uninformed person creates an incentive for an informed person to reveal relevant private information. (p. 302)

Search activity The time spent looking for someone with whom to do business. (p. 170)

Self-interest The choices that are best for the individual who makes them. (p. 4)

Separating equilibrium The outcome when signaling provides full information to a previously uninformed person. (p. 297)

Short run The time frame in which the quantities of some

resources are fixed. In the short run, a firm can usually change the quantity of labor it uses but not its technology and quantity of capital. (p. 348)

Shutdown point The point at which price equals minimum average variable cost and the quantity produced is that at which average variable cost is at its minimum. (p. 377)

Signal An action taken by an informed person (or firm) to send a message to less-informed people. (p. 448)

Signaling When an informed person takes an action that sends information to uninformed persons. (p. 296)

Single-price monopoly A monopoly that must sell each unit of its output for the same price to all its customers. (p. 402)

Slope The change in the value of the variable measured on the y-axis divided by the change in the value of the variable measured on the x-axis. (p. 27)

Social interest The choices that are best for society as a whole. (p. 4)

Social interest theory The theory that regulation achieves an efficient allocation of resources. (p. 420)

Strategies All the possible actions of each player in a game. (p. 466)

Subsidy A payment by the government to a producer to cover part of the cost of production. (pp. 181, 229, 257)

Substitute A good that can be consumed in place of another good. (p. 88)

Substitute in production A good that can be produced in place of another good. (p. 95)

Supply The relationship between the quantity supplied and the price of a good when all other influences on selling plans remain the same. (p. 92)

Supply curve A graph of the relationship between the quantity supplied of a good and its price when all the other influences on selling plans remain the same. (p. 93)

Supply schedule A list of the quantities supplied at each different price when all the other influences on selling plans remain the same. (p. 93)

Tariff A tax imposed on a good when it is imported. (p. 223)

Taxable income Total income minus a personal exemption and a standard deduction (or other allowable deductions). (p. 196)

Tax incidence The division of the burden of a tax between the buyer and the seller. (p. 190)

Time-series graph A graph that measures time on the x-axis and the variable or variables in which we are interested on the y-axis. (p. 22)

Total cost The cost of all the factors of production used by a firm. (p. 355)

Total fixed cost The cost of the firm's fixed factors of production— the cost of land, capital, and entrepreneurship. (p. 355)

Total product The total quantity of a good produced in a given period. (p. 349)

Total revenue The amount spent on a good and received by its

seller and equals the price of the good multiplied by the quantity of the good sold. (p. 120)

Total revenue test A method of estimating the price elasticity of demand by observing the change in total revenue that results from a price change (with all other influences on the quantity sold remaining unchanged). (p. 121)

Total surplus The sum of consumer surplus and producer surplus. (p. 153)

Total utility The total benefit that a person gets from the consumption of a good or service. Total utility generally increases as the quantity consumed of a good increases. (p. 322)

Total variable cost The cost of the firm's variable factor of production— the cost of labor. (p. 355)

Tragedy of the commons The overuse of a common resource that arises when its users have no incentive to conserve it and use it sustainably. (p. 278)

Tradeoff An exchange—giving up one thing to get something else. (pp. 8, 63)

Transactions costs The opportunity costs of making trades in a market or conducting a transaction. (pp. 157, 248)

Trend A general tendency for the value of a variable to rise or fall over time. (p. 22)

Tying arrangement An agreement to sell one product only if

the buyer agrees to buy another, different product. (p. 475)

Unit elastic demand When the percentage change in the quantity demanded equals the percentage change in price. (p. 114)

Unit elastic supply When the percentage change in the quantity supplied equals the percentage change in price. (p. 124)

Utility The benefit or satisfaction that a person gets from the consumption of a good or service. (p. 322)

Utility-maximizing rule The rule that leads to the greatest total utility from all the goods and services consumed. The rule is: 1. Allocate the entire available budget. 2. Make the marginal utility per dollar equal for all goods. (p. 324)

Value of marginal product The value to a firm of hiring one more unit of a factor of production, which equals the price of a unit of output multiplied by the marginal product of the factor of production. (p. 485)

Vertical equity The requirement that taxpayers with a greater ability to pay bear a greater share of the taxes. (p. 207)

Voucher A token that the government provides to households, which they can use to buy specified goods or services. (p. 258)

Wages Income paid for the services of labor. (p. 37)

Index

Photo Credits

The Pearson Series in Economics

Abel/Bernanke/Croushore
*Macroeconomics**

Bade/Parkin
*Foundations of Economics**

Berck/Helfand
The Economics of the Environment

Bierman/Fernandez
Game Theory with Economic Applications

Blanchard
*Macroeconomics**

Blau/Ferber/Winkler
The Economics of Women, Men and Work

Boardman/Greenberg/Vining/ Weimer
Cost-Benefit Analysis

Boyer
Principles of Transportation Economics

Branson
Macroeconomic Theory and Policy

Brock/Adams
The Structure of American Industry

Bruce
Public Finance and the American Economy

Carlton/Perloff
Modern Industrial Organization

Case/Fair/Oster
*Principles of Economics**

Caves/Frankel/Jones
World Trade and Payments: An Introduction

Chapman
Environmental Economics: Theory, Application, and Policy

Cooter/Ulen
Law & Economics

Downs
An Economic Theory of Democracy

Ehrenberg/Smith
Modern Labor Economics

Ekelund/Ressler/Tollison
*Economics**

Farnham
Economics for Managers

Folland/Goodman/Stano
The Economics of Health and Health Care

Fort
Sports Economics

Froyen
Macroeconomics

Fusfeld
The Age of the Economist

Gerber
*International Economics**

Gordon
*Macroeconomics**

Greene
Econometric Analysis

Gregory
Essentials of Economics

Gregory/Stuart
Russian and Soviet Economic Performance and Structure

Hartwick/Olewiler
The Economics of Natural Resource Use

Heilbroner/Milberg
The Making of the Economic Society

Heyne/Boettke/Prychitko
The Economic Way of Thinking

Hoffman/Averett
Women and the Economy: Family, Work, and Pay

Holt
Markets, Games and Strategic Behavior

Hubbard/O'Brien
*Economics**

*Money, Banking, and the Financial System**

Hughes/Cain
American Economic History

Husted/Melvin
International Economics

Jehle/Reny
Advanced Microeconomic Theory

Johnson-Lans
A Health Economics Primer

Keat/Young
Managerial Economics

Klein
Mathematical Methods for Economics

Krugman/Obstfeld/Melitz
*International Economics: Theory & Policy**

Laidler
The Demand for Money

Leeds/von Allmen
The Economics of Sports

Leeds/von Allmen/Schiming
*Economics**

Lipsey/Ragan/Storer
*Economics**

Lynn
Economic Development: Theory and Practice for a Divided World

Miller
*Economics Today**

Understanding Modern Economics

Miller/Benjamin
The Economics of Macro Issues

Miller/Benjamin/North
The Economics of Public Issues

Mills/Hamilton
Urban Economics

Mishkin
*The Economics of Money, Banking, and Financial Markets**

*The Economics of Money, Banking, and Financial Markets, Business School Edition**

*Macroeconomics: Policy and Practice**

Murray
Econometrics: A ModernIntroduction

Nafziger
The Economics of Developing Countries

O'Sullivan/Sheffrin/Perez
*Economics: Principles, Applications and Tools**

Parkin
*Economics**

Perloff
*Microeconomics**

*Microeconomics: Theory and Applications with Calculus**

Perman/Common/McGilvray/Ma
Natural Resources and Environmental Economics

Phelps
Health Economics

Pindyck/Rubinfeld
*Microeconomics**

Riddell/Shackelford/Stamos/Schneider
Economics: A Tool for Critically Understanding Society

Ritter/Silber/Udell
*Principles of Money, Banking & Financial Markets**

Roberts
The Choice: A Fable of Free Trade and Protection

Rohlf
Introduction to Economic Reasoning

Ruffin/Gregory
Principles of Economics

Sargent
Rational Expectations and Inflation

Sawyer/Sprinkle
International Economics

Scherer
Industry Structure, Strategy, and Public Policy

Schiller
The Economics of Poverty and Discrimination

Sherman
Market Regulation

Silberberg
Principles of Microeconomics

Stock/Watson
Introduction to Econometrics

Introduction to Econometrics, Brief Edition

Studenmund
Using Econometrics: A Practical Guide

Tietenberg/Lewis
Environmental and Natural Resource Economics

Environmental Economics and Policy

Todaro/Smith
Economic Development

Waldman
Microeconomics

Waldman/Jensen
Industrial Organization: Theory and Practice

Weil
Economic Growth

Williamson
Macroeconomics

1974	1975	1976	1977	1978	1979	1980	1981	1982	1983	1984	1985	1986
2.8	2.7	2.3	2.0	2.1	2.2	1.8	2.0	1.8	1.3	1.6	1.5	1.4
1.4	1.5	1.4	1.6	1.5	1.7	2.4	2.9	2.5	1.9	1.8	1.5	1.0
4.7	4.3	4.4	4.4	4.6	4.7	4.4	3.9	3.7	3.7	3.9	4.1	4.4
12.3	11.5	12.1	12.5	12.7	12.3	11.3	11.0	10.0	9.8	10.3	9.8	9.5
8.8	8.8	8.9	8.8	8.6	8.6	8.5	8.5	8.2	7.8	7.4	7.2	6.6
3.8	4.1	4.1	4.1	4.1	3.8	4.0	4.1	4.5	4.4	4.3	4.2	4.1
6.9	6.9	6.6	6.5	6.6	6.6	6.5	6.4	6.3	6.1	6.3	6.2	6.1
8.7	8.9	9.0	9.0	8.9	8.6	8.3	8.2	8.3	8.5	8.6	8.7	8.7
3.3	3.0	3.2	3.2	3.2	3.2	3.1	2.9	2.7	2.7	2.8	2.7	2.7
11.8	12.0	11.7	11.8	11.9	11.8	12.3	12.5	13.1	13.4	13.4	13.6	14.0
—	—	—	—	—	—	—	—	—	—	—	—	—
—	—	—	—	—	—	—	—	—	—	—	—	—
—	—	—	—	—	—	—	—	—	—	—	—	—
—	—	—	—	—	—	—	—	—	—	—	—	—
—	—	—	—	—	—	—	—	—	—	—	—	—
36.5	36.0	36.1	35.9	35.7	35.6	35.2	35.2	34.7	34.9	35.1	34.9	34.7
4.8	4.7	4.5	4.2	4.1	3.8	3.8	3.7	3.6	3.5	3.2	2.8	2.6
0.9	1.0	1.0	1.0	1.0	1.1	1.1	1.2	1.3	1.1	1.0	1.0	0.8
5.0	4.5	4.4	4.6	4.8	4.9	4.7	4.5	4.3	4.3	4.6	4.8	4.8
22.5	20.9	21.1	21.1	20.9	20.8	19.9	19.7	18.7	18.2	18.4	17.8	17.2
66.9	68.9	69.0	69.1	69.2	69.5	70.4	70.9	72.2	72.9	72.8	73.7	74.5
4.43	4.73	5.06	5.44	5.88	6.34	6.85	7.44	7.87	8.20	8.49	8.74	8.93
14.43	14.08	14.24	14.40	14.54	14.48	14.33	14.23	14.19	14.22	14.19	14.18	14.18
759	802	975	895	820	844	891	933	884	1,190	1,178	1,328	1,793
2,474	2,389	2,745	2,368	2,028	1,928	1,865	1,785	1,595	2,065	1,970	2,155	2,846
8.6	8.8	8.4	8.0	8.7	9.6	11.9	14.2	13.8	12.0	12.7	11.4	9.0
−0.5	−0.6	2.7	1.6	1.7	1.3	2.8	4.8	7.7	8.1	9.0	8.3	6.8
438	449	513	577	653	737	807	927	949	1,009	1,122	1,224	1,300
454	535	576	623	685	763	883	1,001	1,111	1,210	1,312	1,439	1,539
−16	−87	−62	−46	−32	−27	−76	−74	−161	−202	−190	−216	−239
344	395	477	549	607	640	712	789	925	1,137	1,307	1,507	1,741

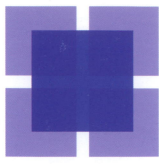

Microeconomic Data

These microeconomic data series show some of the trends in what, how, and for whom goods and services are produced — the central questions of microeconomics. You will find these data in a spreadsheet that you can download from your MyEconLab Web site.

		1987	1988	1989	1990	1991	1992	1993	1994	1995	1996	1997
WHAT WE PRODUCE												
Percentage of gross domestic product												
1	Agriculture, forestry, fishing, and hunting	1.7	1.6	1.7	1.7	1.5	1.6	1.4	1.5	1.3	1.5	1.3
2	Mining	1.5	1.4	1.4	1.5	1.3	1.1	1.1	1.0	1.0	1.1	1.1
3	Construction	4.6	4.6	4.5	4.3	3.8	3.7	3.7	3.9	3.9	4.0	4.1
4	Durable goods	10.2	10.2	9.9	9.4	9.0	8.9	8.9	9.2	9.2	9.0	9.1
5	Nondurable goods	6.9	7.0	7.0	7.0	6.9	6.8	6.7	6.7	6.8	6.4	6.3
6	Utilities	2.6	2.4	2.5	2.5	2.5	2.5	2.5	2.5	2.5	2.3	2.2
7	Wholesale trade	6.0	6.2	6.2	6.0	6.0	6.0	6.0	6.3	6.2	6.3	6.3
8	Retail trade	7.4	7.2	7.1	6.9	6.8	6.8	6.9	7.0	7.0	7.0	6.9
9	Transportation and warehousing	3.2	3.2	3.0	2.9	3.0	2.9	3.0	3.1	3.1	3.0	3.1
10	Finance, insurance, real estate, rental, and leasing	17.7	17.8	17.8	18.0	18.4	18.6	18.6	18.4	18.7	18.8	19.2
11	Professional and business services	8.7	9.1	9.4	9.8	9.7	9.9	9.9	9.9	10.0	10.4	10.8
12	Information	3.9	3.8	3.8	3.9	3.9	4.0	4.1	4.2	4.2	4.3	4.2
13	Educational services, health care, and social assistance	6.0	6.1	6.3	6.7	7.1	7.3	7.3	7.2	7.2	7.1	6.9
14	Arts, entertainment, recreation, accommodation, and food services	3.2	3.3	3.3	3.4	3.4	3.4	3.4	3.3	3.4	3.4	3.5
15	Other services, except government	2.4	2.4	2.4	2.5	2.4	2.4	2.5	2.4	2.4	2.4	2.4
HOW WE PRODUCE												
16	Average weekly hours	34.8	34.6	34.5	34.3	34.1	34.2	34.3	34.5	34.3	34.3	34.5
Employment (percentage of total)												
17	Agriculture	2.6	2.5	2.4	2.3	2.3	2.3	2.1	2.2	2.2	2.0	1.9
18	Mining	0.7	0.7	0.7	0.7	0.7	0.6	0.6	0.6	0.5	0.5	0.5
19	Construction	4.9	4.8	4.8	4.7	4.3	4.1	4.2	4.4	4.4	4.5	4.6
20	Manufacturing	16.8	16.6	16.3	15.8	15.4	15.1	14.8	14.6	14.4	14.1	13.9
21	Services	75.0	75.4	75.9	76.5	77.3	77.9	78.3	78.3	78.5	78.8	79.0
FOR WHOM WE PRODUCE												
22	Wage rate (dollars per hour)	9.14	9.44	9.80	10.20	10.52	10.77	11.05	11.34	11.65	12.04	12.51
23	Real wage rate (2005 dollars per hour)	14.10	14.08	14.08	14.12	14.06	14.06	14.11	14.19	14.28	14.48	14.78
24	Stock price index (Dow Jones)	2,276	2,061	2,509	2,679	2,929	3,284	3,522	3,794	4,494	5,743	7,441
25	Real stock price index (2005 dollars)	3,511	3,074	3,606	3,707	3,915	4,288	4,499	4,746	5,507	6,906	8,793
26	Interest rate Aaa (percent per year)	9.4	9.7	9.3	9.3	8.8	8.1	7.2	8.0	7.6	7.4	7.3
27	Real interest rate (percent per year)	6.5	6.3	5.5	5.5	5.2	5.8	5.0	5.9	5.5	5.5	5.5
GOVERNMENT IN THE ECONOMY												
28	Government revenue (billions of dollars)	1,414	1,514	1,640	1,725	1,775	1,861	1,966	2,112	2,236	2,404	2,584
29	Government expenditure (billions of dollars)	1,622	1,700	1,821	1,977	2,077	2,234	2,304	2,374	2,480	2,583	2,658
30	Government surplus(+)/deficit(−) (billions of dollars)	−208	−187	−182	−252	−301	−373	−338	−262	−245	−180	−74
31	Government debt (billions of dollars)	1,890	2,052	2,191	2,412	2,689	3,000	3,248	3,433	3,604	3,734	3,772

1998	1999	2000	2001	2002	2003	2004	2005	2006	2007	2008	2009	2010
1.1	1.0	1.0	1.0	0.9	1.0	1.2	1.0	0.9	1.0	1.1	0.9	1.1
0.9	0.9	1.1	1.2	1.0	1.2	1.3	1.5	1.7	1.8	2.2	1.7	1.9
4.4	4.6	4.7	4.8	4.6	4.6	4.7	4.8	4.9	4.7	4.3	3.8	3.4
8.9	8.6	8.4	7.4	7.2	6.9	6.9	6.9	6.9	6.7	6.5	6.1	6.6
6.2	6.0	5.8	5.7	5.5	5.5	5.6	5.5	5.4	5.4	5.0	5.1	5.2
1.9	1.8	1.7	1.7	1.7	1.7	1.8	1.6	1.8	1.8	1.8	1.9	1.9
6.3	6.2	6.2	6.0	5.8	5.7	5.8	5.7	5.7	5.8	5.7	5.5	5.5
7.1	7.0	6.9	6.8	6.9	6.9	6.7	6.6	6.5	6.3	5.8	5.8	5.9
3.1	3.1	3.0	2.9	2.8	2.9	2.9	2.9	3.0	2.9	2.9	2.8	2.8
19.3	19.6	20.1	20.9	20.9	20.8	20.3	20.6	20.7	20.6	20.7	21.5	21.1
10.5	10.8	11.2	11.4	11.3	11.3	11.3	11.6	11.7	12.1	12.3	12.0	12.1
4.4	4.7	4.2	4.4	4.7	4.6	4.8	4.7	4.4	4.5	4.5	4.5	4.6
6.8	6.8	6.8	7.1	7.4	7.6	7.6	7.5	7.6	7.7	8.0	8.6	8.7
3.7	3.8	3.8	3.8	3.9	3.8	3.8	3.8	3.8	3.9	3.7	3.6	3.6
2.9	2.8	2.9	2.5	2.7	2.6	2.6	2.8	2.6	2.3	2.6	2.6	2.2
34.5	34.4	34.3	34.0	33.9	33.7	33.7	33.7	33.9	33.8	33.6	33.1	33.4
1.8	1.7	1.6	1.6	1.6	1.6	1.5	1.5	1.4	1.3	1.3	1.3	1.3
0.5	0.5	0.4	0.5	0.4	0.4	0.4	0.5	0.5	0.5	0.6	0.5	0.5
4.8	5.0	5.1	5.1	5.1	5.1	5.2	5.4	5.6	5.5	5.2	4.5	4.2
13.7	13.2	12.9	12.3	11.5	11.0	10.7	10.5	10.3	10.0	9.7	8.9	8.8
79.2	79.7	80.0	80.6	81.4	81.9	82.1	82.2	82.3	82.7	83.3	84.7	85.2
13.01	13.49	14.02	14.54	14.97	15.37	15.69	16.13	16.76	17.43	18.08	18.62	19.04
15.20	15.53	15.80	16.03	16.24	16.33	16.21	16.13	16.24	16.41	16.65	16.97	17.15
8,626	10,465	10,735	10,189	9,226	8,994	10,317	10,548	11,409	13,170	11,253	8,876	10,663
10,078	12,050	12,099	11,231	10,007	9,554	10,660	10,548	11,052	12,398	10,363	8,089	9,607
6.5	7.0	7.6	7.1	6.5	5.7	5.6	5.2	5.6	5.6	5.6	5.3	4.9
5.4	5.6	5.5	4.8	4.9	3.6	2.8	1.9	2.4	2.7	3.4	4.3	3.8
2,762	2,939	3,168	3,156	3,001	3,071	3,296	3,692	4,028	4,229	4,086	3,729	3,983
2,735	2,875	3,022	3,221	3,423	3,625	3,827	4,110	4,320	4,637	5,023	5,351	5,539
27	64	147	−65	−422	−553	−531	−418	−292	−408	−937	−1,622	−1,556
3,721	3,632	3,410	3,320	3,540	3,913	4,296	4,592	4,829	5,035	5,803	7,545	9,019

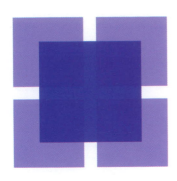

Microeconomic Data

These microeconomic data series show some of the trends in what, how, and for whom goods and services are produced — the central questions of microeconomics. You will find these data in a spreadsheet that you can download from your MyEconLab Web site.

		1963	1964	1965	1966	1967	1968	1969	1970	1971	1972	1973
WHAT WE PRODUCE												
Percentage of gross domestic product												
1	Agriculture, forestry, fishing, and hunting	2.8	2.5	2.6	2.5	2.3	2.1	2.2	2.1	2.1	2.3	3.2
2	Mining	1.2	1.1	1.1	1.0	1.0	1.0	0.9	1.0	1.0	1.0	1.0
3	Construction	4.4	4.5	4.5	4.5	4.5	4.5	4.6	4.6	4.7	4.7	4.8
4	Durable goods	14.7	14.7	15.3	15.4	14.8	14.8	14.4	12.7	12.4	12.7	13.0
5	Nondurable goods	10.5	10.4	10.3	10.3	10.0	10.0	9.7	9.4	9.1	8.9	8.7
6	Utilities	4.1	4.1	4.0	3.9	3.9	3.9	3.9	4.0	4.0	4.0	3.9
7	Wholesale trade	6.6	6.6	6.5	6.5	6.5	6.5	6.5	6.6	6.5	6.6	6.6
8	Retail trade	8.9	9.1	9.0	8.8	8.9	9.1	9.1	9.2	9.2	9.1	9.0
9	Transportation and warehousing	3.5	3.5	3.5	3.4	3.3	3.2	3.2	3.2	3.2	3.3	3.3
10	Finance, insurance, real estate, rental, and leasing	11.9	11.8	11.7	11.4	11.6	11.6	11.7	11.9	12.1	12.0	11.7
11	Professional and business services	—	—	—	—	—	—	—	—	—	—	—
12	Information	—	—	—	—	—	—	—	—	—	—	—
13	Educational services, health care, and social assistance	—	—	—	—	—	—	—	—	—	—	—
14	Arts, entertainment, recreation, accommodation, and food services	—	—	—	—	—	—	—	—	—	—	—
15	Other services, except government	—	—	—	—	—	—	—	—	—	—	—
HOW WE PRODUCE												
16	Average weekly hours	40.5	38.5	38.7	38.5	37.9	37.7	37.6	37.0	36.8	36.9	36.9
	Employment (percentage of total)											
17	Agriculture	8.8	8.2	7.5	6.7	6.1	5.8	5.4	5.3	5.1	5.0	4.9
18	Mining	1.1	1.1	1.1	1.0	1.0	0.9	0.9	0.9	0.9	0.9	0.9
19	Construction	4.9	5.0	5.0	4.9	4.7	4.7	4.9	4.9	5.0	5.1	5.2
20	Manufacturing	25.1	25.0	25.2	25.8	25.5	25.2	24.9	23.8	22.8	22.7	23.0
21	Services	60.0	60.8	61.2	61.6	62.7	63.3	63.9	65.1	66.1	66.3	66.1
FOR WHOM WE PRODUCE												
22	Wage rate (dollars per hour)	2.46	2.53	2.63	2.73	2.85	3.02	3.22	3.40	3.63	3.90	4.14
23	Real wage rate (2005 dollars per hour)	12.76	12.92	13.19	13.31	13.49	13.71	13.93	13.97	14.21	14.63	14.71
24	Stock price index (Dow Jones)	715	834	911	874	879	906	877	753	885	951	924
25	Real stock price index (2005 dollars)	3,707	4,259	4,569	4,261	4,160	4,113	3,792	3,095	3,462	3,566	3,284
26	Interest rate Aaa (percent per year)	4.3	4.4	4.5	5.1	5.5	6.2	7.0	8.0	7.4	7.2	7.4
27	Real interest rate (percent per year)	3.2	2.8	2.7	2.3	2.5	1.9	2.1	2.8	2.4	2.9	1.9
GOVERNMENT IN THE ECONOMY												
28	Government revenue (billions of dollars)	165	170	184	207	222	256	288	292	309	354	397
29	Government expenditure (billions of dollars)	169	178	189	215	243	268	286	313	340	371	401
30	Government surplus(+)/deficit(–) (billions of dollars)	–4	–8	–5	–8	–21	–12	2	–21	–31	–17	–4
31	Government debt (billions of dollars)	254	257	261	264	267	290	278	283	303	322	341